STEP BY ST
GARDENING

Series Editor
ALAN TITCHMARSH

Greenhouse Gardening

Adrienne Wild

Ward Lock Limited · London

CW01618773

© Ward Lock Ltd 1985

First published in Great Britain in 1985
by Ward Lock Limited, 82 Gower Street,
London WC1E, a Pentos Company.

All Rights Reserved. No part of this publication may be reproduced, stored in a retrieval system, or transmitted, in any form or by any means, electronic, mechanical, photocopying, recording, or otherwise, without the prior permission of the copyright owners.

House editor Denis Ingram
Designed by Bob Swan

Text filmset in Monophoto Plantin 110
by MS Filmsetting Limited,
Frome, Somerset

Printed and bound in Italy
by New Interlitho SpA, Milan

British Library Cataloguing in Publication Data

Wild, Adrienne
Greenhouse gardening.—
(Step-by-step gardening series)
1. Greenhouse gardening
I. Title II. Series
635′.0483 SB415
ISBN 0-7063-6267-5

CONTENTS

ACKNOWLEDGEMENTS

(Key: t = top, m = middle, b = bottom, l = left, r = right)

All the line drawings are by Nils Solberg.

The drawings on pp. 6(tl, bl & r); 9(m); 11(m & b); 13(3); 15(t); 19(2); 21(3); 23(2); 25(t); 29(t & m); 31(t & b); 33(t); 35(b); 37 (mr & b); 39 (b); 40(3); 52(b); 53(2); 55(l); 59(4); 60(2); 61(2); 63(tl, bl & r); 67(5); 77(3); 78(m & b); 79(t & m); 81(2); 83(t & b); 86(3); 87(3); 88(2); 89(3); 90(2); 93(tl & r); & 94 are after illustrations the copyright of which belongs to *Practical Gardening* magazine.

The drawings on pp. 9(bl & r); 25(ml, mr, br); 27(t); 39(t); 47(m & b); 49(3); 52(t); 59(2); 56(2); 57(2); 69(4); 74(2); 79(b); & 85(b) are after drawings on pp. 6, 5; 17, 21, 19; 21; 31; 68, 66; 88, 89; 52; 78; 86; 85, 28; 92; 80; 69; & 46 respectively in *The Royal Horticultural Society's Encyclopaedia of Practical Gardening: Growing under Glass*, K. A. Beckett, Mitchell Beazley, 1981.

The drawings on pp. 6(m); 27(b); 45(tl, ml & r, br); 73; 76(2); & 82(t) are after the drawings on pp. 14; 16; 30, 31; 67; 51; & 40 respectively in *Gardening Under Glass*, K. A. Beckett, Octopus, 1982. The drawings on pp. 42(l); 66(2); & 67(t(2) & b(2)) are after the drawings on pp. 6; 80; & 81, 82 respectively in *The Royal Horticultural Society's Encyclopaedia of Practical Gardening: Plant Propagation*, P. McM. Browse, Mitchell Beazley, 1979.

The drawings on pp. 16(t & m) & 43 are after the drawings on pp. 18 & 32 respectively in *Greenhouse Gardener*, D. Shelton, Sundial, 1979. The drawings on p. 75(2) are after the drawings on pp. 40 & 41 respectively in *The Royal Horticultural Society's Encyclopaedia of Practical Gardening: Fruit*, H. Baker, Mitchell Beazley, 1980.

The drawings on pp. 86 & 87 are after drawings the copyright of which belongs to *Greenhouse and Garden* magazine. The drawings on pp. 11(t); 15(bl, br); 29(b); 33(b); & 37 are after illustrations appearing in promotional literature of Edenlite Ltd.; Birmid Qualcast Ltd.; Genesis Ltd.; Halls, Homes and Gardens; & Brannon Ltd., respectively.

Publishers Note

Measurements are generally cited in imperial followed by the metric equivalent in parentheses. In a few instances, owing to pressure on space, the metric equivalent has been omitted.

FOREWORD
BY ALAN TITCHMARCH

Sooner or later you'll simply have to get a greenhouse. When you're irritated at the price of bedding plants or tomatoes, and tired of being rained on in the garden, the prospect of a bit of under-cover potting is irresistible.

But where do you start? What's the best kind of greenhouse for your needs, and how can you equip it and heat it without investing in a second mortgage? Adrienne Wild will put your mind at rest and fire you with the enthusiasm you need to succeed. She has advice on the construction of your miniature Crystal Palace, where to put it, and how to make it work for you through the year, producing a succession of flowers, fruits and vegetables that will satisfy your appetite and cheer your eyes.

Having a greenhouse is a bit like having a family pet – it will need a bit of attention every day – but when you've tasted your own melons, cucumbers and tomatoes, raised your own garden plants for a fraction of the price charged in the nursery, and simply had the satisfaction of watching plants grow happily out of the way of foul weather, you'll wonder how you ever managed before your greenhouse came along.

There's another advantage, too. It's a superb place to sneak off to when you want to escape the clamouring family: half an hour in the greenhouse is a real reviver!

Design features

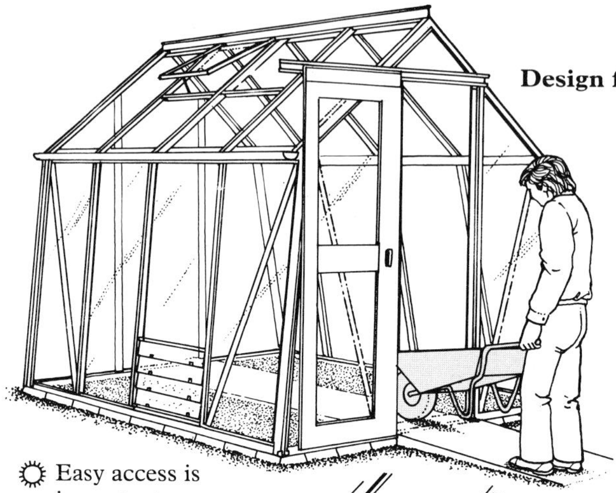

Easy access is important.

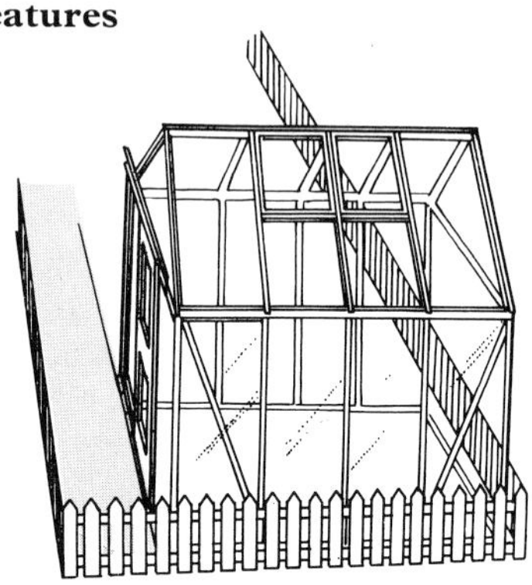

In a confined space a sliding door is preferable.

Barrels of rainwater are the next best thing to a mains water supply.

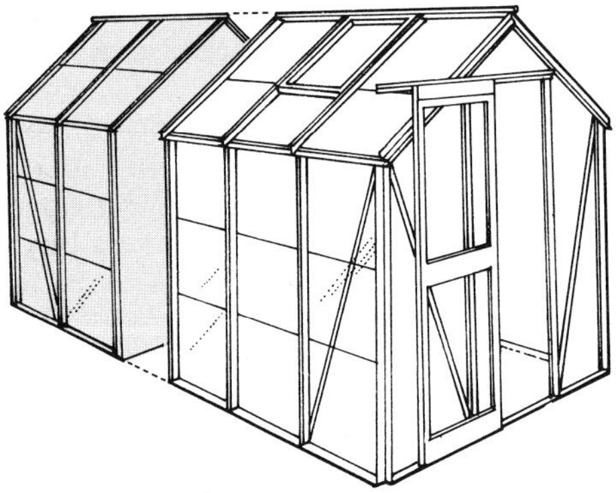

Some greenhouses are extendable.

Others can be partitioned inside.

1
BUYING A GREENHOUSE

Design features

Buying a greenhouse will completely change your hobby by opening up exciting new avenues of gardening that you have never been able to enjoy. No longer will you have to battle with the climate to raise your own plants from seed and cuttings, you will be in complete control and able to provide the optimum conditions to sow or take cuttings just when you like.

Before you buy, shop around and check what design features are fitted as standard by the different manufacturers, and make sure that you clearly understand what you will be getting for your money. The cheapest greenhouse is not always the best buy as often the glass is not included in the kit. Many firms however, include not only the glass but a prefabricated base and even staging in with the price, so what seems to be an expensive model can very often work out to be cheaper. The first thing to check for is an adequate number of ventilators. You cannot have too many, especially if you want to grow alpines. Another necessity is adequate room for access. Few standard greenhouses have a door sufficiently wide enough to take a wheelchair and neither will you be able to get your wheelbarrow in to where you are working – it's helpful if you can, especially in a very long greenhouse.

Entrances and doors

☼ To get in without scraping your knuckles in the process the entrance should be at least 2 ft 6 in (36 cm) wide. For safe and easy access the base of the doorway should be flat, if an integral base is fitted this will not be the case and you may find that you have to install a ramp.

☘ The type of door used is an important consideration too. There are models with hinged or sliding doors and although on a windy site the sliding type is an advantage as it will not swing open or slam shut, some do tend to come off their runners if you pull them too vigorously or get jammed if dirt gets in the track. They may be your only choice, though, if the greenhouse has to go in a tight corner of the garden and there is no space for the door to open outwards.

If you have no water supply laid on to the greenhouse, guttering will be an advantage to trap rain water. In some cases guttering is fitted as standard; if it is not, check that it can be installed later. (With a curved-eave design or dome-shaped greenhouse there are no eaves on which guttering can be fixed.)

Size

You should always choose the largest greenhouse you can afford and accommodate. In a very small greenhouse it is difficult to maintain optimum conditions as the slightest change in the weather causes the temperature to soar or fall immediately. Go for extra width rather than length; you will need the same size path in whichever size you buy and in a narrow house this means using valuable border or bench space.

❁ If cost is the limiting factor, choose a house which can be extended, then if you find yourself wanting more space you will not need to go out and buy a new greenhouse. When you erect the greenhouse remember to leave enough space for the extension.

Some models can be partitioned inside too, and this may be worth considering if you intend to grow a number of plants with different temperature and humidity requirements.

Greenhouse shape

There are many greenhouse shapes available nowadays, but by far still the most popular is the traditional rectangular box with a span roof. This shape is available in both wood and aluminium with either brick or wood cladding or glass to ground. They can be bought in almost any size, the smallest useful size being 6 ft × 8 ft (1.8 m × 2.5 m) with a height of about 7 ft (2.1 m) to the ridge and 4 ft 6 in to the eaves.

A greenhouse with glass right down to the ground allows in more light and is essential for growing tall plants like tomatoes, cucumbers and chrysanthemums and when cultivating the soil border. For these crops the height of the greenhouse, especially to the eaves, is critical if they are to attain their full growing height without being impeded.

If you only intend to use the house for propagation and pot plants and have no use for the space under the staging, other than for storing pots and trays, it would be sensible to choose a half-clad design. This would save you money on the heating bills as less heat will escape through brick or wood cladding than it will through glass.

Some greenhouses, however, have clip-on cladding and this will give you year round adaptability.

A modification of the traditional design is the **Dutch light** house. This has sloping sides made from extra large panes of glass, so light transmission is much improved. They are available in wood and aluminium. The sloping sides, however, mean that there is a loss of headroom, so unless you have an extra wide house you will find it practical to grow tomatoes and such like on one side only as too much space would otherwise be taken up.

The **mansard** or **curvilinear shape** has become increasingly-popular with the serious amateur grower who wants to produce crops in the winter and propagate mostly in the spring. The shape of the greenhouse is such as to provide a range of glass panes at various angles to trap as much light (and solar heat) as possible. The design is also available as a lean-to model with glass to ground or half cladding.

A **polythene** covered greenhouse or tunnel is of less value for winter and spring propagation but can be a great boon for summer crops and growing salads and cut flowers all year round.

The addition of curved eaves to the traditional design has earned the greenhouse a more prominent place in the garden, close to the house. The main disadvantage with this type of house is that guttering cannot be fixed and there is no headroom for shelves on the side walls. These houses are only available in aluminium.

A stylish greenhouse with a more rustic charm is the wooden **hexalight**. The many sides make it open to the angle of the sun from all directions, but it is really only suitable for pot plant collections. Several such houses can be linked together to make an attractive feature in the garden.

Similar, but in aluminium only, is the octagonal **gazebo** greenhouse. Here light transmission is also good, but space is limited inside and the house is only suitable for display and perhaps raising a few plants from seeds and cuttings.

The **geodesic dome** has a certain space age appeal and would fit in well with an ultra modern house and garden rather than a country cottage. Light transmission is improved with this design as the panes of glass face in

Greenhouse shapes

Straight sided, glass to ground.

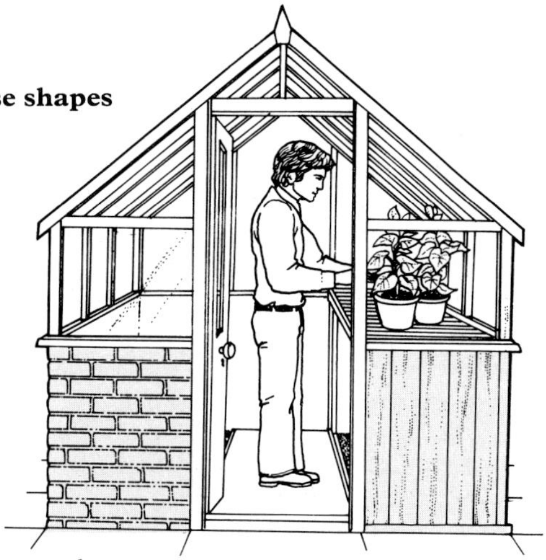

Half-clad design, wood or brick.

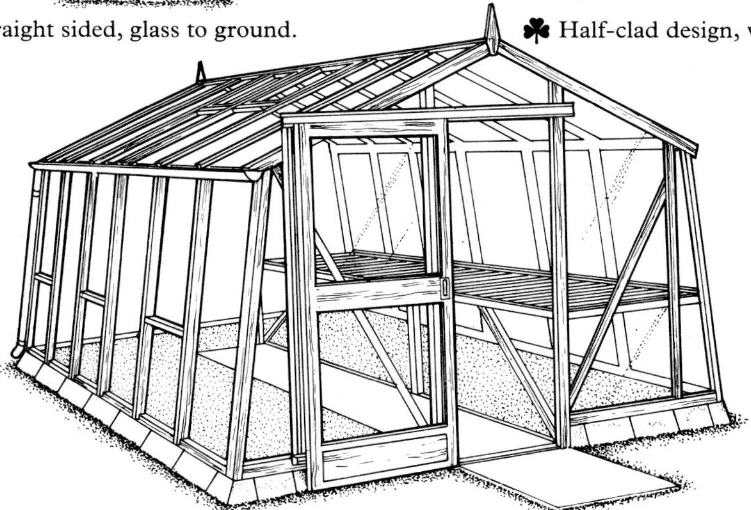

Dutch greenhouse—sloping sides.

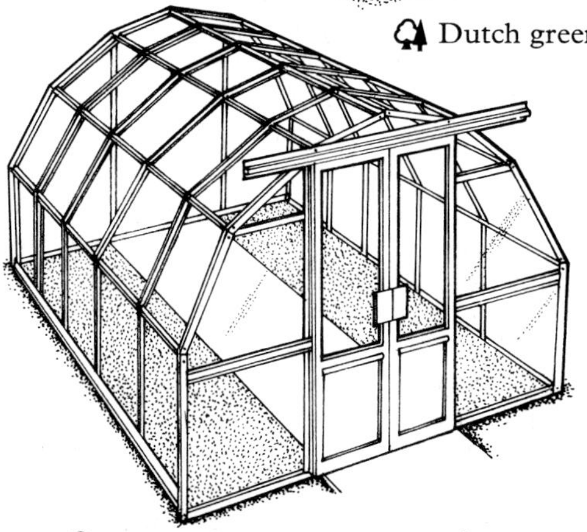

Mansard: glass panes at various angles.

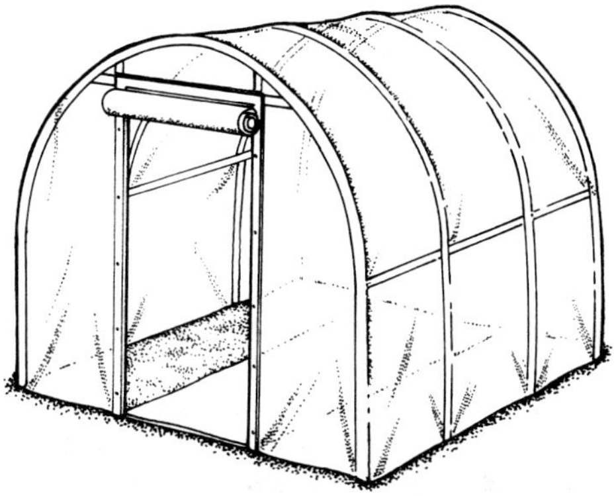

Polythene: cheap but not long lasting.

all directions. Tall crops, such as tomatoes, however, are virtually impossible to grow except in the centre. As a show house for pot plants, an outdoor garden room, and for propagation it is ideal.

Space-savers

A free standing greenhouse can take up quite a lot of valuable space and the cost of installing electricity to the bottom of the garden, to use a fan heater and propagator in the greenhouse for a couple of months a year, can be quite outrageous.

☼ Lean-to conservatories are therefore overtaking greenhouses in popularity. These are fitted to the side of the house and will, in fact, improve the insulation of your home by protecting it from the worst of the weather. The best advantage though, apart from dry access in bad weather, is that they can be heated by a radiator linked to your central heating system. Heat conservation is good too, as the brick wall will retain solar warmth and release it at night. This may cause problems in south facing lean-to's in the summer though, unless plenty of ventilation is applied.

Lean-to's are available in various styles with half cladding or glass to ground. They may have a three quarter span or single pitched roof, curved eaves or be mansard shaped. Some have a lower pitched roof specially designed for bungalows where the house eaves are low. And extra small sizes, 4 ft (1.2 m) wide, are available for situations where space is at a premium. They can be used as an extra room furnished with houseplants. In this case choose a model with solid lower panelling as it will be warmer and safer, especially where children are playing.

Lean-to's can, of course, be kept simply for growing. Ventilate carefully if the site is exposed and to prevent draughts include plenty of louvred side-wall ventilators. Painting the back wall white will improve the light intensity, which is essential if the lean-to is fixed to the shadiest side of the house.

Shelves can be fixed to the wall to utilize as much growing space as possible, or you can grow climbers – a south-facing lean-to makes a splendid vinery, the fruit being trained on the rear wall.

☘ Even in a small garden you can enjoy the pleasures of growing under glass. Miniature models that fit onto a patio or balcony are now available. Most of the designs are lean-to and the plants are tended from the outside through the open doors. The houses come in various sizes, the smallest being capable of holding one growing bag of tomatoes and the largest providing room enough for several growing bags plus shelves for pot plants. These are available in aluminium only.

Free standing models in wood make an attractive feature for the very small back yard or balcony, but they are only suitable for raising plants from seeds and cuttings or housing small collections of pot plants. There is very little headroom, so you will have to grow dwarf varieties of tomatoes. Flooding the market at the moment are vertical frames. These are made from tubular aluminium, or occasionally soft wood, and are clad with polythene. They are completely mobile, but are not truly weather resistant so are really only suitable for summer crops and do not offer the same opportunities for growing all the year round that a greenhouse does.

Space-savers

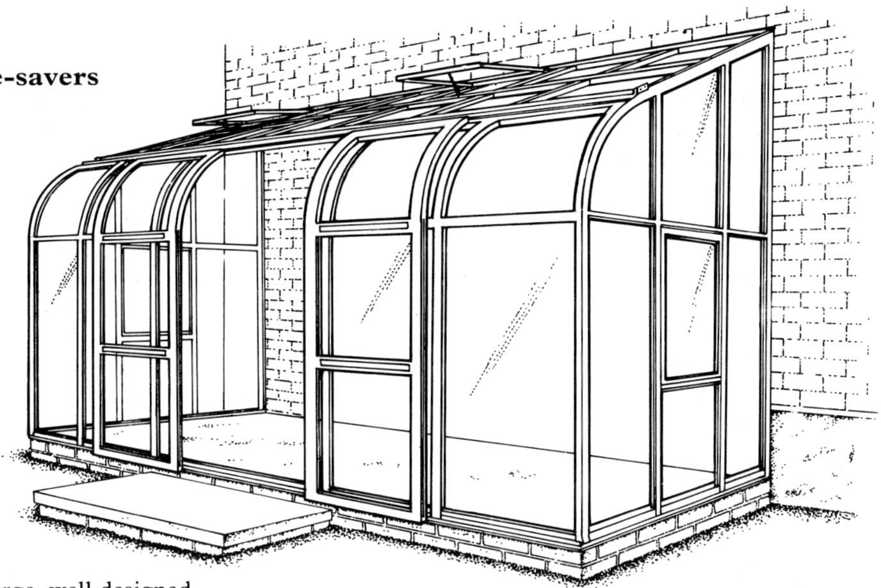

☼ A large, well designed lean-to; can be used either as an extra room or exclusively for growing plants.

♣ Miniature lean-to; access is through the sliding door.

Miniature free-standing model suitable for backyard or balcony.

Wood v. aluminium

The choice of structural materials is today usually limited to aluminium alloy and wood, although in the past steel and even concrete have been used. Of the two, aluminium is by far the most popular being lightweight, very strong and needing virtually no maintenance. Wooden houses are available in both hard and soft timbers and it is best to invest in one made from a good quality timber such as western red cedar. If you choose a soft timber, such as Baltic pine, the cash saving may not be so appealing when you have to treat it with a preservative every year.

Aluminium greenhouses

1 There is a large selection in a variety of styles to choose from, ranging from a budget-priced, traditional shape to luxurious, unconventional designs.
2 Lightweight yet very strong.
3 ☼ Very easy to erect from prefabricated pieces that are bolted together.
4 Less superstructure, so larger panes of glass are used and more light can enter.
5 Often equipped with an integral-baseplate that obviates the need for foundations.
6 Sophisticated glazing systems mean that glass fits snugly, reducing draughts and drips, and aluminium greenhouses are easier to glaze as spring-loaded clips are used instead of putty. Some of the more expensive models have the glass held in place by a continuous capping. This is secured to the framework and clamps the glass very tightly.
7 There is no fear of them rotting and warping and no problems with wood-boring pests. Aluminium must not be put in contact with steel though, otherwise it will corrode.
8 An aluminium greenhouse is virtually maintenance free.
9 They are easier to dismantle and transport if you are moving house. Small sized greenhouses are sold over the counter as packaged kits which can be taken home on the roof rack of a car.

Wood greenhouses

1 Wooden houses are sometimes quicker and easier to erect as they may be sold in pre-glazed panels that only need to be bolted together. (Glazing with putty can be quite difficult to master.)
2 ♣ Wooden greenhouses are not always fitted with an integral base, so foundations need to be prepared and a damp proof material installed.
3 Wood is a poor conductor compared with aluminium, which tends to transmit cold air through the framework from outside and create condensation on the metal. A wooden greenhouse is therefore, slightly warmer and costs marginally less to heat.
4 They have a more resilient structure and the glass is less likely to be broken by strong winds.
5 Wood is the best choice for heavily polluted areas which are not smokeless zones as it resists sulphur fumes, but it can become badly discoloured with soot, which in the long run is more unsightly. Wooden greenhouses are the best choice for coastal areas, where aluminium tends to corrode more readily, leaving the shiny surface with a flaky, grey matt coating.
6 In a wooden greenhouse you can fix shelves using ordinary wood screws without any difficulty. Use brass

screws or other non-corroding types in houses made from cedarwood.

7 There is no need to buy expensive 'supportive' accessories; polythene sheet insulation and twine plant supports can be held in place with drawing pins and ordinary cup hooks.

8 The most attractive feature of a wooden greenhouse is that it blends more easily into a garden setting. (There are aluminium greenhouses available that are coated with bronze or white paint, which is baked onto the surface and will not flake or blister, to make them more aesthetically appealing.)

9 ♣ The most off-putting thing about a wooden greenhouse is that it needs treating with a preservative every year if it is to last any length of time. Unprotected wood will become damp and eventually decay and this process can happen in next to no time with soft wood timbers. Pine and redwood greenhouses are usually pressure treated with preservative; if they are not they will need painting before they are erected.

Natural wood colour preservatives are more rustic and blend easier into the garden setting. Do not use creosote as this gives off fumes which are toxic to plants. Choose one of the new weather-resistant preservatives. Cedar greenhouses are naturally very durable but still require some protection from the elements. Linseed oil, brushed on when the wood is dry, will preserve the wood and retain the beauty of the wood's natural colour.

☼ Aluminium houses are easy to erect.

☘ Laying damp-proof course.

♣ The annual preservative treatment.

Glass v. plastic materials

The materials from which your greenhouse is made determine the cost, but it is actually what you are going to grow, how long you want the greenhouse to last and what you want it to look like that will determine what you will purchase. It's no good buying a cheap polythene tunnel to grow orchids or an expensive aluminium glasshouse for a few tomato plants. Polythene clad greenhouses are mainly used as a replacement for cold frames, for growing salad crops in the summer and over wintering stock plants, so are not a real substitute for glass.

Glass: plus points

1 Glass is more aesthetically appealing.
2 It admits about 90% of the available light. Good quality 24 oz horticultural glass should be used for maximum light transmission.
3 Glass traps solar warmth. The Sun's rays are converted to heat radiation when they hit objects in the greenhouse. This heat is trapped and released during the night.
4 Glass is highly resistant to scratching.
5 Glass can be easily shaded to prevent temperatures from soaring.

Glass: minus points

1 Glass is very expensive.
2 It is very brittle and will easily break.
3 Glass is very heavy; hence a substantial structure is required to support its weight.

Plastic (PVC, Terylene and 600 gauge polythene): plus points

1 Plastic films are the cheapest materials used for covering greenhouses.
2 An advantage only in summer is the fact that more condensation builds up and this diffuses strong sunlight (a sort of shading) and improves growing conditions by raising the humidity.
3 Lightweight, compared with glass, so a less substantial structure is required.
4 Plastic greenhouses are simple to erect and can be easily dismantled and moved to another site.

Plastic: minus points

1 Plastic materials have a short life span – two to three seasons.
2 Plastic films deteriorate with exposure to sunlight, lose their transparency and become brittle. Polythene which has been specially treated with an ultraviolet inhibitor has a longer life.
3 Plastic films do not trap long radiation and at night it can be colder inside the greenhouse than outside.
4 Condensation can be a problem.
5 Polythene houses are difficult to ventilate.
6 Insurance companies will often refuse cover for a polythene greenhouse; unless the polythene is stretched tight it can act like a sail and cause the house to blow away if it is not securely anchored.
7 In windy conditions the material can easily rip.

Rigid plastics (Acrylic, glass fibre, PVC):

These have all the attributes of plastic films, but can also compare more favourably with glass.

Plus points:

1 Long lasting.
2 Half the weight of glass.

3 They can be easily cut and some can be curved for special effects.

Their price is the most off-putting feature, nearly twice that of glass.

Fixing glazing materials

☼ For a tunnel greenhouse the polythene cover is stretched over the framework and secured in a trench backfilled with heavy soil.

Glass must be stored in a dry place in an upright position and always handled with gloves on.

♣ In an aluminium greenhouse the glass is bedded on to rubber seals to give a tight fit.

♠ Spring loaded clips are used to hold the glass in place.

Glaze according to the manufacturers instructions, starting with the roof first so that you don't fall through the side panes.

Wooden houses are more difficult to glaze. The glass is bedded onto linseed putty and secured in place with glazing sprigs.

☼ Securing polythene cover with soil.

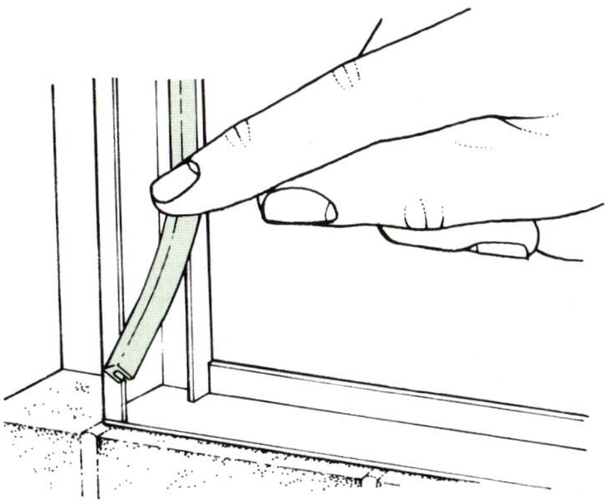

♣ Rubber seals ensure a tight fit for the glass.

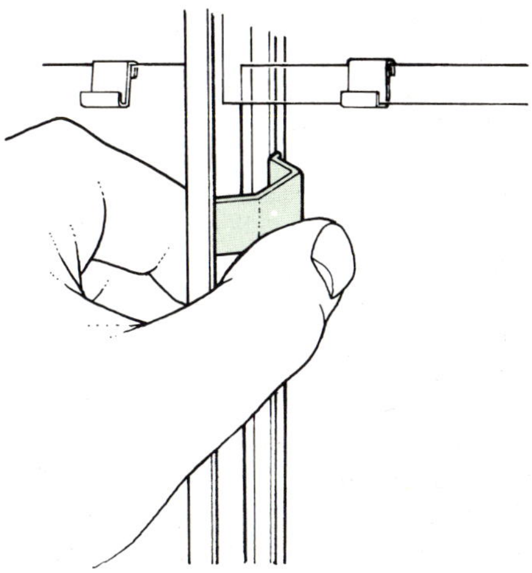

♠ Fitting a spring-loaded clip.

2
THE CORRECT SITE

☼ The site should be neither too sheltered . . .

☘ . . . nor too exposed.

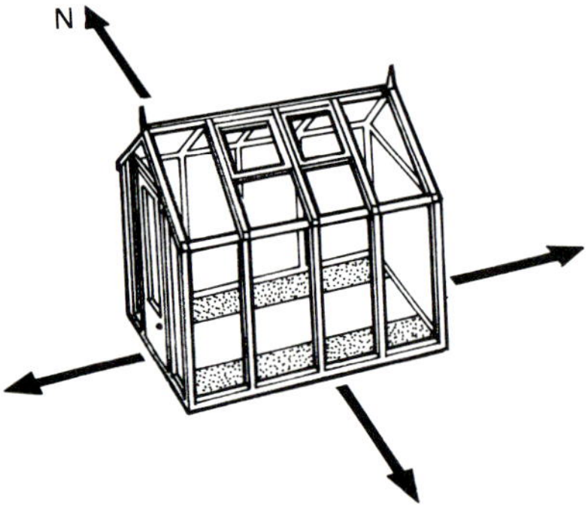

Consideration should be given to the orientation of the house.

Before you erect a greenhouse you should check with your local authority to see if you need planning permission. If you are a tenant ask your landlord first. Sometimes lean-to models are classed as a rateable extension to your home, but your local greenhouse dealer should advise you on this. The location of the greenhouse is very important if you are to get the best out of it. It will not matter how well designed it is to catch the available light from all angles if it is placed in a dark, damp corner of the garden. The place to put your greenhouse is in a well drained, open and sunny position. Badly drained ground will cause many problems, especially in the winter when the cold, damp air will encourage fungal disease, so if necessary drain the site first. If the greenhouse has to be put in the shade of next door's house then you will be limited in what you grow unless you install a sophisticated lighting system.

Neither too sheltered . . .

☼ Always keep a greenhouse away from trees, especially evergreens; not only will they cast shade, but they can also cause extensive damage if branches fall or if the roots lift the foundations. Bird droppings and falling leaves in the autumn will make a filthy mess too, and pests and diseases that take refuge there may in turn attack your greenhouse plants.

Nor too exposed . . .

☘ Avoid a site that is too open and exposed to cold winds as this would mean increased fuel bills, for the amount of heat normally lost through the glass can be as much as doubled. If necessary install a windbreak. Erect a fence or plant a hedge at a distance which is at least four times the height of the greenhouse on the north, north-east or north-west side; on any other side shadows will be a problem. A windbreak will be truly effective up to ten times its height, which means that a 4 ft (1.2 m) hedge will provide shelter for up to 40 ft (12 m). Fast-growing hedges should be avoided as they will soon create shade. Suitable plants would be beech, hornbeam, quickthorn and privet; avoid at all costs Leyland's cypress.

Make sure that any fencing you use is open weave, a solid barrier such as a brick wall makes the wind swirl over the top and causes turbulence on the other side. A windbreak does not stop wind from entering a garden, just slows it down to a more acceptable level. Wire mesh and netting can also be used to some effect and are particularly useful as a temporary measure until the hedge has grown sufficiently.

The lowest part of the garden should be avoided as frosty air will run down the slope and collect at the bottom. In a sloping garden level up the highest point and erect the greenhouse there.

Orientation

As regards the orientation of the greenhouse, it will depend very much on what you intend to grow and the time of the year when you will be the busiest.

A greenhouse with its ridge running east to west is the usual recommendation for general growing, and is essential if you want to grow plants through the winter and do most of your propagation in spring. In the summer, however, overheating can become a problem, so it will be more than necessary to install extra ventilators plus apply plenty of shading in the hottest months.

If you place the ridge running in the opposite direction, north to south, during the winter months the low angle of the sun entering through one side of the greenhouse will cause the glazing bars to cast shadows, thus reducing the amount of valuable light. Positioning the staging wrongly will also cast shade.

In the summer and autumn months, however, each side of the greenhouse will receive an equal amount of sunshine in the course of a day, so the environment will be easier to manage.

With a lean-to greenhouse you may have no choice in the siting. An east or west facing wall is preferable. A north facing wall will be very shady and restrictive in what you can grow. South facing too, can be equally difficult as it will get very hot during the summer and the plants will need to be heavily shaded to prevent them from scorching.

Water and electricity are also two important considerations when choosing a suitable site. The further the greenhouse is from the supply, the more work and expense there will be to install them.

3
ERECTING A GREENHOUSE

Erecting a modern, prefabricated greenhouse is something that the average person can tackle without too much difficulty. Manufacturers supply detailed step by step instructions which on the whole are easy to follow. The first job to do when the greenhouse is delivered is to read the instructions thoroughly.

Check that all the necessary parts have been supplied and that you have the right tools at hand to do the job. Usually a spanner and screw driver are all that are needed.

The greenhouse should not be erected on freshly dug ground unless the soil has been well consolidated first.

Most modern alloy greenhouses have an integral base which can be laid direct on the ground, doing away with any elaborate foundations. On a very windy site ground anchors can be used for added security. These are pegs which are bolted to the base on each of the four corners and set in concrete pits.

If the greenhouse is not supplied with its own foundations you will have to prepare a concrete or brick base to stand it on. The simplest way to make a solid foundation without involving any wooden shuttering is to dig a 6 in (15 cm) deep ditch to the size of your greenhouse and line this with hollow concrete building blocks, carefully levelled and squared. Then infill the hollow centres and bind the bricks together with cement.

[1] To install an integral base, mark out the position of the greenhouse using pegs and a taut line. To get a perfect right angle, so that the greenhouse will sit square, use the 3:4:5 triangle method. For a greenhouse 6 × 8 ft (1.8 × 2.4 m) the diagonal line between the corner pegs, which are making the length and width, should be 10 ft (3 m) exactly (2 × 3:4:5 ft) if you have a perfect right angle at the corners. A special set square, using this equation, can be made from wood to help in all your building work.

The method of erecting a greenhouse depends on the type. An aluminium greenhouse is supplied in *bits* ready for bolting together.

[2] When you are ready to erect the greenhouse lay out all the parts on the lawn, putting together the pieces that are to construct the various sections. Grease all the nuts, bolts and screws to be used; then, if at a later date you want to move the greenhouse, they will be fairly easy to undo. Follow the manufacturer's instruction to the letter for you may find that bolts will need to be fed into the glazing channels for later use when you are fitting ventilators. Assemble the sections on the lawn, bolting them together only finger tight at this stage.

Two people will be needed to join the sides together, as the aluminium could buckle if the partially erected structure collapses. Bolt the assembled sides and ends together then lift the structure on to the foundations and square up the building checking that it is level and square from corner to corner. Tighten all the nuts and bolts so that the building is rigid before you bolt the ridge in place.

If you are erecting a lean-to make sure it sits vertical to the wall and that the corners are perfectly square.

Glazing

Do not start to glaze the greenhouse unless you know that you can finish the job in the same day. Wind will funnel through a partly glazed house and could cause breakages.

Choose a dry, calm day to glaze the

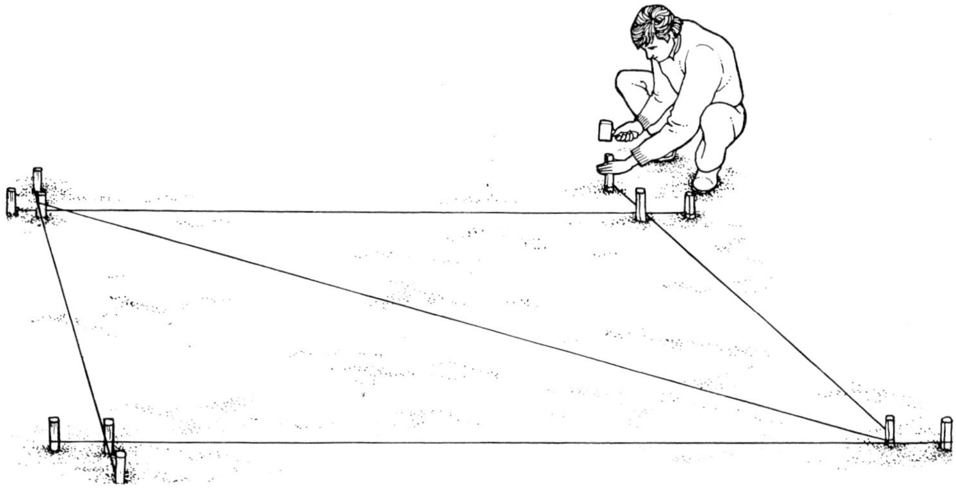

[1] Marking out the position of the house.

[2] Lay out all the components.

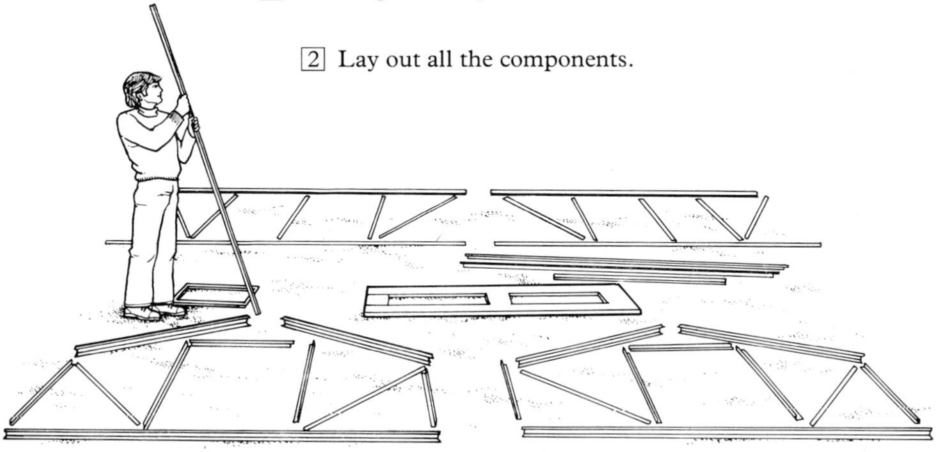

greenhouse. Wear well-fitting gloves when handling glass. Dust down the glazing bars before putting the sealing strips in place. Start with the roof first and check the alignment of the house is correct by placing a pane of glass in position and adjusting the framework accordingly. Start at the bottom of the section and work upwards overlapping each pane by at least $\frac{1}{4}$ in (6 mm) so that rain water is shed effectively. Some wooden greenhouses are sold in six ready-glazed sections that only need bolting together. If you have to glaze the greenhouse yourself have the glass pre-cut to size as it can be quite difficult to master a glass cutting tool with accuracy.

Before you start the job, keep the putty at room temperature so that it becomes pliable and easy to work. Alternatives to putty are the non-hardening mastic compounds. Before you handle putty moisten your hands to prevent it from sticking and leaving you in a tacky mess. Apply the putty to the glazing bars with your thumb in a spreading action. Place the bottom pane of glass in first and secure it in position with glazing sprigs. Position the next pane, resting it in top of the sprigs. After each section is completed trim off excess putty both inside and outside.

4
EQUIPMENT

Ventilation

Oxygen is one of the most essential ingredients that plants need to live. They breathe it in, like us, and utilize it to manufacture their own food in a process called photosynthesis. In the greenhouse the air can soon become stuffy if ventilation is not adequate. Opening a window to allow in air is not enough to prevent a stagnant atmosphere, a complete air change is needed on a regular basis to keep plants happy and healthy. Under stress they can soon become candidates for pest and disease attack. The only time it is recommended to keep the ventilators closed down completely is during damp, foggy weather, when the moisture-laden air will encourage disease. On bright sunny days the temperature in the greenhouse will naturally soar, so unless plenty of ventilation is given the plants will have to absorb a great deal of hot air and in an effort to cool themselves down will lose essential water from their leaves in a process of evaporation called transpiration.

Left to suffer like this for a long period, the plants will eventually collapse and maybe die from exhaustion. Simple physics tells us that warm air naturally rises, so ridge ventilation is essential for heat to escape. The size of these ventilators however, is critical if they're to have any effect on cooling the temperature.

A greenhouse should be adequately fitted with ventilators. The area of glass that opens to give ventilation must equal at least one fifth to one sixth of the total floor space. For example, in a 10 × 8 ft (3 × 2.5 m) greenhouse with a ground area of 80 sq ft (7.7. sq m), one fifth equals 16 sq ft (1.5 sq m). Hence four 2 × 2 ft (60 × 60 cm) ridge ventilators would be adequate, providing they were capable of opening fully to that area. Many of the greenhouses on the market are fitted with too few ventilators as standard; if this is the case, install extra ones. Place the ventilators alternately on each side of the roof, so that those sited on the leeward side can be opened during windy weather without admitting cold draughts.

☼ Air is more effectively changed and circulated if side ventilators are included as well as ridge ones. This is because buoyant warm air flows up through the ridge whilst cool air drawn up through the side ventilators creating what is called a 'chimney effect' making air exchange quicker.

☘ The outside temperature is never constant and in a small greenhouse the slightest fluctuation outside can effect the environment drastically. The ventilators therefore need to be suitably adjusted to maintain a constant temperature whenever the occasion arises. This can pose a problem for busy gardeners who are not always on the spot to give them the necessary attention. In this case automatic ventilator openers are a great boon. Some are electrically operated, working on a thermostat which is housed separate to the ventilators and is sensitized by sunlight or heat, but most work by a built-in cylinder arm filled with mineral oil. As the temperature rises the oil expands, forcing back a piston, which pushes open the ventilator to which the unit is attached.

The temperature at which the ventilators open can be set to anything between 55°F (13°C) and 85°F (30°C). You should adjust the control knob so that they open and close five degrees higher or lower than the temperature required, so that they are not operating continually at the slighest fluctuation.

For an automatic ventilator arm to work efficiently, it must be strong enough to lift the weight of the ventilator. You ought to check how high the automatic arm is capable of lifting the ventilator; you may be losing inches of opening space and will therefore need extra ventilators installed.

A thermostatically controlled extractor fan can also be installed to help maintain a good growing environment. Humidity is kept low and a stuffy atmosphere is avoided because stale air is extracted at one end of the greenhouse whilst fresh is drawn in and across from the other end.

Low humidity is especially important during the winter because in cold temperatures excess moisture in the air leads to condensation and a higher risk of fungal diseases. A crack of ventilation must be applied all year round, and even at night during the winter when the greenhouse is being heated by paraffin or gas. Oxygen is needed for the fuels to burn properly and toxic fumes must escape otherwise plants will be damaged.

In a polythene tunnel it is difficult to ventilate properly. The best way is to put a mesh covered door at either end of the tunnel and rely on natural exchange.

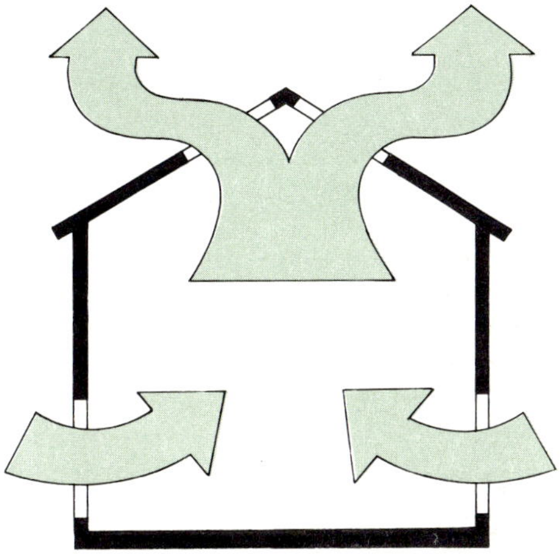

Side ventilators help air flow.

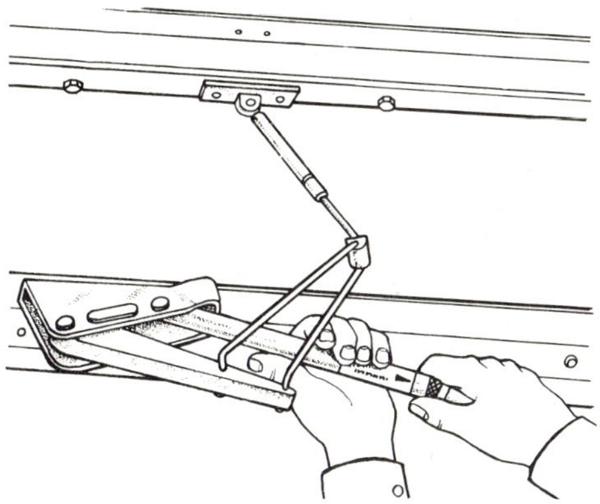

Adjusting an automatic ventilator opener.

Mesh-covered door for polythene tunnel.

Shading

Good light is essential for healthy plant growth, but during the summer months it can be too intense and the plants will soon become scorched and badly damaged. In summer, therefore, some sort of shading will be necessary and this will also help to prevent plants from drying out so quickly, saving your time watering, and it will stop the temperature from soaring. Once the sun's rays have penetrated the glass they are converted to heat and trapped inside, so an unshaded and badly ventilated greenhouse can soon become an oven where plants will shrivel within a day. Very often it is too high a temperature that causes crops to fail. Tomatoes especially suffer and if the temperature rises above 80°F (32°C) the red pigment fails to form properly so the fruit either remains yellow or ripens unevenly, a condition known as greenback. Another problem occurring where there's excessive sunlight is that water droplets lying on the foliage and fruit will act as minute lenses and focus the sun's rays, causing them to blister. During the early spring the sunlight will not be too intense to injure mature plants, but the delicate leaves of seedlings and soft stem cuttings can be bleached or scorched brown.

Covering them with paper on bright days will provide sufficient protection and can be quickly removed if the day turns out dull. As soon as the days lengthen and the weather becomes more reliably bright a permanent shading should be installed.

Paint

☼ The cheapest form of shading comes in the form of a paint that is applied to the outside of the glass. Specially formulated proprietary brands are your best bet and these are available in both green and white shades. Research has shown that the white paints work best as they reflect back a much greater range of light. One to recommend is Coolglass (pbi), which has electrostatic properties that make it cling to the glass even in the heaviest rainstorms, yet at the end of the season it can be easily wiped off with a dry duster. Most of the other proprietary brands need to be washed off and during wet weather may need re-applying several times. Every precaution should be taken when applying them to avoid glass breakage. To reach difficult parts use a sprayer with a lance and to wash it off in the autumn use a squeeze mop and soapy water.

Blinds

External blinds are the most satisfactory form of shading since they can be rolled up out of the way if the weather is dull. They can be fitted to both wood and aluminium houses, but must not be fixed over the ventilators as they will obstruct the air flow.

☘ The slatted type of roller blinds, with wooden or plastic laths, are best for they filter the sun's rays rather than block them out altogether. The blinds also deflect the heat before it actually enters the greenhouse so are very effective in keeping the temperature down. Plastic netting recommended for shading will similarly break up the direct rays of the sun and provide a dappled shade which plants enjoy. It is sold in rolls and fixing can be tricky. The best way is to fix one end at the top of the greenhouse and drape the rest to the ground securing it at regular intervals. Ordinary stretch curtain wires, fastened to hooks, which themselves are fixed to the frame, make ideal supports.

Internal blinds are not so effective in preventing the temperature from soaring, but they do have the advantage in that they stay clean and will not blow away. They can also be used in the winter to help minimize the heat loss at night.

These blinds are often sold as automatically controlled units, operated by a thermostat which is activated by sunlight or temperature and sets off the electric current to roll or unroll as necessary. Some of the modern insulating materials can be left in place all year round to protect plants from strong sunlight in the summer. These are ideal for when the summer season is very short as less valuable gardening time will be taken up installing insulation or shading materials.

A more attractive way to provide shade in the greenhouse would be to grow summer flowering climbers, such as sweet peas and runner beans, outside against the sunniest side of the house. Keep them about 18 in (45 cm) away from the glass so that they do not interfere with the ventilators. Train them up a wire mesh support and keep on top of pests and diseases as heavy infestations will spread to your greenhouse plants. This method is ideal for a small garden where the greenhouse is very much a feature. Inside the greenhouse you should position plants where they will be happiest. Sun loving plants placed near the glass will act as a canopy for those requiring more shade. For pot plants use a tiered staging, this way you will not only be able to display them to their best effect, but also sensitive plants can be put in the shade of the decking above.

Heating 1

If, during the winter, the temperature outside drops to about 20°F (−7°C), there is likely to be several degrees of frost inside the greenhouse. If you are trying to overwinter plants which are not frost hardy, such as geraniums and fuchsias, then you are sure to lose them unless you heat the structure.

The running costs are the most important consideration when choosing a heating system, although the cost of the equipment and installation will be a deciding factor. Before you set out to buy a heater you will need to know

☼ Applying shading paint.

☘ Slatted roller blind.

what size you require. Each heater has a different heat output, so you need to know that the one you choose is capable of raising the temperature of your house sufficiently, based on the lowest winter temperatures in your region.

You have to calculate the degrees of heat needed to *lift* the temperature to the required minimum. For example, if the outside temperature is 30°F (−1.1°C) inside, the heater needs to be capable of raising the temperature by at least 20°F (11°C). This figure should be adjusted to take into consideration the amount of heat lost through the surface of the glass. This is calculated by multiplying the surface area of the roof and walls by that which is lost through the superstructure. An average greenhouse loses 1.4 British Thermal Units (BTU's) through the superstructure. The total figure – temperature lift plus the heat loss – amounts to the BTU rating of the size of the heater that you require. Some heaters are sold with a kilowatt (kW) rating. The most popular sizes of heater are: 1.25 kW = 4262 BTU's; 2.2 kW = 8530 BTU's; 3 kW = 10,236 BTU's.

Heating by electricity

Electricity is a very efficient method of heating the greenhouse. The heaters are clean, can be controlled automatically by an independent thermostat, which switches on and off as required, and need little or no maintenance. The great disadvantage, though, is that installing electricity to the bottom of the garden can be very costly. This can be justified to some extent by the number of electrically operated gardening aids – propagators, watering and ventilation systems, that can subsequently be used.

Electrical installations should be made by a qualified electrician. The damp atmosphere in the greenhouse can make faulty wiring lethal. An isolated mains switch, preferably with a circuit breaker, should be fitted in the greenhouse. This will allow you to switch the electricity off independently of the house. The circuit breaker will do this automatically when there is excess current arising in the circuit from a faulty appliance and the electricity supply will not be renewed until this is corrected. Purpose-designed control panels and light fittings, which are sealed from moisture absorption, should be installed.

If electricity is being taken to the greenhouse by underground cable make sure that it is properly armoured and buried in a trench at least 18 in (45 cm) deep to prevent accidental damage when digging. Overhead cables must be properly tensioned and positioned well clear of tall hedges.

There are basically two types of electrical heating systems available: tubular pipes and fan heaters.

Tubular heaters are made from non-rusting aluminium and are usually rated at 60 watts per ft (30 cm). The tubes can be placed singly or in tiers about 1 ft (30 cm) above the soil level around the perimeter of the greenhouse. They are very efficient at distributing the heat evenly, but plants placed right next to them can become scorched.

Fan heaters can either be wall mounted or stood on the floor but, if they are positioned badly, cold spots will be found. The recommended position is on the floor about 1 ft (30 cm) from the end wall with the blower pointing slightly down so that it does not burn any plants close by. Some models work on a convector system where warm air sets up convection

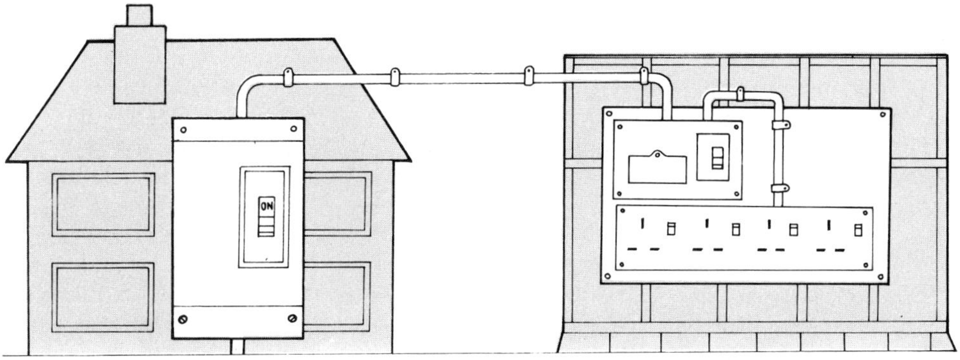

Installing electricity in the greenhouse is a job for the professional.

Underground cables must be properly armoured and buried.

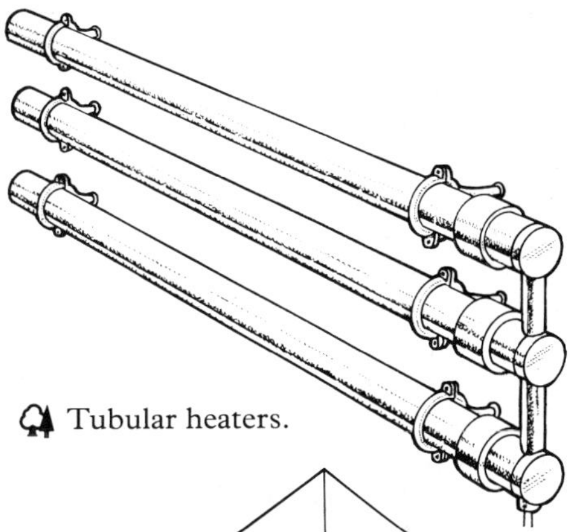

Tubular heaters.

currents and displaces cold air.

A dry heat is produced and this can be an advantage in winter, when a damp greenhouse will encourage fungal diseases. The fan keeps the air moving to maintain a buoyant atmosphere and can be run with or without the heating element, so can be used during the summer months to aid ventilation. A thermostat is built into the fan and accurately controls the temperature without wasting any heat. Fan heaters are useful for the cool greenhouse where frost protection is the aim.

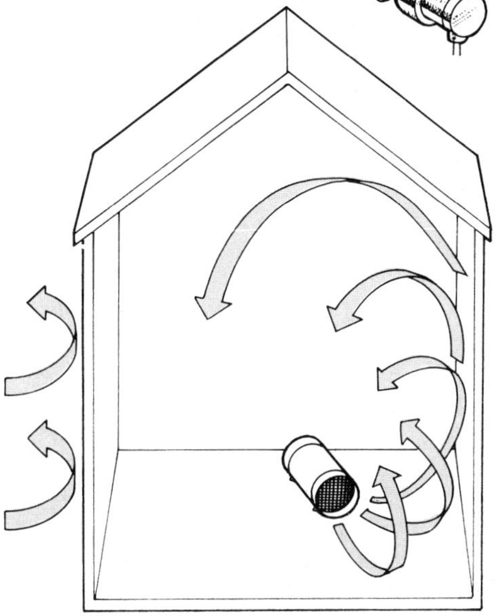

Fan heater.

Heating 2

It is not always possible to take electricity down the garden and in this case other fuels need to be considered for heating the greenhouse. At one time hot water pipes, fired with a solid fuel boiler, were widely used, but today now that smaller greenhouses are being heated, boilers are not well favoured as they are rather bulky and expensive to install and run.

☼ Boilers must have an outside flue discharge to get rid of the harmful fumes produced in the combustion process. In some cases the boiler needs to be positioned outside on the leeward side of the greenhouse. The water filled pipes are positioned along the walls on the inside of the greenhouse and take up valuable growing space. All boiler systems are fitted with a thermostat but because the pipes take a long time to cool, temperature control is not very accurate and overheating can become a serious problem.

Gas, both natural and propane (not butane) and paraffin are by far the most popular systems today.

Gas

Natural gas is a non-poisonous fuel and so an outside chimney is not necessary. It is the cheapest system to run, but installation is very expensive. All of the gas heaters available are fitted with a flame failure device as a safety precaution. This cuts off the gas supply if the pilot light is extinguished accidentally.

☘ The majority are also fitted with a built-in thermostat and are not very effective in maintaining the desired temperature evenly throughout the house. The better models of gas heaters have an independent thermostat that can be sited anywhere in the greenhouse. It is usually quite difficult to assess when a bottle of gas is near empty. The weight of the cylinder will give you an idea.

Continuous burning can be achieved with bottle gas by installing an automatic change-over valve. This comes into operation as soon as one bottle is empty.

Oxygen is required for the combustion process by gas and paraffin, so it is necessary to leave a ventilator slightly open when the heater is in use. Open ventilators will allow heat to escape, and as much as 5% extra heat loss must be added to your running-cost calculations. Burning gas and paraffin adds moisture and carbon dioxide to the air. This is beneficial to plants and can increase growth if heating is operative during the day, for they are used in the process of photosynthesis, which is how plants manufacture food in their leaves under the influence of sunlight.

At night these benefits are nil and the moist atmosphere can become more of a problem, creating condensation and 'damping off' if the temperature is cool. If insufficient air is provided the process of combustion will be incomplete and harmful fumes will ensue.

Paraffin

❃ The least sophisticated heater is the small paraffin burner. The larger stoves are of more value and if they can be fitted with extension pipes will distribute heat quite evenly through the house. The major fault with paraffin heaters is that very few are fitted with a thermostat, so controlling the temperature has to be achieved manually by regulating the flame.

It is essential too that you keep the wick clean, free from carbon, and trimmed with scissors to ensure even burning otherwise the heater will

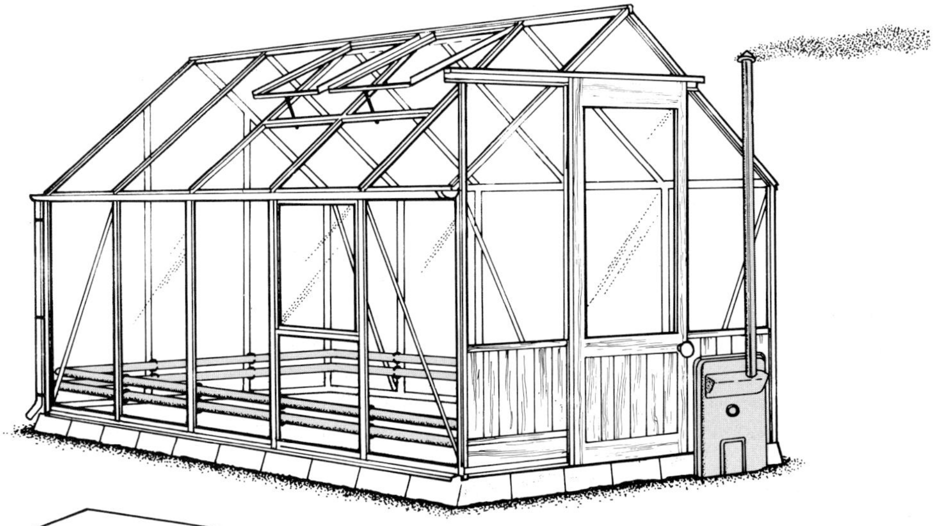

☼ Solid-fuel boiler.

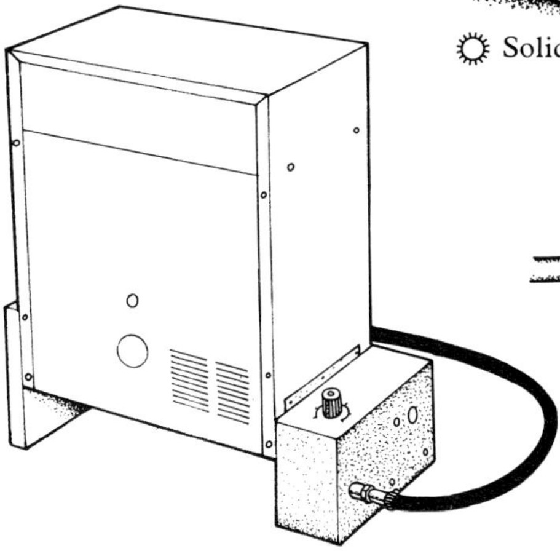

☘ A typical, modern gas heater.

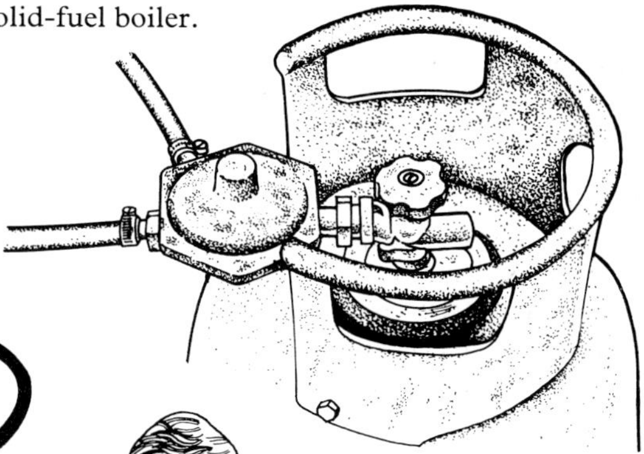

Automatic change-over valve for bottle gas.

smoke and leave your plants covered in a black oily soot. Only a high grade of paraffin should be used and it must never be allowed to burn dry otherwise the wick will smoke and the toxic fumes will kill your plants.

To save you having to check the paraffin level every night, you can connect most models of heater to a reserve tank with an automatic feed. Some paraffin heaters include a water tray for fume absorption, but because there will be plenty of moisture in the air from the combustion process filling it will lead to fungal diseases.

Paraffin heater connected to reserve tank.

Heat conservation

Conserving a warm, cosy environment is of utmost importance during the winter months when artificial heating is being used to keep your plants unharmed on frosty nights. If you do not take steps you will literally be throwing money out of the window, at least 250 BTU's per hour is lost through the glass – more than 50 pence worth of heat per night, depending on the fuel.

☼ First of all you should make sure that all the ventilators and door fit snugly. Then check that each pane of glass is in the right position, that none has slipped leaving gaps, and repair any broken panes.

More heat will be lost from a house that is glazed down to the ground, so if you are not using the area under the staging for growing, fix some insulation material to the inside of the glass. Ready made insulating panels, which just clip into place, are available. These will not fit all greenhouses so good alternatives are polystyrene ceiling tiles or hessian sacks filled with screwed up newspaper.

Double glazing

Above the bench fix a clear double-glazing material on to the inside of the glass. Do not fix it to the outside as it will become damaged and soiled by the weather. Leave a 1–2 in (2.5–5 cm) gap between the glass and material to ensure that a static layer of air is trapped between the two layers. Cover the ventilators separately so that they can be opened on sunny days and when gas or paraffin heaters are used. Double glazing will reduce light transmission, with some materials by as much as 20%, therefore it is essential to keep the glass perfectly clean so that maximum light can enter.

There are various materials that can be used for double glazing. Glass is the best because it admits most light, but it is not commonly used as it is expensive and difficult to fix. Polythene is most widely used material because it is cheap and easy to fix.

☘ In a wooden greenhouse polythene can be held in place with staples or drawing pins. About a 40% saving of the heat lost through the glass can be achieved with thin polythene, but light levels can be reduced by as much as 15% and more when the effect of light on the polythene causes it to discolour and turn brittle. With careful installation ordinary polythene can be used for about three seasons.

A better quality insulating polythene has a double skin and air bubbles trapped between the two layers. It is in effect triple glazing. Manufacturers claim that up to 60% of heat will be saved, so fuel costs will be lower. This material is more expensive than ordinary polythene but is more durable and does not deteriorate quite so quickly with the effect of sunlight. Special clips are needed to fix insulating materials in aluminium greenhouses. These fit into the glazing channels and should hold the material away from the glass.

Overlapping the material is essential to create a *sealed unit*. If air can move between the two layers the insulating effect is reduced. There are a number of rigid plastics that can also be used. They are second to glass for light transmission and a heat saving of more than 60% can be achieved. They are very expensive but will last 15–20 years if used for 12 months of the year, so I am sure that you can at least double their life-span if they are only used during the winter months.

♧ Partitioning the greenhouse and

heating only the area filled with tender plants must provide the biggest saving of all. In some greenhouses a permanent partition can be fixed after erection and this would be useful if you prefer to grow a number of plants that have completely different requirements all year round, such as orchids and cacti. Temporary partitions can be installed by fixing up a curtain of insulating material; bubbled polythene or rigid plastic would be best.

In the early spring when light becomes crucial for propagation, the double glazing should be taken off the sides of the greenhouse, so that the sun, whilst still at a low angle can enter unimpeded. You can leave the material on the roof to trap warm air as it rises. If it is the spring before you usually start to grow anything in the greenhouse it would be worth considering installing a thermal screen. For the last ten years commercial growers have been using them and have made substantial savings in fuel costs as well as heat loss.

The screen fits across the plants at gutter level and is only drawn over the plants at night to act as a blanket, which traps warm air. The screen needs to be made from an open weave insulating material to allow excess moisture to escape, for if the plants are in full growth, high humidity levels will be found below the screen.

During the day the seedlings and cuttings will receive the maximum available light for growth, but you can also make use of this light to retain heat. During the day long-wave radiation is trapped and held in store by the pots, trays, compost, plants, floor etc. then released at night. By filling the greenhouse with more things to trap the heat you will use less fuel at night to keep the temperature above freezing.

☼ Draught-proofing the door.

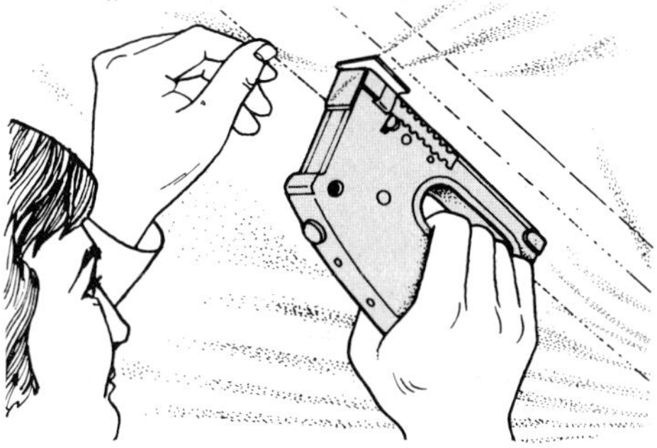

♣ Stapling polythene to framework.

♠ Partitioning the house saves fuel bills.

Watering

Watering is the most skilful job you have to tackle in the greenhouse. In the summer months plants growing in pots, trays and growing bags will be almost drying out as fast as you can water them. During the winter on the other hand, the same plants will die if they are so much as shown the watering can more than once a week. The first thing you must learn therefore, is how to recognize when a plant needs water. A plant which is in a happy state has plump, dark green healthy leaves and shows signs of new growth. If the same plant was left to suffer from lack of water the leaves would become dull and floppy and the new growth may shrivel. Left sitting in the heat of the mid-day sun in this state the plant would eventually collapse completely and probably die.

Similar symptoms occur when a plant has been overwatered. If this is the case the compost will be saturated, maybe under a dry crusty surface layer, and smell 'earthy' due to the decaying roots. You should never let your plants reach either stage.

The mechanics of finding out when a plant needs watering are relatively simple. If the soil looks and feels dry, is light in colour and the pot feels very light when weighed in the hand, the plant is ready for watering. If the compost is *just moist* and sticks together nicely when pinched between your finger and thumb, or dampens a piece of newspaper if pressed onto the surface, leave the plant alone.

If water can actually be squeezed from the compost then you are on the verge of overwatering and the plants should be allowed to dry out before they are next watered. If you are looking for a second opinion on your judgement and are growing in clay pots you can use the old fashioned pot-tapping method to see if your plants need a drink.

Using a cork fixed to a cane, tap each pot and listen. If the pot is dry it will give out a ringing sound and when moist a dull thud.

A more up-to-date method is the moisture meter. This will work in both plastic or clay pots and any soil type. It consists of an electronic probe, operated by a battery, and indicates with a meter reading the state of the soil and whether it needs watering.

A mains supply of water connected at the greenhouse would be ideal and necessary if you want to install a sophisticated mist propagating unit or an automatic trickle irrigation system. If laying mains water on at the greenhouse is out of the question, then collecting rain water may be preferable to a long hose. Guttering will need to be fixed to the greenhouse eaves with a down pipe leading into a water butt. To prevent the rain water from becoming polluted during storage a lid should be fitted to the butt.

Most plants will benefit from watering with rainwater and especially lime haters, such as azaleas and primulas, as it is slightly acid, termed *soft*. Many gardeners prefer to water plants with 'aired' water; they reckon cold water straight from the tap gives them a check. To keep tanks of water in good condition add some potassium permanganate (enough to make the water colour pink), this will help prevent water borne diseases.

In the greenhouse a watering can is is an essential. You will need one, even if you water with a hose, to feed plants or apply insecticides. Look out for a good quality can with a long reach spout.

Are your plants thirsty? Testing (*a*) the old-fashioned way . . .

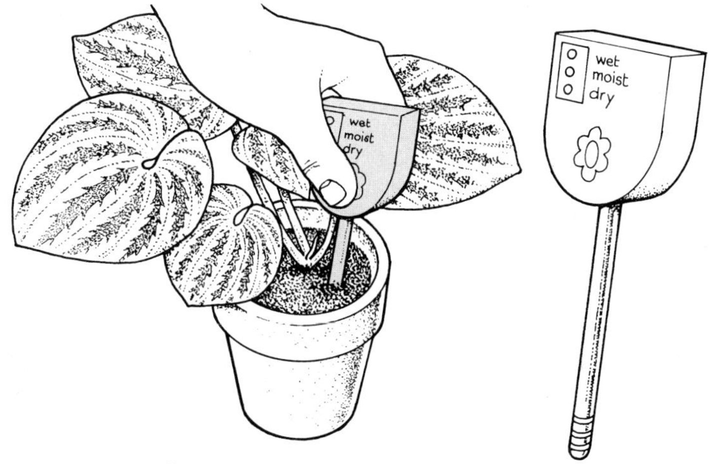

. . . and (*b*) by moisture meter.

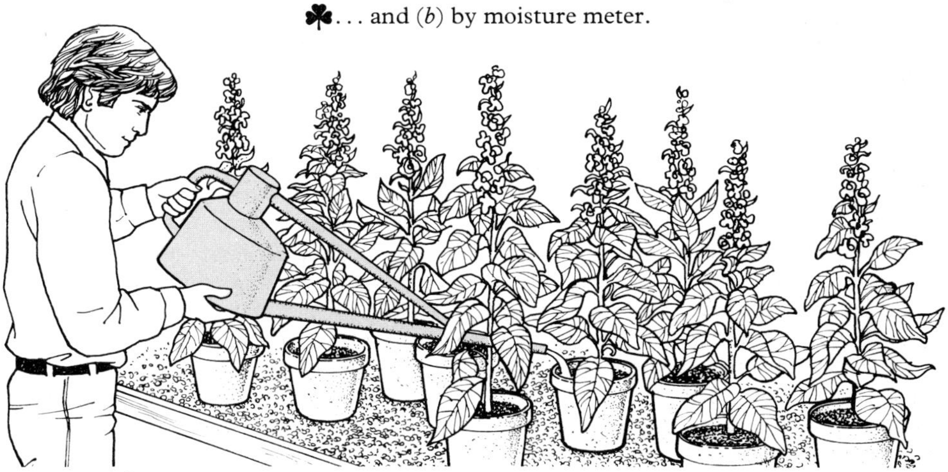

A watering can with a long reach is a must for the greenhouse.

Automatic watering

If you are out at work all day or have your greenhouse on an allotment some distance from the house, coping with the plants' watering needs, especially during the summer, can be rather difficult. Automatic watering can solve this problem, and not only from the practical side; plants too will benefit for they can be kept continually *just moist*. Erratic watering can cause many problems – flower buds dropping from your pot plants, and both cracked fruit and blossom end rot on tomatoes, to name but a few. There are many automatic watering systems to choose from and all offer different advantages.

☼ The most popular type is based on capillary attraction. Trays of sand or a sheet of moist fibre matting are kept moist by a water supply from a header tank or from a bowl of water. No electricity is needed. The staging must be kept perfectly level. Solid staging is needed for matting and it should be lined with polythene. Plastic pots with plenty of drainage holes are more effective than clay types which dry out too easily from the sides. Water is drawn up by the compost as required, provided the compost is watered in when the pots are first placed on the bench.

The disadvantages of using sand are that it is very heavy (the trays, filled with a 2–3 in (5–7.5 cm) layer), it can clog the pots' drainage holes and, when covered with algae, needs sifting, washing and eventually replacing. Matting on the other hand is lightweight, can be cut to fit the shape of the bench, and is quite cheap. Algae can be a problem and will shorten the life of the matting. White coloured matting is affected more than the brown type but it can be sprayed with an algicide to reduce the problem.

Clay granules, the sorts used by houseplant growers in hydroponics, are a good alternative to sand and matting. They are relatively lightweight, will last a life time and hold up to 10 times their own volume with water.

Drip nozzles

♣ Other methods of automatic watering involve systems of small bore tubes connected to a header tank or the end of a hose pipe. This system is very flexible and can be installed and re-adjusted to suit your plant spacing. Each tube, sometimes called spaghetti line, is placed in the compost of an individual pot or growing bag and fixed with a clip. Water runs through the tubes and is released in a steady slow trickle from drip nozzles, which are completely adjustable to suit your plant needs. Any unwanted nozzles can be turned off completely. This is a superb system for general growing where a number of plants with different requirements are being grown. The system can be fully automated if linked to a water supply by a solenoid valve and time clock. An electronic water controller is the best type to install for it turns the water on or off according to the weather conditions.

A supplementary watering system consists of overhead **spray lines** which provide a fine mist to all plants in line of fire and is ideal for damping down to raise the humidity in the summer. Plants like tomatoes and cucumbers will benefit most from this treatment as it assists fruit setting. Make sure that the plants are well shaded if you are spraying the foliage because drops of water will act as lenses in the bright sun and cause the leaves to scorch.

Automatic watering systems are best used during the growing season only.

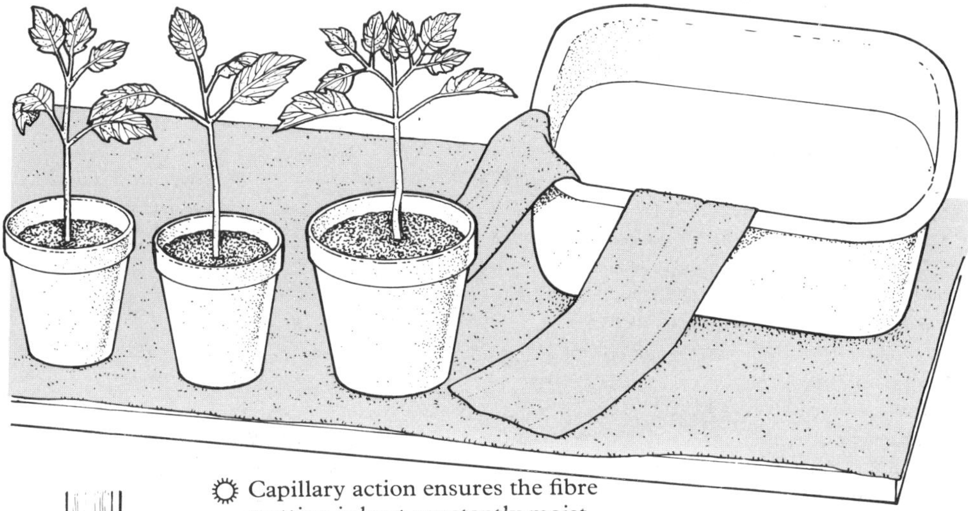

☼ Capillary action ensures the fibre matting is kept constantly moist.

☘ Automatic watering activated by a drip-control valve.

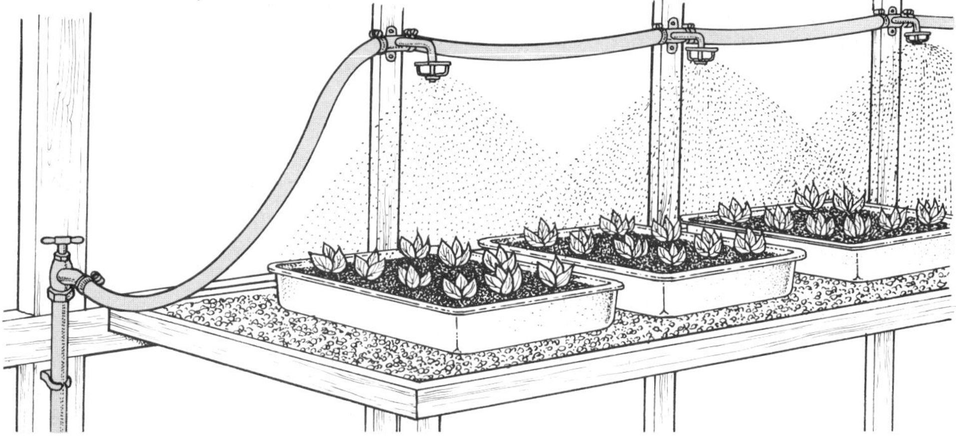

Overhead spray lines provide a fine mist.

Lighting
In the winter months when daylight is poor, or in a shady greenhouse, better conditions for growth can be achieved by installing some form of artificial lighting. Light is essential for plants to produce the food necessary for growth. A spectrum of light is split into a rainbow of colours: violet; indigo; blue; green; yellow; orange and red and each has a different effect on plants. The blue and violet range promote foliage growth, whereas the red spectrum of light encourages flowers. It is a combination, however, of the blue and red light that is necessary for photosynthesis, the process by which plant leaves manufacture their own food. Both are absorbed by the chlorophyll (green pigment in the leaf), to break down carbon dioxide into sugars. The green light is reflected back. In good light therefore, growth is strong, but on dull days it almost stops. Seedlings sown in late winter and early spring and raised under lights will produce sturdy, well-developed plants quickly.

Supplementary lighting is useful too, for encouraging many plants to flower at the *wrong* time. Chrysanthemums, for example, will only initiate their flower buds when the days are short during the winter months. If they receive more than 12 hours of daylight they will not flower but continue to grow. By blacking out the natural daylight in the summer months, to lengthen the nights, and supplementing daylight in the winter to raise new plants by a strict time table, they can be grown to flower all year round. There are 'long day' plants too, and these will only naturally flower in the summer, so additional lighting will need to be given in the winter to extend their season. Some plants are 'day-neutral', whereby light has no effect on flowering; hence if they are sown at regular intervals throughout the year, a continuous show of flowers can be had for twelve months. Ordinary tungsten filament lamps (domestic light bulbs) are not much use for promoting growth, they are low in the blue and violet areas and too high in the yellow, orange and red zones. They can be used, however, for increasing the day length.

Artificial lighting
☼ Two 100 watt bulbs at 6 ft (1.8 m) apart and 18 in (45 cm) above the plants will be enough to illuminate plants on a 3 ft (90 cm) wide bench down one side of a 8 × 12 ft (2.4 × 3.6 m) greenhouse. Connect the lighting to a time switch to provide at least 12 hours and no more than 15 hours of daylight. Fluorescent tubes have more benefits to plant growth – they are much richer in foliage-producing blue rays and do not distribute as much heat so there is less risk of plants becoming scorched. Ordinary daylight or cool white tubes can be used, but special growers' tubes, which are rich in both growth- and flower-promoting colours, are available and give best results.

♣ A single 5 ft (1.5 m) warm white fluorescent 80 watt tube positioned 2 ft (60 cm) above the plants will illuminate an area (4 ft 6 in × 1 ft (1.35 × 30 cm). Three tubes mounted 8 in (20 cm) apart will illuminate a bench 4 ft 6 in × 3 ft (1.35 × 90 cm).

Fluorescent tubes can also be fixed under the staging to utilize the maximum growing space. The bench should be a minimum of 2 ft 6 in (75 cm) high to allow sufficient headroom. Make sure that electrical fittings are completely safe and protected from water dripping onto them.

☼ Artificial lighting by (*a*) two 100-watt bulbs or . . .

♣ . . . (*b*) a single 5 ft (1.5 m) fluorescent 80-watt tube.

Recording equipment

To maintain ideal growing conditions in the greenhouse you will have to monitor what is happening to the environment throughout the day and make the necessary adjustments to the temperature and humidity levels.

A **thermometer** is an indispensable piece of equipment. A maximum-minimum type is preferable as this will indicate the highest and lowest temperatures that have been reached in the time since you last looked. From this reading you will be able to check that automatic ventilators are working efficiently and that your heating system is adequate. After each reading the thermometer should be reset, a magnet is usually used to pull the indicator back down to the mercury level, although the more expensive models have a push button readjustment. To make sure your thermometer is giving you the true picture it should be placed in a central position in the greenhouse out of direct sunlight and protected from draughts.

If you are growing in the border soil it would be useful to have a soil thermometer to check when conditions are right for sowing and planting. At a depth of 8 in (20 cm), if temperatures fall below 42°F (5.5°C), most plants cease to grow.

If you only intend to heat the greenhouse to keep the frost out, a frost forecast thermometer will be of use. This same piece of equipment, a dry and wet bulb **hygrometer,** is used for measuring the relative humidity.

The instrument consists of two similar thermometers: one, the dry bulb, gives the air temperature, whereas the other, the wet bulb, indicates the evaporation rate. The wet bulb is covered with a sleeve of muslin which is kept moist in a tube of water. If the air is dryish the wet bulb will always read less than the dry bulb. The drier the air and the lower the temperature the greater the risk of frost. (Battery operated temperature sensors, which sound a warning bell when the temperature drops below 39°F (4°C) are an alternative frost detector.)

In the winter the relative humidity (amount of water vapour in the air) should not exceed 35% otherwise disease will prevail. In the summer most plants benefit from a moist atmosphere with a relative humidity (RH) of 70–85%. Humidistats, which indicate the moisture level in percentage terms, are available.

To raise the humidity of the air and create a buoyant atmosphere in the greenhouse you can damp down the walls, floor and staging and leave an open tank of water in a sunny position to evaporate into the air. Automatic humidifiers, which usually consist of a fan blowing out a mist of water activated by air moisture, are a great boon where tropical plants are being grown. Most automatic equipment, ventilators, propagators and heaters are only as good as the thermostat controlling them. These are sensitive to temperature change and can be set to the temperature required.

Built in rod thermostats are alright for propagators but where the whole greenhouse air space is to be heated or ventilated an independent thermostat is more effective.

They are best positioned in a central part of the greenhouse at about plant level and should be shaded from direct sun and kept clear of draughts.

Other pieces of equipment that you might find of use in plant management are moisture and light meters.

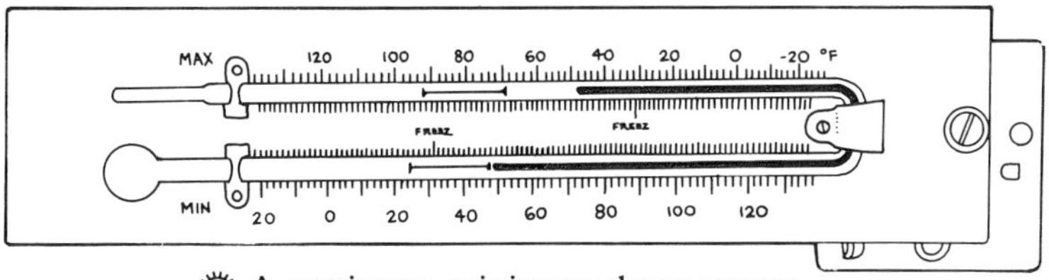

A maximum-minimum thermometer.

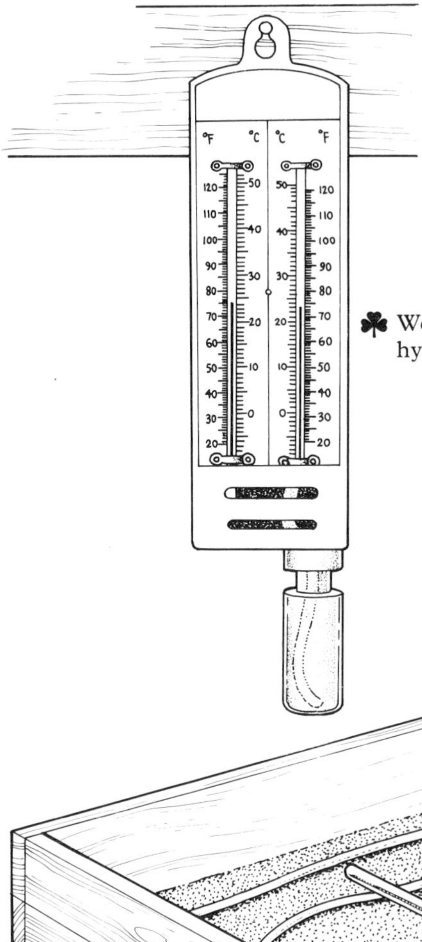

Wet-and-dry bulb hygrometer.

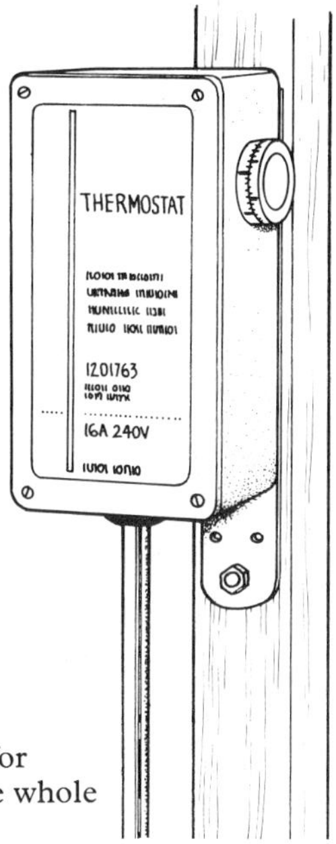

A thermostat for monitoring the whole greenhouse.

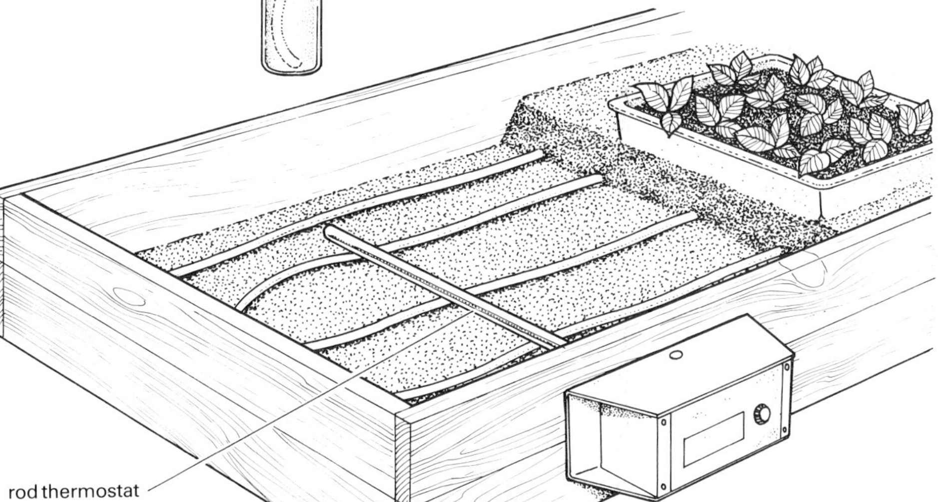

Rod thermostat in propagating tray.

Propagators

There is little point in having a greenhouse and not raising some of your own plants from seed and cuttings. You may think that it is only plants from hot countries that need the protection of glass to encourage germination, and that everything but the soft stem cuttings of perennials and shrubs can be rooted in the garden. This isn't true, for nearly all our favourite bedding plants, as well as many vegetables, have to be started in the warmth if they are to be ready for planting outside to flower or mature before the first frost in the autumn. In some places the frost-free growing season lasts only 12–15 weeks.

Both seeds and cuttings require a warm, moist environment to germinate or root. In the summer months seeds and cuttings will grow quite happily without artificial heat, provided you keep the air around them moist. If the atmosphere is dry, tender seedlings will dehydrate, and cuttings will lose so much water from their leaves that they will collapse and shrivel. Maintaining a moist atmosphere around the plants can be effected simply by covering the pot with a polythene bag. The bag should not touch the leaves and can be supported with a wire or cane framework.

Some pots and trays can be fitted with plastic domes and the better ones have ventilators so that you can release excess condensation, to prevent 'damping off' disease, and gradually harden the plants off until they can be stood, uncovered, on the greenhouse bench. During the late winter and early spring when the bulk of the seed sowing is done, you will have to turn on the heating to raise the temperature sufficiently for germination. This can be quite costly and not very economical if you are only raising a few trays of bedding plants. It would be cheaper to buy them from the garden centre.

Instead you would be better off investing in a heated propagating unit, preferably one fitted with a lid. These are usually electrically powered and consist of a heated base, which is thermostatically controlled within a range of 55–80°F (13–27°C), and are fitted with a glass or plastic dome-shaped lid.

If there is no electricity in your greenhouse, but you still need a propagator, there are a couple of paraffin models you can try. If you intend to propagate only a handful of plants the paraffin heater, which is purpose built with a shelf above the stove, to take a couple of seed trays, will be ideal. It is usually thermostatically controlled and has the advantage of heating the greenhouse at the same time. The fuel tank is small though, and will need re-filling quite often.

Larger paraffin-fired propagators are fitted with soil-warming tubes. A heat exchange unit is connected to the chimney of a large paraffin heater and from this a series of plastic pipes are fixed. The pipes are set out 4 in (10 cm) apart on a level bench and are filled with water from a reservoir tank at the other end of the run. The water in the tubes is in turn warmed-up by the heat rising up the chimney from the stove. A reliable thermostat is built in. The pipes are covered with about 4 in (10 cm) of sand or peat/sand compost if you want to root direct.

This system is completely adaptable to virtually any shape and size of bench. The heater whilst in use as a propagator will offer good frost protection for the rest of the plants being grown.

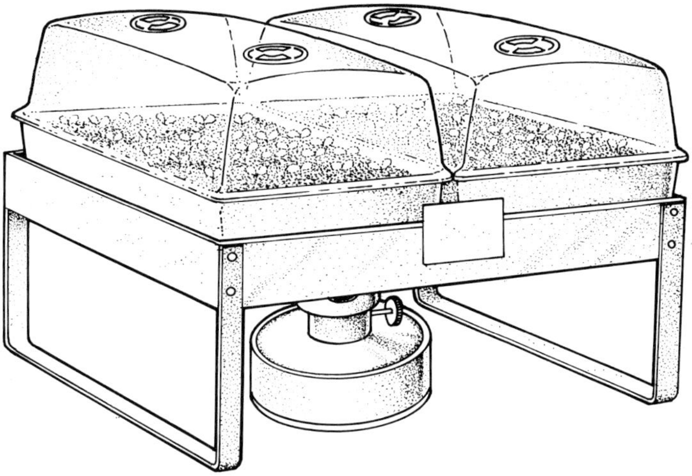

Two seed-tray propagators heated by paraffin burner.

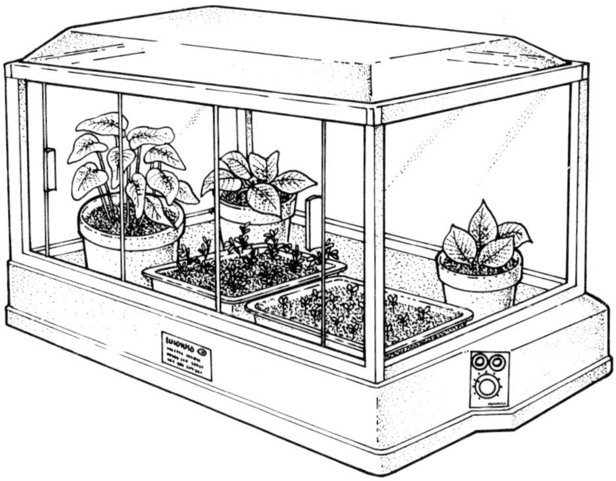

A more sophisticated unit with a thermostatically-controlled heated base.

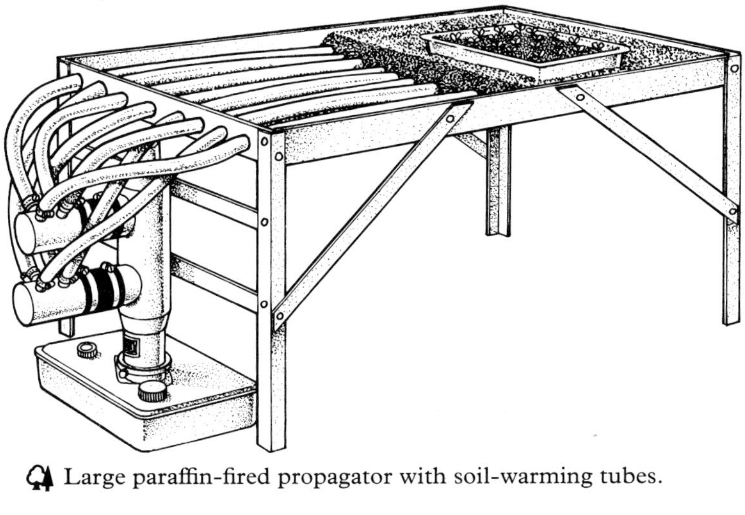

Large paraffin-fired propagator with soil-warming tubes.

Heated bench and mist units

It is much cheaper to make your own heated propagating unit and it can be constructed to any size to cope with any number of plants you want to raise at home. If the unit is to be situated on the staging make sure that the latter is sturdy enough to take the weight.

To start with you will need to make a wooden frame about 8–10 in (20–25 cm) deep. If preserving soft timber treat it with a non-toxic paint (creosote will not do, the fumes will kill off the plants). If you are not intending to heat the rest of the greenhouse during the winter, you could make the frame deeper and fasten a couple of rows of soil warming cable around the sides. Place them near to the top of the frame, to warm the air around the plant leaves, then you will probably be able to overwinter a few tender pot plants on the heated bench.

[1] Lay in the bottom of the frame about 1 in (2.5 cm) of gravel for drainage and top this with a 1 in (2.5 cm) layer of washed sharp sand.

[2] Place the soil warming cables

[1] Firming a layer of sharp sand.

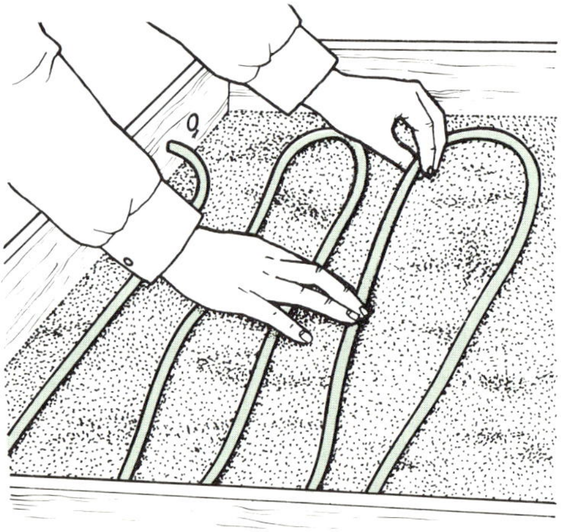

[2] Laying the cables on the sand.

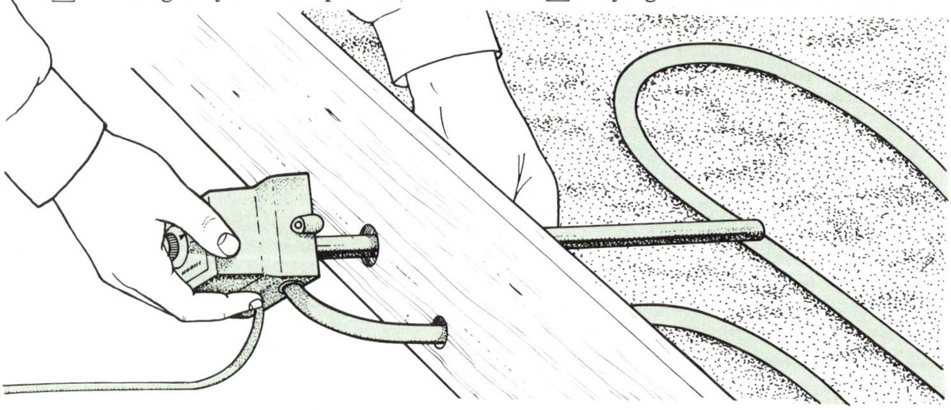

[3] Installing the rod thermostat.

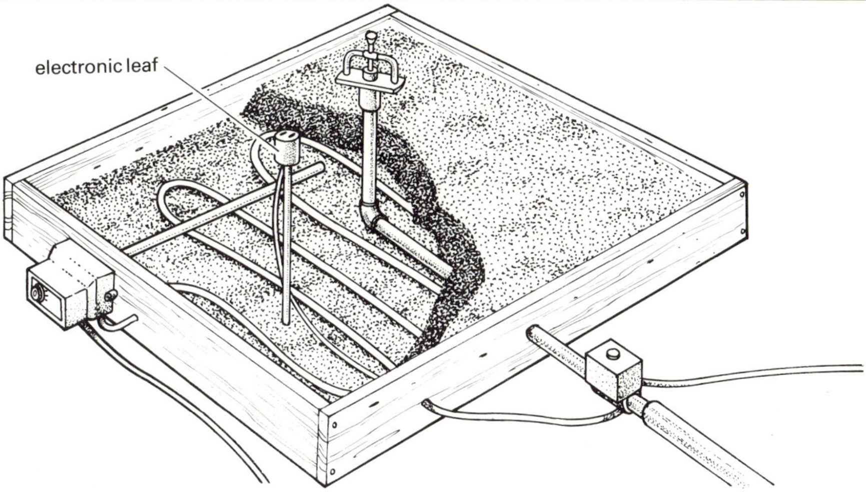

☼ An automatic mist unit, activated by an electronic 'leaf'.

(with a loading of 15 watts per sq ft) in a zig-zag fashion up and down the length of the frame. Make the loops about 4 in (10 cm) apart. The spaces between the cable should be of equal width, for even distribution of heat, and the cable must not be allowed to cross at any point.

[3] Install a rod thermostat about 4–5 in (10–12.5 cm) from the top of the frame so that it will adjust the temperature accordingly in the area nearest the base of the cuttings.

Cover the cable with a 2 in (5 cm) layer of sand and top with a 4–5 in (10–12.5 cm) layer of peat/sand compost so that you can root direct. You could make a tunnel type of lid for the unit, clear polythene draped over wire hoops, or better still install a mist jet.

Misting the cuttings and seedlings regularly with water is beneficial, providing a high humidity around the leaves to prevent them from drying out. Light, which is so important for growth, is not reduced and plenty of air can get to the plants. Under these conditions they usually develop faster than in ordinary closed propagators. Plants such as rhododendrons which are difficult to root, are often more successfully propagated under mist. Mist systems are available in kit form to fix to your existing heated bench and usually suit a 3 ft (90 cm) wide bench.

Mist units

☼ More sophisticated mist units operate by an artificial 'leaf' (an electronic device) which sits among the seeds and cuttings at about the same height. When the surface of the 'leaf' dries out the water is switched on automatically. Other systems work by a time switch, giving a spray, say, every 10–15 minutes, this can be a disadvantage in dull weather, unless the time switch is solar activated – triggered by sunlight.

Misting does not promote disease as you might expect, but actually prevents some, such as powdery mildew. It can however, by constant *watering* cause the nutrients to leach out of the compost, so it may be necessary, if the foliage turns pale, to give them a dilute foliar feed. Algal growth can also be a problem, but this can be easily controlled with one of the proprietary algicides.

Staging and shelves

Some staging will be necessary in the greenhouse if you are going to be growing plants in pots and propagating from seeds and cuttings.

☼ Ideally it should be designed to suit your needs, taking into consideration your height and reach. Most staging is manufactured to a standard height: 2 ft 6 in (75 cm) and in two widths: 2 or 3 ft (60 or 90 cm). More important, to some degree, is that the staging must be suitable for the growing techniques you want to adopt and the nature of the plants concerned.

☘ If you want to provide an attractive display area for flowering pot plants, tiered staging is the best. Place this on the side of the greenhouse where it will cast the least shade on other plants. Staging which is made up of several decks has the advantage of allowing you to grow plants with different light requirements effectively, thus cutting down the need to shade. Using supplementary lighting, the lower decks can be utilized for propagation, to provide you with more valuable growing space. Pots and trays can be neatly stacked there too, so the overall appearance of the greenhouse will be improved.

Before you buy any staging you should look into what is recommended for the watering system you intend to use. Capillary matting, for example, needs to be used on solid staging. If you prefer to use sand instead of matting, the staging will need to be extra strong and made up of a series of trays. During the winter months, an open mesh staging would be more beneficial, allowing fresh air and heat to circulate freely,

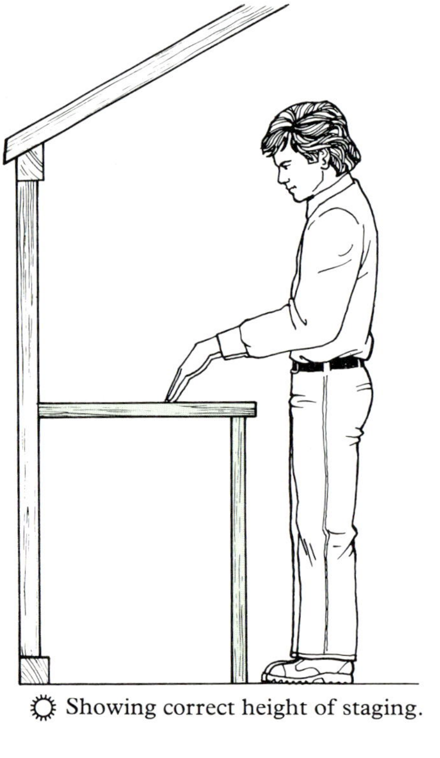

☼ Showing correct height of staging.

☘ Tiered staging for displaying pot plants.

Fold-down staging (*left*) offers flexibility in use of space.

and excess water to drain away. The length of time the staging will be in use each year is another point to think about. Some staging needs to be built in as a permanent fixture, whereas other units are mobile.

Fold-down staging has become very popular as it can be quickly taken down to allow space for tomatoes and chrysanthemums. If the staging is easily mobile but has to be stored elsewhere make sure that room is available in a dry building.

The materials from which the staging is made usually determine its cost and durability. Aluminium is widely used; it is quite expensive but maintenance free and will last a life time. It can be fabricated into almost any design and although it is lightweight it is still very strong. Most fold-down staging designs can be easily dismantled and stored.

Wood, although better at retaining heat, has to be regularly treated against rot and needs scrubbing regularly to prevent it from harbouring pests and diseases.

DIY staging can be easily made from wood. Trestle legs with a non-fixed slatted decking is the best design and can be stored without taking up too much space.

Shelves can be a great asset where space is limited. They can either be fixed to the walls, suspended from the roof or both, depending on the design of the greenhouse. Adequate brackets should be used to support the weight of the shelf when it is laden with pots and trays. For aluminium greenhouses special brackets are available which slot into the glazing channels.

Pots and trays

For raising your own plants from seeds and cuttings and when growing plants for display in the greenhouse containers are essential. The amount of money you will need to spend on them will depend on the type of plants you are growing. In other words, you will not need to buy expensive durable pots for plants which are to be planted outside within a couple of months of sowing, for these plastic cups will probably do, provided you make adequate drainage holes. Slow-growing plants will need to be grown in something stronger, in clay or rigid plastic pots that will not deteriorate after years of use.

Clay pots come in a tremendous size range, thumb pots, half pots and pans plus gigantic pots 30 in (75 cm) across and more. They are expensive to buy, however, so have lost some popularity to plastic, now also available in similar sizes, but for plants that prefer sharp drainage clay pots are still preferred. They are better draining than plastic pots as their porous nature allows the water to escape through the sides as well as the hole in the bottom.

Plastic pots must have plenty of drainage holes otherwise overwatering can be a problem. Plastic pots are more effective than clay for capillary water systems, as an even moisture in the pot can be easily maintained. They can be cleaned easier too, all you need is a cloth and some warm soapy water; no scrubbing is necessary. The strength and durability of plastic depends entirely on the polymer used in manufacture and the thickness of the pot.

Thin plastic vacuum-formed pots and trays are now becoming very popular. They are inexpensive and ideal for temporary use but they are not very strong.

The pots in this range are usually square-shaped, and can be supplied with a carrying tray. This makes them a great space-saver, for they can be packed pot thick on the bench without leaving any unusable gaps.

Black polythene bag pots are useful temporary pots, especially for plants which take several months to develop. They are quite durable but difficult to clean and so not re-usable. They are best removed from the plant by slicing with a knife. If you try to pull them off you may damage the rootball.

Black bitumen pots, made from vegetable matter bound together with bitumen, are superb for raising bedding plants and vegetables. This is because the entire pot can be planted out, so that root disturbance is nil. The roots grow through the pot walls and the pot eventually decays. Similar pots are made from peat and some are impregnated with fertilizers. Peat pots must be soaked before planting out – if they are dry the rootball will not be able to absorb moisture from the surrounding soil.

Popular for propagation are compressed peat pots. They expand when saturated with water and have a ready-made planting hole which is ideal for direct sowing and cuttings. Expanded polystyrene is being used more and more in horticulture; the insulating properties mean that minimum temperatures can be maintained without hindering growth.

Polystyrene compartmentalized trays are useful for space sowing large seeds and cuttings. The large drainage hole in the bottom of each cell allows the plants to be pushed out of the tray simultaneously, with the rootballs intact, by means of a pegged key plate.

Pots and trays

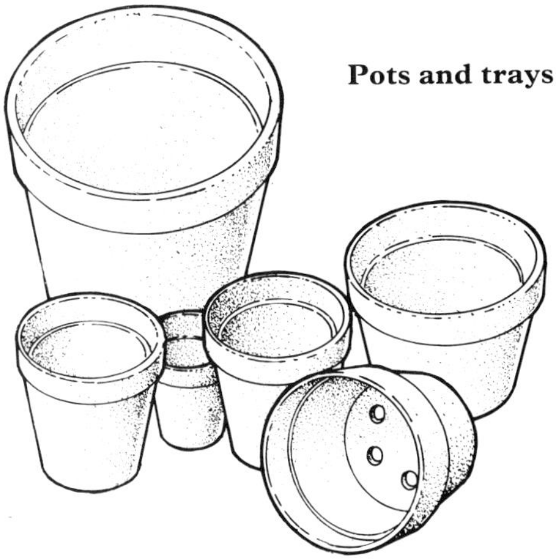

A selection of plastic pots.

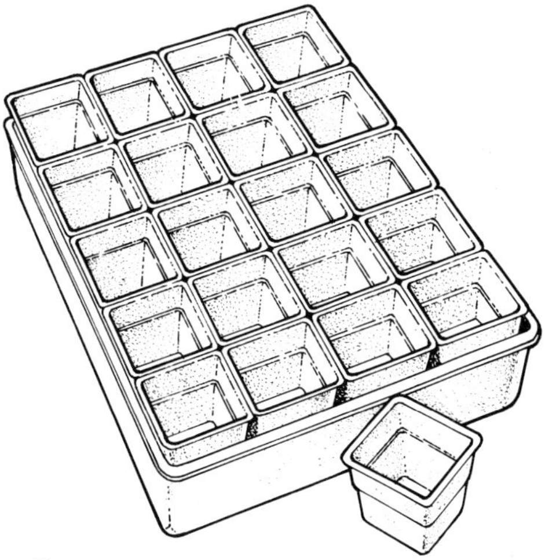

Square-shaped pots eliminate space wastage between pots.

Polythene bag pots.

Bitumen pots.

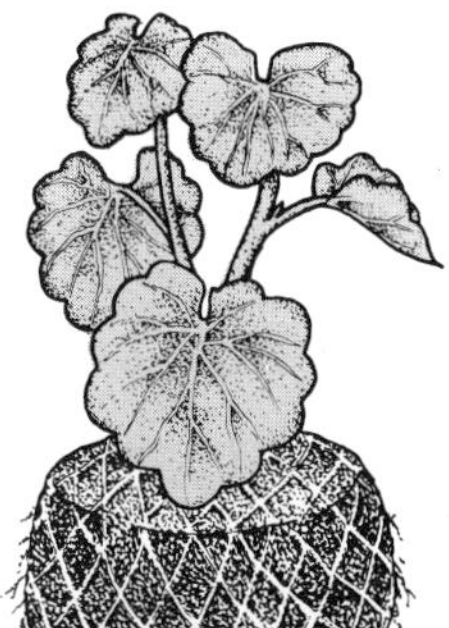

Compressed peat pot.

Polystyrene compartmentalized tray.

5
YEAR ROUND GREENHOUSE USE

Cold greenhouse: flowers/food
What you can grow in your greenhouse depends entirely on the temperature maintained, and although it is quite true to say that the warmer the greenhouse is, the greater the choice of plants that can be grown, it is not sensible to believe that there is nothing worthwhile that can be grown in a cold, unheated greenhouse during the winter. The high cost of fuel has meant most gardeners are unprepared to heat their greenhouse from the first frost in autumn until the last in late spring, especially if it is just used to overwinter a few geraniums and fuchsias. In this case it is cheaper to throw them out and start afresh each year. You have to keep the greenhouse full to justify such a large expense and maybe by late winter or early spring it will be worth considering turning on the heater to raise all your bedding and vegetable plants. A temperature of about 60°F (15°C) will have to be provided for about eight weeks until the plants are ready for going outside. You have to plan ahead for the remaining months of cold weather, when the plants in the greenhouse will be vulnerable to frost, so a list of possible hardy plants should be drawn up when you make your annual seed order. Make sure that any tender plants you sow in the spring are summer flowering or fruiting annuals to avoid filling the house with 'risk' plants. It can be both expensive and heart breaking to have to throw away quantities of good quality plants.

To give a colourful display during the drabbest months you can force winter and spring flowering shrubs and herbaceous perennials. Select some of the more choice shrubs such as azaleas, camellias and daphne plus showy perennials like *Incarvillea delavayi*, *Dicentra spectabilis*, *Helleborus niger* and *Bergenia*.

[1] Container-grown plants can be bought, but if you are lifting plants from the garden do so in the autumn when growth has slowed down. Use a lime-free compost for rhododendrons and other plants that prefer an acid soil and pot them into a container that will just comfortably take the roots. Bring the plants into the greenhouse, in batches to stagger flowering, and stand them in a well-lit position. Give them plenty of ventilation and keep them moist.

[2] After flowering move the plants to a sheltered part of the garden. Plunge the pots to their rims and do not allow them to dry out. During the summer apply a liquid feed once a week until growth ceases. In the autumn top dress with compost – remove the top 1–2 in (2.5–5 cm) and replace with fresh. Most plants can be forced gently each year, but for best results bring them into the greenhouse every other year.

Hardy annuals and biennials make wonderful pot plants too. Some of the most popular ones are: bellis, calendula, myosotis, polyanthus and auricula. The annuals are sown in late summer at fortnightly intervals to give a continual show of flowers from mid-winter until spring. Biennials, such as myosotis and bellis are sown in spring to flower from autumn onwards.

☼ When the seedlings are large enough to handle they are pricked out into trays. Myosotis and calendulas especially are best planted three to a 5 in (12.5 cm) pot. They are grown cool and during the summer can be put in the garden frame to make room for other plants. Other flowering plants such as sweet peas, sown in the autumn and grown as cordons, stocks, sweet williams, wallflowers and *Anemone* 'St Brigid' and 'De Caen' not only make a good show of colour but provide plenty of good quality blooms for cutting and arranging at a time when plants in the garden are looking a little weather-beaten.

Sow stocks in the autumn and when the time is right for pricking out discard the dark green leaved seedlings as these will only produce plants with single flowers. Prick out the pale-coloured seedlings, which produce double blooms.

It is not easy to combine food growing with flower production, especially if the staging is needed for pot plants and is taking up room which would otherwise be used by tall vegetables. In the summer a cold greenhouse can be used for growing tomatoes, cucumbers, melons, peppers, French beans and aubergines, provided the right varieties (those which tolerate lower temperatures) are chosen. These will have to be raised in heat but can be planted in an unheated greenhouse in the spring. Other summer salads which can be sown and grown to maturity in a cold greenhouse include beetroot, lettuce and radish.

[1] Potting the plant in the autumn.

[2] Plunging the potted plant, after flowering, into the garden soil.

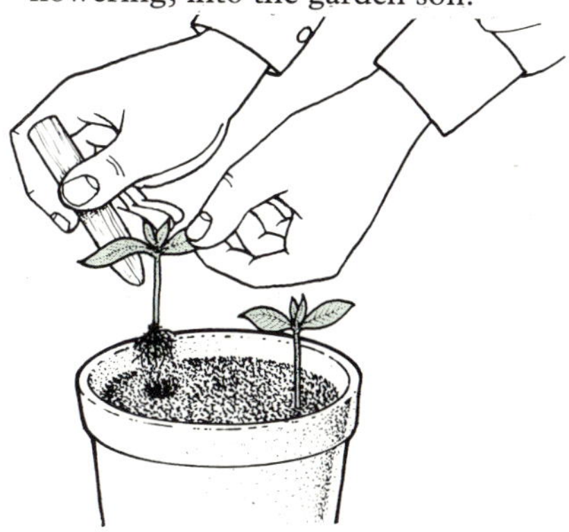

☼ Pricking out seedling.

Cold greenhouse: miniature flowering plants

Bulbs are ideal candidates for the cold greenhouse – any of the hardy garden varieties can be potted and forced into flower without heat. Daffodils, hyacinths and tulips are already popular, but there are many more which are equally rewarding and deserve space on the greenhouse bench. The miniatures especially are worth considering if you have a small greenhouse as you can pack more types into a tiny space to give a superb display of colour.

Dwarf bulbs to recommend are:

Miniature daffodils (narcissus) These are planted in the same fashion as the large varieties: 1–2 in (2.5–5 cm) apart with their noses above the compost.

Chionodoxa Plant in shallow bowls ½ in (13 mm) apart, 1 in (2.5 cm) deep.

Scilla Plant the bulbs close together 1 in (2.5 cm) deep.

Eranthis Plant the bulbs close together ½ in (13 mm) deep.

Erythronium Plant the bulbs immediately on arrival. Put them 3 in (7.5 cm) deep and close together.

Galanthus Plant the bulbs 2 in (5 cm) deep, close together.

Iris reticulata Plant in flower pots 2–3 in (5–7.5 cm) deep, 3 in (7.5 cm) apart.

Muscari Plant the bulbs close together, 1 in (2.5 cm) deep.

Crocus Plant in shallow bowls 1–2 in (2.5–5 cm) deep, 1 in (2.5 cm) apart.

Fritillaria Handle the bulbs carefully. Plant them 1½ in (4 cm) deep, pencil width apart.

Plunge the bulbs (bury them in a pit backfilled with peat) in a cool part of the garden and bring them into the greenhouse when the shoots are about 1 in (2.5 cm) long. A fine sowing of grass seed on the compost makes an effective backcloth for some of the larger flowering bulbs, such as crocus, snowdrops and daffodils.

Alpines

Alpines or rock garden plants can also be included to increase the range of miniature plants and extend the colour right through the spring and early summer when frosts may still prevail. These plants can be grown from seeds or cuttings. Many alpine seeds, especially primulas and cyclamen, are best sown when they are ripe as they deteriorate within months if left. Many germinate in late summer or autumn, but some need a period of freezing cold before they will sprout.

Most cuttings are taken in the spring from soft new growth, but woody plants can also be taken in summer and autumn from ripe shoots. To start a collection you can buy pot-grown plants – spring is the best time, for good specimens are usually available then. Alpines are best displayed in pans or half pots as they are usually very shallow rooting and do not require a deep container. They require good drainage, so clay pots are preferable and a gritty compost must be used. John Innes No 1 with extra grit added is ideal.

[1] A layer of coarse grit should be put on top of the compost, to help keep the plants cool and to improve surface drainage and prevent the crown of the plant from rotting.

[2] For an effective display and to keep the plant roots cool and from drying out too quickly, the pots can be plunged to their rims in a 6 in (15 cm) deep layer of 50:50 mix of gravel and coarse sand, but make sure that your staging is sturdy enough to take the weight. Plunging the pots will also help

protect the plant roots from frost damage during winter.

[3] The plants can be watered from below by keeping the pebbles moist, but remember to lift them occasionally to prevent them from rooting into the plunge mix.

Plenty of ventilation must be given all year round; fix ventilators on both sides and eaves. In summer shading must be applied to protect plants from strong sunlight. It's best to use slatted blinds as these allow air to circulate and keep the glass cool. They also filter light so growth is not affected too much. Alpines should be moved to a well-ventilated frame in late spring to allow other plants to be grown in the greenhouse.

Alpine plants suitable for growing under glass are: androsace, especially the cushion forming species; *Aquilegia* 'Blue Berry'; *Artemisia assoanam*; *Asperula nitida*; *Campanula* 'Joe Elliot'; *C. petrophila*; *Dianthus alpinus* and varieties; *Dionysia aretioides*; *Draba bryoides*; *D. mollissima*; *Geranium farreri*; *Helichrysum milfordae*; *Leontopodium alpinum*; *Lithodora oleifolium*; *Phyteuma comosum*; primula, especially European alpine kinds; saxifraga, especially early flowerers; *Synthyris stellata* and *Teucrium aroanium*.

[1] Adding coarse grit to improve surface drainage.

[2] Plunging potted alpine into 50:50 coarse sand and grit.

[3] Water the plants from below by keeping the gritty mix moist.

Cold greenhouse: foliage plants
In a cold conservatory the effect of an exotic plant room can still be created by growing bold, striking plants. Foliage plants particularly are essential in creating this effect and will provide a good backcloth to show off flowering plants to their best advantage.

In the large conservatory big shrubby plants can be grown and *Fatsia japonica*, especially the variegated form, is a must for creating the 'tropical feel'. It has large glossy leaves which are deeply lobed and in the autumn produces clusters of white flowers. Grow the plant in an 8 in (20 cm) pot of John Innes No 2 potting compost. × *Fatshedera lizei*, a cross between fatsia and hedera, is also suitable for a cold greenhouse. It has quite a sprawling habit and is best trained up a moss pole.

The hardy palm *Trachycarpus fortunei* is fairly slow growing and ideal for the smaller conservatory. It is evergreen and has large fan-shaped leaves on the ends of sharply toothed stalks. Yellow fluffy flowers appear in spring and are followed by blue-black grape-like fruits.

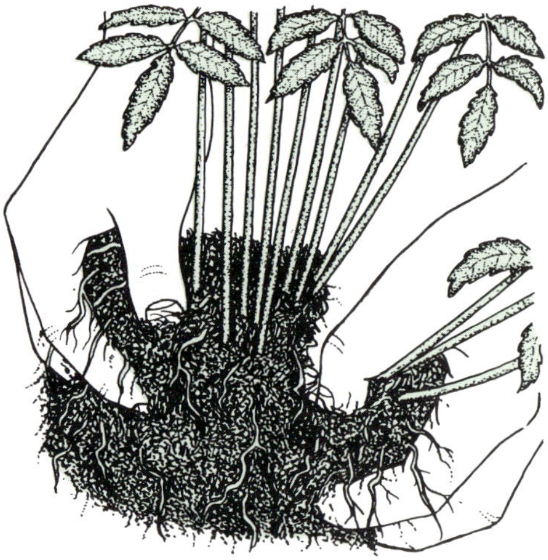

☼ Dividing the fern rootball.

Ferns
For the small, shady greenhouse, hardy ferns can be grown to provide some greenery. They can be displayed on decked staging, the deep shade lovers under the bench, or grown in a more natural rocky outcrop feature if room permits. Given space for the roots to roam freely, they will make better specimens.

The method of building a rock garden is the same as for outside. Choose pieces of weathered rock, which are in scale with the greenhouse size, and arrange them with their strata running in the same direction so that cracks and crevices are left for planting.

Pot culture is simpler for the small greenhouse. The size of the pot depends on the vigour of the plant, but you should choose one that is just one size larger than the rootball and pot on regularly. Do not allow the plant to become pot bound otherwise growth will become stunted. The compost should be kept moist at all times and if clay pots are used plunging them in sand will prevent the compost from drying out too quickly. Use a well-drained compost and in the case of acid lovers omit lime and water with rain water. Provide ventilation at all times and for those ferns which prefer a moist atmosphere, damp down regularly to raise the humidity. Shade the glass in summer to prevent scorching and to keep the plants cool. In the spring large plants which have produced several crowns may be divided.

☼ Remove the pot and loosen the rootball to separate as many of the roots as possible, making it easier to divide the rootball by hand. If necessary use two table forks back to back or a sharp knife, to tease the crowns apart keeping the plant roots intact. Pot up the divisions separately, water well and keep them shaded for a few days.

Ferns are mainly propagated from spores and the hardy varieties can be sown in a cold greenhouse. Growing conditions must be strictly hygienic to prevent the delicate plants from becoming swamped by moss and algae.

[1] The spores are sown thinly on the surface of a prepared pan of peat-based seed compost and are covered with a sheet of glass. The condensation which forms will help maintain a moist atmosphere and should not be removed. Water the pans from below.

[2] In anything up to six months a green film will appear on the surface of the compost followed several weeks later by scale-like leaves (prothalli).

[3] Some months later tiny fern fronds will emerge from the prothalli and when these are large enough to handle they can be pricked out. Small plants can be pricked out in clumps and divided later. Keep them covered with a piece of glass and do not allow them to dry out. When the ferns have developed sufficiently move them into small pots. It may take up to two years from sowing to potting.

Hardy varieties suitable for growing under glass: *Adiantum* species; *Asplenium* species; *Athyrium* species; *Blechnum penna-marine*; *B. tabulare*; *Cryptogramma crispa*; *Phyllitis scolopendrium*; and *Polystichum* species.

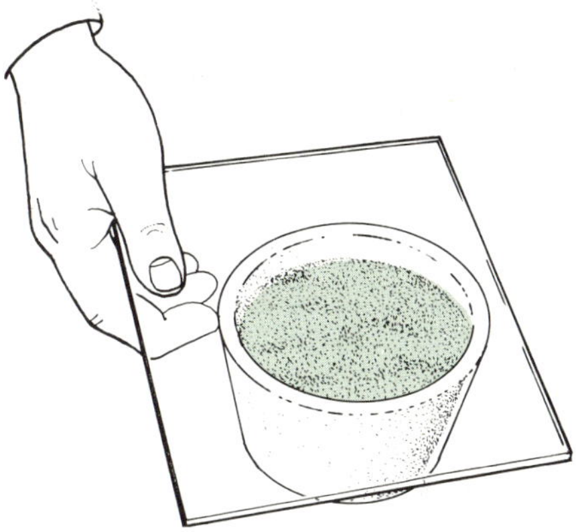

[1] Fern spores sown in compost.

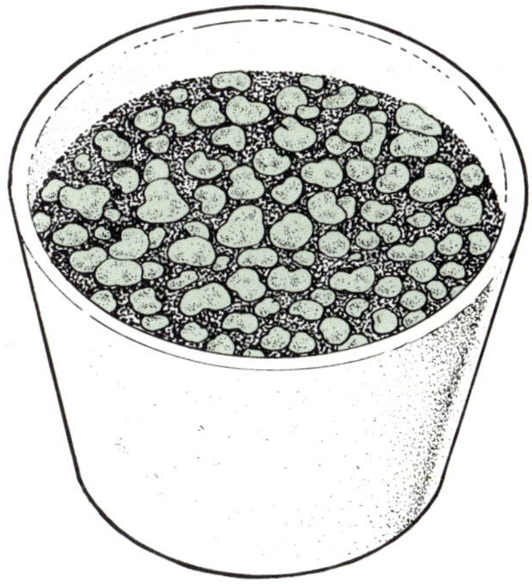

[2] Green-film stage of germination.

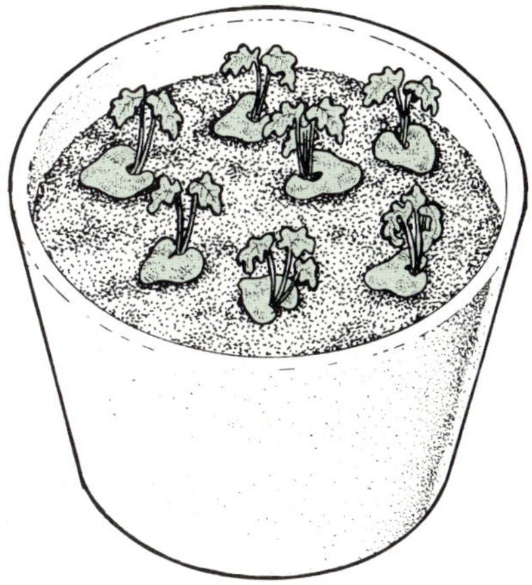

[3] Fronds emerging from the prothalli.

Overwintering plants are watered sparingly.

Many overwintering plants need attention to avoid leaf loss.

Cool greenhouse 1: Overwintering plants

A cool greenhouse, where the temperature is kept above freezing but not allowed to rise much above 45°F (7°C), gives you more scope to grow a wider variety of plants. You can also overwinter successfully summer-flowering half-hardy plants, sometimes referred to as 'risk' plants, which can spend the summer in the garden but are otherwise susceptible to frost damage. Plants in this category are overwintered by a variety of methods.

Some plants, like fuchsias, heliotropes and hydrangeas are allowed to rest completely. After flowering, water is gradually withheld and when the wood is ripe and the leaves have fallen no more water should be given, other than to prevent the root ball from becoming dust dry, until growth is restarted in the spring. Straggly shoots on dormant plants can be pruned to maintain a good shape.

Autumn-rooted cuttings plus standard fuchsias, pelargoniums and abutilons must not be allowed to lose their leaves. The plants must be kept growing by maintaining adequate warmth, at least 45°F (7°C), and sufficient moisture.

Plants which overwinter as bulbs, tubers or rhizomes, such as achimenes and begonias, are allowed to rest as soon as the foliage begins to die back naturally. They will not flower in future unless the bulb or rhizome is properly 'ripened' in the summer sun, therefore keep them growing by regularly watering and feeding them until growth slows down. At this stage reduce the watering and feeding so that the compost dries out slowly. Then turn the pots on their sides and store the dried-off plants under the staging. Keep them clear of drips. Large tubers, such as begonias and gloxinias, that can be easily removed from the dry soil can be loosely stored in paper bags or an open tray until spring.

Dahlia tubers are lifted from the garden after the first frost has blackened the stems. The foliage is trimmed back to 3–4 in (7.4–10 cm) from the tubers and the cleaned-up tubers are placed upside down in trays to allow the sap to drain before they are stored upright in boxes of dry peat.

Summer-flowering **chrysanthemums** are similarly stored in frost free conditions during the winter. The plants are lifted in the autumn and growth is cut back to within 6 in (15 cm) of the crown. They are arranged upright in boxes of peat and stored in a cool, airy position in the greenhouse. As soon as the temperatures begin to rise, water carefully and shoots will sprout from the base of the crown. The shoots can be used for cuttings. Winter-flowering chrysanthemums, grown in pots for cut flowers or exhibition purposes, are brought into the greenhouse before the first frost. After flowering these, too, are cut back and saved for cuttings.

The greenhouse atmosphere must be carefully controlled to prevent any loss of resting plants, so you will have to be careful how you mix the plants being grown. It is essential to ventilate freely when the temperature allows and avoid excess humidity as dormant plants are very prone to fungal attack.

To help protect plants dip them in a solution of benomyl; allow bulbs, rhizomes and tubers to dry thoroughly before storing. Alternatively dust plants with a fungicide powder.

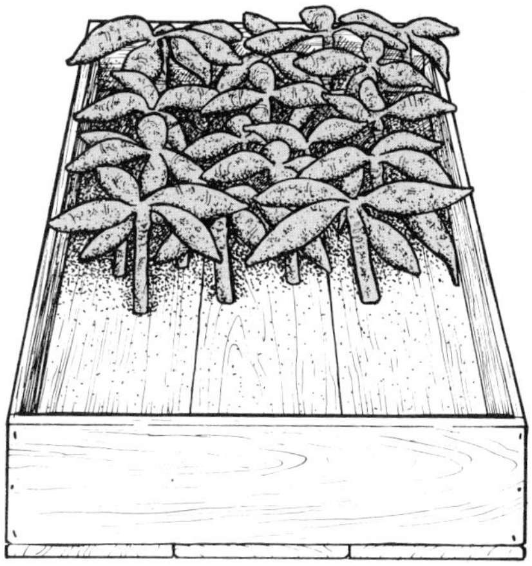

Storing dahlia tubers in boxes of dry peat.

Summer-flowering chrysanthemums are similarly stored in boxes of peat.

Cool greenhouse 2

The majority of plants which can be grown satisfactorily in the cold greenhouse will respond well to some gentle heat by flowering or fruiting earlier. The range of shrubs and perennials can also be increased to include 'risk' plants which in some areas, or in very bad winters, are not perfectly hardy in the garden. Higher temperatures are still needed for germinating half-hardy plants in the spring and a heated propagator will be invaluable for raising those which can be grown on cool after they have germinated. Without a propagator most of the seed sowing and your attempts to put roots on cuttings will have to be delayed until the temperatures become naturally warm. Most of the popular winter- and spring-flowering plants, notably calceolaria, cyclamen, cineraria, *Primula malacoides*, *P. obconica* and schizanthus, can be sown in mid-summer or early autumn. All are grown annually from seed, although cyclamen when sown in the summer take 15–16 months to flower, but they can also be grown from corms to flower in less than nine months.

☼ When potting cyclamen make sure that the top half of the corm is just above the surface of the compost.

♣ During the summer months winter-flowering plants can be put in the cold frame to make room for tomatoes, aubergines and peppers or melons and cucumbers, but they must be brought back indoors before the first frost.

On your list of flowering pot plants

☼ Potting cyclamen.

♣ Winter-flowering pot plants in cold frame during summer.

Potting freesia corms.

Pinching out antirrhinum side shoot to ensure one large flower.

you can also include some tender bulbs as well as the hardy garden varieties. For colour in the spring and early summer grow clivia, lachenalia, freesia and nerine.

Freesias can be grown from seed to flower the same year but a heated propagator will be needed in the spring. Alternatively grow them from corms potted in the autumn. Plant six good-sized corms to a 6 in (15 cm) pot. Position them 2 in (5 cm) apart and cover them with 1 in of compost.

Lachenalias and nerines are planted 2 in (5 cm) apart, just below the surface of the compost. None of these bulbs needs to be plunged outside, just keep them cool and shaded from bright sunshine.

Apart from freesias there are plenty of other flowers suitable for cutting and arranging that can be grown in gentle heat. Antirrhinums are excellent for this, sow them in late summer, whilst the temperature is still warm enough for germination: 65°F (18°C). Grow them singly in 5 in (12.5 cm) pots and either pinch out the growing tips to produce a bushy plant or for prize-size blooms nip out the side shoots to produce one large flower per plant.

Perpetual carnations can be brought into flower all the year round, provided the temperature is sufficiently high. At 50°F (10°C) they will bloom freely, at 45°F (7°C) both growth and flower production will slow down, but at less than 45°F (7°C) they can be successfully overwintered yet will not flower.

Warm greenhouse

Most gardeners are not prepared to provide stove conditions all the year round for tropical plants. Heaters are usually just switched on temporarily, for three to four months, to provide an adequate temperature for propagation. A far greater range of plants can be grown though, if you can raise the temperature to 55°F (13°C) plus. In a lean-to conservatory where the heating is supplied by the domestic boiler this may be easy to do. The plant family *Gesneriaceae* takes in many popular house plants including African violets (saintpaulia) and Cape primrose (streptocarpus), but because most of them enjoy a warm humid atmosphere they grow much better in a greenhouse where damping down will not ruin your soft furnishings. Other gesneriads which can be grown in your garden room are gloxinia, smithiantha, achimenes and columnea. These enjoy shade and can be grown in a conservatory fixed to the north side of the house.

Begonias

Other plants which enjoy a warm shady greenhouse are begonias. In the begonia family there are 900 species and all of them are suitable for growing in a greenhouse, so it is possible to enjoy a very large collection of plants. They are divided into three groups according to their root system – rhizomatous, tuberous and fibrous. The tuberous varieties are popular for their big flowers, which can be almost the size of dinner plates.

[1] The tubers are started into growth in spring (a temperature of 60–65°F (15–18°C) is needed) by embedding them hollowside uppermost in trays of moist peat.

[2] As soon as the leafy shoots are produced they are potted on individually into 4–6 in (10–15 cm) pots according to the size of tuber.

If the plants are required for exhibiting, remove all but one swelling bud and restrict this to two or three shoots. Water them freely during the growing season, being careful not to wet the corm, and apply a liquid feed every two weeks until the flowers fade. After flowering reduce watering and when the foliage has died down cease watering altogether.

Many of the foliage varieties are popular houseplants but like the gesneriads they too enjoy a warm humid atmosphere, and need a minimum temperature in the region of 55°F (13°C).

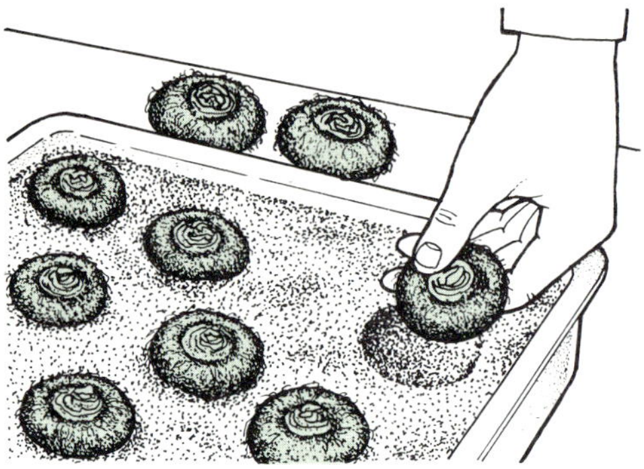

[1] Begonia tubers embedded in moist peat.

[2] Leafy-shoot stage—potting on.

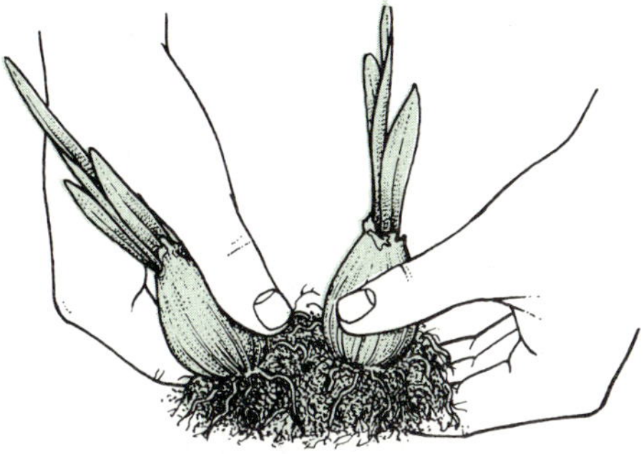

☼ Separating orchid pseudobulbs.

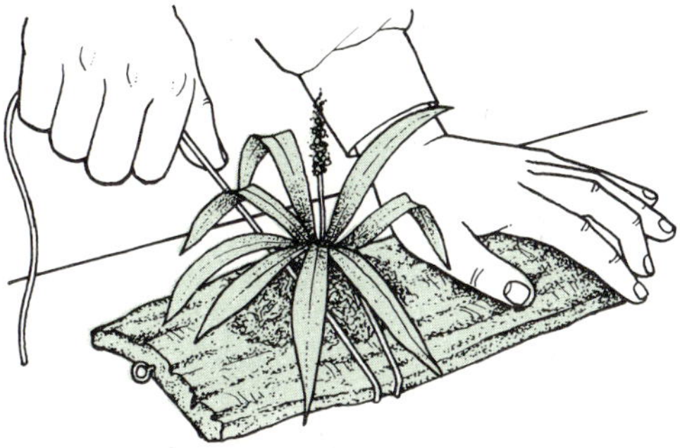

♣ Securing epiphytic orchid to bark.

Orchids

Orchids are the most popular exotics, but there are a number of species that will tolerate lower conditions, so to begin with you can select varieties that require a minimum temperature of 45°F (7°C). The hot-house varieties prefer 60–70°F (15–21°C) but there are others which will tolerate lower temperatures of 55–60°F (13–15°C).

Most orchids are epiphytic plants, found growing on trees and rocks in the wild, others are terrestrial and grow in the open ground. There are two distinct types of growth. Some plants produce pseudobulbs – swollen bulbous stems growing above ground which carry the leaves and flowers.

☼ These orchids can be propagated by removing the older pseudobulbs and potting them up. Other orchids produce a single flowering stem clothed with leaves.

Orchids enjoy a humid atmosphere, but plenty of ventilation must be applied to prevent the air from becoming stagnant. They enjoy good light but during the summer need shading from the scorching sun. The plants need plenty of water and regular feeding throughout the summer. In the autumn the one with pseudobulbs become dormant so little or no water will be needed. Potting should be done in spring, when the plants are not in flower. Terrestrial orchids can be grown in pots containing a 50:50 mixture of sphagnum moss peat and shredded bark.

♣ Epiphytic orchids can be grown on pieces of cork bark. Line the bark with moist sphagnum moss and lay the plant roots out, cover with more moss and secure the plant in place with thin nylon thread. Cattleyas are the most popular of the intermediate warm-blooded orchids. Cymbidiums, another favourite, can be grown slightly cooler.

Tropical plants are best grown as collections, either by family or regions of origin, because it is essential that the growing conditions you provide are ideal for all the plants. Once you start mixing too many sorts of plants, few of them will grow happily.

6
SEED SOWING AND CUTTINGS

Seed sowing

There is no cheaper way to fill your garden with plants than to raise them yourself from seed. There is virtually nothing you cannot grow if you can create the optimum conditions for germination. Not all seeds need the protection of glass to germinate. On the seed packet it will tell you exactly where to sow them and if they require any *treatment* to speed up germination.

Generally speaking, seeds which have a very hard seed coat need either softening by soaking in warm water, chipping with a sharp knife or abrading with sand paper to make the seed permeable to water and gases that are necessary for germination. Many tree and shrub seeds and most alpines require a period of cold (a winter spent outdoors in a pot of compost) before they will begin to sprout.

Seeds that have a fleshy outer coating, such as cotoneaster, need to be squashed and mixed with moist sand or peat, then put in a pot and left in an exposed position outside for the winter. When the weather warms up in the spring, the seeds will begin to germinate and can be sown direct.

You must provide ideal conditions for growth otherwise the seeds may rot before they emerge. Soil temperature is more critical than air temperature and a heated propagator will provide the best environment for plants that need no protection of glass.

Before you prepare a large seed tray, check the number and size of the seeds enclosed in the packet. This will tell you how to handle them and what size of container to use. Large seeds can be picked up individually and sown 2 in (5 cm) apart or in compartmentalized trays. They can be left in position until ready for potting, thus doing away with the need to prick out. Root disturbance will be cut to the minimum when transplanting, so there will be little check to growth.

Dust-like seed can be mixed with some dry silver sand to bulk up the seed. This mixture can be shaken, like salt and pepper on the surface of the compost. The seed is not covered with a sifting of compost. Burying seeds too deep will either prevent germination or cause the seeds to 'damp off'.

1 Prepare your tray or pot. Fill to the brim with seed compost and tap the container on the bench to settle the mixture. Press the compost gently with your fingers, especially in the corners, and top up with compost the areas that are low.

Firm and level the compost gently with a presser board, made from a smooth piece of wood. Water the tray from below in a shallow tray of water. Remove the container as soon as the surface of the compost is moist and allow to drain. Alternatively, water the tray from above using a can fitted with a fine rose.

2 Sow the seeds thinly and evenly, in two directions, on the surface of the compost.

3 Just cover the seeds with a light sifting of compost. Do not cover tiny seeds. Label each tray and for future reference enter it in your 'growing diary'. Here write details of sowing, germination and potting dates plus any feeding and other treatment you give.

4 Put the pots and trays of seed in a warm place to germinate. Most seeds require a temperature of 60–65°F (15–18°C) for good germination. Maintain a dark, moist atmosphere by covering them with a pane of glass and

newspaper or polythene. Wipe off the condensation regularly. Check the seeds daily and if any have started to sprout bring them into the light.

Vegetables and bedding plants that are only in the greenhouse temporarily can be sown in peat blocks. These are made with a special tool and blocking compost. Vegetables, such as cabbage, lettuce, beetroot and onions can be sown several seeds to a block – multiple seeding. They are transplanted at twice the normal distance but give you far more edible-sized plants.

[1] Firming compost with presser board.

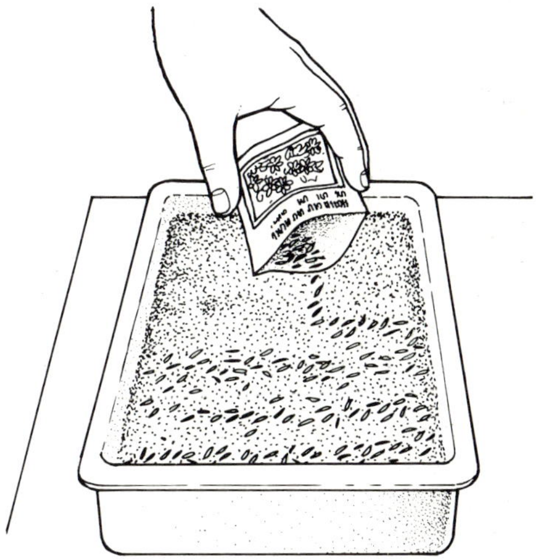

[2] Sowing the seeds.

[3] Covering the seeds with sieved compost.

[4] Cover tray with glass pane and newspaper.

Seedlings: pricking out

Most seeds need putting in a dark place to germinate. As soon as there are visible signs of growth they should be brought immediately into a well-lit, but not sun-scorched position. If they are left in the dark the seedlings will become drawn and remain white as they will not be able to produce any food in their leaves. Bring them into the light and the green pigment present will work with sunlight to provide many of the essential nutrients required for growth. In many plants the first leaves produced are unlike the mature leaves and are known as the seed leaves or cotyledons. In most cases these will be either a pair of rounded cotyledons, or one grass-like cotyledon. The mature leaves do, in some plants, appear first, this is where the seed germinates below ground before sending up a shoot.

As soon as the seedlings are large enough to handle, not later than when the first true leaves have expanded, they should be pricked-out. If they are left, they will become weak and drawn as the result of overcrowding. Deep seed trays should be used. Wash them thoroughly then fill them with some peat-based potting compost. If you prefer, use a loam-based compost such as John Innes No. 1. Firm the compost gently with your fingers, paying particular attention to the corners, and press level with a wooden block to leave the compost $\frac{1}{2}$ in (13 mm) below the rim of the tray. Water the seedlings in before you prick them out so that they are easier to lift. If the compost is dry the roots will stick to the sides of the pot and break off when moved.

[1] Taking care not to damage their roots, prise some seedlings from the tray. Take out just a few at a time and keep them shaded from bright sun otherwise they will shrivel and die. Tease the seedlings apart with a dibber, handling them at all times with their

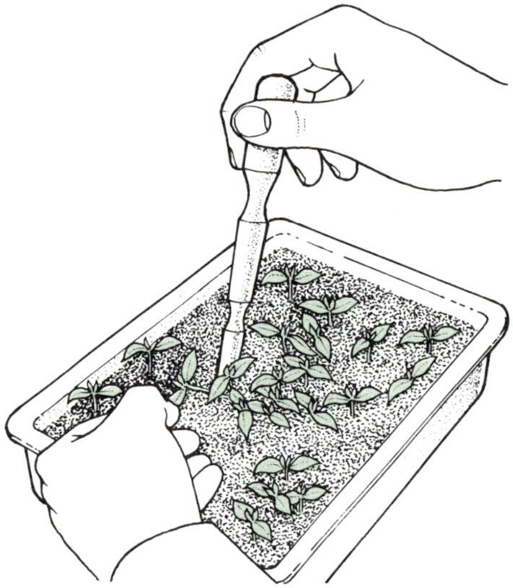

[1] Prising seedlings from their original compost.

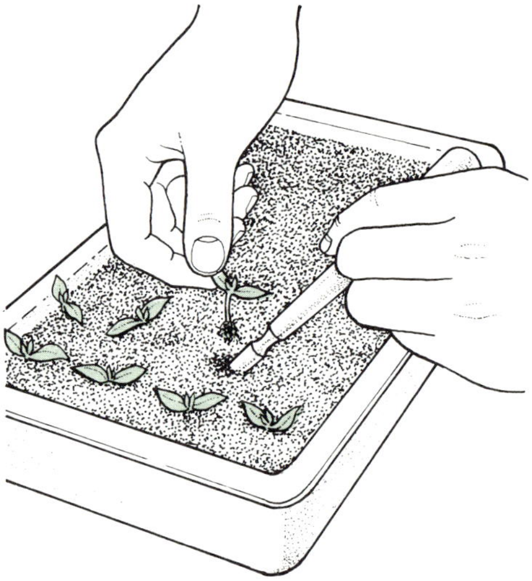

[2] Inserting seedlings in new tray.

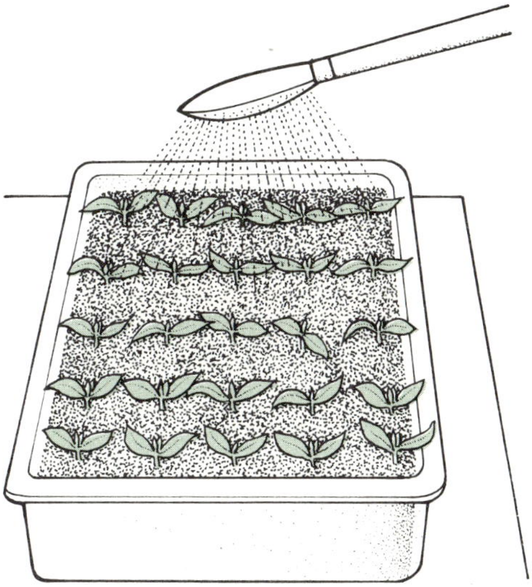

[3] Watering seedlings with fine rose.

[4] Mature seedling being potted up.

seed leaves and not their stems which bruise and snap easily. Select seedlings of similar size and vigour for one tray. Mark out the positions of the rows along one end and side of the tray, placing the seedlings $1\frac{1}{2}$–2 in (4–5 cm) apart.

[2] With your dibber make a hole deep enough to allow the roots to drop to the bottom and so that the seed leaves are just above the level of the compost. Firm them in by pressing the compost gently around them. Take care not to damage the roots and stem. Label each tray individually and place them in a well lit position.

[3] Water the seedlings in using a can fitted with a fine rose. Shade them from bright sun. As soon as the seedlings are touching each other and have about four or five true leaves they are ready for potting up. If they are left too long cramped together, growth will be poor as they become starved of nutrients. The seedlings are moved from the tray and carefully separated so that each plant has a good size root ball.

[4] They are then potted individually into small pots, about a 3 in (7.5 cm) is adequate, but it should be large enough to take the root ball and allow some development.

Over-potting can be disastrous as it will encourage rotting. A small plant sitting in too much cold wet compost does not have sufficient roots to draw up the excess moisture. As soon as a pot is filled with roots the plant should be moved to the next size container. From a 3 in (7.5 cm) move it to a 5 in (12.5 cm) pot and from a $3\frac{1}{2}$ or 4 in (7.5 or 10 cm) to a 6 in (15 cm) pot. Richer potting composts are used for potting on and when a plant has been in its final pot for about a month regular weekly feeding should be given during the growing season.

Cuttings

Stem cuttings

The most important method of greenhouse propagation, next to seed sowing, is that of stem cuttings. Many of the bedding plants, such as fuchsias and geraniums are propagated this way, plus chrysanthemums and dahlias as well as flowering pot plants like hydrangeas. All of these are grown from cuttings taken from the soft shoots during the growing season. No specialist equipment is essential, but for those taken in the spring and autumn a heated propagator is an advantage in rooting them quickly. Hardy plants can also be grown from softwood cuttings taken in the spring, but because most of them can be rooted equally as well from ripe wood cuttings taken in the summer and autumn outside, it is not worth letting them take up valuable space in the greenhouse.

All cuttings should be taken from healthy vigorous shoots where the growth is fairly firm. Flowering shoots, or those which are about to flower, are not recommended as a first choice as the plant will have used a lot of energy in producing the flower and so will probably take longer to root. Selected shoots should be removed from the parent plant and put in a polythene bag to prevent them from drying out. The snag left behind on the parent plant should be trimmed clean to just above a leaf joint to prevent it from rotting back. This heading back will also encourage more shoots to act as cuttings material.

[1] Trim the cutting, using a sharp knife or razor blade, just below a leaf joint to make it 2–4 in (5–10 cm) long. The tissue around the leaf joint is much harder and so more resilient to rot. Remove the leaves from the lower half of the cutting. If the plant has large leaves either slice off half the blade (e.g. hydrangeas) or roll them and secure with an elastic band (e.g. rubber plants) so you can put more cuttings in a tray and prevent them from flopping over.

[2] Dust the cut base with a hormone rooting powder.

[3] Insert the cuttings in trays or place four around the edge of a 4½ in (12 cm) pot to half their length and water them in using a can fitted with a fine rose.

[4] Place the cuttings in a heated propagator and maintain a temperature of about 60–65°F (15–18°C). The soft growth from which the cutting is made will quickly dehydrate unless kept in a moist atmosphere; hence cover the propagator with a lid or place a polythene bag over the cuttings. Support the bag above the leaves with canes and remove excess condensation daily to prevent it from running back into the compost and making it soggy.

As soon as the cuttings show signs of growth, roots will usually have formed and the cuttings will be ready for potting on individually. Transfer the cuttings to 3 in (7.5 cm) pots of potting compost. Keep them warm and shaded for the first few days until they have settled in, then move them to a well-lit position on the staging.

When the plants are 3–4 in (7.5–10 cm) tall pinch out the growing tip to encourage a bushy habit. As soon as the pots are filled with roots, move the plants into larger containers. From a 3 in (7.5 cm) pot put them into a 5 in (12.5 cm) pot. If the plants are over potted there is a much greater risk of over watering them.

Stem cuttings

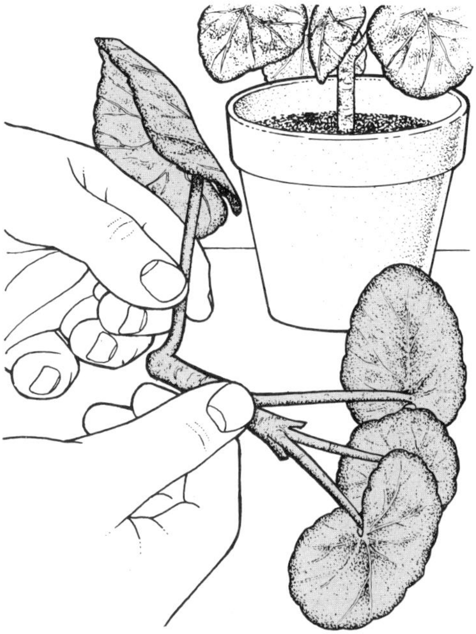

[1] Removing leaves from lower half of cutting.

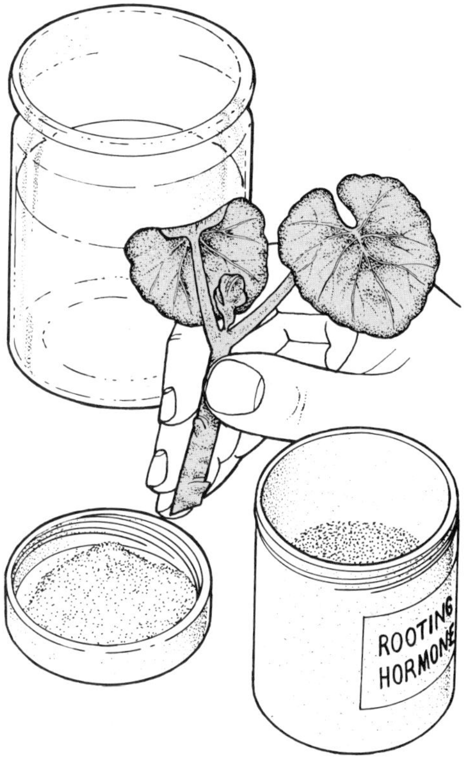

[2] Dusting cutting with hormone powder.

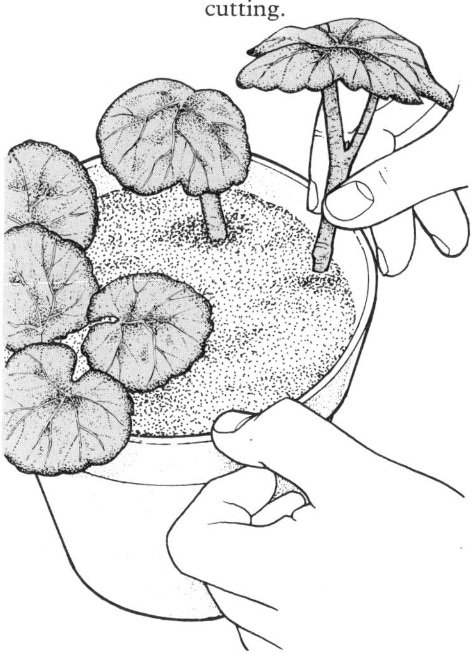

[3] Cuttings inserted into pot of compost.

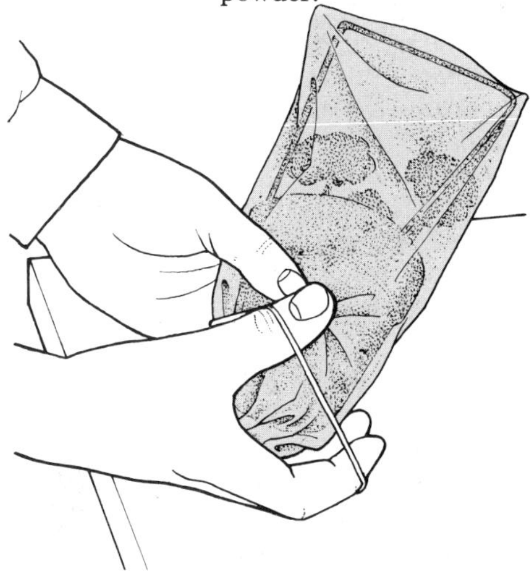

[4] Cover potted cuttings to avoid dehydration.

Leaf cuttings

The natural habit of a plant indicates how it can be propagated. Some plants do not have obvious stems but produce offsets or several crowns which can be removed or divided. The leaves of many plants will also root, but only optimum conditions, a soil temperature of 70°F (21°C) and a moist atmosphere, will guarantee successful results, so the warmth and protection of a covered propagator, or greenhouse is needed. Leaf cuttings are taken in the spring and summer when the plant is growing. There are three techniques used according to the type of plant.

The long, narrow leaves of plants such as **streptocarpus**, the Cape primrose, are cut into sections. Only healthy mature leaves should be used and cut into pieces 1½–2 in (3–5 cm) long so that each piece contains a central vein. Mark the end of the cuttings nearest to the parent plant, to indicate the top and bottom.

☼ Insert the cuttings to half their length 1 in (2.5 cm) apart in trays of cuttings compost. The roots and shoots will grow from the central vein.

Saintpaulias (African violets) produce new plants freely when propagated from the complete leaf with its stalk attached.

[1] A healthy leaf is removed from a plant and the stalk trimmed to about 1½ in (3 cm) long.

[2] No rooting powder needs to be applied; the cutting is inserted into a tray or pot of compost so that the base of the leaf blade just touches the surface of the compost.

[3] Insert pairs of leaves back to back to prevent them from lying on the damp compost and rotting off.

[4] A new plant usually arises from the place where the stalk joins the leaf.

There are two ways in which you can propagate **Begonia rex:**

One method involves cutting a mature leaf into inch-square sections each containing part of the main vein. These are inserted upright to half their length in trays of moist compost. To prevent the sections from damping-off spray them with a fungicide before putting them in a closed propagator or covering them with a polythene bag.

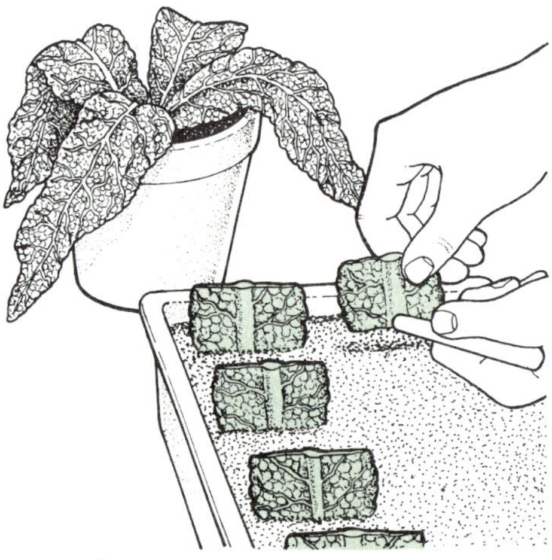

☼ *Streptocarpus*—leaf cuttings.

♣ *Begonia rex*, showing one way of producing leaf cuttings.

[1] *Saintpaulia*—removing leaf and stalk.

[2] Cutting inserted into compost tray.

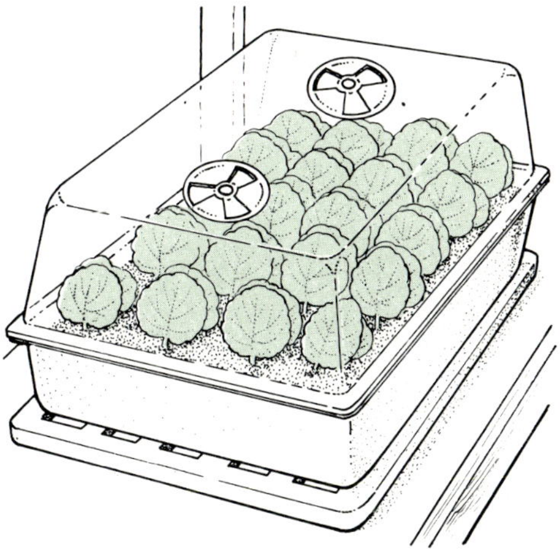

[3] Pairs of leaves inserted back-to-back for support.

[4] Emergence of new plant.

☘ The other method involves removing a healthy mature leaf from the parent plant and slicing the main veins across on the underside of the leaf. The leaf is then secured with pegs cut-side down on a tray of moist cuttings' compost. Small plantlets will appear from the cut areas.

Rooting leaf cuttings will take several months and they do not want to be potted on immediately there are signs of growth. They need to be gradually hardened off to the normal greenhouse environment. This is done by applying a little ventilation to the propagator. Gradually increase the amount and at the same time lower the soil temperature, until the lid can be removed totally. Pot the plantlets on only when they are large enough to handle and stand them in a well-lit position on the greenhouse staging.

7
SPRING-FLOWERING BULBS

There is nothing simpler and more rewarding than persuading bulbs to flower in pots. The spring-flowering bulbs are by far the most popular ones grown as these can be planted in late summer to provide colour in what can otherwise be a dull time – the middle of winter. Bulbs which force well are: hyacinths, tulips, narcissi, crocuses, lilies and lily-of-the-valley. For extra early displays of narcissi and hyacinths *prepared* bulbs will have to be bought. These have been harvested earlier by the growers and stored for specific periods under strict temperature controls so that the flower growing inside the bulb is advanced.

There are a variety of ways of growing bulbs indoors. The most common method is to use pots of bulb fibre, but some, such as *Narcissus* 'Paper White', will grow well in a shallow dish of moist pebbles. Hyacinths can also be grown equally as well in special bulb vases filled with water.

Any type of container can be used for growing bulbs, and one 3–4 in (7.5–10 cm) deep and 8 in (20 cm) in diameter is best to allow a reasonable root run.

[1] In pots without drainage holes a few pieces of charcoal should be placed in the bottom to prevent the compost turning sour.

[2] Part fill the container with enough bulb fibre or potting compost so that when the bulbs are placed on top their noses are about 1 in (2.5 cm) below the rim. Place larger bulbs 2 in (5 cm) apart and smaller ones 1 in (2.5 cm) apart.

[3] Cover the bulbs with fibre or compost, leaving just the tips of their 'noses' exposed. Avoid firming compost too hard or the roots will find it hard to penetrate and the bulbs will tend to be pushed up out of the pot.

[4] Water the plants well and place the pots in a cool dark place where the temperature does not exceed 40°F (7°C). A plunge bed in a shady part of the garden or darkened cold frame are ideal. Wrap the pots in black polythene and cover with 6 in (15 cm) layer of sand, peat or ashes. Protect the bulbs from being eaten by mice and slugs.

[5] Leave the bulbs in the plunge bed until the shoots are 1 in (2.5 cm) tall. This will take 8–10 weeks. Remove the black polythene and bring them into a cool greenhouse where the temperature does not exceed 50°F (10°C). Place them in subdued light at first, then after a week transfer them to a well-lit position. Within a month the flower shoots will appear and as soon as they are well formed the temperature can be increased to 65°F (15°C).

A number of lily bulbs, such as *L. auratum*, *L. speciosum* and *L. longiflorum* are available in the shops during the winter for early spring flowering. These should be planted immediately you get them home in 6 in (15 cm) pots of well drained compost. Plunge them in the garden and cover them with some loose peat. When the top growth has reached 3 in (7.5 cm) bring them into the cold greenhouse. Water them sparingly and when the plants are fully in bud the temperature should be raised to 65°F (18°C).

Lily-of-the-valley can be planted in pots 2 in (5 cm) apart with their noses just above the compost. They should be put in a warm, dark place where a temperature of 60–70°F (15–21°C) is maintained. They must not be allowed to dry out. When the top growth has reached 2–3 in (5–7.5 cm) gradually move them into full light. Shade them at all times from direct sunlight.

1 Adding charcoal to prevent souring of compost.

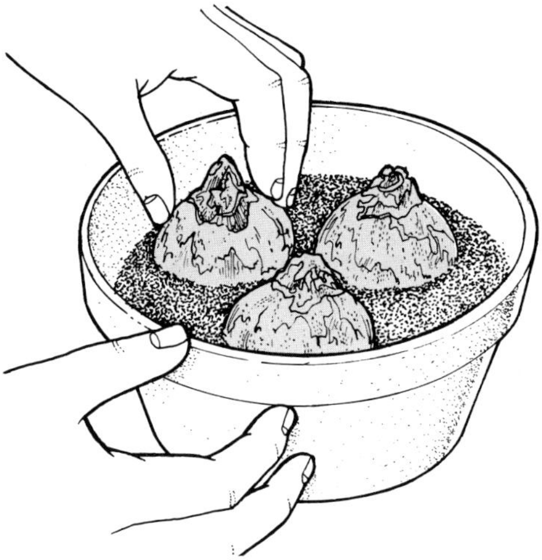

2 Placing bulbs in container.

3 The prepared pot is labelled.

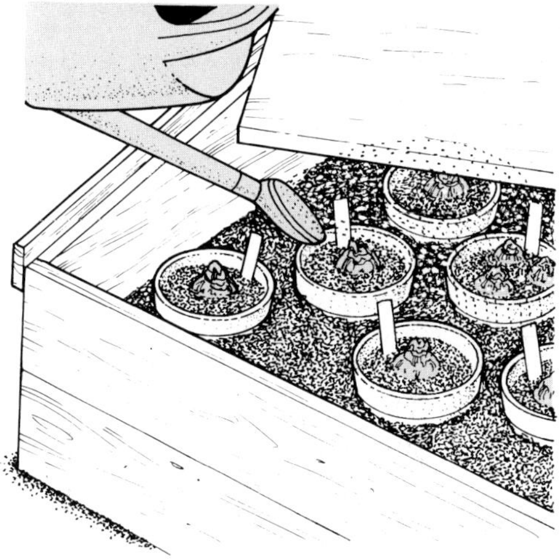

4 The potted bulbs are placed in a darkened cold frame.

5 After 8–10 weeks, bring pots into a cool greenhouse.

8
SUMMER BEDDING PLANTS

Most of the summer bedding plants grown in tubs, baskets and borders to give a splash of colour in the garden have to be started off under glass. The majority are seed raised, others are propagated by cuttings.

From cuttings

Cuttings of geraniums, fuchsias, coleus, heliotropes etc, are usually taken in the autumn before the bedding plants are lifted at the end of the summer bedding season. No bottom heat is needed to root the cuttings at this time but the plants will need to be overwintered carefully and kept above freezing. Spring cuttings can also be taken but a propagator will be essential for rooting and the plants produced will not be quite as large.

From seed

Most bedding plants grown from seed will germinate satisfactorily in temperatures of 60–65°F (16–18°C). The speed of germination varies but if optimum conditions are given most will have sprouted within less than a month. As soon as the seedlings are large enough to handle they must be pricked out to lessen the risk of damage to their roots and a check to growth. The plants should be grown on at a slightly lower temperature, not less than 55°F (13°C), so they are gradually hardened to the outside temperatures. Correct timing is essential if you are to get your plants ready for flowering when they are planted out.

Most plants are ready for planting out within 12–15 weeks of sowing. If plants are ready too soon the fertilizer added to the compost will have been used or leached out through watering and plants will start to show signs of starvation. If the leaves turn yellow water them with a half-strength liquid fertilizer. Remove any flowers which are premature.

[1] Before the plants are put in the garden they need to be acclimatized to colder conditions otherwise they will suffer a check to growth. This hardening off process usually takes 2–3 weeks. Move them from the greenhouse and into a cold frame.

[2] Keep the frame light closed for the first few days. Then open it by an increasing amount each day, but close it down at night.

If a frost is forecast cover the frame with some sheets of sacking or cover the plants with newspaper.

[3] As the nights get warmer leave the lights open so that eventually they can be left off altogether.

[4] Ready for planting out.

Bedding plants from seed

Ageratum Sow, on the surface, late winter/germination takes about 3 weeks.

Antirrhinum Sow, on the surface, mid-winter/germination takes about 3 weeks.

Aster Sow late winter/germination takes about 3 weeks.

Begonia (fibrous) Sow, on the surface, mid-late winter/germination about 3 weeks.

Dahlia (bedding vars.) Sow late winter/germination 2–3 weeks.

Dianthus Sow mid–late winter/germination 2–3 weeks.

Geranium (F_1 hybrids – correct Pelargonium) Sow mid winter at 70–75°F (21–24°C)/germination takes about 2 weeks.

Impatiens Sow late winter/germination about 3 weeks.

Lobelia Sow, on the surface, mid–late

1 Hardening off by moving plants to cold frame.

2 Increase ventilation day by day.

3 Eventually remove the lights completely.

4 Planting out.

winter/germination 3 weeks/prick out seedlings in clumps of four or five.

Marigolds Sow in late winter/germination 1–2 weeks.

Mimulus Sow late winter/germination 2–3 weeks.

Nemesia Sow late winter at 50–68°F (10–20°C)/ germination 2–3 weeks.

Nicotiana Sow late winter/germination 2–3 weeks.

Pansy Sow early–mid winter/germination 2–3 weeks.

Petunia Sow, on the surface, mid–late winter/germination about 2 weeks.

Salvia Sow mid–late winter/germination 2–3 weeks.

Tagetes Sow in late winter/germination 1–2 weeks.

Verbena Sow mid winter/germination 3–4 weeks.

9
CLIMBERS: SMALL GREENHOUSES

There are few plants which will benefit their neighbours during the summer as much as climbers. Not only do they give wall-to-wall colour, but the shade they cast will also provide a canopy for plants that would otherwise scorch in bright sun. They will help to raise the humidity in the greenhouse, which is beneficial for most plants. However, during the winter months these advantages disappear, so only annuals and deciduous climbers should be grown. Winter flowering and evergreen species are best grown only on the house wall in a lean-to conservatory. Before you grow a climber on a wall, render the brickwork to give it a smooth finish, so there are no nooks and crannies where pests may lurk, and give the wall a coat of white emulsion paint. This will not only make it look good but will help to reflect light. Some climbers are too vigorous for the small greenhouse but can be restricted to some degree by being grown in containers, which will restrain the roots and therefore shoot growth. Careful pruning also helps but remember that summer pruning can, in fact, stimulate growth.

If the plants are to be grown in the border soil, this should be dug deeply and prepared thoroughly before planting. Supports, whether wooden trellis or lengths of wire run along the walls of the greenhouse, should be placed in position first so that they can be used as soon as they are needed.

[1] Dig the planting hole about 2 ft (60 cm) square and, in the case of vigorous climbers, line it with paving slabs to restrict root growth.

[2] Add some peat and general fertilizer to the backfill to improve its condition, if the soil is clayey add some extra grit. If the soil is very poor replace it totally with fresh compost – choose a John Innes mix which will dry out less rapidly than a peat-based compost. If the climber is planted beneath slatted staging, make sure that the soil is well drained to cope with the drainage water, which will drip through.

[3] Plant the climber to the level at which it was grown in the pot.

[4] Replace the backfill soil, firm it gently with your feet and give the plant a good soaking.

[5] Tie the climber into the support with soft string. Do not train it flat against the glass, keep it at least 2 in (5 cm) away to allow air to circulate freely behind. This will also make it easier to spray against pests and diseases and the foliage is less likely to become scorched in bright sun.

Bougainvillea is one of the most popular deciduous summer flowering climbers for a cool greenhouse.

Cobaea scandens, better known as the cup and saucer vine because of its quaint flowers which turn from green to purple during the summer, is a vigorous perennial climber which is best grown as an annual in a small greenhouse. Seed is sown in late winter.

Ipomoea (morning glory) is a well-loved climber grown from seed to flower the same year.

Jasminum polyanthum has white flowers, which are heavily scented, and appear in winter. It grows well in temperatures as low as 40°F and is best trained on the back wall of a lean-to.

Lapageria rosea is another favourite winter-flowering climber that will tolerate cool, shady conditions.

Thunbergia alata (black-eyed Susan) is fast growing and usually treated as an annual. The seeds are sown in late winter and the plants will be in flower by mid-summer.

1 Inserting paving slabs to restrict root growth.

2 Add peat and fertilizer to the backfill.

3 Planting the young climber.

4 Firming in the plant.

5 Tying the climber on to the support wires.

10
GROWING FOR FOOD

Food: forcing and sowing for early crops

Vegetables can be sown early under glass, if the temperature is maintained about 50°F (10°C), to give them a head start, for they can be planted out immediately the weather turns warmer and will be ready for harvesting several months before those sown direct. Plants to treat this way are: broad beans, runner beans, leeks, marrows, onions, celeriac, celery, Brussels sprouts, summer cabbage, calabrese, summer cauliflower, cucumbers (outdoor), sweetcorn and tomatoes. Out of season sowings can also be made to ensure that you have fresh vegetables through the autumn, winter and early spring.

Globe carrots can be sown in growing bags and the seedlings transplanted 4 in (10 cm) apart. Celery can be sown during the summer for cropping in mid-winter. Lettuce can be produced all the year round and in a temperature of 50°F (10°C) supplies of salad onions and radish can be maintained during the winter. Early potatoes can be produced in spring when prices of new potatoes in the shops are high. Choose early varieties, such as 'Epicure' and 'Sharpe's Express'.

[1] Sprout potatoes in mid-winter, by standing them upright in egg trays so that the dormant growth buds are exposed to the light.

[2] In about 2–3 weeks shoots will appear and the tubers can then be planted in large pots – five to a 12 in (30 cm) pot. Half fill the pot with John

[1] Sprouting potato tubers.

[2] Planting the sprouted tubers.

Innes No. 3 compost or loamless equivalent, lay out the potatoes and cover them with a thick layer of compost.

As the shoots emerge, top-dress several times until the compost is level with the top of the pot.

Other choice crops to force in a slightly heated greenhouse are **rhubarb, chicory, seakale** and **endive.** Two-year-old rhubarb crowns are lifted from the garden in mid-winter and brought into the greenhouse to force new edible shoots. They are replanted in a dark place, such as under the staging in deep boxes of peat, where they are not exposed to any light. The sticks are ready for cutting when they are 10 in (25 cm) long. At the end of the season throw away the crowns as they will be exhausted and no use for forcing again.

☼ **Chicory** and **seakale** are similarly dug up from outside in early winter. The leaves are cut off and the remaining roots, which can be trimmed, are potted up so that the top of the roots are level with the compost. Take care to leave at least 1 in (2.5 cm) of the leaf bases intact. They are covered with an upturned plant pot to completely exclude light and the blanched shoots are harvested regularly, the chicons are used in salads and seakale is eaten boiled, almost in the same way as asparagus.

Sow **endive** in late summer and early autumn and grow in pots or the open ground. When the plants are fully grown cover them with an upturned pot to blanch the leaves. Endive is a good alternative to lettuce and can be grown in a cold or cool greenhouse.

Herbs can be kept in tip-top condition, ready for use, all year round in a cold or cool greenhouse. Sow basil, chives, borage, marjoram, mint, parsley, sage and thyme in pots during the summer outside and bring them into the greenhouse in the autumn. Cut them regularly to encourage fresh shoots.

☼ Forcing chicory by covering potted-up roots with an upturned pot.

Food: out of season plants

Lettuce can be grown all year round under glass, but it is only when the shop prices are high during the winter that it is worth giving space for them in your greenhouse. After all they can be grown equally as well outside during the summer. A cold greenhouse is all that is needed, but you must choose a variety that will grow well in the reduced light and short days of winter. Sow small batches at fortnightly intervals from late summer onwards for a continuous supply of lettuce ready for cutting. Cool temperatures 55–60°F (13–15°C) are needed for germination and as soon as the seedlings are large enough to handle they are pricked out individually into 3 in (7.5 cm) pots. A moist, slightly acid soil ensures a crisp heart to a lettuce so a peaty compost should be used in growing bags or pots and the plants must never be allowed to dry out as they will flag beyond recovery.

Plant lettuces as shallowly as possible 8–12 in (20–30 cm) apart to allow a free circulation of air around the leaves and access for watering the soil without splashing the foliage. Soggy leaves will lead to fungal attack.

Another food crop worth considering as a special out of season treat is the **strawberry.** Growing under glass will mean that there are fruits for picking at least six weeks before the fruit is seen in the shops at a reasonable price.

It is best to choose early varieties and buy pot-grown runners in late summer. You can establish your own plants outside by pegging down four or five runners on each strawberry plant into sunken pots of compost. This is done in early summer and for better plants it is best if you do not allow the strawberry plants to flower and fruit. Leave the plantlets attached to the parent plant and only detach them once they are well rooted. Pot them on in late summer and stand them in a cool place until they are established, then put them in full sun. During the winter protect the plants from harsh drying winds.

[1] In mid-winter, move them into a cold greenhouse with a temperature of 40–50°F (4–10°C). Stand them on a shelf where they will receive plenty of light, and water them only when the compost is dry.

[2] Most strawberries are self-fertile but because there are no pollinating insects about you will have to do the job by hand. A soft, dry paint brush can be used to transfer pollen from one flower to another. To help the fruit swell, water freely and apply a liquid feed once a week. As the fruit starts to

[1] Watering overwintering strawberry plants.

[2] Pollinating the flowering plants.

[1] Pruning the grape vine.

[2] Thinning the bunches of fruits.

colour-up ventilate freely and reduce watering to prevent botrytis (grey mould) from rotting the fruit. After the fruits have been picked set the plants out in the garden and do not use them for forcing again.

Most **grapes** can be grown in a cool or even cold greenhouse, although many of the Muscat varieties do perform best in one that is heated.

The traditional method is to grow them direct in the greenhouse border but they will produce a dense canopy during the summer so that only shade-loving plants can be grown beneath them. Raising bedding and vegetable plants in the spring will not be too difficult for they will be planted outside before the grape's leaves have unfolded to cast too much shade but you will be limited in your choice of summer crops. In a small greenhouse it is only advisable to grow a grape vine in a pot so that the growth is somewhat restricted. In a 12–14 in (30–35 cm) pot of rich compost a reasonable crop of six or seven small bunches can be expected. Train the vine on a wire framework.

[1] Each year cut back the main stems to half their length in the autumn and prune the fruiting spurs back to two buds leaving one every 12–18 in (30–45 cm). Rub out completely those seen sprouting in between. In the spring when growth starts pinch back the shoots, which develop from the leaf axils, to one leaf. From now on tie in all the new growth and only remove that which becomes congested.

[2] When the fruits start to swell thin out the bunches. Use a long-bladed pair of scissors and do not touch the fruit. Remove the smallest fruit first and thin them to leave ½ in (13 mm) space between the fruits. Ventilate the greenhouse freely to maintain a temperature no higher than 55°F (13°C). Water the plant well and give a liquid feed at regular intervals when the grapes are swelling. After the fruit is harvested, stand the plant outside for the wood to ripen and bring it back indoors as soon as the leaves have fallen.

Food: compatible plants 1

The greenhouse is of just as much value for growing things to eat as it is for growing things to look at. You will have to be careful, though, how you mix the crops as you should put together only those with similar requirements. If you try to keep too many different plants happy none of the results will be very rewarding. Commonly grown vegetables with contrasting needs in temperature and humidity are tomatoes, which enjoy a cool, dry atmosphere and cucumbers, which prefer a warm, moist environment. Peppers and aubergines will grow well alongside tomatoes, whereas melons are much happier with cucumbers. Permanent plants such as grapes are a little more difficult to accommodate alongside many plants as they cast a lot of dense shade. Figs, peaches and nectarines however, provide a more dappled shade making them compatible with tomatoes and many flowering plants.

Tomatoes are undoubtedly the most popular greenhouse crop. They need reasonably good light for strong growth and early ripening. For fruits to be ripe before the prices drop in the shops, seed should be sown in mid-winter – a temperature of 70°F (21°C) will be needed for germination and the plants are grown on at about 65°F (18°C). Sowings can also be made in late winter for growing on in an unheated greenhouse and ripening by mid-summer. Germination usually takes about two weeks and as soon as the seedlings are large enough to handle they are pricked out into individual 3 in (7.5 cm) pots. The plants are set out in their final position when they are either 8–12 in (20–30 cm) tall or when a couple of flowers on the first truss have started to open. They need to be watered well and staked immediately to prevent them from flopping.

[1] As soon as the side shoots are 1 in (2.5 cm) long pinch them out. To help the fruit to set, raise the humidity by damping down the path and misting the open flowers with tepid water. If temperatures are low, spray the plants with a proprietary hormone 'setting' compound to aid fertilization. A dilute

[1] Tomatoes: pinching out sideshoots.

[2] Pinching out the growing tip.

liquid feed should be given with every watering after the first fruit has set.

[2] Pinch out the growing tip after the eighth flower truss to *check* growth and encourage the fruit to ripen before the end of the season.

When the plant reaches 4–5 ft (1.2–1.5 m) remove the lower leaves beneath the first truss to allow air to circulate and to encourage ripening of the lower trusses. Spray against pests and diseases and keep the plants well watered to prevent disorders such as blossom end rot and cracked fruit.

Capsicums are today a very popular ingredient of salads and savoury dishes. Seeds are sown individually in small pots during late winter in a cool temperature of 50–55°F (10–13°C).

[1] As soon as the plants are well rooted, but not pot-bound, they are planted 18 in (45 cm) apart in growing bags or 7 in (18 cm) pots. To assist fruiting spray the open flowers.

[2] Start to feed the plants as soon as the first fruits have set.

Pick the peppers as soon as they are ripe to encourage others to develop.

☼ Aubergines: spraying open flowers to aid fruit setting.

[1] Capsicums: planting young plants in a growing bag.

[2] Liquid-feeding the maturing plants.

Aubergines require similar treatment to peppers. They are propagated from seed raised in a slightly higher temperature of 65–70°F (18–21°C). This is reduced to 60–65°F (15–18°C) for growing on.

☼ To help the fruit to set, spray the open flowers on sunny days. If you require large fruits, leave only six to develop and remove the rest.

[1] Melon: sowing seeds.

[2] Setting out plants at 4-leaf stage.

[3] Tying-in the maturing plant to wire supports.

Food: compatible plants 2

Melons and **cucumbers** both like hot, humid conditions and can be grown successfully together.

[1] Their seeds are large and are sown, on edge, in 3 in (7.5 cm) pots during mid-winter where a temperature of 75°F (22°C) is maintained. Germination takes only a few days.

Sowing can be delayed until the weather warms up or lower temperatures can be provided but germination will take longer and fruiting will be later. Ideally maintain 70°F (21°C) during the life of the crop. At temperatures less than 55°F (13°C) growth will be poor.

[2] Set the plants out 2 ft (1.2 m) apart before they become pot bound, usually at the four-leaf stage. Growing bags and pots will guarantee successful results or you can grow the plants in the open ground for better yields, providing it is well prepared and disease free. Melons should be planted so that the top of the roots are slightly exposed to reduce the risk of collar rot. Cucumbers can be planted deeper as roots can form on the stems. They should be mulched to conserve moisture.

[3] [4] Train melons upright so they take up less room. Allow the main stem to grow to 3 ft (90 cm) then remove the growing tip. Tie in the side shoots to horizontal wires placed in rows 9 in (23 cm) apart. Remove the tips when the shoots reach 18 in (45 cm). Cucumbers can be similarly trained. Tie the main stem to a cane and tie in the upper side shoots to horizontal wires.

Remove the lowest six or seven side shoots to encourage larger fruits. Pinch out the growing tips of the shoots as soon as the second leaf has formed.

Stop further lateral shoots which develop, after the first true leaf has formed.

[5] Traditional varieties of cucumbers carry both male and female flowers. If cross-pollination takes place, bitter and seedy fruit may be produced. To prevent this pick off the male flowers every day before they are fully open. To recognize which is which, the female flowers all have a miniature cucumber behind them, whereas the males have very short stalks. This should be carried out daily. Modern 'labour-saving' all-female varieties are also available.

With melons the female flowers have to be pollinated before the fruits will develop. This is done by picking off a fully open male flower, removing the petals and pushing its pollen coated stamens into the centre of a female flower. The female flowers are easily identified by the miniature melon already forming behind the bloom. One and maybe more male flowers are needed to pollinate each female flower, but allow only one fruit to form on each side shoot and remove the rest.

[6] As the melons get heavier support them to the horizontal wires in a string net.

When the fruits have started to swell feed both cucumbers and melons weekly and do not allow the compost to dry out. As soon as the melons have swelled to full size reduce watering otherwise they may split. Ripe melons give off a strong, distinctive aroma and can easily be damaged at this stage.

Maintain the temperature around 60–65°F (15–18°C) nearer to harvesting to improve the flavour of the fruit. Damp down the path and foliage regularly to increase the humidity. Treat pests and diseases as soon as they occur.

[4] Tying in the side shoots.

[5] Removing a male flower.

[6] String net to support the mature fruit.

11
COMPOSTS

Ordinary garden soil is quite unsuitable for plants growing in pots. It seldom has a good open texture, nor enough fibrous matter to make it well drained. It usually contains weed seeds, pests and diseases – a definite recipe for disaster. A good usable potting compost must be sterile, with no harmful organisms, 'open' to allow free drainage and passage of air (the roots need to breathe too) and contain a well-balanced supply of nutrients.

To achieve this only the best ingredients must be used and a reliable recipe followed. In the 1930's the John Innes Institute developed a few standard mixes in which all common plants can be grown. The ingredients are as follows:

Loam, such as that found under mature meadows (this can be made at home by stacking turves); sphagnum moss peat, which is granular and free from dust; washed coarse sand, not builders' sand. The loam must be shredded and freshly sterilized, at a temperature of 180°F (82°C) for 30 minutes, then allowed to cool before being mixed with the peat and sand. Small electric sterilizers are available for use at home.

For the John Innes Seed mix you will need the following:

2 parts by volume of sieved loam
1 part by volume of sphagnum peat
1 part by volume of coarse horticultural sand

To every 8 gallons (40 litres) of the mixture add:

1½ oz (42 gm) superphosphate and ¾ oz (21 gm) of finely ground chalk. Leave the chalk out if the compost is for lime hating plants*.

The standard John Innes Potting mix is made up from:

7 parts by volume of sieved loam
3 parts by volume of sphagnum peat
2 parts by volume of coarse horticultural sand

For No 1 compost, which is suitable for seedlings and young plants, you will need to add to every 8 gallons (40 litres) of the mixture 4 oz (113 gm) of the base fertilizer and ¾ oz (21 gm) of ground chalk*. John Innes base is made up by mixing equal parts by weight of superphosphate and hoof and horn, plus half a part of sulphate of potash. For No 2 compost, suitable for most pot plants, add twice as much fertilizer and for No 3, used for very vigorous or large plants, use three times as much.

[1] The ingredients should be laid out on clean paving or concrete in a sandwich fashion: layers of loam, peat, sand and fertilizer.

[2] In the same way you would mix cement, the compost is turned three or four times so that all the ingredients are evenly mixed.

Proprietary brands of John Innes compost are available but due to the reduced availability in good loam, poor quality types are often sold. Look out for those carrying the seal of the John Innes Manufacturers' Association.

The most widely used composts today are the soil-less types. These are usually based on sphagnum peat and either perlite, coarse sand or vermiculite with nutrients added. Polystyrene granules can also be used to 'open up' the compost to allow good aeration and drainage. They also help in retaining heat in the compost so fewer problems of root rot can be expected. Ingredients need to be chosen carefully as peat will dry out very quickly and can be difficult to moisten again. Most proprietary

[1] Compost making: making layers of peat, loam, sand and fertilizer.

brands have a wetting agent added to overcome this problem. At home a dash of washing-up liquid added to the mixture will work quite well. When horticultural perlite is used instead of sharp sand it makes the compost easier to moisten as it readily absorbs water.

Horticultural vermiculite is another alternative to sand. It has similar qualities to perlite and is especially useful to make a proprietary brand of compost go further. Add vermiculite at the rate of half by volume to a loam-less compost to make it free draining and easily wettable. Vermiculite can also be used on its own for root cuttings, which essentially require good drainage.

[2] The ingredients are thoroughly mixed together.

12
POTTING AND FEEDING

[1] Potting on: removing the plant from its container.

[2] The plant in its new larger pot.

[3] Firming the plant in its new compost.

As soon as the days lengthen and the temperature rises in the spring, plants seem to take a turn for the better and produce plenty of fresh green leaves and strong vigorous stems. If a plant does not have enough room to expand below ground at the same time then it will suffer from lack of nutrients and maybe drought. A pot bound plant needs frequent watering. After several months in the same pot a vigorous plant will probably be ready for moving into a larger pot. To check if this is the case you will need to take the plant out of its pot – water the plant first and it will be easier to remove.

[1] Take the pot off by spreading your fingers over the surface of the soil and inverting the pot. Gently knock the rim on the edge of the staging to help loosen the plant. If the soil is a mass of roots winding round in circles, tease them carefully apart to encourage them to spread into the fresh compost. Choose a pot only a couple of inches larger in diameter than the existing one. Using a pot that is several sizes bigger can lead to overwatering and root rot.

[2] Place a little compost in the base of the pot so that the plant sits about $\frac{1}{2}$ in (13 mm) below the rim. Backfill with compost.

[3] Firm the compost around the edge with your fingers. Add more compost to fill the gaps then tap the pot on the bench to settle the level. Water the plant in well using a can fitted with a fine rose.

Place the freshly potted plants in a shady part of the greenhouse for a few days to let them settle in their new pots, then move them into a well-lit position on the staging.

When plants have reached a good-sized pot and you do not have space to move them on, they will need an annual top dressing and feeding regularly to keep them happy. Top dressing is done in the spring and the top inch or so of compost is scraped away and replenished with fresh. When a plant has been in the same spot for more than a month it will have used all the nutrients in the compost, so will need feeding. Most of the fertilizers formulated for pot grown plants are 'complete' ones – they contain all the main nutrients: Nitrogen (N), phosphate (P) and potash (K) plus trace elements. The use of the feed in your growing programme will depend on the proportions of nutrients in each brand of fertilizer. Some are higher in nitrogen, many are balanced and others contain higher proportions of phosphates and potash. Nitrogen is the leaf maker and most foliage plants require a high nitrogen feed through the summer. Phosphates encourage root growth and to a lesser degree help to harden plants against disease and low temperature. Potash is essential to produce full-sized flowers and top-grade fruit.

Liquid feeds are best for potted plants. These should be diluted and applied according to the maker's instructions. If plants are overfed they will equally suffer.

Solid, dry, slow-release fertilizers are useful for busy gardeners who cannot spare the time to feed their plants once a week. They are sold in stick, granule and tablet form and are applied at the beginning of the season. A little of the nutrient is dissolved every time the plant is watered.

Foliar feeds are useful more as a tonic, a plant pick-me-up for neglected specimens. They can also be used to supplement ordinary feeding for fast growing plants. They are diluted in water and sprayed on to the leaves.

Follow liquid-feed manufacturer's instructions carefully.

Inserting a solid fertilizer stick.

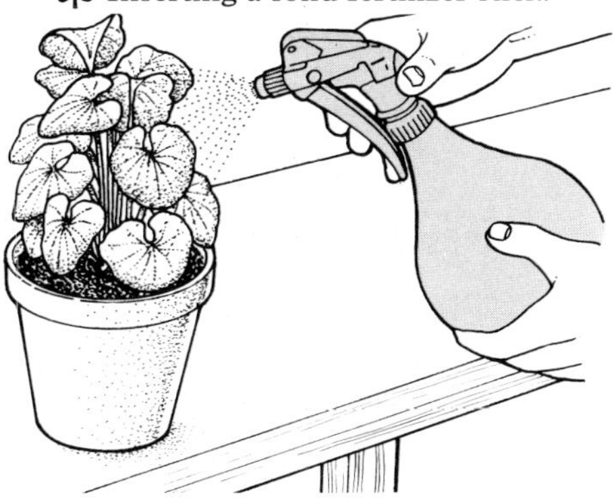

Foliar feeds are sprayed on to the leaves.

13
GROWING SYSTEMS

There are several methods by which you can grow plants under glass. Pots are the obvious choice for display work, but for seasonal crops like tomatoes the border soil is often used. This is because the roots are not restricted and plants can grow to a much bigger size, and produce more trusses of fruit. Growing in the ground can be more risky than in containers of compost, for unless you are sure that the soil is completely pest and disease free, is well drained and contains no toxic substances the plants will be of no use at all. If one type of crop is grown in the same soil year after year the yields often deteriorate due to soil sickness. To prevent this from happening it would be best to rotate your crops, but if you lack the space to do this or are only growing tomatoes the best plan would be to replace the top 12 in (30 cm) of soil with fresh compost every other year or sterilize it. Sterilizing the borders may be quite difficult to do if the greenhouse is never empty. It has to be cleared of plants completely for a specified time and the borders cannot be planted up for anything up to two months. If you cannot afford a gap in your growing programme other methods of growing your tomatoes and cucumbers will have to be sought.

Ring culture is a popular alternative to the open ground, the roots are given quite a free run so yields are similar but the problems of soil-borne pests and diseases are eliminated.

[1] Dig a trench, to a spade's depth in the soil border of the greenhouse.

[2] Lay plastic sheeting in the trench and then backfill with gravel.

[3] Plant the tomatoes in bottomless 8 in (20 cm) pots of loam-based compost such as John Innes No. 3. The idea is that the feeding roots are confined to the pot whereas the bulk of the roots search for water and anchor the plants securely in the gravel. The plants, once established, are watered via the gravel.

[1] Ring culture: digging out the trench.

[2] Plastic-lined trench filled with gravel.

A liquid feed is poured into the pot of compost once a week.

The watering and feeding requirements can be quite difficult to assess at first, but once the roots are growing happily through the substrate the bed can be soaked and left on hot days without fear of it drying out to the detriment of the plants. The moisture will also help create a humid atmosphere which is beneficial in the summer.

Growing bags have overtaken both the open soil and ring culture methods of growing seasonal crops. This is mainly because they are clean and convenient to use, they can be placed on a concrete floor and you do not need a greenhouse to use them. Any number of plants can be successfully grown in them from strawberries and cucumbers to bedding plants, but they are most popularly used for tomatoes. Yields may not be quite as good as the other systems because the restricted root run usually produces smaller plants. The standard compost used makes them completely reliable providing they are kept well watered. If they are allowed to dry out the peat-based compost is difficult to re-wet.

3 Feeding roots in pot; anchoring roots in gravel.

☼ A cut-open growing bag ready for planting.

☼ Before you plant up the bag cut out the area marked by the manufacturer or, to conserve as much moisture as possible, just cut a slit crossways in the marked area and plant so that the polythene fits close to the stems.

Automatic watering systems specifically designed for growing bags are available. Some are trays with water channels and capillary matting. Others consist of small bore tubes, fitted with drip nozzles that can be closed if necessary, which are pegged into the compost. Water is supplied from a header tank which is topped up manually.

Feeding is necessary as with other growing systems and solid sticks of fertilizer are useful for they are slow release and feed the crop for a whole season. Liquid feeds especially formulated for growing bags are applied on a weekly basis during the growing season.

14
SUPPORT SYSTEMS

Many greenhouse plants need staking to prevent them from flopping, because the soft growth that tall plants, such as tomatoes and chrysanthemums, make during the growing season is not sturdy enough to hold them upright. Bamboo canes, now also plastic coated steel ones, and string are most frequently used, but it is really only useful if the cane can be pushed into the pot or ground deep enough so that it can support the weight of the top growth.

☼ For plants up to 2 ft (60 cm) tall or larger ones growing in an 8 or 10 in (20 or 25 cm) pot, a cane is usually quite sufficient, but it is best inserted when the plant is potted in the first instance even though the growth at this stage may not require staking. If inserted when the roots fill the pot there is a likelihood that they will be damaged and open to infection and growth will be checked.

♣ Twist ties and wire clips are convenient to use, especially for fast-growing plants like chrysanthemums and carnations, but the tie must always look inconspicuous for display work, so with plants that have a dainty habit stick to soft green string or raffia. Tie the plant loosely to the cane so there is room for the stems to expand without being bruised or cut by the string.

For plants with a straggly habit or grassy foliage, such as bulbs, three canes can be inserted around the edge of the pot and looped with string. More effective, though, are pea sticks as they help to retain some of the natural shape of the plant. Where top-heavy crops such as tomatoes and cucumbers are growing in pots (and especially in growing bags where there is no depth to push in a cane securely) another system of support has to be adopted.

✿ For growing bags special metal frames are available. The growing bag sits on the wire base to hold the frame firm and canes are pushed in slots in the top. This arrangement is very useful if you are growing tomatoes in the centre of the greenhouse where the plants cannot easily be tied into the framework. At the sides of the greenhouse string alone can be used.

◊ A length of strong, durable string

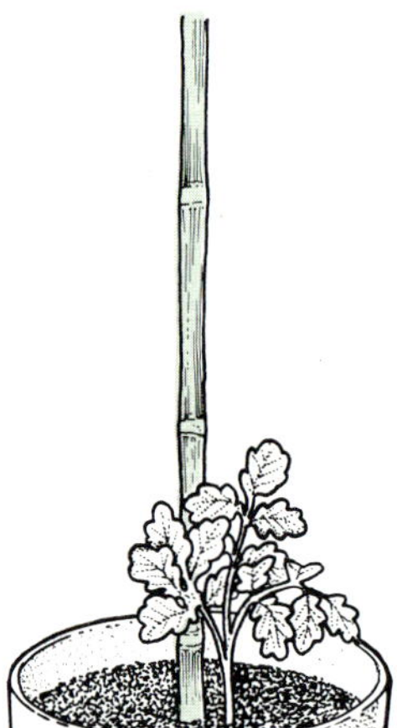

☼ Single-cane support.

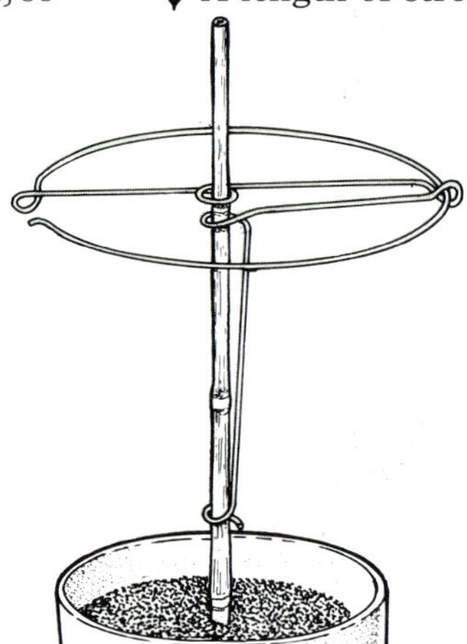

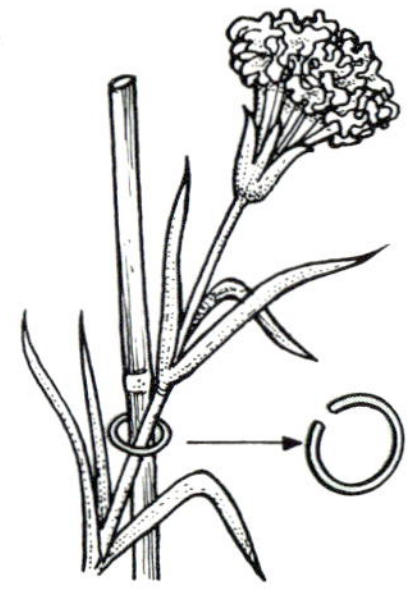

♣ Wire twist tie and clip.

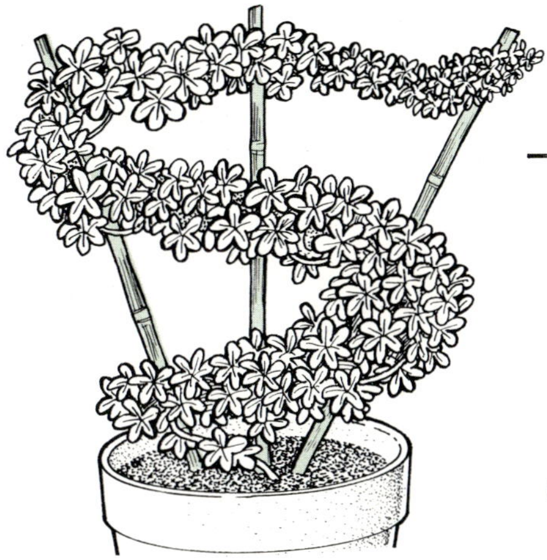

Three-cane support.

Use of string as plant support.

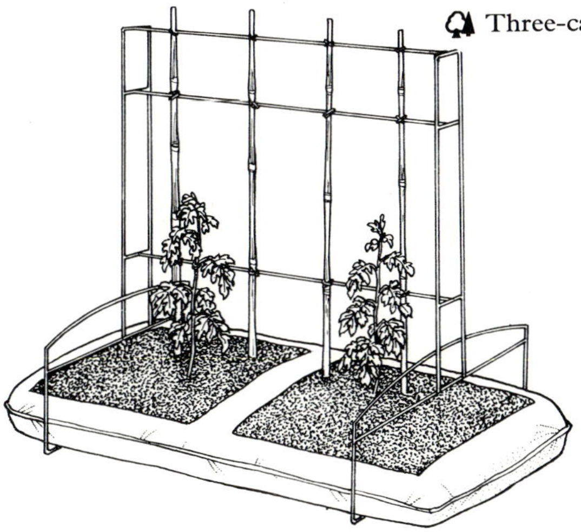

Metal support frame for growing bag.

is tied to a hook, embedded in the soil and then wound clockwise round the stem and secured to the greenhouse frame. In aluminium greenhouses special clips which fit into the glazing bars are available, or strings can be tied to a piece of wire running across the eaves. As the plant grows the string is twisted round the stem. For permanent climbing plants a more substantial support system is required. Taut wires stretched across the sides of the greenhouse are ideal for plants with shrubby growth, such as vines. The wires need to be placed in rows 10 in (12.5 cm) apart and in the case of aluminium greenhouses are secured to the glazing bars with special clips.

Young climbers and annual varieties can be supported in pots with a framework of canes. Lightweight canes are arranged in a fan-shape and are tied together with soft string. Plastic frames of a similar design are also available.

15 HYGIENE

To be sure of healthy plants and to prevent troublesome pests and diseases,strict cleanliness is an essential part of greenhouse management. During the growing season faded flowers and dead leaves should be removed, algae checked and weeds hoed out of the borders as soon as they are seen. Debris and weeds will harbour pests and diseases ready to infect your plants. The glass should be kept crystal clear; dirty glass can affect light transmission by as much as 20%, which will reduce the growth rate of plants tremendously in winter. Once a year the greenhouse framework should be given a good scrub. Autumn is usually the best time as most of the summer crops are over and much clearing-out is necessary.

[1] The shading paint on the outside of the glass will need washing off, too. If you have been shading in the summer with external roller blinds, they should be cleaned, removed and stored in a dry building. If they are left in place all year round they may become damaged by the weather.

[1] Autumn cleaning: washing off the shading paint.

[2] Plants that are left in the greenhouse after clearing out the spent crops should be placed outside, if it is a mild day, or put in the house until the greenhouse has been cleaned. Start the job first thing in the morning so that you can put them back before nightfall.

[3] Use a strong disinfectant in the water to scrub down the framework. Make sure that you clean all the nooks and crannies where overwintering eggs and spores may be lurking. Scrub the staging also and if the plants have been standing on gravel or sand give this a wash too. Throw away capillary matting that is green with algae.

[4] If you have been growing plants in the border soil and have been troubled with soil-borne pests, fork it over and water with a chemical sterilizer. This is best done before the soil temperature drops below 50°F (10°C) for best results. Empty the greenhouse of plants and apply the chemical as instructed. Cover the soil with polythene sheeting and keep the ventilators closed. Keep out of the greenhouse

[2] Remove all plant debris from ground surface.

3 Scrub down framework with disinfectant.

4 Sterilize the border soil.

5 Clean the glass inside and out with warm, soapy water.

for the interval recommended by the manufacturers. Afterwards open the ventilators and door wide to let the fumes escape more quickly. Then fork over the border; do not plant anything in the borders until the recommended time has elapsed. This can be anything from one to eight weeks.

5 Clean the glass on the inside and out with a sponge and warm soapy water. A long-handled squeeze mop is useful for reaching the roof. Where the panes of glass overlap, dirt and algae tend to collect, this can be dislodged with a kitchen knife or metal label. Plants which are to be put back into the greenhouse should be checked for pests and diseases and fumigated if necessary. Pots should be thoroughly washed and wiped over before standing them on the clean bench.

16
PESTS AND DISEASES

Whether the climate in the greenhouse is warm and moist, cold and damp or hot and dry, pests and diseases will flourish. You therefore have to try your utmost to prevent attack by growing in optimum conditions, with strict attention to hygiene.

☼ Making a solid floor out of brick or concrete will prevent weed growth or a 2 in (5 cm) layer of gravel will restrict it. Weeds harbour troublemakers ready to infect your plants.

☘ A small outbreak of pests and diseases may be controlled by hand picking and removing infected leaves, but if many plants become infected chemicals will have to be used. It is essential to good husbandry that you are able to recognize at least the commonest pests and diseases, plus the symptoms plants show when they are present. This will help you to get rid of them as easily as possible before they ruin your plants.

Aphids (greenfly) attack most common plants. They feed by piercing the plant tissue and sucking the sap. This causes the plant to become weak and the resulting growth can be stunted, distorted and discoloured. They also produce a sticky excrement called honeydew which attracts sooty mould, which will cover the leaves and block out light. Virus disease may also be transmitted by aphids due to their action of feeding.

Controlling aphids on a small scale can be done by washing them off with luke warm soapy water. They can also be controlled by a variety of chemicals such as pirimicarb and malathion.

Whitefly, tiny moth-like insects, suck the sap from the foliage, which weakens the plant and affects growth. They also excrete honeydew. The young flies are 'scales' and are difficult to control as they have a waxy coating which prevents the penetration of spray chemicals. A systemic insecticide should be used to kill the feeding adults, and this must be repeated at intervals to catch the maturing scales.

Leaf miners are the larvae of insects which lay their eggs inside the leaves of a number of plants, particularly chrysanthemums and cinerarias. The larvae

☼ Making a solid floor, brick or concrete.

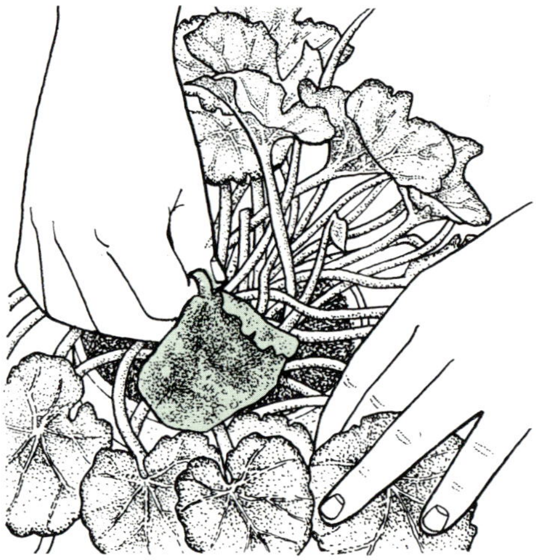

☘ Removing an infected leaf.

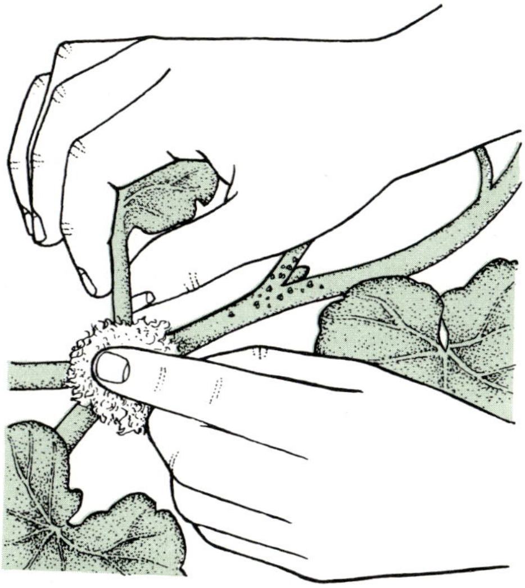

Removing mealy bugs with cotton wool soaked in meths.

are creamy coloured grubs which tunnel and feed inside the leaf leaving narrow snake-like marks behind them. If there are only a few infested leaves, remove and burn them. In more serious cases spray fortnightly with malathion or HCH.

Mealy bugs are soft, oval flattish insects without wings. They resemble small woodlice and are covered with a white or pinkish waxy woolly coating. They can be found in the axils of the leaves and buds. Both the adults and young suck sap from the leaves and excrete honeydew. Attacked plants make poor growth, their leaves turn yellow and drop. Rub them off with cotton wool soaked in methylated spirit. Alternatively use a systemic insecticide for continual control.

Red spider mites are a serious problem where conditions are hot and dry. They are minute – you will need a hand lens to see them. Both the adults and young feed on the undersides of the leaves causing a yellow speckling to appear on the upper surface. The leaves eventually turn bronze and fall. These withering leaves are often covered with a fine silk webbing. Attacked plants are usually stunted.

Damping down the path and misting the foliage helps to check small infestations.

Chemical control should be applied regularly and the chemical should be changed frequently to prevent pests from becoming immune. Chemicals to use are: derris, malathion and demeton-S-methyl. Red spider mites cease to breed when the weather turns cold. They overwinter in the greenhouse framework, so it must be scrubbed thoroughly every autumn.

Scale insects look like waxy brown blisters on the leaves and stems. Apart from the young, which crawl, they are quite immobile and feed by sucking the plant sap. This causes loss of vigour, stunting of young growth and yellowing foliage. They also excrete honeydew. Remove the scales by hand, with cotton wool dipped in methylated spirits, or use a systemic insecticide.

Thrips (thunderbugs) are usually found on the underside of leaves, young shoots and in flowers. They feed by scraping the surface tissues and sucking sap. Damaged areas can be identified by a silver mottling, which may later turn brown. In severe cases the leaves become distorted. Thrips will transmit viruses and should be controlled with HCH or demeton-S-methyl.

Blackleg is a disease that commonly destroys cuttings and is caused by fungi and bacteria present in the soil or water. To control the disease pay strict attention to greenhouse hygiene and use sterilized composts. Add potassium permanganate to stored water to purify it. Destroy affected cuttings.

Damping-off is caused by parasitic fungi that attack seedlings and causes them to collapse and die. The fungi live on dead and decaying matter in the soil and tend to attack overcrowded seedlings, especially if they are growing in a wet, compacted soil. High temperatures also favour the disease. Check attacks by watering with Chestnut compound (pbi), captan or zineb.

Grey mould usually infects plants through open wounds and is encouraged especially in winter, when plenty of moisture is left lying overnight on flower and foliage. Overcrowded plants in the greenhouse create the ideal conditions. Good hygiene prevents trouble. To control use thiram or zineb.

Pest and disease controls

Fungicides and insecticides are available in many forms – as liquids applied to the soil, as liquids sprayed onto the foliage, as dusting powders and fumigant smokes. Fumigants are most suitable to use as a precautionary measure and a combined insecticide/fungicide can be used all year round at regular intervals to protect your plants from attack. Fumigants are popular mainly because they can be applied quickly to a greenhouse full of plants. But you must check that none of the plants you are growing is susceptible to damage (a full list will be on the packet) and it would be best to wait until seedlings are growing well in their first pot before you risk treating them. Fumigants are applied at a measured rate depending on the cubic capacity of the greenhouse. This is calculated by the formula: length × width × height, midway between eaves and ridge. The manufacturer's instructions will indicate what volume each cone or pellet will treat. Fumigating is best done in the later afternoon or on dull days, several hours after the plants have been watered. Never fumigate plants which are dry at the roots.

Beforehand damp down the path and benches, taking care not to wet any plant foliage. This will create a moist atmosphere and make the smoke hang longer. Seal any gaps with tape or sacking to make the greenhouse smoke-tight.

☼ Close the ventilators, then light the fumigant and shut the door securely behind you. The morning after fumigating the greenhouse, open the ventilators and door wide to allow the fumes to escape. Do not work in the greenhouse for at least an hour.

Liquid chemicals

Liquid chemicals should be handled with care and only stored in their original containers out of the reach of children.

Pest and disease controls

☼ Fumigation: sealing the door.

♣ Use gloves and face mask when applying liquid chemicals.

Grow nasturtiums between tomatoes to repel whitefly and greenfly.

Rubber gloves and a face mask should be worn when mixing and using chemicals.

There are two ways in which insecticides work. Some kill insects on contact whereas others are systemic, absorbed by the plants, and kill feeding insects over a few weeks. Spraying should only be done on dull days otherwise the plants may scorch. It is essential, with contact insecticides especially, to see that all parts of the plant are covered. Dusts and smokes are most effective for curing diseases. Red spider mite and whitefly in particular are very difficult pests to control. They breed so quickly that unless you spray regularly to catch the eggs as the adults emerge the problem escalates. Regular spraying can lead to other problems, plant damage, insect immunity to the chemical and delayed harvesting. For these reasons other methods of control are sought.

Biological control

Growing nasturtiums in between tomatoes is a tried and tested method of repelling whitefly and greenfly. Other companion plantings have been tried but scientific proof of their worth is still awaited.

Using natural predators and parasites for control is most effective and extensively used by commercial growers. The natural enemies of whitefly and red spider mite are available from specialist suppliers. Whitefly is controlled by a tiny parasitic wasp called *Encarsia formosa*.

These chalcid wasps lay eggs in the whitefly larvae, which are seen as motionless scales on the underside of the leaves. When parasitized they turn black and the larvae is killed. Within a couple of weeks the wasps hatch out and continue to take care of eggs, larvae and future generations.

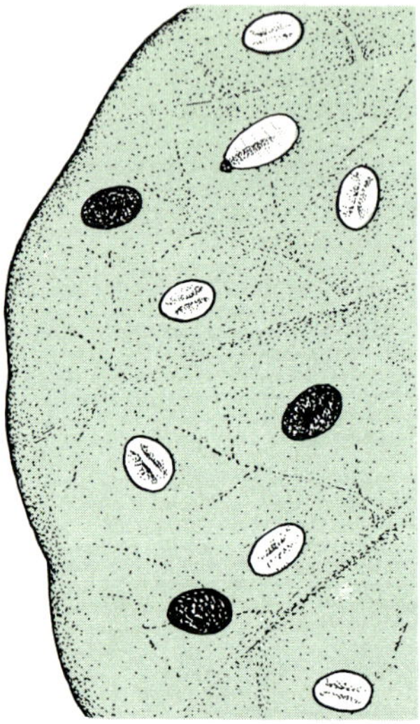

Biological control: the eggs of the chalcid wasp parasitize whitefly larvae.

Red spider mites are controlled by a predatory mite called *Phytoseiulus persimilis*. These can eat up to seven adults and 20 eggs a day. Once all the pests have been cleared both *Encarsia* and *Phytoseiulius* will die, so they are only worth investing in if the plants are badly infested. They can seldom be kept going in the greenhouse through the winter. Other natural enemies to control mealy bugs and leaf miner may be available in the near future to amateur gardeners.

INDEX

CW01618765

Photographies : p. 1 : À la terrasse d'un café, place des Vosges ; pp. 2-3 : Sous la tour Eiffel ; p. 8 : Le Louvre et sa pyramide.

SOMMAIRE

COMMENT UTILISER

Musée du Jeu de Paume

Carte p. 123

Palais du Louvre, 107, rue de Rivoli

Fermé lun.

01 44 55 57 50

€

Palais-Royal-Musée du Louvre, Tuileries, Pyramides

RENSEIGNEMENTS

Des informations sur les principaux sites à visiter figurent en marge des pages (voir la légende des symboles sur le dernier rabat de la couverture). Lorsque la visite est payante, le tarif des entrées est indiqué par le symbole €.

€	moins de 5 euros
€€	de 5 à 10 euros
€€€	de 10 à 15 euros
€€€€	de 15 à 20 euros
€€€€€	plus de 20 euros

58

CODE COULEUR

Chaque quartier est identifié à l'aide d'une couleur afin de faciliter la navigation dans le guide. Ce même principe est appliqué dans la partie **Informations pratiques.**

TABLEAUX SYNOPTIQUES

Vous trouverez des tableaux à la fin du guide (pp. 240-243 et pp. 249-251) pour vous aider à choisir hôtels et restaurants. Classé par ordre de prix, quartier, niveau de prestation, chaque établissement est précédé d'un numéro qui renvoie à une notice explicative dans les pages suivantes. Nos enquêteurs ont établi ces listes selon des critères objectifs, mais aussi selon leur coup de cœur.

HÔTELS

N°		tél.	prix	ch
3	À LA VILLA DES ARTISTES	01 43 26 60 86	¥¥¥	59
4	ARTUS HÔTEL	01 43 29 07 20	¥¥¥	25
16	AU MANOIR ST-GERMAIN-DES-P.	01 42 22 21 65	¥	32
47	BALZAC	01 44 35 18 00	¥¥¥	70
66	BEAUMARCHAIS	01 53 36 86 86	¥¥¥	29+2s
17	BEL-AMI	01 42 61 53 53	¥¥	115
39	BRIGHTON	01 47 03 61 61	¥¥	64+1s
40	CAMBON	01 44 58 93 93	¥¥¥	32+8s
5	COLBERT	01 56 81 19 00	¥	36+3s
41	COSTES	01 42 44 50 00	¥¥¥	80+3s

Détails de tableaux synoptiques réduits

SAINT-GERMAIN & MONTPARNASSE

16 – AU MANOIR SAINT-GERMAIN-DES-PRÉS
★★★★ €€€
TÉL. : 01 42 22 21 65
FAX : 01 45 48 22 25
153, BOULEVARD SAINT-GERMAIN – 75006
SAINT-GERMAIN-DES-PRÉS
Face à Saint-Germain-des-Prés et des célèbres cafés de Flore et des Deux-Magots, se tient l'élégant Manoir.

17 – HÔTEL BEL-AMI
★★★★ €€€€
TÉL. : 01 42 61 53 53
FAX : 01 49 27 09 33
7/11, RUE SAINT-BENOÎT – 75006
SAINT-GERMAIN-DES-PRÉS
Les amateurs de design seront comblés dans cet hôtel entièrement rénové. Mélange de style, harmonie des couleurs, matières nobles, maîtrise de la lumière… le Bel-Ami est vraiment très chic.

18 – HÔTEL FERRANDI
★★★ €€€
TÉL. : 01 42 22 97 40
FAX : 01 45 44 89 97
92, RUE DU CHERCHE-MIDI – 75006
SAINT-PLACIDE
Le Ferrandi est un trois étoiles qui a tout d'un grand hôtel. De belles réceptions richement meublées et décorées en style Restauration, des chambres spacieuses et des salles de

Nom du quartier et code couleur

Numéro, nom de l'hôtel et indication de tarif

Adresse, téléphone, fax, métro le plus proche

Bref commentaire sur l'hôtel

RESTAURANTS

Les restaurants sont classés par ordre de prix, pour que vous n'ayez pas de mauvaises surprises au moment de l'addition. À chaque nom de restaurant correspond un chiffre qui renvoie à un bref commentaire. Le téléphone figure également car il vaut mieux réserver dans les bons restaurants. Hors de France métropolitaine, composez le 00 33 avant les dix chiffres.

RESTAURANTS

	moins de 20 €	tél.	métro
82	AU PIED DE FOUET	01 47 05 12 27	Sèvres-Babylone
29	BISTROT BEAUBOURG	01 42 77 48 02	Rambuteau
79	CHARTIER	01 47 70 86 29	Grands Boulevards
83	CHEZ GERMAINE	01 42 73 28 34	Duroc
106	CHEZ GLADINES	01 45 80 70 10	Corvisart
101	CHEZ TOINETTE	01 42 54 44 36	Abbesses
45	L'AS DU FALLAFEL	01 48 87 63 60	Saint-Paul
96	LE GALILÉO	01 47 20 91 30	Kléber
46	LE PETIT FER À CHEVAL	01 42 72 47 47	Saint-Paul/Hôtel-de-Ville

CARTE DE SITUATION

Les monuments marquants du quartier

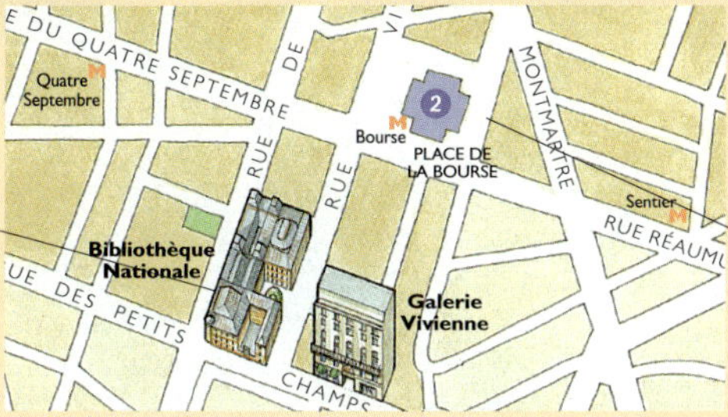

Bâtiments ou lieux intéressants

ITINÉRAIRE DE PROMENADE

Site intéressant sur l'itinéraire

Itinéraire

Les chiffres en rouge renvoient aux lieux et bâtiments mentionnés dans le texte

Départ de promenade

Sens de la promenade

- Un encadré indique le point de départ et d'arrivée de la promenade, sa durée, son kilométrage et les lieux incontournables. Lorsque deux itinéraires sont proposés, le second est tracé en orange.

CARTE D'ESCAPADE

Autres lieux conseillés

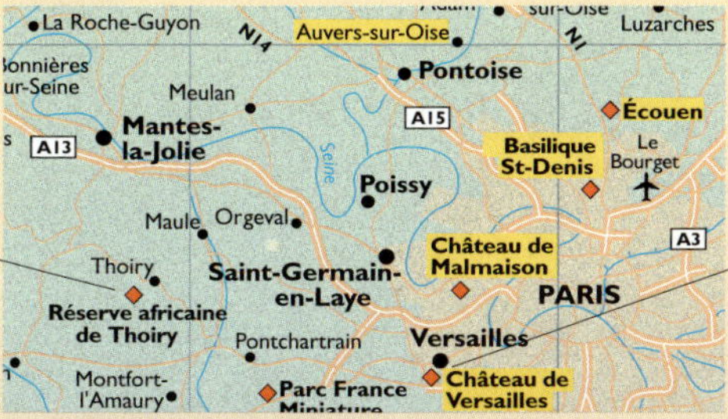

Lieu conseillé, faisant l'objet d'une description dans le guide

PAVILLON SULLY

Histoire et culture

Détail d'une statue de la basilique Saint-Denis.

Paris aujourd'hui

« VILLE LUMIÈRE », « LA PLUS BELLE VILLE DU MONDE », « CAPITALE DE LA MODE », VOIRE « capitale du monde », Paris est une ville superlative qui ne laisse aucun visiteur indifférent. Doté d'une incroyable richesse culturelle, Paris n'est pas une ville musée. En effet, les Parisiens se réapproprient de plus en plus l'espace public. Le Paris d'aujourd'hui, ce sont les quais fermés aux voitures le dimanche, les gigantesques promenades en rollers, les parties de football sur les pelouses de l'hôtel des Invalides…

PREMIER CONTACT

Quand on arrive dans une ville que l'on connaît uniquement par les livres, on court à l'endroit que par avance l'esprit a magnifié. À Florence, les premiers pas vous précipitent au Palazzo Vecchio ; à Moscou, au Kremlin ; à Athènes, au Parthénon. Où trouver à Paris aujourd'hui cette image ? La tour Eiffel ? L'Opéra ? Le Sacré-Cœur ? Les Champs-Élysées si célèbres à travers le monde ? Oui, sans doute. Mais d'abord le fleuve, la Seine, et l'un de ses ponts, celui du Carrousel ou celui des Arts.

C'est à cet endroit que l'on prend conscience que Paris, plus que toutes les autres capitales européennes, est d'abord une ville royale. Tout y reflète noblesse et grandeur : rive droite, l'immense palais du Louvre modelé à travers les siècles par les plus grands architectes ; rive gauche, l'ancien collège des Quatre-Nations, qui abrite l'Académie française, et l'hôtel de la Monnaie, chef-d'œuvre d'Antoine ; le Pont-Neuf (le plus vieux pont de Paris) d'où Henri IV à cheval contemple les deux ravissantes maisons de briques roses qui s'élèvent au débouché de la place Dauphine construite sous son règne.

Au loin, les tours du palais de Justice évoquent les derniers rois capétiens tandis que la flèche de la Sainte-Chapelle, les tours de Notre-Dame et le dôme du Panthéon (ex-église Sainte-Geneviève) rappellent que la religion catholique a profondément marqué le paysage parisien. Nulle part on ne trouve une pareille harmonie entre la nature et les œuvres des hommes, un équilibre aussi juste entre les pierres, les arbres, l'eau et le ciel. Nulle part on ne pénètre mieux dans l'intelligence de Paris.

La promenade que proposent les célèbres bateaux-mouches est une agréable façon de prendre contact avec Paris. De jour mais plus encore de nuit, la vue est spectaculaire.

Mais le Paris d'aujourd'hui ne se résume pas au spectacle enchanteur des rives de la Seine (inscrites sur la liste du patrimoine mondial par l'Unesco) ou à celui des admirables perspec-

tives qui ont tracé leurs sillons dans la capitale. Il recèle aussi, au hasard des rues de ses 80 quartiers, des trésors, humbles ou somptueux, qu'un promeneur à l'œil un tant soit peu exercé découvre avec ravissement : vieux puits dissimulé dans une cour aux pavés disjoints, antiques maisons à colombages, vestiges des remparts qui pendant des siècles ont ceinturé Paris, porches aux heurtoirs ciselés, vieilles enseignes, inscriptions des noms de rues sculptées à même le mur des maisons…

Le Marais, le Quartier latin, Saint-Germain-des-Prés sont des lieux de prédilection pour ceux qui cherchent les témoignages du passé. C'est également dans ces antiques quartiers que se sont installés nombre des créateurs que compte la capitale. Boutiques de mode et de décoration, ateliers, galeries, espaces multimédias, cafés sont incontournables pour sentir les tendances du moment. Et puis, brusquement, au détour d'une rue : un jardin princier ou un square étriqué où hêtres pourpres, noyers du Japon, chênes verts, platanes d'Orient, marronniers, saules pleureurs, micocouliers de Provence, entre autres, ombragent des parterres fleuris. Il y a 450 000 arbres à Paris, plantés dans 3 000 ha d'espaces verts entretenus par 2 000 jardiniers.

PARIS ET SA RÉGION

Paris n'est pas pour autant une ville-musée, même si ses innombrables musées eux-mêmes comptent parmi les principales raisons de son rayonnement. Paris est une ville de pouvoir. Capitale de la France depuis quinze siècles, la ville a joué un rôle essentiel dans la mise en place de l'État français moderne qui s'est développé à partir des Capétiens. Depuis les années 1980, une politique de décentralisation a été menée, mais, à bien des égards, la France reste dépendante de sa capitale dont les autres régions peinent à se démarquer.

Baigné par la Seine, Paris est situé au milieu du plus grand bassin sédimentaire d'Europe occidentale. Cet espace géographique – la région Île-de-France – concentre sur à peine 2 % du territoire national plus de 15 % de la population et 30 % du PIB français global.

L'agriculture, bénéficiant de sols riches, y est très productive et les industries mécaniques et électroniques sont historiquement très puissantes, mais c'est le secteur tertiaire qui est l'activité dominante, employant 79,1 % de la population active francilienne. Pas moins de 65 % des entreprises françaises ont leur siège social en Île-de-France, signe de la prédominance de cette région dans l'économie française.

VIVRE À PARIS

En 1914, Paris comptait 4 millions d'habitants, il n'en abrite plus que 2,2 millions aujourd'hui. Les bureaux ont supplanté les appartements d'habitation, entraînant une forme de pénurie et une hausse du coût des loyers. De nombreux Parisiens aux revenus modestes ou recherchant une surface habitable plus grande ont dû déménager en banlieue, dont la population a doublé depuis les années 1960. Toutefois, le RER (Réseau express régional) permet une liaison rapide avec le centre de Paris.

D'une façon générale, les habitants (dont 15 % d'étrangers) affichent un niveau de vie et de qualification supérieur à la moyenne nationale. Les Parisiens ont tendance à s'identifier à leur quartier, qu'il s'agisse des très chics VIe, VIIe, VIIIe et XVIe arrondissements ou des quartiers plus animés et multi ethniques comme Belleville ou Ménilmontant.

Et si traditionnellement les arrondissements de l'est sont plus populaires que ceux de l'ouest, un certain rééquilibrage en faveur de l'est est en train de s'accomplir. C'est le cas des ZAC de Bercy (Palais omnisports, ministère de l'Économie et des Finances) et de Tolbiac (autour de la bibliothèque François-Mitterrand). Certains quartiers naguère populaires des Xe, XIe, XIIe, XVIIIe arrondissements sont maintenant très recherchés par les « bourgeois-bohème », cette couche de la population parisienne, aisée et jeune, issue du monde de l'informatique, des médias, de la publicité…

La réhabilitation de l'habitat ancien et celle des quartiers déshérités est donc à l'ordre du jour à Paris. L'ère du gigantisme semble révolue. Les architectes sont plus soucieux d'alignements, de perspectives, de jeux de correspon-

Les Bains, haut lieu de la nuit parisienne : là où les « beautiful people » viennent faire la fête.

dance avec les bâtiments voisins. L'ambiance du quartier, son histoire, le tracé de ses rues sont mieux pris en considération, de même que les problèmes ayant trait à la circulation.

Se déplacer à Paris

Le flot des voitures et la pollution qui en résulte menacent en effet de plus en plus la qualité de vie des Parisiens, au point que la municipalité en a fait l'une de ses priorités. Les Parisiens ont ainsi récemment découvert de nouveaux couloirs de bus élargis aux vélos tandis que les automobilistes voient leur espace réservé se réduire comme peau de chagrin. Utiliser sa voiture à Paris se rapproche du parcours du combattant avec embouteillages, recherche désespérée d'une place de stationnement et contraventions garanties. Débrouillards, les Parisiens ont recours à d'autres solutions pour se déplacer. Les plus classiques sont bien évidemment les transports en commun, qui sont plutôt efficaces. Le métro parisien compte 14 lignes, parcourt 211 km et s'arrête à 380 stations. Ses rames transportent 9 millions de voyageurs par jour. Le maillage de stations est très serré et la RATP a fait beaucoup de progrès

dans l'accueil de ses usagers (sécurité, propreté, décoration magnifique de certaines stations comme celles de Louvre-Rivoli, des Tuileries ou des Abbesses). La toute récente ligne 14 permet de relier le centre de Paris à la bibliothèque François-Mitterrand en un temps record. Les autobus sillonnent 354 km de lignes et s'arrêtent à 8 359 endroits de Paris et de sa proche banlieue. Ils sont les grands bénéficiaires des couloirs réservés. D'autres Parisiens, plus individualistes, se risquent à prendre leur vélo, mais la plupart des amateurs de deux-roues ont choisi de se déplacer en scooter. À chaque feu rouge, coursiers et cadres dynamiques pressés se retrouvent au coude à coude en une bruyante pétarade.

D'autres Parisiens encore profitent de la bonne qualité des revêtements des trottoirs pour s'adonner aux joies de la « glisse » en skateboard ou en rollers. Le dimanche sur les quais ou le vendredi soir, lors de la rituelle balade en rollers qui compte près de

Vue panoramique depuis la tour Eiffel : au centre le dôme des Invalides.

25 000 fanatiques, la rue leur appartient, tout comme aux cyclistes.

Si tout cela va décidément trop vite pour vous, n'oubliez pas que Paris est avant tout une ville où il faut se promener à pied. Contrairement à Londres ou Berlin, qui sont des mégapoles, Paris ne fait que 10 km sur 10, et de nombreux ponts permettent facilement de passer d'une rive à l'autre. Flânez, musardez, le nez au vent, mais ayez un œil sur les trottoirs. Ce n'est que récemment (et bien tardivement) que la municipalité a décidé d'infliger de fortes amendes aux propriétaires de chiens incivils. Enfin, n'oubliez pas de vous livrer au moins une fois à l'une des activités favorites des Parisiens : s'installer à une terrasse de l'un des 12 000 cafés que compte la ville et regarder les passants en savourant un « ballon de rouge ». ■

L'histoire de Paris

Deux mille ans d'histoire ont démontré toute la justesse de la devise de Paris *Fluctuat nec mergitur* (« Il flotte mais ne sombre pas »). La ville a prouvé à maintes reprises sa capacité à renaître de ses cendres aux pires moments de son existence : attaques barbares au cours du IIIe siècle, guerre de Cent Ans, épidémies de peste aux XIVe et XVe siècles, guerres de Religion au XVIe siècle, siège par les Prussiens, embrasement de la Commune (1870-1871), occupation allemande de 1940 à 1944. Quels que soient les futurs enjeux, Paris, fort de son patrimoine et de sa prépondérance culturelle, reste et restera sans aucun doute le foyer du rayonnement de la France dans le monde entier.

Les Celtes

Le site de Lutèce *(Lutetia)* a été occupé de 5 000 ou 4 000 av. J.-C. jusqu'au premier âge du fer (800-700 av. J.-C.). Les hommes du néolithique se regroupaient sur l'actuelle île de la Cité ainsi que sur la saillie rocheuse de la rive gauche qui servait de poste d'observation. L'île est ensuite abandonnée, sans doute après des modifications climatiques.

Lorsque, en 52 av. J.-C., les *Parisii* se font laminer par les légions romaines de Labienus, ils sont installés au creux de ce méandre de la Seine depuis déjà deux siècles. Sur la route de l'étain et du vin, ils en maîtrisent l'acheminement fluvial et surtout développent un art de la métallurgie remarquable. Les Romains, fidèles à leurs méthodes, reconstruisent et donnent un nouvel essor à Lutèce. Les rustiques habitations gauloises cèdent la place à des alignements de maisons bordant les rues. Une nouvelle ville s'étend sur la rive gauche de part et d'autre des actuelles rue Saint-Jacques et rue Saint-Martin. Les Romains construisent également des thermes dont seuls subsistent ceux situés à l'angle des actuels boulevards Saint-Michel et Saint-Germain, un théâtre à l'emplacement du lycée Saint-Louis, un temple consacré à Jupiter et à Tibère (sur le site de Notre-Dame), un forum dans la rue Soufflot, des arènes rue Monge, un aqueduc et des tavernes servant des bières et du vin. Enfin, une enceinte est érigée autour de la ville au cours du IIe siècle ap. J.-C.

Vers 250, Lutèce devient un siège épiscopal grâce aux efforts de saint Denis, le premier évêque de la ville, qui s'attire ainsi la méfiance des Romains. Selon la légende, Denis aurait été battu, jeté aux lions et crucifié. Refusant d'abjurer sa foi, il aurait été décapité au mont des Martyrs (qui deviendra Montmartre). Il se serait alors relevé, aurait ramassé sa tête et l'aurait transportée jusqu'à un village au nord de Paris. La basilique Saint-Denis a été construite précisément à l'emplacement de la tombe du martyr et Denis est célébré depuis comme le saint patron de la France.

Chrétiens et barbares

En 313, l'édit impérial de Constantin fait du christianisme la religion d'État. Son neveu Julien dit l'Apostat séjourne à Lutèce en tant que préfet et, en 361, sa légion le proclame empereur. Par décret, Lutèce est nommée Paris et devient ville impériale. À ce titre, elle se développe considérablement. Au cours du Ve siècle, Lutèce, malgré l'affaiblissement du pouvoir impérial, est un État indépendant relativement épargné par les invasions barbares. Pourtant, en 451, le bruit court qu'Attila et ses Huns sont en

Ci-dessus : Détail d'une pièce fondue par les *Parisii*. À droite : Scène de semailles au pied du palais du Louvre, construit par Charles V (miniature des *Très Riches Heures du Duc de Berry*).

marche vers Paris, le peuple prend peur et se prépare à fuir. Une jeune femme gallo-romaine de Nanterre, nommée Geneviève, persuade les habitants de rester et de prier Dieu. Par chance pour Geneviève, Attila se détourne vers la Loire pour attaquer les Wisigoths. Les Parisiens saluent cette fortune providentielle comme un miracle, d'autant que la jeune femme ne s'arrête pas là : elle organise l'acheminement de

Jeanne d'Arc mène l'assaut sur Paris, en septembre 1429. *(Les Vigiles de Charles VII).*

vivres pour la ville affamée, fait élever la première basilique dédiée à saint Denis et vraisemblablement joue un rôle considérable dans la conversion au christianisme du nouveau maître de la région, Clovis.

Clovis, dont le grand-père Mérovée a aidé le romain Aetius à repousser les Huns, assoit progressivement son pouvoir sur la majeure partie de la Gaule romaine. Il s'appuie pour cela sur le clergé catholique et certains notables gallo-romains. Il s'arroge même le titre de proconsul, afin de bien montrer le lien institutionnel qu'il entend incarner entre l'empire déchu (476) et la monarchie franque à venir.

En 486, Clovis triomphe de généraux romains récalcitrants à Soissons. Il épouse en 491 une catholique, Clotilde, fille de Chilpéric, roi des Burgondes, et se fait baptiser à Reims. Clovis fait de Paris la capitale de son royaume en 508. Trois ans plus tard, il meurt et son royaume est divisé entre ses quatre enfants. L'un des descendants de Clovis, Dagobert (628-639), accorde de larges privilèges à l'abbaye Saint-Denis. La ville devient alors un centre commercial et culturel important.

La dynastie mérovingienne s'étiole en intrigues intestines et ses représentants n'exercent bientôt plus la réalité du pouvoir. Pépin le Bref, maire du Palais, entend par la prise du pouvoir en 751, mettre un terme au règne des rois « fainéants ». Son fils Charlemagne devient le roi des Francs en 768 et, en trente ans, parvient à reconquérir la majeure partie de l'ancien Empire romain d'Occident. En décembre 800, il est couronné empereur à Rome et choisit Aix-la-Chapelle comme capitale du Saint-Empire. À sa mort, le grand empire est alors divisé en trois royaumes qui ont bien du mal à organiser une résistance efficace contre les invasions barbares, dont celle des Vikings. En 885, ceux-ci assiègent Paris. Les tergiversations de l'empereur, loin de la ville, livrent les Parisiens à eux-mêmes. Eudes, comte de Paris, organise leur défense et livre bataille. L'île de la Cité est sauvée, mais pas les faubourgs. Reconnaissants, les dignitaires mandatés par les Parisiens élisent Eudes « roi des Francs » en 888. Cent ans plus tard, à la mort du roi carolingien Louis V, son petit-neveu Hugues Capet installe la dynastie comtale sur le trône de France.

Le Moyen Âge

Famille parisienne, les Capétiens exercent leur pouvoir depuis Paris, rendant ainsi à la ville un prestige qu'elle n'a plus connu depuis Clovis. La rive droite devient le domaine du commerce. Les puissantes abbayes Saint-Denis et Saint-Germain contribuent tout autant au développement de la ville, que l'abbé Suger, ministre de Louis VI et de Louis VII, qui commande la construction de la nouvelle basilique Saint-Denis, en 1136. De cet édifice, il se dégage la volonté de son commanditaire, qui fait de la basilique la nécropole royale et impose une nouvelle esthétique, élancée et baignée de lumière, le gothique.

Le domaine royal double au cours du règne de Philippe Auguste (1180-1223). L'île de la Cité, aisément défendable, concentre tous les pouvoirs : temporel avec le Palais et spirituel depuis que le rêve de pierre de Maurice de Sully s'est matérialisé en la cathédrale Notre-Dame (1163). Au même moment, les maîtres des écoles épiscopales revendiquent une plus grande indépendance vis-à-vis de l'évêque et désertent le cloître de Notre-Dame pour s'installer sur la rive gauche, à proximité de l'abbaye Saint-Victor. Maîtres et étudiants investissent la montagne Sainte-Geneviève, fondent l'*Universitas* qu'ils placent sous la tutelle du pape Innocent III qui la reconnaît en 1210. Le Quartier latin est né. Philippe Auguste, qui porte un grand intérêt à Paris, fait paver ses rues principales, construit un marché aux Halles et pose les fondations du Louvre. Paris compte alors 50 000 habitants et, pour les protéger, Philippe Auguste fait élever une enceinte autour de la ville, dont il reste des vestiges dans le Quartier latin et dans le Marais.

Le petit-fils de Philippe Auguste, Louis IX, le dernier roi chevalier (1126-1270), fait construire la Sainte-Chapelle, véritable châsse de lumière pour les reliques de la sainte Croix et de la couronne d'épines du Christ. Au cours du règne de Philippe IV le Bel (1285-1314), se développe une administration laïque dont les offices occupent peu à peu tout le vieux palais de la Cité. Cette affluence de notables aisés favorise le développement des arts décoratifs (orfèvrerie, vitraux, enluminure…). Philippe IV fait du Parlement de Paris une cour de justice (mais pas un corps gouvernemental) et convoque la première assemblée. Il bâtit également la magnifique salle des Gens d'Armes à la Conciergerie. Ses trois fils accèdent successivement au trône à sa mort en 1314. Le dernier fils, Charles IV, meurt en 1328 sans laisser d'héritier mâle.

Édouard III d'Angleterre (petit-fils de Philippe IV) revendique alors le trône français, arguant d'une ascendance capétienne plus directe que celle du régent en titre Philippe VI de Valois. L'installation du Valois sur le trône de France et le refus d'Édouard de prêter hommage à ce dernier pour ses possessions en terre française précipitent la France et l'Angleterre dans la guerre de Cent Ans. La guerre exige de gros sacrifices, essentiellement supportés par Paris, siège du pouvoir et principale ville marchande du royaume. Le traité de Brétigny en 1360 marque une rémission, après les humiliations et la terreur de la peste noire qui caractérisent les décennies précédentes. Rémission qui se matérialise par le grand train que mènent certains princes. Le quartier du Marais est leur fief. Pourtant en 1358, exaspérés par la misère et la faim, les Parisiens s'arment et se choisissent un chef: le prévôt des marchands, Étienne Marcel. Ils investissent le palais de l'île de la Cité, égorgeant quelques conseillers du futur roi Charles V. Cet événement aurait tellement traumatisé Charles V (1364-1380) qu'il déplacera la résidence royale au Louvre. Il embellit la ville en faisant construire des jardins, des palais et des hôtels particuliers, et dote le palais du Louvre

En 1358, Étienne Marcel, à la tête de ses partisans, prend le palais de l'île de la Cité.

d'une bibliothèque de 843 manuscrits enluminés. Il élargit également les murs de la ville et fait bâtir la forteresse de la Bastille à l'est de Paris, non pour défendre la ville mais pour la mater le cas échéant et assurer le chemin qui conduit, depuis le Louvre, à la résidence royale de Vincennes.

La guerre reprend cependant. À l'issue de la bataille d'Azincourt en 1415, les Anglais, alliés aux ducs de Bourgogne, sont vainqueurs. De 1420 à 1436, ils occupent Paris et Henri VI d'Angleterre est sacré roi de France à Notre-Dame en 1431. La ville assiégée connaît alors une période de famine et de rebellions et doit faire face aux meutes de loups qui l'assaillent. Au terme d'une reconquête progressive, Charles VII (1422-1461) reprend finalement Paris en 1436. La guerre s'achève en 1453.

La France connaît une forte prospérité au cours de la fin du XVe siècle et jusqu'au début du XVIe siècle. La maison de Valois retrouve son autorité. L'imprimerie est introduite. Les

François Ier, entré dans la postérité pour sa victoire à Marignan et ses châteaux de la Loire, a également beaucoup œuvré pour l'embellissement de Paris.

monuments du gothique flamboyant, comme l'église Saint-Séverin, l'hôtel de Sens et l'hôtel de Cluny, se multiplient dans Paris.

La Renaissance

François Ier (1515-1547), grand protecteur des arts et des lettres, fait de Paris sa résidence en 1528. La ville devient plus cosmopolite et des artistes comme Léonard de Vinci et Benvenuto Cellini travaillent à sa cour. François Ier fait rénover le Louvre par Pierre Lescot et Jean Goujon, édifie de magnifiques châteaux à Chambord, Blois et Fontainebleau et commande l'Hôtel de Ville au Boccador. C'est à partir de cette époque qu'un urbanisme ordonnancé commence à modeler la ville. Les successeurs de François Ier poursuivent l'embellissement de Paris : le style Renaissance s'exprime dans la fontaine des Innocents (Jean Goujon), l'église Saint-Eustache – synthèse du gothique persistant et du langage décoratif de la Renaissance – et le palais des Tuileries. Ce bel élan se brise sur les convulsions de la fin des Valois. La Réforme gagne la France et bientôt la déchire en de sanglantes guerres. À Paris, elle recrute plutôt ses partisans dans les classes les plus élevées de la société – savants, artistes, princes et riches marchands – tandis que le peuple reste plutôt catholique. Le 24 août 1572, le massacre de la Saint-Barthélemy signifie, par le sang versé des Huguenots, le choix du peuple parisien. Un choix qui le pousse à résister au roi de France, Henri III, et à Henri de Navarre, son héritier direct et protestant de foi.

Lorsqu'en 1589 Henri III est assassiné, Henri de Navarre devient roi, fondant ainsi la dynastie des Bourbons. Les portes de Paris lui sont cependant fermées, tenues par le parti catholique. Seule son abjuration du protestantisme en 1593 lui permet de conquérir Paris et de reconstruire l'unité du pays. Un an plus tard, il est sacré roi à Chartres et entre dans la capitale le 22 mars 1594. Henri IV cherche alors à consolider le pouvoir royal. Il fait achever le Pont-Neuf, le premier pont de Paris sans habitations ni magasins mais pourvu de trottoirs et de bancs. Avant d'être assassiné rue de la Ferronnerie en 1610, il a encore le temps de faire bâtir la place Dauphine puis la place Royale, aujourd'hui place des Vosges, dont les hautes toitures en pavillon et l'usage combiné de la brique et de la pierre définissent pour de longues décennies un nouveau « style français ».

Lorsque le dauphin Louis est couronné roi de France sous le nom de Louis XIII en 1610, il n'a que 8 ans. Sa mère Marie de Médicis, aidée de Concini, lui confisque le pouvoir jusqu'à sa majorité en 1617. À cette date, Louis XIII appelle Armand du Plessis, bientôt cardinal et duc de Richelieu. En accord avec le roi, celui-ci jette les fondements de l'absolutisme royal. Il fait bâtir le Palais-Cardinal (le Palais-Royal), reconstruire la Sorbonne et fonde l'Académie française. La réforme catholique encourage la construction de couvents, de chapelles et d'églises comme le Val-de-Grâce, bâti en 1638 pour célébrer la naissance « miraculeuse » du fils de Louis XIII et d'Anne d'Autriche, le futur Louis XIV.

Louis XIV, le Roi-Soleil

Celui-ci hérite du trône à l'âge de 5 ans en 1643. Anne d'Autriche et le cardinal Mazarin assurent la régence, consolident le pouvoir central en alourdissant notamment les impôts. En 1648, la levée d'un nouveau tribut soulève le Parlement contre Mazarin. Les bourgeois soutiennent les parlementaires dans leur Fronde et menacent directement la stabilité de l'État, d'autant que l'aristocratie s'empare de la révolte pour formuler son opposition à la centralisation du pouvoir. Les troupes du prince de Condé vont jusqu'à assiéger Paris et bloquer l'approvisionnement en nourriture. La révolte échoue. La monarchie et Mazarin sortent affermis de cette période troublée.

À la mort de Mazarin, Louis XIV exerce désormais seul le pouvoir. Il se lance dans une série de guerres pour assurer la suprématie de la France en Europe. Dans un premier temps, il délègue au successeur de Mazarin, Jean-Baptiste Colbert, le soin de remplir les caisses de l'État et de rendre Paris plus sûr. Le poste de lieutenant général de police, dont La Reynie est l'un des plus brillants représentants, est créé. Ce dernier organise notamment l'assainissement de la ville et impose aux Parisiens d'enduire leurs colombages de plâtre afin de freiner la progression des incendies. Louis XIV s'efforce de continuer à faire de Paris une véritable capitale en s'inspirant d'un idéal classique, qui s'exprime magistralement place Vendôme, place des Victoires, aux Invalides, à l'Observatoire, ou à la manufacture des Gobelins.

Cependant le Roi-Soleil conserve un souvenir cuisant de la Fronde qui, enfant, l'a contraint à se réfugier à Saint-Cloud. Il commande donc la construction d'un château à Versailles, et s'y installe avec sa cour en 1682. Le pouvoir politique est ainsi écarté des risques des mouvements de rue et de l'humeur ombrageuse des Parisiens. Louis XIV réduit les grands féodaux au rang de courtisans suspendus aux faveurs royales. Mais le financement des guerres et des extravagances royales, ainsi que l'exil d'artisans et de marchands de grand talent après la révocation, en 1685, de l'édit de Nantes, réduisent à néant le renouveau économique organisé par Colbert.

À la mort de Louis XIV en 1715, la cour et le jeune roi Louis XV (1715-1774) reviennent à Paris. La régence de Philippe d'Orléans marque le retour en faveur de la grande noblesse. Les Parisiens cherchent à oublier l'austérité de la fin du règne de Louis XIV. C'est la période des peintures de Watteau, de Fragonard... L'économie, sous la houlette du cardinal de Fleury, est relancée, la monnaie stabilisée. Ce dernier favorise les échanges avec l'outre-mer et améliore les transports, ce qui permet d'accroître le développement commercial du royaume. Paris s'étend sur les deux rives et surgissent de nouveaux et « nobles » faubourgs (quartiers situés en dehors des anciens murs) de Saint-Germain et de Saint-Honoré. À la mort de Fleury en 1743, Louis XV décide de ne pas le remplacer. Il fait bâtir la place Louis XV (aujourd'hui place de la Concorde), l'église Sainte-Geneviève (aujourd'hui le Panthéon), l'École militaire et le Champ-de-Mars.

Intelligent, timide, Louis XV exerce le pouvoir en désabusé. Ses maîtresses se succèdent, tandis que la réalité du pouvoir revient à des corps d'administrateurs, dont certains sont très brillants. Néanmoins ouvert aux idées nouvelles,

Louis XIV fit de Paris une véritable capitale en s'inspirant d'un idéal classique, qui s'exprime magistralement dans la place Vendôme, la place des Victoires ou aux Invalides.

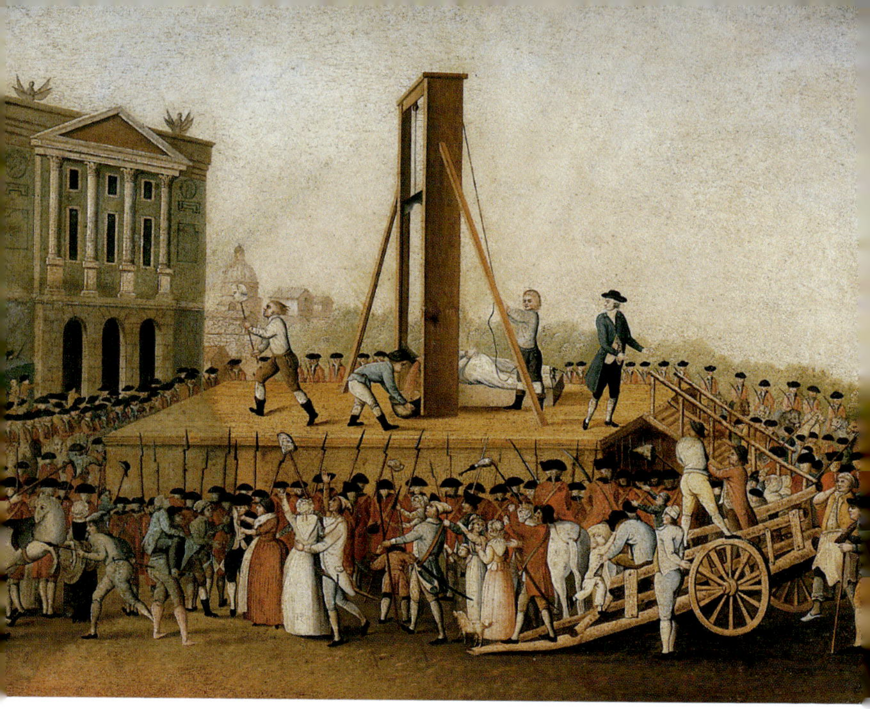

L'exécution de la reine Marie-Antoinette le 16 octobre 1793, place de la Révolution, aujourd'hui place de la Concorde.

Louis XV tente une vaste réforme, à la fin de son règne. Aidé du triumvirat d'Aiguillon, Maupeou et Terray, il remanie les parlements, renverse les alliances diplomatiques et entreprend un vaste programme de réformes judiciaires et économiques. Sa mort, en 1774, ruine ces efforts. Le XVIIIe siècle est profondément politique. La réflexion des « philosophes », à la suite de Montaigne, de Descartes et de Locke, s'engage sur le meilleur gouvernement, sur les structures sociales. Vers 1750, les idées révolutionnaires en matière de science ou de philosophie circulent dans les salons tenus par des femmes influentes comme Madame Geoffrin. Elles s'expriment aussi dans les pages de la monumentale *Encyclopédie* de Diderot et d'Alembert qui font appel aux esprits les plus brillants de leur temps pour affirmer la prééminence de la connaissance et de la raison sur l'obscurantisme et les préjugés. Le premier volume est publié en 1751.

Ces idées gagnent la rue. Le règne de Louis XVI avait commencé dans une relative stabilité en 1774, mais suite aux atermoiements de celui-ci et au retour de la crise économique, les contestations s'expriment de manière plus virulente. Le parlement de Paris devient l'un des principaux opposants et se perçoit comme le défenseur des libertés. Louis XVI tente de promulguer des réformes et de gagner la faveur du peuple, en nommant Jacques Necker, personnage populaire, au poste d'Intendant général des Finances en 1777. Mais le royaume est au bord de la banqueroute en raison des dépenses engagées au cours de la guerre de l'Indépendance américaine.

En 1785, Louis XVI prend la décision de faire construire un mur autour de la ville pour permettre aux fermiers généraux de mieux percevoir l'octroi, taxe sur les marchandises entrant dans la ville. Les pavillons d'entrée sont pour la plupart dessinés par Ledoux à l'imitation des villas palladiennes – il en reste quatre : les rotondes de Chartres et de la Villette, et les barrières du Trône et d'Enfer. La colère populaire gronde, d'autant que les 600 000 habitants de la capitale connaissent la faim et la pénurie, étouffent l'été et ne peuvent se déplacer à pied sec l'hiver.

La Révolution française

Ne parvenant pas à résoudre la crise financière, Louis XVI est contraint de convoquer les états généraux pour tenter de lever de nouveaux impôts. Les états généraux rassemblent les trois ordres fondateurs de la monarchie : le clergé (*qui orant*, ceux qui prient), la noblesse (*qui pugnant*, ceux qui se battent) et le tiers (*qui laborant*, ceux qui travaillent). Ce dernier est très disparate, il comprend aussi bien le bas clergé et le peuple que les bourgeois. La réunion des états généraux le 5 mai 1789 (pour la première fois depuis 1614) est l'occasion d'exprimer le profond désir de réforme de ces derniers. Les bourgeois détiennent en effet la réalité du pouvoir économique depuis largement un siècle sans pour autant que le pouvoir politique leur soit accessible. Représentant 96 % de la population, les députés du tiers état se proclament « Assemblée nationale » le 17 juin 1789.

Louis XVI impose de fermer la salle de réunion et les députés se retrouvent dans une autre salle de Versailles, au Jeu de paume, où ils jurent le 20 juin de rester ensemble jusqu'à ce que la constitution du royaume soit établie. Le 11 juillet, Necker est démis de ses fonctions et remplacé par le favori de la reine Marie-Antoinette, le baron de Breteuil. La révolte populaire de Paris va prendre de vitesse l'Assemblée : les Parisiens, exaspérés par la faim depuis les récoltes désastreuses de 1788 et la flambée des prix, surtout du pain, prennent les armes et marchent sur la Bastille, symbole du pouvoir monarchique de Paris. Refusant de se rendre, le gouverneur est tué et sa tête montrée dans Paris, plantée au bout d'une pique, en signe de victoire. La commune est proclamée. Louis XVI se rend à l'Hôtel de Ville où il accepte de porter la cocarde tricolore du nouveau gouvernement municipal dirigé par Bailly. Les esprits ne sont pas pour autant apaisés. En octobre, les Parisiens en colère marchent sur Versailles pour protester contre le prix élevé du pain et ramènent de force la famille royale à Paris, qu'ils enferment aux Tuileries.

Sous la houlette des clubs politiques qui se sont installés dans les couvents nouvellement mis à la disposition de la nation, l'Assemblée nationale ébauche une constitution limitant le pouvoir monarchique, que Louis XVI est contraint d'accepter après sa tentative désastreuse de fuite à l'étranger le 20 juin 1791. En 1792, l'exaspération des Parisiens contre le gouvernement entraîne la radicalisation des sans-culottes (appelés ainsi car ils portaient un pantalon à rayures par opposition à la culotte). Le 10 août 1792, une demande de destitution de Louis XVI est rejetée, provoquant leur fureur. Ils attaquent alors les Tuileries et une commune insurrectionnelle remplace la commune élue légalement. Le mois de septembre qui suit ensanglante Paris. La monarchie est abolie le 22 septembre 1792, le premier jour de l'an I de la République française selon le nouveau calendrier révolutionnaire. La guillotine dresse son spectre sinistre. Le Comité de salut public mène, d'une poigne de fer, une impitoyable chasse aux traîtres et impose un strict rationnement alimentaire sur Paris.

Deux ans de Terreur ont raison de la dictature de Robespierre et le 9 thermidor de l'an II, elle est renversée. La Convention nationale qui a été élue pour établir une nouvelle constitution met en place un directoire composé de cinq membres. En butte à des divergences internes, il doit faire appel à l'armée pour conserver son pouvoir. Le Directoire est renversé par un coup d'État en novembre 1799. Napoléon Bonaparte est proclamé Premier consul.

La Révolution et les régimes qui l'ont suivie ont profondément marqué la capitale. De nombreuses églises et couvents sont rasés, certaines maisons de nobles émigrés saisies ou détruites. Mais cette période a surtout confirmé et marqué la prééminence politique de Paris et de sa population sur le reste de la France. Ce sont essentiellement les mouvements populaires parisiens qui ont précipité les événements, et c'est à Paris que tout a été organisé et que la centralisation a été confirmée politiquement et administrativement. Le résultat paradoxal en est la méfiance tenace que le pouvoir politique national entretient à l'égard des Parisiens : dès 1796, la Convention réforme l'administration de Paris de sorte que toute centralisation entre les mains exclusives des Parisiens soit impossible. Bonaparte, sous le Consulat, fait de même : Paris dépend directement du pouvoir politique central.

Napoléon Ier a organisé avec tout le faste qu'il convient son couronnement dans la cathédrale Notre-Dame de Paris, le 2 décembre 1804.

Paris, capitale de l'Empire

La popularité de Bonaparte augmente au fur et à mesure que la paix s'installe. La France redevient rapidement un État puissant et centralisé. Paris, meurtri par dix années de convulsions insurrectionnelles, attend moins de la prospérité retrouvée une floraison de palais que la réorganisation de son approvisionnement en eau, celle de sa voirie et de sa police. Bonaparte dote Paris d'un préfet, le double d'un préfet de police, méfiant à l'égard de ses citoyens trop turbulents. S'il songe une fois l'empire établi (2 décembre 1804) à embellir sa capitale, la plupart de ses projets restent lettre morte, comme le titanesque palais du roi de Rome qui aurait dû coiffer la colline de Chaillot. Percier et Fontaine poursuivent néanmoins le chantier séculaire du Louvre – dont les collections sont complétées grâce au butin rapporté de l'étranger –, ouvrent une voie rigoureusement ordonnancée, la rue de Rivoli ; Chalgrin s'attelle à l'érection de l'Arc de Triomphe de l'Étoile, et Vignon à celle de l'église de la Madeleine. Le pont d'Iéna est également construit ainsi que l'Arc de Triomphe du Carrousel et le palais de la Bourse. La ville est aussi largement équipée et modernisée : les premiers éclairages au gaz apparaissent dans les rues, le réseau d'égouts est considérablement agrandi, des quais le long de la Seine sont aménagés et les rues sont numérotées. Enfin l'approvisionnement de la ville est réorganisé : le marché historique des Halles devient le point central de tout un réseau de marchés, des abattoirs sont créés et le canal de l'Ourcq est percé pour acheminer de l'eau potable à Paris.

Après une série de campagnes militaires couronnées de victoires, Napoléon connaît de sévères revers sur les champs de bataille européens (notamment en Russie en 1812). L'Europe tout entière est coalisée contre la France. Au début de 1814, Paris est occupé par les troupes autrichiennes, prussiennes et britanniques, qui sont des alliées de la Russie. Napoléon, déchu, est alors exilé sur l'île d'Elbe. Le roi Louis XVIII (R. : 1814-1824 ; frère de Louis XVI) est placé sur le trône avec l'aide de Talleyrand, mais le retour d'exil de Napoléon le pousse à fuir en 1815. L'aventure napoléonienne dure cent jours, une ultime bataille menée à Waterloo marque sa fin. Napoléon est reconduit en exil sur la lointaine île de Sainte-Hélène par le gouvernement britannique. Louis XVIII remonte sur le trône pour dix ans, avant que son frère Charles X ne lui succède.

Paris sous les barricades

Ni Louis XVIII ni Charles X n'ont la volonté de changer Paris. C'est l'initiative privée qui va modifier la ville. La bourgeoisie de la finance conquiert de nouveaux quartiers (Saint-Georges, François Ier, Europe), tandis que le quartier Saint-Germain demeure le bastion de l'élite aristocratique. L'avènement des Bourbons marque aussi le « siècle des préfets ». Ces derniers, le comte de Chabrol dans un premier temps (1812-1830), puis le comte de Rambuteau (1833-1848), perçoivent assez rapidement les enjeux du développement de la ville. L'industrialisation de la région draine un flot constant d'ouvriers, de domestiques et de petits artisans qui viennent grossir les quartiers centraux de la Cité et de Saint-Merri.

Le nombre d'habitants passe de 700 000 en 1817 à 1 280 000 en 1857. La plupart d'entre eux s'entassent dans les quartiers du centre et vivent dans l'insalubrité la plus totale : la tuberculose, et sporadiquement le choléra, font des ravages. Ces quartiers, ainsi que les faubourgs à l'est (le faubourg Saint-Antoine), deviennent les foyers de la contestation politique.

Trois jours en 1830 suffisent pour balayer les Bourbons et pour installer la branche cadette des Orléans sur le trône de France. Le préfet Rambuteau élabore un programme visant à adapter Paris à son époque. L'industrialisation va croissante, de nouveaux besoins apparaissent, le chemin de fer se développe dans toute la France. La gare Saint-Lazare est inaugurée en 1837. Une loi de 1842 dessine le tracé du réseau ferré français : la plupart des lignes convergent vers Paris. En 1841, Thiers décide de ceindre Paris de fortifications : elles englobent les villages de Paris en pleine expansion dont Austerlitz, Vaugirard, Passy, Montrouge, Montmartre et Belleville. Seize bastions détachés doublent l'enceinte.

Le 23 février 1848, une insurrection à Paris provoque la chute de Louis-Philippe et de la monarchie de Juillet. La IIe République est aussitôt proclamée. L'Assemblée constituante lance de nombreuses réformes (abolition de l'esclavage, instauration du suffrage universel, garantie de la liberté d'expression…) et surtout crée les Ateliers nationaux à Paris qui reprennent les chantiers lancés par le préfet Rambuteau.

C'est d'ailleurs la décision de fermer ces Ateliers, jugés trop coûteux par le gouvernement, qui jette au mois de juin 1848 les ouvriers parisiens dans les rues au cri de « Du pain ou du plomb ! » L'insurrection est matée au prix d'une impitoyable répression.

Napoléon III remet au baron Haussmann (le troisième en partant de la gauche) les décrets d'annexion à Paris des communes limitrophes.

Paris remodelé par Haussmann

À la fin de 1848, les élections permettent à Louis Napoléon Bonaparte (neveu de Napoléon Ier) d'accéder à la présidence française. Le conflit entre le Prince-Président, qui ne peut briguer un second mandat, et l'Assemblée conduit au coup d'État du 2 décembre 1851. L'établissement de l'Empire réalise la conjonction d'un régime autoritaire et l'instrumentalisation politique du capital industriel. Une politique de grands travaux est lancée, dont Paris est le principal bénéficiaire. Les raisons sont multiples, mais les premières sont d'ordre sanitaire, les autres d'ordre stratégique : Napoléon III veut faire de Paris la vitrine du régime impérial et le pivot de sa politique internationale.

Pour ce faire, il appelle le baron Haussmann, préfet de la Seine, pour superviser les principaux travaux et leur financement (voir p. 160). Celui-ci, avec une belle audace, taille

Le Paris de la Belle Époque : de belles avenues, des inventions, et des Expositions universelles...

dans le vif. Il fait percer un nouveau réseau de circulation afin de désengorger le vieux Paris, fait recouvrir les rues d'alsphate et crée des trottoirs. Il confie à Belgrand le soin d'agrandir le réseau des égouts et d'acheminer de l'eau potable. Le paysagiste Alphand est, quant à lui, chargé de créer des espaces verts en périphérie – bois de Boulogne et de Vincennes – comme au centre – les Buttes-Chaumont, les parcs Montsouris et Monceau. Les architectes Garnier et Baltard conçoivent l'Opéra, l'église Saint-Augustin... De nouvelles gares sont inaugurées, caractérisées par leurs charpentes métalliques (gares de l'Est et du Nord). Le baron Haussmann fait également construire quelque 100 000 immeubles entre 1852 et 1870 le long des nouvelles avenues. À la fin du Second Empire, Paris est une vitrine pour les salons industriels et l'économie connaît un bel essor. Toutefois, la période d'euphorie est brutalement interrompue par la guerre désastreuse de 1870 entre la France et la Prusse.

À la suite de la défaite militaire de Napoléon III à Sedan le 2 septembre 1870, le régime impérial s'effondre et une nouvelle république est proclamée, le 4 septembre 1870. Sa première tâche : conduire la guerre contre les Prussiens. Fin septembre, les troupes de la capitale comprennent 500 000 soldats (dont les deux tiers sont quasiment inexpérimentés). Bien que 30 000 bovins et 180 000 moutons aient été parqués en prévision dans le bois de Boulogne, les Parisiens assiégés sont affamés durant l'hiver. Les chevaux, les chiens, les chats, les rats et même certains animaux du jardin des Plantes sont abattus pour être consommés. Le gouvernement d'Adolphe Thiers négocie un armistice temporaire avec Bismarck, le 28 janvier 1871.

La Commune de Paris

De nombreux Parisiens considèrent cet armistice comme une trahison et la défiance qu'exprime Thiers à leur égard en envoyant des troupes se saisir des armes restées dans la garnison de Montmartre les mécontentent. L'insurrection gronde et rapidement s'organise en une Commune. Sa principale revendication est d'avoir un gouvernement municipal à Paris au sein d'une République démocratique française. Elle rend obligatoire l'école primaire et met en place des coopératives d'ouvriers.

Pour mettre fin à la Commune, Thiers et l'armée régulière cantonnée à Versailles entreprennent la reconquête au prix de cinq semaines de combats meurtriers. Au terme de la Semaine sanglante (du 22 au 28 mai), on dénombre 25 000 tués parmi les ruines de monuments inestimables.

La IIIe République n'a de cesse que d'effacer la lutte fratricide qui marque son avènement. On tergiverse longtemps sur le sort du palais des Tuileries et de l'Hôtel de Ville, incendiés mais restaurables. Le premier est abattu, le second est reconstruit. La colline de Montmartre est coiffée de la basilique du Sacré-Cœur. Enfin, l'accueil des Expositions universelles de 1878 et 1889 contribue au prestige du régime par l'étalage des forces recouvrées de la nation.

Paris au XXe siècle

Les travaux engagés dans Paris par le baron Haussmann sont poursuivis à la Belle Époque. Le tournant du siècle est marqué par l'Exposition de 1900. Cette même année, la première ligne de métro est inaugurée joignant la porte

Place de l'Opéra, le 1er mai 1915. Des « poilus » en permission achètent un brin de muguet.

de Vincennes à la porte Maillot. Artistes et écrivains se retrouvent à Paris et jettent les bases de l'époque moderne. En architecture, Hector Guimard est peut-être celui qui présente la version la plus aboutie de l'Art nouveau.

Le déclenchement de la guerre met brutalement un terme à cet essor. Le 2 septembre 1914, les Allemands ne se trouvent qu'à une vingtaine de kilomètres de Paris. Cinq jours plus tard, 4 000 hommes sont envoyés au front en taxis. À la suite de la bataille de la Marne, la retraite allemande est ordonnée et une éprouvante guerre de tranchées commence. En quatre ans, 746 bombes tombent sur Paris. De la forêt de Saint-Gobain, à 140 km de Paris, la Grosse Bertha propulse plus de 300 obus de plus de 180 kg chacun sur la ville. Au lendemain du traité de Versailles en 1919, qui entérine la fin de la guerre, le principal défi pour les Français est la reconstruction.

À Paris, les fortifications de Thiers sont rasées. À leur place, il est prévu de construire des logements sociaux et de constituer une ceinture « verte » de parcs, de stades et de piscines. Si les espaces verts ont tardé à se matérialiser, les immeubles de brique aux toits rouges ont rapidement circonscrit Paris d'une « ceinture rouge ». Ces premières années d'après-guerre sont aussi les Années folles, marquées par le besoin presque compulsif de rompre avec le passé et de jouir de la vie, et par une reprise économique remarquable, sauf en Allemagne. Traumatisés par la guerre et ses conséquences, artistes et intellectuels sont convaincus qu'il est urgent et nécessaire de tout renouveler. Paris est, avec Berlin, l'une des premières capitales européennes où résonnent les accents du jazz, importé des États-Unis. Le music-hall fait aussi son apparition.

Le krach boursier de 1929 et la crise économique freinent cet élan en même temps qu'il exacerbe les dissensions politiques. Ainsi à Paris, sur la place de la Concorde, les forces de droite rassemblent le 6 février 1934 les mécontents, des anciens combattants aux fascistes, pour dénoncer la corruption du gouvernement. Une émeute éclate : la police tue 15 personnes et fait 1 500 blessés dont plusieurs anciens combattants. Cinq jours plus tard, les syndicats organisent une grève générale pour soutenir la démocratie. Les Parisiens renouent avec le débat politique et reprennent possession de la rue en de grands défilés.

Le 3 septembre 1939, la France et la Grande-Bretagne déclarent la guerre à l'Allemagne. Durant la « drôle de guerre » qui s'ensuit, les musées et les monuments de Paris sont vidés de leurs œuvres d'art. Des camions entiers quittent le Louvre pour Chambord ; les vitraux de la Sainte-Chapelle sont démontés, des sacs de sable protègent les principaux monuments. L'attaque allemande du 10 mai 1940 et sa fulgurante réussite forcent de nombreux Parisiens à fuir. Paris perd son statut de capitale politique et, le 14 juin, est déclaré ville ouverte.

Paris vit dès lors à l'heure allemande. Une nouvelle fois, les Parisiens vont connaître la ter-

reur, le rationnement et les privations. Les troupes d'occupation investissent hôtels et bâtiments publics pour installer leurs services et leur administration (la Gestapo rue Lauriston, rue des Saussaies et avenue Foch). La signalisation est en allemand et la croix gammée flotte au-dessus de l'Hôtel de Ville et de la tour Eiffel.

26 août 1944, Charles de Gaulle vient de descendre triomphalement les Champs-Élysées. Sur la place de la Concorde, la foule des Parisiens acclame son héros.

Les premières manifestations de contestation ne tardent pas, certaines exprimées ouvertement comme ces étudiants qui s'en vont fleurir la tombe du soldat inconnu le 11 novembre 1940, d'autres, plus discrètement, par la formation des premiers réseaux de résistance, encouragés par l'appel du 18 juin 1940 du général de Gaulle. Les persécutions contre la communauté juive culminent avec la rafle du Vel' d'Hiv en juillet 1942 : plus de 12 284 personnes, dont 3 451 enfants, sont rassemblées dans ce stade du XVe arrondissement puis déportées.

Le débarquement allié le 6 juin 1944 donne le signal de la mobilisation pour libérer le territoire français, et Paris au premier chef. Les Forces françaises de l'intérieur déclenchent une insurrection, le 16 août. Les services publics se déclarent en grève, les barricades bloquent les rues. Les combats font plus de 5 000 morts en six jours. Le soir du 24 août, un détachement de la 2e division blindée du général Leclerc entre dans Paris et se dirige vers l'Hôtel de Ville. Le 25 août, c'est la 2e division blindée tout entière qui libère la ville avec la 4e division d'infanterie américaine. Le drapeau français est hissé au-dessus de la tour Eiffel et les cloches de tout le monde libre font écho à celles de Paris pour célébrer sa libération. Le gouverneur allemand, le général von Choltitz, signe le lendemain en gare de Montparnasse la capitulation allemande, sans avoir exécuté l'ordre de réduire la ville en poussière comme Hitler l'avait exigé.

Le Paris contemporain

Charles de Gaulle apparaît comme l'homme qui doit gouverner la France d'après-guerre, mais, en 1946, il s'éclipse brusquement lors des tractations politiques précédant l'instauration de la IVe République. Le régime ne parvenant plus à maîtriser la situation en Algérie, il est rappelé en 1958. À peine investi du pouvoir, de Gaulle s'attelle à la constitution de la Ve République, règle la question coloniale, avec pour point d'orgue l'indépendance de l'Algérie en 1962. Intact au sortir de la guerre mais exsangue, Paris est lui aussi touché par la vague de modernité des années 1950-1960. Les nouvelles constructions, répondant à un fonctionnalisme exigeant, sont surtout des bâtiments commerciaux et administratifs et leurs architectes sont parmi les plus renommés au monde. C'est aussi l'époque des tours dont la plus célèbre est la celle de Montparnasse. Cette tranquille confiance est brutalement remise en cause en 1968, lorsque les étudiants français, Parisiens en tête, investissent à nouveau la rue, exprimant leur volonté de briser la rigidité de

La Grande Arche de la Défense, de Johan Otto von Spreckelsen, est tout simplement colossale. C'est un cube évidé qui fait plus de 100 m de côté. La cathédrale Notre-Dame et sa flèche tiendraient sans difficulté sous la voûte !

la société. « Il est interdit d'interdire ! » clament-ils en élevant des barricades dans le Quartier latin. Émeutes et grève générale paralysent la France.

Dix mois après ces événements, le général de Gaulle démissionne et Georges Pompidou est élu président. Ce dernier est l'un des premiers présidents à renouer avec les grands projets urbanistiques concernant Paris. Passionné d'art contemporain, il fait construire à proximité du quartier des Halles un vaste centre culturel, qui porte aujourd'hui son nom.

Valéry Giscard d'Estaing poursuit cet effort en faisant aménager la gare d'Orsay en un musée consacré à l'art de la fin du XIXe siècle, et le parc de La Villette. En 1981, François Mitterrand devient le premier président socialiste de la Ve République. Sept ans plus tard, il est réélu. Durant ses deux mandats, il lance une série de grands travaux dans la capitale qui lui confère un statut résolument international (le Grand Louvre, l'Opéra-Bastille, l'Institut du monde arabe, la nouvelle Bibliothèque nationale qui désormais porte son nom…). ■

Les arts

PARIS, LA VILLE LA PLUS VISITÉE AU MONDE, DOIT SA RÉPUTATION DE GRANDE CAPITALE artistique à ses monuments et à son histoire. Cette ville trépidante jouit surtout de son riche héritage culturel et ne cesse d'attirer les grands noms de la littérature, de la peinture, de la danse, du théâtre et de l'opéra.

LA LITTÉRATURE

Paris a toujours été et demeure un puissant pôle d'attraction pour les écrivains en quête de reconnaissance et d'inspiration au cœur de la société européenne.

Paris, un foyer ancien de la culture

La fondation de l'Université au XIIIe siècle a très largement contribué au développement et au rayonnement intellectuels de la ville, d'autant plus que cette dernière est restée très longtemps le seul centre culturel d'envergure de la France du Nord. L'université attire les étudiants de toute la France, ils viennent de province étudier dans les facultés le grec, le latin, la philosophie, la médecine; d'autres sont sur place comme François Villon (1431-1463). Turbulent, aventureux mais aussi profondément religieux et pessimiste, celui-ci est l'un des poètes les plus marquants de son époque, dépeignant cette vie estudiantine du Quartier latin. Un peu plus tard, Rabelais (1483-1553) laissera souvent transparaître son agacement devant les Parisiens et leurs attitudes, mais il n'en demeure pas moins que deux de ses héros, et non des moindres, Pantagruel et Gargantua, font leurs études à Paris!

La fondation par François Ier et Guillaume Budé du Collège des lecteurs royaux contribue à faire de Paris le foyer intellectuel du royaume et marque la reconnaissance par le pouvoir royal de la recherche artistique. Ronsard et les poètes de la Pléiade étudient le grec en son sein et favorisent, sur des fondements humanistes, la rénovation des formes littéraires. Ce renouveau des lettres antiques s'inscrit dans une démarche de retour aux formes originelles, et n'exclut ainsi nullement le recours à la langue vernaculaire, comme le démontre magistralement la *Défense et Illustration de la langue française* de Joachim du Bellay (1549).

Au XVIIe siècle, les institutions officielles se renforcent (fondation de l'Académie française en 1634) mais perdent le monopole de la production intellectuelle. Des aristocrates fortunés ouvrent des salons. L'un des plus célèbres est celui de l'hôtel Rambouillet: Catherine de Vivonne, marquise de Rambouillet, reçoit des gens de bonne compagnie pour y discuter littérature en présence de familiers dont Voiture, Saint-Amant... Louis XIV lui-même s'institue protecteur des arts et des lettres et, à partir des années 1660, attire en sa cour de Versailles tant d'artistes que bientôt les salons littéraires tombent en désuétude. Il fonde, en 1680, la Comédie française. Sous l'impulsion du pouvoir royal, la fixation de la langue française (Vaugelas, Malherbe) a en effet favorisé l'essor d'un théâtre brillant: Pierre Corneille puis Jean Racine revisitent de leur art la tragédie grecque, tandis que Molière épingle ses contemporains dans leurs travers les plus secrets.

Le XVIIIe siècle

Ni Louis XV ni Louis XVI ne prétendent à un tel mécénat durant leur règne. Les salons sont relancés et, avec les cafés (le Procope), reprennent la tradition du débat d'idées. Mesdames de Lambert, de Tencin et du Deffant accueillent ainsi Montesquieu, Marivaux, Fontenelle, Voltaire, Diderot dans leurs salons. Les débats, tout au long du siècle, sont fortement teintés de philosophie politique et marqués par le progrès des sciences comme l'illustre *Encyclopédie* de Diderot et d'Alembert.

À la même époque, héritiers des libertins du XVIIe siècle qui prétendaient au droit de soumettre toute vérité au libre examen, les écrits de Choderlos de Laclos, de Crébillon fils et surtout de Sade poussent jusqu'à l'immoralisme cette attitude et font scandale.

La pyramide qui abrite l'accès au musée du Louvre a été dessinée par l'architecte I. M. Pei. Inaugurée en 1989, elle a été créée dans le cadre du projet « Grand Louvre », lancé par le président François Mitterrand et destiné à aménager la totalité du palais en un musée.

Sur cette photo figurent presque tous les représentants du surréalisme (de gauche à droite en haut) : Paul Éluard, Hans Arp, Yves Tanguy, René Crevel ; (en bas) Tristan Tzara, André Breton, Savaldor Dalí, Max Ernst et Man Ray.

Le XIXe siècle

Après la Révolution, si Paris n'est plus tout à fait le lieu de résidence privilégié des écrivains, il demeure néanmoins le lieu où leur art trouve sa consécration. La fin du XVIIIe siècle a favorisé un nouveau genre littéraire, le roman, et quelles que soient les sensibilités littéraires qui les animent – romantisme, réalisme, naturalisme ou encore symbolisme –, les écrivains du XIXe siècle prennent de plus en plus part à la vie politique tandis que le cercle de leurs lecteurs s'élargit. Certains font parfois de Paris le véritable personnage principal de l'ouvrage comme Victor Hugo dans *Notre-Dame de Paris*, Eugène Sue dans *Les Mystères de Paris*, d'autres en font le cadre privilégié de leurs études de mœurs comme Balzac ou Zola. Les poètes sont désormais vus sous un autre jour. Certains, comme Charles Baudelaire, Théophile Gautier, Gérard de Nerval ou Paul Verlaine, choquent la société en mettant en exergue les facettes les plus sombres de la nature humaine et sont même poursuivis en justice pour leurs œuvres.

Le XXe siècle

Paris devient une terre d'asile pour des intellectuels et artistes de toute l'Europe, comme Karl Marx, Richard Wagner et Heinrich Heine. Dans les cafés, de Montmartre à Montparnasse, les nouveaux courants artistiques, littéraires, philosophiques, politiques et institutionnels dominent les conversations, ce qui renforce la réputation de pôle artistique et intellectuel de Paris.

Les belles lettres continuent de se démocratiser à la Belle Époque. À côté des romans dits populaires dans la plus pure tradition romanesque française, les tenants de l'introspection et de l'engagement politique tiennent le haut du pavé : Maurice Barrès, Henri Bergson, Anatole France ou Romain Rolland sont les auteurs les plus lus de cette période. Marcel Proust sublime cette démarche d'introspection en décrivant avec subtilité la comédie mondaine parisienne. C'est aussi l'époque du théâtre de boulevard, où, en marge des courants idéaliste, mystique – représenté par Paul Claudel –, ou plus classique comme les pièces d'Edmond Rostand, des auteurs comme Courteline et Feydeau ridiculisent sans pitié les mœurs bourgeoises.

Les poètes sont peut-être les plus radicaux dans leur approche de la modernité, rejetant ou exploitant les références du passé. Incontestablement le plus remarquable de sa génération, est Guillaume Apollinaire qui fera partie, comme

Charles Péguy, des nombreuses victimes, de la Première Guerre mondiale.

L'entre-deux-guerres est dominé par l'engagement politique toujours plus marqué des écrivains français, notamment André Gide, André Malraux, Roger Martin du Gard, Jean Cocteau. Les surréalistes, dans une approche radicale de la création artistique, ouvrent une voie féconde. Aragon, Soupault, Breton, Vitrac et Prévert multiplient les expériences, tandis que Céline publie ses premiers brûlots. Le théâtre est dominé par Montherlant, Giraudoux ou Guitry. Durant la Seconde Guerre mondiale, certains entrent en résistance (Éluard, Camus), d'autres adhèrent au principe de collaboration (Céline, Brasillach), d'autres encore montrent une grande indécision. Des imprimeries clandestines publient sous le manteau des œuvres comme le récit de Vercors, *Le Silence de la mer*, aux éditions de Minuit, ou le poème enflammé de Paul Éluard, *Liberté*.

Après la guerre, l'épuration met sur le devant de la scène une nouvelle génération d'écrivains et d'intellectuels, parmi lesquels Jean-Paul Sartre, Albert Camus, Boris Vian et Simone de Beauvoir. Un théâtre d'un type nouveau se développe à travers les pièces de Samuel Beckett, Arthur Adamov et Eugène Ionesco qui travaillent dans la même veine que leur précurseur Antonin Artaud.

Dans cette effervescence, autour des éditions de Minuit, se détache un groupe de romanciers. Tout sauf une école littéraire, le Nouveau Roman désigne des auteurs qu'unit le refus. Nathalie Sarraute, Alain Robbe-Grillet, Claude Simon ou Michel Butor refusent en effet de se laisser enfermer dans le récit et explorent à leur manière toutes ses possibilités.

Cette période marque aussi la consécration de la « rive gauche » parisienne, de l'esprit de Saint-Germain-des-Prés. Maurras, Apollinaire, les surréalistes, Gide, Picasso ou Saint-Exupéry avaient fait leur fief de ce quartier de cafés, bien avant Jean-Paul Sartre et Simone de Beauvoir… De cette époque, il ne reste rien, sinon une étrange nostalgie.

Seules quelques maisons d'édition prestigieuses, telles des gardiennes de cette époque révolue, continuent de croire une fois l'an, à l'occasion des remises des prix littéraires, que ce passé vit encore. Les lieux de la créativité se sont aujourd'hui largement diversifiés.

Jean-Paul Sartre fut un archétype de l'intellectuel français de la rive gauche.

LA PEINTURE ET LA SCULPTURE

Au même titre que pour les autres arts, Paris a été un foyer de développement de la peinture et de la sculpture, et cela depuis des siècles. D'abord étroitement liées au pouvoir politique et au principe du mécénat, ces deux disciplines se sont émancipées de cette tutelle, consacrant Paris durant le XIXe siècle et la première moitié du XXe comme l'un des tout premiers lieux de création artistique au monde.

Les débuts

La peinture et la sculpture profitent du grand élan de construction qui marque le Moyen Âge. Les peintres sont sollicités par les autorités religieuses, parfois par les monarques ou les princes pour dessiner les vitraux des églises et les sculpteurs pour orner leurs façades ou leurs intérieurs. Un grand réalisme caractérise les deux arts, que seule l'influence italienne de la Renaissance vient peu à peu adoucir.

Si les peintres français du XVIe siècle ont franchement adopté le maniérisme italien et si l'art du vitrail a atteint son apogée au même moment, la sculpture, magistralement représentée par Jean Goujon, conserve des références très françaises, annonçant déjà le classicisme. Les commanditaires ont changé, ce sont désor-

mais principalement les rois et les princes qui sollicitent les services de ces artistes pour orner leurs châteaux et palais.

La fondation en 1648 de l'Académie de peinture et de sculpture permet de rassembler les plus grands artistes du moment au service de la monarchie absolue. Le Brun, Le Sueur, mais aussi Vouet contribuent à définir les règles de la peinture. En sculpture, Paris est largement bénéficiaire des commandes que passe Louis XIV à Girardon, à Coustou, ou encore à Coysevox pour l'embellir ; au XVIIIe siècle, Pigalle ou Bouchardon continuent d'agrémenter la ville d'œuvres monumentales.

Les peintres, quant à eux, à la suite de Mignard, accentuent encore la touche maniériste. Watteau illumine ses compositions avec des couleurs douces. La Tour dans ses portraits et Chardin dans ses scènes de genre montrent la même délicatesse. À la fin du XVIIIe siècle, deux tendances se dessinent en peinture : l'une incarnée par David qui illustre le retour au classicisme, l'autre par Fragonard dont les portraits annoncent une sensibilité romantique.

La gare Saint-Lazare peinte par Claude Monet en 1877.

Le XIXe siècle est riche en mouvements et ruptures. Géricault et Delacroix adhèrent au romantisme avec une vigueur renouvelée. Les Salons officiels sont alors le lieu de tous les débats. C'est par réaction à l'académisme ambiant qu'en 1863, Manet et Fantin-Latour décident de réunir en une seule exposition tous les peintres refusés au Salon annuel. Ces peintres en dissidence manifestent un même goût pour les plaisirs de la vie quotidienne et pour un dessin d'après nature. Ces principes sont bientôt exploités par les peintres impressionnistes : ceux-ci plantent leurs chevalets sur les lieux de composition et laissent la couleur envahir la toile en touches délicates.

À la fin du XIXe siècle, une démarche toujours plus poussée sur l'utilisation de la couleur et une intériorisation de plus en plus grande de la réalité animent les peintres. Comme en littérature, le symbolisme s'impose chez certains des plus grands peintres de cette époque.

Après Degas, Monet, Pissarro et Cézanne, les pointillistes continuent en effet à exploiter la couleur, au point que la nature devient symbole comme chez Puvis de Chavannes. Van Gogh peint avec de la couleur à l'état pur, et privilégie l'expression du réel plutôt que sa représentation. Gauguin et Cézanne, quant à eux, rejettent en partie l'héritage de l'impressionnisme et recherchent davantage à peindre le volume. Lorsque Gauguin s'installe à Pont-Aven, bientôt suivi par Sérusier et Bernard, sa démarche est clairement symboliste et elle influence la génération suivante de peintres, les nabis. Ces derniers, dont les plus grands représentants sont Denis, Bonnard et Vuillard, revendiquent la supériorité de la couleur sur le sens et la forme.

En sculpture, Rodin impose son génie de toute sa puissance. L'expressivité, la recherche du mouvement et la sensualité caractérisent son œuvre, dégagée de tout académisme. Ses sculptures, en dehors du musée qui leur est consacré, ornent

Dans la cour du musée Rodin, la sculpture *Les Bourgeois de Calais*.

Paris en de nombreux endroits. Ses successeurs, dont certains furent ses élèves comme Bourdelle, ont eux aussi travaillé pour la ville de Paris.

Le XXe siècle

En 1906, le Salon d'Automne de 1906 présente les œuvres des peintres Derain, Vlaminck, Matisse et Van Dongen, rapidement surnommés les fauvistes. L'ensemble de leurs œuvres manifeste avec éclat l'autonomie de la couleur et l'intervention des émotions et réactions de l'artiste comme composantes à part entière du tableau. Cette démarche, avec l'étude des volumes, annonce les mouvements d'avant-garde de ce début du XXe siècle et l'art non figuratif. L'exploration des volumes aboutit sur les toiles de Braque et de Picasso à une véritable décomposition de ceux-ci. Dans les années 1920-1930, le surréalisme offre encore de nouvelles possibilités aux peintres, fondamentalement subversives. Le rêve, l'absence de logique et l'inconscient envahissent les toiles de Dalí, de Ernst, de Magritte, de Picabia et de Duchamp…

La sculpture et la peinture de l'après-guerre en France sont fortement caractérisées par l'abstraction et la diversité. Chaque artiste exploite à

sa manière cette voie nouvelle. Certains, comme les peintres Riopelle, Mathieu ou Soulages, travaillent sur la matière et le chromatisme. D'autres, comme les sculpteurs César ou Arman, s'emparent des objets de la vie quotidienne. De plus en plus souvent, les artistes sont sollicités dans le cadre d'une réflexion urbanistique, tel Buren dans la cour du Palais-Royal...

Voir l'art à Paris

Les nombreux musées de la ville apportent une belle contribution à l'exposition des artistes contemporains. Mais le meilleur moyen de voir les

Tous les soirs, la tour Eiffel scintille pendant les dix premières minutes de chaque heure, de la tombée de la nuit à 2 heures du matin (1 heure en hiver), grâce à 20 000 ampoules. Au fond, le Trocadéro.

œuvres artistiques contemporaines est encore de courir les quelque 500 galeries d'art qu'abrite la capitale. De nombreuses publications fournissent des informations sur les expositions, notamment l'hebdomadaire *Pariscope*, *Zurban*, la revue mensuelle *Beaux-Arts*, le *Guide des Galeries*, *Art Press*, *Nova* ou encore *Technikart* et *Le Journal des Arts*.

***La Revue blanche*, bi-mensuelle, l'une des nombreuses revues de la Belle Époque.**

Les galeries du quartier Saint-Germain, de la Bastille et du Marais se sont réunies pour publier une lettre d'informations où figurent les lieux et dates des vernissages. Ces galeries, avec celles du VIIIe arrondissement, juste derrière les Champs-Elysées, présentent pour la plupart des artistes classiques, reconnus. Pour voir les nouveaux artistes, mieux vaut se rendre du côté de la Bastille, rue Keller et rue Vieille-du-Temple, où les galeries sont nombreuses. Saint-Germain n'a jamais été le cœur de la peinture parisienne, mais vous passerez un agréable après-midi à visiter la dizaine de galeries regroupées autour de la rue de Seine et de la rue Guénégaud. Plusieurs galeries consacrées, à l'origine, à l'art conceptuel, se sont regroupées rue Louise-Weiss, dans le XIIIe arrondissement, juste derrière la Bibliothèque François-Mitterrand.

Les ateliers portes ouvertes

Vous avez aussi la possibilité d'admirer les œuvres à l'extérieur des galeries. Plusieurs artistes exposent dans l'un des squares de Montmartre et de nombreux groupes ou associations d'artistes organisent des journées portes ouvertes pour permettre au public de visiter leurs ateliers (habituellement en mai et en octobre). *Le Génie de la Bastille* est la première de ces associations, mais d'autres se sont installées dans la banlieue d'Ivry, de Montreuil et de Montrouge où de nombreux artistes ont emménagé pour fuir les loyers élevés des ateliers de la capitale.

L'ARCHITECTURE

L'un des charmes de Paris est de présenter une composition étonnamment harmonieuse de bâtiments de style et d'époque très différents. La configuration actuelle de cette ville très cosmopolite a été modelée par des préoccupations sociales, économiques et politiques. Depuis ses premiers habitants installés sur l'île de la Cité, elle s'est développée le long de la Seine, qui peut être considérée comme la plus belle avenue de Paris. Excepté sous le régime de la Commune à la fin du XIXe siècle, la ville n'a pas souffert de destructions majeures depuis de nombreux siècles. En revanche, elle n'a cessé de se rebâtir sur elle-même, et cette perpétuelle régénération favorise la confrontation directe de styles très divers : l'Institut du monde arabe veille sur le chevet de Notre-Dame tandis que la tour Eiffel toise l'École militaire.

L'architecture moderne

Les innovations techniques et la nouvelle esthétique prônées par Le Corbusier ont contribué à l'avènement d'un style plus géométrique et plus fonctionnel, propre au mouvement moderniste postérieur à la Première Guerre mondiale. Les réalisations de Le Corbusier sont rares à Paris bien que son influence ait été considérable.

Le Paris d'après 1945 a été marqué par de vastes chantiers visant à remplacer des quartiers entiers par des tours impersonnelles, comme ce fut le cas dans le XIXe arrondissement et plus tard, sur les quais de Seine dans le XVe arrondissement. Les vastes chantiers lancés par les présidents de la Ve République, notamment François Mitterrand, ont contribué au rayonnement international de Paris, grâce à la participation de grands architectes étrangers (Pei, Ghery, Piano et Rogers, Ott...) pour la pyramide du Louvre, la Grande Arche de la Défense, le Centre Georges Pompidou, le musée d'Orsay ou encore l'Opéra-Bastille. D'autres bâtiments, comme l'Institut du monde arabe ou les tours austères de la nouvelle Bibliothèque François-Mitterrand, créations françaises, illustrent cet intérêt pour les arts contemporains.

LE CINÉMA

Aller au cinéma est une composante essentielle de la vie parisienne. Dans un système éducatif pourtant peu enclin à la frivolité, les étudiants ont la possibilité de suivre des études de cinéma dans les universités où le film est considéré comme un sujet tout aussi sérieux que la littérature ou la trigonométrie.

L'État encourage la fréquentation des cinémas en offrant des réductions aux étudiants, aux retraités, aux militaires, aux familles nombreuses et aux chômeurs. Un Parisien va en moyenne un peu plus d'une fois par mois au cinéma. Il dispose de 378 salles et de plus de 70 000 places. Jusque dans les années 1980, la moitié des spectateurs voyaient des films français, puis les films des studios américains se sont largement imposés. Depuis la fin des années 1990 cependant, la production française reconquiert des parts de marché. Une nouvelle génération de réalisateurs avec des films à grand spectacle ou des œuvres plus intimistes réussit à drainer et à fidéliser le public français.

Un peu d'histoire

Jusqu'à la Première Guerre mondiale, la France était le premier producteur de films dans le monde. Le cinéma naît en France, le 28 décembre 1895, dans le Salon indien du Grand Café, boulevard des Capucines, où plusieurs petits films sont projetés pour la première fois en public par les frères Lumière, grâce à leur ingénieux cinématographe. La technique se développe vite. Les premiers cinéastes sont bientôt capables de présenter des films qui durent davantage que quelques minutes et certains commencent à explorer les diverses possibilités qu'offre ce nouvel art.

L'illusionniste Georges Méliès multiplie les effets spéciaux pour ses centaines de films aux trucages inventifs. Max Linder, maître et inspirateur de Charlie Chaplin, est à l'origine d'une multitude d'innovations comiques pendant l'époque du cinéma muet. Couronnant et dépassant cet art naissant, l'atypique *Napoléon* d'Abel Gance est le film le plus marquant de cette époque pionnière. Nombre de ces œuvres du cinéma muet ont été sauvées de la destruction ou de l'oubli par un cinéphile passionné, Henri Langlois. Il est parvenu à réunir une remarquable collection qui va constituer le fonds de la Cinémathèque française (voir p. 182).

Avec l'avènement du parlant à la fin des années 1920, la production française connaît un nouvel essor, illustré avant la guerre par des

Le premier film de la Nouvelle Vague : *À bout de souffle* (1960) de Jean-Luc Godard avec Jean Seberg et Jean-Paul Belmondo.

réalisateurs tels que Renoir, Carné, Duvivier… C'est la persistance jusqu'aux années 1950 d'un certain classicisme qui, par réaction, déclenche la Nouvelle Vague. Nourris par une solide culture cinématographique dispensée par la Cinémathèque de Langlois, Jean-Luc Godard, François Truffaut, Jacques Rivette, Éric Rohmer et Claude Chabrol s'affranchissent des contraintes d'une production traditionnelle, allègent leur matériel en même temps qu'ils font appel à une toute jeune génération de comédiens. Avec sa collection de films, la Cinémathèque française a été une véritable école expérimentale pour ces jeunes critiques et réalisateurs.

Les Français cinéphiles

La France a une longue expérience de la critique cinématographique. Les revues *Positif* et *Cahiers du Cinéma,* qui existent depuis bientôt un demi-siècle, se font parfois l'écho de points de vue clairement antagonistes. Les magazines culturels comme *Télérama, Les Inrockuptibles, Technikart,* ou *Nova* tout comme la presse généraliste quotidienne ou hebdomadaire, consacrent une large place aux critiques de films et aux portraits de réalisateurs.

Paris offre un choix impressionnant de films, de la dernière superproduction hollywoodienne au documentaire tourné en super-8 ou DV qui trouve toujours un écho dans les médias. Bien que le cinéma d'art et d'essai demeure bien plus vivant à Paris qu'ailleurs dans le monde, les grandes chaînes de distribution, telles que Gaumont et Pathé, mettent en péril la survie des salles indépendantes. Certaines salles historiques demeurent, comme le Studio 28, à Montmartre, où a eu lieu en 1928 la première d'*Un chien andalou,* chef-d'œuvre surréaliste de Luis Buñuel et de Salvador Dalí. Au Grand Rex, magnifiquement décoré, vous pourrez visiter les coulisses et monter dans l'ascenseur situé derrière le grand écran pendant la projection d'un film. Paris possède 2 grands écrans hémisphériques : celui de la Géode à La Villette et le plus grand écran IMAX-OMNIMAX du monde, le Dôme de la Défense.

LE THÉÂTRE

Depuis que les Confrères de La Passion ont créé le premier théâtre de Paris en 1547, dans l'hôtel du duc de Bourgogne (consultez la plaque commémorative au 29, rue Étienne-Marcel), les arts dramatiques se sont diversifiés. Ils vont désormais du théâtre de rue, en été, aux grandes pièces représentées partout, du petit sous-sol aux scènes somptueuses. La culture contestataire des années 1960 et le programme de décentralisation d'André Malraux, alors ministre de la Culture, ont réussi à élargir le public du théâtre qui connaît une popularité croissante.

Cette récente révolution n'a toutefois pas entamé le prestige de la Comédie-Française créée par Louis XIV en 1680, sept ans après la mort de Molière. Dans ce panthéon de la culture française, sont représentés aussi bien les grands classiques de Molière, de Corneille et de Racine que les pièces d'auteurs modernes tels

que Jean Genet, Marguerite Duras, Tom Stoppard et quelques autres.

Le théâtre contemporain

Des metteurs en scène comme Ariane Mnouchkine, Peter Brook, Robert Cordier, Patrice Chéreau auparavant au théâtre des Amandiers sortent des sentiers battus et expérimentent de nouvelles formes théâtrales.

Au Théâtre du Soleil, Mnouchkine utilise le vaste espace d'un dépôt d'armes désaffecté pour éveiller la curiosité du public avec des pièces évocatrices et colorées. Les mises en scène des pièces de Shakespeare, Bernard Koltès, David Mamet et Sam Shepard par Robert Cordier et Lesley Chatterley dans leur théâtre intimiste se caractérisent par un traitement violent, érotique et multilingue.

Cet usage non conventionnel de l'espace, caractéristique de nombreux théâtres parisiens, attire des metteurs en scène étrangers tels que l'Anglais Peter Brook, directeur du théâtre des

Bouffes du Nord. Avec Micheline Rozan, il a fondé le Centre international de recherche théâtrale (CIRT), en 1970 et le Centre international de créations théâtrales, en 1974. Il dirige des pièces de Shakespeare, met en scène le *Mahabharata,* une œuvre du théâtre classique indien, et du vaudeville, dans un vieux théâtre délabré maintenu à dessein en l'état.

LA DANSE

Capitale européenne incontestée de la danse, Paris offre un choix important de festivals, de manifestations et de spectacles qui couvrent toutes les formes de danse, du tango et du ballet au hip-hop et à la danse contemporaine.

Le ballet

L'Opéra Garnier, siège du Ballet de l'Opéra national de Paris, est presque exclusivement dédié à la danse depuis 1990. Des subventions du ministère de la Culture permettent d'accueillir des productions grandioses telles que *Roméo et Juliette*, le *Lac des Cygnes* et *Raymonda,* ainsi que les ballets de Roland Petit et de Kenneth MacMillan. Depuis 1973, Carolyn Carlson, Angelin Preljocaj, Jean-Claude Gallotta et Merce Cunningham, pionniers de la danse moderne, ont réactualisé son répertoire.

La danse contemporaine

Le Théâtre de la Ville, propriété de la ville de Paris, consacre une place importante à la danse contemporaine. Il accueille presque chaque année Pina Bausch et son Wuppertaler Tanztheater, ainsi que d'autres habitués du lieu comme la chorégraphe belge Anne Teresa De Keersmaeker et sa compagnie Rosas. La recherche d'une nouvelle expression artistique

***Le Fabuleux Destin d'Amélie Poulain* (2001) de Jean-Pierre Jeunet a connu un grand succès populaire. Ici l'héroïne (Audrey Tautou) fait des ricochets sur les eaux du canal Saint-Martin.**

produit souvent des œuvres agressives, à forte connotation sexuelle, ponctuées de silences, de grognements, de hurlements sur fond de *world music*. De la poésie, des textes et des projections de diapositives accompagnent souvent les spectacles de danse contemporaine.

Le programme varié du Festival d'automne offre une excellente occasion de suivre l'évolution de cet art sur tout le globe. Toutefois, les amateurs peuvent assister toute l'année à des spectacles de danse indienne donnés par Bharatha Natyam, une école originaire du sud de l'Inde, ou Kathak (danse classique hindoue du Nord). La Maison de la Culture du Japon propose des spectacles de Jiuta Mai ou danse des geishas, ainsi qu'un programme varié de cinéma, de théâtre et d'expositions. Le premier festival de hip-hop a eu lieu en 1996 à la Grande Halle de la Villette.

L'OPÉRA

L'Académie royale de musique et de danse, fondée en 1669, appelée depuis Opéra de Paris, a œuvré pendant des décennies pour les arts dramatique et lyrique à l'instar de la Comédie française. Lorsque l'Opéra national de Paris-Bastille a ouvert ses portes en 1990, il a repris l'essentiel du programme lyrique du palais Garnier. La combinaison ingénieuse de la musique et du

L'Opéra de Paris impose sa singulière silhouette dessinée par Charles Garnier.

mime dans les théâtres de foire parisiens est à l'origine de la création de l'Opéra-Comique, il y a de cela deux cents ans. Le bâtiment qui l'abrite, la salle Favart, a ouvert le 7 décembre 1898. De nombreux opéras dont *Carmen* de Georges Bizet et *Pelléas et Mélisande* de Claude Debussy y ont été créés. Cette salle, loin d'être à la pointe de la technique, s'accorde néanmoins agréablement au théâtre lyrique. En revanche, l'immense Opéra-Bastille est conçu pour s'adapter à des représentations grandioses ou plus modestes.

Le Théâtre musical de Paris (ancien Théâtre du Châtelet, entièrement rénové) a rouvert ses portes en septembre 1999. Il doit sa réputation à la qualité des metteurs en scène et des chefs d'orchestre invités et ses opéras n'ont rien à envier aux théâtres les plus célèbres. Sur les six manifestations de la saison, une au moins est contemporaine.

Le Théâtre des Champs-Elysées, où fut créé *Le Sacre du Printemps* de Stravinsky en 1913, offre un cadre raffiné (sa façade de marbre et les intérieurs magnifiques valent à eux seuls la visite) aux compagnies de danse et aux orchestres. Il accueille également le concours du Nouveau Festival international de danse de Paris. ■

Les îles sont le cœur même de Paris. L'île de la Cité, regardée comme la nef tutélaire des Nautes, a longtemps été le siège du pouvoir royal, judiciaire et ecclésiastique. Quant à l'île Saint-Louis, véritable joyau du Grand Siècle, elle a conservé la plupart de ses hôtels aristocratiques.

Les îles

Détail du portail du Jugement dernier (Notre-Dame de Paris).

Les îles

Jadis, le lit de la Seine était presque deux fois plus large. Les caprices du fleuve formaient alors de nombreux îlots, parfois simples bancs de sable impraticables. La régulation des flots en a submergé beaucoup, d'autres ont été intégrés aux berges si bien qu'il ne reste que deux îles : l'île de la Cité et l'île Saint-Louis.

L'ÎLE DE LA CITÉ

Victor Hugo écrivait dans *Notre-Dame de Paris* que « l'île de la Cité était la tête, le cœur et l'essence de Paris. » En effet, l'île de la Cité est le lieu de naissance de la ville et peut être considérée comme le centre géographique de Paris, lui-même le centre culturel de la France, voire du monde selon certains…

C'est son emplacement stratégique qui a déterminé son essor. Les Romains, les Francs puis les rois capétiens ont chacun agrandi le site initial. Dès l'âge du bronze, elle a formé un gué sur la très importante route commerciale qu'empruntait le transport de l'étain anglais en direction de l'Europe centrale et de la Méditerranée. Elle a également servi de refuge en temps de guerre. Au cours de la *pax romana, Lutetia* (Lutèce) s'est étendue sur la rive gauche. Cet âge d'or a duré près de trois cents ans jusqu'aux invasions germaniques. Lutèce s'est alors retranchée sur l'île de la Cité, laquelle a toujours été un centre adminis-

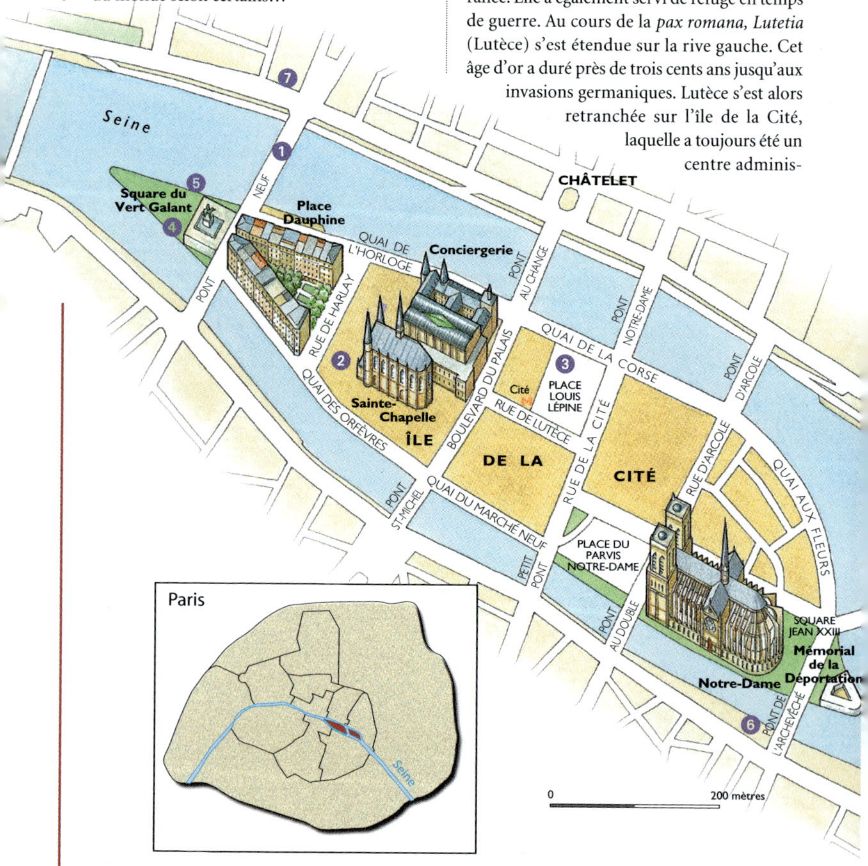

Les élégantes façades de l'île Saint-Louis surplombent la Seine.

tratif et religieux de poids. Le siège originel du gouverneur romain est aujourd'hui le Palais de Justice où, 2000 ans plus tard, les juges exercent toujours leur fonction. La Conciergerie (la prison révolutionnaire; voir p. 60) et la célèbre Sainte-Chapelle (voir pp. 56-59) se trouvent au sein même de l'île.

Malgré l'affluence des visiteurs, surtout sur le parvis de Notre-Dame, l'île de la Cité ménage encore quelques havres pleins de charme. C'est le cas du marché aux fleurs de la place Louis-Lépine, du square du Vert-Galant à la pointe ouest de l'île et des rues étroites qui donnent sur le quai aux Fleurs, comme la rue des Ursins avec son immeuble gothique, résidence de l'Aga Khan, qui possède une façade intéressante et constitue un étonnant pastiche d'éléments architecturaux d'origines diverses. En bas de la rue des Chantres, vous disposez d'une superbe perspective sur la flèche de Notre-Dame (voir pp. 48-53). La promenade le long du chevet de la cathédrale permet d'admirer les magnifiques arcs-boutants: que vous veniez le soir lorsqu'ils sont illuminés, ou au lever du jour dans la lumière douce du printemps, il s'agit toujours d'une des plus belles vues de la ville.

Les îles

1 Pont-Neuf 2 Palais de Justice
3 Marché aux Fleurs 4 Statue Henri IV
5 Embarcadère des vedettes du Pont-Neuf 6 Embarcadère des bateaux parisiens Notre-Dame
7 La Samaritaine 8 Berthillon

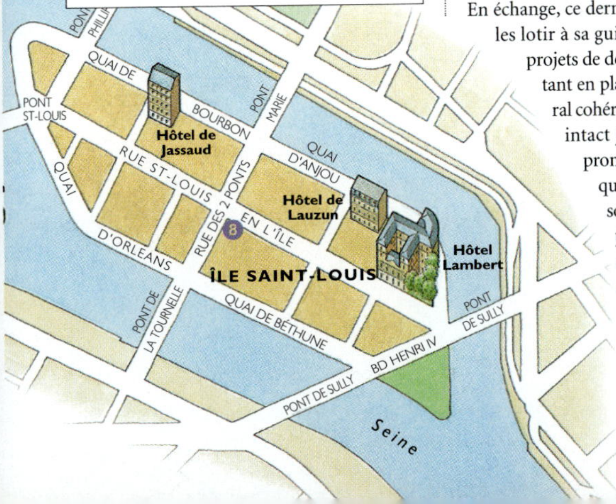

L'ÎLE SAINT-LOUIS

Les deux îles n'ont pas la même histoire ce qui explique leur caractère différent. L'île Saint-Louis n'existait pas jusqu'au XVIIe siècle. À la place, il y avait deux îlots, l'île aux Vaches et l'île Notre-Dame, l'une et l'autre inhabitées. En 1614, Louis XIII chargea Christophe Marie de réunir les deux îlots et de les relier aux berges. En échange, ce dernier obtint l'autorisation de les lotir à sa guise. C'est l'un des premiers projets de développement planifié, mettant en place un ensemble architectural cohérent qui soit parvenu presque intact jusqu'à nous. Il fait bon se promener dans les rues et sur les quais pour en admirer les trésors: les voitures n'y circulent pas aisément, et il n'y a aucune station de métro, aucun grand magasin ni cinéma dont la fréquentation engendrerait une trop grande affluence. ■

Notre-Dame de Paris

La cathédrale Notre-Dame est l'un des symboles forts de Paris. Comme la ville, elle s'élève le long des rives de la Seine et sa façade ouest se dresse comme une « vaste symphonie de pierre » selon Victor Hugo. Récemment ravalée, elle se dresse dans toute sa magnificence.

Carte p. 46
Place du Parvis-Notre-Dame, île de la Cité
01 42 34 56 10
Cité, RER: Saint-Michel

Tours
€€
(gratuit 1er dim. de chaque mois)

Trésor
Fermé dim.
€

Crypte archéologique
€
(gratuit 1er dim. et tous les jours pour les moins de 27 ans et les plus de 60 ans)

L'emplacement même de la cathédrale est riche en histoire. Elle se dresse sur les vestiges d'un temple gallo-romain dédié à Jupiter, d'une église du IVe siècle et d'une basilique du VIe siècle, dans les fondations de laquelle ont été retrouvées douze pierres ayant servi à la construction du temple romain. Au XIIe siècle, la basilique était en ruine et l'évêque de Paris, Maurice de Sully, décide de la remplacer par une superbe cathédrale capable de rivaliser avec la basilique Saint-Denis. Le pape Alexandre III pose, en 1163, la première pierre de ce qui allait devenir l'un des chefs-d'œuvre de l'architecture gothique. L'ouvrage avance rapidement grâce aux sommes récoltées par l'évêque auprès du roi, du clergé, de la noblesse et même des pauvres. Lorsqu'elle est achevée, la cathédrale supplante tous les autres monuments religieux élevés en l'Île-de-France.

LA RESTAURATION

L'apparence actuelle de Notre-Dame est en grande partie due au travail de restauration effectué au XIXe siècle. Aux XVIIe et XVIIIe siècles, le style gothique est passé de mode et la cathédrale en subit les conséquences. Sous Louis XIV (1643-1715), le chœur est partiellement détruit, les vitraux du XIIIe siècle sont remplacés par des vitres transparentes, dont les bords sont peints en bleu et or, puis le jubé et les tombes disparaissent (un fragment du jubé « La Descente aux limbes » se trouve au Louvre).

Au cours de la Révolution, la cathédrale est pillée et transformée en temple de la Raison puis de l'Être suprême. Les cloches, sauf le gros bourdon de la tour sud, sont fondues pour en faire des canons, et les 28 statues des rois d'Israël et de Juda qui ornent la façade ouest sont prises par les révolutionnaires pour des statues des rois de France et jetées à bas. Par miracle, 21 de ces têtes ont été retrouvées et sont maintenant conservées au musée de Cluny (voir pp. 66-67), sauf celle du roi David qui se trouve au Museum of Art à New York.

En 1804, la cathédrale est dans un tel état de délabrement que, lors du couronnement de Napoléon Ier, de grands tapis et tapisseries sont placés dans toute la cathédrale pour dissimuler les dommages.

Comme Victor Hugo l'écrit dans *Notre-Dame de Paris*, en 1831 : « Sur la face de cette vieille reine de nos cathédrales, à côté d'une ride on trouve toujours une cicatrice. *Tempus edax, homo edacior.* Ce que je traduirais volontiers ainsi : le temps est aveugle, l'homme est stupide. » La publication du roman de Victor Hugo a encouragé les efforts pour sauver la cathédrale et réunir les fonds pour sa restauration.

De 1845 à 1864, l'architecte Eugène Viollet-le-Duc restaure la cathédrale en la dénaturant. C'est ainsi que les culées des arcs-boutants de la nef sont surmontées d'offensants édicules, que la façade sud du transept est chargée d'éléments nouveaux et désastreux et qu'une flèche haute de 90 m est dressée.

LES PORTAILS

Trois portails ornent la façade ouest de Notre-Dame. De gauche à droite se dressent le portail de la Vierge, le

La rose sud de Notre-Dame comporte en son centre une représentation du Christ entouré des douze apôtres, de saints et d'anges.

LÉGENDE DU BOURDON
Le bourdon de la tour sud ne sonne qu'en de rares occasions. La légende prétend que, lors de sa refonte en 1686, les Parisiennes sont venues sacrifier leurs bijoux en or et en argent en les ajoutant au bronze fondu. Cela expliquerait l'exceptionnelle pureté de son fa dièse. ■

portail du Jugement dernier (ci-dessous) puis le portail de Sainte-Anne. Les statues décorant les portails étaient autrefois peintes en couleurs vives et placées sur un fond doré, et composaient une bible illustrée. Le portail de Sainte-Anne possède les plus anciennes statues, datant de 1170 environ. Les portails ouvrent sur cinq nefs ; le long de chaque collatéral se répartissent sept chapelles complétées par celles qui donnent sur le chœur. Les portails sont encadrés de deux grandes tours (la tour nord est légèrement plus grande que la tour sud), chacune possédant des fenêtres en ogive de plus de 15 m de haut. Une galerie, connue sous le nom de galerie des Chimères (statues ajoutées par Viollet-le-Duc), relie les deux tours.

LES GRANDES ROSES

La taille et les vitraux des trois grandes roses témoignent de la splendeur de l'architecture gothique. La rose nord de 13 m de diamètre, dont les vitraux du XIIIe siècle sont quasiment intacts, représente les personnages de l'Ancien Testament entourant la Vierge. La rose sud, de même diamètre, qui fait face

La rose ouest, celle de la façade.

Le portail du Jugement dernier.

à la Seine, a été en grande partie restaurée en 1737. Elle représente le Christ entouré de saints, d'apôtres et d'anges. Les travées de la nef et les rosaces de la galerie ont été refaites en 1965 par Jacques Le Chevallier qui a remplacé les vitraux sombres du XIXe siècle par de nouveaux vitraux colorés de rouge et de bleu.

LES SCULPTURES

Les sculptures de la clôture du chœur, œuvre de Jean Ravy, ont servi de sources d'inspiration aux ivoiriers, aux miniaturistes et aux peintres. De part et d'autre du maître autel, on a conservé une *Pietà* et une statue de Louis XIII par Coustou ainsi que celle de Louis XIV par Antoine Coysevox. La très belle madone du XIVe siècle, dite *Notre-Dame de Paris*, s'appuie au pilier sud-est du transept.

La rose sud.

Vue depuis la flèche.

Page ci-contre : La nef de Notre-Dame est éclairée sur les côtés par sept verrières. Un transept court mène au chœur qui a conservé des stalles en bois sculpté du XVIIIe siècle.

Ci-dessous : Les gargouilles ont une fonction décorative et utilitaire : elles permettent d'évacuer l'eau des toits. Leurs motifs grotesques ont souvent frappé l'imagination des visiteurs.

Le trésor de la cathédrale comprend la Couronne d'épines, un Clou sacré et un fragment de la Vraie Croix (voir pp. 56-59). Ces reliques ne sont exposées qu'une fois par an lors de la semaine sainte. Il renferme également d'autres reliques, notamment la tunique de saint Louis, un fragment de sa mâchoire et une côte. L'orgue du début du XVIIIe siècle, situé sur le mur ouest, a été restauré en 1868 et de nouveau en 1992. Il compte 6000 tuyaux, 110 registres et 5 claviers : c'est le plus grand orgue de France. La vue sur la flèche, les arcs-boutants et la ville est tout à fait remarquable depuis le sommet de la tour sud (accès par l'extérieur de l'édifice).

LE PARVIS DE NOTRE-DAME

Le parvis actuel est six fois plus grand qu'il ne l'était au Moyen Âge. Un marquage de pierre indique le nom des anciennes rues, comme la rue Neuve Notre-Dame. À l'emplacement actuel de la statue de Charlemagne se trouvait l'ancien Hôtel-Dieu, maintes fois agrandi et reconstruit et dont on relève les traces depuis le IXe siècle. Au Moyen Âge, les patients n'étaient pas séparés par sexe ou par maladie et il pouvait y avoir jusqu'à six personnes par chambre. L'élargissement du parvis et le dégagement latéral de la cathédrale ont déporté l'hôpital sur la berge nord de l'île, dans un vaste édifice néo-florentin construit entre 1868 et 1877.

LA CRYPTE ARCHÉOLOGIQUE

Avant de partir, n'oubliez pas de visiter la crypte pour vous faire une idée juste des fortifications gallo-romaines sous le parvis. À gauche, se trouvent les ruines des salles qui utilisaient un système de chauffage appelé hypocauste. ■

Une promenade dans les îles

Les deux îles, toutes proches, sont pourtant très différentes. L'île de la Cité, vivante et animée, possède de nombreuses merveilles architecturales dont la cathédrale Notre-Dame. L'île Saint-Louis en revanche, plus petite et plus calme, exhale une ambiance de village ; ses rives sont bordées d'hôtels particuliers qui sont autant de témoins muets des splendeurs du Grand Siècle.

Il faut partir du « point zéro » qui se trouve sur le parvis de Notre-Dame 1 pour admirer la cathédrale dans toute sa splendeur gothique, qu'elle soit nimbée de brume ou éclairée par le soleil. Ce point du kilomètre zéro, datant de 1769 (même si l'étoile en bronze est récente), est le point à partir duquel sont mesurées toutes les distances exprimées au départ de Paris ou de France.

Lorsque vous arrivez au bout du parvis, suivez le quai du Marché Neuf puis tournez à droite dans le boulevard du Palais pour admirer la Sainte-Chapelle 2 (voir pp. 56-59), un joyau de l'architecture gothique.

Revenez sur vos pas et tournez à droite sur le quai des Orfèvres. Vous passez devant le célèbre 36, quai des Orfèvres, siège de la Police judiciaire, un lieu mythique pour tous les amateurs des romans de Simenon. Passez devant le Palais de Justice sur votre droite puis, après avoir traversé le Pont-Neuf, le plus vieux pont de Paris, vous arrivez au square du Vert-Galant. Une vue magnifique s'offre alors à vous sur le Louvre à votre droite, l'hôtel de la Monnaie à votre gauche. Remontez sur le Pont-Neuf, saluez le bon roi Henri IV caracolant sur son cheval, et prenez la rue Henri-Robert qui débouche sur la place Dauphine 3. Il s'agit de l'une des rares zones de Paris à avoir échappé aux travaux d'urbanisme du baron Haussmann. Les maisons donnant sur la place datent, pour la plupart, du règne de Louis XIII. C'est là que les acteurs Yves Montand et Simone Signoret habitaient autrefois. Tournez à gauche dans la rue de Harlay au bout du square, puis à droite sur le quai de l'Horloge. Continuez jusqu'à la Conciergerie 4 (voir p. 60) où la plus ancienne horloge de Paris (1370) fonctionne toujours.

Suivez maintenant le quai de la Corse jusqu'au marché aux fleurs. Les étals regorgent de camélias, d'orchidées, de jasmins et de bambous. Le dimanche, il s'y tient également un marché aux oiseaux. Continuez le long du quai aux Fleurs, tournez à droite dans la rue de la Colombe, puis à gauche dans la rue des Ursins avant de rejoindre le quai aux Fleurs.

Continuez jusqu'au Mémorial de la Déportation 5 (square de l'Île-de-France ; tél. : 01 46 33 87 56 ; métro : Cité). Les murs sont recouverts de pierres provenant de tous les massifs montagneux de France. Deux escaliers étroits et raides s'enfoncent jusqu'à un parvis triangulaire entouré de hauts murs. L'eau de la Seine qui coule juste derrière des barreaux de fer et une

Le marché aux fleurs de l'île de la Cité avec les tours de la Conciergerie en arrière-plan.

herse aux pointes acérées créent une profonde impression de claustration. À l'intérieur de la crypte, le long des murs des deux galeries latérales, se succèdent une série de petites niches où sont mentionnés les noms des différents camps de concentration et qui contiennent des urnes remplies de la terre des camps et des cendres des crématoriums. Une autre galerie, longue et obscure, est tapissée de facettes de verre symbolisant les dizaines de milliers de déportés partis de France. Face à l'entrée, un tombeau renferme les restes d'un déporté inconnu recueillis au camp du Struthof.

L'ÎLE SAINT-LOUIS

Traversez le pont Saint-Louis pour rejoindre l'île du même nom. L'intérêt de cette île est de présenter une grande homogénéité architecturale. En effet, la quasi-totalité des bâtiments datent du XVIIe siècle et les plus beaux hôtels, ainsi que l'église baroque Saint-Louis en l'Île, sont dus à un seul architecte: Louis Le Vau.

La vue depuis les quais est splendide et si vous vous êtes gourmand, allez donc chez Berthillon au 31, rue Saint-Louis en l'Île pour déguster leurs fabuleuses glaces et innombrables sorbets. Vous pouvez également aller admirer l'hôtel de Jassaud (6) au 19, quai de Bourbon (la sculptrice Camille Claudel a vécu là, dans un atelier donnant sur la cour), ainsi que l'hôtel de Lauzun (7) au 17, quai d'Anjou. Édifié en 1657 par Le Vau, il sera acheté trente ans plus tard par le duc de Lauzun. À la fin du XIXe siècle, cet hôtel devient le refuge de Théophile Gautier et de Charles Baudelaire qui y a écrit, en 1857, la majeure partie de ses *Fleurs du Mal*. L'hôtel Lambert (8) au 2, rue Saint-Louis en l'Île est également une œuvre de Le Vau. L'élément original de cet hôtel réside dans la galerie de 23 m de long où Le Brun a peint l'apothéose d'Hercule et son mariage avec Hébé. ■

Voir aussi carte pp. 46-47
Parvis de Notre-Dame
4,3 km
4 heures
Hôtel Lambert

À NE PAS MANQUER

- Notre-Dame
- Sainte-Chapelle
- Square du Vert-Galant
- La Conciergerie
- Marché aux Fleurs
- Mémorial de la Déportation
- Hôtel de Jassaud (île Saint-Louis)
- Hôtel de Lauzun (île Saint-Louis)

LES GRANDES INONDATIONS

Vous remarquerez ici ou là des inscriptions qui indiquent le niveau atteint par la Seine, rappelant que Paris a connu une sévère inondation en 1910. ■

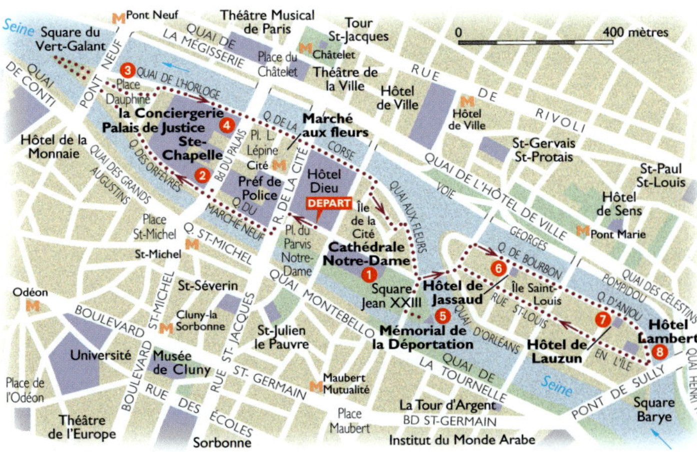

La Sainte-Chapelle

www.monum.fr

Carte p. 46
4, boulevard du Palais, île de la Cité
01 53 40 60 80 (sam.-dim.)
01 53 40 60 97 (lun.-ven.)
€€
Cité, Saint-Michel, Châtelet

LA SAINTE-CHAPELLE EST UN VÉRITABLE JOYAU AU CŒUR DE PARIS. C'est l'un des plus beaux fleurons du style gothique. Elle est reconnue comme un chef-d'œuvre en matière d'architecture et de vitraux.

Louis IX a fait bâtir cette chapelle entre 1242 et 1248. L'architecte présumé est Pierre de Montreuil, mort en 1267. Ce « reliquaire » a été construit pour abriter les reliques de la Passion (un morceau de la Vraie Croix et la Couronne d'épines) que le roi avait achetées en 1239 à Baudouin II, l'empereur de Constantinople. Si Louis IX était sans conteste un homme pieux (il a été canonisé 27 ans après sa mort), les motifs qui l'ont poussé à faire bâtir la Sainte-Chapelle étaient aussi politiques. Louis était âgé de 12 ans seulement à la mort de son père, Louis VIII. Sa mère, Blanche de Castille, a exercé la régence jusqu'à

Les verrières de la chapelle haute constituent une véritable Bible en images, illustrant des scènes de l'Ancien et du Nouveau Testament.

sa majorité. Son accession au trône a été contestée et, à une époque où la monarchie se réclamait du droit divin, la Couronne d'épines (la relique la plus importante de toutes) représentait un véritable symbole pour affermir la légitimité du roi. En effet, cette relique avait une telle valeur (bien que n'ayant jamais officiellement été reconnue par le Vatican) qu'elle a coûté trois fois plus cher que la construction de la Sainte-Chapelle elle-même. Elle fut rapportée en France et placée dans la chapelle, dans une magnifique châsse détruite à la Révolution. Cependant, la plupart des reliques ont été sauvées et sont conservées dans le trésor de Notre-Dame de Paris (p. 51).

LA CHAPELLE BASSE

L'édifice comprend deux chapelles superposées : la chapelle basse, plus sombre mais richement décorée de peintures murales, était réservée aux serviteurs, tandis que la chapelle haute était destinée à l'usage exclusif de la famille royale, des dignitaires et des souverains étrangers. Le rouge et le bleu de la chapelle basse datent du XIXe siècle, époque à laquelle des ten-

La chapelle basse a été fortement endommagée durant la Révolution. Elle a fait l'objet d'une restauration au XIXᵉ siècle.

tatives ont été faites pour retrouver la décoration médiévale d'origine. Les fenêtres sont étroites car la chapelle basse doit supporter le poids de la chapelle haute. Les pierres tombales des XIVᵉ et XVᵉ siècles, incrustées dans le dallage, ont mal résisté aux 900 000 visiteurs annuels.

LA CHAPELLE HAUTE

La chapelle haute est d'une beauté à couper le souffle : c'est une véritable cathédrale de lumière. Les quinze baies (15 m de haut chacune) de la verrière, composées de 1 113 pièces, déversent leur flot lumineux à dominante bleue et rouge. Leurs vitraux sont les plus anciens de Paris et deux tiers d'entre eux datent du XIIIᵉ siècle. À l'exception des trois vitraux derrière l'autel (saint Jean l'Évangéliste, la Passion et saint Jean-Baptiste) et du vitrail situé à droite en entrant dans la Chapelle (histoire des saintes reliques), tous les autres vitraux dépeignent des scènes de l'Ancien Testament.

Le style de la rose est différent des vitraux. Commandée par le roi Charles VIII, elle a été réalisée en 1485 et représente l'Apocalypse. Une paire de jumelles n'est pas inutile pour mieux voir les vitraux du niveau supérieur. Chacune des verrières doit être lue de gauche à droite et de bas en haut (sauf nᵒˢ 6, 7, 9, 11). Certains vitraux ont été détruits pendant la Révolution. À partir de 1791, le bâtiment fut converti tour à tour en club, puis en dépôt de farine et d'archives. Les vitraux détruits ont été remplacés au XIXᵉ siècle par des copies exactes.

LES SCULPTURES

Devant chaque faisceau de colonne, sous un dais, un apôtre est sculpté. Seulement deux d'entre eux sont du XIIIᵉ siècle, les autres sont des copies. Les deux alcôves situées de chaque côté de la chapelle étaient réservées au roi Louis (à gauche) et à sa mère (à droite). On suppose que la femme de Louis, la reine Marguerite, éclipsée par sa belle-mère, devait se tenir à côté de son époux. Le roi entrait par la porte principale qui communique avec les appartements royaux de la Conciergerie. ■

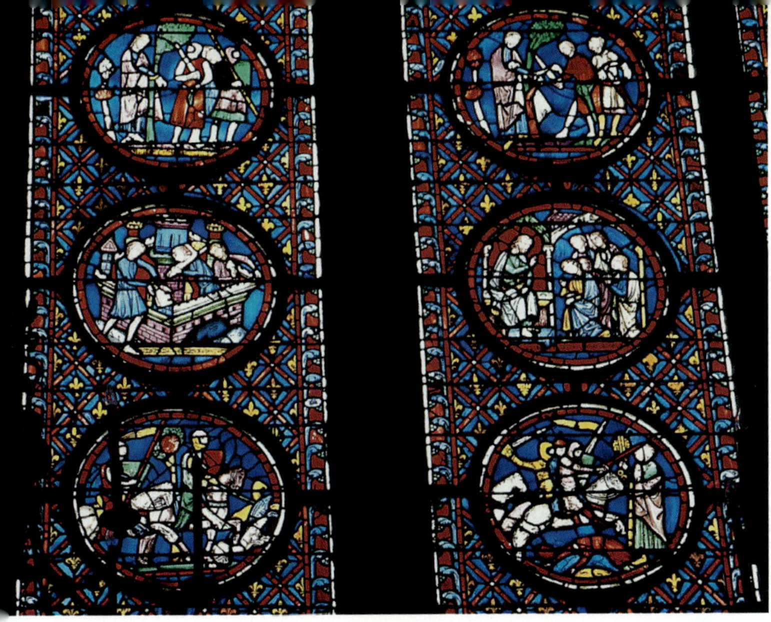

La chapelle haute, avec ses murs de verre.

Les vitraux

Au Moyen Âge, l'Église reconquiert la société civile. Pour dispenser à la population une éducation religieuse, elle fait couvrir ses édifices de scènes bibliques. Les vitraux comme les sculptures font alors office de pages d'un grand manuel permettant de « lire » et de comprendre l'enseignement du Livre. Les scènes sont conçues pour être lues de gauche à droite et de bas en haut.

La technique du vitrail est très ancienne : les Romains utilisaient déjà du verre dans les thermes et maîtrisaient la fabrication de vases et de coupes en verre coloré. La technique alliant le verre coloré à une armature métallique n'a été découverte que plus tard. Avec le développement de l'arc-boutant et de la voûte gothique, les murs n'étaient plus les seuls soutiens des bâtiments et les bâtisseurs ont pu percer de larges ouvertures entre les piliers et les doter de vitraux.

Les techniques de base pour réaliser des vitraux ont peu évolué : le verre transparent et coloré est découpé selon un modèle puis peint avec de la grisaille avant d'être cuit dans un four. Les pièces sont ensuite assemblées à l'aide d'armatures métalliques afin de créer des mosaïques. Aux XIIe et XIIIe siècles, un nombre limité de couleurs était utilisé et les maîtres verriers juxtaposaient le rouge et le bleu lumineux pour créer une variété de teintes semblable à celle des bijoux. Au milieu du XVe siècle, ils ont commencé à imiter les peintures et les fresques en modelant les formes pour créer un effet tri dimensionnel. Le verre est toujours aussi magnifique mais il a perdu de son caractère si particulier. Il ne s'agit plus d'une mosaïque transparente de couleurs brillantes mais plutôt d'une reproduction semi-opaque d'un tableau sur verre. ■

LES VITRAUX DURANT LES GUERRES

Au cours des deux Guerres mondiales, tous les vitraux de la Sainte-Chapelle et de Notre-Dame ont été démontés et mis à l'abri. ■

www.monum.fr

La Conciergerie

Carte p. 46
2, bd. du Palais
01 53 40 60 80 (sam.-dim.)
01 53 40 60 97 (lun.-ven.)
€€
Cité, Saint-Michel, Châtelet

DEPUIS LE XIVe SIÈCLE, LA CONCIERGERIE FAIT PARTIE DU PALAIS royal avant de devenir la première prison de Paris. Pendant la Révolution, c'est là que les « ennemis du peuple » étaient enfermés avant d'être conduits à l'échafaud. Elle est actuellement englobée dans le Palais de Justice.

Philippe IV le Bel (1285-1314) fit construire la plupart des bâtiments de l'époque médiévale qui existent toujours, bien qu'amplement rénovés au XIXe siècle. Après le transfert de la résidence royale au palais du Louvre (voir p. 124) par Charles V, le palais devient, sous la responsabilité du concierge, un officier chargé de l'intendance, une prison. La tour crénelée du XIIIe siècle, dite tour Bonbec, a longtemps été utilisée comme lieu de torture.

L'ARCHITECTURE MÉDIÉVALE PROFANE

L'imposante salle des Gens d'Armes, au bout de la cour lorsque vous empruntez l'entrée principale, quai de l'Horloge, est l'un des plus beaux exemples d'architecture médiévale profane. Cette salle servait de réfectoire au nombreux personnel employé au service du roi (2 000 personnes). Son chauffage était assuré par 4 vastes cheminées encore en place. La « rue de Paris », à l'extrémité ouest de la salle, était l'endroit le plus sinistre de la Conciergerie. Ce nom provient de ce que les prisonniers qui y étaient entassés sous la Terreur étaient destinés au bourreau Sanson appelé « Monsieur de Paris ».

À l'étage, la salle des Pas perdus est aujourd'hui le hall dans lequel les avocats et leurs clients attendent leur audience.

LE SIÈGE DU TRIBUNAL RÉVOLUTIONNAIRE

Pendant la Révolution, le Tribunal révolutionnaire siège dans une des salles du Palais de Justice (la Grand Chambre, aujourd'hui la Ire Chambre du tribunal civil) et condamne près de 2 780 personnes à mourir sous le couperet de la guillotine. Des cellules ont été reconstituées dans les locaux de la Conciergerie. Les conditions de détention dépendaient étroitement de la bourse des prisonniers : les plus pauvres (les « pailleux ») se contentaient de dormir sur de la paille ; les prisonniers « à la pistole » dormaient sur de véritables lits, tandis que les prisonniers de marque disposaient de leurs meubles dans une cellule individuelle. Une chapelle expiatoire a été aménagée dans une partie de la cellule de Marie-Antoinette (dont seul l'ancien carrelage subsiste). Une exposition permanente retrace également l'histoire de la prison et présente ses « hôtes » les plus prestigieux. ■

LES CHEMINÉES MÉDIÉVALES

Chaque cheminée des cuisines avait une fonction : l'une était réservée aux soupes, la deuxième aux ragoûts, la troisième aux viandes ; quant à la quatrième, on ignore son usage. ■

Le mécanisme de l'horloge de la tour de l'Horloge (Palais de Justice) est le plus ancien de Paris.

Les érudits du Moyen Âge enseignaient en latin ; de là le nom du quartier où la vie universitaire du royaume s'est concentrée pendant des siècles... La tradition s'est maintenue, comme l'attestent la Sorbonne et le Collège de France ainsi que les dizaines de librairies, de cafés et les maisons d'édition qui y sont installés.

Le Quartier latin

Un des superbes vitraux Renaissance de l'église Saint-Étienne-du-Mont.

Le Quartier latin

DEPUIS LA FONDATION DU COLLÈGE DE LA SORBONNE, AU XIIIe SIÈCLE, LE QUARTIER LATIN est le cœur de la vie intellectuelle parisienne. Principal centre du savoir de l'Europe occidentale médiévale, le quartier doit son nom au fait que l'enseignement universitaire était uniquement dispensé en latin. Lors des événements de mai 1968, les étudiants révoltés privèrent le Boul' Mich' de ses pavés. Aujourd'hui, l'animation règne encore en permanence même si les étudiants se sont assagis. Librairies spécialisées, cafés, restaurants à petits prix jalonnent ce haut lieu historique.

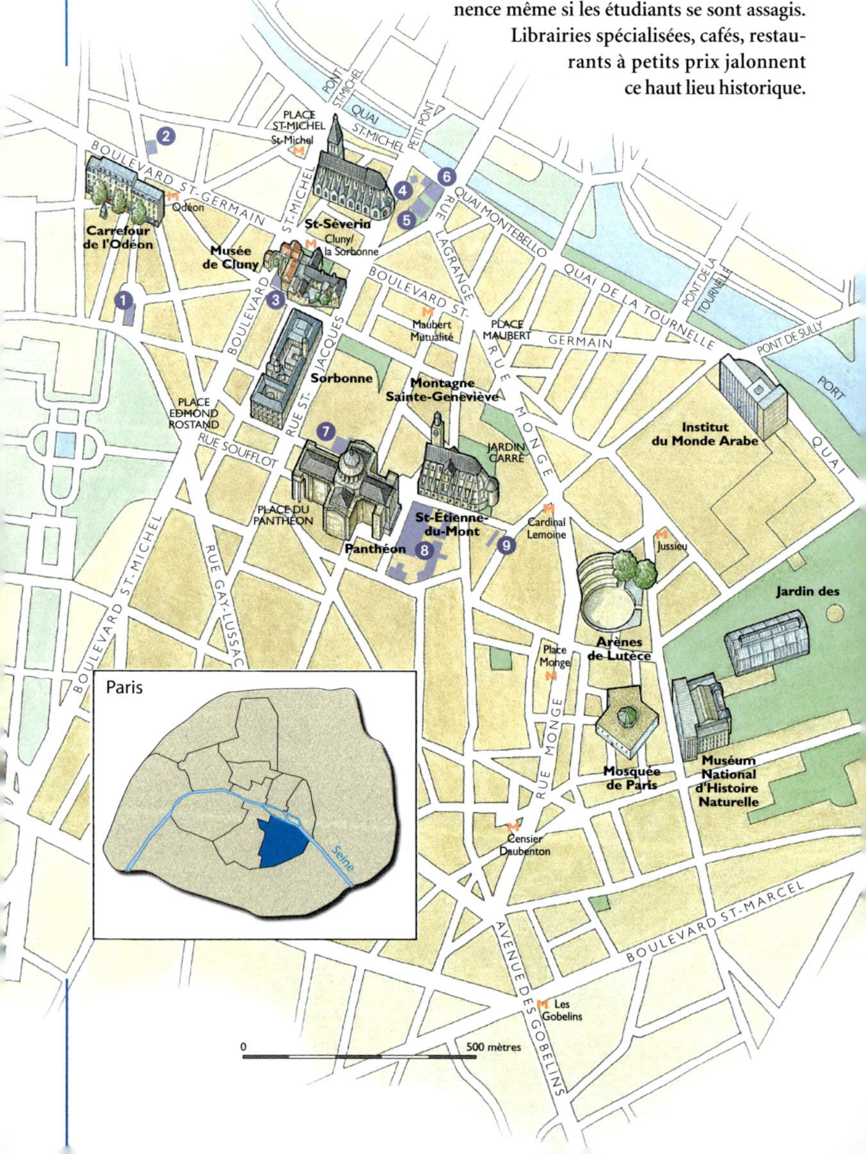

Le Quartier latin regroupe les quartiers de Saint-Séverin, de la montagne Sainte-Geneviève et de la place Saint-Michel, où la fontaine de l'architecte Davioud met en scène le saint terrassant un dragon. Lors de votre première visite, évitez d'aborder le quartier par le boulevard Saint-Michel, dont les fast-foods et les magasins de vêtements risquent de ternir la réputation mythique qui l'auréole. Traversez plutôt la Seine à hauteur de Notre-Dame, pour découvrir le square Viviani, aux pelouses ornées de vestiges de la cathédrale. Derrière ce square se niche Saint-Julien-le-Pauvre, l'une des plus anciennes églises de Paris ; tout à côté, rue de la Bûcherie, la célèbre librairie anglaise Shakespeare and Company ne manquera pas d'attirer les anglophiles. Certains noms de rues, comme la rue de la Parcheminerie (anciennement rue des Escrivains), témoignent de la tradition littéraire qui imprègne le quartier. Remontez ensuite vers la place Maubert où se tenaient, jusqu'à la Première Guerre mondiale, la « bourse aux mégots » (tabac issu de mégots) et le « marché aux rogatons » (restes provenant des grands restaurants). À présent, tous les mardis et samedis matin, un marché très animé propose des produits de toute première fraîcheur.

LE QUARTIER LATIN

1 Odéon-Théâtre de l'Europe
2 Café Procope 3 Thermes gallo-romains 4 Caveau des Oubliettes
5 Saint-Julien-le-Pauvre 6 Square Viviani 7 Bibliothèque Sainte-Geneviève 8 Lycée Henri IV
9 Vestiges de l'enceinte de Philippe-Auguste

On trouve dans le Quartier latin des petites rues pleines de charme et très animées.

Le Quartier latin est un haut lieu historique de Paris. Des ruines romaines, comme les arènes de Lutèce (voir p. 76) ou les bains publics du IIIe siècle situés dans l'enceinte du Musée national du Moyen Âge-Thermes de Cluny (voir pp. 66-67), jalonnent le parcours qui vous mènera jusqu'à la montagne Sainte-Geneviève, ainsi baptisée parce que c'est là qu'au XIe siècle fut dédié un sanctuaire à la sainte patronne de la capitale. Vous y découvrirez Saint-Étienne-du-Mont, l'unique église parisienne à avoir conservé son jubé. L'édifice se dresse sur l'emplacement de la basilique Saint-Pierre-et-Saint-Paul, qui commémorait jadis l'unité du pays. Juste à côté, s'élève le Panthéon (voir p. 69), conçu à l'origine pour remplacer l'antique église Sainte-Geneviève, mais transformé sous la Révolution en temple destiné « aux grands hommes » (il abrite aussi une femme d'exception : la physicienne Marie Curie).

À l'est, sur l'autre versant de la colline, la place de la Contrescarpe rappelle le remblai du fossé qui entourait l'enceinte de Philippe-Auguste. Non loin, le grand marché en plein air de la rue Mouffetard vous enchantera par son amoncellement de fruits, de légumes, de fromages et de volailles de toutes sortes.

Encore plus à l'est, se trouve la Grande Mosquée de Paris (voir p. 74), construite à proximité du jardin des Plantes (voir pp. 70-71). Enfin, l'édifice moderne de l'Institut du monde arabe de l'architecte Jean Nouvel (voir p. 75) domine la Seine et le square Tino-Rossi (voir p. 205), dont les sculptures s'alignent le long du quai. ■

Saint-Séverin et la montagne Sainte-Geneviève

Église Saint-Séverin
Carte p. 62
1, rue des Prêtres-Saint-Séverin
01 46 34 23 09
Saint-Michel

Bibliothèque Sainte-Geneviève
Carte p. 62
10, place du Panthéon
01 44 41 97 97
www-bsg.univ-paris1.fr
Fermé dim.
Luxembourg (RER B), Maubert-Mutualité

Fortifications Philippe-Auguste
Carte p. 62
3, rue Clovis
Cardinal-Lemoine

CES DEUX QUARTIERS SONT PARMI LES PLUS ANCIENS DE LA CAPITALE. Certaines de leurs rues datent du Moyen Âge, comme la rue du Fouarre et la rue Galande, ont conservé de nombreuses maisons anciennes.

LE QUARTIER SAINT-SÉVERIN

Le philosophe et théologien Pierre Abélard (1079-1142) est un des personnages historiques les plus célèbres du quartier (voir p. 114, le récit de sa malheureuse aventure avec Héloïse). Expulsé du couvent de Notre-Dame à la suite d'une querelle philosophique, il vint s'établir sur la rive gauche en drainant 3000 étudiants dans son sillage.

Les petites rues autour de l'église Saint-Séverin existaient déjà au temps des Gallo-Romains. La rue de la Huchette porte le même nom depuis huit cents ans; la rue du Chat-qui-Pêche est l'une des plus courtes de Paris; la rue Galande, au XVIIIe siècle, était bordée de cabarets mal famés. Toutes ont gardé un charme désuet, et offrent de jour comme de nuit une animation quasiment permanente.

L'église Saint-Julien-le-Pauvre

La rue Galande débouche sur Saint-Julien-le-Pauvre. Construite entre 1165 et 1220, c'est une des trois églises les plus anciennes de Paris. À l'origine, les pèlerins y faisaient étape sur le chemin de Saint-Jacques-de-Compostelle, en Espagne. Au bas Moyen Âge, des étudiants y tenaient des réunions mouvementées.

Saint-Julien-le-Pauvre conserve d'admirables chapiteaux romans. Le chœur, fermé par une iconostase de bois, ainsi que les icônes rappellent que l'église est affectée au rite catholique melkite (liturgie de Saint-Jean Chrysostome).

Le square Viviani et l'église Saint-Séverin

Juste à côté s'étend le square Viviani, d'où l'on découvre une superbe vue sur Notre-Dame. Le jardin est agrémenté d'une fontaine contemporaine inspirée par saint Julien et d'un robinier, dit faux acacia, qui du haut de ses 400 ans passe pour être le plus vieil arbre de Paris. Ne manquez pas l'église Saint-Séverin, l'une des plus belles de la capitale. De style gothique flamboyant, elle se caractérise par de hautes voûtes noyées dans une lumière tamisée, par une abside aux vitraux éclatants et par un magnifique double déambulatoire.

LA MONTAGNE SAINTE-GENEVIÈVE

Sur la montagne Sainte-Geneviève (voir p. 76), parcourue de rues aussi tortueuses qu'escarpées, s'étendait probablement le forum gallo-romain.

Des vestiges de **thermes,** en bon état de conservation, se dressent à l'angle de la rue des Écoles et du boulevard Saint-Michel. Contournez-les par l'est, remontez la rue de Cluny et longez le square Paul-Painlevé, qui sépare le **musée de Cluny** (voir pp. 66-67) de la **Sorbonne** (voir p. 68). À l'angle de la rue des Écoles et de la rue de la Sorbonne s'élevait le monastère où étudia François Villon. À la fois poète et mauvais garçon, celui-ci fut expulsé de Paris pour avoir assassiné un prêtre, en 1455. La Sorbonne abrite plusieurs universités. Plus haut dans la rue Saint-Jacques, vous parviendrez au **Panthéon** (voir p. 69), dont

les derniers agencements datent de 1812. Sur le côté nord de la place du Panthéon, la **bibliothèque Sainte-Geneviève,** la seule grande bibliothèque monastique parisienne qui ait traversé la Révolution, est désormais une bibliothèque universitaire abritée dans un beau bâtiment construit par Labrouste en 1850. Derrière le Panthéon se dresse **Saint-Étienne-du-Mont** (voir p. 74), l'une des églises les plus curieuses, par le mélange de ses styles, de la capitale. Sur l'autre trottoir, le prestigieux **lycée Henri IV** occupe le site d'une basilique construite par Clovis au VIe siècle, après sa victoire sur les Wisigoths. Par la suite y fut édifiée la célèbre abbaye Sainte-Geneviève. Plus bas, dans la rue Clovis, subsiste un mur de l'**enceinte de Philippe-Auguste.** ■

Le chevet de l'église Saint-Julien-le-Pauvre, un lieu où sont donnés de nombreux concerts. À droite, un robinier, l'un des plus vieux arbres de la capitale.

Intérieur du Panthéon. Réalisée par Soufflot, cette église d'inspiration hellénistique (plan en croix grecque, colonnades corinthiennes…) est devenue un monument dédié à la mémoire des personnalités les plus illustres de la Nation.

Le musée de Cluny

www.musee-moyenage.fr

Carte p. 62
6, place Paul-Painlevé
Répondeur : 01 53 73 78 00 ou 01 53 73 78 16

Fermé mar.
€€
Saint-Michel, Odéon

LE MUSÉE NATIONAL DU MOYEN ÂGE-THERMES DE CLUNY SE compose de deux musées : d'une part, l'hôtel de Cluny, un bâtiment du XVe siècle qui abrite les collections médiévales et les célèbres tapisseries de *La Dame à la licorne* ; d'autre part, les bains publics de l'époque gallo-romaine.

L'HÔTEL DE CLUNY ET LES THERMES

Rebâti de 1485 à 1500 afin d'héberger les prélats de la riche abbaye bourguignonne de Cluny lors de leurs déplacements à Paris, cet édifice médiéval est un des plus anciens exemples d'architecture civile parisienne. Il s'organise autour d'une cour pavée. On y accède par un escalier extérieur en tourelle, caractéristique des grandes demeures de l'époque.

L'Hôtel de Cluny est bâti au voisinage immédiat des vestiges de bains gallo-romains (datant des IIe et IIIe siècles). Les thermes se composaient de trois grandes salles bordées de magnifiques mosaïques : le ***caldarium*** (« étuve »), aujourd'hui en ruine ; le ***tepidarium*** (réservé aux bains tièdes), dont les baignoires étaient encastrées dans des alcôves ; et le ***frigidarium*** (« pièce froide »). Les murs et le sol du caldarium étaient chauffés par des tuyaux de plomb et de terre cuite alimentés par des fourneaux souterrains. Haut de 13,50 m, le *frigidarium* est intact ; on y donne aujourd'hui des concerts de musique médiévale. Il est si bien conçu qu'il y fait toujours frais, même en été. Le sous-sol voûté, où était aménagée la **chaufferie**, se visite certains jours (renseignez-vous à l'entrée).

LES COLLECTIONS

Les premières salles sont consacrées aux tapisseries, à la ferronnerie et aux coffres. Vous accédez aux thermes romains par la salle 8, qui abrite l'étonnante galerie des « Rois » (21 têtes [sur 28] des statues des rois qui figuraient sur la façade principale de Notre-Dame, voir pp. 48-53). Pendant la Révolution, les émeutiers prirent ces sculptures pour celles des rois de France et les décapitèrent. En fait, il s'agissait de personnages bibliques… On avait perdu espoir de les retrouver lorsque, en 1977, elles ont réapparu lors de travaux rue de la Chaussée-d'Antin. Cet ensemble constitue désormais un des trésors de la salle, où sont également exposées des sculptures romanes. Daté du Ier siècle, le *Pilier des Nautes* est la plus ancienne œuvre en pierre de la ville. Il se dresse dans un angle de la salle voisine, près du frigidarium, et témoigne de l'importance des « marchands de l'eau » dès le début de l'histoire de Paris. Ce sont eux qui ont financé la construction des bains publics de Cluny.

À l'étage, vous admirerez de précieux objets de métal, dont la *Rose d'or de Bâle,* une délicate pièce de fer forgé réalisée en 1330, et des retables exceptionnels. La salle 13 est une rotonde conçue afin de mettre en valeur la pièce la plus célèbre du musée : la série des tapisseries de *La Dame à la licorne* (vers le XVe siècle, Pays-Bas). Les cinq premières seraient des allégories des cinq sens. La sixième s'orne de la mystérieuse devise « À mon seul désir » qui symboliserait le renoncement au plaisir des sens. Très fréquente dans l'iconographie médiévale, la licorne incarne la pureté et la chasteté : elle se défend avec férocité si on l'attaque, et ne se laisse apprivoiser qu'au contact d'une vierge.

Une visite au **jardin médiéval** s'impose : plantes condimentaires, jardin des simples et autres plantes cultivées au Moyen Âge. ■

Les tapisseries

Dans l'Europe du Moyen Âge, les tapisseries étaient tendues sur les murs de pierre froids et humides. Faciles à transporter, elles permettaient de décorer châteaux et églises tout en y retenant la chaleur. D'ordinaire, leur thématique était centrée sur l'histoire, la mythologie et la Bible. Leur somptueuse texture et leurs motifs complexes révélaient la richesse de leurs propriétaires. La première œuvre issue d'un atelier parisien à nous être parvenue est un ensemble de tentures intitulé *L'Apocalypse d'Angers* (vers 1375). Après la défaite d'Azincourt, Arras devient le grand centre de production de la tapisserie de lice, notamment grâce au mécénat des ducs de Bourgogne. En 1662, Colbert crée la Manufacture royale des meubles et des tapisseries de la Couronne qui succède à celle de la famille Gobelin. Des pièces d'une rare perfection ont été tissées dans ses ateliers. La Manufacture nationale des Gobelins continue de produire des chefs-d'œuvre selon des méthodes ancestrales. Ceux-ci sont réservés à la décoration des bâtiments publics (ambassades et palais nationaux). Il est possible d'effectuer une visite guidée de la manufacture. (Tél. : 01 44 61 21 69). ■

« À mon seul désir », telle est l'inscription énigmatique qui figure sur la sixième tapisserie de la série de *La Dame à la Licorne*, l'une des plus belles pièces des collections du musée de Cluny.

La Sorbonne et le Collège de France

La Sorbonne
Carte p. 62
47, rue des Écoles
01 40 46 22 11
Visite sur demande
Saint-Michel, Maubert-Mutualité

Collège de France
Carte p. 62
11, place Marcellin-Berthelot
01 44 27 12 11
www.college-de-france.fr
Visite sur demande
Saint-Michel, Maubert-Mutualité

La façade et la coupole de la chapelle de la Sorbonne reflètent l'idéal mystique des Jésuites.

Hauts lieux de la culture et de l'intelligence, la Sorbonne et le Collège de France sont des institutions séculaires qui offrent encore aujourd'hui le libre accès à un enseignement de qualité.

LA SORBONNE

En 1257, Robert de Sorbon, chapelain de Saint Louis, crée un collège pour offrir hébergement et enseignement à seize étudiants en théologie. Ce collège, très prospère et célèbre, prend au cours de sa longue histoire, des positions très tranchées. La Sorbonne s'oppose en effet aux Templiers, soutient l'Angleterre pendant la guerre de Cent Ans, condamne les philosophes au XVIIIe siècle… Sept siècles après sa création, elle devient le symbole de la révolte estudiantine de mai 1968.

Les bâtiments ont été reconstruits par Nenot à la fin du XIXe siècle. En revanche la chapelle, construite par Lemercier qui abrite le magnifique tombeau du cardinal de Richelieu (par Girardon), date du XVIIe siècle. Elle peut se visiter dans le cadre d'expositions temporaires, et le 4 décembre, jour anniversaire de la mort du prélat. La grande cour est ouverte au public.

LE COLLÈGE DE FRANCE

Conçu en 1530 par François Ier comme un véritable contre-pouvoir laïque opposé à l'Université, le Collège de France permettait aux érudits d'étudier – en français – l'hébreu, le grec et les mathématiques.

Resté fidèle au concept de liberté de l'enseignement auquel il doit sa création, le Collège de France accueille (dans la limite des places disponibles) gratuitement et librement tous les auditeurs – étudiants ou autodidactes – lors de cours professés par les plus grands spécialistes dans des domaines aussi variés que la biologie moléculaire, la sociologie ou la civilisation byzantine. ■

Le Panthéon

DÉDIÉ « AUX GRANDS HOMMES » PAR « LA PATRIE RECONNAISSANTE » en 1791, le Panthéon a été bâti sur ordre de Louis XV. En 1744, le roi, malade, jure de faire élever une nouvelle église et de la consacrer à sainte Geneviève si celle-ci le guérit. Rétabli, il confie, en 1754, à Germain Soufflot le soin de concevoir un vaste sanctuaire où « la légèreté de la construction des édifices gothiques » s'unirait à « la pureté et la magnificence de l'architecture grecque ».

Carte p. 62
place du Panthéon
01 44 32 18 00
€€
Cardinal-Lemoine

L'immense structure conçue par Soufflot était, pour l'époque, une prouesse audacieuse. Il fallut, dans un premier temps, combler les puits et les carrières dont le sous-sol était truffé. En 1764, la pose de la première pierre eut enfin lieu, en présence du monarque, mais le sanctuaire ne fut achevé qu'en 1790, année où le nouveau gouvernement abolit les ordres monastiques. Proclamé « temple à la Nation », il a ensuite servi de dernière demeure à l'écrivain Voltaire, au philosophe Jean-Jacques Rousseau et à l'homme politique Mirabeau. Sous la Restauration, il recouvrit son statut d'église. Il est enfin devenu le cénotaphe des grands hommes du pays en 1885, à l'occasion des funérailles de Victor Hugo (voir encadré ci-dessous). Ses murs sont ornés de peintures, dont certaines exécutées par Puvis de Chavannes relatent les grandes actions de sainte Geneviève. La crypte contient, parmi d'autres, les tombeaux d'Émile Zola (1830-1902), du résistant Jean Moulin (1899-1943), de la physicienne Marie Curie (1859-1906) et, depuis 2002, celui d'Alexandre Dumas (1802-1870). ■

La seconde calotte de l'impressionnante coupole du Panthéon (haute de 83 m) est décorée d'une fresque d'Antoine Gros : *L'Apothéose de sainte Geneviève* (1811).

Victor Hugo

Victor Hugo (1802-1885) occupe une place exceptionnelle dans la littérature française du XIXe siècle. Engagé politiquement, on dit que ses œuvres, par leurs idées sociales, inspirèrent des révolutions, notamment celle de 1830. Ses pièces de théâtre ont éclairé l'art dramatique en le libérant du carcan qui l'entravait depuis l'époque de Racine et de Corneille. En 1851, après avoir tenté de contrer le coup d'État de Napoléon III et s'estimant menacé, Victor Hugo s'exile. Il ne rentre en France que dix-huit ans plus tard, en 1870. Lors de son décès, en 1885, un demi-million de personnes sont descendues dans la rue pour le pleurer. Sa dépouille mortelle est restée exposée en grand apparat sous l'Arc de Triomphe. On l'a ensuite transportée au Panthéon sur le corbillard des pauvres, pour marquer sa solidarité avec les petites gens. Ironie du sort, Hugo a toujours détesté ce monument qu'il comparait à une pièce montée, du fait de ses trois coupoles superposées. ■

www.mnhn.fr

Le Jardin des Plantes

Carte pp. 62-63
36, rue Geoffroy-Saint-Hilaire
01 40 79 56 01
Fermé mar.
€€
Gare d'Austerlitz, Jussieu

Le plus ancien jardin de Paris – après les Tuileries – n'a pas été conçu pour l'agrément de ses riverains, mais dans l'intérêt des botanistes, des médecins et des herboristes.

Créé en 1635, le « Jardin royal des plantes médicinales » de Louis XIII n'acquiert sa notoriété qu'en 1739, grâce à son directeur, Georges Buffon, qui lui conféra une vocation scientifique universelle. Le Jardin devient alors un vaste laboratoire où de grands naturalistes français ont travaillé. Bon nombre d'entre eux ont donné leur nom aux rues voisines. En 1793, il est transformé en muséum d'histoire naturelle. Durant les trente années suivantes, il a accueilli une grande diversité d'animaux.

La Grande Galerie de l'évolution du muséum d'Histoire naturelle illustre superbement la théorie de l'évolution et de la sélection naturelle.

LE MUSÉUM NATIONAL D'HISTOIRE NATURELLE

En 1965, la galerie zoologique a fermé en raison de son état de délabrement, pour ne rouvrir ses portes qu'en 1994. Elle a fait l'objet d'une rénovation de grande ampleur supervisée par les architectes Paul Chemetov et Borja Huidobro. Les résultats sont spectaculaires : sous un éclairage théâtral, les visiteurs pénètrent dans la Grande Galerie de l'évolution (niveau 1), une sorte d'arche de Noé dans laquelle tout un bestiaire naturalisé semble progresser vers le centre du bâtiment. Au niveau inférieur (niveau 0), les animaux marins sont suspendus comme s'ils étaient encore en train de nager et un squelette de baleine long de 16,50 m flotte au-dessus des têtes. Le niveau 2 est consacré à la « galerie de l'Homme », et le niveau 3 à « l'évolution de la vie ». La rénovation du musée a respecté la structure métallique d'origine en l'incorporant avec brio au nouvel ensemble. Une salle de la Découverte (niveau 1) permet aux enfants de moins de 12 ans de se familiariser avec les fossiles et les sciences naturelles, pendant que leurs aînés étudient les objets présentés dans les autres galeries.

LES JARDINS

Deux imposantes serres construites entre 1830 et 1833 se dressent à l'extérieur. La serre australienne (fermée au public), appelée aussi serre des plantes utiles, abrite une flore originaire de la Méditerranée et d'Australie (fougères, ficus...) On y trouve également le jardin d'hiver qui accueille les végétaux des pays chauds (bananiers, palmiers). La serre mexicaine, appelée aussi serre aux cactées, regroupe plusieurs milliers d'espèces de cactées et d'autres plantes dites « succulentes », et d'arbres venus d'Afrique australe ainsi que de Madagascar.

À l'entrée du musée, trois majestueuses allées bordées d'arbres traversent des parterres de fleurs méticuleusement agencés. Ailleurs, le naturel l'emporte sur le formalisme géométrique. Au nord s'étendent la ménagerie et un labyrinthe du XVIIIe siècle. Celui-ci livre accès à un kiosque de bronze, la gloriette de Buffon, qui est la plus vieille structure métallique de Paris (vers 1786). Un grand cèdre planté en 1734 s'élève sur un versant du labyrinthe.

Le jardin alpin (fermé d'octobre à mars) est aménagé tout près de là. Difficile à trouver, ce havre discret est situé trois mètres au-dessous des autres sites, de façon à offrir un terrain plus varié. Les botanistes y ont recréé un paysage de vallées et de collines miniatures, où la température peut varier considérablement d'un point à l'autre. Deux mille espèces végétales classées par régions prospèrent dans ce milieu.

LA MÉNAGERIE

Ce jardin zoologique figure parmi les plus anciens du monde. À son ouverture, en 1794, il était peuplé d'animaux issus des collections royales. Il est devenu si prisé du public que l'arrivée d'une girafe (la première à fouler le sol français) dans son enceinte a attiré, en 1827, près de 600 000 Parisiens. Habitués aux équipements modernes, les actuels visiteurs n'en restent pas moins sensibles à son charme rustique. Mais le manque de fonds donne parfois à certaines installations une piètre allure. Sans se laisser décourager, les soigneurs consacrent leur attention aux petits primates, aux reptiles, aux rapaces et à quelques tigres. ■

Ménagerie

Carte p. 62

57, rue Cuvier

€€

Le Douanier Rousseau (1844-1910) observa la végétation des serres du Jardin des Plantes pour la transposer de façon fantastique dans ses peintures.

Le Paris souterrain

La vie parisienne est aussi animée sous terre qu'en surface. Le site le plus fréquenté est celui des catacombes (voir Denfert-Rochereau, p. 86), mais on trouve aussi des cryptes moins connues dans des lieux inattendus : sous la colonne de Juillet, place de la Bastille (voir p. 119), où sont enterrées les victimes des révolutions de 1830 et de 1848, ou sous l'église Saint-Sulpice (voir p. 83). La ville recèle un réseau d'égouts qui se visite, un abri antinucléaire et une cachette de Résistants aménagés sous la Sorbonne, quantité de carrières, de rivières ou de canaux, et même un lac situé sous la place de l'Opéra. N'oublions pas le métro ni le RER, locataires permanents des sous-sols parisiens.

Carrières, égouts et réserves d'eau

Paris est fait du gypse et du calcaire extraits de son sous-sol. À elle seule, la rive gauche abrite 299 km de galeries (fermées au public). L'exploitation intensive des carrières a entraîné des affaissements de terrain. Bien que cette pratique ait cessé et que de nombreux immeubles soient désormais renforcés, plusieurs bâtiments menacent de s'effondrer dans des quartiers comme Montmartre. On tente actuellement de combler les anciennes carrières de calcaire, dont les fissures sont en permanence surveillées par une équipe de spécialistes.

Si vous effectuez la visite des égouts (voir p. 165), vous découvrirez le musée le plus malodorant de la capitale. En contrepartie, vous saurez tout des systèmes d'évacuation et de traitement des eaux usées, de monsieur Poubelle (qui a donné son nom au conteneur d'ordures ménagères présent dans chaque foyer), et des diverses techniques de purification. En général, les égouts courent sous le milieu des petites rues et sous les trottoirs des avenues. Ils sont désignés par des plaques portant le nom des voies situées à l'air libre. Les canalisations maîtresses renferment les tuyaux réservés à l'eau potable à usage privé ou industriel ; les tubes pneumatiques, grâce auxquels les services postaux acheminaient les lettres et les petits paquets (deux d'entre eux sont toujours en service) ; les conduites d'air comprimé et les câbles du téléphone, du télégraphe ou des feux qui régulent la circulation automobile.

Page de droite, en haut : La construction de la première ligne de métro débuta en 1900. Aujourd'hui, la capitale en compte quatorze.

La première fontaine publique alimentée en eau de source a été inaugurée en 1184, mais c'est le baron Haussmann (voir p. 160) qui a mis en place le système moderne. En 1852, son bras droit, Eugène Belgrand, a commencé à détourner le cours des sources qui offrent aujourd'hui une eau potable à la moitié de la ville. L'autre moitié est alimentée en eaux retraitées. Les Parisiens disposent également de celle qui est pompée dans la Seine et la Marne. Partiellement enfoui, le réservoir Montsouris a une capacité de 3,25 millions de mètres cubes ; il assure l'approvisionnement de l'est de Paris. Pour prouver aux consommateurs la pureté absolue de ses eaux, une expérience fut faite : on y introduisit des truites, celles-ci évoluèrent, sur ce fond turquoise, comme dans leur milieu naturel.

Le métro

À Paris, le métro est le moyen de transport en commun le plus rapide. Ses stations constituent les principaux repères pour se déplacer dans la ville. Lors de sa construction, des os, des dents et des défenses de mammouth ont été mis au jour près du cimetière de Montmartre et sous le square Montholon. Les premiers travaux ont été dirigés par Fulgence Bienvenüe qui a également conçu les plans, établis pour desservir Paris *intra muros.*

On dénombre précisément 380 stations. Saint-Lazare est la plus animée, Abbesses la plus profonde, et Châtelet-Les-Halles celle qui compte le plus de correspondances. À la fin des années 1960, on a décoré celle du Louvre (station Louvre-Rivoli) de copies d'œuvres conservées au musée, ce qui a lancé la mode des stations thématiques. À Varenne, ne manquez pas les répliques du musée Rodin ; à Bastille, les reproductions de la prise de la forteresse ; à Arts et Métiers, les objets associés aux prouesses du génie civil ; enfin, à Porte Dauphine et Abbesses, les « bouches » de style Art nouveau. ■

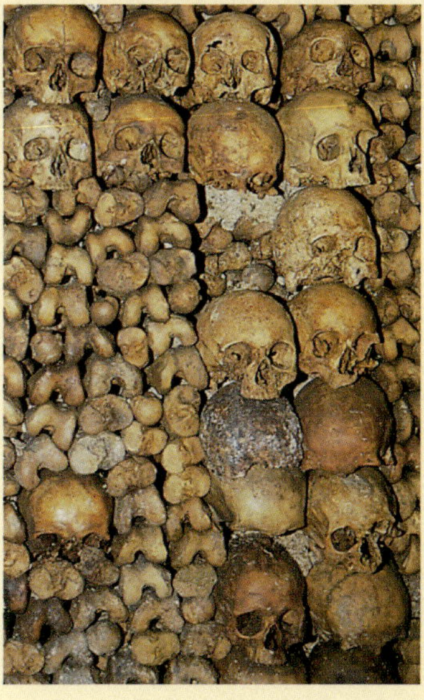

Ci-dessus : Bouche de la station de métro Porte Dauphine, réalisée par Hector Guimard, dans le plus pur style Art nouveau.
À gauche : Au début du XIXe siècle, les ossements des catacombes ont été empilés pour faciliter la visite du public.

Autres sites à visiter

SAINT-ÉTIENNE-DU-MONT

Méconnue du grand public, Saint-Étienne-du-Mont est une des églises les plus monumentales et les plus originales de la capitale. Dotée d'une façade à trois frontons superposés et de différents styles (influences italiennes, tradition gothique et formes antiques), ainsi que d'un intérieur asymétrique, elle abrite le seul jubé («balcon surmonté d'un crucifix et séparant la nef du chœur») qui ait subsisté à Paris. Les épitaphes de Jean Racine et de Blaise Pascal dans la première chapelle du déambulatoire, de très beaux vitraux du XVIe siècle, une tribune d'orgues superbement ouvragée, une chaire baroque soutenue par une figure de Samson et une châsse de cuivre doré qui contient un fragment du tombeau de sainte Geneviève comptent parmi les principales œuvres qu'elle abrite.

Selon la légende, Geneviève aurait fait recouvrer la vue à sa mère en lui lavant les yeux avec l'eau d'un puits; cette scène est représentée sur un vitrail du sanctuaire. Jusqu'à la Révolution, pendant laquelle on a fondu les reliques et brûlé la dépouille de la sainte en place de Grève, un reliquaire constellé de pierreries faisait l'objet d'une intense vénération. Lors des crues et des épidémies, il était porté en procession à Notre-Dame après une journée de pénitence.

Flanqué de deux escaliers ajourés en spirale, le jubé à la décoration inspirée de la Renaissance italienne est une pièce magnifique. La galerie des Charniers est décorée de splendides vitraux des XVIe et XVIIe siècles.

Carte p. 62 place Sainte-Geneviève ☎ 01 43 54 11 79 Fermé 12h-14h lun.-ven. et 12h-14h30 dim. Ⓜ Cardinal-Lemoine

LA MOSQUÉE DE PARIS

Fréquentée par une communauté musulmane principalement d'origine algérienne, la plus grande mosquée de Paris se compose d'un centre cultuel, d'où s'élance un minaret à décor blanc et vert (26 m de haut), de l'Institut musulman, où l'on enseigne la langue arabe et la culture arabo-islamique, d'un salon de thé, d'un restaurant et de bains turcs.

Inauguré en 1926 pour commémorer l'effort de guerre des musulmans, l'édifice est l'œuvre de trois architectes français: Charles Heubès, Robert Fournez et Maurice Mantout. Les meilleurs artisans tunisiens, marocains et algériens ont été sollicités pour la décorer de marbre, de faïences, de mosaïques, de damas et de fontaines en porphyre. Le grand patio s'inspire de celui de l'Alhambra de Grenade, en Espagne; vous y remarquerez des boiseries d'eucalyptus et de cèdre, une frise en mosaïque où sont inscrits des versets coraniques et une belle fontaine qui servait aux ablutions.

Carte p. 62 place du Puits-de-l'Ermite (mosquée) ou 39, rue Geoffroy-Saint-Hilaire (pour le salon de thé, les bains turcs, le restaurant et la boutique) ☎ 01 45 35 97 33 / www.mosquee-de-paris.com Ⓜ Censier-Daubenton

Le minaret de la Mosquée de Paris est le point de mire des fidèles...

Le jubé de Saint-Étienne-du-Mont constitue une curiosité architecturale. C'est l'unique église parisienne à l'avoir conservé.

L'INSTITUT DU MONDE ARABE

Inauguré en 1987, ce bâtiment d'acier et de verre est l'aboutissement d'un projet franco-arabe visant à promouvoir les échanges culturels entre l'Occident et le monde islamique. Vingt États arabes ont participé à sa construction. Il comprend des espaces d'expositions permanentes et temporaires, une bibliothèque, une librairie, des salles de conférences, un auditorium, ainsi qu'un restaurant et un café aménagés sur son toit en terrasse (à elle seule, la vue qu'on y découvre mérite le déplacement).

L'admirable architecture, conçue par Jean Nouvel, se veut symbolique du concept de carrefour. La façade nord (dite « occidentale »), qui longe la Seine, est formée d'un mur transparent, lisse et brillant.

Celle de la cour reflète l'influence arabe classique en réinterprétant sur le mode high-tech le traditionnel moucharabieh (« panneau de bois ajouré »). Contrôlés par ordinateur, 1 600 prismes d'aluminium s'ouvrent et se ferment pour réguler le flot de lumière qui y pénètre. La collection permanente occupe trois niveaux et présente les nombreuses innovations scientifiques et culturelles des savants arabes.

Carte p. 62 1, rue des Fossés Saint-Bernard Fermé lun. 01 40 51 38 38/ www.imarabe.org € Jussieu, Cardinal-Lemoine, Sully-Morland

LE CARREFOUR DE L'ODÉON

Dominé par la statue du révolutionnaire Georges Jacques Danton (érigée sur l'emplacement même de sa demeure, où il fut arrêté en mars 1794 avant d'être guillotiné), le carrefour de l'Odéon, de son vrai nom place Henri-Mondor, est l'endroit le plus animé du Quartier latin. À deux pas, rue de l'Ancienne-Comédie, le café Procope (fondé en 1686), l'établissement le plus ancien de ce genre à Paris, rappelle son passé glorieux : Diderot et d'Alembert y ont entrepris la rédaction de leur célèbre *Encyclopédie* en 1727, et Benjamin Franklin, représentant des États-Unis, s'y détendait avant d'aller négocier une alliance avec Louis XVI. Avant de continuer dans cette direction, ne manquez pas de découvrir, place de l'Odéon, le bel édifice néo-classique qui abrite le théâtre de l'Europe (encore désigné par les Parisiens sous son ancien nom de Théâtre de l'Odéon), construit en 1782 par Peyre et de Wailly. En 1784, c'est là qu'eut lieu la première du *Mariage de Figaro* de Beaumarchais. Jugée subversive, cette pièce a valu à son auteur un an d'emprisonnement. L'ensemble des rues qui rayonnent depuis la place date de la même époque.

En retournant rue de l'Ancienne-Comédie, vous rejoindrez la très animée rue Saint-André-des-Arts, mélange de belles façades et d'édifices pittoresques. Et, au hasard de votre promenade, vous découvrirez les vestiges du passé : balcons en fer forgé, portes basses, petits hôtels particuliers, passages au charme provincial… Ne manquez pas la cour de Rohan (vous pouvez y accéder par la rue du Jardinet) qui, au XVᵉ siècle, faisait partie de l'hôtel des archevêques de Rouen. Elle constitue, en fait, une succession de trois petites cours bordées d'élégants édifices. À noter, un bâtiment Renaissance, dans la deuxième cour, qui fut la demeure de Diane de Poitiers. Vous pouvez ensuite rejoindre la cour du Commerce-Saint-André qui possède encore une tour intacte de l'enceinte érigée par Philippe-Auguste. C'est aussi dans cette cour que le docteur Guillotin essaya sur des moutons, en 1790, sa « philanthropique machine à décapiter », et que Marat y imprimait *L'Ami du peuple*…

Les arènes de Lutèce accueillent aujourd'hui promeneurs et joueurs de boules.

LES ARÈNES DE LUTÈCE

Au voisinage des immeubles modernes de l'université de Jussieu s'étendent les vestiges des arènes de Lutèce. On suppose que cet amphithéâtre romain du IIᵉ siècle, conçu pour accueillir jusqu'à 15 000 spectateurs, était le deuxième par la taille en Gaule. Ses bâtisseurs ont tiré parti de la pente de la colline pour y aménager 35 gradins de pierre. Ils ont installé la scène face à l'ouest, de sorte que les acteurs bénéficient des derniers rayons du soleil. L'ensemble a conservé peu de traces de son lointain passé, car les Parisiens y ont prélevé un grand nombre de pierres pour ériger les murs de l'île de la Cité. Au fil des siècles, les débris ont envahi l'espace. Au XIXᵉ siècle, la plupart des habitants pensaient que les arènes relevaient plus de la légende que de la réalité. En 1869, les aménagements engagés rue Monge par le baron Haussmann ont mis au jour leur infrastructure. Il les a fait déblayer et en a détruit à peu près les deux tiers pour y établir un dépôt d'autobus. En 1883, Victor Hugo a mené campagne en faveur de la sauvegarde du site, qui a été restauré en 1917. À l'heure actuelle, seul environ un tiers des arènes est d'origine.

Carte p. 62 ✉ 49, rue Monge Ⓜ Cardinal-Lemoine ■

Autrefois hauts lieux de la vie intellectuelle et artistique de la capitale, les quartiers de Saint-Germain et de Montparnasse conservent encore les traces de ce passé prestigieux et restent parmi les endroits les plus animés de la rive gauche.

Saint-Germain et Montparnasse

Angelots ornant l'un des balcons de la rue de la Gaîté, à Montparnasse.

Saint-Germain et Montparnasse

Le légendaire quartier de Saint-Germain-des-Prés s'est développé à partir du IXe siècle autour d'une des plus célèbres abbayes bénédictines du pays. Il abrite aujourd'hui quantité de cafés littéraires, de librairies et de galeries d'art. Autre lieu mythique, Montparnasse a longtemps été la terre d'élection des artistes et des intellectuels.

L'église Saint-Germain-des-Prés formait le cœur d'une abbaye dont les terres occupaient l'emplacement des actuels VIe et VIIe arrondissements et s'étendaient à l'est jusqu'au Petit-Pont. Ce sanctuaire roman, le plus ancien de Paris, abrite la dalle funéraire de René Descartes, penseur, mathématicien et père de la philosophie moderne. C'est au Café de Flore voisin, plusieurs siècles plus tard, qu'un autre grand philosophe, Jean-Paul Sartre, le théoricien de l'existentialisme, aimait s'installer pour écrire ou bavarder avec la romancière Simone de Beauvoir et leurs amis. D'autres intellectuels, dont Raymond Aron, allaient prendre un verre aux Deux-Magots ou se restaurer à la brasserie Lipp, faisant ainsi du quartier le symbole de la vie intellectuelle parisienne.

Montparnasse a été le berceau de ce qui allait devenir dans les années 1920 l'École de Paris. Modigliani, Utrillo, Max Jacob, Apollinaire, Paul Fort s'y sont installés dès 1900. Le bouillonnement artistique et intellectuel qui règne alors dans ce coin de bohème attire peintres, poètes, écrivains, musiciens et exilés politiques du monde entier.

Ernest Hemingway, Francis Scott Fitzgerald, John Dos Passos, Henry Miller ont fréquenté ses brasseries et ses bars; James Whistler a vécu dans les parages; Lénine a joué aux échecs à la Closerie des Lilas; Trotski avait ses habitudes à la Rotonde; Hart Crane a été arrêté pour avoir boxé un serveur du Sélect; et Kiki, la très exotique « reine de Montparnasse », séduisait tout ce petit monde par sa voix rocailleuse et sa silhouette sensuelle.

De nombreux peintres et sculpteurs ont vécu et travaillé à la Ruche, une cité d'artistes installée passage de Dantzig. Parmi eux, beaucoup étaient originaires d'Europe centrale, tels Constantin Brancusi, Ossip Zadkine, Chaïm Soutine et Marc Chagall. Vivant parfois dans un grand dénuement, certains d'entre eux passaient des heures entières au café pour échapper au froid.

Connue pour rester ouverte tard le soir, la librairie-galerie d'art La Hune est toujours en activité, comme ses dizaines de concurrentes du quartier. Saint-Germain-des-Prés a longtemps regroupé la plupart des grandes maisons d'édition françaises. Mais investi par les commerces de luxe de la rive droite, ce sanctuaire de la littérature tend aujourd'hui à se transformer en temple de la consommation : ainsi Armani s'est installé à la place de l'illustre Drugstore Publicis, Cartier a remplacé un grand disquaire spécialisé en musique classique, Louis Vuitton s'est établi 6, place Saint-Germain-des-Prés, et le Flore lui-même a créé sa boutique d'accessoires.

SAINT-GERMAIN ET MONTPARNASSE

❶ Tour Montparnasse ❷ Closerie des Lilas ❸ Marché Saint-Germain ❹ École nationale supérieure des Beaux-Arts

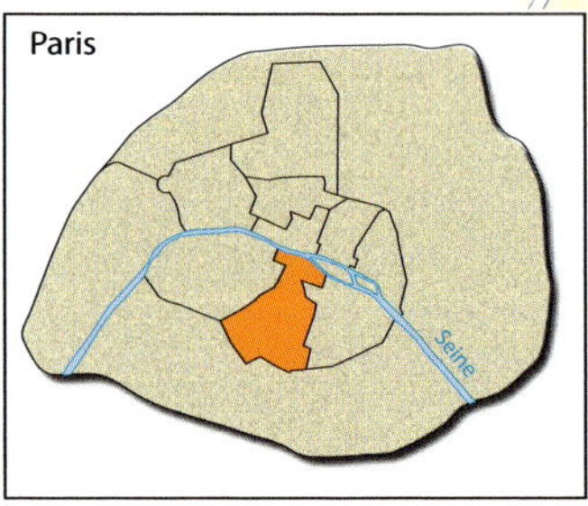

La visite du quartier n'en reste pas moins agréable. Ne manquez pas les nombreuses galeries d'art qui bordent les rues de Seine, Bonaparte et des Beaux-Arts, ni les musées Delacroix et de la Monnaie.

N'oubliez pas non plus de faire une pause face au bassin octogonal du jardin du Luxembourg, ni de contempler, du pont des Arts, le soleil qui se couche sur la Seine en éclairant de ses derniers rayons les coupoles dorées de l'Institut de France.

Et si vous voulez avoir une idée de ce qu'était la vie dans le quartier autrefois, faites un tour au Sélect et à la Closerie des Lilas (voir p. 88). ■

L'église Saint-Germain-des-Prés

Carte p. 79
3, place Saint-Germain
01 55 42 81 33
Saint-Germain-des-Prés

SUR LES CONSEILS DE SAINT GERMAIN, FUTUR ÉVÊQUE DE PARIS, LE roi mérovingien Childebert Ier ordonna en 543 la construction d'une basilique et d'un monastère dédiés à saint Vincent et à la sainte Croix. L'abbaye, devenue l'une des plus prestigieuses du royaume des Francs, reçut les sépultures des rois mérovingiens. Rattachée à l'ordre de saint Benoît au VIIe siècle, elle a bénéficié de donations considérables, et son domaine s'est étendu sur plus de 30 000 ha.

L'église Saint-Germain-des-Prés abrite la dépouille mortelle du philosophe René Descartes. Son crâne est conservé au musée de l'Homme (voir p. 182).

Détruite par les Normands, l'église abbatiale a été rebâtie autour de l'an 1000 dans le style roman. Son clocher du XIe siècle est le plus ancien de la ville. Le chœur gothique, du XIIe siècle, a été consacré en 1163 par le pape Alexandre III, tandis que débutait le chantier de Notre-Dame-de-Paris. Pour mieux affirmer l'indépendance du sanctuaire, l'évêque de Paris, Maurice de Sully, a été tenu à l'écart de la cérémonie. En 1245, l'église s'est agrandie de la chapelle de la Vierge et du cloître, dont on peut voir les vestiges dans le square voisin. Le palais abbatial, édifié en 1586, s'élève rue de l'Abbaye.

UNE HISTOIRE MOUVEMENTÉE

En juin 1789, les révolutionnaires prennent d'assaut la prison de l'abbaye pour libérer les soldats qui ont refusé de tirer sur les ouvriers insurgés du faubourg Saint-Antoine. L'année suivante, l'abbaye est définitivement transformée en prison et l'église devient un entrepôt de salpêtre.

En 1792, elle est l'un des principaux théâtres des massacres de Septembre. Pendant la Terreur, Charlotte Corday y a été emprisonnée après l'assassinat de Marat. En 1794, quinze tonnes de poudre stockées dans le réfectoire explosent, dévastant la quasi-totalité des bâtiments conventuels (on a toutefois pu sauver quelques-uns des 50 000 volumes et des 7 000 manuscrits de sa bibliothèque). Rendue au culte, l'église a été restaurée au XIXe siècle, en grande partie grâce aux efforts de Victor Hugo. Hippolyte Flandrin, un élève d'Ingres, a réalisé une série de fresques sur les murs de la nef et du chœur. Les colonnettes de marbre de la primitive église Saint-Vincent ont été réutilisées pour orner le triforium du chœur. Dans le square qui borde l'église au nord, vous pouvez admirer une tête de femme en bronze de Picasso. ■

Le musée Delacroix

Delacroix était fasciné par l'Orient.

Carte p. 79
6, rue de Furstemberg
01 44 41 86 50
Fermé mar.
€€
Saint-Germain-des-Prés

www.musee-delacroix.fr

Aménagée à l'emplacement de la cour d'honneur de l'abbaye, la place Furstemberg est l'une des plus romantiques de Paris. Au n° 6 se situe le musée Eugène Delacroix, immeuble dans lequel le peintre a vécu jusqu'à sa mort, en 1863. Il avait quitté le IXe arrondissement pour y emménager en 1857, alors qu'il réalisait les peintures murales de l'église Saint-Sulpice.

Créé en grande partie grâce à l'action des peintres Paul Signac et Maurice Denis, le musée abrite 22 études à l'aquarelle pour les fresques peintes par Delacroix au plafond de la bibliothèque du Palais-Bourbon. Présentée dans l'appartement et l'atelier de l'artiste, la collection comporte des tableaux plus petits et des sujets religieux (*L'Annonciation, La Mise au tombeau* et *La Montée au calvaire*). La deuxième version de *L'Enlèvement de Rébecca* est la plus importante des œuvres exposées. Le musée présente aussi des souvenirs personnels et des œuvres des amis du peintre. ■

L'institut de France

Carte p. 79
23, quai de Conti
01 44 41 44 41
Saint-Michel

www.institut-de-france.fr

Face au pont des Arts s'élève le palais de l'Institut, couronné de sa célèbre coupole. Dessiné par Louis Le Vau, l'édifice abritait à l'origine le collège des Quatre-Nations, fondation posthume de Mazarin (1661), destiné à recevoir des écoliers des quatre provinces rattachées depuis peu à la France. Depuis 1805, le palais est le siège des cinq académies.

L'Académie française, la plus ancienne et la plus connue, a été fondée par le cardinal de Richelieu, en 1635. Ses 40 membres, surnommés les « Immortels », ont pour tâche principale la rédaction et la réactualisation d'un *Dictionnaire de la langue française*. L'aile orientale du bâtiment est occupée par la bibliothèque Mazarine, la première bibliothèque publique du royaume. Dans l'ancienne chapelle, se trouve le tombeau du cardinal Mazarin, exécuté par Coysevox.

À proximité de l'Institut, l'École nationale supérieure des Beaux-Arts (14, rue Bonaparte) est installée depuis 1816 sur l'emplacement de l'ancien couvent des Petits-Augustins (dont il ne reste que la chapelle), construit sur ordre de Marguerite de Valois en 1608 ; ses jardins sont ouverts au public (fermés le samedi et le dimanche). ■

www.senat.fr

Le palais du Luxembourg

Carte p. 79
rue de Vaugirard
01 42 34 20 00
Pour le palais, visites guidées uniquement, 1er dim. de chaque mois, sur rendez-vous auprès de la Caisse nationale des Monuments historiques (places limitées). Tél. : 01 44 54 19 49. Pour le jardin, du lever du soleil à la tombée de la nuit.
Saint-Sulpice, Odéon, Luxembourg

Au XIXe siècle, il était possible de louer des journaux pour deux heures dans les jardins du Luxembourg, et des écrivains publics y proposaient leurs services.

Pour la plupart des Parisiens, le nom de « Luxembourg » évoque le beau parc à la française de 29 ha, seul véritable espace vert du VIe arrondissement, et non le palais du même nom qui abrite le Sénat depuis 1852. Depuis des générations, ce jardin reste en effet l'un des plus prisés des habitants de la capitale.

UN PALAIS À L'ITALIENNE

L'édifice et son parc ont été créés par Marie de Médicis au début du XVIIe siècle, après l'assassinat de son époux Henri IV. Nostalgique du palais Pitti où elle avait passé son enfance florentine, elle demanda à Salomon de Brosse de bâtir une demeure à l'italienne sur un terrain acheté au duc de Luxembourg. Conservant l'hôtel de Luxembourg, devenu le Petit Luxembourg (actuellement résidence officielle du président du Sénat), l'architecte a élevé une somptueuse construction de style français avec des touches d'inspiration florentine.

Pour la décorer, la reine commanda à Rubens 24 peintures monumentales (aujourd'hui exposées au Louvre) la représentant dans les grands moments de sa vie. En 1630, à la suite de la journée des Dupes, elle dut s'exiler sur ordre de son fils Louis XIII, alors qu'elle n'habitait son palais de rêve que depuis cinq ans.

UN PARC À LA FRANÇAISE

Les vergers, les vastes parterres, les 2 000 ormes plantés par ses soins témoignent de la passion que Marie de Médicis vouait à son jardin. Redessiné au XIXe siècle il a conservé son plan d'origine, mêlant tradition française et anglaise dans l'art du jardin. Toujours parfaitement entretenu, il offre au regard des perspectives harmonieuses et une riche palette de couleurs.

Ombragé de platanes centenaires, le long bassin de la fontaine Médicis est l'un de ses plus beaux ornements. De nombreuses statues se dressent çà et là, dont l'original de la *Liberté* de Bartholdi. Les enfants ont le choix entre un parc à jeux qui leur est réservé, des promenades en poney, des balançoires, des toboggans, un théâtre de marionnettes à l'ancienne ou un manège réalisé d'après les plans de Charles Garnier (l'architecte de l'Opéra). ■

Saint-Sulpice et son quartier

LORSQUE LES RAYONS DU SOLEIL PRINTANIER ÉCLAIRENT LES FLEURS roses des marronniers, la place Saint-Sulpice est l'une des plus jolies de Paris. Assis à l'une des tables en terrasse du Café de la Mairie, où les écrivains Albert Camus et Georges Perec avaient leurs habitudes, vous apprécierez mieux la monumentale fontaine des Quatre-Évêques (de Joachim Visconti, 1844) et l'imposante église Saint-Sulpice.

L'ÉGLISE

Saint-Sulpice est un édifice majestueux et austère, dont la construction s'est échelonnée sur plus de cent trente-cinq ans (d'où la différence de style des deux tours de part et d'autre de la façade à colonnade). La pose de la première pierre a eu lieu en 1646. Il était alors question de relever un sanctuaire du XIIIe siècle, mais les travaux durent s'arrêter vingt ans plus tard par manque de fonds.

Au XVIIIe siècle, la construction a repris et s'est poursuivie jusqu'en 1778, année d'achèvement de la tour nord. La chapelle des Saints-Anges, que Delacroix a mis dix ans à décorer, est le joyau de l'église. Les représentations tourmentées de *La Lutte de Jacob avec l'ange* et d'*Héliodore chassé du Temple* sont les derniers chefs-d'œuvre de l'artiste.

LES RUES AVOISINANTES

À l'ombre du sanctuaire, au 36, rue Saint-Sulpice, se tenait une célèbre maison close ; l'établissement a disparu, mais l'étroite façade à colonnade ainsi que les carreaux de faïence jaunes et verts signalent encore l'endroit.

Les rues qui entourent Saint-Sulpice abritent des boutiques d'art liturgique et de nombreuses librairies, certaines catholiques comme la Procure, ou anglaises comme le Village Voice. Elles cèdent cependant de plus en plus la place à de luxueuses boutiques de mode.

Idéal pour le lèche-vitrines, le quartier s'étend jusqu'à Sèvres-Babylone, où trône le Bon Marché. Récemment rénové, ce grand magasin est devenu un lieu moderne et élégant. À elle seule, l'épicerie fine du rez-de-chaussée mérite le déplacement. Derrière Saint-Sulpice s'étend le marché Saint-Germain, dont les galeries couvertes sont occupées par des boutiques de vêtements et de décoration. On est loin de la célèbre foire qui s'y tenait au Moyen Âge… ■

Église Saint-Sulpice

Carte p. 79
place Saint-Sulpice
01 46 33 21 78
Saint-Sulpice, Odéon

La fontaine des Quatre-Évêques sur la place Saint-Sulpice.

Les cimetières

Pendant des siècles, les Parisiens ont enterré leurs morts au cimetière des Innocents, en plein cœur de la capitale, non loin du quartier animé des Halles. Le site a servi de nécropole à plus de 20 paroisses, notamment à celles qui en étaient dépourvues, aux indigents et aux malades décédés à l'Hôtel-Dieu. Les inhumations avaient lieu dans des fosses communes qui pouvaient contenir jusqu'à 1 500 corps. Lorsque l'une d'elles était pleine, on en creusait une autre à côté.

À la fin du XVIIIe siècle, l'intolérable puanteur qui s'en dégageait a contraint les autorités à transférer, par convois entiers, les restes de presque six millions de défunts aux catacombes situées près de Denfert-Rochereau. L'opération a duré quinze mois. Les cimetières aménagés dans la ville ont été fermés, et ceux du Père-Lachaise, de Montparnasse et de Montmartre les ont remplacés.

Le cimetière du Père-Lachaise

Le Père-Lachaise attire davantage de visiteurs (plus de 2 millions par an) que tous les autres cimetières parisiens. Son nom lui vient du père de La Chaise, le confesseur de Louis XIV, qui résida de 1665 à 1709 dans le domaine des jésuites, alors propriétaires des lieux.

En 1803, l'architecte Alexandre Brongniart fut chargé d'aménager le site pour en faire un cimetière. S'inspirant des jardins anglais, il a imaginé un paysage romantique et pittoresque, doté d'une végétation abondante et d'une statuaire funéraire exubérante. Le cimetière a ouvert ses portes le 21 mai 1804 ; onze ans plus tard, il ne comptait que 2 000 tombes. D'astucieux responsables municipaux projetèrent alors d'y transférer les dépouilles mortelles de personnages célèbres, certains que, le snobisme aidant, les futurs défunts viendraient les rejoindre. En 1817, les restes de Molière, du poète Jean de La Fontaine, mais aussi d'Héloïse et d'Abélard (voir p. 114) y ont été inhumés. L'opération fut efficace : en 1828, le cimetière abritait plus de 33 000 tombes et la municipalité s'est vue dans l'obligation de l'agrandir.

Aujourd'hui, ses 44 ha font de lui le plus grand espace vert de la ville (à condition d'en exclure les bois de Boulogne et de Vincennes). Il se compose de plusieurs divisions numérotées. La partie basse, qui a été classée Monument historique, se présente comme un enchevêtrement de tombes et d'arbres, traversé de sentiers de terre et d'allées pavées. La partie haute, en revanche, obéit à un plan parfaitement géométrique.

À l'entrée, procurez-vous un plan qui vous permettra de repérer les tombes les plus connues. Pour parvenir jusqu'à elles, vous devrez souvent vous aventurer hors des grands axes. Vous découvrirez quantité de sépultures intéressantes, les plus curieuses n'étant pas nécessairement celles qu'occupent des célébrités. Ne manquez pas celles de Frédéric Chopin et d'Oscar Wilde (à l'origine, le personnage sculpté sur la tombe de l'écrivain irlandais avait une anatomie parfaite, mais un vandale anonyme l'a castré). La dernière demeure de Jim Morrison, le chanteur des Doors, est devenue un sanctuaire pour ses fans. Près du mur des Fédérés, attardez-vous devant les émouvants monuments élevés à la mémoire des Français morts dans les camps de concentration nazis.

187 et 197 E3-F3 ✉ 8, boulevard de Ménilmontant ☎ 01 55 25 82 10
Ⓜ Père-Lachaise, Philippe-Auguste

Le cimetière Montparnasse

Le site, occupé depuis 1654 par la nécropole d'une abbaye, n'est devenu cimetière municipal qu'en 1824. Divisé en deux, les Petit et Grand Cimetières, il est en superficie le troisième de la capitale. À première vue moins romantique que le Père-Lachaise, il est découpé par des allées en damier, bordées de tombeaux où reposent de nombreux intellectuels et artistes français. L'art funéraire y atteint des sommets d'originalité : dominant une énorme chauve-souris, le buste du poète Charles Baudelaire contemple son propre corps sculpté en contrebas ; sur la sépulture de la famille Pigeon, l'une des plus extravagantes, le couple est allongé sur un grand lit de bronze et de pierre. Des sculptures de Brancusi, qui est enterré sur place, ornent certains édifices (voir *Le Baiser*). Serge Gainsbourg, Jean-Paul Sartre et Simone de Beauvoir sont également inhumés ici.

La tombe d'Oscar Wilde (ci-dessus), dans le cimetière du Père-Lachaise (à gauche). Ci-dessous : Le cimetière Montmartre, où sont enterrés les compositeurs Offenbach et Berlioz, et le danseur russe Nijinski.

79 et 196 D2 3, boulevard Edgar Quinet 01 44 10 86 50 Raspail, Edgar-Quinet

Le cimetière de Montmartre
Ancienne carrière de plâtre devenue fosse commune pendant la Révolution, c'était jadis un endroit sinistre. Créé en 1798, fermé puis rouvert en 1825, le cimetière abrite aujourd'hui les tombeaux de nombreuses personnalités, dont Edgar Degas, Offenbach, Louis Jouvet, Dalida et François Truffaut.
187 et 196 C4 20, avenue Rachel
01 43 87 64 24 Place de Clichy ■

Denfert-Rochereau

Dans le XIVe arrondissement, deux places étoilées, dans l'axe de la route d'Orléans, ont un rôle déterminant : au sud, la place Victor-Basch et, plus au nord, la place Denfert-Rochereau sont des carrefours qui orientent le flux des automobiles vers l'intérieur de la capitale.

Le lion d'origine a été taillé à même le roc par Bartholdi à Belfort.

Les catacombes

- place Denfert-Rochereau
- 01 43 22 47 63
- Fermé lun.
- €
- Denfert-Rochereau

Au centre de la place Denfert-Rochereau trône le *Lion de Belfort*, copie en bronze du lion sculpté par Bartholdi en hommage au courage des Alsaciens lors de la guerre de 1870. Au 261, boulevard Raspail, ne manquez pas la Fondation Cartier (tél. : 01 42 18 56 50, fermé le lun.). Construite en 1994 par l'architecte Jean Nouvel, cette élégante structure de verre et d'acier située dans un magnifique jardin accueille des expositions d'art contemporain.

Les Catacombes (entrée : place Denfert-Rochereau) constituent la plus étrange nécropole de Paris. Ces anciennes carrières abritent près de six millions de squelettes retirés au XVIIIe siècle des cimetières paroissiaux et des Innocents saturés. Les galeries bordées d'ossements s'étendent sur des kilomètres sous les rues de Paris. À l'entrée de l'ossuaire, une inscription avertit le visiteur : « Arrête ! C'est ici l'empire de la mort. » ■

Les fontaines Wallace

C'est à sir Richard Wallace que les Parisiens doivent leurs premières fontaines d'eau potable. La santé publique étant devenue une grande préoccupation sous le Second Empire et la IIIe République, la première fontaine Wallace fut inaugurée en 1871, boulevard de La Villette. Ces élégantes fontaines de fonte verte se composent de quatre cariatides (la Simplicité, la Charité, la Sobriété et l'Abondance), qui soutiennent un dôme surmonté d'un dauphin. Elles sont typiques du mobilier urbain du XIXe siècle, comme les bancs, les lampadaires et les colonnes Morris au dôme en bulbe, où sont présentées les affiches des pièces de théâtres et des concerts. ■

La Ruche n'était guère luxueuse, mais au moins offrait-elle un toit aux artistes désargentés.

La Ruche

- 2, passage de Dantzig
- 01 44 24 96 96
- La visite des ateliers est laissée à la discrétion de leurs occupants.
- Quai de la Gare

Ce bâtiment polygonal est une des plus anciennes cités d'artistes à être encore en activité. Il s'agit à l'origine du pavillon des Vins construit par Gustave Eiffel pour l'Exposition universelle de 1900. Le sculpteur Alfred Boucher, premier maître de Camille Claudel, l'a récupéré et installé à cet endroit afin d'y accueillir de jeunes artistes. Le grand escalier dessert des ateliers disposés en alvéoles (d'où le nom de « Ruche »).

Haut lieu de la création artistique, la Ruche a hébergé de nombreux artistes, dont Fernand Léger, Modigliani, Chaïm Soutine, Marc Chagall, Zadkine, Brancusi, ainsi que des écrivains comme Guillaume Apollinaire, Max Jacob et Blaise Cendrars. Bon nombre d'entre eux y ont trouvé refuge en période de vaches maigres.

Le lieu a connu un certain déclin après la Première Guerre mondiale, mais une nouvelle génération d'artistes est venue s'installer après 1945. Sauvé de la démolition grâce à l'intervention d'un comité présidé par Chagall, ce monument, aujourd'hui classé, continue à bourdonner d'activité. ■

L'Observatoire de Paris

- Carte p. 79
- 61, avenue de l'Observatoire
- 01 40 51 21 70
- Fermé le week-end. Visites guidées le 1er sam. du mois (fermé en août) sur demande écrite (joindre une enveloppe timbrée pour la réponse).
- Port-Royal

Fondé en 1667 par Louis XIV et achevé en 1672, l'Observatoire de Paris est le plus ancien du monde à être encore en service. Œuvre de Claude Perrault, l'édifice a été conçu comme un reflet du cosmos : son plan médian a été axé sur le méridien de Paris, les quatre faces du corps principal sont orientées vers les quatre points cardinaux, et les murs des deux tours octogonales de sa façade sud indiquent la position du Soleil lors des solstices d'hiver et d'été.

C'est dans cet observatoire qu'a été cartographiée la surface de la Lune (1679), conçu le système métrique appliqué aux poids et mesures (1791), mesurée la vitesse de la lumière (XVIIIe siècle), et que Le Verrier a permis par ses calculs de découvrir Neptune (1846).

Bien qu'il abrite toujours un centre de recherches en astronomie et ses services annexes, vous pouvez visiter le bâtiment, qui comporte un petit musée. ■

www.obspm.fr

Une promenade dans Montparnasse

Certes, Montparnasse n'est plus le haut lieu artistique qu'il était dans la première moitié du XXe siècle, mais des traces de ce passé subsistent encore dans bien des endroits, des grandes brasseries du boulevard aux ateliers d'artistes des petites rues voisines, et font de ce quartier un lieu encore très vivant de jour comme de nuit.

Commencez votre promenade au métro Raspail et prenez la rue Campagne-Première 1. Au n° 31, un magnifique immeuble d'ateliers est décoré de hautes fenêtres et de carreaux de céramique. Le photographe américain Man Ray y vivait avant d'emménager avec sa maîtresse Kiki à l'Istria.

Situé juste à côté, cet hôtel a accueilli de nombreux créateurs, dont les peintres Francis Picabia et Marcel Duchamp, le poète autrichien Rainer Maria Rilke, ainsi que le compositeur Erik Satie. Paul Verlaine a habité sur l'autre trottoir, au n° 14 (la maison a disparu) ; lorsqu'il en est parti, il a laissé sa chambre à son compagnon Arthur Rimbaud.

Au n° 9, franchissez la porte qui donne accès aux ateliers aménagés au fond de la cour pavée. Avant la Première Guerre mondiale, quantité d'artistes ont quitté Montmartre pour Montparnasse, où les loyers étaient plus bas, et sont venus chercher l'inspiration dans les cafés du boulevard du même nom. Les peintres italiens Giorgio De Chirico et Modigliani, l'Anglais James Whistler et Rainer Maria Rilke ont compté parmi les occupants de cet immeuble.

Remontez à droite le boulevard du Montparnasse et dirigez-vous vers l'enseigne mauve de la Closerie des Lilas 2, où se retrouvaient peintres et écrivains. À son arrivée à Paris, en 1924, Ernest Hemingway y a passé de longs moments à écrire « La Grande Rivière au cœur double » (une nouvelle du recueil intitulé *Paradis perdu*), et bien d'autres œuvres. Sur le comptoir d'acajou, une plaque de cuivre indique la place où il avait l'habitude de s'installer. Le décor de boiseries, de lampes rouges et de miroirs est toujours aussi intime et feutré qu'autrefois.

Devant la Closerie se dresse une statue du maréchal Ney, héros des guerres révolutionnaires et napoléoniennes, érigée à l'endroit même où il a été fusillé, en 1815. Hemingway vivait non loin de là, au 113, rue Notre-Dame-des-Champs (tournez à gauche en sortant de la Closerie pour poursuivre la promenade), au-dessus d'une scierie aujourd'hui disparue (même le numéro de la maison s'est volatilisé : on passe directement du 111 au 115).

Tournez encore à gauche dans la rue de Chevreuse. Au croisement du boulevard du Montparnasse, un restaurant a remplacé le Jockey, un cabaret où se produisait Kiki, modèle d'artistes et chanteuse légendaire.

Prenez à droite le boulevard du Montparnasse. Le célèbre *Balzac* de Rodin (voir p. 172) se dresse au carrefour Vavin.

Traversez le boulevard et empruntez la rue Delambre. Kiki se rendait souvent au n° 5, où le peintre japonais Foujita occupait un atelier équipé d'une baignoire et d'eau chaude (équipements rares en ce temps-là !) Au n° 10, l'Auberge de Venise, appelée « le Dingo » dans les années 1920, était fréquentée par les expatriés. C'est là qu'Hemingway a fait la connaissance de son compatriote F. Scott Fitzgerald. Arrivé à la place Edgar-Quinet, prenez à droite la rue du Montparnasse. Plus bas à gauche, le Falstaff (transformé en simple brasserie) était le bar préféré de Samuel Beckett, Kiki, Man Ray, Fitzgerald et Hemingway.

Remontez à droite le boulevard du Montparnasse. Un peu plus loin se tiennent quatre des cafés les plus connus du monde : d'un côté

Le *Balzac* de Rodin, présenté au Salon de 1898, fut très mal accueilli par la critique du moment.

La Coupole, rénovée en 1988, a conservé son splendide décor des années 1920.

du boulevard, le Sélect (qui a su conserver l'ambiance feutrée et l'esprit d'autrefois) et la Rotonde et, sur le trottoir d'en face, le Dôme (aujourd'hui reconverti en un luxueux restaurant de poissons) et la Coupole (voir p. 253) ❸. Ce dernier établissement, qui doit son nom à la coupole de verre qui éclairait jadis la salle, reste un authentique lieu de mémoire de Montparnasse, même si un immeuble de bureaux s'est construit au-dessus. ■

Voir aussi carte pp. 78-79
Raspail
2,1 km
Environ 2 heures
Vavin

À NE PAS MANQUER

- Closerie des Lilas
- Le *Balzac* de Rodin
- La Coupole
- Le Sélect

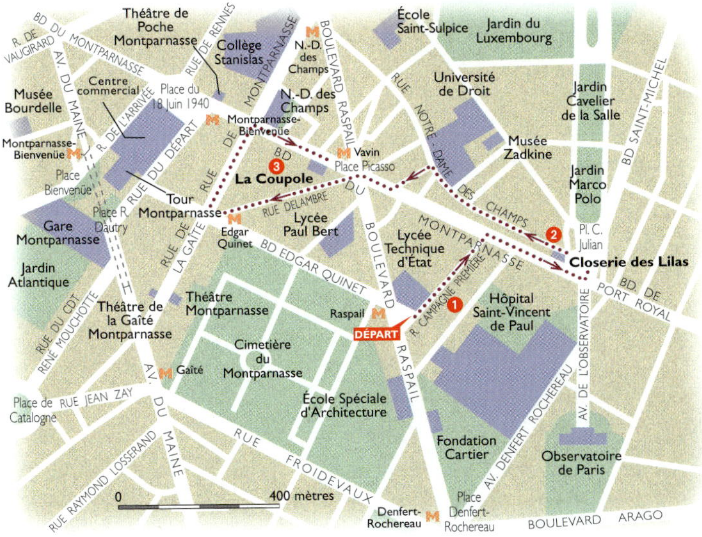

Autres sites à visiter

LE CARRÉ RIVE GAUCHE

Les plus grands antiquaires parisiens se concentrent dans quelques rues du VIIe arrondissement. Délimité par le quai Voltaire et les rues des Saints-Pères, de l'Université et du Bac, le Carré Rive gauche abrite une trentaine de magasins associés où l'on propose du mobilier, des objets d'art et des tableaux de grande qualité. Dans chaque vitrine est exposé un objet exceptionnel, lié à un thème choisi chaque année en vue de la semaine « du Carré Rive gauche » de la mi-mai.

L'HÔTEL DE LA MONNAIE

Cette imposante bâtisse néo-classique du XVIIIe siècle, dessinée par l'architecte Jacques Antoine et première manifestation marquante du style Louis XVI, a été jusqu'en 1973 le centre de la fabrication monétaire en France. Les locaux abritent aujourd'hui des ateliers de frappe des médailles et des poinçons ainsi qu'un musée. La passionnante visite guidée retrace l'historique de la frappe des monnaies et permet de comprendre comment l'argent peut faire ou défaire des royaumes, renforcer le pouvoir et imposer une idéologie.

Carte p. 79 11, quai de Conti 01 40 46 55 35/www.monnaiedeparis.fr Fermé lun. € Saint-Michel, Pont-Neuf, Odéon

LE MUSÉE BOURDELLE

Le travail de ce sculpteur du début du XXe siècle n'a pas été immédiatement reconnu à son époque. Quelques expositions aux États-Unis et au Japon ont suffi à lui forger une réputation mondiale. Puisant son inspiration dans ses origines rurales et dans les styles médiévaux, il a notamment sculpté les bas reliefs du Théâtre des Champs-Élysées. Ce musée est, en fait, son domicile, réaménagé, mais vous pourrez voir son atelier dans l'état où il l'a laissé et admirer nombre de ses œuvres.

18, rue A.-Bourdelle 01 49 54 73 73/ www.bourdelle.paris.fr Fermé lun. et jours fériés Montparnasse-Bienvenüe

LE MUSÉE ZADKINE

Dans cette petite maison, située à quelques rues du Luxembourg, le sculpteur d'origine russe Ossip Zadkine a vécu de 1928 à sa mort, en 1967. Elle est restée presque intacte depuis. Les sculptures sont réparties dans cinq salles et dans le jardin. Plusieurs pièces maîtresses sont exposées, dont la maquette du célèbre *Monument à la ville détruite*, œuvre à la fois tourmentée et triomphante, commandée par la ville de Rotterdam en souvenir de la Seconde Guerre mondiale.

Carte p. 79 100*bis*, rue d'Assas 01 55 42 77 20 ; www.paris.fr/musees/zadkine Fermé lun. Port-Royal, Vavin, Notre-Dame-des-Champs

LA TOUR MONTPARNASSE

Vous ne pouvez manquer cette construction de 58 étages, haute de 210 m. Le plus haut des édifices d'acier et de verre d'Europe se dresse sur l'emplacement de l'ancienne gare. Au sommet est aménagé un restaurant panoramique, d'où la vue est exceptionnelle. rue de l'Arrivée 01 45 38 52 56/www.tour-montparnasse.com €€ Montparnasse-Bienvenüe ■

Sculptures dans le jardin du musée Zadkine.

À la place du plus grand marché de Paris, appelé les Halles, se tient maintenant un énorme complexe en partie souterrain sous lequel se croisent pas moins de 8 lignes de métro et de RER. Alentour, le quartier a conservé par contraste un peu de son cachet.

Le Châtelet et les Halles

Le centre Georges Pompidou.

Le Châtelet et les Halles

MÊME SI LE QUARTIER A PERDU UN PEU DE SON ÂME, CERTAINES PETITES RUES QUI entourent le Châtelet et les Halles sont comme les venelles pavées du vieux Paris : encombrées, mal famées et malodorantes, mais pleines de vie.

Pendant cinq siècles, les négociants des Halles et les habitants du quartier cohabitent avec le fameux cimetière des Innocents, jusqu'à ce que celui-ci, débordant, soit transféré dans les catacombes actuelles. L'odeur parfois insupportable n'empêche pas mimes, bateleurs, jongleurs, musiciens, écrivains publics, prostituées, mendiants et voleurs d'y trouver refuge.

LE CHÂTELET

Les abords de la place du Châtelet (voir p. 95) étaient connus pour l'insécurité qui y régnait. Le quartier était associé à

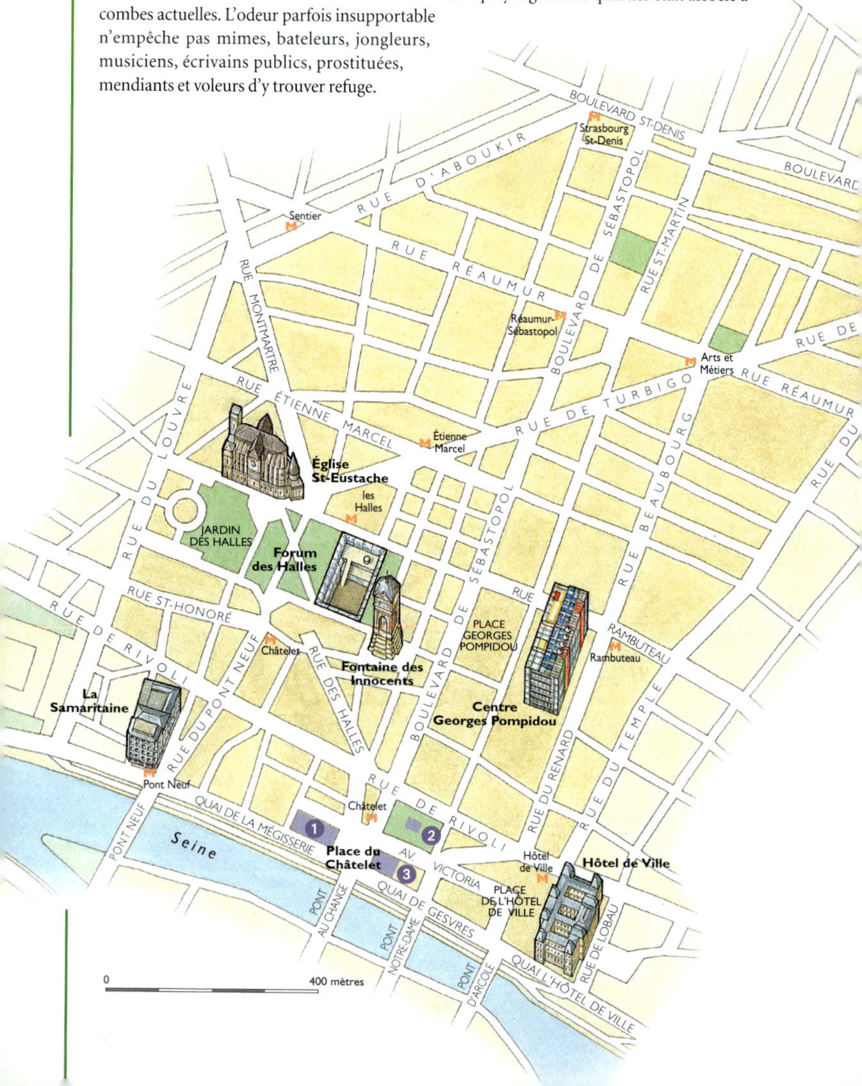

la puissante guilde des bouchers, aux tanneries et à la sinistre geôle du Grand Châtelet, qui abritait, entre autres instruments de torture, une cellule en forme de cheminée dans laquelle les prisonniers ne pouvaient s'asseoir. À la vue de cette place, aujourd'hui flanquée de théâtres et agrémentée d'une fontaine dont la base s'orne de sphinx, qui pourrait imaginer son ancien aspect? Érigée au XVIe siècle au profit de la confrérie des bouchers, la tour Saint-Jacques (un clocher de style gothique flamboyant qui dominait l'église Saint-Jacques-de-la-Boucherie) était une étape importante des pèlerins de Saint-Jacques-de Compostelle. En 1648, Blaise Pascal y reproduit les expériences barométriques qu'il avait menées dans le Puy-de-Dôme. Entourée d'un square, la tour sert aujourd'hui de station météorologique (fermée au public).

LE CHÂTELET ET LES HALLES

❶ Théâtre musical de Paris ❷ Tour Saint-Jacques ❸ Théâtre de la Ville

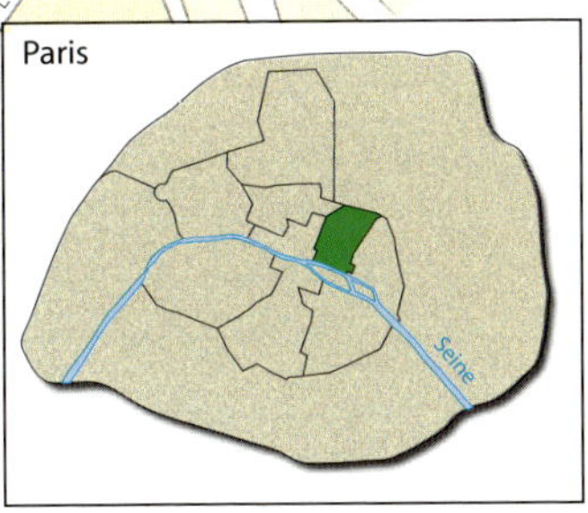

Jusqu'à la Révolution, des abattoirs se dressent quai de la Mégisserie. Cette belle artère est désormais bordée de jardineries et d'animaleries.

Contrastant avec la réputation douteuse du Châtelet, la rue Saint-Denis a connu une splendeur dont la croissance a été proportionnelle à celle de la basilique éponyme. Lorsque les rois de France faisaient leur entrée, cette voie s'ornait de fontaines d'où s'écoulait du vin. Aujourd'hui, elle a pour ornementation des fast-foods, des boutiques de vêtements et des sex-shops. La partie nord du quartier est célèbre pour ses hôtels de mauvaise réputation…

À la Samaritaine (voir p. 95), un grand magasin de 5 étages situé rue de la Monnaie, – « on trouve tout » disait un slogan publicitaire célèbre –, on trouvait effectivement tout, du matériel informatique aux jouets, en passant par la confection pour enfants et les articles de sport, avant sa fermeture pour travaux de rénovation en mai 2005.

LES HALLES

Les Halles (voir p. 98), où tous les produits de bouche français se sont vendus pendant huit siècles, attirent toujours les badauds, qui se rassemblent autour de la fontaine des Innocents (à l'emplacement du cimetière du même nom, voir p. 102), dans les jardins, sur les terrasses, tout au long de la rue Saint-Denis ou aux environs de l'église Saint-Eustache (voir p. 102). En 1969, le marché a été transféré à Rungis, au sud de Paris.

Froid, moderne et en grande partie souterrain, le complexe commercial et culturel du Forum des Halles, qui a remplacé le marché, manque cruellement de charme. Le cœur du quartier s'est déplacé à l'est, vers l'édifice bariolé du centre Georges Pompidou (également appelé « Beaubourg », voir pp. 96-97) et le bâtiment néo-Renaissance de l'Hôtel de Ville (voir p. 94). Au XIIe siècle, Beaubourg est un village protégé par la muraille de Philippe Auguste; le secteur conserve un peu de ce passé médiéval, notamment dans ses petites rues. Au XVIIe siècle, les hôtels borgnes du IIe arrondissement n'ont pas encore proliféré sur l'emplacement de la cour des Miracles (voir p. 99). À travers la description qu'il en fait, Victor Hugo nous propose cette terrible vision de la vie parisienne au Moyen Âge: « *[…] égout d'où s'échappait chaque matin, et où revenait croupir chaque nuit ce ruisseau de vices, de mendicité et de vagabondage toujours débordé dans les rues des capitales […]; immense vestiaire, en un mot, où s'habillaient et se déshabillaient à cette époque tous les acteurs de cette comédie éternelle que le vol, la prostitution et le meurtre jouent sur le pavé de Paris.* » ■

Les statues présentes sur la façade néo-Renaissance de l'Hôtel de Ville sont autant d'allégories des villes de France. On dénombre également 108 personnalités, toutes parisiennes (excepté l'architecte italien le Boccador).

L'Hôtel de Ville

Siège de la mairie de Paris, l'Hôtel de Ville fut incendié lors de la Commune et reconstruit dans un style néo-Renaissance. La place du même nom a été le témoin d'une histoire riche et rocambolesque.

Carte p. 92
Place de l'Hôtel de Ville (entrée du public au 29, rue de Rivoli)
01 42 76 40 40
Visites guidées uniquement. Individuels : 1er lun. de chaque mois à 10h30 Groupes : lun. apr.-midi et ven. (tél. : 01 42 76 50 49). Les groupes se rassemblent 5, rue Lobau
Hôtel-de-Ville, Châtelet

L'activité marchande des bateliers de la Seine a joué un rôle essentiel dans l'essor de Paris. C'est de cette puissante guilde – qui contrôlait et gérait le commerce sur la Seine, l'Oise, l'Yonne et la Marne – que naîtra l'administration municipale. Ainsi, au milieu du XIIIe siècle, saint Louis instaure le « Parloir aux Bourgeois », un gouvernement citadin dirigé par le prévôt des marchands et composé des principaux échevins élus par les habitants. La corporation serait à l'origine du blason de Paris avec son navire et sa devise *Fluctuat nec mergitur* (« Il flotte, mais ne sombre pas »).

Jusqu'au milieu du XIVe siècle, la place du Châtelet abrite le « Parloir aux Bourgeois ». En 1357, Étienne Marcel transfère cette administration pour l'installer dans la maison aux Piliers, place de Grève (actuelle place de l'Hôtel de Ville). Mais sous François Ier, la maison aux Piliers tombe en ruine. La construction d'un nouvel édifice, sur les plans de l'architecte italien le Boccador, commence en 1533 pour ne s'achever qu'au XVIIe siècle. Incendié en mai 1871, l'Hôtel de Ville est reconstruit de 1874 à 1882. Le bâtiment a été le théâtre de révolutions, de célébrations et d'exécutions. En 1789, Louis XVI y a agrafé à sa coiffure la cocarde tricolore. Sous la Révolution, Robespierre y trouve un dernier refuge avant d'être guillotiné, le 27 juillet 1794.

À l'époque de Noël, une superbe crèche est aménagée sur son parvis. L'intérieur de l'Hôtel de Ville est somptueux. On y admire notamment : les lambris dorés (remarquez les sept essences différentes de bois utilisées dans le salon Bertrand), le grand escalier décoré de fresques (*L'Été* et *Le Printemps*) de Puvis de Chavannes et les plafonds peints à la gloire de la IIIe République.

L'eau reste associée au site grâce aux fontaines réalisées en 1980 par François-Xavier Lalanne. Elles flanquent le bel édifice qui abrite souvent des expositions temporaires. ■

La place du Châtelet

Aujourd'hui agrémentée de deux théâtres en vis-à-vis, d'une imposante fontaine et offrant une belle vue sur la Seine, la place du Châtelet n'a presque rien gardé de son passé, ni de sa geôle ni des coupe-gorge qui l'environnaient. Seuls les noms de certaines rues (de la Lingerie, de la Ferronnerie) témoignent de l'époque où ferronniers et lingères y exerçaient leur métier.

Le nom de la place rappelle la forteresse du Grand Châtelet, érigée par Louis VI le Gros vers 1130 pour protéger l'accès à l'île de la Cité. Plus tard, la prévôté, la prison et les tribunaux s'y installent. Démolie à partir de 1802, la place accueille, en 1862, deux édifices construits par Davioud : côté Louvre, le Théâtre musical de Paris (ancien Théâtre du Châtelet) et, côté Hôtel de Ville, le Théâtre de la Ville (ancien théâtre Sarah-Bernhardt), qui attirent l'un et l'autre un large public dans le quartier. La fontaine du Châtelet, dite aussi du Palmier (1808), commémore les victoires de Napoléon Ier. ■

LE PONT-AU-CHANGE

Le Pont-au-Change est situé face à la place du Châtelet. Il est habité, à partir de 1305, par des orfèvres et des changeurs, d'où son nom de « Pont-aux-Changeurs » à la fin du XIVe siècle. ■

La Samaritaine

Ce grand magasin, qui porte le nom de la pompe qui ornait le Pont-Neuf de 1609 à 1813, occupait, avant sa fermeture pour travaux, plusieurs bâtiments, dont chacun témoigne des styles architecturaux de la période 1900-1930. Le magasin 1 est un immeuble 1900, construit dans un style révolutionnaire par Frantz Jourdain ; il se caractérise par son ossature métallique et ses immenses fenêtres de métal riveté (matériau jugé vulgaire à l'époque). Réalisé de 1926 à 1928, le magasin 2 est remarquable par sa façade Art déco. Enfin, l'édifice construit en 1930 s'orne d'une frise insolite et d'un majestueux escalier. La date de sa réouverture et sa destination future ne sont pas encore connues. ■

Carte p. 92
75, rue de Rivoli
01 40 41 20 20
Pont-Neuf

La Samaritaine.

Le centre Georges Pompidou

Rénové depuis peu, le Centre Pompidou est un des endroits les plus fréquentés de la capitale. Construit en plein cœur de Paris, ses tuyaux et conduits aux multiples couleurs tranchent sur la grisaille des toits voisins. Véritable fer de lance de l'architecture contemporaine, ce complexe artistique érigé en 1977 par Richard Rogers et Renzo Piano a injecté une tonalité avant-gardiste dans un des plus vieux quartiers de la ville, tout en suscitant une âpre controverse.

Victime de son succès, Beaubourg (ainsi que l'appellent les Parisiens) a été obligé de fermer ses portes durant deux ans et d'investir près de 100 millions d'euros dans des travaux de rénovation et de réorganisation. Résultats : les espaces consacrés aux expositions, permanentes ou temporaires, se sont considérablement développés ; la BPI (Bibliothèque publique d'information, aux 1er, 2e et 3e niveaux) s'est agrandie, équipée d'ordinateurs et bénéficie dorénavant d'une entrée indépendante ; des salles de théâtre, de danse et de cinéma ont ouvert en sous-sol ; la galerie du Musée, la galerie d'Arts graphiques et la collection de Nouveaux Médias sont venues enrichir le Centre ; et un luxueux restaurant *(Georges)*, géré par la famille Costes, s'est installé au sommet de cet édifice à 6 niveaux. Vous y trouverez toujours : le CCI (centre de la Création industrielle), spécialisé en architecture, en urbanisme et en communication visuelle ; l'IRCAM (institut de Recherche et Coordination acoustique et Musique), installé sous la place Igor Stravinsky, consacré à l'exploration du monde sonore ; la Cinémathèque, qui présente des festivals et des films rares ; l'atelier des enfants, pour « développer le sens artistique » des 6-12 ans ; ainsi que des salles de conférences, de séminaires et de débats. En revanche, les travaux ont nui au caractère démocratique du lieu. Vivement critiqué par les concepteurs du bâtiment, le nouveau règlement impose aux visiteurs de payer pour emprunter l'escalator qui les conduit au toit en terrasse. En contrepartie, le ticket de 7 euros donne accès au musée national d'Art moderne (MNAM).

L'atelier Brancusi

À sa mort, en 1957, le sculpteur d'origine roumaine Constantin Brancusi légua, dans son testament, son atelier à l'État français, à condition que celui-ci reconstitue entièrement le lieu. D'abord transféré de l'impasse Ronsin, dans le XVe arrondissement, au Palais de Tokyo, l'atelier a été rebâti sur l'esplanade (la Piazza) du Centre Pompidou, en 1977. Il abrite des esquisses, des œuvres de bronze et de pierre, des plâtres originaux, mais aussi un lit, une armoire, des outils, et des maquettes. Des expositions temporaires y sont organisées. ■

LE MUSÉE NATIONAL D'ART MODERNE

C'est un des musées d'Art moderne les plus riches au monde : 45 000 œuvres des débuts du XXe siècle à nos jours, sont réparties sur 2 étages. À la suite des travaux de rénovation, l'espace d'exposition a doublé. L'accrochage des créations contemporaines est renouvelé tous les 18 mois, et celui des galeries d'Art moderne tous les ans. Le 1er étage du musée (4e niveau) est consacré à l'art contemporain (de 1960 à nos jours). Vous y trouverez aussi bien la présentation de grands mouvements artistiques (pop art, arte povera…) que d'artistes isolés (Klein, Dubuffet…), et une création contemporaine très diversifiée (vidéos, installations, design, architecture). Au 2e étage du musée (5e niveau), la section d'Art moderne (1905-1960) présente les grands courants artistiques : des œuvres fauvistes (Matisse, Derain) aux cubistes (Braque, Picasso), en passant par le mouvement « dada » (Marcel Duchamp). Puis suivent les peintres abstraits (Kandinsky, Delaunay, Klee), les expressionnistes (Soutine, Chagall, Modigliani), les surréalistes (Dalí, Miró, Magritte), jusqu'à la peinture américaine des années 1960 (Pollock, Rothko). En règle générale, les sculpteurs, dont les œuvres sont exposées sur les trois terrasses prolongeant le musée, et les peintres contemporains français sont particulièrement bien représentés, de même que le mobilier et le design. À noter, parmi les nouvelles acquisitions du musée : *Le Dresseur d'animaux*, de Francis Picabia. ✉ 19, rue Beaubourg ☎ 01 44 78 12 33 Ⓜ Châtelet ■

Les couleurs des ascenseurs, escalators, tuyaux et conduits situés à l'extérieur du centre Georges Pompidou répondent à un code : bleu pour l'air conditionné, vert pour l'eau, jaune pour l'électricité et rouge pour les visiteurs.

Les Halles

Carte p. 92

Le Jardin des enfants (de 7 à 11 ans)

Forum des Halles, 105, rue Rambuteau

01 45 08 07 18

Les adultes ne sont pas admis (sauf sam. de 10 h à 14 h)

Les Halles

LE FORUM DES HALLES N'EST PLUS QUE LE PÂLE REFLET DU LÉGENDAIRE « ventre de Paris » décrit par Zola, où mille petits métiers pittoresques proliféraient la nuit pour garnir les pavillons des meilleurs produits de la France rurale avant leur ouverture à l'aube.

Philippe Auguste fait édifier les premières halles entre 1181 et 1183. Il finance en partie les travaux par la vente des biens confisqués aux juifs expulsés du quartier en 1182. Petit à petit, négociants et artisans viennent s'y établir et de splendides demeures se construisent alentour. Au milieu du XIVe siècle, les commerçants y ouvrent boutique trois fois par semaine. En 1851, Louis Napoléon Bonaparte charge l'architecte Victor Baltard d'édifier des « parapluies » avec « du fer, rien que du fer », pour abriter les marchandises. De 1854 à 1912, 10 pavillons du même métal furent bâtis, complétés par deux autres en 1936.

***Le Carreau des Halles*, par Victor Gabriel Gilbert (1880, huile sur toile).**

Mais en 1969, les installations vétustes et insuffisantes, les problèmes de circulation automobile et de salubrité publique contraignent les autorités à transférer l'ensemble à Rungis, au sud de Paris. Seuls deux pavillons échappent à la destruction, l'un d'eux est remonté à Nogent-sur-Marne et l'autre… à Tokyo ! En 1979, la construction du Forum des Halles ranime le quartier. Aujourd'hui, les couloirs tentaculaires de la station de métro et de RER Châtelet-Les Halles sont sillonnés de banlieusards et d'acheteurs. Des badauds venus de tous les horizons arpentent les galeries du complexe souterrain aménagé sur quatre niveaux, qui comporte, outre les nombreuses boutiques, un espace d'expositions de photographies, un gymnase, une piscine, une serre tropicale, des salles de cinéma, une vidéothèque, une discothèque de prêt, ainsi qu'un centre consacré à la musique et à la danse.

De la promenade en haut du bâtiment Lescot, vous découvrirez une vue des manèges, du jardin, de l'église Saint-Eustache et du bâtiment rond de la Bourse du commerce, un ancien marché au grain dont l'étrange colonne servait d'observatoire à Ruggieri, l'astrologue de Catherine de Médicis. De là, vous pourrez accéder à la maison des conservatoires municipaux de musique, de danse et d'art dramatique, à la Maison de la poésie, au Pavillon des Arts, qui abritent des expositions temporaires, ainsi qu'à une bibliothèque pour enfants.

Devant l'église Saint-Eustache, le jardin des Halles, conçu par F.-X. Lalanne, est idéal pour y prendre quelque repos. Des topiaires en forme d'éléphants flanquent l'accès au Jardin des enfants. Les petits peuvent se faufiler dans des tunnels, grimper sur des balançoires de corde et « nager » dans un bassin rempli de ballons multicolores et entouré de palmiers, de bambous et de lilas. ■

HUMILIATION PUBLIQUE

Non loin de l'église Saint-Eustache, se dressait, au XIVe siècle, un pilori. C'est là que voleurs, malfaiteurs et autres gredins étaient exposés à la vindicte du peuple. ■

LE FORT DES HALLES

Pour avoir droit à l'appellation de « fort » des Halles, il fallait être capable de porter 200 kg sur une distance de 50 mètres. ■

Les façades en verre du Forum des Halles et leurs jeux de miroirs donnent à l'entrée des 4 niveaux souterrains du centre commercial et culturel un aspect théâtral.

La cour des Miracles

Aux XVe, XVIe et XVIIe siècles, la population française, touchée par les guerres et la peste, compte de nombreux mendiants. À Paris, ceux-ci se réfugient dans les ruelles protégées par l'enceinte de Charles V. Dans la journée, certains mendient en feignant d'être estropiés, aveugles ou orphelins, et d'autres s'infiltrent dans la foule aux côtés des escrocs et des voleurs. La nuit, ils disparaissent dans les venelles comme étant touchés par une guérison miraculeuse, d'où l'expression « cour des Miracles ». En 1667, le lieu, situé à la lisière du quartier, est fermé par les forces de police, devant lesquelles les estropiés sont les premiers à s'enfuir… ■

Les marchés de Paris

Les amateurs de couleur locale prendront plaisir à passer une matinée dans un des nombreux marchés de la capitale. Laissez-vous tenter par les étals de fruits, de légumes ou de fromages…

Chaque quartier a son marché. Quelques-uns sont encore établis dans des bâtiments prévus à cet effet. Certains sont permanents et d'autres ne se tiennent que deux ou trois matinées par semaine. À l'ouverture, les clients sont moins nombreux et les denrées plus fraîches. En revanche, on peut faire des affaires avant la fermeture, lorsque les marchands bradent leurs derniers produits.

Les marchés permanents et temporaires

Les marchés permanents sont fermés le dimanche après-midi et le lundi, ainsi que quelques heures au moment du déjeuner. Celui d'Aligre, sur la place du même nom, est l'un des moins chers, des plus vivants et des plus denses de la ville. On y vend aussi bien des produits exotiques (piment rouge et épices d'Afrique du Nord) que des fripes. Un autre marché haut en couleur s'étend dans le bas de la rue Mouffetard, il est à lui seul un véritable spectacle.

Si vous aimez le chic « rive gauche », rendez-vous au marché de Buci, dans les rues de Buci et de Seine ; le dimanche matin, vous y verrez une clientèle très « parisienne » se presser parmi des étals chargés de victuailles coûteuses et raffinées. Si vous préférez le chic « rive gauche tendance bio », le marché du boulevard Raspail n'attend que vous : vous y trouverez des volailles élevées en plein air et nourries au grain, des légumes cultivés sans engrais chimiques et des fromages artisanaux. Parmi les autres rues qui disposent d'un marché permanent, citons la rue Montorgueil, une extension des anciennes Halles, la rue du Poteau (XVIIIe arr.), un endroit trop méconnu, et la rue Poncelet (XVIIe arr.).

Le plus grand marché temporaire s'installe sur le boulevard Richard-Lenoir dans la matinée du jeudi et du dimanche. Là, comme rue de la Convention (XVe arr.) ou avenue de Versailles (XVIe arr.), les gens du quartier s'adressent à leurs marchands habituels. Prenez toutefois le temps d'étudier le rapport qualité-prix de chacun. Si vous recherchez des denrées très exotiques, allez vous promener au marché

Qu'ils soient dans les quartiers chics ou plus populaires, les marchés de Paris présentent souvent des étals soignés, plus attrayants pour les clients.

Le marché des timbres et des cartes postales se tient tous les jeudis, samedis et dimanches à l'angle de l'avenue de Marigny et de l'avenue Gabriel, à deux pas des Champs-Élysées.

de Belleville (XIXe arr.) dans la matinée du mardi et du vendredi.

Les marchés spécialisés

Paris regroupe aussi de nombreux marchés spécialisés. Le marché aux fleurs (voir p. 54) s'étend à l'ombre du palais de Justice, dans l'île de la Cité. Le dimanche, un marché aux oiseaux s'y tient, et l'air résonne des trilles des canaris ainsi que des sifflements des mainates. Le quai de la Mégisserie, sur l'autre rive de la Seine, est bordé de jardineries et d'animaleries.

Les bibliophiles ou les curieux peuvent flâner au marché du livre ancien et d'occasion de la rue Brancion (XVe arr.), dans le parc Georges-Brassens, le samedi et le dimanche. Les vrais amateurs arrivent de bonne heure pour repérer les ouvrages intéressants. Le quartier situé au pied de Montmartre est spécialisé dans le textile. Deux grands magasins s'y dressent : au Marché Saint-Pierre (2, rue Charles-Nodier), on vend sur 5 niveaux des soieries, des lainages et des tissus d'ameublement à des prix bas. Juste en face (5, place Saint-Pierre), Reine est son concurrent direct. De nombreuses petites boutiques dans les rues voisines regorgent d'accessoires de mercerie et de chatoyants rouleaux de tissus de toutes les origines et de toutes les qualités. ■

LES PRINCIPAUX MARCHÉS

- Marché d'Aligre (XIIe arr.)
  Ⓜ *Ledru-Rollin*
- Marché de la rue Mouffetard (V[e] arr.)
  Ⓜ *Censier-Daubenton*
- Marché de Buci (VIe arr.)
  Ⓜ *Odéon*
- Marché biologique (VIe arr.)
  Ⓜ *Sèvres-Babylone*
- Marché de la rue Montorgueil (IIe arr.)
  Ⓜ *Les Halles ou Étienne-Marcel*
- Marché de la rue du Poteau (XVIIIe arr.)
  Ⓜ *Jules-Joffrin*
- Marché de la rue Poncelet (XVIIe arr.)
  Ⓜ *Ternes*
- Marché du boulevard Richard-Lenoir (XIe arr.)
  Ⓜ *Bastille ou Richard-Lenoir*
- Marché de Belleville (XIXe arr.)
  Ⓜ *Belleville*
- Quai de la Mégisserie (Ier arr.)
  Ⓜ *Hôtel-de-Ville ou Châtelet*
- Marché du livre ancien de la rue Brancion (XVe arr.)
  Ⓜ *Porte de Vanves ou Plaisance*
- Marché Saint-Pierre (XVIIIe arr.)
  Ⓜ *Barbès-Rochechouart ou Anvers.* ■

Autres sites à visiter

LA FONTAINE DES INNOCENTS

Achevée par Jean Goujon en 1549 sur un dessin de Pierre Lescot, cette fontaine est la seule de style Renaissance à Paris. Elle est transférée, en 1787, de l'angle de la rue Saint-Denis à son emplacement actuel. Sous ses délicats bas-reliefs se rassemblent amoureux, adeptes de skateboard, punks et clochards. Bien que la place soit envahie par des enseignes de restauration rapide et de magasins de vêtements, un charme bon-enfant continue de s'y exprimer par le biais de musiciens de rue et d'excellents mimes.

L'ÉGLISE SAINT-EUSTACHE

Construite entre 1532 et 1637 sur les plans de Notre-Dame, l'église Saint-Eustache est d'abord une petite chapelle vouée à sainte Agnès. Elle prend ensuite le nom d'un général romain, converti après avoir vu une croix apparaître entre les bois d'un cerf (la tête de l'animal est sculptée sous la pointe du pignon qui agrémente la belle façade du transept Renaissance).

Bon nombre de personnages historiques y ont laissé leur trace. C'est là que Molière est baptisé (1622), que Louis XIV fait sa première communion (1649), que Jean Colbert, ministre des Finances du Roi-Soleil, est inhumé (dans une des chapelles du chœur, se trouve son tombeau dessiné par Le Brun et sculpté par Coysevox et Tuby). Fléchier y prononce, en 1676, l'oraison funèbre de Turenne. Les obsèques de La Fontaine s'y déroulent en 1695. Berlioz y dirige la première exécution de son *Te Deum,* en 1885, et Liszt celle de sa *Messe solennelle,* en 1886. L'excellente acoustique de l'église a toujours servi la musique d'orgue et le chant choral. Les vitraux réalisés au XVIIe siècle par Antoine Soulignac, d'après des cartons de Philippe de Champaigne, sont remarquables. Le sanctuaire s'orne également de peintures de l'école de Rubens *(Les Pèlerins d'Emmaüs)* et de Simon Vouet *(Martyre de saint Eustache),* ainsi que d'une sculpture naïve de Raymond Mason, intitulée *Le Départ des fruits et légumes du cœur de Paris* (1969).

Non loin, les fleuristes, bouchers et commerçants de la rue Montorgueil rappellent l'animation qui régnait jadis au marché des Halles. Des créateurs de mode ont investi la rue du Jour. Ne manquez pas, dans cette même venelle, le splendide portail de l'hôtel des abbés de Royaumont. Quant aux noctambules, ils se retrouvent au Pied de Cochon, véritable institution où l'on sert une généreuse cuisine jusqu'à l'aube.

Carte p. 92 ✉ 2, impasse Saint-Eustache ☎ 01 42 36 31 05/www.st-eustache.org Ⓜ Les Halles

Au Pied de Cochon ✉ 6, rue Coquillière € €€ ☎ 01 40 13 77 00/www.pieddecochon.com ■

La sculpture moderne de Henri de Miller, *Écoute*.

Lorsque vous flânerez sur les places, dans les jardins et parmi les élégants édifices du Marais, vous aurez le sentiment d'évoluer dans un vaste musée à ciel ouvert.

Le Marais et la Bastille

Motif du portail d'entrée de l'hôtel des Ambassadeurs de Hollande.

Le Marais et la Bastille

Jusqu'au XIIe siècle, le quartier, inondé à chaque crue de la Seine, est une terre marécageuse. Lorsque des moines s'y installent, suivis par la communauté juive, le marais est défriché et mis en culture. Les seigneurs établissent alors leurs « courtilles » (maisons de campagne de la noblesse). Au XIVe siècle, les ordres monastiques quittent le quartier et vendent leurs terres aux aristocrates désireux de se doter d'une demeure hors de la ville.

Le musée Carnavalet, fleuron du Marais, renferme la mémoire de Paris.

À la fin du XVe siècle, la vieille noblesse, dite « d'épée », est solidement implantée dans le quartier du Marais, annexé à la ville par la construction de l'enceinte de Charles V. Au XVIe siècle, la noblesse dite « de robe » – formée de la bourgeoisie intellectuelle et financière qui achète ses titres de noblesse au roi, lui procurant ainsi de confortables revenus – l'y rejoint.

C'est au début du XVIIe siècle, sur ordre de Henri IV, qu'est créée la place Royale (actuelle place des Vosges, voir pp. 106-107), véritable lieu d'agrément et de festivités. Courtisans et seigneurs construisent aux alentours de superbes demeures, les fameux hôtels particuliers, comme ceux de Sully (voir p. 116), de Rohan (qui fait aujourd'hui partie des Archives nationales, voir p. 117), Salé (occupé par le musée Picasso, voir pp. 110-111) ou encore Carnavalet (voir p. 113). Mais sous Louis XVI, la noblesse, avide de nouveautés, quitte le quartier pour s'installer dans les faubourgs Saint-Honoré et Saint-Germain. Le Marais tombe alors dans un discrédit total.

Artisans et petits commerçants occupent les nobles bâtiments et recouvrent les jardins d'appentis et de constructions parasitaires. Dans les années 1960, une vaste entreprise de rénovation est lancée par André Malraux, alors ministre de la Culture. Le plus grand soin est apporté à la réhabilitation des bâtiments, si bien que le quartier a conservé de superbes portes, d'intéressantes fenêtres ouvragées, de délicieuses cours intérieures et de précieuses sculptures (*Les Chevaux du Soleil* de l'hôtel de Rohan, notamment). Sous les plaques bleues qui indiquent les noms de rues, les appellations d'origine sont restées gravées dans la pierre. Les grands témoins du passé, tels les fragments de l'enceinte de Philippe Auguste ou le portail de l'hôtel de Soubise (anciennement de Clisson), ont été précieusement conservés. Créateurs de mode et yuppies se sont ensuite emparés du quartier. Cette mainmise a apporté au décor une touche tantôt kitsch, tantôt glaciale qui n'est pas sans lui nuire. La reconversion du hammam de la rue des Rosiers, dans le quartier juif, en café branché illustre on ne peut mieux l'évolution du Marais. ■

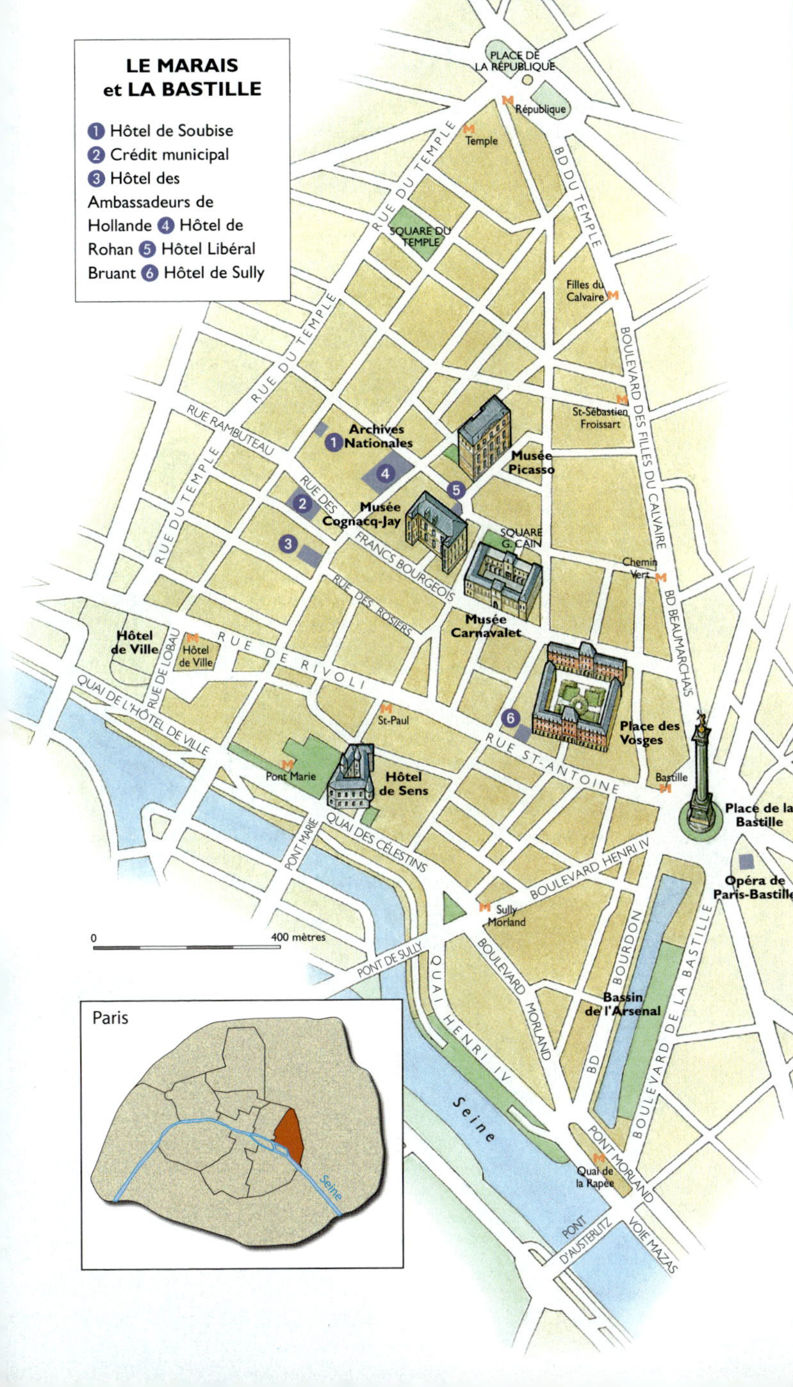
LE MARAIS et LA BASTILLE
1 Hôtel de Soubise
2 Crédit municipal
3 Hôtel des Ambassadeurs de Hollande
4 Hôtel de Rohan
5 Hôtel Libéral Bruant
6 Hôtel de Sully
PLACE DE LA RÉPUBLIQUE
République
Temple
RUE DU TEMPLE
SQUARE DU TEMPLE
BD DU TEMPLE
Filles du Calvaire
BOULEVARD DES FILLES DU CALVAIRE
St-Sébastien Froissart
RUE RAMBUTEAU
Archives Nationales
Musée Picasso
RUE DES FRANCS BOURGEOIS
Musée Cognacq-Jay
SQUARE G. CAIN
Chemin Vert
BD BEAUMARCHAIS
RUE DES ROSIERS
Musée Carnavalet
Hôtel de Ville
RUE DE LOBAU
RUE DE RIVOLI
QUAI DE L'HÔTEL DE VILLE
St-Paul
RUE ST-ANTOINE
Place des Vosges
Bastille
Place de la Bastille
Pont Marie
Hôtel de Sens
PONT MARIE
QUAI DES CÉLESTINS
BOULEVARD HENRI IV
Opéra de Paris-Bastille
Sully Morland
PONT DE SULLY
QUAI HENRI IV
BOULEVARD MORLAND
BD BOURDON
Bassin de l'Arsenal
BOULEVARD DE LA BASTILLE
Seine
PONT MORLAND
Quai de la Rapée
PONT D'AUSTERLITZ
VOIE MAZAS
0
400 mètres
Paris
Seine

La place des Vosges

Carte p. 105
Bastille, Chemin Vert, Saint-Paul

Rebaptisée « place des Vosges » en 1800, l'ancienne place Royale a été la première grande place de Paris. Bordée de trente-six pavillons de brique (neuf de chaque côté) agrémentés d'arcades et de toits d'ardoise à forte pente, elle s'étend sur l'emplacement de la maison royale des Tournelles. Cette imposante bâtisse, entourée de jardins clos par un mur doté de nombreuses tourelles (« tournelles »), est longtemps restée la résidence des rois de France. À la mort de Louis d'Orléans, en 1407, elle devient propriété de la Couronne.

Ci-dessus : Le pavillon de la Reine, érigé au nord de la place des Vosges.

Lorsque Charles VI quitte l'hôtel Saint-Pol pour s'installer à l'hôtel des Tournelles, la Cour le suit et le quartier alentour se développe. Il comprend alors plusieurs demeures, des chapelles, des bains, des cloîtres, des parcs et jardins, des bosquets, un labyrinthe et même des prés (d'où le nom de la rue du Foin). Par la suite, l'hôtel des Tournelles accueille Charles VII, Louis XI, Charles VIII, Louis XII, François Ier et Henri II. Mais quatre ans après le décès de ce dernier, survenu en 1559 lors d'un tournoi organisé sur le cours Saint-Antoine (près de l'actuelle place des Vosges), son épouse Catherine de Médicis prend en horreur la résidence royale, ordonne sa destruction et s'installe au Louvre. La place devient alors un marché aux chevaux.

Après avoir voulu y construire des ateliers de soierie pour limiter la dépendance de la France vis-à-vis des importations des étoffes italiennes, Henri IV ordonne la construction de la place Royale en 1605, et offre ainsi à Paris l'espace de fêtes qui lui manque. Érigé au sud, face à celui de la Reine, le pavillon du Roi sert de modèle à tous les autres. Henri IV est assassiné en 1610, et c'est deux ans plus tard qu'a lieu l'inauguration de la place. Cet événement coïncide avec la célébration de deux fastueux mariages : celui de Louis XIII, successeur d'Henri IV, avec Anne d'Autriche, et celui d'Élisabeth de France avec le futur Philippe IV d'Espagne. Mille trois cents cavaliers défilent au son de 150 trompettes, et de 80 musettes, hautbois et violons. La nuit venue, des porteurs de torches envahissent les rues, tandis que des feux d'artifice et des fusées éclatent au-dessus de la Bastille.

Plus tard, la place devient l'étape des émissaires étrangers sur le chemin du Louvre. De grandes familles (Rohan, Bassompierre, Dangeau, Loménie de Brienne…) s'y installent. Chaque édifice a son histoire. Au n° 1, le pavillon du Roi – construit grâce à l'argent de la Couronne – a été donné en location, sans jamais être occupé par un seul souverain. Le n° 1*bis* a vu naître, en 1626, madame de Sévigné, la célèbre épistolière. Le marquis de Favras, accusé d'avoir projeté l'enlèvement de Louis XVI et l'assassinat de La Fayette, commandant de la Garde nationale, habite au n° 4 en

Une grande variété de restaurants coexiste sous les arcades de la place des Vosges, du plus typique au plus raffiné.

1789. Le n° 6 est la demeure de Victor Hugo, de 1832 à 1848. Il y rédige *Les Chants du crépuscule* et *Ruy Blas*; au début du XXe siècle, l'endroit est transformé en musée *(Tél. : 01 42 72 10 16, fermé lun.)*, où est conservé le lit à baldaquin dans lequel l'écrivain est mort. Au n° 7, s'ouvre un passage qui est emprunté, au XVIIe siècle, par le duc de Sully, propriétaire de l'hôtel du même nom, pour aller de chez lui à la place Royale. Au n° 8 sont hébergés, au milieu du XIXe siècle, les écrivains Théophile Gautier et Alphonse Daudet. Au n° 9, la grande tragédienne Élisabeth Félix, dite « Rachel », y passe l'année 1857; aujourd'hui, le restaurant L'Ambroisie y est établi. Le cardinal de Richelieu réside, de 1615 à 1623, au n° 21.

En 1818, la statue de Louis XIII qui orne le jardin planté de tilleuls remplace l'œuvre de bronze que Richelieu y avait fait dresser en 1639. Chose rarissime à Paris, on peut s'allonger sur les pelouses. Le dimanche après-midi, ne manquez pas de faire du lèche-vitrine sous les arcades qui résonnent de toutes sortes de musiques. ■

Les rues de Paris

Pendant des siècles, il est difficile de circuler dans les rues sombres et boueuses de la ville. Elles ne portent pas de noms et leurs maisons ne sont pas numérotées. Apparues au XVe siècle, les enseignes font office d'adresses. Taillées dans des plaques métalliques, elles sont suspendues à de longs bras de fer. Elles accentuent l'obscurité des rues et, les jours de grand vent, s'avèrent aussi bruyantes que dangereuses. Au milieu du XVIIIe siècle, leur taille a diminué et elles sont fixées au-dessus des portes. Le musée Carnavalet (voir p. 113) en possède une intéressante collection.

Les noms de rues

En 1728, la municipalité décide d'indiquer les noms des rues aux croisements. Tantôt des plaques donnent l'information, tantôt celle-ci est gravée dans la pierre des immeubles d'angle. En 1844, apparaissent les plaques d'émail bleu toujours en usage. De nombreuses rues sont baptisées ou rebaptisées en l'honneur de marchands ou de résidents célèbres (Galande), de villages des environs (Charonne, Belleville), d'églises, de professions (Coutellerie), de points de repère comme les fontaines ou les marchés aux chevaux (cul-de-sac du Ha ! Ha !, aujourd'hui Cul-de-Sac-Royale-Saint-Antoine), d'enseignes (Chat-qui-Pêche, Pot-de-Fer), d'événements ou de dates historiques (Quatre-Septembre), de héros, de victoires, de chefs, voire de stations de métro. En 1994, celles situées aux abords de la Bibliothèque nationale de France-François-Mitterrand reçoivent des noms d'écrivains (François-Mauriac, Raymond-Aron).

La Révolution balaie toute allusion à la religion ou à la monarchie. Après la Première Guerre mondiale, la rue de Berlin devient la rue de Liège. Il arrive que certains noms choquent les habitants : la rue du Pélican, jadis haut lieu de la luxure, s'appelait à l'origine « rue du Poil-au-Con »... D'autres évoluent par le biais d'un jeu sur les mots : en 1868, la rue de la Croix devient la rue Delacroix.

L'éclairage de la Ville lumière

En 1318, seuls trois sites sont dotés d'une lanterne : la forteresse du Grand Châtelet, la tour de Nesle (à laquelle les bateliers se repèrent) et le cimetière des Innocents (signalé par la « lanterne des morts »). Dans la première moitié du XVIe siècle, Louis XII, François Ier et Henri II ordonnent qu'une chandelle soit placée derrière une fenêtre de chaque maison ; cette mesure n'empêche pas l'assassinat dans les rues de la ville de plusieurs personnes par nuit. En 1662, un éclairage portatif permet à ceux qui le souhaitent de se déplacer : des hommes munis de torches en cire (ils font payer chaque couche de cire consumée) ou de lampes à huile accompagnent les Parisiens jusqu'à leur porte, même si les clients habitent à l'étage.

Sous Louis XIV (1643-1715), 3 000 lanternes sont installées, bientôt remplacées par des réverbères à huile. En 1837, la capitale en compte 13 000, que 240 allumeurs font fonctionner au crépuscule ; l'opération ne dure que trois quarts d'heure. Sous la Restauration, l'usage du gaz se propage rapidement ; en 1845, on dénombre 8 000 becs de gaz. La place de l'Opéra est éclairée à l'électricité en 1878. Tout récemment les ponts ont été dotés de projecteurs à halogène pour mettre en valeur leurs sculptures. Contrairement aux règles traditionnelles de l'éclairage des monuments, la tour Eiffel est illuminée de l'intérieur et clignote dix minutes chaque heure dès la tombée de la nuit.

Une ville peinte

On voit bien mieux Paris en marchant lentement. Chemin faisant, levez les yeux vers les balcons fleuris, les pilastres, les cariatides et les mosaïques. La ville est couverte de fresques, une forme de décoration née dans les années 1930 avec les réclames peintes sur les murs (la boisson chocolatée Banania ou « Dubo, Dubon, Dubonnet », encore visible rue de Sèvres). Dans les années 1970, des peintres sont chargés de réaliser des œuvres en trompe-l'œil. Citons notamment les ruines égyptiennes de la rue de Torcy, dans le XVIIIe arrondissement, la serre peinte en bleu et violet du 60, rue de Reuilly, dans le XIIe arrondissement, l'homme gravissant l'escalier de la rue Étienne-Marcel, dans le Ier arrondissement, et le rayonnage de bibliothèque géant du 52, rue de Belleville, dans le XXe arrondissement. ■

À gauche : Détail de la place des Victoires, inaugurée en 1686, et dédiée à Louis XIV.

À droite : Lampadaire ouvragé de la place de la Concorde. Ci-dessous : La rue Norvins est une des principales rues de Montmartre menant à la place du Tertre. Au fond, on aperçoit le dôme blanc du Sacré-Cœur.

Le musée Picasso

www.musee-picasso.fr

Carte p. 105
Hôtel Salé, 5, rue de Thorigny
01 42 71 25 21
Fermé mar.
€€
Gratuit le premier dim du mois
Saint-Sébastien Froissart, Saint-Paul, Filles du Calvaire

Derrière une impressionnante entrée flanquée de sphinx se cache la plus grande collection d'œuvres de Picasso au monde. Un génial « touche-à-tout » qui a instillé sa fraîcheur et son inventivité à chaque forme d'art qu'il a abordée. Cette visite s'impose à quiconque s'intéresse à la création au XXe siècle.

L'HÔTEL SALÉ

Le musée est installé dans un superbe hôtel particulier, construit par Jean Boullier entre 1656 et 1659 pour Pierre Aubert de Fontenay, qui avait fait fortune en levant l'impôt sur le sel (la gabelle). C'est tout naturellement et avec une certaine malice que le peuple parisien nomma l'édifice hôtel Salé. Le goût ostentatoire du propriétaire se manifeste par le grand escalier de fer forgé, au-dessus duquel deux personnages portent une guirlande de fruits d'où pendent des médaillons, et par le salon de Jupiter, orné de chérubins et de festons.

À la mort d'Aubert, le bâtiment accueille, entre autres, l'ambassade de Venise et l'archevêque de Paris Leclerc de Juigné, qui se fait un devoir de recouvrir la nudité des sculptures. Fuyant Paris en carrosse sous les jets de pierres des révolutionnaires, le cocher de l'archevêque eut un mot célèbre : « J'ai peur, Monseigneur, que nous soyons deux à perdre notre siège ! » Pillé sous la Révolution, l'hôtel est vendu, puis loué à l'École centrale des Arts et Manufactures, puis à l'école des Métiers d'Art. La ville de Paris en fait l'acquisition en 1964, avant de le louer à l'État, qui envisage d'y créer un musée du Costume. Mais à la suite du décès de Picasso en 1973 et la dation faite par ses héritiers, l'hôtel Salé devient, trois ans plus tard, un musée consacré à l'artiste. Choix judicieux : la demeure correspond aux goûts du maître en matière d'architecture…

L'hôtel Salé, qui abrite le musée Picasso, date du XVIIe siècle.

L'HOMME ET L'ARTISTE

Pour plaisanter, Picasso aimait se présenter comme le plus grand collectionneur de Picasso au monde. Il est vrai qu'il conserva de son vivant une grande partie de sa propre production. Né à Málaga en 1881, il gagne la France à l'âge de 23 ans, après avoir fréquenté dans son pays l'école des beaux-arts. Il ne quitte alors plus son pays d'adoption, à part quelques courts déplacements à l'étranger. En 1934, après un bref séjour dans sa patrie, il jure de ne jamais y retourner tant que Franco serait au pouvoir.

Après sa mort, le 8 avril 1973, survenue à Mougins (Alpes-Maritimes), ses héritiers règlent les droits de succession en œuvres d'art. L'État sélectionne les pièces qui constituent aujourd'hui le gros de la collection du musée. L'institution abrite 203 tableaux, 158 sculptures, 28 tableaux-reliefs, 16 collages en papier, 88 céramiques, ainsi que plus de 3 000 gravures et dessins. La période couverte débute en 1895 *(La Fillette aux pieds nus)* et s'achève à la fin de la vie du peintre. Certaines œuvres gardées par l'artiste avaient été exposées lors de manifestations temporaires, mais quantité d'autres n'avaient été vues de personne, même de ses proches. Parmi ces dernières, très peu étaient détériorées ou inachevées. Visiblement, Picasso prenait grand soin de sa collection, car même les assemblages cubistes les plus fragiles sont restés en bon état.

Le musée se caractérise par le grand nombre d'œuvres qu'il expose et par leur qualité. Accompagnées de commentaires détaillés, elles retracent la carrière du peintre de façon chronologique : sa période bleue, consécutive au décès de son ami Casagemas ; sa période rose, marquée par une accentuation des volumes, ainsi que par une simplification et une disproportion des traits typiques de l'art ibérique ; son choc face à la découverte des arts africain et océanien, lors d'une exposition organisée au musée de l'Homme, au Trocadéro ; son cheminement entre le cubisme aux volumes simplifiés d'un Cézanne et sa propre traduction, plus complexe, de ces mêmes volumes ; son incorporation d'objets quotidiens, ou « éléments du réel », à ses compositions, afin que le spectateur s'identifie plus facilement à elles (du jamais vu dans l'histoire de l'art) ; son œuvre thématique, centrée sur le Minotaure, la crucifixion et la corrida ; enfin, son glissement de la peinture et de la sculpture vers le collage et le tableau-relief, ces nouvelles formes reprenant les caractéristiques des précédentes.

Son don quasi inégalé pour le croquis s'exprime dans la représentation de ses modèles préférés (Dora Maar, son épouse Jacqueline, Marie-Thérèse) sous tous les angles imaginables. Sont également exposés ses objets d'art primitif et sa collection privée, composée d'œuvres de Paul Cézanne, d'Henri Matisse, de Georges Braque, d'André Derain, de Pierre Renoir et du Douanier Rousseau. Le mobilier et les chandeliers sont de Diego Giacometti, le frère d'Alberto. ■

Un des portraits de Dora Maar par Picasso, *Femme assise aux bras croisés* (1937).

Le quartier juif

Carte p. 105
Épicentre : rue des Rosiers
Saint-Paul

S'IL FAUT EN CROIRE GRÉGOIRE DE TOURS, LES JUIFS ÉTAIENT DÉJÀ établis à Paris au VIe siècle. Commerçants ou artisans, ils étaient arrivés, pensait-on, dans le sillage des Romains. Le premier quartier juif de la capitale n'est apparu qu'en 1119, dans la rue de la Juiverie (l'actuelle rue de la Cité).

LA RUE DES ROSIERS

La rue des Rosiers était l'ancien chemin de ronde de l'enceinte de Philippe Auguste. Les jardins qui l'agrémentaient étaient plantés de nombreux rosiers, d'où son nom. ■

L'histoire de la communauté juive parisienne est faite d'expulsions et de réintégrations successives. En 1182, Philippe Auguste chasse les juifs hors de la ville. Ils reviennent pour s'installer, certains rive gauche, d'autres rue Saint-Bon sur la rive droite. À la même époque, un autre quartier se forme à l'est, entre la rue des Rosiers et la rue aux Juifs (aujourd'hui rue Ferdinand-Duval). En 1394, Charles VI bannit à nouveau les juifs de la ville. Revenus au début du XVIIIe siècle, ils obtiennent la citoyenneté française, en 1791. En 1871, ils sont au nombre de 25 000.

À la fin du XIXe siècle, une nouvelle vague de juifs venus d'Europe de l'Est et d'Europe centrale s'établit dans la rue des Rosiers et ses alentours. De 1950 à 1962, des séfarades arrivent d'Égypte, d'Algérie, de Tunisie et du Maroc pour grossir les rangs d'une communauté qui commence à déborder des limites du quartier historique. Aujourd'hui, le coin le plus traditionnel du quartier est la partie ouest de la rue des Rosiers. Vous pourrez y déguster chez Jo Goldenberg (au n° 7) ou chez Finkelsztajn (au n° 27) des *flanken* (harengs), du bortsch et autres spécialités d'Europe centrale et de Russie. Non loin de leurs magasins, au 10, rue des Hospitalières-Saint-Gervais, se dresse l'ancienne école de garçons juifs, d'où 160 élèves ont été emmenés en déportation, lors de la Seconde Guerre mondiale. On peut lire maintenant ces mots gravés sur le mur : « N'oubliez pas. »

Ouvert depuis peu, dans l'hôtel Saint-Aignan (*71, rue du Temple, tél. : 01 53 01 86 60, www.mahj.org, fermé sam.*), le musée d'Art et d'Histoire du Judaïsme offre un panorama du patrimoine juif, notamment de l'éducation et des rites. Il renferme également des œuvres de Soutine, Chagall et Modigliani. ■

Dessins, adages et maximes ornent la devanture de Chez Marianne, épicerie fine et restaurant de ce quartier.

Le musée Carnavalet

Consacré à l'histoire de Paris, ce musée est aménagé dans l'hôtel Carnavalet, un édifice de style Renaissance construit en 1548 pour Jacques des Ligneris, président au Parlement de Paris. Il est acquis par la veuve du tuteur d'Henri III, un certain Kernevenoy, surnommé « Carnavalet » par francisation de son nom breton. En 1677, la célèbre marquise de Sévigné le loue. Elle y réside jusqu'à sa mort, en 1696.

Carte p. 105
23, rue de Sévigné
01 44 59 58 58
Fermé lun.
€€ pour les expositions temporaires
Saint-Paul, Chemin Vert

www.paris.fr/musees

LE MUSÉE

En 1866, lors des travaux d'aménagement de la ville, Haussmann suggère à l'administration d'acquérir l'hôtel Carnavalet, afin d'y entreposer les éléments décoratifs extraits des immeubles démantelés. L'hôtel est agrandi par le transfert, pierre par pierre, de différents bâtiments parisiens, tel le pavillon qui enjambait la rue de Nazareth, dans l'île de la Cité. Les collections du musée (peintures, sculptures, mobilier) sont réparties dans deux bâtiments : l'hôtel Carnavalet abrite la section concernant la période des origines de Paris à 1789 ; l'hôtel Le Peletier de Saint-Fargeau (29, rue de Sévigné), celle allant de la Révolution à nos jours.

LES COLLECTIONS

Agencées selon un ordre chronologique, les salles présentent des ensembles décoratifs et de nombreuses œuvres d'art, et même des vestiges gallo-romains. Pêle-mêle, vous y verrez la reconstitution de la chambre de Marcel Proust, un modèle réduit de la guillotine, un fragment de la Bastille, ainsi que des objets jadis détenus par Voltaire et Rousseau. Ne manquez pas le plafond peint par Charles Le Brun à l'hôtel de La Rivière (salle 21), la collection Bouvier (salles 37 à 48) et la statue pédestre de Louis XIV, par Coysevox, dans la cour d'honneur. Expositions temporaires et concerts sont organisés (consultez le calendrier des manifestations). ■

ENSEIGNES

Le musée Carnavalet possède une belle collection d'enseignes. Sous l'Ancien Régime, celles-ci servaient à identifier les maisons. ■

Le style Art nouveau est illustré par la boutique du bijoutier Fouquet décorée par Mucha et reconstituée au musée Carnavalet.

La ville de l'amour

À Paris, le temps semble ne pas compter pour les amoureux. La passion a suscité des liaisons qui ont résisté à l'oubli, comme celles des sculpteurs Auguste Rodin et Camille Claudel (voir p. 172) ou des écrivains Henry Miller et Anaïs Nin.

L'amour accompli dans la mort : Héloïse et Abélard

Vers 1118, Fulbert, chanoine de Notre-Dame, accueille chez lui, dans l'île de la Cité, le théologien Pierre Abélard (1079-1142). En contrepartie, il charge son invité d'instruire sa nièce Héloïse, une jeune fille de 17 ans. Malgré leur différence d'âge (l'érudit en avait 39), professeur et élève s'éprennent l'un de l'autre et se marient en secret. Scandalisé, Fulbert fait émasculer Abélard. Morte vingt-quatre ans après son amant, Héloïse émet le souhait d'être couchée dans le cercueil où il repose. Une religieuse contrarie ce projet en déposant le corps de la défunte ailleurs. Le vœu de l'amoureuse se réalise en 1817, année où les deux dépouilles mortelles sont réunies dans une tombe néo-gothique du cimetière du Père-Lachaise (voir p. 84).

L'amour adultère : Henri II et Diane de Poitiers

Si les initiales de Henri II (1547-1559) et de Catherine de Médicis, gravées sur l'aile sud de la Cour carrée du Louvre, semblent témoigner d'une grande dévotion entre le roi et la reine, elles expriment en réalité le profond attachement de Henri II pour sa maîtresse Diane de Poitiers, de 20 ans son aînée. Les deux C entrelacés au H doivent en effet être lus comme des D. Sans aucun pouvoir jusqu'à la mort de son époux, la reine s'est ensuite vengée en expulsant Diane de son cher château de Chenonceau, dans la vallée de la Loire.

L'amour malheureux : Napoléon et Joséphine

Napoléon Bonaparte (1769-1821), maître de la majeure partie de l'Europe, a eu du mal à conquérir celle qu'il aimait. Le 9 mars 1796, il s'unit à Joséphine de Beauharnais au cours d'une cérémonie civile. Pour son épouse, une aristocrate veuve en quête de soutien financier et de sécurité politique en ces temps troublés de l'après-Révolution, cette union n'est qu'un simple mariage de raison. En revanche, pour le futur empereur passionnément épris, c'est une véritable affaire de cœur.

Une des nombreuses lettres qu'il adresse à son élue se clôt sur ces phrases : « Tu pars à midi, je te verrai dans trois heures. En attendant, *mio dolce amor,* un millier de baisé [sic !] ; mais ne m'en donne pas, car il brûle [sic !] mon sang. » Le couple passe ses meilleurs moments au château de la Malmaison (voir p. 232). Napoléon répudie Joséphine en 1809 au motif qu'elle ne peut lui donner d'héritier. Il continue néanmoins à financer son train de vie extravagant, tout en la suppliant de réduire ses dépenses. Malgré cela, elle a trois millions de francs de dettes à sa mort, en 1814.

L'amour romantique : George Sand et Frédéric Chopin

Le XIXe siècle est celui des romantiques. George Sand, née Amandine Aurore Lucie Dupin en 1804, est l'une des figures marquantes de cette époque. Après s'être séparée de son mari, elle mène une vie de bohème, à Paris. Après une liaison tumultueuse et éphémère avec le poète Alfred de Musset, elle vit sa plus célèbre histoire d'amour avec le compositeur polonais Frédéric Chopin.

Tous deux font partie de la communauté de peintres et d'écrivains qui résident dans le quartier de la Nouvelle Athènes, au sud de Montmartre. Atteint par la tuberculose, Chopin ne supporte plus la dévorante sollicitude maternelle de sa compagne et il rompt en 1847. Le musée de la Vie romantique *(16, rue Chaptal, Tél. : 01 55 31 95 67, fermé lun., métro : Saint-Georges ou Pigalle)* fait revivre l'illustre couple en exposant des objets ayant appartenu à Chopin et en recréant le salon de George Sand.

L'amour charnel : Henry Miller et Anaïs Nin

Le film *Henry et June* (1990) est consacré aux déboires du ménage à trois formé dans les années 1920 par l'écrivain américain Henry Miller (1891-1980), son épouse June, ainsi

Ci-dessus : Détail de *La Rose de Malmaison* (1867), peinture de Hector Viger du Vigneau. On y voit l'impératrice Joséphine, entourée de ses amies et de ses belles-sœurs, recevoir une rose de Napoléon, en gage de son amour.

qu'Anaïs Nin (1903-1977), femme de lettres née en France et connue pour ses textes érotiques. Le trio se lance dans une exploration du libertinage qui donne naissance à une nouvelle forme de littérature, illustrée par *Tropique du Cancer*, l'ouvrage scandaleux de Miller, et par *Vénus Erotica* et le *Journal* d'Anaïs Nin, où celle-ci relate ses expériences sexuelles. Au 18, villa Seurat, Miller loua une maison qu'il partagea parfois avec sa maîtresse. ■

Héloïse et Abélard, représentés par Jean de Meung dans une miniature du XIVe siècle intitulée *Le Roman de la Rose, le Testament* (Musée de Condé, Chantilly ; voir p. 232).

Madame de Sévigné donne de vivantes descriptions de la vie aristocratique sous Louis XIV (ici, la cour d'honneur du musée Carnavalet) dans des lettres adressées à sa fille.

Une promenade dans le Marais historique

Le quartier le mieux préservé de Paris concentre tant de richesses historiques et architecturales qu'il faut prévoir plusieurs jours pour visiter ses musées, ses hôtels particuliers, ses places et ses différents sites.

Au départ de la place de la Bastille, remontez la rue Saint-Antoine. Après avoir dépassé la statue de Beaumarchais, tournez à droite dans la rue de Birague pour rejoindre la place des Vosges 1 (voir p. 106). Franchissez la voûte du pavillon du Roi et faites le tour de la place par la droite, en flânant sous les arcades où s'ouvrent boutiques et galeries d'art. Chemin faisant, veillez à ne pas manquer les résidences d'hommes célèbres. Au n° 7, empruntez le passage couvert qui débouche sur les jardins de l'hôtel de Sully, devenu le Centre européen de la photographie, où la Caisse nationale des Monuments historiques et des Sites a ses locaux. Le soir, si ce passage est fermé, prenez la rue de Birague pour regagner la rue Saint-Antoine.

Reprenez celle-ci à droite, puis tournez encore à droite dans la rue Caron. Vous arriverez sur la place du Marché-Sainte-Catherine, où un prieuré d'augustins se dressait au XIIIe siècle. Traversez-la et bifurquez à gauche dans la paisible rue de Jarente. Le n° 6 livre accès à un charmant décor villageois. De là, descendez à droite la rue de Sévigné, puis remontez, à gauche, la rue des Francs-Bourgeois. Au Moyen Âge, la rue Elzévir (alors appelée « rue des Poulies ») tirait son nom des pièces mécaniques qui surplombaient les ateliers des tisserands. Au n° 23 de la rue des Francs-Bourgeois, une boulangerie de la Belle Époque est devenue un élégant magasin de chaussures.

Vous pouvez visiter le musée Carnavalet 2 (voir p. 113) avant de reprendre la rue des Francs-Bourgeois dans le même sens. Remarquez la ravissante tour de guet quadrangulaire dont la base s'orne des lettres SC. Marquant la limite du domaine du couvent Saint-Catherine-du-Val-des-Écoliers, jadis propriétaire du secteur, elle fait partie d'une des plus anciennes demeures du Marais, l'hôtel de Lamoignon, où est aménagée la bibliothèque historique de la Ville de Paris. Hector Guimard a construit la synagogue du 10, rue Pavée ; à l'avènement du nazisme, l'architecte se réfugia aux États-Unis avec son épouse, une juive américaine. Tournez à droite dans la rue Payenne. Agrémenté de fragments de monuments détruits, le ravissant square Georges-Cain s'étend près du Musée lapidaire de Paris, abrité dans l'ancienne orangerie de l'hôtel Carnavalet. Au n° 11, sur le trottoir d'en face, admirez la façade de l'hôtel de Donon **3**, devenu le musée Cognacq-Jay (voir p. 120). Juste à côté se dresse le Centre culturel suédois, au toit en forme de coque de bateau renversée, où a vécu la gouvernante des enfants de la reine Marie-Antoinette. La cour du n° 13 est particulièrement avenante en été.

Prenez à gauche la rue du Parc-Royal, qui longe le square Léopold-Achille, et dirigez-vous vers la place de Thorigny. L'hôtel de Libéral Bruant, au 1, rue de la Perle, a été transformé en un musée de la Serrurerie où sont exposés des loquets, des poignées de portes et des attaches métalliques (dont de superbes pièces provenant de châteaux royaux), de la période romaine à la Belle Époque. En vous engageant à droite dans la rue de Thorigny, vous pourrez vous rendre au musée Picasso **4** (voir pp. 110-111). Rebroussez chemin et reprenez la rue de la Perle dans le même sens. Faites un crochet à gauche, dans la rue Vieille-du-Temple, pour admirer l'hôtel de Rohan **5**, qui s'orne des magnifiques *Chevaux du Soleil* de Robert Le Lorrain (ouvert lors d'expositions temporaires et de visites guidées). Revenez vers la rue des Quatre-Fils, qui prolonge la rue de la Perle après le croisement de la rue Vieille-du-Temple,

Voir aussi p. 105
Place de la Bastille
2,4 km
Environ 3 heures
Rue des Rosiers

À NE PAS MANQUER

- Place des Vosges
- Place du Marché-Sainte-Catherine
- Musée Carnavalet
- Square Georges-Cain
- Musée Picasso
- Rue des Rosiers

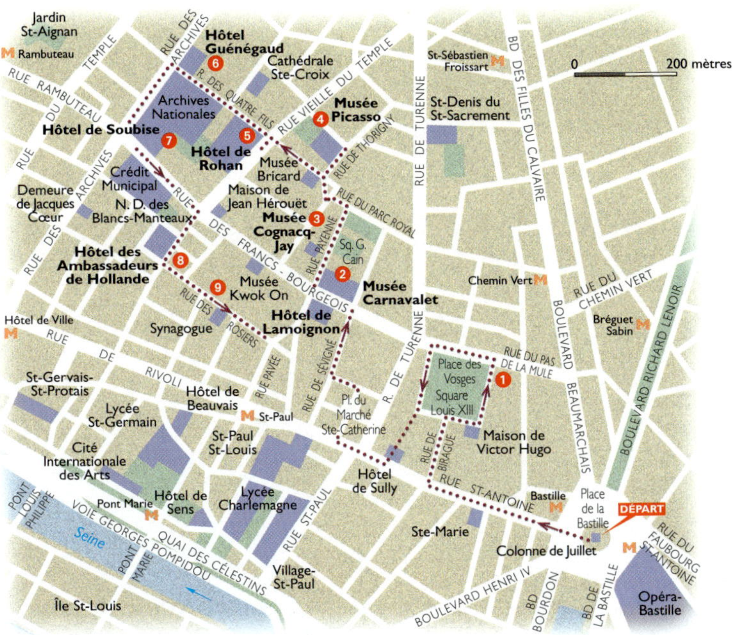

et gagnez l'hôtel Guénégaud 6, sur le côté droit. Dotée d'un beau jardin à la française, cette demeure du XVIIe siècle, où est aménagé le musée de la Chasse et de la Nature *(entrée au 60, rue des Archives, tél. : 01 42 72 86 42, fermé lun., métro : Rambuteau)*, est le seul hôtel particulier de Mansart à être demeuré intact. Descendez à gauche la rue des Archives.

Au n° 58 s'élève le portail de l'hôtel de Clisson 7 (maintenant hôtel de Soubise), l'un des plus anciens vestiges de la capitale, que flanquent deux tourelles gothiques. Construit de 1372 à 1375 sur un terrain ayant appartenu aux templiers, il livrait accès au manoir d'Olivier de Clisson, connétable de France et compagnon d'armes de Du Guesclin. Au XVIe siècle, le manoir tombe aux mains de la puissante famille des Guise, à qui il sert de quartier général pendant les guerres de Religion ; le massacre de la Saint-Barthélemy y a sans doute été programmé. François de Rohan, prince de Soubise, fait reconstruire par Delamair en 1709, à l'emplacement de l'hôtel de Guise démoli, un magnifique hôtel superbement décoré par Boffrand. Au début du XIXe siècle, l'hôtel devient propriété de l'État. En 1808, Napoléon y installe les Archives nationales.

Tournez à gauche dans la rue des Francs-Bourgeois. Sur le trottoir de droite, au n° 8, s'élève le Crédit municipal, ou Mont-de-Piété. À la fois organisme de prêt sur gages, hôtel des ventes et banque, il a été fondé en 1777. À droite, dans la cour, se dressent les vestiges d'une des tours dont Philippe Auguste a hérissé sa muraille il y a huit siècles. Leur préservation est due à l'intervention de Victor Hugo. Reprenez la rue des Francs-Bourgeois jusqu'à la gracieuse tour Renaissance qui s'élève à l'angle de la rue Vieille-du-Temple. Elle orne la demeure de Jehan Hérouet, le trésorier de Louis XII.

À droite, dans la rue Vieille-du-Temple, ne manquez pas la porte du n° 47, où Renaudin a sculpté deux têtes de Méduse : c'est celle de l'hôtel Amelot de Bisseuil, aussi appelé « des Ambassadeurs de Hollande » 8, où Beaumarchais a écrit *Le Mariage de Figaro*. S'il n'a jamais abrité de diplomates, l'édifice a servi de résidence au chapelain protestant de l'ambassade des Pays-Bas, qui y a célébré un service religieux de 1720 à 1727, après la révocation de l'édit de Nantes. Un parent de Benjamin Franklin s'y est marié, et la fille de Necker (la future madame de Staël) y a reçu le baptême protestant, en 1766. Sonnez à la porte et l'on vous laissera peut-être entrer pour admirer Romulus et Remus, un bas-relief de 1660, ainsi que quatre grands cadrans solaires. En sortant, continuez à descendre la rue Vieille-du-Temple et bifurquez à gauche dans la rue des Rosiers 9 (voir p. 112), qui forme le cœur du quartier juif. Des traces de l'enceinte de Philippe Auguste sont visibles aux n°s 8, 10 et 14. ■

La librairie du Marais, rue des Rosiers, a longtemps fourni à la communauté juive livres et objets de culte.

La place de la Bastille

DE JOUR, LE GÉNIE DE LA LIBERTÉ RESPLENDIT AU SOLEIL ET, DE nuit, la colonne de Juillet illuminée brille comme un fanal. La place, et surtout ses ruelles alentour, est un passage obligé de la vie nocturne parisienne. Conçue pour le peuple, elle est toujours le théâtre de manifestations politiques et sociales. Le 14 juillet, la fête nationale, commémore la prise de la Bastille. La veille, les Parisiens dansent dans les bals de rue en levant les yeux vers les feux d'artifice ; le jour même, un défilé militaire est organisé aux Champs-Élysées.

Carte p. 105
Bastille

Cette place porte le nom de l'un des bâtiments les plus symboliques de l'histoire française. Dotée de huit tours, de douves, d'un pont-levis et de murailles crénelées, la forteresse de la Bastille a été bâtie au XIVe siècle notamment pour protéger l'hôtel Saint-Pol, où résidait Charles V. Le Café français (3, place de la Bastille) est aménagé à l'endroit où se dressait la porte de la forteresse au Moyen Âge. Des pavés indiquent l'emplacement exact de l'édifice, qui n'a joué de rôle militaire que pendant la Fronde. À l'époque de Richelieu, elle commence à faire office de prison.

Aux XVIIe et XVIIIe siècles, plusieurs personnages illustres y séjournent dans des conditions de confort surprenantes : le cardinal de Rohan y donne un dîner de 20 couverts ; le marquis de Sade y fait livrer le vin de ses terres de Provence ; et Voltaire en vante la cuisine à sa sortie. Jugeant sa gestion trop coûteuse, Necker, ministre des Finances de Louis XVI, décide de l'abattre pour la remplacer par une esplanade. Les révolutionnaires mènent son projet à bien.

LA COLONNE DE JUILLET

La colonne de Juillet s'inspire de celle de Trajan, à Rome. Elle rappelle le souvenir des morts de la révolution de juillet 1830. Sa base est entourée d'une galerie où reposent les victimes des affrontements de 1830 et de 1848. ■

La colonne de Juillet, au centre de la place, et à l'arrière-plan l'Opéra-Bastille. Ce dernier a été conçu pour être accessible à tous, aussi bien par ses tarifs relativement peu élevés que par son acoustique identique à tous les niveaux de rang.

Autres sites à visiter

LE BASSIN DE L'ARSENAL

Des bateaux de plaisance sont amarrés dans un bassin creusé sur l'emplacement d'une partie des douves de la Bastille. L'extrémité sud du canal Saint-Martin passe sous la place ; un joli jardin borde sa rive est.

Carte p. 105 Entre les boulevards Bourdon et de la Bastille Ⓜ Bastille

L'HÔTEL DE SENS

Cette belle demeure mi-civile, mi-militaire est l'une des rares grandes résidences privées qui nous soient parvenues du Moyen Âge. Érigée vers 1475 en bordure de Seine, elle est un bel exemple du style apparu entre la période gothique et la Renaissance. Elle a été conçue par Tristan de Salazar, archevêque de Sens, et Martin Chambiges, qui a dessiné le transept de la cathédrale de cette ville. En 1605, Henri IV y loge son ex-épouse, la reine Margot. Le boulet de canon lancé sur la bâtisse pendant la révolution de 1830 est resté encastré dans le pignon proche de la tour gauche. En 1911, la ville de Paris acquiert l'édifice, dont la restauration commence en 1929. En 1961, on y installe la bibliothèque des Arts décoratifs et des Beaux-Arts (dite Forney, en raison du legs de l'industriel de ce nom), dont la belle salle de lecture est ouverte au public. La façade ouest de l'hôtel donne sur un très joli jardin de buis, créé par la Ville de Paris et dont la décoration florale est modifiée tous les ans.

Carte p. 105 1, rue Figuier ☎ 01 42 78 14 60 fermé dim.-lun. Ⓜ Saint-Paul

LE MUSÉE COGNACQ-JAY

Les collections d'Ernest Cognacq et de son épouse Louise Jay, léguées à la ville de Paris en 1928, sont abritées dans le bel hôtel de Donon, devenu le musée Cognacq-Jay. Fragonard, Boucher, Chardin, Reynolds, Guardi, Canaletto et Watteau y croisent du mobilier du XVIIIe siècle et une exceptionnelle collection de tabatières.

Carte p. 105 Hôtel de Donon, 8 rue Elzevir ☎ 01 40 27 07 21 fermé lun € Gratuit, sauf expositions temporaires : € Ⓜ Saint-Paul, Rambuteau, Chemin Vert

LA MAISON EUROPÉENNE DE LA PHOTOGRAPHIE

Installé dans l'hôtel Henault-de-Cantobre du XVIIIe siècle, ce musée détient une collection de 12 000 clichés contemporains. Les accrochages sont régulièrement renouvelés et de nombreuses expositions temporaires y sont organisées.

Carte p. 105 5-7, rue de Fourcy ☎ 01 44 78 75 00 fermé lun.-mar. € Gratuit, sauf expositions temporaires : € Ⓜ Saint-Paul ■

Le bassin de l'Arsenal, creusé en 1806 et équipé de 9 écluses, relie le canal Saint-Martin à la Seine.

Par l'originalité de sa pyramide high-tech et la richesse de ses collections, le musée du Louvre se démarque nettement de la bonne centaine de musées qu'on dénombre à Paris. La capitale n'a pas reculé devant la dépense pour s'offrir un chef-d'œuvre, qui est aussi le plus grand espace d'exposition au monde.

Le Louvre et le Palais-Royal

Un des versants de la pyramide du Louvre.

Le Louvre et le Palais-Royal

Bien que la monarchie ne soit plus qu'un lointain souvenir, presque tout la rappelle dans ce quartier. Avant de devenir un musée, le Louvre était une forteresse destinée à protéger Paris des invasions. Pendant environ six siècles, il est resté une résidence royale où chaque monarque a modifié, agrandi et rénové l'œuvre de ses prédécesseurs. Le Palais-Royal, habité par la famille d'Orléans jusqu'en 1830, abrite maintenant le Conseil d'État, le Conseil constitutionnel et le ministère de la Culture.

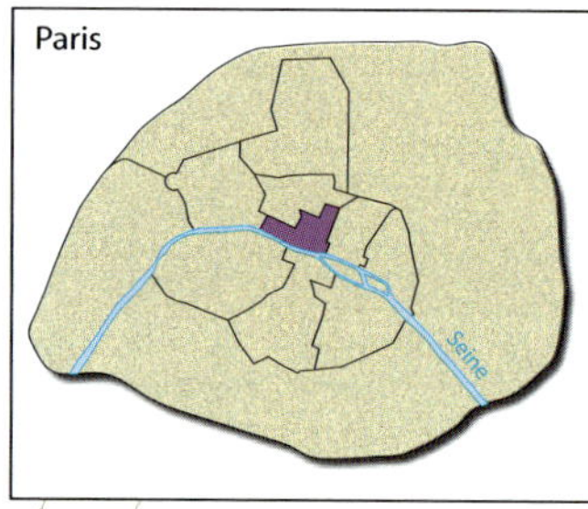

L'expansion du Louvre a entraîné celle des rues voisines. Ses jardins se sont étendus à l'ouest. La jonction s'est opérée avec le palais des Tuileries, édifice construit au-delà des murs de la ville. On a ensuite aménagé le Palais-Royal (voir p. 141), donné au roi par le cardinal de Richelieu. Enfin, on a percé la rue de Rivoli (voir p. 142).

Les fonds du musée du Louvre et de la Bibliothèque nationale ont été formés à partir des collections royales. En 1373, Charles V rassemble 973 ouvrages dans son château du Louvre. Ses livres sont dispersés à sa mort, mais ses successeurs reconstituent l'ensemble. L'idée de créer une vraie bibliothèque nationale prend naissance sous Louis XIV, lorsque Jean-Baptiste Colbert, son ministre des Finances, regroupe la collection royale dans un somptueux édifice, rue de Richelieu. Au fil du temps, le fonds se développe et le manque d'espace se fait de plus en plus sentir. Il est finalement décidé de construire la nouvelle Bibliothèque nationale, quai François-Mauriac. Achevé en 1997, le nouveau bâtiment rassemble la majeure partie des imprimés tandis que les estampes, photographies, cartes, médailles et partitions restent dans les anciens locaux.

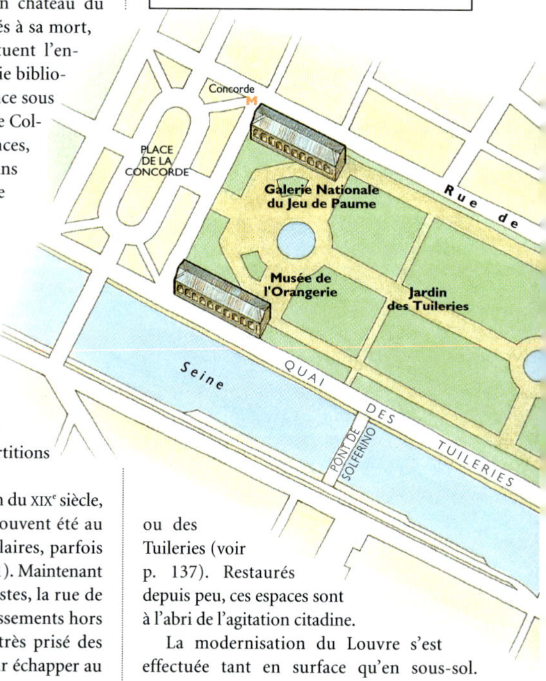

De la fin du XVIIIe siècle à la fin du XIXe siècle, le Louvre et ses environs ont souvent été au cœur des manifestations populaires, parfois violentes (1792, 1830, 1848, 1871). Maintenant bordée de magasins pour touristes, la rue de Rivoli conserve quelques établissements hors pair, comme l'hôtel Meurice, très prisé des riches Anglais au XIXe siècle. Pour échapper au brouhaha des rues avoisinantes, vous pouvez vous réfugier dans les jardins du Palais-Royal ou des Tuileries (voir p. 137). Restaurés depuis peu, ces espaces sont à l'abri de l'agitation citadine.

La modernisation du Louvre s'est effectuée tant en surface qu'en sous-sol. En 1989, l'édification de la pyramide de Pei (l'entrée principale) a constitué la première étape de ce grand remodelage. Aménagé sous le musée et au-delà, l'élégant complexe du Carrousel du Louvre est une véritable ville qui regroupe des boutiques, un parking et un espace de restauration. Faisant référence à celle de Pei, une pyramide de verre inversée éclaire toute cette partie souterraine.

LE LOUVRE ET LE PALAIS-ROYAL

1 Carrousel du Louvre 2 Colonnes de Buren 3 Le Louvre des Antiquaires 4 Bibliothèque nationale, site Richelieu 5 Banque de France 6 Bourse du Commerce

Le jardin des Tuileries se déploie d'est en ouest entre le Louvre et la place de la Concorde sur laquelle s'ouvre son entrée principale. Celle-ci est flanquée de deux musées ; à gauche, la Galerie nationale du Jeu de paume (voir p. 141), où sont exposées des œuvres contemporaines ; à droite, le musée de l'Orangerie (voir p. 140), qui abrite les célèbres *Nymphéas* de Monet, ainsi que des œuvres de Soutine, Cézanne et Renoir.

La terrasse du Bord de l'Eau constitue, tout le long du quai des Tuileries, une charmante promenade dominant la Seine. ■

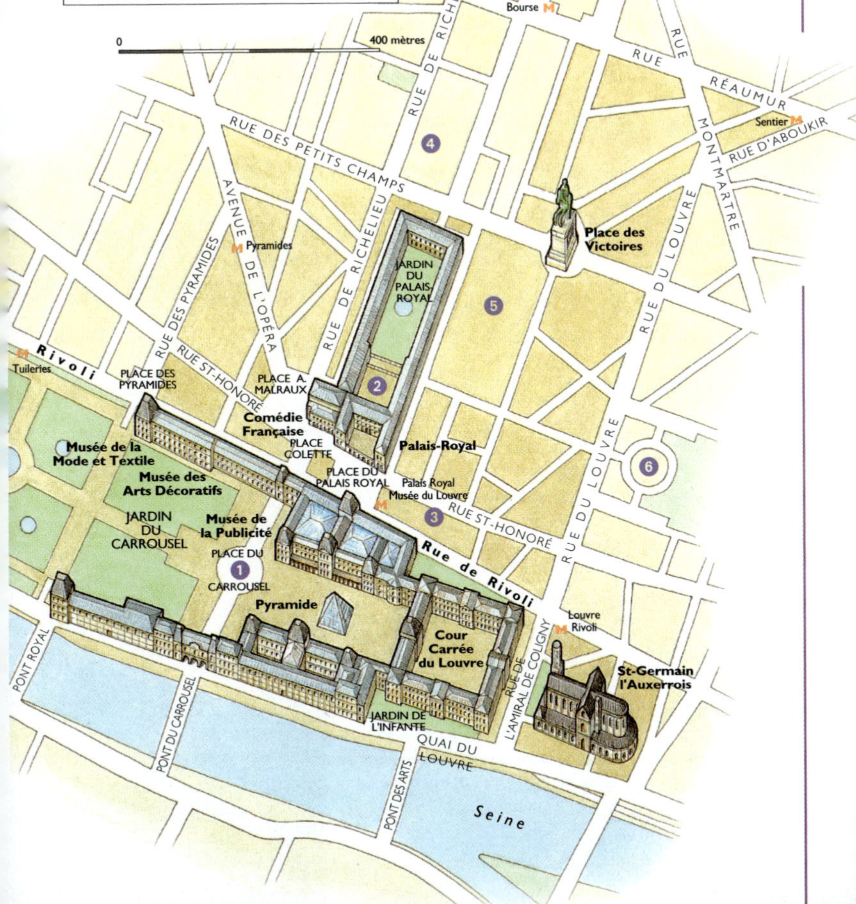

Le musée du Louvre

Carte p. 123
Entrée principale : Pyramide du Louvre, Cour Napoléon. Autres entrées : Galerie du Carrousel, Porte des Lions
01 40 20 50 50. Répondeur : 01 40 20 51 51.
Fermé mar. Nocturnes lun. et mer.
€€. Réduction à partir de 15 h et dim. Gratuit pour les moins de 18 ans et le 1er dim. de chaque mois. Visite guidée : €. Audioguide : €€ Pour éviter les files d'attente, achetez vos billets à l'avance (Tél. : 08 92 68 46 94).
Palais-Royal-Musée du Louvre

Lancé par le président François Mitterrand en 1981, le projet de modernisation du Louvre a véritablement métamorphosé le musée. La pyramide de verre, œuvre de Pei, procure espace et lumière, et lui offre surtout une entrée principale qui manquait cruellement. La réorganisation des collections et des salles fait de la visite de cet immense musée un agréable lieu de promenade.

C'est en 1190 que le roi Philippe Auguste, partant pour la croisade, ordonne la construction d'une forteresse destinée à la protection de la rive droite de la ville. Celle-ci est élevée vers 1200 et un donjon entouré d'un fossé en marque le centre (actuelle Cour Carrée). Au XIVe siècle, Charles V fait transformer le Louvre en résidence par son architecte Raymond du Temple. François Ier décide de démolir une partie de la vieille forteresse, dont le donjon, et de construire un palais sur ses fondations. Les travaux, confiés à Pierre Lescot assisté du sculpteur Jean Goujon, introduisent le style de la Renaissance italienne à Paris. Puis Catherine de Médicis, à la mort de son époux Henri II, en 1559, ordonne la construction d'un deuxième palais, les Tuileries, qu'elle souhaite relier par un passage couvert au Louvre.

En 1594, Henri IV décide de faire du Louvre le lieu symbolique de la monarchie. Les aménagements et les projets sont nombreux ; le « Grand Dessein » (réunir en un seul ensemble les deux palais) ne sera cependant réalisé que par Napoléon III. En 1608, Henri IV, souhaitant donner une dimension artistique au Louvre, installe des artistes dans une partie du palais et met à leur disposition de vastes ateliers.

Les travaux d'embellissement et d'extension se poursuivent sous les règnes de Louis XIII et de Louis XIV, même si ce dernier quitte Paris pour Versailles, laissant le Louvre, à l'exemple de Henri IV, à des artistes et aux Académies. Le 10 août 1793, le Muséum central des Arts est inauguré au Louvre, la République mettant ainsi à exécution une idée qui avait germé au siècle des Lumières.

C'est Napoléon Ier et Napoléon III qui achèvent les constructions de ce nouveau temple des arts. Mais en 1871, lors du soulèvement de la Commune, le palais des Tuileries est incendié ; ses ruines seront rasées en 1882. Le Louvre et ses collections

« J'ai presque tout le Louvre en tête : salle par salle, peinture par peinture » (Alberto Giacometti, d'après les *Dialogues du Louvre*, 1972). ■

échappent par miracle à l'incendie. En 1981, le projet « Grand Louvre » est lancé. Les travaux de restauration et de restructuration sont une magnifique réussite, même si l'inauguration en 1989 de la pyramide en verre de Ieoh Ming Pei, qui abrite la nouvelle entrée principale du musée, a suscité de vives polémiques. Cet ajout s'inscrit pourtant dans une problématique connue: de tout temps, les architectes ont dû intégrer des éléments aux formes nouvelles dans des ensembles déjà disparates.

LES COLLECTIONS

Outre les salles d'Histoire du Louvre et le Louvre médiéval, le musée du Louvre se compose de sept départements: Antiquités grecques, romaines et étrusques, Antiquités égyptiennes, Antiquités orientales-Arts d'Islam, Peintures, Sculptures, Objets d'Art et Arts graphiques. Ils se répartissent dans trois sections principales, correspondant aux trois directions partant du hall Napoléon (sous la pyramide): Sully (Cour Carrée), Richelieu (l'aile parallèle à la rue de Rivoli) et Denon (celle qui borde la Seine). Malgré la réorganisation des locaux, la visite du musée peut se révéler délicate. Si vous êtes novice, munissez-vous d'un dépliant gratuit ou du guide intitulé *Destination Louvre: visite guidée*, tous deux disponibles dans le hall d'accueil. Repérez plusieurs œuvres que vous ne voulez pas manquer, comme la *Victoire de Samothrace* ou *La Joconde*, ou délimitez quelques périodes de l'histoire de l'art, et commencez votre parcours.

Prenez comme point de départ les fondations de la forteresse de Philippe Auguste (accès direct aux Antiquités égyptiennes).

Une étonnante caractéristique: la pyramide en verre de Ieoh Ming Pei a quasiment les mêmes proportions, en réduction, que la pyramide de Kheops, à Gizeh.

À droite : La stèle du *Harpiste* (vers 1069-664 av. J.-C.) représente un musicien jouant de la harpe devant le dieu Soleil à tête de faucon.

À gauche : Un des esclaves sculptés par Michel-Ange pour le tombeau du pape Jules II.

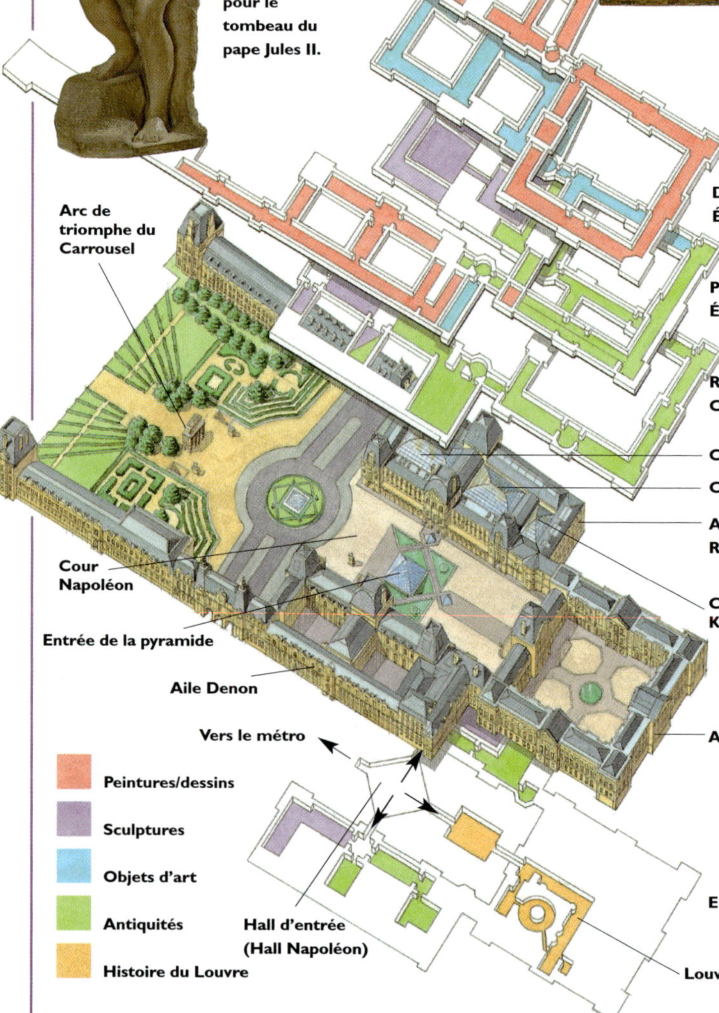

ANTIQUITÉS

Les trésors égyptiens du Louvre sont réunis à l'entresol de l'aile Denon (salles A à C), ainsi que dans l'aile Sully (salles 1 à 30). Les antiquités grecques, étrusques et romaines se trouvent à l'entresol de l'aile Denon (salles 1 à 3), ainsi qu'au rez-de-chaussée et au 1er étage des ailes Denon et Sully (salles A, B et 4 à 44).

Les antiquités égyptiennes

La collection, la plus importante au monde après celle du musée du Caire, obéit à un agencement thématique au rez-de-chaussée (salles 1 à 19) et chronologique (de la préhistoire à la conquête romaine) au 1er étage (salles 20 à 30).

Un grand sphinx monolithe en granit rose marque l'entrée du département (salle 1), où Nakhthorheb (salle 2) vous attend. Les huit salles qui suivent illustrent, à travers des œuvres d'art et des objets usuels, la vie quotidienne des Anciens égyptiens : le Nil (salle 3), l'agriculture (salle 4), l'élevage, la chasse et la pêche (salle 5), l'écriture (salle 6), les arts et l'artisanat (salle 7), la maison (salle 8), la parure (salle 9) et, enfin, les loisirs (salle 10). Ne manquez pas, salle 4, les superbes bas-reliefs du mastaba (tombeau) d'Akhethétep, sépulture civile de la Ve dynastie (vers 2350 av. J.-C.). Les salles 11 à 19 sont consacrées aux temples et aux rites funéraires de l'ancienne Égypte. La salle 12 est impressionnante par l'aspect monumental des portiques, colonnes et statues de l'époque avec, entre autres, les colosses de Séthi II et Ramsès II. En descendant dans la crypte d'Osiris (salle 13), vous aurez un bon aperçu des pratiques religieuses des Égyptiens. Enfin, la salle 19 vous présentera toutes sortes d'animaux momifiés (du crocodile long de 3 m au minuscule scarabée).

À l'étage, la collection est classée par ordre chronologique. La première salle (n° 20) marque la fin de la préhistoire en Égypte, appelée époque de Nagada. Admirez le *Poignard du Gebel el Arak* (vers 3200 av. J.-C.), un des tout premiers bas-reliefs. Ne manquez pas non plus la superbe *Stèle du Roi-serpent*, dans la salle 21 consacrée à l'époque thinite. L'Ancien Empire (2700-2200 av. J.-C.), salle 22, est représenté par le célèbre *Scribe accroupi*, statue en calcaire peint au réalisme époustouflant.

Le Moyen Empire (2000-1700 av. J.-C.), salle 23, et le Nouvel Empire (1550-1200 av. J.-C.), salles 24 à 28, ont laissé les plus beaux chefs-d'œuvre. La salle 25 célèbre le règne d'Aménophis IV-Akhénaton et de son épouse Néfertiti. C'est l'époque où la rupture s'opère avec les traditions ancestrales. Akhénaton professe un dieu unique, le dieu-soleil Aton, l'art se libère et devient plus naturel et plus familier. C'est l'âge d'or de la création artistique en Égypte. Ne manquez pas la tête colossale d'Akhénaton et le torse en quartzite rouge que l'on attribue à Néfertiti. Attar-

Fragment de la statue colossale en grès d'Akhénaton (1353-1337 av. J.-C.). Le long nez et les lèvres sensuelles sont caractéristiques de la période artistique sous le règne de ce pharaon qui n'adorait qu'un seul dieu, Aton.

Le père de l'égyptologie

Jean-François Champollion (1790-1832) est considéré comme le père de l'égyptologie. Il a joué un rôle fondamental dans le déchiffrement des hiéroglyphes de la pierre de Rosette, permettant ainsi de dévoiler les mystères de la langue des pharaons.
En 1826, il fut le premier conservateur du département égyptien du Louvre. ■

ÉTYMOLOGIE DU MOT LOUVRE

Personne ne connaît le sens du mot « LOUVRE ». Certains suggèrent qu'il faut en chercher l'origine soit dans le mot « léproserie », soit dans le mot saxon « lower », signifiant habitation fortifiée, à moins qu'il ne rappelle tout simplement les loups qui pullulaient dans la région. ■

Peinture de l'intérieur d'un sarcophage (1552-1199 av. J.-C.) représentant la personne décédée entourée de Maat, déesse de la vérité et de l'ordre divin (à droite), et d'Anubis, le dieu égyptien de la mort (à gauche).

LES INCANTATIONS POUR L'AU-DELÀ

Le *Livre des morts* ne faisait aucune allusion à une vie nouvelle après la mort. Ce n'était qu'une longue série d'incantations et de conseils pour aider à braver les périls de l'au-delà. ■

dez-vous, salle 27, devant le relief de calcaire peint, où Séti Ier est en compagnie de la déesse Hathor. Enfin, les deux dernières salles (29 et 30) marquent la fin de l'Égypte pharaonique (1000-30 av. J.-C.) avec notamment l'invasion perse. Ne manquez pas la *Triade d'Osorkon II* (salle 29), magnifique bijou en or mettant en scène Osiris, Isis et Horus.

Le parcours chronologique se poursuit, à l'entresol de l'aile Denon, avec les antiquités de l'époque romaine (salle A) et de la culture chrétienne copte (salles B et C). Dans la première salle, de nombreuses statues funéraires et des momies voisinent avec les extraordinaires portraits de défunts découverts dans le Fayoum, dont le style est si réaliste qu'on les a longtemps crus faux. L'art copte est rassemblé de l'autre côté de la cour Visconti. Les tissus confectionnés au IIe siècle comptent parmi les nombreux trésors cachés du Louvre. Le châle de Sabine, pièce aux coloris éclatants, constitue l'un d'eux.

La salle de Baouit (salle C) abrite une reconstitution de l'église copte éponyme (VIe-VIIe siècle). Ce sanctuaire découvert en 1900 n'est, croit-on, qu'un élément d'un monastère aujourd'hui disparu.

Les antiquités grecques

La collection couvre trois époques: l'art grec archaïque (3000 à 480 av. J.-C.), l'art grec classique et la Grèce hellénistique (323 à 31 av. J.-C.).

La galerie de l'entresol (Denon, salles 1 à 4) est consacrée à la période préclassique, riche d'un précieux savoir-faire se nourrissant au contact d'autres civilisations. Sculptures, vases, céramiques, figurines, motifs funéraires ou votifs et inscriptions sont des pièces majeures de l'évolution de l'art grec archaïque. Ne manquez pas les idoles cycladiques (salle 1a), la *Dame d'Auxerre* (vers 630 av. J.-C., salle 1d), superbe statuette en calcaire dont l'austérité témoigne du style dorien, ou encore la *Coré de Samos* (vers 565 av. J.-C., salle 1e), provenant du temple d'Héra et dont le raffinement du vêtement traduit l'inspiration ionienne.

Au rez-de-chaussée (Denon et Sully), les salles 4 à 17 sont consacrées à la Grèce classique et hellénistique. Après 450 av. J.-C., la puissance d'Athènes ne cesse de croître et des politiques de prestige assurent le développement artistique de la cité. Une nouvelle esthétique s'élabore avec la conquête du mouvement. Cette nouvelle forme d'art est apparue dans les métopes (plaques sculptées) du temple de Zeus à Olympie (salle 4). Le fragment de la frise du Parthénon (vers 440 av. J.-C.), où des jeunes filles s'apprêtent à faire une offrande à leur déesse protectrice Héra, est tout aussi remarquable.

La période hellénistique, qui débute à la mort d'Alexandre le Grand (323 av. J.-C.), introduit un art plus volontiers décoratif, où l'enfance et la vieillesse retiennent l'attention et où les sentiments, de la joie à la douleur, acquièrent droit d'expression. La salle 12 renferme l'une des pièces majeures du Louvre, la *Vénus de Milo* (vers 100 av. J.-C.), qui marque le retour au classicisme de certaines œuvres de la période hellénistique. Découverte sur l'île de Milos (Milo) en 1820, l'expression douce du visage, l'attitude sereine et l'admirable jeu du drapé font de ce marbre l'un des chefs-d'œuvre de la statuaire antique.

C'est en haut du grand escalier Daru que vous découvrirez *La Victoire de Samothrace* (début du IIe siècle av. J.-C.), figure de proue d'un bateau commémorant une victoire navale, témoignage éblouissant de l'art hellénistique.

La visite se poursuit au premier étage (Sully) avec la salle des Bronzes (n° 32) – ne manquez

La Victoire de Samothrace, Victoire ailée, découverte en morceaux sur l'île de Samothrace en 1863, se dresse, telle une déesse de la victoire poussée par les vents, sur un piédestal sculpté en forme de proue de navire.

TRÉSORS EN TEMPS DE GUERRE

Évacués au cours des deux conflits mondiaux, les trésors du Louvre furent mis dans des caisses sans marque et cachés dans des endroits sûrs. Beaucoup d'entre eux furent placés au château de Chambord. Le 1er septembre 1939, la plupart des œuvres avaient quitté Paris. ■

pas la *Tête de jeune homme* dite « de Bénévent » –, la salle Henri II-Orfèvrerie romaine (n° 33), célèbre pour son trésor de Boscoreale, composé de monnaies, bijoux d'or et vaisselle d'argent découverts près de Pompéi après l'éruption du Vésuve (79 ap. J.-C.), et la salle des Verres grecs et romains (n° 34).

Enfin, la galerie Campana (salles 39 à 47) offre une impressionnante collection de vases grecs, dont les motifs sont de véritables témoignages de la vie quotidienne de la Grèce antique. Vers 530 av. J.-C., le remplacement de la technique dite « de la figure noire » (silhouette noire sur fond rouge) par celle dite « de la figure rouge », par le peintre Andokidès, révèle le raffinement de l'art pictural de l'époque.

Les antiquités étrusques

Les antiquités étrusques (Denon, salle 4, salles 18 à 20) sont l'œuvre d'artistes d'Étrurie, région d'Italie centrale qui connut son apogée au VIe et au tout début du Ve siècle av. J.-C. L'art étrusque s'inspire à la fois des arts oriental et grec, mais son originalité s'affirme dans la céramique, le bronze et la terre cuite.

Le *Sarcophage des époux* (vers 520-510 av. J.-C., salle 18) est un joyau du Louvre. Cette urne en terre cuite représente un couple, souriant et enlacé, qui participe au banquet divin. À demi étendue, à la différence des femmes grecques qui ne pouvaient pas assister aux banquets, la femme verse quelques gouttes d'huile parfumée (offrande qui faisait partie du rite funéraire des Étrusques) sur la main tendue de son époux. Les bustes, les mains, les drapés ou encore les détails du mobilier révèlent un artiste de grand talent.

Les antiquités romaines

Si les sculpteurs romains n'ont cessé de copier leurs prédécesseurs grecs, ils ne se sont pas contentés de réaliser des versions édulcorées des œuvres de l'époque hellénistique. L'Empire s'étendait sur de nombreux pays aux cultures très diverses, et Rome abritait quantité d'artistes étrangers. Après s'être approprié certains éléments étrusques et grecs,

Le *Sarcophage des époux* en terre cuite, datant du VIe siècle av. J.-C., fut découvert à Cerveteri en Italie. Il reflète à la fois le style grec archaïque et les gracieuses formes de l'art étrusque.

les Romains ont adapté leur style à des sujets moins mythiques, plus factuels, en l'occurrence la glorification de l'État et des grandes familles.

Le réalisme se substituant peu à peu à l'idéal classique de la beauté, le portrait a acquis une tout autre dimension. Ce genre était si prisé qu'on sculptait souvent les têtes à part, avant de les fixer sur des corps produits en série (voir la statue d'Auguste, dans la salle 27).

Les riches Romains décoraient leurs demeures de fresques et de mosaïques aux couleurs vives. Parmi ces dernières, celle qui orne le sol de la salle 31, la *Mosaïque des saisons*, d'époque constantinienne (elle date du IVe siècle), provient d'une villa d'Antioche.

PEINTURES

Les tableaux du Louvre se répartissent ainsi : les œuvres françaises produites entre le XIVe et le XIXe siècle, les œuvres italiennes, celles d'Europe du Nord, et celles des autres pays européens.

La peinture française

Accrochés au premier étage de l'aile Denon, ainsi qu'au deuxième étage des ailes Sully et Richelieu, les tableaux français appartiennent à toutes les grandes époques, du haut Moyen Âge et de la Renaissance au milieu du XIXe siècle (la production ultérieure est exposée au musée d'Orsay, voir pp. 174-178).

Les salles 1 et 2 (Richelieu) sont consacrées au XIVe siècle, et la collec-

***La Mort de Sardanaple* (1827), par Eugène Delacroix, montre le souverain assyrien contemplant, après sa défaite, le massacre de ses femmes et la destruction de ses trésors par ses esclaves.**

Par son caractère dramatique, et par le contraste entre les parties éclairées et les parties sombres, le *Radeau de la Méduse* de Géricault, est caractéristique du style des peintres de l'école romantique.

L'ÉQUIPE DU LOUVRE

Une équipe de 1 600 conservateurs, gardiens et techniciens travaille au Louvre. Près de 60 conservateurs veillent sur les 350 000 œuvres d'art, dont « seules » 30 000 sont exposées. ■

tion s'ouvre sur le *Portrait de Jean le Bon* (vers 1350), la première peinture exécutée sur chevalet.

Le XVe siècle (salles 3 à 6) est représenté, entre autres, par la *Pietà de Villeneuve-lès-Avignon* d'Enguerrand Quarton, et *Charles VIII* de Jean Fouquet, où l'on sent déjà les premières influences de la Renaissance. Au XVIe siècle (salles 7 à 16), les nombreux artistes italiens invités par François Ier, tels Léonard de Vinci, le Rosso, le Primatice, bouleversent la peinture française qui passe de l'art médiéval au maniérisme.

Le XVIIe siècle (salles 11 à 34) est marqué par les peintres dits « caravagesques », tendant au luminisme de Caravage et au réalisme. Parmi ceux-ci, notons, tout particulièrement : Nicolas Poussin, dont un quart des œuvres est présent au Louvre (salles 13, 14, 16, 18), Le Lorrain (salle 15), Georges de La Tour (aile Sully, salle 28), Le Sueur et Le Brun (salles 31 et 32). Le Louvre possède de superbes œuvres de Watteau (salle 36), Boucher (salle 46) et Fragonard (salle 48), qui comptent parmi les plus grands peintres du XVIIIe siècle. Le XIXe siècle (salles 55 à 73) est également bien représenté avec, entre autres, Ingres (salle 60), Géricault (salle 61), Delacroix (salle 62) et Corot (salle 73), qui préfigure les impressionnistes.

La collection d'œuvres françaises ne se limite pas à cette suite chronologique. Les salles 75 et 77 du premier étage de l'aile Denon regroupent des toiles de grand format typiques de deux écoles picturales opposées du XIXe siècle : le néoclassicisme et le romantisme.

Certains peintres ont vigoureusement défendu leurs qualités respectives : la beauté idéalisée, froide et rationnelle de la première est représentée par *Le Serment des Horaces* (1784) et *Le Sacre* de Napoléon Ier (1804) de Jacques Louis David ; l'émotion et l'individualisme de la seconde sont illustrés par *La Mort de Sardanapale* (1827) d'Eugène

RETOUR AUX COULEURS ORIGINALES
Les restaurateurs de l'œuvre de Véronèse *Les Noces de Cana* ont retrouvé les teintes originales du tableau grâce aux nouvelles technologies d'analyse des couleurs et aux rayons X. Il y a quelques années le manteau vert du personnage au premier plan était rouge. ■

Delacroix. Les romantiques s'inspiraient des événements de leur temps. Ainsi, Théodore Géricault a fait scandale en peignant *Le Radeau de la Méduse* (salle 77) après le naufrage de ce navire en juillet 1816, et en y abordant les thèmes du cannibalisme et de la trahison.

La peinture européenne

Les peintures d'Europe du Nord (Allemagne, Flandres et Pays-Bas), du XIVe au XVIIe siècle, sont regroupées au 2e étage de l'aile Richelieu. Vous découvrirez les peintres primitifs flamands avec, entre autres, Jan Van Eyck, qui mit au point la technique de la peinture à l'huile, et sa célèbre *Vierge au chancelier Rolin*, et Jérôme Bosch *(La Nef des fous)*. Bruegel le Vieux et Lucas de Leyde illustrent assez bien la Renaissance flamande du XVIe siècle, tandis que Dürer et Cranach sont les dignes représentants de l'école germanique. La galerie Médicis renferme une époustouflante série de toiles (d'une surface totale de 275 m^2) de Rubens, commandées par Marie de Médicis pour décorer le palais du Luxembourg. Elle s'orne aussi de quelques peintres hollandais du XVIIe siècle, dont la ravissante *Bethsabée au bain* de Rembrandt, ou *La Dentellière* et *L'Astronome*, deux chefs-d'œuvre de Vermeer de Delft.

Giotto et Cimabue annoncent la collection des peintres italiens des XIIe, XIVe et XVe siècles (aile Denon, 1er étage, salles 1 à 11). Ne manquez pas le *Saint François d'Assise recevant les stigmates* de Giotto, qui affirme, au début du XIVe siècle, le parti pris réaliste de l'école de Florence. Puis vous décou-

Léonard de Vinci, archétype du génie de la Renaissance, fut à la fois un peintre et un homme de science. *La Joconde* marque l'apogée de ses multiples talents. Le portrait, qui représente Mona Lisa, épouse de Francesco del Giocondo, fut peint en 1503. Mais Léonard ne le signa pas et ne le remit pas aux époux Giocondo qui l'avaient commandé. Il le garda et il ne le quitta plus. À sa mort, survenue en 1519, le tableau entra dans les collections de François Ier.

vrirez Fra Angelico, Botticelli, Paolo Uccello, Pisanello, Piero della Francesca avant d'accéder à la Grande Galerie où Léonard de Vinci occupe la place d'honneur. Vous pourrez admirer plusieurs de ses œuvres, dont *La Vierge, l'Enfant Jésus et sainte Anne, La Vierge aux rochers* ou encore *Saint Jean Baptiste.* Enfin, la fameuse salle des États abrite *La Joconde*, célébrissime portrait de Mona Lisa, *Les Noces de Cana* de Véronèse, couvrant un mur entier, et quelques-uns des plus beaux tableaux italiens du XVIe et du XVIIe siècle.

ANTIQUITÉS ORIENTALES

Cette collection, l'une des plus célèbres du musée, se divise en quatre sections : la Mésopotamie, l'ancien Iran, le Levant (rez-de-chaussée des ailes Richelieu et Sully, salles A à D et 1 à 21) et les arts islamiques (entresol de l'aile Richelieu, salles A et 1 à 11).

La section islamique regroupe des œuvres très variées (tapis, armes, céramiques, miniatures, etc.) qui, par leur raffinement et leur stylisation extrêmes, sont les témoignages d'une maîtrise exceptionnelle des techniques de l'art.

Dans la section des pays du Levant, ne manquez pas, parmi les tombeaux phéniciens, le *Sarcophage en forme de momie d'Eshmunazor II*, roi de Sidon (Ve siècle av. J.-C.), témoignage de l'influence égyptienne en Syrie, et *Aphrodite à la tortue*, superbe portrait funéraire datant du IIe siècle ap. J.-C. La collection mésopotamienne et celle d'Iran offrent une quantité impressionnante d'œuvres en provenance d'empires déchus, comme celui de Babylone.

Enfin, la cour Khorsabad renferme de superbes bas-reliefs assyriens, provenant du palais de Sargon II, roi d'Assyrie (720 av. J.-C.). Les deux étonnants taureaux ailés à cinq pattes (pour être regardés aussi bien de face que de profil) étaient une partie du décor de la troisième porte de l'enceinte de Khorsabad.

SCULPTURES

Sous les grandes verrières des cours Puget et Marly, vous découvrirez les sculptures de plein air qui décoraient les parcs royaux aux XVIIe et XVIIIe siècles, et le château de Marly, une des résidences de Louis XIV. Admirez, notamment, les célèbres *Chevaux de Marly* de Coustou, qui se dressaient à l'entrée des Champs-Élysées et furent remplacés, en 1984, par des moulages. Les salles qui ouvrent sur la cour Marly rassemblent les sculptures françaises du XIIe siècle, puis des époques romane et gothique. Bon nombre d'entre elles ornaient les églises du pays. Le *Tombeau de Philippe Pot* (XVe siècle, salle 10), où huit hommes encapuchonnés portent le corps du défunt, est d'une originalité stupéfiante.

L'aile Denon abrite une série de sculptures allemandes, hollandaises, espagnoles et italiennes. Parmi ces dernières, remarquez les deux *Esclaves* de Michel-Ange, chefs-d'œuvre ina-

La cour Marly a été utilisée pour mettre en valeur les chefs-d'œuvre de la sculpture française du XVIIIe siècle. Y sont, notamment exposés les groupes équestres sculptés pour le château de Marly par Coysevox (*La Renommée* et *Mercure*, 1702) et par Coustou (*Les Chevaux de Marly*, 1783).

chevés conçus entre 1513 et 1520 pour le tombeau du pape Jules II.

OBJETS D'ART

Les pièces rassemblées dans ces salles datent de la période comprise entre le Moyen Âge et le XIXe siècle. Quantité d'objets anciens proviennent de la basilique Saint-Denis (voir p. 220), mais le département s'est agrandi à la suite de dons et de legs. Le terme « objets d'art », qui s'applique aussi bien aux accessoires religieux et aux émaux qu'aux tapisseries, aux bijoux et au mobilier, désigne en fait les objets « quotidiens » du clergé et de la noblesse. Ils sont tous présentés au premier étage des ailes Richelieu et Sully, ainsi que dans la somptueuse galerie d'Apollon, dans l'aile Denon, qui renferme les joyaux de la Couronne. N'hésitez pas à pénétrer dans les appartements Napoléon III, au décor étourdissant d'or, de cristaux et de velours, conçu par l'architecte Lefuel. Une partie des collections d'art premier du futur musée du quai Branly (ouverture prévue en 2006) sont exposées ici.

DESSINS ET GRAVURES

On connaît peu les expositions temporaires organisées dans ce département des Arts graphiques et l'on ignore s'il est possible de voir tout ce qu'il détient. Réunie au 1er étage de l'aile Denon (salles 8 à 10), la collection comporte quelque 120 000 œuvres qui couvrent presque toutes les périodes de l'histoire de l'art, dont des manuscrits enluminés, des dessins de Léonard de Vinci, des esquisses réalisées par Delacroix au Maroc et des études de Rembrandt. La boutique de chalcographie, qui propose des gravures réalisées à partir de plaques de cuivre originales, est plus accessible. Elle se situe sous la pyramide. ■

Les somptueux appartements Napoléon III de l'aile Richelieu, qui regorgent de meubles dorés recouverts de velours rouge et d'immenses lustres de cristal, furent restaurés et ouverts au public en 1983.

Trois musées d'art

Carte p. 123
Palais du Louvre, 107, rue de Rivoli
Fermé lun.
01 44 55 57 50
€
Palais-Royal-Musée du Louvre, Tuileries, Pyramides

Le musée de la Publicité possède des affiches, telle celle du Chat Noir, nom du cabaret qui vit naître la tradition montmartroise des chansonniers. Des artistes fameux, comme Aristide Bruant, s'y produisirent.

Trois musées sont aménagés dans les ailes de Rohan et de Marsan du Louvre : le musée des Arts décoratifs, le musée de la Mode et du Textile, ainsi que le musée de la Publicité, tous trois gérés par l'UCAD (Union centrale des Arts décoratifs). Leurs espaces d'exposition ont été récemment rénovés et réaménagés, et se présentent sous leur meilleur jour.

LE MUSÉE DES ARTS DÉCORATIFS

Installé dans l'aile de Marsan du Louvre depuis 1905, ce musée possède une extraordinaire collection d'objets (céramique, verrerie, bijoux, mobilier, dessins, jouets, etc.) retraçant l'art de vivre du Moyen Âge à nos jours. Les peintures et sculptures proviennent essentiellement de monastères et d'églises.

Actuellement en travaux, le musée est fermé au public. Sa rénovation s'achèvera en 2006. Il présentera alors plus de 4 500 objets. Seule se visite aujourd'hui la galerie des bijoux. Environ 1 200 pièces exposées offrent un panorama exemplaire de l'histoire du bijou et de la joaillerie, du Moyen Âge à nos jours.

LE MUSÉE DE LA MODE ET DU TEXTILE

Le musée retrace l'évolution de la mode vestimentaire à travers les âges. Des costumes en usage pendant trois siècles (du XVIIe au XIXe), des accessoires et des tissus rares y voisinent avec les œuvres des maîtres de la haute couture du XXe siècle et de créateurs contemporains, tels Poiret, Dior, Lanvin ou Schiaparelli. Ses collections sont visibles au cours d'expositions temporaires, renouvelées tous les 6 mois environ.

Le musée comporte aussi un centre de documentation ouvert aux chercheurs, aux professionnels et, sur rendez-vous, au grand public.

LE MUSÉE DE LA PUBLICITÉ

Naguère établi dans le Xe arrondissement, le musée de la Publicité a été créé en 1978. Il abrite les affiches de la bibliothèque de l'UCAD, dont le fonds s'est étoffé au fil des ans grâce à de nombreux dons. On y voit aujourd'hui quelque 40 000 œuvres venues du monde entier, dont les premières datent de la moitié du XVIIIe siècle et les dernières de 1949, auxquelles s'ajoutent 45 000 affiches contemporaines offertes par les agences et leurs concepteurs, ainsi que 20 000 films publicitaires récents. ■

Le jardin des Tuileries

Le jardin des Tuileries ouvre la « Voie triomphale », superbe perspective linéaire qui débute avec l'Arc de triomphe du Carrousel, se poursuit avec l'obélisque de Louksor, érigé sur la place de la Concorde, puis avec l'Arc de Triomphe de l'Étoile, pour s'achever avec la Grande Arche de la Défense, huit kilomètres plus loin.

Carte pp. 122-123
Palais-Royal, Tuileries, Pyramides, Concorde

Construit pour Catherine de Médicis afin d'agrémenter son palais des Tuileries, le jardin, où fêtes royales et feux d'artifice rivalisent de beauté, devient rapidement un lieu de promenade à la mode. En 1664, Le Nôtre est chargé de son embellissement par Colbert. On lui doit, entre autres, la magnifique perspective de l'allée centrale.

Dans le cadre de la rénovation du Grand Louvre (1981), les espaces verts adjacents ont été redessinés pour mieux mettre en valeur l'axe est-ouest et relier les parvis du nouveau musée à la place de la Concorde. Le plan d'origine a été repris. Ce dernier prévoyait l'aménagement, près du Louvre, d'un jardin classique, de plus en plus boisé au fur et à mesure qu'on approcherait de la Concorde. Ornée de l'Arc de triomphe du Carrousel voulu par Napoléon Ier, la partie orientale du lieu est délimitée par les deux longues ailes du musée. Des parterres y ont été replantés. Des cafés, des promenades en poney et une fête foraine estivale font des Tuileries un véritable jardin d'agrément.

Près du Louvre, un espace planté de haies d'ifs s'orne de vingt bronzes d'Aristide Maillol. ■

Les Tuileries nous ramènent aux temps passés : les enfants pilotent leurs bateaux sur les bassins et, un peu partout dans le jardin, des fauteuils de métal peint en vert attendent les visiteurs.

Ponts et quais de Paris

À la tombée de la nuit, lorsqu'on se tient sur le pont de la Concorde et qu'on voit d'un côté l'Assemblée nationale s'illuminer et de l'autre la silhouette imposante de la Madeleine se dessiner au loin, on comprend pourquoi Paris est surnommée « la Ville lumière ». Et lorsqu'on flâne le long des quais en admirant ses trente-six autres ponts, on découvre à quel point tout converge en ces lieux : les amoureux et les voitures, mais aussi l'histoire, la politique et l'art. La splendeur et les traditions de la capitale se reflètent (au sens le plus littéral du terme) dans les eaux de la Seine.

L'île de la Cité est reliée à la ville par huit ponts, et l'île Saint-Louis par cinq. Enjambant le fleuve derrière Notre-Dame, une passerelle, le pont Saint-Louis, permet de se rendre de l'une à l'autre. Construit à la pointe est de l'île Saint-Louis, le pont Sully doit son nom au célèbre duc, ministre et ami d'Henri IV, qui a géré d'une main de maître les finances du royaume à la fin du XVIe siècle.

Le plus vieux et le plus récent

Le Pont-Neuf, majestueux ouvrage jeté entre les quais des Grands Augustins et de la Mégisserie, coupe l'extrémité ouest de l'île de la Cité. Ses douze arches en font l'un des plus beaux de Paris. Contrairement à ce que son nom indique, c'est aussi le plus ancien et le premier à être bordé de trottoirs et non d'habitations. La statue équestre en bronze de Henri IV, détruite à la Révolution, a été rétablie en 1818. Devenu le cœur de la ville, le Pont-Neuf fut longtemps un lieu de promenade à la mode. En 1985, l'artiste américain Christo l'a « emballé » de kilomètres de tissu ; plus tard, lors d'une fête de la Musique, le styliste japonais Kenzo l'a décoré de cent mille fleurs. Le pont Charles-de-Gaulle, inauguré en 1998, traverse la Seine entre le pont d'Austerlitz et le pont de Bercy.

Passerelles artistiques

Situé une centaine de mètres à l'ouest, le pont des Arts est une passerelle au plancher de bois sur laquelle les amoureux aiment se retrouver au coucher du soleil. Il s'étend dans l'axe de la coupole dorée de l'Institut de France, édifié par Louis Le Vau, le grand architecte du Louvre. Longue de 106 m, la passerelle de Solférino est le fruit d'un projet ambitieux qui visait à relier le Louvre au musée d'Orsay par le jardin des Tuileries et la Seine. Cet ouvrage moderne de métal est doté d'une passerelle à deux niveaux en bois exotique. C'est le seul auquel on puisse accéder depuis la rue et les rives du fleuve.

Le plus photogénique

Le pont Alexandre-III, qui porte le nom du tsar qui en a posé la première pierre en 1896 (voir p. 150), fait face aux Invalides. Il est chargé d'une profusion de chevaux ailés, de chérubins, de nymphes, d'épées et où l'or a été répandu à profusion (l'ensemble a été redoré en 1989 et repeint en 1997). C'est le plus connu et le plus photographié des ponts parisiens.

Les plus anglo-saxons

Les abords du pont de l'Alma et le tunnel qui les traverse attirent aujourd'hui les touristes désireux de voir l'endroit où Diana, princesse de Galles, est morte en 1997.

Le pont de l'Alma est décoré d'une statue de zouave, un soldat du Second Empire, qui permet de mesurer le niveau de la Seine. Lors de la grande crue de 1910, l'eau est montée à hauteur de sa barbe.

Au pied du pont, sur la rive droite, se dresse la flamme dorée de la statue de la Liberté, moulée sur l'original de New York. Un modèle réduit de la statue accueille les bateaux lorsqu'ils arrivent en vue du pont de Grenelle.

À l'ouest, la Seine reflète les étais métalliques du pont de Bir-Hakeim. Le film *Le Dernier Tango à Paris*, avec Marlon Brando, lui vaut un statut quasi mythique depuis les années 1970. ■

Page de droite, en haut : Le pont de la Tournelle (tel qu'il figure dans une peinture de 1646) a été reconstruit plusieurs fois en bois, avant d'être élevé en pierre en 1656.

Page de droite, en bas : Le Pont-Neuf est le plus vieux pont de Paris. Henri III en posa la première pierre en 1578, mais il ne fut inauguré que trente ans plus tard.

Ci-dessous: Des décennies durant, le zouave sculpté au pied du pont de l'Alma a permis de mesurer le niveau des eaux de la Seine.

Le musée de l'Orangerie

Carte p. 122
Jardin des Tuileries, place de la Concorde
01 42 97 48 16
9h45-17h15. Fermé mar.
€€
Concorde

Monet fut inspiré par des gravures japonaises représentant des fleurs, montrées lors des expositions universelles de 1878 et 1881. Il commença à peindre des nénuphars au tournant du siècle.

Les *Nymphéas* de Claude Monet ont fait la renommée du musée de l'Orangerie dans le monde entier. Mais il abrite aussi quelques autres chefs-d'œuvre, de l'époque impressionniste jusqu'aux années 1930, qui méritent le détour.

Construit en 1853, cet édifice était censé protéger des rigueurs de l'hiver les orangers qui bordaient les allées des Tuileries. Transformé en lieu d'exposition au début du XXe siècle, il a récemment fait l'objet d'importants travaux de rénovation. Il renferme la collection de Paul Guillaume, grand amateur d'œuvres de l'école de Paris, propriétaire d'une galerie dès 1914 et ardent défenseur d'avant-gardistes tels que Soutine ou Utrillo.

L'ensemble témoigne de la qualité visionnaire de son détenteur : on y voit 22 Soutines, 14 Cézannes, 28 Derains, 24 Renoirs, ainsi que des Matisses, Modiglianis, Utrillos et Picassos. En 1977, Domenica, l'épouse de Guillaume, fait don de ces œuvres à l'État, à condition que la collection ne soit pas dispersée.

Au rez-de-chaussée, les *Nymphéas* de Claude Monet (1840-1926) et sept autres grandes compositions constituent le clou de l'exposition. Elles reflètent le travail incessant de l'artiste pour rendre la lumière et ses subtiles tonalités. Après l'armistice de 1918, Monet lègue à l'État cet ensemble unique et choisit lui-même le lieu où les exposer après sa mort. Souvent surnommée « la chapelle Sixtine de l'impressionnisme », la série de salles ovales conçues pour abriter les œuvres est inaugurée en 1927, moins d'un an après la mort du peintre. ■

La Galerie nationale du Jeu de paume

Napoléon III fait élever cet édifice entre 1861 et 1862 pour y pratiquer le jeu de paume (l'ancêtre du tennis). Reconverti en lieu d'exposition en 1909, le bâtiment a été réquisitionné par les nazis qui voulaient y entreposer provisoirement les œuvres dont ils s'étaient emparés. Juste après la guerre, il devient l'un des plus beaux musées impressionnistes du monde. En 1986, la collection est transférée au musée d'Orsay. Depuis lors, ses vastes salles lumineuses accueillent des expositions temporaires d'artistes contemporains français et internationaux (Dubuffet, Tàpies, Arman...). ■

Carte p. 122
Jardin des Tuileries, place de la Concorde
01 47 03 12 50
Fermé lun.
€€
Concorde

www.jeudepaume.org

Le Palais-Royal

Le palais (et non les jardins qui s'étendent derrière lui) est élevé par le cardinal de Richelieu en 1636, d'où son premier nom de Palais-Cardinal. Louis XIV, enfant, y habite. Sous la Régence, Philippe d'Orléans y organise ses célèbres « soupers ». Louis-Philippe Joseph d'Orléans, à court d'argent, réduit le jardin et fait construire des bâtiments à arcades pour y abriter des boutiques qu'il loue. En 1784, le nouveau Palais-Royal est ouvert au public en grande pompe. Il ne tarde pas à attirer commerçants, intellectuels et amateurs d'établissements mal famés. En 1830, après être monté sur le trône, le très puritain roi Louis-Philippe ferme cet antre du vice, forçant les Parisiens épris de mode à s'en éloigner.

Incendié sous la Commune, puis restauré, l'ancien palais est aujourd'hui occupé par différentes institutions gouvernementales. De nombreuses personnalités (Colette au 9, rue de Beaujolais; Cocteau au 36, rue de Montpensier) ont habité ce havre de paix en plein cœur de Paris.

Il y a quelques années, l'érection des colonnes blanches et noires de Daniel Buren à l'extrémité sud du site a suscité une très vive controverse. Dans sa partie nord, le Grand Véfour, célèbre restaurant datant du XVIIIe siècle, attire toujours une clientèle fortunée.

Entre les deux, les jardins entourés d'arcades abritent des boutiques de livres anciens, de médailles militaires, de porcelaines et d'élégants salons de thé. ■

Carte p. 123
Place du Palais-Royal
Palais-Royal-Musée du Louvre

Les colonnes de Buren dans la cour principale du Palais-Royal ont fait couler beaucoup d'encre.

Médaillons de mosaïque et arabesques décorent de nombreuses arcades de la rue de Rivoli.

Autres sites à visiter

LA COMÉDIE-FRANÇAISE

Fondée en 1680 par Louis XIV et établie dans ces locaux depuis 1799, la compagnie théâtrale financée par l'État présente des pièces françaises classiques et modernes dans une des plus belles salles parisiennes.

Carte p. 123 Place Colette 01 44 58 15 15/www.comedie-française.fr Palais-Royal-Musée du Louvre

LA PLACE DES VICTOIRES

En 1686, le maréchal de La Feuillade, un brillant courtisan, demande à Hardouin-Mansart de dessiner une place pour servir d'écrin à une statue de Louis XIV. Fondue à la Révolution, une nouvelle statue a été érigée en 1822. Cette ravissante place abrite aujourd'hui des boutiques de créateurs de mode.

Carte p. 123 Louvre-Rivoli, Bourse

LA RUE DE RIVOLI

Toujours encombrée de touristes en raison de sa proximité avec le Louvre, cette artère a été percée sous Napoléon Ier, qui voulait doter la ville d'un autre axe est-ouest afin de réduire les encombrements de la rue Saint-Honoré. Achevée en 1835, la rue à arcades représentait une innovation car elle protégeait les piétons des intempéries et de la circulation. De nos jours, des boutiques de souvenirs occupent le rez-de-chaussée de la plupart des immeubles. De somptueux hôtels de luxe, tel le Meurice, s'y sont installés. La rue de Rivoli se prolonge jusqu'à l'Hôtel de Ville, en face duquel se trouve l'un des plus célèbres grands magasins de Paris, le BHV (pour Bazar de l'Hôtel de Ville).

Carte pp. 122-123 Concorde, Tuileries, Palais-Royal-Musée du Louvre

SAINT-GERMAIN-L'AUXERROIS

Érigée face à la colonnade du Louvre, cette église, paroisse des rois de France, se caractérise par son harmonie d'ensemble qui en fait un des grands monuments gothiques de la ville. Le porche, d'inspiration bourguignonne (vers 1435) est unique à Paris.

Carte p. 123 place du Louvre Louvre-Rivoli ■

Pour tous les événements historiques et les grandes commémorations, les Parisiens se retrouvent sur l'avenue des Champs-Élysées, longtemps appelée la Voie triomphale.

Les Champs-Élysées

Détail d'une statue ornant une des fontaines de la place de la Concorde.

Les Champs-Élysées

Si vous visitez Paris pour la première fois, ne manquez pas l'avenue des Champs-Élysées, symbole de la splendeur parisienne. Depuis l'Arc de Triomphe ou la place de la Concorde, ses lumières étincelantes s'offrent à vous. Ancien lieu de promenade de la haute société, ce sont désormais les cinémas, les fast-foods, les grands magasins de la culture et de la mode qui attirent une foule bigarrée sur ce qu'il est convenu d'appeler « la plus belle avenue du monde ».

Au XVIIe siècle, les Champs-Élysées étaient une avenue bordée sur chaque côté de quatre rangées de grands arbres. C'est sous le Second Empire (1852-1870) que ce quartier prit sa physionomie actuelle. De retour de Londres où il avait été impressionné par les travaux d'urbanisme du prince régent (le futur George IV) et de l'architecte Nash, Napoléon III décida de donner à la capitale française de l'espace et de la verdure. Il confia à Adolphe Alphand le soin de redessiner les Champs-Élysées.

Dans les jardins, celui-ci fit édifier des théâtres, des salles de concert et des panoramas, tableaux circulaires en trompe-l'œil qui représentaient souvent des scènes de batailles et donnaient aux promeneurs l'impression d'être au cœur de l'action. Certains des bâtiments existent toujours, comme le théâtre du Rond-Point, où s'installèrent au début des années 1980 Jean-Louis Barrault et Madeleine Renaud. Ne manquez pas dans ce quartier le théâtre de Marigny, et surtout le théâtre des Champs-Élysées (13, avenue Montaigne), construit en 1913 par les frères Perret et célèbre pour ses fresques de Bourdelle et ses sculptures de Denis. C'est encore l'une des meilleures salles de concert de Paris.

LE BERCEAU DE LA HAUTE COUTURE

La haute couture a été créée dans le VIIIe arrondissement de Paris par l'Anglais Charles Worth, sous le Second Empire, et reste fermement ancrée dans le quartier des Champs-Élysées. Paul Poiret, ancien disciple de Jacques Doucet (l'autre couturier innovateur de l'époque), ouvrit une boutique sur ce qui est devenu l'avenue Franklin D. Roosevelt. Son style révolutionnaire, qui donnait aux femmes une liberté de mouvement toute nouvelle, sonna le glas des corsets inconfortables et s'afficha dans les boutiques qui jalonnent encore l'avenue Montaigne et l'avenue George-V. Dans la rue du Faubourg-Saint-Honoré, parallèle aux Champs-Élysées, se trouvent de nombreuses galeries d'art et boutiques de luxe, dont Hermès au n° 24. Au n° 55 se dresse le palais de l'Élysée, résidence officielle du président de la République française depuis 1873. Ce palais initialement construit pour le comte d'Évreux, fut acheté par la maîtresse de Louis XV, Madame de Pompadour, qui y investit une fortune pour le faire agrandir et redécorer selon son goût raffiné. Il est ouvert au public à l'occasion de la Journée du Patrimoine.

LE PETIT ET LE GRAND PALAIS

Ces deux bâtiments ainsi que le pont Alexandre-III sont des vestiges de l'Exposition universelle de 1900. Le Petit Palais, récemment rénové, abrite la très importante collection d'art de la ville de Paris. Réouverture prévue fin 2005. ■

LES CHAMPS-ÉLYSÉES

❶ Théâtre des Champs-Élysées ❷ Théâtre du Rond-Point ❸ Théâtre Marigny ❹ Palais de l'Élysée ❺ Hermès ❻ Louis Vuitton ❼ Le Lido ❽ Centre national de la photographie ❾ Embarcadère des bateaux-mouches ❿ Maxim's ⓫ Musée Nissim-de-Camondo ⓬ Ambassade de Belgique ⓭ Ambassade du Canada

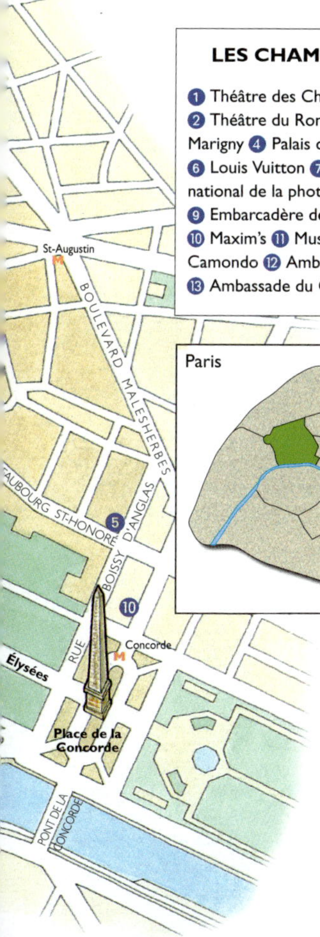

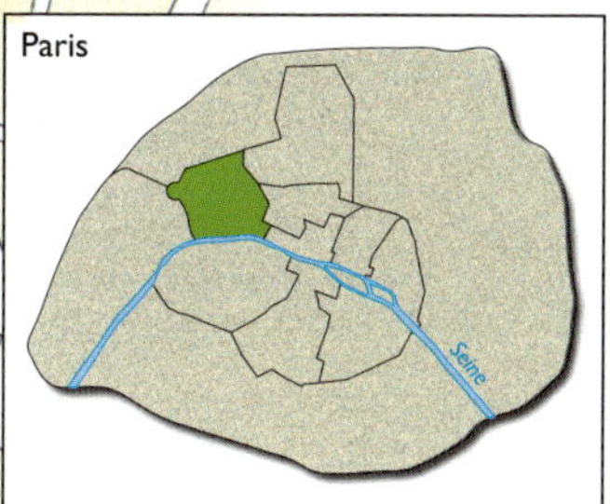

La place de la Concorde

Carte p. 145
Concorde

Principal lieu des exécutions capitales sous la Révolution, l'actuelle place de la Concorde est une vaste esplanade que de nombreux aménagements ont peu à peu modelée. Elle offre une vue spectaculaire sur les Champs-Élysées et l'Arc de Triomphe.

L'obélisque est flanqué de deux fontaines : au nord, la navigation fluviale, au sud, la navigation maritime. Des statues, symbolisant les huit plus grandes villes de France, sont placées sur les guérites d'angle.

L'actuelle place de la Concorde a été réalisée en 1757, par l'architecte Jacques Ange Gabriel, pour recevoir la statue équestre de Louis XV.

Contrairement aux autres places de Paris (comme la place Vendôme et celle des Victoires) fermées sur elles-mêmes, celle-ci laisse intacte la vue sur les Champs-Élysées, sur le jardin des Tuileries et sur la Seine. Ses deux palais à colonnades et frontons antiques, qui abritent aujourd'hui l'hôtel Crillon et le ministère de la Marine (où Marie-Antoinette possédait autrefois un appartement secret), y sont des œuvres exemplaires de l'architecture du Grand Siècle.

La statue de Louis XV fut détruite en 1792 et la place, qui portait jusqu'alors le nom du roi, fut rebaptisée place de la Révolution. Pendant la Terreur, plus de 1 200 personnes y furent guillotinées, dont les souverains Louis XVI et Marie-Antoinette, ainsi que Robespierre.

L'OBÉLISQUE

Après avoir changé de nom plusieurs fois, la place devint la place de la Concorde. Louis-Philippe y fit ériger deux fontaines et des statues représentant les principales villes de France et fit placer en son centre un obélisque vieux de 3 300 ans (le jumeau de celui qui orne l'entrée du temple de Louqsor), offert à la France en 1829 par le vice-roi d'Égypte.

En 1836, des milliers de Parisiens assistèrent à l'érection de l'obélisque par l'ingénieur Lebas et son équipe de 120 hommes. Les différentes phases de cet exploit sont gravées sur le socle de l'obélisque. *Les Chevaux de Marly*, statues de Coustou, encadrent l'entrée des Champs-Élysées. Mais ce ne sont que des copies, les originaux sont au Louvre.

Traverser la place pour se rapprocher de l'Obélisque nécessite un certain courage ; il vous faudra en effet franchir un flot quasi ininterrompu de voitures. ■

L'avenue des Champs-Élysées

De la place de la Concorde au Rond-Point, l'avenue est bordée d'allées plantées d'arbres tandis que du Rond-Point à l'Arc de Triomphe, les « Champs » deviennent une vaste avenue commerciale.

En 1667, lorsque André Le Nôtre trace les Champs-Élysées, il les conçoit comme le prolongement des jardins des Tuileries. Les champs et les sous-bois alentour fourmillaient alors de truands...

Pendant l'occupation de Paris qui suivit la défaite napoléonienne à Waterloo en 1815, les armées coalisées se répartirent la ville. Les Britanniques s'installèrent dans les jardins des Tuileries et sur la place de la Concorde et les Russes, le long des Champs-Élysées. Le noble alignement d'arbres de Le Nôtre fut sévèrement mis à mal par la soldatesque.

Vers 1830, l'architecte Jacques Hittorff commença à aménager cette zone inhabitée de Paris. Plus de 1 200 lampes à gaz furent installées pour éclairer jardins à la française, fontaines, restaurants et cafés-concerts. Deux grands restaurants sont les vestiges de cette époque : Ledoyen et Laurent. Les jardins du palais de l'Élysée (la résidence présidentielle) bordent le côté nord de l'avenue Gabriel. Juste avant le Rond-Roint (sur le côté droit), se tient le marché aux timbres (mer. et sam. mat.).

Après le Rond-Point, s'étend « la plus belle avenue du monde », passage obligé de tous les grands événements (victoires militaires, politiques ou sportives, défilé du 14 juillet, arrivée du Tour de France, départ du marathon...) Sur de larges trottoirs constamment entretenus par des « hommes en vert » juchés sur des engins improbables, la foule descend et remonte les Champs-Élysées avec, çà et là, des points de fixation : la queue pour accéder à une des nombreuses salles de cinéma, la vitrine d'une boutique à la mode, un fast-food plein quel que soit le moment de la journée. Cette avenue attire une foule bigarrée de flâneurs, touristes d'un jour venus de banlieue pour voir et être vus, cinéphiles, couples endimanchés, amoureux enlacés, cadres dynamiques, visiteurs des antipodes... ■

Carte pp. 144-145

Ⓜ Concorde, Champs-Élysées-Clemenceau, Franklin D. Roosevelt, George-V, Charles-de-Gaulle-Étoile

En 1871, lorsque Bismarck entra à la tête des troupes prussiennes dans Paris, l'avenue des Champs-Élysées l'impressionna tant qu'il décida de faire construire une avenue semblable à Berlin, qui porte aujourd'hui le nom de Kurfürstendamm.

La mode française

La France est la capitale mondiale du luxe, notamment dans les domaines de la mode et de la parfumerie. Malgré la concurrence des couturiers new-yorkais, londoniens et milanais, Paris reste le siège de la haute couture et tient à conserver sa réputation.

Paris, capitale de la mode

Bien que l'avenue des Champs-Élysées se soit laissée massivement envahir par les marques franchisées du prêt-à-porter international, le VIIIe arrondissement, de l'avenue Montaigne au faubourg Saint-Honoré, mérite plus que jamais son surnom de « triangle d'or ». L'avenue Montaigne est à elle seule un magnifique écrin pour la haute couture parisienne, bordée d'arbres et de boutiques de luxe parmi lesquelles celles de Dior, Chanel, Ungaro, Prada et Helmut Lang. En passant par l'avenue Matignon et ses galeries d'antiquités aux allures de musées, vous rejoindrez un autre lieu de la mode parisienne : la rue du Faubourg-Saint-Honoré.

À l'angle de la rue d'Aguesseau, le cavalier majestueux dressé sur le toit de l'incontournable maison mère d'Hermès veille sur le luxe français. Face à lui, la maison Lanvin et son Café bleu habillent et restaurent les hôtes des ambassades voisines, et Cartier a ouvert une boutique à la façade d'ardoise dessinée par J.-M. Wilmotte. Aucun des grands noms de la mode ne manque à l'appel de cette rue prestigieuse où Jaques Fath, Sonia Rykiel, Christian Lacroix, Versace, Gucci, Chloé et bien d'autres encore offrent aux regards des passants leurs précieuses vitrines.

À quelques pas de là, près de la place Vendôme et ses bijoutiers, l'hôtel Costes accueille mannequins et célébrités. Le restaurant, décoré par José Garcia, mérite qu'on s'y arrête avant d'affronter quelques mètres plus loin la « faune » de la boutique Colette, temple moderne de la consommation qui fait et défait la mode au rythme de ses vitrines et de ses choix d'accessoires.

« La mode est pour la France ce que les mines du Pérou sont pour l'Espagne », disait

Défilé de la collection Printemps-Été 2004 de Sonia Rykiel.

Colbert, preuve que la mode est bel et bien ancrée depuis des siècles dans la culture française. Seules 10 maisons bénéficient de l'appellation juridique « haute couture » en 2005. Celle-ci impose d'employer 20 salariés participant à la production ou à la création, de présenter deux collections par an à Paris, chacune

Synonyne d'élégance, la maison Chanel que dirige Karl Lagerfeld ne cesse de se renouveler.

composée d'au moins 25 modèles qui doivent êtres réalisés à la main et sur mesure. Les collections de Balmain, Chanel, Dior, Lacroix, Versace, Ungaro, Féraud, Givenchy, Hanae Mori, Jean-Paul Gaultier, Scherrer, Torrente, Yves Saint Laurent attirent à Paris chaque saison plus de 1 000 journalistes français et étrangers et génèrent 1 500 pages rédactionnelles dans la presse du monde entier.

Entre art et consommation, la mode est plus que jamais à la page et sa démocratisation n'a plus de frontières. Fini le temps où l'on entrait chez Chanel en rougissant. Les marques se sont affranchies et les couturiers ont su se diversifier en développant en parallèle la création de prêt-à-porter, de parfums et d'accessoires qui constituent la quasi-totalité de leur chiffre d'affaires. Aujourd'hui la « mode » n'est plus synonyme de « mode française » ; le langage est le même à Tokyo, Londres, Milan ou New York. Les stylistes britanniques règnent en maîtres sur la création de maisons bien françaises comme John Galliano chez Dior ou Alexander McQueen chez Givenchy. Même si Hambourg ou Londres ont supplanté Paris en termes de créativité, si Milan ou New York sont les places financières de la mode internationale, Marie-Antoinette et ses robes extravagantes, Coco Chanel et sa « petite robe noire », la beauté de la ville ainsi que la réputation d'élégance et de chic des Parisiennes font de la ville la capitale incontestable des amoureux de la mode, du luxe et de la haute couture. ■

Le pont Alexandre-III.

Le Grand et le Petit Palais

Galeries nationales du Grand Palais
- Carte p. 144
- 3, avenue du Général-Eisenhower
- 01 44 13 17 17 wwww.rmn.fr/galeriesnationalesdugrandpalais
- Fermé mar.
- Selon les expositions
- Champs-Élysées-Clemenceau

Palais de la Découverte
- Av. Franklin-D.-Roosevelt
- 01 56 43 20 20 www.palais-decouverte.fr
- Fermé lun.
- €€
- Champs-Élysées-Clemenceau

Petit Palais
- Av. Winston- Churchill
- 01 44 51 19 31
- €€
- Champs-Élysées-Clemenceau

Après le succès de l'Exposition universelle de 1889, il fut immédiatement décidé d'en préparer une autre. L'exposition de 1900 nous a légué deux palais conçus en hommage à l'art français, véritables témoignages de la Belle Époque.

LE GRAND PALAIS

Le Grand Palais (1897-1900) est une immense structure de fer et de verre ornée d'une façade de pierre due à Charles Girault. La sculpture de bronze représentant le char d'Apollon tiré par des chevaux volants, la ferronnerie extravagante et l'immense verrière sont typiques du style Art nouveau de l'époque.

Depuis son inauguration jusque dans les années 1960, le Grand Palais a accueilli de nombreuses expositions et salons officiels comme le Salon d'automne, et jusque plus récemment le Salon du livre, le Salon de l'automobile et la Foire internationale d'art contemporain… En 1964, André Malraux, ministre de la Culture du général de Gaulle, décida d'y créer les Galeries nationales d'expositions temporaires. Le but était de présenter des œuvres majeures illustrant les diverses formes de la création.

Le **Palais de la Découverte,** sous le même toit, est un espace de vulgarisation scientifique. Son planétarium et un grand nombre d'expériences permettent à tous de mieux comprendre les lois de la science.

LE PETIT PALAIS

Édifié à la même époque et par le même architecte que le « Grand », le Petit Palais était destiné à accueillir la rétrospective de l'art français au cours de l'Exposition universelle de 1900. Ce palais majestueux, avec sa colonnade ionique et son vaste porche, devrait abriter dès sa réouverture de prestigieuses collections : tableaux flamands et hollandais ; objets d'art de la période 1900 (verres de Gallé notamment) et des porcelaines chinoises.

LE PONT ALEXANDRE-III

Ce pont de structure métallique et orné de sculptures dorées est dédié à l'amitié franco-russe. Le tsar Nicolas II posa la première pierre en 1896. Il ouvre une belle perspective sur l'esplanade des Invalides. ■

L'Arc de Triomphe

La place entourant l'Arc de Triomphe demeure l'Étoile pour tous les Parisiens en raison des douze avenues qui partent de son centre. Pourtant, elle a été rebaptisée « place Charles-de-Gaulle » en 1970. L'Arc de Triomphe, symbole de la puissance militaire napoléonienne, est un monument incontournable, qui domine, du Louvre à la grande Arche de la Défense, la plus longue perspective de Paris.

Carte p. 144
Place Charles-de-Gaulle
01 55 37 73 77
€€ (musée compris)
Charles-de-Gaulle-Étoile

En 1806, Napoléon confia à l'architecte Jean-François Chalgrin la réalisation d'un monument en l'honneur de la Grande Armée et de la victoire d'Austerlitz. Conforme à la grandeur napoléonienne, l'Arc de Triomphe, haut de 50 m et large de 45 m, est le plus grand édifice de ce genre qui ait jamais été construit. Son édification s'acheva en 1836.

Parmi ses bas-reliefs, vous noterez le célèbre *Départ des volontaires,* dit *La Marseillaise,* de François Rude, représentant un personnage ailé qui conduit les soldats à la bataille. Ses frises illustrent le départ (côté est) et le retour (côté ouest) des armées françaises.

Les douze avenues rayonnantes qui entourent l'Arc de Triomphe et les douze hôtels qui flanquent la place ne faisaient pas partie du projet initial. Ces aménagements ont été réalisés sur l'initiative du baron Eugène Haussmann (voir p. 160). Le résultat est impressionnant, y compris sous un aspect que ce dernier n'avait sans doute pas du tout envisagé : les douze avenues qui convergent vers cette place créent aujourd'hui d'énormes embouteillages.

Au fil des ans, la symbolique de l'Arc de Triomphe s'est enrichie d'autres grands moments de l'histoire de France. Avant d'être déposées aux Invalides, les cendres de Napoléon passèrent sous la voûte, tout comme le cortège funèbre de Victor Hugo. Le 26 août 1944, le général de Gaulle s'inclina sur la tombe du Soldat inconnu en présence de centaines de milliers de Parisiens. Par ce geste, il effaça magistralement l'image des défilés impies des troupes allemandes sous l'Occupation.

Un passage souterrain situé du côté des numéros pairs des Champs-Élysées permet d'accéder sans danger à l'arche, dont le dernier étage offre une vue panoramique sur la perspective Grande Arche de la Défense – Pyramide du Louvre. En sous-sol, se trouve un petit musée abritant une exposition sur la construction du monument et quelques objets et documents concernant Napoléon et la Première Guerre mondiale. ■

Sur l'Arc de Triomphe sont gravés les noms des plus grandes victoires militaires de l'histoire française et ceux des 666 généraux qui se battirent durant les guerres de la Révolution et de l'Empire.

Autres sites à visiter

L'AVENUE MONTAIGNE

L'avenue Montaigne, où était donné l'un des plus célèbres bals populaires au milieu des années 1800, est maintenant bordée de boutiques de luxe, d'hôtels somptueux et de maisons de haute couture dont celles de Christian Lacroix ou de Christian Dior. À juste titre elle pourrait prendre le surnom de sa rivale, « la plus belle avenue du monde ». carte p. 144 Ⓜ Franklin D. Roosevelt, Alma Marceau

LA CATHÉDRALE ALEXANDRE-NEVSKY

Cette cathédrale orthodoxe russe surmontée de dômes en forme de bulbe a été bâtie en 1861 selon un plan en croix grecque. L'intérieur est orné de fresques et d'icônes superbes, et le tympan est couvert de mosaïques sur fond doré. carte p. 144 12, rue Daru 01 42 27 37 34 ouvert mar. ou ven. 15 h-17 h Ⓜ Ternes, Courcelles

LE MUSÉE JACQUEMART-ANDRÉ

Ce magnifique musée est situé dans l'hôtel particulier d'Édouard André et de son épouse, Nélie Jacquemart, qui à sa mort l'a légué à l'Institut de France. Il est le résultat de toute une vie, celle du couple qui a consacré son temps et sa fortune à constituer sa collection d'objets d'art. Célèbre pour ses œuvres de la Renaissance italienne, cette collection comprend une gigantesque fresque de Tiepolo, *Henri III reçu à Venise par le doge Contarini*, et le *Saint Georges tuant le dragon* d'Uccello. Vous pourrez également admirer quantité de peintures françaises et flamandes, notamment *Les Pèlerins d'Emmaüs, Amalia Van Solms* et *Docteur Tholinx* de Rembrandt. Rénové en 1997, le bâtiment illustre parfaitement le type d'architecture en vogue au XIXe siècle. Outre les trésors qu'il recèle, ce musée présente l'intérêt d'avoir conservé dans leur disposition d'origine les collections des André. carte p. 144 158, boulevard Haussmann 01 45 62 11 59/www.musee-jacquemart-andré.com €€ Ⓜ Miromesnil, Saint-Philippe du Roule

LE PARC MONCEAU

Ce parc n'est pas vraiment tout proche des Champs-Élysées mais reste dans l'esprit Second Empire, époque à laquelle le quartier est devenu à la mode. Avec ses espaces verts pittoresques, ses grottes, ses rocailles et ses folies extravagantes (maisons de plaisance), il a conservé une partie de son aura bourgeoise du XIXe siècle. Au 63, de la rue de Monceau, ne manquez pas le **musée Nissim-de-Camondo** qui, dans un hôtel particulier construit à la manière du Trianon, abrite une belle collection de mobilier et de tableaux des maîtres du XVIIIe siècle. carte p. 144 boulevard de Courcelles Ⓜ Monceau, Courcelles ■

En 1769, le duc de Chartres achète un hectare de terre dans la plaine Monceau. Ce sera le début de la « folie » de Chartres, transformée en parc à l'anglaise en 1861.

Les Grands Boulevards, de la Madeleine à la Bastille, furent créés par Louis XIV à l'emplacement de l'enceinte fortifiée. Ils longent l'Opéra, les grands magasins et plusieurs théâtres et salles de spectacles.

Les Grands Boulevards

Détail ornemental de la façade de l'Opéra-Garnier.

Les Grands Boulevards

Les Grands Boulevards commencent près du quartier de la Madeleine, à l'ouest, et vont jusqu'à la Bastille, à l'est. Ces grands axes constituent un centre culturel et commercial qui comprend l'Opéra-Garnier, des théâtres, des galeries, des maisons de couture, des boutiques de luxe, des épiceries fines et des cafés.

« *Là est la vie !* », déclara Honoré de Balzac à propos des Grands Boulevards. Le lieu, très couru au XIXe siècle après la fermeture des tripots et des maisons closes du Palais-Royal par Louis-Philippe, regroupait à l'ouest la bourgeoisie, tandis que les artisans et la bohème se rassemblaient à l'est. Les Grands Boulevards (« boulevard », du nom donné en langage militaire au terre-plein d'un rempart) furent créés sur l'ordre de Louis XIV de 1660 à 1705 après une série de victoires militaires qui rendirent les fortifications de la ville, déjà en fort mauvais état, inutiles. Une partie des remparts de Charles V (entre la Bastille et la porte Saint-Denis), de Charles IX et de Louis XIII (entre la porte Saint-Denis et l'actuelle Madeleine) fut rasée et les douves comblées pour construire de larges voies publiques.

Le boulevard des Capucines, le boulevard des Italiens et l'avenue de l'Opéra convergent vers l'Opéra-Garnier (voir p. 157), l'un des plus grands opéras du monde, mis en valeur par la place de l'Opéra conçue par le baron Haussmann (voir pp. 160-161). L'édifice est également l'une des plus belles illustrations du style Napoléon III. Dans le quartier, l'empereur réinstalla sur la colonne Vendôme, au centre de la place Vendôme (voir p. 156), une statue de son oncle (Napoléon Ier) vêtu à la façon de Jules César. La Grèce antique inspira également plusieurs édifices, réalisés à l'initiative de Napoléon Ier, dont l'église de la Madeleine, temple à la gloire de la Grande Armée, et la Bourse, temple de la finance.

Le quartier de la Madeleine (voir p. 156), où commencent les Grands Boulevards, est devenu quant à lui un temple du luxe. La rue de la Paix et la place Vendôme, lieux aristocratiques et tranquilles jusqu'à la fin du XIXe siècle, attirèrent ensuite des joailliers et des couturiers, dont l'Anglais Charles Frédéric Worth, qui fut le premier à présenter ses créations sur un modèle vivant – sa femme. Jeanne Lanvin, autre pionnière de la mode, ouvrit une boutique au n° 22, de la rue du Faubourg-Saint-Honoré, en 1890, où elle créa des vêtements pour sa fille.

Nombre d'artistes fréquentèrent les Grands Boulevards. La première exposition impressionniste eut lieu au 35, boulevard des Capucines, et les courts métrages des frères Lumière furent projetés pour la première fois au n° 14 (actuel hôtel Scribe) du même boulevard. Des musiciens tels que Lully (compositeur de la Cour qui établit l'opéra français au XVIIe siècle) vécurent non loin des anciennes salles de musique de Paris, comme la salle Louvois qui fut démolie par Charles X après l'assassinat, en 1820, de son fils, le duc de Berry, au terme d'une représentation du *Carnaval de Venise*.

À la place de cet ancien opéra, se trouve désormais l'élégant square Louvois, près de l'ancienne Bibliothèque nationale, rue de Richelieu (voir p. 159). De l'autre côté de la rue, vous pourrez visiter les galeries Vivienne et Colbert, deux des passages couverts construits au XIXe siècle.

La place Vendôme réunit les plus grands joailliers du monde, le mythique hôtel Ritz et le ministère de la Justice. Plusieurs épiceries de luxe, notamment Fauchon, Hédiard et la Maison de la Truffe, sont rassemblées autour de la Madeleine et de son célèbre marché aux fleurs. ■

LES GRANDS BOULEVARDS

1 Église Notre-Dame-de-l'Assomption
2 La Bourse 3 Passage des Panoramas
4 Passage Jouffroy 5 Passage Brady
6 Les Galeries Lafayette 7 Le Printemps
8 Olympia 9 Hôtel Drouot 10 Théâtre des Variétés 11 Gare Saint-Lazare
12 Consistoire de Paris 13 Hôtel Ritz
14 Opéra-Comique

L'église de la Madeleine

Carte p. 154
place de la Madeleine
01 44 51 69 00
Madeleine

L'église Sainte-Marie-Madeleine, appelée communément « la Madeleine », est l'un des monuments les plus célèbres de Paris. Sa façade est composée de 52 colonnes corinthiennes plus hautes (20 m) que celles de n'importe quel temple grec ou romain. Commencée en 1764, suivant les plans d'aménagement de la place Louis-XV (actuelle place de la Concorde) par Jacques Ange Gabriel, l'église fut ensuite rasée pour être remplacée par un bâtiment conçu sur le modèle du Panthéon. La Révolution interrompit les travaux, qui reprirent en 1806, lorsque Napoléon Ier décida de bâtir un temple à la gloire de la Grande Armée. Il en passa commande à Vignon. La structure existante fut une nouvelle fois détruite et l'édifice actuel s'éleva lentement. Enfin, en 1814, Louis XVIII rendit au monument sa fonction d'origine et le dédia à son frère guillotiné, Louis XVI. L'intérieur, faiblement éclairé par les trois coupoles aplaties qui surmontent les trois travées de la nef et une abside semi-circulaire, renferme quelques tableaux et sculptures de maîtres. Ne manquez pas dans le narthex *Le Baptême du Christ* (sur l'extrême gauche), chef-d'œuvre de François Rude. En plus du service religieux habituel, cette église accueille de nombreux concerts de musique, classique ou non. ■

La place Vendôme

Carte p. 154
Opéra

Conçue par Louvois pour rivaliser avec la place des Vosges et accueillir la statue équestre de Louis XIV par François Girardon, la place Vendôme, anciennement place Louis-le-Grand, fut construite par Boffrand et Hardouin-Mansart, de 1685 à 1720.

La place Vendôme accueille les plus grands joailliers (ici, Chaumet).

En 1792, la statue royale fut détruite et remplacée dix-huit ans plus tard par la colonne Vendôme en hommage aux campagnes victorieuses de Napoléon. Les bas-reliefs de bronze ornant la colonne de pierre, inspirée de la colonne de Trajan, à Rome, furent réalisés à l'aide des 1 200 canons saisis lors de la bataille d'Austerlitz (1805). Pendant la Commune, le peintre Gustave Courbet dirigea une manifestation qui mit à bas la colonne. Arrêté, jugé, il fut contraint de financer sa reconstruction. La statue triomphante de Napoléon en César n'a pas bougé depuis.

Ouvert sur la place en 1898, le Ritz fut le premier hôtel à disposer de baignoires individuelles. Francis Scott et Zelda Fitzgerald y vécurent dans les années 1920. Coco Chanel en fit sa « maison » pendant plus de trente ans et mourut dans ses murs. Plus récemment, c'est en ce lieu que la princesse Diana passa sa dernière soirée avec Dodi Al-Fayed. ■

L'Opéra-Garnier

Le palais Garnier, entrepris sous Napoléon III et achevé sous la IIIe République, accueille essentiellement des ballets, les opéras étant joués en priorité à l'Opéra-Bastille. Hanté par le souvenir de l'attentat dont il fut la cible en 1858, rue Le Peletier, l'empereur décida de transférer l'opéra, qui se trouvait dans la même rue, sur un site plus ouvert et plus sûr. L'architecte Charles Garnier, alors âgé de 35 ans, remporta le concours pour l'édification du nouveau bâtiment. Il affronta 169 concurrents, dont Viollet-le-Duc.

Carte p. 154
place de l'Opéra
01 40 01 17 89. Musée: 01 53 79 37 40
Billets et réservation: 08 92 89 90 90
Fermé aux visiteurs dim. et tous les autres jours en cas de représentations en matinée
€€
Opéra

www.opera-de-paris.fr

Lors de l'inauguration de l'Opéra par Mac-Mahon en 1875, l'impératrice Eugénie émit quelques réserves: « *De quel style s'agit-il? Ce n'est ni grec ni Louis XVI.* » Ce à quoi Garnier aurait répondu: « *Mais, Majesté, c'est… du Napoléon III!* »

Baroque, éclectique et particulièrement extravagant avec son dôme surmonté d'un Apollon et ses statues de femmes portant des lampadaires, l'édifice est en effet typique de l'architecture du Second Empire. Le groupe sculpté de Carpeaux, *La Danse*, situé à droite de l'entrée et dont l'original se trouve désormais au musée d'Orsay, fut qualifié d'« ignoble saturnale » et considéré comme un « outrage à la pudeur ». Le pavillon de l'Empereur (rue Scribe), reconnaissable aux nombreux aigles dont il est orné, comportait un accès direct à la loge impériale, qui abrite aujourd'hui un musée et une bibliothèque.

L'Opéra, aux boiseries dorées, aux sols de marbre et aux murs ornés de fresques, possède un foyer et un escalier grandioses. La salle de cinq niveaux ne compte que 2 131 places, dont certaines sont aveugles, mais la scène peut accueillir jusqu'à 450 artistes. Il est possible d'admirer le plafond peint par Chagall en 1964, lorsqu'il n'y a ni représentation ni répétition.

Vous pouvez aussi vous laisser tenter par le miel issu des ruches situées sur les toits de l'Opéra. Il est en vente à la boutique… à prix d'or. ■

En plus d'abriter le *Fantôme* de Gaston Leroux, l'Opéra-Garnier eut droit à un élevage de truites dans son lac souterrain.

Une promenade sur les Grands Boulevards

En flânant sur les Grands Boulevards, anciennes promenades bordées d'arbres réalisées au XVIIe siècle, vous vous imprégnerez peu à peu de l'atmosphère qui y régnait.

Débutez votre promenade place de l'Opéra, en partant du mythique Café de la Paix, construit au XIXe siècle par Charles Garnier, où Émile Zola et Guy de Maupassant avaient leurs habitudes. Visitez ensuite l'Opéra-Garnier ❶ (voir p. 157).

En sortant de l'Opéra, prenez le boulevard des Capucines, à droite. C'est à l'hôtel Scribe, au n° 14, que les frères Lumière effectuèrent la première projection de leurs courts métrages, dont *L'Arrivée d'un train en gare de La Ciotat*. Au n° 28, l'Olympia, une des premières salles de concert parisiennes, accueillit, entre autres, Édith Piaf, Jacques Brel et les Beatles.

Continuez tout droit sur le boulevard des Capucines jusqu'à l'église de la Madeleine ❷ (voir p. 156). Sur le côté est, ne manquez pas les toilettes publiques de style Art nouveau, lambrissées et ornées de vitraux et de céramiques aux motifs floraux jaunes et verts (fermées entre 11 h 30 et 12 h 30). Faites le tour de l'église en passant par le marché aux fleurs pour aller chez Fauchon, au n° 26 de la place de la Madeleine, l'épicerie fine la plus célèbre de Paris. Au n° 21, de l'autre côté de l'église, Hédiard propose de façon plus discrète des fruits et des légumes exotiques, dont six différentes sortes de poivres, d'excellents thés et les premiers fruits de la saison. Également sur la place de la Madeleine, la Maison de la Truffe (n° 19) et Caviar Kaspia (n° 17), renommé pour son caviar et sa vodka au poivre.

Retournez devant la façade de l'église. Marcel Proust vécut au n° 9, de la place de la Madeleine, au-dessus de l'actuel restaurant Lucas Carton, aussi célèbre pour sa cuisine que pour ses boiseries Art nouveau attribuées à Majorelle. Descendez ensuite la rue Royale ❸ jusqu'à la cité Berryer, qui abrite un bon caviste. Découvrez au passage le salon de thé Ladurée, le restaurant Maxim's, le fleuriste Lachaume, la cristallerie Lalique et l'orfèvrerie Christofle, fleurons du luxe français.

Prenez la rue Saint-Honoré, à gauche. Entrez au Nain bleu (n° 408), le magasin de jouets le plus chic de Paris. Plus loin, sur la droite, se dresse l'église Notre-Dame-de-l'Assomption ❹ (l'église polonaise de Paris), bel édifice du XVIIe siècle. Poursuivez et coupez par le passage situé juste avant la rue de Castiglione, à gauche, pour rejoindre la place Vendôme, qui mène à la rue de la Paix. Cette rue, prestigieuse dès sa création (début du XIXe siècle), s'appelait rue Napoléon avant d'être rebaptisée lors de la signature du traité d'Amiens en 1802.

La galerie Vivienne date de 1823. Elle est éclairée par des verrières et bordée de commerces.

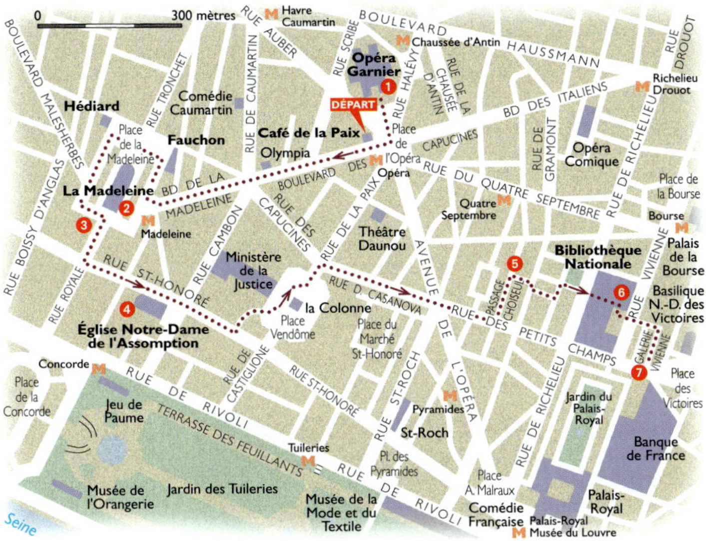

Au début de la rue de la Paix, prenez la rue Danielle-Casanova. À votre droite dans la rue du Marché-Saint-Honoré, une construction de verre et d'acier abrite quelques galeries et des boutiques de luxe. Continuez jusqu'à la rue des Petits-Champs et, au n° 40, prenez le passage de Choiseul **5** sur votre gauche. Construite en 1825 par l'architecte Tavernier, cette galerie au toit de verre présente avant tout un intérêt architectural.

Prenez le passage Sainte-Anne, à droite, puis la rue Cherubini pour rejoindre le square Louvois. Traversez la rue de Richelieu et entrez dans la cour de l'ancienne Bibliothèque nationale (*58, rue de Richelieu, tél. : 01 53 79 59 59, fermé dim.*) **6**. Des expositions temporaires permettent d'admirer certains des trésors de cette bibliothèque, fondée à partir des collections royales en 1666.

Les livres ont été transférés à la Bibliothèque nationale de France-François-Mitterrand, (située le long de la Seine dans le XIIIe arrondissement), mais les collections spécialisées, les dessins, les gravures et la bibliothèque d'histoire de l'Art s'y trouvent encore. Tournez à droite et entrez dans le bâtiment principal où vous découvrirez, à travers des portes vitrées, la spectaculaire salle de lecture édifiée autour d'une fine structure de fonte par Henri Labrouste en 1868. Suivez le couloir du bâtiment principal et sortez par les jardins. Traversez la rue Vivienne et gagnez la galerie du même nom **7**, ouverte en 1823. Dotée d'un somptueux décor, elle abrite des boutiques de prestige dont un salon de thé (A Priori Thé) qui propose chaque dimanche un brunch. La galerie Colbert, parallèle à la première, abrite le restaurant Grand Colbert, à la décoration de style Belle Époque. ■

Voir aussi carte pp. 154-155
➤ Café de la Paix, place de l'Opéra
2,6 km
3 heures
➤ Galerie Vivienne, rue Vivienne

À NE PAS MANQUER

- Palais Garnier
- Toilettes Art nouveau
- Hédiard
- Ancienne Bibliothèque nationale
- Galerie Vivienne

Il est conseillé de faire cette promenade au cours de la journée afin de pouvoir profiter des boutiques des passages qui ferment vers 19 h.

Le renouveau urbain au XIXe siècle

À l'aube du XIXe siècle, la France entre dans une ère de révolution industrielle qui transforme la société et modifie complètement le visage de Paris.

L'impact de la révolution industrielle

Le développement du chemin de fer contribua à la métamorphose de la ville. Il fallait non seulement régler le problème de l'implantation des gares et de leur accès aux points névralgiques de la capitale, mais aussi canaliser le flux croissant de visiteurs éphémères. Les architectes intégrèrent ces gares, de vastes bâtiments industriels, en utilisant de nouveaux matériaux, comme la fonte et la feuille de verre. Le métal était léger, résistant et flexible, et le verre laissait passer une lumière uniforme. Les structures de fer et de verre étaient donc parfaites pour les musées, les gares et les marchés. Les premiers passages de Paris furent créés sur ce modèle, tout comme les Halles.

Au milieu du XIXe siècle, alors que la révolution industrielle était à son apogée, de nombreux travailleurs affluèrent dans la capitale. Lorsque Louis Napoléon Bonaparte accéda au pouvoir, en 1848, la population de Paris avait doublé et la ville connaissait de sérieux problèmes de logement, d'approvisionnement en eau, de ramassage des ordures et de transport. Outre ces exigences sanitaires, Napoléon avait également une ambition esthétique : il voulait faire de la capitale la vitrine de son règne. S'inspirant des grands parcs et des larges avenues de Londres, où il avait vécu en exil, il envisagea alors un nouveau Paris, dont il confia la réalisation au préfet de la Seine, Georges Eugène Haussmann. Ces travaux d'aménagement allaient, par la même occasion, détruire de vieux quartiers parisiens, véritables foyers révolutionnaires, et faciliter, par de larges avenues, l'intervention de la troupe contre d'éventuelles barricades. En 1830 et en 1848, les rebelles parisiens avaient, en effet, pu élever, dans un dédale de ruelles, des barricades en plein cœur de la ville, provoquant ainsi la chute de Charles X et de Louis-Philippe.

Portrait du baron Haussmann (1809-1891), qui occupa le poste de préfet de la Seine pendant dix-sept ans.

Les transformations d'Haussmann

Le projet d'Haussmann de relier les grandes gares par de larges avenues coïncida avec une nouvelle vision de Paris. La bourgeoisie montante voulait vivre, travailler et se détendre dans le centre de la ville. Haussmann lui donna accès aux théâtres, aux musées, aux bibliothèques et aux magasins. Toute la structure urbaine fut démolie et remodelée. Les conséquences sociales de ce bouleversement furent encore plus brutales. Ceux qui n'étaient pas assez riches pour se loger dans les nouveaux quartiers furent refoulés à la périphérie de Paris ou dans les faubourgs.

L'un des principaux objectifs visait à faciliter la circulation, ce qu'Haussmann parvint à obtenir en taillant de larges artères à travers la ville (notamment l'avenue de l'Opéra, le boulevard Saint-Germain et le boulevard Haussmann) et en créant de grandes places, comme la place de la République. Les nouvelles avenues étaient souvent conçues de façon à mettre en valeur un monument (l'Opéra-Garnier, au bout de l'avenue de l'Opéra, par exemple). L'aspect radical du renouveau urbain fut très contesté, Paris étant devenu un gigantesque chantier. À l'exception des principaux monuments, la majeure partie de l'île de la Cité fut détruite. Des bâtiments séculaires disparurent.

Haussmann avait des méthodes brutales, mais sa vision d'une ville reliant ses éléments entre eux était une approche révolutionnaire de l'urbanisme. Près de 25 000 maisons furent détruites et remplacées par 50 boulevards et rues, 75 000 bâtiments nouveaux et 2 parcs : le parc Montsouris et le parc des Buttes-Chaumont. Égouts, trottoirs, écoles, hôpitaux et marchés fleurirent de toutes parts. Les nouvelles rues furent bordées de bâtiments qui se distinguaient par leur cohérence et leur unité architecturale (des codes définissaient chaque élément d'architecture, depuis les portes jusqu'aux corniches).

Haussmann réorganisa également la structure politique et administrative de la ville. Il annexa la périphérie comprise entre l'ancienne barrière d'octroi et les fortifications du XIXe siècle, portant Paris de 12 à 20 arrondissements et accroissant la population de 600 000 habitants. Haussmann amorça un bouleversement si radical et si profond qu'il fallut, au terme de sa longue administration, encore près d'un demi-siècle pour l'achever.

Le modèle de ville ainsi défini devait s'expatrier à travers toute l'Europe, et même au-delà (comme à Buenos Aires). ■

Les douze avenues rayonnantes de la place Charles-de-Gaulle reflètent la vision d'Haussmann.

Autres sites à visiter

AUTRES PASSAGES ET GALERIES

Les passages et galeries aux toits de verre – ce qui donne, dit-on, une lumière d'aquarium – traversent les Grands Boulevards du nord au sud, reliant un quartier à un autre. Ces rues couvertes permettaient aux passants de faire leurs achats sans craindre d'être éclaboussés par les véhicules. Au début du XIXe siècle, Paris en comptait plus de cent mais aujourd'hui une vingtaine subsistent.

Le passage des Panoramas

Le passage des Panoramas est le premier à être éclairé au gaz (le plus ancien est néanmoins le passage du Caire avec ses trois têtes d'Hathor rappelant l'égyptomanie qui suivit les campagnes napoléoniennes en Égypte). Ouvert en 1800, il tire son nom des panoramas (tableaux circulaires en trompe-l'œil) de Rome, de Londres et d'autres capitales qui en décoraient autrefois l'entrée. Il donne accès à un labyrinthe de galeries : galerie Saint-Marc, galerie des Variétés et galerie Feydeau. Admirez l'enseigne impressionnante de l'atelier de gravure Stern (créé en 1840) au n° 47 et le décor Napoléon III du salon de thé L'Arbre à Cannelle.

Carte p. 155 Entrée au 11, boulevard Montmartre Grands Boulevards

Le passage Jouffroy

Adjacent au musée Grévin, ce passage très fréquenté abrite des boutiques remplies de figurines artisanales et de cannes à pommeaux d'ivoire taillés en forme de chien ou de lion couché, des salons de thé et des bistros. Il débouche sur le passage Verdeau, où vous trouverez des livres et des lithographies.

Carte p. 155 12, boulevard Montmartre Métro : Richelieu-Drouot

Le passage Brady

Avec ses épices, ses fruits, ses légumes et ses petits restaurants, le passage Brady semble mener directement en Inde et en Asie du Sud-Est.

Carte p. 155 Entre le 46, rue du Faubourg-Saint-Denis et le 43, rue du Faubourg-Saint-Martin Château d'Eau

LE MUSÉE GRÉVIN

Le musée Grévin, musée de cire créé à la fin du XIXe siècle, eut beaucoup de succès à une époque dépourvue de télévision et d'images médiatiques. Cette tradition s'est maintenue et, aujourd'hui, parmi les mannequins de cire, vous reconnaîtrez Serge Gainsbourg accoudé au bar, Zinedine Zidane, Johnny Hallyday, ou encore la somptueuse Naomi Campbell et de nombreux personnages historiques (Charlemagne, Napoléon Ier et Marat dont le corps, poignardé, gît dans une baignoire). Vous effectuerez un véritable voyage dans le temps grâce aux salles historiques allant de la terrible période de la peste noire à la reconstitution plus contemporaine d'un café parisien, en passant par la vie à la cour de Versailles. Les visiteurs se laissent rapidement prendre au jeu, surtout s'ils sont accompagnés par des enfants.

Carte p. 155 10, boulevard Montmartre 01 47 70 85 05/www.musee-grevin.com €€ Grands Boulevards

Le passage des Panoramas.

Le VIIe arrondissement, où les ambassades, les ministères et les antiquaires occupent d'anciens hôtels particuliers, affiche une élégance tranquille, dominée par le monument parisien le plus connu : la tour Eiffel.

La tour Eiffel et les Invalides

À l'aplomb de la tour Eiffel.

La tour Eiffel et les Invalides

LE VIIE ARRONDISSEMENT, SITUÉ À L'OUEST DE SAINT-GERMAIN-des-Prés, est jalonné d'hôtels particuliers pour la plupart reconvertis en ambassades ou en ministères. Il abrite de nombreux musées et le site touristique le plus couru de Paris : la tour Eiffel.

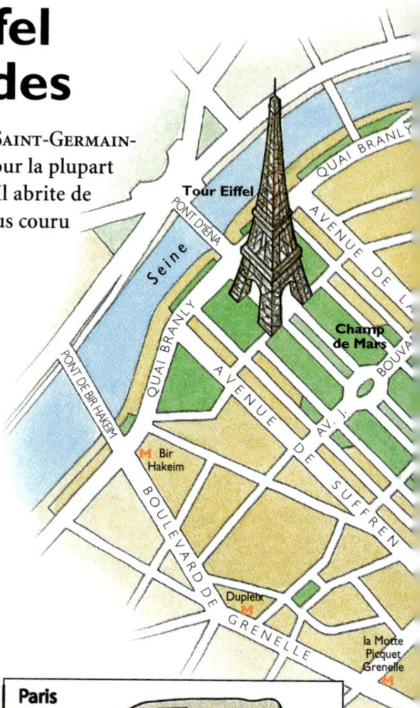

Au début du XVIIe siècle, cette zone éloignée du centre ville, difficile d'accès, est une vaste étendue de terre inhabitée. Un bac, instauré au XVIe siècle pour acheminer les matériaux nécessaires à la construction des Tuileries, transporte les passagers de l'autre côté de la Seine. Le pont le plus proche est le Pont-Neuf, en amont. Le pont Royal est bâti en 1689 pour remplacer le pont Rouge, passerelle construite en 1632. Il relie la rue du Bac, sur la rive gauche, aux jardins des Tuileries (voir p. 137), facilitant ainsi l'accès à la rive droite.

La mort de Louis XIV, en 1715, inaugure une période de développement du quartier. Tous les nobles qui avaient suivi le roi à Versailles se réjouissent de retourner à Paris. Ils sont nombreux à s'installer dans ce quartier champêtre situé à proximité de la route de Versailles (actuelle rue de Sèvres), et font construire d'élégantes demeures, pour la plupart confiées aux soins de grands architectes : Aubert, Courtonne, Boffrand. Jusqu'aux années 1880, le quartier reste le bastion de l'aristocratie légitimiste, alors que les beaux quartiers de la rive droite, tenus par la haute finance, sont plutôt orléanistes.

Désormais, la plupart de ces bâtiments abritent des ambassades ou des ministères. Le Palais-Bourbon, construit pour la duchesse de Bourbon (la fille de Louis XIV et de Madame de Montespan), accueille aujourd'hui l'Assemblée nationale (voir p. 169), l'hôtel Matignon, 57, rue de Varenne, est la résidence officielle du Premier ministre. L'ancien hôtel Biron, 77, rue de Varenne, est devenu le musée Rodin (voir pp. 172-173), où on peut visiter l'atelier de l'artiste ou faire une promenade dans les jardins ornés de ses sculptures.

Autre grand musée, le musée d'Orsay (voir pp. 174-178) est consacré à l'art du XIXe siècle et renferme certaines des peintures impressionnistes les plus célèbres du monde. À côté, se trouve le musée de la Légion d'honneur, moins connu, qui rassemble toute une collection d'insignes de l'ordre institué par Napoléon. L'empereur est à jamais lié au quartier puisque son tombeau se trouve sous le dôme doré des Invalides (voir p. 170).

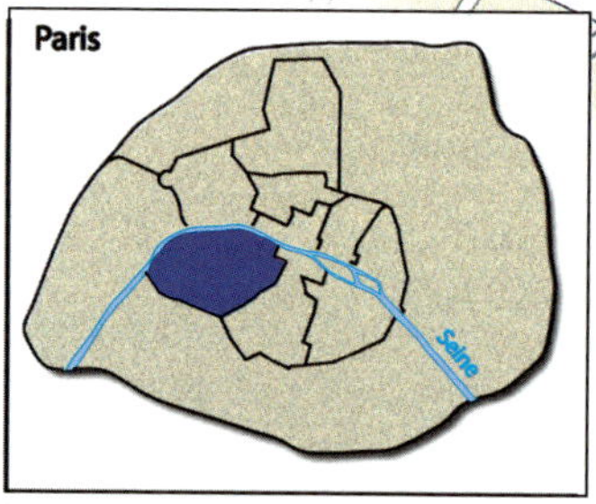

LA TOUR EIFFEL ET LES INVALIDES

❶ Façade du 29, avenue Rapp ❷ Entrée des égouts ❸ Rue Cler ❹ Hôtel Matignon ❺ Le Bon Marché ❻ Cinéma La Pagode ❼ Ambassade de Suisse

Le monument le plus célèbre du monde, la tour Eiffel (voir p. 166), s'élève à 300 mètres au-dessus de la pelouse du Champ-de-Mars (voir p. 168), dans la partie ouest du quartier.

Le bâtiment de l'Unesco, situé juste derrière l'École militaire (voir p. 168), a été conçu par une équipe internationale d'architectes. Lors de son inauguration, en 1958, on le dit révolutionnaire. Sa collection d'œuvres d'art reflète les ambitions de l'institution : un immense mobile de Calder et une sculpture de Henry Moore, *Silhouette au repos*, ornent l'esplanade, tandis que l'intérieur contient des œuvres de Karel Appel, Jean Arp, Matta et Picasso. Les jardins japonais, conçus par Isamu Noguchi, ont été restaurés en 1998.

Si vous préférez les endroits à échelle plus humaine, ne manquez pas le marché de la rue Cler, et la façade du 29 avenue Rapp, bel exemple d'architecture Art nouveau et chef-d'œuvre de l'architecte Jules Lavirotte. Ou encore, la Pagode au 57, rue de Babylone, la salle de cinéma-salon de thé le plus insolite de Paris. Pour une vue souterraine de la ville, visitez les célèbres égouts (voir p. 72), dont l'entrée se trouve place de la Résistance, en face du pont de l'Alma, sur la rive gauche.

Le Musée des Arts Premiers du quai Branly, doit ouvrir ses portes en 2006 et regrouper les collections de l'ancien Musée de l'homme et celles du Musée des Arts d'Afrique et d'Océanie. ■

www.tour-eiffel.fr

La tour Eiffel

Emblème de l'Exposition universelle de 1889, la tour Eiffel, vertement décriée par ses détracteurs aurait dû être déboulonnée à la fin des festivités. Heureusement, l'apparition de la TSF lui sauva la mise.

Élevée de 1887 à 1889 par Gustave Eiffel, à l'occasion de l'Exposition universelle de 1889 qui marque le centenaire de la Révolution française, la haute tour de fer annonce le XXe siècle. La réalisation paraît hardie, mais pour l'ingénieur, c'est la suite naturelle de ses précédentes constructions; il vient d'achever le viaduc de Garabit (1884) lorsqu'il lance son projet. Les 15 000 composants en métal de la future tour sont préfabriqués et numérotés pour l'assemblage, et la quasi-totalité des 2,5 millions de rivets sont déjà en place avant qu'elle soit montée. Grâce à cette rigueur, à la qualité de l'expertise et à l'intervention de 300 métallurgistes ayant travaillé d'arrache-pied sept jours par semaine pendant vingt-six mois (sans le moindre accident mortel), le plus haut monument du monde est achevé sept jours avant l'ouverture de l'Exposition. Son poids: 7 000 t, auxquelles il faut ajouter 50 t de peinture. Sa hauteur: 300 m.

La tour Eiffel, alors fortement décriée, est qualifiée de « chandelier creux » et de « colonne disgracieuse de boulons et de tôle ». Guy de Maupassant, qui n'en supporte pas la vue, prend ses repas au *Jules-Verne*, restaurant situé au deuxième étage, déclarant que c'est le seul endroit dans toute la ville où il ne peut pas la voir. Elle devait normalement être démontée, l'Exposition universelle une fois terminée, comme nombre d'infrastructures semblables, mais elle est sauvée par la TSF (télégraphie sans fil), sa hauteur lui permettant de jouer le rôle d'antenne et de réaliser les premiers essais radiotéléphoniques.

La tour offre une vue superbe, qui peut s'étendre jusqu'à 70 km par temps clair. Le prix de l'ascension varie en fonction de l'étage et selon que vous prenez l'ascenseur ou l'escalier, qui mène jusqu'au deuxième étage. Parmi les 5 millions de visiteurs qui affluent chaque année, les Parisiens sont rares… ■

Carte p. 164
Champ-de-Mars
01 44 11 23 23
de € à €€
Bir-Hakeim, Trocadéro, RER C: Champ-de-Mars-Tour Eiffel

Ci-dessus: Les étapes de l'édification de la tour Eiffel. À droite: Son nouvel éclairage la fait pétiller chaque heure pendant 10 mn, jusqu'à 2 h du matin (1 h en hiver).

Le Champ-de-Mars et l'École militaire

Carte p. 165
École militaire, avenue de La Motte-Picquet
École Militaire, RER C: Champ-de-Mars, Tour Eiffel

Ouvrant sur le Champ-de-Mars, l'École militaire couvre une superficie de 116 520 m^2. Depuis sa création, elle a conservé sa fonction, abritant aujourd'hui les écoles militaires d'enseignement supérieur.

Construite en 1752, sur proposition de Madame de Pompadour et du financier Pâris-Duvernay, l'École militaire initie à l'art de la guerre quelque 500 cadets de la noblesse désargentée. Le jeune Napoléon Bonaparte y passe un an (1784-1785). Le Champ-de-Mars est alors utilisé comme terrain de manœuvres par les élèves de l'école.

Le 14 juillet 1790, le Champ-de-Mars accueille la fête de la Fédération. Un an plus tard, des manifestants réclamant la déchéance de Louis XVI y sont tués sur ordre de Bailly, le maire de Paris. À la fin du XVIIIe siècle, le Champ-de-Mars est transformé en champ de courses de chevaux, sport importé d'Angleterre, et garde, peu ou prou, cette fonction jusqu'en 1855.

Les urbanistes qui ont travaillé sur Paris ont toujours eu un penchant pour les longues perspectives. Depuis l'École militaire (fermée au public), vous pourrez admirer la vue sur le Champ-de-Mars et, dans le même axe, la tour Eiffel et les ailes déployées du palais de Chaillot. ■

De nombreux bâtiments furent construits à l'occasion de l'Exposition universelle de 1900, dont le pont Alexandre-III (au premier plan).

Les Expositions universelles

La Grande-Bretagne crée l'événement avec le Crystal Palace, construit, à Londres, en 1851, pour la première *Great Exhibition*, destinée à exposer les produits et le savoir-faire technique britanniques. Les Français préparent à leur tour leur foire mondiale. Une série de cinq expositions s'ensuit, dont la première eut lieu en 1855 (voir p. 150). La plus grande fut celle de 1889, où se pressèrent 28 millions de visiteurs émerveillés par le scintillement des bâtiments de fonte et de verre jalonnant le site et par l'époustouflante tour Eiffel. ■

L'Assemblée nationale

Alors que le Sénat siège au palais du Luxembourg (voir p. 82), l'Assemblée nationale occupe le Palais-Bourbon. Les visiteurs peuvent assister aux débats qui se tiennent dans l'hémicycle, depuis des tribunes qui leur sont réservées. La très belle bibliothèque, dont les coupoles s'ornent du cycle de *L'Histoire de la Civilisation*, peint par Delacroix, ne se visite qu'en de rares occasions.

Le Palais-Bourbon fut une demeure aristocratique. Il est maintenant un symbole de la République française.

Le Palais-Bourbon, qui accueille les 577 députés (au complet dans les grandes occasions) de l'Assemblée nationale, est construit entre 1722 et 1728 sur ordre de la duchesse de Bourbon. Elle cède une partie de sa propriété à son amant, le marquis de Lassay, qui bâtit le magnifique hôtel mitoyen, qui porte son nom. À la mort de la duchesse, Louis XV achète le palais en 1756, pour le revendre en 1764 au prince de Condé qui l'embellit, y intègre l'hôtel de Lassay et le rebaptise Petit-Bourbon. Sous la Révolution, en 1790, les biens du prince – qui a émigré – sont confisqués et le palais sert au Conseil des Cinq-Cents. Une salle des débats semi-circulaire est construite à la place des salles de réception et la restructuration est d'une telle ampleur que seule la cour donne une idée du palais d'origine.

C'est à Napoléon que le monument doit aujourd'hui sa colonnade. Sa façade ne correspondant pas au style de la place de la Concorde, l'empereur approuve, en 1806, le projet de l'architecte Poyet qui préconise d'ajouter un péristyle à fronton pour faire pendant à celui de la Madeleine, située de l'autre côté de la Seine. Sculpté par Cortot, il est flanqué de deux bas-reliefs par Rude (à droite) et Pradier (à gauche) et des statues de Sully, Colbert, d'Aguesseau et L'Hospital.

L'hôtel de Lassay est la résidence du président de l'Assemblée, depuis 1843. Les appartements, bien que remaniés sous la IIe République, conservent leur ordonnance du XVIIIe siècle, mais l'accès en est interdit au public, excepté lors des Journées du Patrimoine, généralement à la fin du mois de septembre. ■

Carte p.165
126, rue de l'Université
01 40 63 60 00
Visites guidées sur rendez-vous, sam. 10h., 14h. et 15h., sauf en cas de cession parlementaire. Présentez-vous 20 min. à l'avance au 33, quai d'Orsay. Carte d'identité ou passeport exigé.
Assemblée nationale

www.invalides.org

Les Invalides

C'est Louis XIV qui décide la construction du somptueux hôtel des Invalides, établissement destiné aux soldats réformés pour une raison d'âge ou de blessure. Jusque-là, ces malheureux erraient de place en place, souvent réduits à la mendicité. La sollicitude du roi se reflète dans l'architecture à la fois austère et grandiose. C'est, après Versailles, le plus ambitieux chantier du règne, initialement confié à l'architecte Libéral Bruant.

En 1764, les premiers soldats sont hébergés aux Invalides, où la discipline est si rigoureuse que beaucoup d'entre eux ont dû regretter leur liberté, sinon leur pauvreté. La réglementation est stricte et tout écart de conduite entraîne une peine d'emprisonnement, mais les soldats bénéficient d'une pension complète et de soins médicaux. Cette initiative est couronnée de succès. Dès 1690, environ 6 000 hommes y demandent asile, alors qu'il n'est conçu que pour 1 500 pensionnaires. Les monarques de toute l'Europe s'en inspirent pour créer leur propre hôpital militaire.

LE TOMBEAU DE NAPOLÉON

Libéral Bruant se révélant trop timoré dans ses projets, c'est finalement Jules Hardouin-Mansart qui édifie la chapelle royale du bâtiment, en 1706. Son dôme audacieux, récemment restauré, étincelle de tous ses ors, au milieu des toits de zinc de la capitale. En 1840, les cendres de Napoléon Ier y sont déposées et la chapelle devient un mausolée impérial. En 1861, le tombeau en porphyre, œuvre colossale de l'italien Visconti, où repose désormais l'empereur, est édifié dans la crypte funéraire, au centre du dôme.

LES MUSÉES MILITAIRES

Quatre musées se trouvent dans l'enceinte des Invalides. Le musée de l'Armée, fondé en 1905, est l'un des musées militaires les plus complets du monde. Sa collection de peintures, d'armures, d'armes, d'uniformes et de souvenirs couvre les siècles, de l'Antiquité à la Seconde Guerre mondiale. Entre autres trésors, sont exposés l'armure de François Ier et le masque mortuaire de Napoléon. Le musée des Plans et Reliefs abrite, quant à lui, de nombreuses maquettes de villes, de ports et de places fortes confectionnées sur ordre de Louis XIV. Le musée de l'Ordre de la Libération rend hommage à ceux qui ont mérité cette prestigieuse décoration au cours de la Seconde Guerre mondiale. L'Ordre de la Libération a été créé par le général de Gaulle en novembre 1940. Enfin, les nouveaux espaces 1939-1945 retracent les grandes actions de la Résistance et des unités de la France libre et des Alliés. ■

L'hôtel des Invalides

- Carte p. 165
- Esplanade des Invalides
- 01 44 42 37 72
- Fermé 1er janv., 1er mai, 25 déc.
- €€
- Varenne, Latour-Maubourg

Page de droite : Sur le côté est de la cour d'honneur, la cinquième lucarne est encadrée par deux pattes de loup qui forment les armes « parlantes » de Louvois, le ministre créateur des Invalides.

À gauche : Les cendres de Napoléon reposent dans six cercueils emboîtés les uns dans les autres. Un en fer-blanc, un autre en acajou, puis un en plomb, doublé d'un autre en plomb ; pour finir, un cercueil d'ébène protégé par un autre de chêne.

www.musee-rodin.fr

Le musée Rodin

Carte p. 165
77, rue de Varenne
01 44 18 61 10
Fermé lun.
€€
Varenne

UNE GRANDE PARTIE DE L'ŒUVRE D'AUGUSTE RODIN EST EXPOSÉE dans l'hôtel Biron, propriété datant du XVIIIe siècle qui a su conserver le charme et la simplicité de la retraite campagnarde qu'elle fut à l'origine. Outre la collection, présentée dans l'hôtel, nombre de statues jalonnent le parc, agrémenté d'une somptueuse roseraie.

Rodin (1840-1917) est généralement considéré comme le père fondateur de la sculpture moderne. Artiste autodidacte, il a rejeté pendant toute sa vie les conventions académiques.

LE MUSÉE D'UN ARTISTE

Rodin a près de 38 ans lorsque sa première grande œuvre, *L'Âge d'airain*, est remarquée au Salon de 1877. Celle-ci provoque une vive controverse : ses contours sont si parfaits que les critiques accusent le sculpteur d'avoir effectué des moulages directement sur son modèle. Son authenticité est finalement reconnue et le tapage auquel elle a donné lieu fait connaître Rodin. Deux ans plus tard, celui-ci reçoit une commande pour *La Porte de l'Enfer* (œuvre restée inachevée).

Rodin s'est inspiré des personnages de Dante (Chant V ; L'Enfer), Paolo et Francesca, pour sculpter le couple qui figure dans le *Baiser* et sur *La porte de l'Enfer*.

À 45 ans, il a acquis une renommée internationale. Pourtant, presque toutes ses œuvres prêtent à polémique, des *Bourgeois de Calais* (débutés en 1884) à *Victor Hugo* (1890), en raison de leur réalisme et de leur forte charge émotionnelle. La statue de Balzac (1891-1897), dans sa célèbre robe de bure, est d'abord refusée par la Société des gens de lettres parce qu'elle ne répond pas à la commande. Gardée en réserve pendant quarante et un ans, elle est finalement placée au carrefour Vavin, en 1939.

Maison et Atelier de Rodin
Villa des Brillants, 19, avenue Auguste-Rodin, Meudon (au sud-ouest de Paris)
01 45 14 35 00
Ouvert ven., sam. et dim. d'avr. à sept.
€

Camille Claudel

Rodin disait de Camille Claudel : *« Je lui ai montré où trouver de l'or, mais l'or qu'elle a trouvé était en elle. »* Il l'accueille dans son atelier en 1883 en tant qu'élève et en fait rapidement son modèle et sa maîtresse. Il la représente notamment dans *Le Baiser*, *La Porte de l'Enfer* et *Fugit amor*. La liaison qu'ils ont ensemble prend fin en 1898 lorsqu'il est clair que Rodin ne mettra jamais un terme à sa relation avec Rose Beuret.

Camille Claudel se réfugie alors dans son atelier de l'île Saint-Louis, où elle sombre dans la folie.
En 1913, elle est internée dans un hôpital psychiatrique, où elle demeure jusqu'à sa mort, en 1943. Dans son testament, Rodin demande que ses œuvres soient exposées dans son musée. Ce dernier abrite ses plus belles sculptures, notamment *Sakountala*, *La Valse* et *L'Âge mur*, réalisé lors de leur séparation. ■

L'HÔTEL BIRON

En 1753, le maréchal de Biron achète au financier Abraham Peyrenc de Moras l'hôtel de la rue de Varenne, construit en 1731 par Jean Aubert, architecte des grandes écuries de Chantilly. Après la Révolution, l'hôtel accueille l'ambassade de Russie, puis une école confessionnelle. En 1905, laissé à l'abandon, ce n'est plus qu'un bâtiment délabré. L'État achète la propriété et la met à la disposition d'artistes. Matisse, Cocteau, le poète autrichien Rainer Maria Rilke, entre autres, s'y installent. Rodin, par l'intermédiaire de Rilke qui fut son secrétaire, y transfère son atelier en 1908 et rêve d'y créer un musée consacré à son œuvre. Au tout début du XXe siècle, l'État donne son accord. Malheureusement, il meurt avant l'ouverture de son musée, retardée des années durant par des intrigues et des négligences diverses. Rodin fit don de ses œuvres et de ses collections de peintures et de sculptures grecques et romaines à l'État. Ses principales sculptures, ainsi que quelques études, figurent dans le musée.

Sa maison et son atelier de Meudon abritent des milliers de modèles en terre cuite et en plâtre. ■

***La porte de l'Enfer* fut à l'origine commandée en 1888 pour figurer dans un musée des Arts décoratifs, qui devait être construit à Paris.**

Le musée d'Orsay

FONDÉ SUR LE PRINCIPE DE LA PLURIDISCIPLINARITÉ (PEINTURE, sculpture, photographie, arts décoratifs et graphiques), Orsay est à ce titre le musée le plus complet de la seconde moitié du XIXe siècle et du début du XXe siècle.

www.musee-orsay.fr

Carte p. 165
1, rue de Bellechasse
01 40 49 48 84
Fermé lun.
€€
Solférino

Le palais d'Orsay, siège du Conseil d'État et de la Cour des comptes, est incendié en 1871 lors de la Commune. Ses ruines noircies demeurent sur place pendant près de trente ans. À la fin du XIXe siècle, la compagnie ferroviaire d'Orléans acquiert l'emplacement et la gare est construite en un temps record de 1898 à 1900.

Intégrer un terminal ferroviaire à cet élégant quartier, proche du Louvre et des Tuileries, n'est pas aisé. Victor Laloux, dont le projet est retenu par la compagnie, suggère de camoufler les structures de fonte sous une architecture en pierre de taille. Il utilise en outre les technologies les plus avancées : ascenseurs, passerelles, monte-charges, traction électrique. Orsay est la première gare aussi perfectionnée. Un hôtel de 370 chambres, longeant la rue de Bellechasse, la rue de Lille et une partie du quai, est bâti autour de la gare.

La gare et l'hôtel sont inaugurés le 14 juillet 1900. Le hall du bâtiment est si luxueux que le peintre Édouard Detaille le qualifie prophétiquement de « palais des beaux-arts ». Plusieurs gares dans le monde sont construites sur le modèle de celle d'Orsay, notamment le Grand Central Terminal de New York et la Union Station de Washington. Pendant près de quarante ans, les grandes lignes du Sud-Ouest sont

La gare d'Orsay, construite au début du XXe siècle avec un luxe incroyable pour ce type de bâtiment, fut en service durant trente ans, avant d'être transformée dans les années 1960 en musée.

desservies par la gare d'Orsay. Mais, dès 1939, l'électrification du réseau permet la mise en circulation de trains plus longs et les quais de la gare, qu'on ne peut prolonger, deviennent trop courts. Le bâtiment est alors destiné à plusieurs usages.

Centre de tri au cours de la Seconde Guerre mondiale, il est transformé en centre d'accueil des anciens prisonniers de guerre, puis en salle des ventes. En 1962, Orson Welles y tourne *Le Procès,* adaptation du roman de Kafka. Dans les années 1960, le projet de construction d'un complexe hôtelier menace le site, mais l'opinion publique réagit et fait pression pour obtenir son classement parmi les monuments historiques, ce que fait Jacques Duhamel, alors ministre de la Culture, en 1973. En 1977, l'idée d'un musée consacré à l'art du XIXe siècle (de 1848 à 1915), faisant le lien entre le musée du Louvre et Beaubourg, prend corps.

La conception est confiée au cabinet d'architecture ACT et l'aménagement intérieur à l'architecte italienne Gae Aulenti. Les piliers de

Le décor originel de la gare d'Orsay était si somptueux que l'architecte italienne, Gae Aulenti, chargée de sa transformation en musée, préféra conserver la verrière et les plafonds à caissons.

fonte de Laloux sont intégrés au nouveau décor. Le hall d'entrée, à la fois immense et lumineux, est divisé en plusieurs paliers de pierre et bordé de galeries latérales.

Le musée d'Orsay, inauguré par le président François Mitterrand, le 1er décembre 1986, devint le nouveau foyer des œuvres impressionnistes jusqu'alors exposées dans la galerie nationale du Jeu de paume. Le Louvre y transfère des peintures de Salon et des œuvres d'artistes nés après 1820 et le musée national d'Art moderne, des œuvres post-impressionnistes.

LES COLLECTIONS

La période couverte par le musée d'Orsay est très importante dans l'histoire de l'art contemporain. C'est une époque de rupture avec les conventions. De nouveaux thèmes et une approche radicale de la peinture et de la photographie en termes de couleur et de composition apparaissent. La peinture est classée par thèmes ou par écoles en différentes tranches chronologiques.

Au rez-de-chaussée

Les peintres officiels et académiques (1848-1870) occupent le rez-de-chaussée. Dessins affirmés, chairs glabres, scènes édifiantes de la mythologie ou de l'histoire nationale, leurs œuvres, parfois non sans talent, reflètent l'enseignement des maîtres de l'Académie.

Thomas Couture et Alexandre Cabanel illustrent ces sujets classiques chers aux « pompiers » et à leurs très convenables commanditaires. Cependant, certains peintres, appelés les grands classiques, tels Chassériau, Ingres ou Delacroix, assurent la transition avec une peinture moins académique, et produisent des œuvres qui inspireront les impressionnistes. Celles-ci sont exposées dans les premières salles, à droite de l'entrée.

À gauche de l'entrée, l'école de Barbizon réunit des peintres (Charles Daubigny, Jean-Baptiste Corot et Théodore Rousseau) qui abandonnent les conventions académiques pour une idéalisation de la nature.

Le réalisme, mouvement qui marque une rupture radicale avec l'académisme contemporain, est représenté, entre autres, par Honoré Daumier, Jean-François Millet ou encore Gustave Courbet. Les œuvres de ce dernier, exposées dans une salle en rotonde, confèrent aux scènes de la vie quotidienne – comme *Un enterrement à Ornans*– la solennité de la grande peinture d'histoire. Peintre de la nature, Courbet est aussi le maître des chairs vibrantes. À ce titre, le musée conserve une œuvre longtemps cachée, autrefois propriété du psychanalyste Lacan, *L'Origine du monde.*

Le rez-de-chaussée abrite également des œuvres de peintres impressionnistes, Boudin, Bazille, Cézanne, Renoir, Monet, Degas ou Manet, réalisées avant 1870. Ces derniers rejettent les teintes sombres des ateliers de leurs aînés pour des couleurs lumineuses et des compositions vibrantes.

L'allée centrale, au fond, est consacrée à la sculpture néo-classique du XIXe siècle. *La Danse* (1869), de Jean-Baptiste Carpeaux, créée pour la façade de l'Opéra-Garnier, fut considérée comme une « atteinte à la morale »…

Au niveau supérieur

Les escalators mènent directement à l'étage supérieur, qui abrite la plus grande collection de tableaux impressionnistes et post-impressionnistes peints de 1874 à 1886. Après la guerre de 1870, Renoir, Monet et Pissarro, ainsi que Berthe Morisot et Alfred Sisley, se désintéressent des Salons officiels et décident de se grouper pour présenter des expositions libres. La première a lieu en 1874. C'est à cette occasion que le critique Louis Leroy qualifie les exposants d'« impressionnistes » (terme alors péjoratif), pour parodier *Impression soleil levant* de Monet (actuellement au musée Marmottan, voir p. 183). Les artistes adoptent ce nom et continuent d'exposer jusqu'en 1886.

par les critiques, il est aujourd'hui considéré comme le précurseur de la peinture du XXe siècle. Picasso et Matisse ont été fortement influencés par son style.

Cézanne est également représenté dans la salle consacrée à la collection du Dr Gachet, dans la galerie

***Romains de la période de Décadence* de Thomas Couture (1847).**

Dans la première galerie, se trouve la collection Moreau-Nélaton, avec le célébrissime *Déjeuner sur l'herbe* de Manet, chef-d'œuvre du Salon des refusés de 1863. Les salles suivantes sont consacrées à Manet, à James Whistler et au développement de l'impressionnisme avec, entre autres, des œuvres de Degas (*Danseuses bleues*), Monet (*La Gare Saint-Lazare*), Renoir (*Le Bal du Moulin de la Galette*).

Dans la salle Paul Cézanne, vous découvrirez notamment *Les Joueurs de cartes* et *Pommes et Oranges*. L'artiste ne s'intéressait pas tant à la lumière qu'à la structure, à la couleur et à la composition. Ridiculisé

Bellechasse, où sont exposés trois chefs-d'œuvre de Van Gogh : *L'Église d'Auvers-sur-Oise*, *Portrait de l'artiste* et *L'Arlésienne*.

Les œuvres innovantes de la génération suivante – Gauguin et les peintres de l'école de Pont-Aven comme Odilon Redon et Paul Signac – se trouvent dans les autres salles de la galerie Bellechasse. Vous verrez notamment *La Belle Angèle*, *Sur la plage* et Le *Cheval blanc* de Gauguin, *La Bouée rouge* de Signac et les paravents décoratifs de Redon.

Au niveau médian

Les galeries de ce niveau semblent ne comporter que des œuvres de genre

Van Gogh peignit *La sieste de midi* d'après un dessin de Jean-François Millet, durant son internement à Saint-Rémy-de-Provence (1889-1890).

et les peintures monumentales de la République. En réalité, elles abritent un large éventail de peintures, d'objets d'art et de sculptures. Un quart environ de la plate-forme des sculptures est consacré à Rodin. Plusieurs œuvres ont été empruntées au musée Rodin (voir pp. 172-173), notamment les plâtres de *La Porte de l'Enfer* et du *Balzac*. Commandée pour un musée des arts décoratifs qui ne fut jamais construit, *La Porte de l'Enfer* est inspirée de *La Divine Comédie* de Dante.

Les nabis, du nom hébreu « prophète », représentés par Pierre Bonnard, Édouard Vuillard et Maurice Denis occupent plusieurs salles sur le côté sud de ce niveau. Leur principal souci est d'ordre décoratif. Leurs œuvres sont reconnaissables aux aplats et aux répétitions de motifs mineurs, procédés propres aux arts décoratifs.

Plusieurs salles sont également consacrées à l'Art nouveau, mouvement qui se répand dans toute l'Europe sous des étiquettes différentes – Modern Style en Angleterre, Jugendstil en Allemagne et Arte Joven – à la fin du XIXe siècle. Des objets de toutes sortes (chaises, meubles, verrerie et vitraux) illustrent ce qui est une approche radicalement nouvelle de l'esthétique. La salle à manger de Charpentier (environ 1900) faite d'acajou, de chêne et de peuplier, et ornée de motifs floraux, typiques de ce style, en est un superbe exemple.

LA PHOTOGRAPHIE

Le musée possède aussi des milliers d'images datant des débuts de la photographie, présentées à tour de rôle dans les salles d'exposition : Dossier 3 (rez-de-chaussée) et Dossier 5 (niveau supérieur).

Les photographies de J.E. Marcy, précurseur de la décomposition du mouvement, font également partie de la collection. ■

Avec les musées du Trocadéro, le palais de Chaillot et ses belles avenues, le XVIe arrondissement est le quartier résidentiel le plus huppé de la capitale.

Le XVIe arrondissement

Statue du palais de Chaillot.

Le XVIe arrondissement

Quartier résidentiel par excellence, où il est agréable de venir flâner, le XVIe arrondissement abrite aussi de nombreux musées, la plus grande concentration de bâtiments Art nouveau et Art déco, et quelques vestiges de son ancienne vie villageoise. Confortablement niché entre la Seine et le bois de Boulogne, loin du tumulte du centre ville, il séduit encore les familles aisées. La zone attenante aux Champs-Élysées attire banquiers, grands couturiers, multinationales et hôtels de luxe. Le sud de l'arrondissement, notamment les anciens villages de Passy et d'Auteuil, bénéficie d'une tranquille vie de quartier.

Le XVIe arrondissement a toujours été fréquenté par les couches supérieures de la population parisienne. Lorsqu'elle allait de Saint-Germain-en-Laye à Paris, Catherine de Médicis s'arrêtait souvent sur la colline de Chaillot, l'actuel Trocadéro (place semi-circulaire en face du palais de Chaillot), pour aménager le pavillon qu'elle y possédait. Plus tard, les nobles qui se rendaient à Versailles firent d'abord étape à Passy et à Auteuil pour y goûter une atmosphère champêtre.

Le vin et l'eau contribuèrent aussi à l'attrait du site. Le vin produit par les Minimes de Chaillot était réputé dans toute la région. Des vignobles bordaient les collines qui descendaient jusqu'à la Seine. Au XVIIe siècle, les vertus curatives de la source de Passy attirèrent une clientèle fortunée, impatiente de goûter aux plaisirs des cures thermales. Aujourd'hui, cette source fournit encore aux quartiers environnants une eau claire comme du cristal.

DES JOYAUX ARCHITECTURAUX

Plus de la moitié des bâtiments Art nouveau de Paris, dessinés par Hector Guimard, se trouvent dans le XVIe arrondissement, surtout à Auteuil. Plus connu pour les superbes édicules de fer et de verre du métro (notamment celui de la porte Dauphine), Guimard a également conçu le flamboyant Castel Béranger (14, rue La Fontaine). Ce chef-d'œuvre de l'Art nouveau a été achevé en 1898 et primé au concours de façades de la Ville de Paris. Plusieurs autres bâtiments du même architecte se dressent le long de la même rue.

Le style Art déco « dépouillé » fut en faveur dans les années 1920 et 1930. Son chef de file parisien, Robert Mallet-Stevens, conçut une série d'hôtels particuliers dans une rue d'Auteuil qui porte aujourd'hui son nom. Les petites ruelles qui partent de la rue Boileau, notamment la villa Cheysson et la villa Mulhouse, initialement construites pour loger les ouvriers des filatures, sont bordées de maisons charmantes entourées de jardins. Elles sont aujourd'hui très prisées.

Les villages de Passy, d'Auteuil et de Chaillot furent annexés à la ville de Paris en 1859. C'était la grande époque des Expositions universelles (voir p. 168). La colline de Chaillot fut choisie pour la construction d'un immense palais d'inspiration hispano-mauresque à l'occasion de l'Exposition universelle de 1878. Mal aimé des Parisiens, ce monument fut remplacé par l'actuel palais de Chaillot (voir p. 182), construit pour l'exposition de 1937. Bâti dans un style néo-classique et orné de sculptures et de bas-reliefs, il comporte le musées de la marine, celui des monuments et un théâtre. La Cinémathèque française a quitté le palais de Chaillot pour s'installer à Bercy. Sa vaste esplanade est devenue un lieu de rendez-vous des amateurs de glisse sur rollers ou sur skateboard.

À l'est de la colline de Chaillot se trouvent deux grands musées de Paris : le musée Guimet (voir p. 184), consacré aux arts asiatiques, et le très riche musée d'Art moderne de la Ville de Paris (voir p. 182), installé dans le palais de Tokyo, un bâtiment néo-classique construit lui aussi pour l'Exposition universelle de 1937. ■

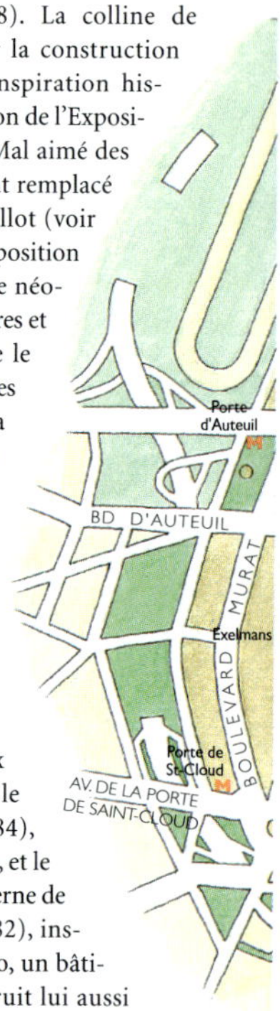

LE XVIE ARRONDISSEMENT

1. Métro Porte Dauphine
2. Castel Béranger
3. Rue Boileau
4. Délégation générale du Québec
5. Arc de Triomphe

Le musée d'Art moderne organise des expositions temporaires, comme celle de Sima, un artiste tchèque.

Le palais de Chaillot et les musées du Trocadéro

Les musées qu'abrite le palais de Chaillot sont relativement méconnus et pourtant très intéressants. Le palais fait l'objet actuellement d'un large remaniement. Le musée de l'Homme déménage, le musée de la Marine reste en les murs et le musée des Monuments français fait peau neuve.

Carte p. 181
Ⓜ Trocadéro

Musées du Trocadéro

Musée de la Marine :
17, place du Trocadéro
01 53 65 69 69
www.musee-marine.fr
Fermé mar.
€

Cité de l'Architecture et du Patrimoine :
1, place du Trocadéro
Ouverture prévue fin 2007

Théâtre national de Chaillot

1, place du Trocadéro
01 53 65 30 00
www.theatre-chaillot.fr

Musée d'Art moderne de la Ville de Paris

11, avenue du Président-Wilson
01 53 67 40 00
Fermé lun.
Ⓜ Iéna

Après avoir savouré la vue depuis l'esplanade sur la tour Eiffel et l'École militaire de l'autre côté de la Seine, vous pourrez visiter l'un des musées des palais de Chaillot ou de Tokyo. La cité de l'Architecture et du Patrimoine regroupera à terme le département des Monuments français, l'Institut français d'architecture et le centre des hautes études de Chaillot. La Cinémathèque française a fermé ses portes pour les rouvrir prochainement à Bercy, mais le Théâtre national de Chaillot présente toujours des classiques de l'art dramatique français.

LE MUSÉE DE LA MARINE

Créé en 1827 par une ordonnance de Charles X, à partir de la collection d'Henri-Louis Duhamel du Monceau, inspecteur général de la Marine française, le musée de la Marine est l'un des plus anciens et des plus riches musées maritimes du monde. Il abrite des pièces exceptionnelles. Ne manquez pas les modèles réduits de navires de guerre et les superbes prototypes de navires à voiles.

LE MUSÉE D'ARTS ET CIVILISATIONS

Le musée d'Arts et Civilisations d'Afrique, d'Asie, d'Océanie et des Amériques ouvrira ses portes en 2006 quai Branly. Il présentera les collections du musée d'Arts d'Afrique et d'Océanie et une partie de celles du musée de l'Homme. Ce dernier ferme ses portes, le reste des collections étant abrité par le musée du Louvre.

LE MUSÉE D'ART MODERNE DE LA VILLE DE PARIS

Le musée d'Art moderne de la Ville de Paris, inauguré en 1961 au palais de Tokyo, présente des artistes de l'école de Paris, ainsi qu'une riche collection d'œuvres fauvistes et cubistes. Dans l'aile ouest, le Site de Création contemporaine (*13, av. du Président-Wilson; tél. : 01 47 23 38 86*) se définit comme « laboratoire d'art contemporain ». ■

Le musée Marmottan-Monet

AUJOURD'HUI CÉLÈBRE DANS LE MONDE ENTIER POUR SES PEINTURES impressionnistes, notamment *Impression soleil levant* de Monet, le musée Marmottan-Monet était initialement consacré à un thème tout à fait différent : l'art napoléonien.

***Bouquet de Fleurs* (1897) est une des toiles peintes par Gauguin à Tahiti que l'on peut admirer au musée Marmottan.**

Carte p. 181
2, rue Louis-Boilly
01 44 96 50 33
fermé lun.
€€
La Muette

Jules Marmottan a constitué, avec l'aide de son fils Paul, les collections de ce musée situé dans un ancien pavillon de chasse qu'il a lui-même réaménagé. Les deux hommes se sont intéressés à l'art napoléonien à une époque (début du XIXe siècle) où tout le monde l'ignorait ou le méprisait. Ils rassemblèrent de superbes meubles de style Empire.

Alors que Jules Marmottan faisait fortune en tant que directeur d'une compagnie houillère, son fils mena une courte carrière de fonctionnaire jusqu'à la mort de son père, qui fit de lui un homme riche. Paul devint ensuite un expert reconnu en matière d'art de l'Empire. À sa mort, en 1932, il légua son pavillon et toute sa collection à l'Institut de France (Académie des Beaux-Arts).

En 1950, Madame Donop de Monchy fit don au musée d'une partie de la collection héritée de son père, le docteur Georges de Bellio. Médecin et ami des peintres impressionnistes, celui-ci avait acquis plusieurs œuvres de Monet, Pissarro, Renoir et Sisley, notamment *Impression, soleil levant* de Monet qui donnera son nom au mouvement.

En 1970, Michel Monet, le fils cadet du peintre, lègue à l'Académie les œuvres de son père restées en sa possession. C'est ainsi que le musée Marmottan possède la plus importante collection au monde d'œuvres de Monet, à laquelle s'ajoute la collection personnelle du peintre ; cette dernière comprend notamment des œuvres de ses amis Boudin, Caillebotte, Guillaumin, Jongkind, Manet, Morisot, Pissarro, Renoir et Rodin.

Au rez-de-chaussée sont exposés des manuscrits médiévaux enluminés, legs de Georges Wildenstein. ■

Autres sites à visiter

LA MAISON DE BALZAC

En 1840, Honoré de Balzac, auteur de *La Comédie humaine*, était au bord de la ruine. Il se retira dans sa maison de Passy, où il vécut sous le pseudonyme de Monsieur de Breugnol. Il avait également la jouissance du jardin dont il goûtait le calme tout en cueillant pour madame Hanska (qu'il épousa juste avant sa mort) les premières violettes « venues au soleil de Paris dans cette atmosphère de gaz carbonique où les fleurs poussent comme des champignons ». Transformée en musée en 1960, cette maison abrite de nombreux objets personnels de l'écrivain, notamment la petite table, un bureau Henri II, sur laquelle il travaillait parfois vingt-quatre d'affilée. Dans une lettre à madame Hanska, Balzac écrivit à propos de cette table : « Elle a été le témoin de mes angoisses, de mes misères, de mes détresses, de mes joies, de tout… »

Carte p. 181 47, rue Raynouard 01 55 74 41 80 ; www.paris.fr/musees/Balzac fermé lun. Passy

Buste d'Honoré de Balzac, l'auteur de *La Comédie humaine*.

LE MUSÉE DES ARTS ASIATIQUES GUIMET

La collection originale du musée appartenait à Émile Guimet (1836-1919), qui rassembla de nombreux objets au cours de ses voyages en Extrême-Orient à la fin du XIXe siècle. Inauguré en 1889, ce musée national, qui vient d'être remarquablement rénové, possède des collections d'une richesse et d'une qualité uniques en Europe. Il a rempli dès 1945 la fonction de département des arts asiatiques du Louvre. Dans un bâtiment annexe, entouré d'un ravissant jardin, se trouvent les collections du Panthéon bouddhique du Japon, ainsi qu'un authentique pavillon de thé.

Carte p. 181 6, place d'Iéna 01 56 52 53 00/www.museeguimet.fr fermé mar. € Iéna

LE MUSÉE DU VIN

À quelques pas du Trocadéro se cache un bâtiment du XVe siècle, qui abrite les caves de l'ancien monastère des Minimes de Chaillot. C'est ici qu'était distillé l'un des crus préférés de Louis XIII. La majeure partie du site fut détruite pendant la Révolution et les Parisiens oublièrent les caves jusque dans les années 1950. Le musée du Vin fut créé en 1984. Vous y découvrirez toutes sortes d'objets destinés à fabriquer ou à goûter le vin. L'entrée est gratuite pour ceux qui mangent dans le restaurant, ouvert uniquement à l'heure du déjeuner.

De somptueuses caves du XVe siècle accueillent un musée et un restaurant.

Carte p. 181 5, square Charles Dickens 01 45 25 63 26/www.museeduvinparis.com fermé lun. €€ (comprenant un verre de vin) Passy ■

Avec ses rues étroites qui serpentent jusqu'au sommet de la Butte, Montmartre a gardé un charme rustique. Le dôme blanc du Sacré-Cœur est visible depuis presque tous les quartiers de Paris.

Montmartre

Montmartre en affiche.

Montmartre

À Paris, rien n'est comparable à Montmartre. Situé au sommet d'une colline que les Parisiens appellent « la Butte », ce quartier, qui s'étend des néons de Pigalle aux rues sinueuses de l'ancien village, dégage une atmosphère unique. La musique, l'art et le vin – ainsi qu'une pointe d'irrévérence envers l'autorité et la tradition – ont alimenté le mythe. Mais les racines de Montmartre sont beaucoup plus anciennes que ses légendaires cabarets du XIXe siècle, y compris le célèbre Moulin-Rouge.

La butte Montmartre a toujours été un lieu de culte : les druides y célébraient déjà leurs rites sacerdotaux. Elle accueillit également deux temples romains (de Mars et de Mercure). Puis, vers 250 ap. J.-C., saint Denis, évêque de Paris, et l'archidiacre Éleuthère s'y firent décapiter. La butte prit le nom de mont des Martyrs, qui devint par déformation Montmartre.

La Butte fut alors jalonnée d'édifices chrétiens, dépendant de l'abbaye royale de Saint-Denis, construite en 1133 par Louis VI et son épouse Adélaïde de Savoie en hommage au saint martyr. Les terres de l'abbaye s'étendaient de l'actuel IXe arrondissement, au sud, jusqu'à l'abbaye elle-même, au nord.

Après la Révolution, les terres de l'abbaye furent vendues et tous les édifices démolis, à l'exception de l'église romane Saint-Pierre-de-Montmartre (voir p. 188). Cette église restera le lieu de culte favori des villageois même après la construction de la basilique du Sacré-Cœur (voir p. 188). En 1871, les Montmartrois, mécontents de la capitulation de Thiers face à la Prusse, refusèrent de restituer les canons entreposés sur la Butte. Les généraux envoyés par Thiers pour récupérer l'armement furent arrêtés et fusillés par les insurgés. Ce drame, qui a déclenché les événements sanglants de la Commune, est aujourd'hui commémoré par une plaque placée derrière la basilique, rue Chevalier-de-la-Barre.

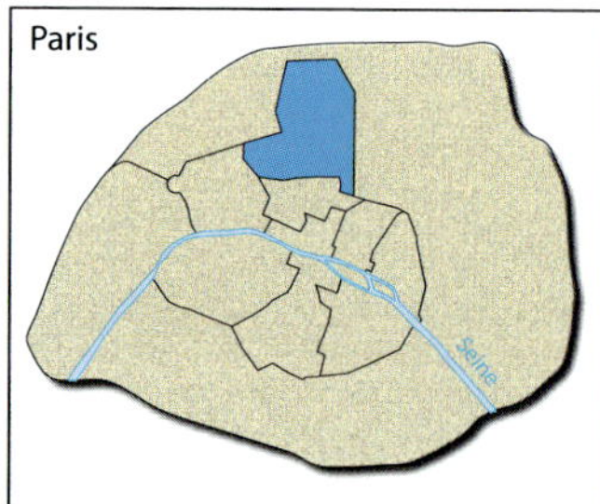

MONTMARTRE

1 Lapin Agile 2 Allée des Brouillards
3 Place des Abbesses 4 Folies-Bergère
5 Place du Tertre

Au cours de la révolution industrielle, les provinciaux affluèrent à Paris pour trouver du travail. Ils s'installèrent dans ce village modeste, dont ils bouleversèrent la structure sociale. À l'époque, la barrière de l'octroi coupait Montmartre du reste de la ville à la hauteur de l'actuelle place Pigalle. Toutes les marchandises entrant dans l'enceinte de Paris

Le début des vendanges est célébré chaque premier samedi du mois d'octobre au vignoble de Montmartre.

étaient taxées. En dehors du mur, le vin – produit en abondance sur la Butte – était donc moins cher. Le village fut annexé à Paris sous Napoléon III et devint ainsi une partie du XVIIIe arrondissement.

À la fin du XIXe siècle, les nombreux cabarets, maisons closes et autres établissements mal famés de Montmartre valurent au quartier une réputation de débauche qui attira artistes, écrivains et bourgeois en quête de sensations. Eugène Delacroix, Hector Berlioz et Vincent Van Gogh s'installèrent sur la Butte pour bénéficier de sa lumière, de son charme et, à l'époque, de ses loyers peu élevés.

Le Montmartre d'aujourd'hui n'a pas beaucoup changé. C'est un mélange de poésie, de sexe et de mercantilisme. Le Moulin-Rouge (voir p. 193) est encore rempli tous les soirs et la place du Tertre est envahie par les portraitistes et les odeurs de crêpes. Mais quelques vestiges d'une époque plus romantique ont survécu dans le dédale de rues bordées d'arbres qui entourent la Butte. Depuis le sommet, la capitale fourmillante semble appartenir à un autre monde. ■

Le Sacré-Cœur

Depuis cent dix ans, des fidèles se relaient vingt-quatre heures sur vingt-quatre dans la basilique du Sacré-Cœur pour prier.

LA BASILIQUE DU SACRÉ-CŒUR, QUI SE DRESSE SUR LE POINT CULMINANT de Paris, est le monument le plus récent et le plus visible de Montmartre. Sa pierre blanche, étincelante malgré la pollution, provient de Seine-et-Marne. Lorsqu'il pleut, elle produit un dépôt de calcin qui rend le monument encore plus blanc.

LA BASILIQUE

Cette basilique romano-byzantine dédiée au Sacré-Cœur de Jésus fut construite à l'initiative de quelques personnalités pour expier les crimes de la Commune de Paris...

Les travaux commencèrent en 1875. L'architecte Paul Abadie (disciple de Viollet-le-Duc) mourut en 1884 et la basilique fut terminée en 1914 par Lucien Magne, qui ajouta le campanile haut de 84 m. La préparation des fondations fut à elle seule un véritable exploit: 83 puits de 45 m de profondeur furent creusés pour accueillir des structures reliées entre elles par des arches souterraines destinées à stabiliser le sous-sol et à compenser les tunnels percés dans les anciennes carrières. Il fallut 28 chevaux pour tirer le chariot transportant la Savoyarde, la cloche du Sacré-Cœur, l'une des plus grosses au monde (19 t). Pour une vue sur l'intérieur de la basilique, montez dans la galerie ornée de vitraux de la coupole. Celle-ci offre également un intéressant panorama de la ville.

L'ÉGLISE SAINT-PIERRE-DE-MONTMARTRE

Les habitants de la Butte ignorent le Sacré-Cœur et continuent de venir prier dans l'église Saint-Pierre, l'une des plus anciennes de Paris, située entre la basilique et la place du Tertre. Après avoir franchi le porche de l'église, qui date du XVIIIe siècle, vous découvrirez une superbe nef d'époque romane (XIIe siècle). ■

Carte p. 187
Ⓜ Anvers, Abbesses, Lamarck-Caulaincourt

Basilique
✉ 35, rue du Chevalier-de-la-Barre
€ Basilique: gratuit. Crypte et dôme: €

Saint-Pierre de Montmartre
✉ 2, rue du Mont-Cenis

La place du Tertre

LA PLACE DU TERTRE ET LES RUES AVOISINANTES SONT BORDÉES DE magasins de souvenirs, de bistros chers et de portraitistes aux talents très inégaux.

LA PLACE DU TERTRE

C'est tôt le matin, avant l'arrivée des foules, que l'on s'imprègne le mieux de l'ambiance du vieux Montmartre. Certaines anecdotes ont la vie longue. Si vous vous arrêtez au restaurant La Mère Catherine, les serveurs vous diront que c'est ici qu'apparut le terme « bistro ». Pendant l'occupation de Paris en 1814, des soldats du Tsar auraient frappé sur la table en criant « *bistro !* », ce qui signifie « vite » en russe.

UN MUSÉE À MONTMARTRE

Le musée du Vieux Montmartre se trouve juste derrière la place du Tertre. À la fin du XIXe siècle, plusieurs artistes (Dufy, Renoir, Suzanne Valadon, mère du peintre impressionniste Maurice Utrillo) vécurent dans ce bâtiment du XVIIe siècle. Les collections du musée recréent l'atmosphère unique du Montmartre d'antan. Ne manquez pas la reproduction de la toile qui fit l'objet d'un célèbre canular de Roland Dorgelès. L'auteur, qui méprisait l'art moderne, avait attaché un pinceau à la queue d'un âne appartenant au propriétaire du bistro dénommé le Lapin Agile. L'œuvre qui en résulta, appelée *Et le soleil se coucha sur l'Adriatique*, fit l'objet d'articles élogieux de la critique !

Place du Tertre

Carte p. 187

Musée du Vieux Montmartre

12, rue Cortot

01 46 06 61 11

fermé lun.

€

Lamarck-Caulaincourt

L'enseigne du Lapin Agile, peinte par André Gill, d'où le jeu de mots le « lapin à Gill ».

Une promenade à Montmartre

Ce quartier bohème a sans doute perdu un peu de son charme mais, en vous promenant dans ses rues pittoresques, vous retrouverez l'atmosphère de l'époque où les plus grands artistes du début du XXe siècle y vivaient.

Ce trajet vous fera gravir des escaliers et des rues en côte ; aussi, si vous préférez, prenez le petit train qui part de la place Blanche (en face du Moulin-Rouge, 82, boulevard de Clichy) pour faire une visite guidée de la Butte en quarante minutes. Sachez toutefois que certains des sites proposés ci-dessous ne sont accessibles qu'à pied.

Commencez par la place Pigalle, dont les cabarets de la fin du XIXe siècle attirèrent de nombreux Parisiens avides de plaisirs canailles. Aujourd'hui, avec les néons des sex-shops, le quartier n'a plus vraiment la même allure.

Longez le boulevard de Clichy en direction de l'est et prenez la rue des Martyrs, à gauche, qu'arpentèrent de nombreux pèlerins catholiques en route vers la basilique du Sacré-Cœur. Vous arriverez au 9, rue Yvonne-le-Tac, où saint Denis aurait été décapité au IIIe siècle. C'est également ici qu'Ignace de Loyola fonda la Compagnie de Jésus, plus connue sous le nom de l'ordre des Jésuites en 1534. Au bout de la rue Yvonne-le-Tac, prenez la rue des Trois-Frères, à droite, puis tournez à gauche devant le théâtre de l'Atelier (1822) sur la place Charles-Dullin.

Les peintres de portrait, omniprésents sur la place du Tertre, ont transformé ce charmant lieu en un des pièges à touristes les plus renommés de la capitale.

Continuez jusqu'à la rue de Steinkerque et tournez à gauche pour découvrir la vue sur le Sacré-Cœur. Cette rue, ainsi que la place Saint-Pierre, sont bordées de magasins offrant la plus grande sélection de tissus de Paris à bas prix. Pour monter jusqu'à la basilique, gravissez les escaliers ou, si vous préférez, prenez le funiculaire, à gauche, pour le prix d'un ticket de métro.

Après avoir admiré la vue et visité la basilique du Sacré-Cœur ❶ (voir p. 188), prenez la rue Azaïs pour rejoindre la place du Tertre (voir p. 189), site touristique incontournable de Montmartre. Prenez le temps d'explorer l'église Saint-Pierre-de-Montmartre ❷ (voir p. 188), l'une des rares églises romanes de Paris.

Descendez la rue du Mont-Cenis (après la rue Sainte-Rustique) pour vous imprégner du charme du vieux Montmartre. Prenez ensuite la rue Cortot, à gauche, où vous pourrez faire une visite du musée du Vieux Montmartre ❸, situé au n° 12 (voir p. 189). En sortant, engagez-vous dans la rue des Saules, à droite, d'où vous verrez le carré de vigne de Montmartre. Une fête des vendanges y a lieu tous les premiers samedis d'octobre. Juste en face, se trouve le légendaire cabaret Lapin Agile ❹ *(22, rue des Saules, tél. : 01 46 06 85 87)*, autrefois fréquenté par Picasso, Apollinaire et Modigliani.

Remontez sur la colline et prenez la rue de l'Abreuvoir, à droite. La maison rose du n° 2 a été immortalisée par le peintre Maurice Utrillo. Poursuivez jusqu'à la mystérieuse allée des Brouillards, où Renoir vécut avec sa famille. D'après la tradition, saint Denis s'arrêta à la fontaine de l'actuel square Suzanne-Buisson, à gauche, pour laver sa tête tranchée avant de poursuivre son chemin. Allez jusqu'à l'avenue Junot ❺ et tournez à gauche. Au n° 15 se trouve un bel exemple d'architecture Art déco réalisé par le Viennois Adolf Loos en 1926. La villa Léandre, au n° 25, constitue un ensemble architectural magnifique également construit en 1926.

Prenez les escaliers au n° 23 et descendez jusqu'à la rue Lepic. Ne manquez pas l'un des deux derniers moulins de la Butte, sur la gauche – le Moulin de la Galette **6**, peint par Renoir, transformé aujourd'hui en restaurant. Prenez la rue d'Orchampt, à droite, pour gagner la place Émile-Goudeau **7**. Le cubisme naquit dans un ancien entrepôt rebaptisé Bateau-Lavoir. On l'appelait la « villa Medicis » de la peinture moderne. Renoir y peignit, en 1885, *La Danse de la Ville* et *La Danse de la Campagne*. Van Dongen, Picasso, Modigliani, Vlaminck, Derain, Braque, Dufy, Max Jacob y travaillèrent ou la fréquentèrent jusqu'en 1914. Les ateliers de ce bâtiment furent ensuite transférés au 6, rue Durantin (à droite).

Longez la rue Durantin et prenez la rue Tholozé, à gauche. Le Studio 28, cinéma situé au n° 10, défraya la chronique en 1930 lorsque des spectateurs choqués lancèrent des œufs et de l'encre sur l'écran lors de la première du film surréaliste de Buñuel, *L'Âge d'or*. Dans le hall, vous pourrez voir les empreintes de Buñuel et de Cocteau. Prenez la rue des Abbesses, à gauche, où vous trouverez plusieurs cafés où terminer agréablement votre promenade. Rejoignez le métro sur la place des Abbesses **8**. ■

Voir aussi carte pp. 186-187
Place Pigalle
4,8 km
2 h 30-3 heures
Place des Abbesses

À NE PAS MANQUER

- Place Pigalle
- Sacré-Cœur
- Place du Tertre
- Saint-Pierre de Montmartre
- Musée de Montmartre
- Allée des Brouillards

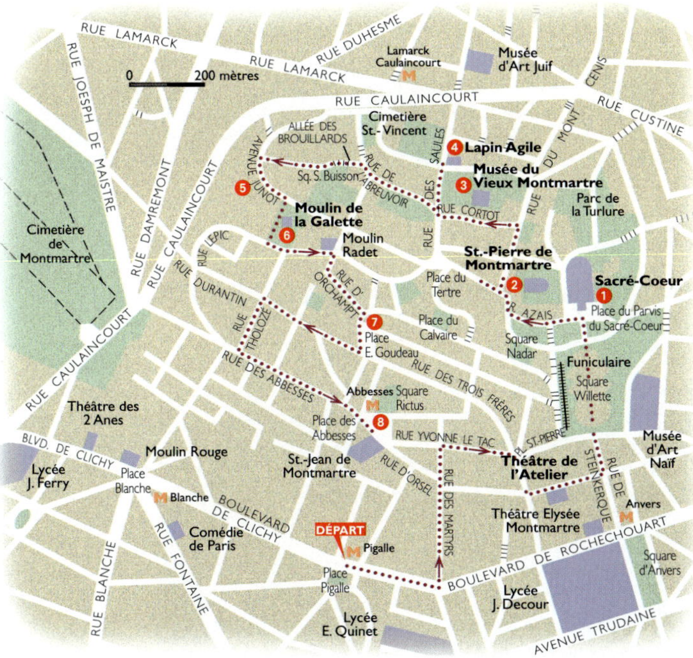

Les cabarets

Paris ne cesse de réinventer l'art de se distraire. Les cafés chantants ou guinguettes, populaires pendant la Révolution, cédèrent la place, dès le Second Empire et la Belle Époque, aux cafés-concerts, ancêtres des music-halls et des cabarets artistiques irrévérencieux qui fleurirent à Montmartre au début du XXe siècle.

Une tradition purement française

Dans les années 1950, des chanteurs comme Léo Ferré et Georges Brassens débutèrent dans les cabarets. Dix ans plus tard, une nouvelle forme d'expression apparut avec les cafés-théâtres, où l'on jouait des comédies satiriques devant un public restreint. Ces cafés-théâtres, dont les premiers furent Le Royal (à Montparnasse) et La Vieille Grille (dans le Quartier latin), lancèrent de nombreux acteurs, tels Coluche, Gérard Depardieu et la troupe du Théâtre du Splendid, dont Thierry Lhermitte, Christian Clavier, Anémone et Gérard Jugnot.

La tradition la plus typiquement française reste néanmoins la revue à grand spectacle, qui recrée les folles nuits de la Belle Époque. Le Crazy Horse *(12, avenue George-V, tél. : 01 47 23 97 90, www.lecrazyhorseparis.com)*, le Lido *(116 bis, avenue des Champs-Élysées, tél. : 01 40 76 56 10, www.lido.fr)* et ses superbes Bluebell Girls proposent des spectacles extravagants avec lasers, vidéo, fontaines et dragons crachant le feu. Le Paradis Latin, situé dans un théâtre conçu par Gustave Eiffel, offre un spectacle de cabaret plus traditionnel.

En 1926, Joséphine Baker conquit le public parisien des Folies-Bergère avec sa grâce et… quelques plumes.

Les sublimes Doriss Girls continuent à entretenir la légende du Moulin-Rouge.

Avec ses jongleurs, ses lutteurs, ses danseurs et ses magiciens évoluant dans des décors exotiques, la salle des Folies-Bergère (*Tél. : 01 44 79 98 98, www.foliesbergere.com*), inaugurée en 1869, est le plus ancien music-hall. Bien qu'il soit associé à Joséphine Baker, celle-ci débuta en réalité dans *La Revue nègre*, au théâtre des Champs-Élysées, en 1925. Née à Saint-Louis, Missouri, la célèbre danseuse noire devint la star des Folies. Dans un décor composé de jambons et de pastèques, elle entrait en scène avec une plume de flamant rose entre les jambes ou une corolle de bananes autour de la taille. Devenue citoyenne française, elle resta en France jusqu'à sa mort, en 1975.

Le Moulin-Rouge

Au Moulin-Rouge (*82, boulevard de Clichy, tél.: 01 53 09 82 82, www.moulinrouge.com*), dont seules les ailes rouges sont d'origine, les Doriss Girls dansent encore le french cancan, auquel le cabaret est associé depuis toujours grâce aux affiches de Jane Avril et d'Yvette Guilbert, dessinées par Toulouse-Lautrec. En réalité, le cancan est apparu à Montparnasse et le Moulin-Rouge serait plutôt le berceau du strip-tease. En 1893, lors du bal des « quat'zarts » organisé tous les ans par les étudiants des Beaux-Arts, un modèle féminin d'artiste, un peu éméché, sauta sur une table et se dévêtit entièrement… Scandalisé par cet outrage à la pudeur, le président de la Ligue contre la licence publique porta l'affaire devant les tribunaux. Le modèle fut arrêté et les étudiants protestèrent en avançant le droit à la « nudité artistique ». Cette anecdote déclencha une avalanche de spectacles osés dans les cabarets du quartier, notamment au Divan Fayouau, où Yvette se déshabillait tous les soirs avant de se mettre au lit sur scène. Dans *La Puce*, une autre demoiselle se contorsionnait avec sensualité pour retrouver une puce qui la démangeait. ■

Le Moulin-Rouge est un lieu mythique du french cancan. À tel point que Hollywood s'est emparé du sujet.

Autres sites à visiter

Gustave Moreau demanda à Albert Lafon de construire ce superbe escalier pour accéder au 4e étage.

LE MUSÉE GUSTAVE-MOREAU

Situé au sud de Montmartre, le musée Gustave-Moreau offre une découverte passionnante de l'atelier et de la maison de l'artiste. Considéré comme un précurseur du mouvement surréaliste, Moreau était un homme réservé, financièrement indépendant, qui préférait enseigner à l'école des Beaux-Arts plutôt que d'exposer ses propres œuvres. Georges Rouault et Henri Matisse sont ses plus célèbres disciples.

De magnifiques tableaux ornent les murs de cette maison de famille ordonnée avec soin. L'escalier en colimaçon très ouvragé est superbe. Les quelque 6 000 œuvres exposées comptent aussi bien des dessins que des aquarelles ou des huiles sur des thèmes mythologiques, comme *Apollon et Pégase*, *Les Licornes* et *La Descente de croix*.

Carte p. 187 14, rue de La Rochefoucauld 01 48 74 38 50 Fermé mar. € Trinité ■

Le vignoble de Montmartre

La Butte était autrefois couverte de vignes mais les vendanges prirent fin dans les années 1920. En 1929, le peintre Poulbot et quelques-uns de ses amis sauvèrent une parcelle de terrain située en face du Lapin Agile des griffes des promoteurs immobiliers en proposant d'y replanter des vignes.

Ignorant qu'il fallait attendre quatre ans avant que les vignes produisent des fruits, le groupe d'amis organisa naïvement une fête des vendanges dès la première année. Alors que la date approchait et que les pieds n'avaient toujours pas de grappes, les vignerons bien intentionnés mais visiblement incompétents furent tirés d'affaire par de grands producteurs qui fournirent plus de 30 tonnes de raisin pour la fête. Aujourd'hui, le carré de vigne produit

environ 300 litres de vin (de qualité incertaine) chaque année. Les bouteilles, dont l'étiquette a été réalisée par un peintre local, sont vendues à la criée au profit du Comité de bienfaisance de l'arrondissement. ■

Paris intra-muros, délimité par le boulevard périphérique, comporte aussi deux grands parcs, quelques anciens villages et l'un des projets urbains les plus ambitieux du monde, le quartier de La Défense.

Autres endroits à découvrir

À la Cité des Sciences et de l'Industrie.

COURBEVOIE
Seine
D7
D1
D908
Île de la Grande Jatte
CLICHY
Porte de St-Ouen
BOULEVARD
Porte de Clichy
BD BESSIÈRES
N13
la Défense
A14
LEVALLOIS-PERRET
Porte d'Asnières
BD BINEAU
BD BERTHIER
BATIGNOLLES
Porte de Champerret
NEUILLY-SUR SEINE
PUTEAUX
Île de Puteaux
AV. CHARLES DE GAULLE
Porte Maillot
WAGRAM
MONCEAU
CLICHY
BD DES BATIGNOLLES
Palais des Congrès
JARDIN D'ACCLIMATATION
PLACE DE LA PORTE MAILLOT
BD DE COURCELLES
PARC DE MONCEAU
Gare St-Lazare
Arc de Triomphe
AV. DE FRIEDLAND
PARC DE BAGATELLE
Porte Dauphine
AVENUE FOCH
CHAMPS-ÉLYSÉES
Palais de l'Élysée
Opéra Garnier
AV. KLÉBER
AV. GEORGE V
AV. DES CHAMPS ÉLYSÉES
La Madeleine
TROCADÉRO
AV. MONTAIGNE
PLACE DE LA CONCORDE
BOIS DE BOULOGNE
Porte de la Muette
AV. DU PRÉS. WILSON
Grand Palais
JARDIN DES TUILERIES
AV. H. MARTIN
Palais de Chaillot
AV. DE NEW YORK
Musée Marmottan
Musée d'Orsay
Tour Eiffel
AV. BOSQUET
Hôtel des Invalides
Hippodrome d'Auteuil
PASSY
PARC DU CHAMP DE MARS
Seine
École Militaire
INVALIDES
Porte d'Auteuil
BD DE GRENELLE
BOULEVARD
A13
Stade Roland-Garros
AUTEUIL
QUAI ANDRÉ CITROËN
GRENELLE
BD DU MONTPARNASSE
BD EXELMANS
Musée Albert Kahn
Gare Montparnasse
D907
JAVEL
AV. DE VERSAILLES
Porte de St-Cloud
Porte de Sèvres
MONTPARNASSE
CIMETIÈRE DE MONTPARNASSE
RASPAIL
BD VICTOR
Porte de Versailles
VAUGIRARD
Quai d'Issy
D10
PLAINE DE VAUGIRARD
la Ruche
DENFERT-ROCHEREAU
Parc des Expositions
BD LEFEBVRE
BOULOGNE-BILLANCOURT
Porte Brancion
PLAISANCE
Porte de la Plaine
BOULEVARD BRUNE
BOULEVARD PÉRIPHÉRIQUE
VANVES
Porte de Châtillon
Porte d'Orléans
MONTROUGE
MALAKOFF
N20
A
B
C
1
2
3
4
5
Paris
Seine

ST-OUEN
ST-DENIS
AUBERVILLIERS
A1
N2
Porte de Clignancourt
Porte de la Chapelle
Porte de la Villette
PÉRIPHÉRIQUE
BOULEVARD NEY
Porte d'Aubervilliers
Cité des Sciences et de l'Industrie
CLIGNANCOURT
PARC DE LA VILLETTE
PANTIN
BD ORNANO
MONTMARTRE
LA CHAPELLE
AVENUE DE FLANDRE
LA VILLETTE
Cité de la Musique
N3
Porte de Pantin
Sacré Cœur
Goutte d'Or
BD BARBÈS
AVENUE JEAN JAURÈS
LE PRÉ ST-GERVAIS
PIGALLE
BD DE LA CHAPELLE
BOULEVARD SÉRURIER
CLICHY
BD DE ROCHECHOUART
Gare du Nord
PARC DES BUTTES-CHAUMONT
Porte des Lilas
Musée de la Vie Romantique
Gare de l'Est
BOULEVARD DE MAGENTA
BOULEVARD DE LA VILLETTE
LES LILAS
GRANDS BOULEVARDS
BELLEVILLE
HAUSSMANN
BD DE STRASBOURG
PÉRIPHÉRIQUE
BD MORTIER
BOURSE
BD DE BELLEVILLE
Porte de Bagnolet
D20
BD ST-MARTIN
RÉAUMUR
PLACE DE LA RÉPUBLIQUE
RÉPUBLIQUE
MÉNILMONTANT
A3
AV. DE L'OPÉRA
Palais-Royal
LES HALLES
BD DE SÉBASTOPOL
BD DE MÉNILMONTANT
BEAUBOURG
Centre Georges Pompidou
CIMETIÈRE DU PÈRE-LACHAISE
Musée Picasso
BOULEVARD DAVOUT
Musée du Louvre
CHÂTELET
LE MARAIS
BASTILLE
Hôtel de Ville
BOULEVARD DE CHARONNE
Île de la Cité
CHARONNE
ST-GERMAIN-DES-PRÉS
Notre-Dame
PLACE DE LA BASTILLE
Porte de Montreuil
Île St-Louis
FAUBOURG ST-ANTOINE
ST-GERMAIN
ARSENAL
Opéra-Bastille
Palais du Luxembourg
QUARTIER LATIN
Jardin Tino Rossi
PLACE DE LA NATION
Château de Vincennes
N34
BD ST-MICHEL
Panthéon
QUAI DE LA RAPÉE
NATION
Porte de Vincennes
JARDINS DES PLANTES
Gare de Lyon
BD SOULT
Seine
Porte de St-Mandé
MOUFFETARD
BD ST-MARCEL
Gare d'Austerlitz
BD DE L'HÔPITAL
BD DE BERCY
ST-MANDÉ
BD DE PORT ROYAL
Palais Omnisports
Palais de la Porte-Dorée
GOBELINS
QUAI DE BERCY
Parc Floral
BD ARAGO
BD VINCENT AURIOL
BERCY
BD PONIATOWSKI
Porte Dorée
ST-JACQUES
PLACE D'ITALIE
Bibliothèque Nationale de France François-Mitterrand
Parc Zoologique
Lac de Daumesnil
BOIS DE VINCENNES
Butte-aux-Cailles
Porte de Bercy
MONTSOURIS
Quai d'Ivry
Parc de Bercy
N4
PARC MONTSOURIS
BOULEVARD MASSÉNA
CHARENTON-LE-PONT
JOURDAN
BD KELLERMANN
IVRY-SUR-SEINE
Cité Internationale Universitaire de Paris
Porte d'Ivry
Seine
A4
Marne
Porte de Choisy
0
1 kilomètre
Porte de Gentilly
Porte d'Italie
A6a
A6b
N7
N6
D
E
F

Autres endroits à découvrir

Un boulevard périphérique ceint la ville de Paris et définit avec précision les limites. De nombreux quartiers des arrondissements situés en bordure du périphérique présentent un grand intérêt, car ils gardent la trace des villages annexés par Haussmann en 1860. Si vous en avez le temps, n'hésitez pas à les visiter.

Le bois de Vincennes.

Avec ses rues pavées étroites, ses passages obscurs et ses petites maisons couvertes de vigne, la Butte-aux-Cailles (voir p. 202) est typique du vieux Paris. Belleville et son hameau Ménilmontant (voir pp. 206-207) abritaient à la fois les vignes des grandes abbayes de Paris et des cafés où les Parisiens venaient boire un verre de guinguet (vin aigrelet) le dimanche. Ces deux quartiers, particulièrement actifs pendant la Commune (voir p. 26), furent des bastions de l'agitation ouvrière, notamment après la réorganisation urbaine du baron Haussmann (voir pp. 160-161) qui chassa le prolétariat du centre ville au XIXe siècle. Avec ses quartiers chinois, arabe, africain et turc et ses marchés ethniques colorés, Belleville a toujours attiré des vagues d'immigrants du monde entier et possède la population la plus cosmopolite de la ville. Les abattoirs de la Villette (voir pp. 208-209) ont fait place à un grand parc, nouveau venu parmi les nombreux espaces verts qui entourent Paris, comme le bois de Vincennes (voir p. 203), à l'est, et le bois de Boulogne (voir p. 199), à l'ouest.

Avec le PC (autobus de la Petite Ceinture), qui suit les boulevards des maréchaux (qui portent les noms des chefs de guerre de l'Empire), vous découvrirez, chemin faisant, les abords de Paris avec ses voies ferrées, ses ports, ses marchés aux puces, sa foire du Trône et sa cité universitaire. ■

Le bois de Boulogne

IMMENSE PARC DE 863 HA, LE BOIS DE BOULOGNE ATTIRE CHAQUE week-end ensoleillé des promeneurs venus de toute la ville. Ses deux lacs (lac Inférieur et lac Supérieur), situés à deux niveaux différents, sont reliés par une cascade.

Le bois de Boulogne tel qu'on le connaît aujourd'hui fut aménagé sur l'ordre de Napoléon III. Le beau monde des quartiers de l'ouest parisien s'y promenait dans la journée, tandis que des individus moins fréquentables s'y rassemblaient le soir – et s'y rassemblent encore (certaines parties du bois sont à éviter après le coucher du soleil).

D'élégantes avenues et des sentiers mènent aux lacs à travers une pinède et plusieurs chênaies. Dans le jardin d'Acclimatation, parc d'attraction pour les enfants, vous aurez le choix entre la promenade, le golf miniature et bien d'autres activités.

Le jardin Shakespeare, au cœur du bois, entoure un petit théâtre en plein air de 300 places (représentations en français et en anglais). Le Pré-Catelan, restaurant romantique (et cher), se trouve juste à côté.

Avec ses 9 000 rosiers, le parc de Bagatelle est aussi spectaculaire au printemps qu'en automne. Il contient, en outre, de superbes variétés d'iris et de nénuphars.

Les serres d'Auteuil, situées dans la partie sud du bois, près du stade Roland-Garros, contiennent des plantes exotiques, une serre tropicale et une palmeraie sous le dôme central. ■

196 A3

Jardin d'Acclimatation

Avenue Mahatma-Gandhi

01 40 67 90 82

www.jardindacclimatation.fr

€

Sablons

Jardin Shakespeare

Route de Suresnes

Porte-Maillot, puis bus n° 244

Parc de Bagatelle

Boulevard Richard-Wallace

01 40 67 97 00

ouvert la journée

€

Pont-Reuilly, puis le bus n° 43 ; ou Porte-Maillot et bus n° 244

Roland-Garros

196 A2

2, av. Gordon-Bennett

01 47 43 48 00

www.fft.fr

Tournoi de tennis, fin mai-déb. juin

€€ (musée ou visite guidée)

Porte-d'Auteuil

Le comte d'Artois (futur Charles X) fit en 1775 le pari de bâtir le palais de Bagatelle en sept semaines et le gagna.

La Grande Arche
196 A4
Parvis de La Défense
01 49 07 27 57
€€
La Défense

La Défense

Avec sa Grande Arche, le quartier de La Défense complète l'immense axe qui traverse Paris d'est en ouest et dégage une atmosphère résolument futuriste.

La Grande Arche est le monument en forme d'arcade qui achève la perspective commençant avec l'Arc de Triomphe.

La Défense est un quartier d'affaires international, à la fois moderne et fonctionnel, conçu en 1950 sur le modèle américain. Sa construction débuta au début des années 1960.

Dans les années 1970, La Défense, peu recherchée par les sociétés, devint le symbole de l'inhumanité de l'architecture moderne. Les années 1980 amorcèrent un renversement de tendance avec la construction de l'immense centre commercial des Quatre-Temps et l'installation du dôme IMAX.

Certains voient la Défense comme un quartier tentaculaire et sans âme ; d'autres apprécient son côté innovant et futuriste. Quoi qu'il en soit, il s'agit de l'un des projets d'urbanisation les plus audacieux d'Europe. À l'origine, les plans rappelaient les structures de certaines villes américaines, mais les architectes allèrent plus loin en éliminant toute circulation automobile. La Défense a donc un niveau en plein air, composé de bureaux et d'immeubles d'habitation reliés par une immense esplanade, et un niveau souterrain qui renferme les réseaux routier, ferroviaire et métropolitain, et plusieurs parkings.

Avec son toit de 230 m de long, le CNIT fut l'un des premiers bâtiments de la Défense. Il a longtemps abrité les foires commerciales, transférées depuis à la porte de Versailles. Entièrement rénové, il est devenu aujourd'hui un centre d'affaires international et de communication.

Béton, verre et acier sont de rigueur, mais l'esplanade est embellie par diverses œuvres d'art, notamment une gigantesque sculpture d'Alexandre Calder, une œuvre de Niki de Saint Phalle et plusieurs fontaines originales. La Grande Arche, dont le toit est situé à 91,5 m du sol, est ouverte au public ; vous pourrez y voir une exposition retraçant sa construction. Ce grand cube vide habillé de marbre de Carrare pourrait contenir Notre-Dame. ■

Les marchés aux puces

«Ma parole, c'est le marché aux puces ! » Cette exclamation d'un visiteur anonyme frappé par ces marchés périphériques de Paris est à l'origine de l'appellation de ces lieux de vente. Paris compte trois principaux marchés aux puces, mais le plus renommé reste celui de Saint-Ouen qui fête ses 116 ans !

Les puces
Sam.-dim.-lun.
De 7 h à 19 h
(sauf Vanves fermé lun.)

www.parispuces.com

Au XIXe siècle, Paris se dote d'une ceinture fortifiée. Au pied de cette enceinte, se regroupe une véritable « cour des miracles » chassée du centre de Paris. Ces chiffonniers, appelés aussi « biffins » ou, plus poétiquement « pêcheurs de lune », récupèrent les rebuts des plus riches et déballent leurs trouvailles sur des couvertures dans la rue. Très vite, les marchés s'organisent et c'est plus particulièrement à Saint-Ouen qu'on prend l'habitude de venir chiner.

Le succès des puces (120 000 visiteurs par week-end à Clignancourt) est dû à la population variée et cosmopolite qui les fréquente, à la diversité des produits, neufs ou d'occasion, qu'on y trouve.

Quelques exemples de ce que vous pourrez y acheter : du mobilier de différentes périodes, des photographies, des gravures et livres anciens, des disques, de la vaisselle, de la peinture, des bijoux, des vêtements neufs ou des fripes, de la ferraille et… des animaux empaillés !

Un dernier conseil avant de vous y rendre : attention aux pickpockets !

Puces de Saint-Ouen
Métro : Porte-de-Clignancourt
Bus : 56, 85, PC

Puces de Vanves
Métro : Porte-de-Vanves
Bus : 58, 95, PC
Ce marché date des années 1920 ; vous y trouverez des vêtements neufs et de la brocante.

Puces de Montreuil
Métro : Porte-de-Montreuil
Bus : PC
Ce marché haut en couleur est très animé et plus spécialisé dans les fripes. ■

On trouve de tout aux puces, il suffit d'être patient et curieux…

La Butte-aux-Cailles

197 DI
Entre la rue de la Butte-aux-Cailles et la rue des Cinq-Diamants
Corvisart

Le passé et le présent coexistent dans ce quartier ouvrier qui était à l'origine l'un des nombreux villages entourant Paris. On y appelait ses habitants les « pieds mouillés », car ils traversaient nu-pieds la Bièvre (désormais détournée sous la rue Corvisart) pour rejoindre Paris intra-muros (de l'autre côté des remparts) sans payer l'octroi. Ce quartier au calme campagnard et aux noms de rues évocateurs – rue des Peupliers, du Moulin-des-Prés, du Champ-de-l'Alouette – contraste avec les hautes tours du quartier de la place d'Italie.

La Butte-aux-Cailles est devenue célèbre le 21 novembre 1783 lorsque le physicien Pilâtre de Rozier fit atterrir son ballon, qui avait quitté le château de la Muette 25 minutes plus tôt, entre le moulin des Merveilles et le moulin Vieux. Il s'agissait du premier vol en ballon, réalisé à une altitude d'environ 945 m. À l'époque, la Butte était un superbe belvédère naturel surplombant les marais, les prairies et les moulins de la vallée de la Bièvre ainsi que les clochers de Paris.

Les habitants de ce quartier furent parmi les premiers à se rebeller pendant la Commune. « Le Temps des cerises » (l'un des rares établissements de Paris géré en coopérative ouvrière) et « Le Merle moqueur » (un bistrot datant de la Commune) ont perpétué jusqu'à nos jours cet esprit libertaire et indépendant. La Butte-aux-Cailles fut le refuge des communards et l'Association des Amis de la Commune se réunit régulièrement pour vendre des livres et des documents se rapportant à cette époque.

Le quartier est également connu pour sa ferme, située près du passage Barrault, qui accueillit les dernières vaches de Paris jusque dans les années 1950. Petites maisons, rues pavées et sinueuses se cachent juste à côté des tours ultra-modernes du quartier chinois et de la place d'Italie, ancien carrefour gallo-romain.

Explorez les rues Buot, Michal, de la Butte-aux-Cailles et des Cinq-Diamants, très pittoresques, la charmante villa Daviel et, plus loin, le square des Peupliers, bordé de maisons bourgeoises.

La piscine de la Butte aux Cailles, située place Verlaine, date de 1924. Disposant d'un bassin couvert et d'un bassin en plein air, elle a été récemment rénovée et repeinte en jaune et rouge. Elle est alimentée par un puits artésien de 570 m de profondeur et reçoit plus de 6 millions de litres d'eau sulfureuse à 27 °C par jour.

Non loin de là, visitez la manufacture des Gobelins (voir p. 67). ■

Le quartier de la Butte-aux-Cailles date du XVIIIe siècle et n'a pas beaucoup changé, avec ses rues pavées et ses étroites impasses pentues.

Le bois et le château de Vincennes

LIEU DE PROMENADE TRÈS APPRÉCIÉ, LE BOIS DE VINCENNES ABRITE un hippodrome, comme au bois de Boulogne, l'Institut international bouddhique et son temple tibétain très coloré, des lacs, un zoo (700 animaux de 70 espèces), un musée, un terrain de jeux et, bien sûr, le château.

Après avoir soigneusement aménagé le bois de Boulogne pour l'offrir à la ville en 1852, Napoléon III décida, en 1860, de faire un geste pour les ouvriers des XIe et XIIe arrondissements en créant un parc identique à l'est de Paris, le bois de Vincennes. Quatre lacs furent creusés et agrémentés d'îles romantiques abritant des restaurants et des grottes secrètes.

Ne manquez pas le grand lac Daumesnil et le parc zoologique attenant (53, avenue de Saint-Maurice, tél. : 01 44 75 20 10). Découvrez également un bâtiment « Art déco » conçu pour l'Exposition coloniale de 1931 et qui abritait jusqu'à peu le musée des Arts d'Afrique et d'Océanie. La collection de masques africains et d'objets d'art océaniens prendra place quai Branly. Au sous-sol se trouve un petit aquarium. Le Parc floral, moins connu, est superbement aménagé. Le terrain de jeux destiné aux enfants propose promenades à cheval, murs d'escalade et piste de kart. Enfin, des pavillons accueillent des expositions temporaires, et des concerts de jazz et de musique classique ont lieu en plein air, au printemps et en été.

Le château de Vincennes, construit par Charles V, fut une résidence royale pendant des siècles. Le musée installé dans le donjon du XIVe siècle est en rénovation jusqu'en 2007. La chapelle du XVIe siècle possède encore de magnifiques vitraux. ■

En 1763, le marquis de Sade fut emprisonné au château.

197 F1
Avenue Daumesnil ou avenue de Gravelle

Institut international bouddhique
40, route de Ceinture du Lac Daumesnil
01 43 41 54 48
Fermé à la visite
Porte-Dorée

Temple tibétain
Route de ceinture du Lac Daumesnil
01 40 04 98 06
www.kagyu-dzong.org
Fermé lun.
Porte-Dorée

Parc Floral
197 G2
Esplanade du château de Vincennes
01 43 43 92 95
www.parcfloraldeparis.com
€
Château-de-Vincennes

Château de Vincennes
Donjon actuellement fermé à la visite
197 G2
1, avenue de Paris
01 48 08 31 20
www.monuments.fr
€€
Entrée libre 1er dim. oct-mai
Château-de-Vincennes

Parcs et jardins de Paris

Les Parisiens se plaignent souvent du manque d'espaces verts dans cette ville dense. Pourtant, plus de 400 parcs, jardins et squares jalonnent le paysage urbain depuis les jardins à la française des Tuileries, réalisés par André Le Nôtre, jusqu'au récent parc André-Citroën, aux couleurs thématiques et aux allures post-modernes, situé à l'ouest du XVe arrondissement.

Les grands parcs parisiens

Jusqu'au XIXe siècle, les grands jardins – Luxembourg, Palais-Royal, Tuileries – faisaient partie du domaine royal. Mais sous le Second Empire, d'immenses parcs ainsi que de petits squares de quartier ont commencé à apparaître dans tout Paris sous l'impulsion d'Adolphe Alphand, paysagiste officiel du préfet Haussmann. Alphand créa le bois de Boulogne, à partir de ce qui restait de la forêt de Rouvray, le bois de Vincennes, les Buttes-Chaumont et le parc Montsouris.

Au début du XXe siècle, les promoteurs utilisèrent les terrains pour construire des logements au détriment de nouveaux parcs. Ce n'est que dans les années 1980 que les autorités s'intéressèrent de nouveau aux espaces verts. Au cours des vingt dernières années, plusieurs parcs, couvrant en totalité 101 ha, furent ouverts aux Parisiens.

Les parcs moins connus

Le parc des Buttes-Chaumont (*rues Botzaris, Manin et de Crimée, métro : Simon-Bolivar ou Buttes-Chaumont*) se situe dans le nord-est de Paris. Son relief abrupt, ses sentiers entrelacés, ses grottes et son célèbre belvédère perché au sommet d'une colline en font un des lieux les plus charmants de Paris. Il comporte un petit lac, ainsi qu'un kiosque où sont donnés des concerts en été, et propose des activités pour les enfants. La vue sur la ville est magnifique.

Le parc Montsouris (*avenue Reille, boulevard Jourdan, RER : Cité-Universitaire*), est situé dans le XIVe arrondissement, au sud de Paris. Avec ses saules pleureurs et son lac que sillonnent quelques cygnes, il est tout aussi romantique que le parc des Buttes-Chaumont, bien qu'il n'occupe pas un site aussi spectaculaire. Pour camoufler les lignes ferroviaires qui l'entouraient, Alphand créa des ravins bordés de pins. De nombreux étudiants résidant à la cité universitaire fréquentent le parc.

Le dernier en date des jardins parisiens est la Promenade plantée, ou Coulée verte, réalisée à l'emplacement d'un ancien viaduc ferroviaire, allant de la place de la Bastille au bois de Vincennes. La première section comprend le viaduc, transformé en jardin surplombant la ville, et la seconde, ouverte aux cyclistes, va du jardin de Reuilly (dans le XIIe arrondissement) au

Jean Cocteau appelait les jardins du Palais-Royal, « la campagne au cœur de Paris ».

Des sentiers entrelacés mènent au belvédère dominant les Buttes-Chaumont.

bois de Vincennes. En dessous, les anciennes voûtes du viaduc abritent une galerie commerciale, le Viaduc des Arts.

Non loin se trouve le parc de Bercy, réalisé sur le site d'anciens entrepôts de vin, à proximité du palais omnisports de Paris Bercy et de l'imposant ministère des Finances. Quelques bâtiments datant du XVIIIe siècle et certains arbres centenaires ont été préservés. Le parc comprend un canal, un verger, un potager et des jardins créés sur le thème des quatre saisons. Sur une des esplanades bordant la Seine ont été érigées de très belles statues de Rachid Khimoune.

Le square Tino-Rossi, jalonné de sculptures contemporaines, offre une belle vue sur la Seine. Il a été réalisé en 1977, en face de l'Institut du Monde arabe.

Les jardins Albert-Kahn (*14, rue du Port, Boulogne-Billancourt, tél. : 01 46 04 52 80, fermé le lun.*), situés en banlieue ouest, font partie des parcs les plus intéressants de la région parisienne. Récemment restaurés, ils renferment un superbe jardin japonais. ■

Notre sélection

Les jardins à la française : Les Tuileries (p. 137), le Luxembourg (p. 82).
Les jardins botaniques : le Parc floral de Vincennes (p. 203) ; les serres d'Auteuil (p. 199) ; le jardin des Plantes (pp. 70-71).
Les jardins romantiques : le parc Monceau (p. 152) ; les Buttes-Chaumont ; le parc Montsouris ; le parc de Bagatelle (voir p. 199) ; le parc du musée Rodin (pp. 172-173).
Les jardins contemporains : le square Tino-Rossi, le parc de Bercy ; le parc de Belleville (p. 207) ; le parc de la Villette (pp. 208-209) ; le parc André-Citroën.
Les grands espaces verts : le bois de Vincennes (p. 203) ; le bois de Boulogne (p. 199). ■

Belleville et Ménilmontant

197 F3

Belleville : centré autour de la rue de Belleville. Ménilmontant : centré autour de la rue de Ménilmontant

Belleville : Belleville ou Pyrénées. Ménilmontant : Ménilmontant

LES DIFFÉRENTES VAGUES D'IMMIGRATION ONT AMENÉ UNE POPULATION très variée dans ces quartiers : Juifs ashkénazes d'Europe centrale, Arméniens et républicains espagnols s'installèrent ici au début des années 1930 et furent suivis par des Juifs séfarades d'Afrique du Nord, des Maghrébins, des Africains, des Cambodgiens, des Thaïlandais, des Vietnamiens et des Chinois. Avec ses restaurants maghrébins, ses boucheries casher et ses cafés turcs, la rue de Belleville dégage une atmosphère particulièrement exotique. Le long du boulevard Ménilmontant, les marchés du mardi et du vendredi reflètent également cette diversité culturelle. À côté de Ménilmontant, un ensemble de résidences modernes et de maisons anciennes est en passe de devenir un des quartiers en vogue de Paris.

En plus du quartier chinois de Belleville (ci-dessus), d'autres se sont développés. Le Triangle de Choisy est le plus connu d'entre eux (voir p. 210).

HIER ET AUJOURD'HUI

Annexé à la capitale en 1860, l'ancien village de Belleville fut l'un des berceaux de l'opposition du Second Empire et le dernier quartier à déposer les armes pendant la Commune. De nombreuses mesures furent prises pour réprimer et contenir l'agitation ouvrière, notamment la division de Belleville en trois arrondissements (XIe, XIXe et XXe). Pendant longtemps, Belleville conserva son cachet de quartier typiquement populaire. Mais il ne cesse de changer en raison de l'immigration et d'innombrables projets de reconstruction et de rénovation qui mettent à mal l'âme de l'ancien village. Les rues sinueuses sont bordées de magasins, d'ateliers, de vieux bistros, de ruelles et de cours intérieures mystérieuses.

Belleville et Ménilmontant sont encore marqués par l'époque où les

Le Café Charbon, une ancienne salle de bal rénovée, est l'un des lieux les plus branchés de Paris. Dans ce quartier Oberkampf, vous trouverez un grand nombre de cafés, de bars et de restaurants.

hommes travaillaient dans les carrières de gypse situées à proximité. Fondé au XVe siècle autour du vignoble exploité par les grandes abbayes de Paris, Belleville était connu pour ses guinguettes, où les Parisiens venaient le dimanche boire le guinguet (vin aigrelet). Les gens modestes, chassés du centre ville par les bouleversements haussmanniens du XIXe siècle, s'y installèrent et la population augmenta considérablement.

Jusqu'en 1914, il y eut à Belleville et à Ménilmontant autant de buvettes, de cafés, de cabarets et de bals musettes qu'à Montmartre. L'Élysée-Ménilmontant (qui n'existe plus aujourd'hui) était l'un des cabarets les plus connus du quartier. C'est ici que Maurice Chevalier fit ses débuts. Édith Piaf est née au 72, rue de Belleville. La discothèque « La Java » possède encore son décor de bal-musette d'origine. La rue des Envierges, bordée de restaurants, de bistros et de cafés chantants, est très animée le soir.

Le sommet de la colline de Belleville, à l'angle de la rue Piat, de la rue du Transvaal et de la rue des Envierges, offre un beau panorama sur la ville. La rue des Cascades rappelle les nombreux ruisseaux de Ménilmontant. La rue Piat menait autrefois à deux moulins et débouche désormais sur le **parc de Belleville,** qui est aménagé le long de la pente escarpée de la colline et offre un magnifique panorama sur Paris.

La **villa Castel**, dont l'entrée se trouve rue du Transvaal, est une petite allée bordée de maisons, où François Truffaut tourna une scène de *Jules et Jim*, en 1962. Chaque année, au printemps, des peintres locaux ouvrent leurs ateliers au public. C'est l'occasion de découvrir des cours intérieures, des ateliers et de charmants petits jardins de ville.

Les rues entrelacées et les passages qui séparent la rue de Belleville de la rue de Ménilmontant sont d'anciennes voies qui reliaient autrefois les vignobles. Avec l'apparition de bars et de cafés branchés, comme Le « Café Charbon », « La Mercerie » ou « La Buvette » (musique africaine et antillaise), la rue de Ménilmontant redevient à la mode, notamment sa partie basse proche de la rue Oberkampf. ■

Le parc de la Villette

197 E4
Quai de la Gironde
Porte-de-Pantin

Cité des Sciences et de l'Industrie
197 E5
30, avenue Corentin-Cariou
01 40 05 70 00
www.cite-science.fr
Fermé lun.
€€
Porte-de-la-Villette

La Géode
197 E5
Au sud de la Cité des Sciences
01 40 05 79 99
Fermé lun.
€€
Porte-de-la-Villette

Le parc de la Villette est l'une des réalisations les plus récentes et les plus réussies de Paris. Il y a à peine quinze ans, des abattoirs s'élevaient au milieu d'un gigantesque no man's land, dans le nord-est de la ville. Aujourd'hui, ce parc de 28 ha comprend la Cité des Sciences et de l'Industrie, la Cité de la Musique, le Zénith (une salle de concert) et la Grande Halle.

LA CITÉ DES SCIENCES ET DE L'INDUSTRIE

Avec plus de 5 millions de visiteurs par an, la Cité des Sciences est l'attraction la plus populaire du parc. Contrairement à la plupart des musées, elle propose de nombreuses expositions interactives. La principale exposition permanente de ce grand bâtiment de 5 étages fait de verre et d'acier, « Explora », permet aux visiteurs de découvrir les galaxies, les volcans, les océans, l'énergie et le son grâce à une multitude de dispositifs novateurs : exploration de l'espace sur ordinateur, simulateurs de vol et Odorama pour tester la perception des odeurs.

Ouverte en 1986, la Cité des Sciences comporte également un planétarium pour voyager dans l'espace, une serre, la Géode (salle de projection hémisphérique de 100 places), l'Argonaute (sous-marin authentique) et le Cinaxe (salle de cinéma mobile). Deux sections ont été réservées aux enfants : la Cité des enfants (de 3 à 12 ans) et la Techno-Cité (à partir de 11 ans) – villages scientifiques où les enfants peuvent

participer à des expositions interactives de 90 minutes (réservation conseillée lors de l'achat de votre billet d'entrée).

LE MUSÉE DE LA MUSIQUE

Le musée de la Musique fait partie de la Cité de la Musique, conçue par Christian de Portzamparc et qui abrite également une salle de concert, un centre de recherche ainsi que le Conservatoire national supérieur de musique et de danse de Paris. Les visiteurs explorent le musée avec un casque qui s'active automatiquement.

AUTRES COMPOSANTES DU PARC

Outre ses musées, ce parc conçu par le Suisse Bernard Tschumi est un endroit idéal pour fuir la ville. Il renferme une superbe bambouseraie, d'extravagantes « folies » (édifices recouverts de métal rouge) dont l'une abrite un centre d'information, une aire de jeux pour enfants avec un grand toboggan en forme de dragon et dix jardins thématiques. Le mobilier du parc a été créé par Philippe Starck. Ne manquez pas la sculpture représentant une bicyclette à moitié enterrée de Claes Oldenburg. En été, tard dans la soirée, des concerts et des séances de cinéma sur écran géant ont lieu en plein air.

Le seul vestige des abattoirs et de la foire aux bestiaux est la **Grande Halle** (*221, avenue Jean-Jaurès, tél.: 01 40 03 75 75, métro: Porte-de-Pantin*), magnifique exemple d'architecture en verre et en fonte. Construite en 1867, l'ancienne halle aux bœufs n'était à l'origine qu'un abri pour les bêtes destinées à être vendues à la foire. Entièrement rénovée, elle comporte aujourd'hui des plates-formes modulables pouvant accueillir des expositions temporaires et des concerts. ■

Une séance à la Géode est une des nombreuses activités du parc de la Villette. Le procédé de projection IMAX permet de placer le spectateur au cœur même de l'image avec un écran hémisphérique de 1 000 m².

Cité de la Musique

197 E4
221, av. Jean-Jaurès
01 44 84 44 84
www.cite-musique.fr
Fermé lun.
€€
Porte-de-Pantin

Autres quartiers

Le canal Saint-Martin et le canal de l'Ourcq relient la Villette à la Seine.

LA GOUTTE-D'OR

À l'est de Pigalle et de Montmartre, se trouve le quartier de la Goutte-d'Or, qui tire son nom du vin très réputé produit autrefois sur ses coteaux. Depuis le XIXe siècle, c'est le quartier le plus modeste et le moins cher de Paris. Au cours des dernières décennies, il est devenu un quartier essentiellement arabe et africain. Ici, les langues, les costumes traditionnels et les cuisines épicées se mélangent, et les rues sont bordées de cafés kabyles.

Faites un tour au marché Dejean (métro : Château-d'Eau) ou au marché à ciel ouvert du boulevard de la Chapelle (lun. et sam.), où vous trouverez de tout à des prix imbattables. Chaque année, lors du festival de musique, la Goutte-d'Or en Fête, ce quartier reçoit des musiciens locaux ainsi que des grands noms du raï, du rap et du hip-hop.

197 D4 Ⓜ Barbès-Rochechouart

LE QUARTIER CHINOIS

À première vue, les tours du XIIIe arrondissement n'ont aucun charme. Pourtant, ce qu'on appelle aujourd'hui le Triangle de Choisy est le centre florissant du quartier chinois de Paris. Environ 30 000 résidents asiatiques y ont importé leur culture, représentée par des magasins en forme de pagode et des centres d'arts martiaux. Ne manquez pas le plus grand supermarché asiatique de France, chez Tang, avenue d'Ivry, et les nombreux restaurants qui proposent tous les types de cuisine asiatique.

197 D1 Ⓜ Tolbiac, Porte d'Ivry

LA « NOUVELLE ATHÈNES »

Nichée entre Pigalle et les Grands Boulevards, la Nouvelle Athènes a accueilli de nombreux artistes du XIXe siècle, comme Théodore Géricault, Eugène Delacroix et Frédéric Chopin. Dans ce quartier, vous pourrez visiter le **musée Gustave-Moreau** (voir p. 194) et le **musée de la Vie romantique** (voir p. 114) *(Maison Renan Scheffer, 16, rue Chaptal, tél. : 01 48 74 95 38, fermé lun.)*. Créé dans l'atelier du sculpteur et peintre Ary Scheffer, ce musée, dissimulé dans un délicieux jardin de roses et de lilas, abrite notamment des objets ayant appartenu à l'écrivain George Sand.

Prenez ensuite le temps d'aller admirer la place Saint-Georges, avec les façades de l'hôtel néo-Renaissance de la Païva et le magnifique hôtel Thiers, qui possède un musée consacré à l'ère napoléonienne *(Bibliothèque Thiers, 27, place Saint-Georges, tél. : 01 48 78 14 33, ouvert jeu. et ven. 12 h-18 h)*.

196 C4 Ⓜ Saint-Georges, Trinité, Pigalle ■

Les canaux de Paris

Avec l'ouverture du parc de la Villette, au nord, et l'aménagement du bassin de l'Arsenal, qui va de la place de la Bastille à la Seine, les canaux de Paris sont redevenus très populaires. Le canal Saint-Martin, qui mène au bassin de la Villette, et le canal de l'Ourcq passent par 9 écluses, 2 ponts tournants et quelques jolies passerelles. Bien que des bateaux naviguent sur ces canaux, une promenade à pied en offre une vision plus typique.

L'hôtel du Nord, qui inspira le titre du célèbre film de Marcel Carné (1938), se trouve au 102, quai de Jemmapes. Sauvé de la destruction dans les années 1980, il est devenu depuis un restaurant très touristique.

Il est possible d'effectuer des croisières en bateaux sur le canal Saint-Martin, le bassin de la Villette et le canal de l'Ourcq (5 km). Vous avez le choix entre plusieurs compagnies ; réservation conseillée. ■

À deux pas de la capitale, se trouvent des abbayes, des châteaux, des forêts et des villes qui ont inspiré des artistes tels que Van Gogh et Monet.

Quelques escapades

Sculpture du Parterre d'eau à Versailles.

Quelques escapades

Des cathédrales et des abbayes médiévales, des palais royaux, certains désormais présidentiels, des châteaux somptueux, des parcs d'attractions, de « vraies » forêts vous attendent aux portes de Paris. Pour toute information sur le réseau ferroviaire d'Île-de-France, composez le 08 91 36 20 20.

Si vous n'êtes jamais allé en région parisienne, ne manquez pas le château de Versailles (voir pp. 214-219), parfait exemple de la grande tradition architecturale française. Rêve de Louis XIV, il fut l'instrument de son pouvoir et de sa politique. Le parc à lui seul vaut l'objet d'une visite. L'Île-de-France est jalonnée d'autres châteaux, comme celui de Fontainebleau (voir pp. 224-225), de style Renaissance, dont la forêt aux alentours ravira les amateurs d'escalade. Le château de Rambouillet (voir p. 226) est l'une des résidences du président de la République. Celui de Vaux-le-Vicomte (voir p. 222) n'était pas un palais royal, mais il était si somptueux que Nicolas Fouquet, le ministre des Finances de Louis XIV, qui l'avait fait bâtir, fut emprisonné pour avoir détourné les fonds

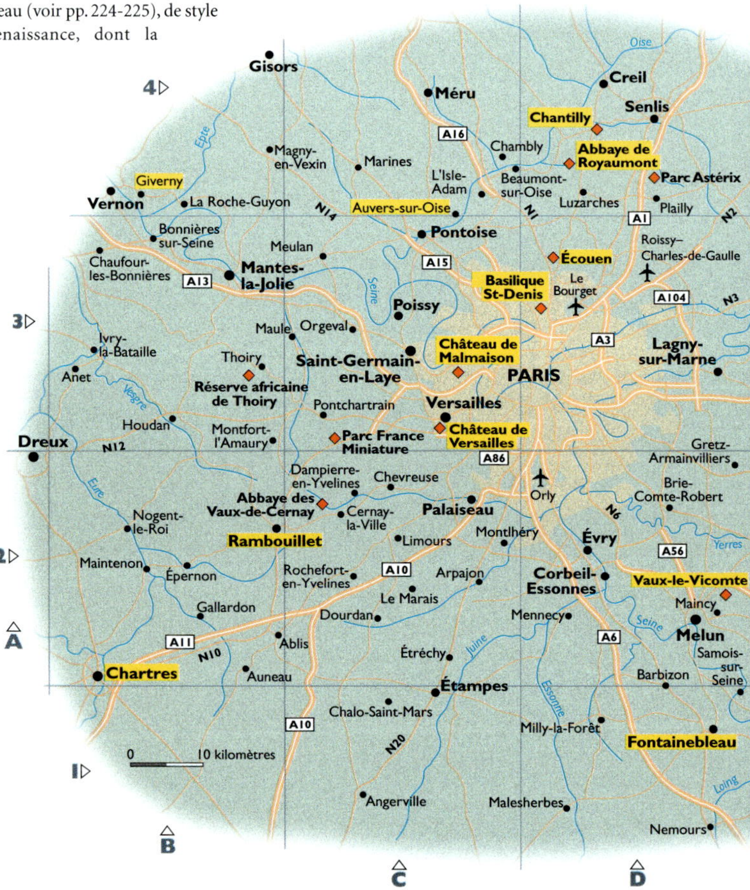

de l'État. Le château de Chantilly (voir p. 232) abrite une superbe collection d'œuvres d'art, notamment des peintures de Raphaël et les splendides enluminures des *Très Riches Heures du duc de Berry* (voir p. 232). Les imposantes écuries, construites au XVIIIe siècle pour loger les 240 chevaux du prince de Condé (transformées en musée du Cheval), comptent parmi les plus belles d'Europe. Le château d'Écouen (voir p. 232) offre un beau témoignage de la Renaissance en France.

Plusieurs sites proches de Paris vous donneront un aperçu du patrimoine médiéval de la région, notamment la forteresse de Blandy (voir p. 222), près de Vaux-le-Vicomte, et la cité de Provins (voir p. 223), où a lieu tous les ans une fête en costume d'époque. À Saint-Denis, se trouve la basilique du même nom (voir p. 220), qui date du XIIIe siècle et fut le premier grand édifice gothique d'Europe. C'est également dans cette ville que se trouve le nouveau Stade de France qui fut le théâtre des exploits de l'équipe de France de football en 1998.

Si vous êtes amateur d'art, ne manquez pas la maison et les jardins de Monet, à Giverny (voir pp. 230-231), où le peintre trouva une éternelle source d'inspiration. La ville d'Auvers-sur-Oise (voir p. 227) témoigne de l'attrait qu'a eu la vallée de l'Oise sur les impressionnistes. Van Gogh vécut et mourut à Auvers (sa tombe jumelée avec celle de son frère Théo est très émouvante). La ville attira plusieurs autres peintres, dont Paul Cézanne et Charles Daubigny.

L'abbaye des Vaux-de-Cernay (voir p. 226), transformée en hôtel de luxe, date du XIIe siècle et apparaît comme un refuge isolé au milieu de la vaste forêt de Rambouillet. Le réfectoire d'origine a été préservé, tout comme l'église dont seul manque le toit.

La cathédrale de Chartres (voir pp. 228-229), joyau de la France médiévale, possède des vitraux du XIIIe siècle uniques au monde. ■

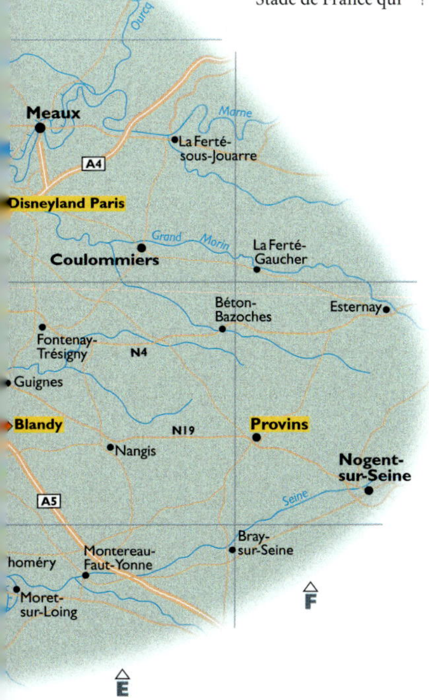

Pour les enfants

Tout le monde a entendu parler de **Disneyland Paris** (voir p. 221), mais il existe aussi d'autres excursions pour les enfants.

La réserve africaine de **Thoiry** *(Tél. : 01 34 87 52 25, www.thoiry.tm.fr/thehp.htm)*, située sur la D11 à l'ouest de Paris, fut l'un des premiers parcs de ce genre à ouvrir ses portes en 1968. Les animaux se déplacent librement et vous pouvez les observer depuis votre voiture. Le parc comporte également un zoo traditionnel et d'autres attractions.

Le **parc Astérix,** situé à Plailly, sur l'A1 au nord de Paris, est un parc à thème avec attractions et spectacles entièrement consacrés au héros gaulois (*Tél. : 08 36 68 30 10, www.parcasterix.fr, fermé mi-oct.-Pâques, RER : ligne B3 Aéroport Charles-de-Gaulle et navette*).

Le **parc France Miniature** (*Tél. : 01 30 16 16 30, www.franceminiature.com ouvert mi-mars-mi-nov.*), situé à l'ouest de Paris après Versailles, n'est pas très connu. Plus de 150 monuments français ont été reconstruits à très petite échelle dans ce parc de 5 ha. ■

Le château de Versailles

La somptueuse chambre de la reine. Les soieries tissées ou brodées de lilas et de plumes de paon ont été restaurées en 1976.

Rien n'est plus étincelant que le château de Versailles. Cet immense palais, construit sous le règne de Louis XIV, témoigne du rayonnement de la France aux XVIIe et XVIIIe siècles.

En 1623, Louis XIII, grand amateur de chasse, fait construire au milieu de la forêt un pavillon si modeste que ses contemporains le qualifient de « misérable manoir dont même un simple châtelain ne tirerait aucune fierté ». À sa mort, en 1643, son fils, Louis XIV, n'a que 5 ans. Il va transformer le modeste pavillon de chasse en un palais éblouissant. Il y dépensa une fortune considérable, faisant appel aux meilleurs artistes

Le remarquable Bassin d'Apollon, point central du parc.

de France : l'architecte Louis Le Vau (puis Jules Hardouin-Mansart), le paysagiste André Le Nôtre et le peintre Charles Le Brun, qui avaient tous travaillé à Vaux-le-Vicomte (voir p. 222).

Le château de Versailles est indissociable de la personnalité du roi (son arrière-petit-fils Louis XV et son arrière-arrière-petit-fils Louis XVI ne firent que quelques modifications mineures) et du rayonnement de la France à cette époque. Il reflète parfaitement les ambitions du Roi-Soleil, dont le règne (1643-1715) incarna la monarchie absolue.

L'INTÉRIEUR

Les Grands Appartements du roi, présentent un ensemble d'une richesse inouïe. Les pièces, ornées d'or et de marbre (extrait de toutes les carrières du royaume), furent disposées comme les planètes gravitant autour du Soleil (emblème du roi). À partir de 1682, Louis XIV s'établit définitivement à Versailles et utilise ces grandes salles pour les cérémonies officielles et les audiences, préférant résider dans des pièces plus petites, constituant l'Appartement du Roi, situées dans une ancienne partie du château, face à la cour de marbre.

À Versailles, tout est régi par « l'étiquette », y compris dans les appartements privés du roi. Les courtisans se disputent jalousement le privilège d'être présents, notamment

Château de Versailles

19 km, au sud de Paris

☎ 01 30 83 78 00

Fermé lun.

€€

Ⓜ En voiture : A13, sortie 14.
En train : de la gare Montparnasse jusqu'à Versailles-Chantiers ; de la gare Saint-Lazare jusqu'à Versailles-Rive-droite.
RER C : Versailles-Rive-gauche

lors des cérémonies du « lever » et du « coucher » royal. La chambre du roi, rouge et or, a été réaménagée telle qu'elle était le 1er septembre 1715, jour de la mort du souverain.

La chambre dorée de la reine est encore plus somptueuse, mais les princesses qui y vécurent (deux reines, deux dauphines et l'épouse du fils aîné du roi) avaient encore moins d'intimité. Elles devaient notamment y accoucher, toujours en public pour éviter que l'on puisse mettre en doute la naissance des héritiers de la couronne. Marie-Antoinette dormit dans cette chambre jusqu'à la nuit du 5 au 6 octobre 1789 où elle dut s'enfuir des appartements envahis par les émeutiers révolutionnaires.

La volonté de grandeur de Louis XIV est particulièrement visible dans la galerie des Glaces (façade ouest du château) : 73 m de long, 10,50 m de large, 12,30 m de haut. C'est ici qu'avaient lieu les grandes fêtes de la cour. Les 17 fenêtres en arcade font face à 17 miroirs, tandis que le plafond voûté (décoré par Le Brun) présente en 30 compositions les moments marquants du règne de Louis XIV jusqu'à la paix de Nimègue. La galerie était garnie d'un somptueux mobilier comprenant des tables, des vases à orangers en argent massif, 41 lustres et torchères qui furent fondus en 1864.

Après la fin de l'Ancien Régime, la galerie des Glaces servit encore de cadre à de grands événements. Le 18 janvier 1871, Bismarck fait proclamer Guillaume Ier empereur d'Allemagne, après la défaite de Napoléon. Le 28 juin 1919 y fut signé le traité de Versailles qui mettait fin à la Première Guerre mondiale.

LES JARDINS

À partir d'un terrain marécageux et escarpé, André Le Nôtre réalisa ce qui est aujourd'hui le plus bel exemple de jardin à la française. À une époque où l'on pensait que l'homme devait maîtriser la nature, le paysagiste entreprit d'immenses travaux de drainage et déplaça des monceaux de terre pour former les terrasses qui vont du parterre d'eau (deux bassins symétriques sous les fenêtres de la galerie de Glaces) au bassin d'Apollon et au Grand Canal.

Le roi était si fier de ses jardins qu'il proposa lui-même un itinéraire pour les visiter. Bien que classiques dans leur conception et organisés autour de deux grands axes en croix, ces jardins sont jalonnés de bosquets, de fontaines, de labyrinthes et autres curiosités comme le bassin de Neptune et les bains d'Apollon.

Les bosquets abritent des fontaines très sophistiquées, créées pour agrémenter les fêtes organisées par Louis XIV. La plus célèbre d'entre elles (en 1664), officiellement don-

Le parterre sud.

Le bassin d'Apollon.

Le plafond de la chapelle royale.

Le salon de Mars.

Avec ses 73 m de long et ses 12,30 m de haut, la galerie des Glaces est la salle la plus prestigieuse du château.

née en l'honneur de l'épouse du roi, Marie-Thérèse, rendait en réalité hommage à la favorite du moment, Mademoiselle de La Vallière. Molière écrivit plusieurs pièces, notamment *Tartuffe,* pour cette fête qui dura une semaine. Ballets, feux d'artifice, jeux d'eau, tournois et banquets éblouirent les courtisans. Aujourd'hui, les « Grandes Eaux », qui ont lieu tous les dimanches de mai à octobre, recréent en musique l'ambiance grandiose de cet événement.

Louis XIV exigeait que les bosquets du parc soient fleuris toute l'année. Grâce à l'ingéniosité de Jean-Baptiste de La Quintinie, il put manger des fraises en mars et de la laitue en janvier. Le Potager du Roy, qui produit fruits et légumes sans discontinuer depuis trois siècles, est également ouvert au public.

LE GRAND TRIANON ET LE PETIT TRIANON

Versailles était trop grand et pas assez intime. Environ 10 000 personnes occupaient le château, sans compter les serviteurs et les soldats, et il n'y avait aucun moyen d'échapper aux courtisans obséquieux ou aux règles strictes de l'étiquette. Le roi demanda à Hardouin-Mansart de bâtir le Grand Trianon en 1687, petit

palais de marbre rose situé dans le parc à quelque distance du château. Confortable, facilement chauffable, le Grand Trianon fut le refuge de Louis XIV. Délaissé par ses successeurs, il fut rénové sous la présidence du général de Gaulle. Une de ses ailes est utilisée pour certaines réceptions officielles et pour accueillir des chefs d'État étrangers.

Après la mort du Roi-Soleil, Louis XV continua à vivre à Versailles. Il fit bâtir le Petit Trianon par Gabriel, de 1762 à 1768, pour y recevoir sa maîtresse, Madame de Pompadour. Lorsque Marie-Antoinette devint reine, elle créa le « Hameau », village de rêve situé sur les bords du Grand Lac du Trianon. Ce village, construit par Mique, comprenait 12 maisons. Le charmant moulin, dont la roue était mue par le cours d'un ruisseau, a été fort bien restauré.

LA VISITE DU CHÂTEAU

Il est impossible de tout voir en une seule journée. Le château compte plusieurs entrées. L'entrée A donne accès aux pièces les plus importantes : la galerie des Glaces, les appartements du roi et ceux de la reine – qui se visitent seul ou avec un guide. Il y a généralement de longues files d'attente à cette entrée. Il est donc conseillé de payer un peu plus cher à une autre entrée, qui donne accès à ces pièces et à d'autres salles du château (comme les appartements du Dauphin, l'opéra, la chapelle et les petits appartements).

Vous pouvez également acheter un ticket pour le Grand Trianon et le Petit Trianon (on peut prendre un petit train qui relie le château aux Trianons). La visite des jardins est gratuite excepté pendant les Grandes Eaux, spectacle musical au cours duquel les 32 bassins et fontaines sont animés. ■

Seuls quelques intimes de la reine Marie-Antoinette étaient admis au hameau, qui constitue une ferme miniature.

Basilique
Carte p. 212 D3
16, rue de Srasbourg
01 48 09 83 54
€€
Métro : Basilique de Saint-Denis. En voiture : A1, 8 km au nord de Paris

Office de tourisme
01 42 43 33 55

Stade de France
09 92 70 09 00

La basilique Saint-Denis

Plus de 800 ans séparent les deux édifices les plus célèbres de Saint-Denis, ville populaire de la banlieue nord de Paris : la basilique bâtie à partir de 1136 par l'abbé Suger, élément phare dans l'évolution de l'architecture gothique, et le tout nouveau Stade de France, où fut disputée la finale de la Coupe du monde de football en 1998. C'est évidemment le premier monument qui vaut le détour…

Lieu de sépulture officiel des monarques français depuis 1122, la basilique Saint-Denis représente un tournant dans l'histoire de l'architecture. La légende médiévale de saint Denis, célèbre martyr chrétien, avait inspiré à sainte Geneviève, patronne de Paris, la construction d'une basilique aux environs de 475 (voir le chapitre consacré à l'histoire de Paris). Charles Martel y fut enterré, tandis que son fils, Pépin le Bref, et son petit-fils, Charlemagne, y furent couronnés.

L'abbaye de Saint-Denis était déjà puissante lorsque l'abbé Suger transforma la basilique mérovingienne en lui ajoutant des voûtes en croisée d'ogives – une innovation pour l'époque. Les bâtisseurs des autres grandes cathédrales qui suivirent, notamment celles de Chartres et de Senlis, s'inspirèrent de ce modèle. Malheureusement, l'église fut très endommagée pendant la Révolution ; les tombeaux furent profanés et les sculptures mutilées. La plupart de ses trésors sont désormais au Louvre.

Tombes de Henri II et de Catherine de Médicis.

LES MONUMENTS FUNÉRAIRES DES ROIS

La crypte illustre la chronologie fascinante de la monarchie française. Autour de 1260, saint Louis fit réaliser des gisants de ses prédécesseurs en remontant jusqu'au VIIe siècle. À partir du XIVe siècle, le cœur et les viscères des rois défunts furent extraits des dépouilles et dispersés dans divers monuments, tandis que leurs corps recevaient une sépulture à Saint-Denis.

Pendant des siècles, presque tous les rois, reines et dauphins furent enterrés à Saint-Denis, de Dagobert à Louis XVIII. Les monuments funéraires les plus intéressants sont ceux de Dagobert, Henri II, Catherine de Médicis, Pépin le Bref, Charles Martel, Louis XII et François Ier. ■

Disneyland Paris

MALGRÉ DES DÉBUTS DIFFICILES, DISNEYLAND PARIS EST AUJOURD'HUI un franc succès. Le parc propose de nombreuses attractions et comprend de magnifiques décors explorant tous les univers traités par Disney, comme le château de la Belle au Bois dormant ou le bateau des pirates de Peter Pan. On est admiratif devant la qualité des reconstitutions et des fabuleuses parades.

213 E3
19 km de Paris à Marne-la-Vallée
01 60 30 60 30
€€€€€
En voiture : A4 direction Nancy-Metz, sortie 14.
En train : RER A, Marne-la-Vallée-Chessy. Navettes des aéroports de Roissy et d'Orly.

www.disneylandparis.com

Si vous voulez faire plaisir à vos enfants, emmenez-les à Disneyland. L'entrée principale conduit à Main Street, bordée de boutiques où vous trouverez tous les produits Disney imaginables. De là, quatre grands axes mènent à différentes attractions thématiques. Les pays imaginaires sont au nombre de quatre. Les petits adoreront « Fantasyland ». Ils pourront faire une promenade en barque dans *It's a small World* ou se perdre dans le *Labyrinthe d'Alice*, inspiré d'*Alice au Pays des Merveilles*. Les plus grands iront tout droit à « Discoveryland », notamment à *Space Mountain*, et *Space Mountain Mission 2* depuis avril 2005, des montagnes russes à couper le souffle où les voyageurs sont littéralement propulsés dans l'espace. Les *Star Tours*, situées à proximité, proposent une simulation de voyage spatial plus vraie que nature. À « Frontierland », de nouvelles sensations vous attendent à *Big Thunder Mountain* et au *Temple du Péril*.

Entre « Fantasyland » et les loopings sauvages, « Adventureland » vous propose un tour de bateau à aubes aux côtés des Pirates des Caraïbes ou une dégringolade fantastique dans un petit train de mine. Ne manquez pas les classiques comme la Disney Parade avec ses chars illuminés et ses personnages en costume toujours prêts à poser pour une photo.

Le parc comprend dix hôtels à thème pour un séjour prolongé ainsi que de nombreux restaurants. À l'extérieur, un complexe où vous entendrez toutes sortes de musique – de la country au jazz – est également à votre disposition.

Dernière née des attractions : les Walt Disney Studios qui initient aux secrets du cinéma et du dessin animé.

Les prix élevés de l'entrée, de la restauration, ainsi que les files d'attentes (qui peuvent dépasser une heure par attraction…) sont là pour vous rappeler que le « royaume » de Disney n'est pas si « magique » que cela. ■

Le château de la Belle au Bois dormant.

www.vaux-le-vicomte.com

Vaux-le-Vicomte

Vaux-le-Vicomte est le monument privé le plus visité en France.

VAUX-LE-VICOMTE EST L'UN DES PLUS BEAUX EXEMPLES DE CHÂTEAU français de style classique. Tous les samedis soirs, de mai à mi-octobre, château et jardin sont illuminés par plus de 1 000 bougies pour une visite aux chandelles.

Vaux-le-Vicomte
- 212 D2; 50 km sud-est de Paris
- 01 64 14 41 90
- Ouvert tous les jours
- €€
- En train: gare de Lyon, arrêt Melun, puis taxi

Blandy-les-Tours
- 50 km au sud-est de Paris
- 01 60 69 96 89
- Ouvert sam. et dim. de mi-oct. à mi-avr. Fermé mer. de mi-avr. à mi-oct.
- €

Le château fut construit pour Nicolas Fouquet, surintendant des Finances de Louis XIV, par des artistes d'exception: l'architecte Louis Le Vau, le peintre Charles Le Brun et le paysagiste André Le Nôtre. Selon les rumeurs de l'époque, les fonds réunis pour le chantier avaient été détournés des caisses de l'État dont Fouquet avait la charge.

Pendant six ans, de 1656 à 1661, Fouquet dépensa sans compter pour la construction de ce superbe château et de ses jardins à la française. En 1661, il convia Louis XIV à une réception grandiose (6 000 personnes étaient invitées) avec feux d'artifice, jeux d'eau sophistiqués, repas succulents servis dans une vaisselle d'or. Louis XIV prit-il ombrage d'un tel luxe ou Colbert, qui convoitait la succession de Fouquet, dénonça-t-il ses malversations? Quinze jours plus tard, Fouquet fut jeté en prison, où il demeura jusqu'à sa mort. Le souverain s'empara ensuite des meubles, des statues et des tapisseries et prit à son service Le Vau, Le Brun et Le Nôtre pour bâtir le château de Versailles.

Ne manquez pas le salon ovale, le plafond peint par Le Brun dans le Salon des Muses, la cuisine restaurée et les jardins en terrasses.

BLANDY-LES-TOURS

À quelques kilomètres à l'est de Vaux-le-Vicomte (carte 213 E2) se trouve Blandy-les-Tours, dernière forteresse médiévale d'Île-de-France, nichée dans une vallée. Il ne manque aux tours de pierre que leurs bannières colorées pour se croire revenu au Moyen Âge. ■

Provins

Un manuscrit enluminé du XIVe siècle illustrant la foire bisannuelle de Provins.

CHAQUE ANNÉE, AU PRINTEMPS ET À L'ÉTÉ, CETTE CITÉ MÉDIÉVALE ramène les visiteurs 800 ans en arrière, au temps des chevaliers en armure, des catapultes défiant les remparts et de la fauconnerie. Des centaines de citadins sillonnent les rues en costumes d'époque.

Provins fut la capitale économique de la Champagne dès le Xe siècle. Au cours de sa foire bisannuelle, qui attirait des commerçants venus de toute l'Europe, la cité achetait de la soie, des épices et de la laine.

Pour partir à la découverte du passé, entrez dans la **Grange-aux-Dîmes** *(située rue Saint-Jean)*, robuste entrepôt élevé au XIIIe siècle, pour une projection audiovisuelle relatant l'histoire de la ville. La Ville-Haute et la Ville-Basse sont criblées de tunnels (le réseau fait près de 9 km) qui relient des dizaines de caves voûtées. Les murs portent les sceaux mystérieux de diverses sociétés secrètes, notamment celle des francs-maçons.

La Ville-Haute, entièrement restaurée, abrite nombre de monuments historiques qui forment le décor d'une grande fête médiévale. Des joutes reconstituent la bataille qui eut lieu en 1230, lorsque le comte Thibaud de Champagne sauva Provins du comte de Picardie, dont les armées assiégeaient la ville. Chaque été, près de 80 rapaces planent au-dessus de la foule en hommage à l'art de la fauconnerie.

L'office de tourisme met à votre disposition une brochure suggérant un circuit en ville le long des remparts du XIIe et XIIIe siècles (soit environ 1 km). La tour César, superbe donjon du XIIe siècle qui surplombe la ville, offre une belle vue sur la Brie. La fête médiévale a lieu lors d'un week-end en juin avant d'autres manifestations, (concerts, son et lumière) pendant l'été. Cette ville, classée au patrimoine mondial de l'Humanité par l'Unesco, mérite votre visite. ■

213 F2
80 km, est de Paris

En voiture : A4 en prenant la sortie n° 13 à Serris, direction Provins (D231) ; En train : gare de l'Est, direction Troyes

Office de tourisme

place H. de Balzac

01 64 60 26 26

Fontainebleau et ses environs

212 D1
60 km au sud-est de Paris

Château de Fontainebleau
01 60 71 50 70
www.musee-chateau-fontainebleau.fr
Fermé mar.
€€
En voiture: A6 sortie Fontainebleau. En train: gare de Lyon jusqu'à Fontainebleau-Avon, puis bus A ou B jusqu'au château

Le week-end, Fontainebleau est l'une des destinations favorites des Parisiens, qui vont faire des promenades, de l'escalade ou du vélo dans la forêt. Si Versailles reflète la gloire d'un seul monarque (Louis XIV), le château royal de Fontainebleau a évolué constamment au cours des règnes de trente souverains français. Tout son charme repose sur la disparité de ses éléments.

LE CHÂTEAU

Attiré par le gibier abondant de la forêt, Louis VII commença à construire un château sur les lieux, en 1137. Ses successeurs, férus de chasse, modifièrent et agrandirent la propriété. François Ier, qui préférait Fontainebleau à ses autres châteaux, effectua les premiers grands travaux en 1530. Il fit appel à des artistes italiens (comme Léonard de Vinci, dont *La Joconde* fut accrochée aux murs du château avant d'être transférée au Louvre) et à des artisans pour faire du modeste pavillon de chasse un magnifique palais maniériste. Les fresques et les stucs de la galerie François Ier datent de cette période. Henri II poursuivit les travaux de son père en créant notamment la salle de bal de 30 m de long – exemple éblouissant du style Renaissance, avec un plafond voûté réalisé par l'architecte Philibert Delorme et des fresques de l'artiste italien le Primatice.

Ne manquez pas le célèbre escalier extérieur dit du « fer à cheval » (1634), construit sous Louis XIII, ainsi que la Cour du cheval blanc ou cour des adieux où Napoléon Ier, après avoir abdiqué, fit ses adieux, le 20 avril 1814, à sa garde impériale avant de partir pour l'exil.

Les emblèmes de plusieurs souverains sont visibles dans différentes pièces: le H et le C entrelacés d'Henri II et de Catherine de Médicis (où il faut lire en réalité un D,

La galerie François Ier, un style renaissance flamboyant.

pour Diane de Poitiers, la maîtresse du roi) ; l'abeille dorée de Napoléon, blasonnée sur velours rouge dans la salle du trône ; et la salamandre de François Ier. Le château comporte également un musée abritant des antiquités chinoises collectionnées par l'impératrice Eugénie et un musée consacré à Napoléon Ier.

LA FORÊT DE FONTAINEBLEAU

Cette forêt de 25 000 ha est traversée par 320 km de sentiers balisés et d'innombrables allées. L'office du tourisme de Fontainebleau fournit des cartes de la forêt et des informations sur les quelques excursions. Bien que le site ne dépasse pas 127 m d'altitude, il est très fréquenté par les amateurs d'escalade. Des vélos tout terrain peuvent être loués sur place. Les principales curiosités sont les gorges d'Apremont et celles de Franchard.

LES SITES ENVIRONNANTS

La région de Fontainebleau a joué un rôle clé dans l'histoire de la peinture. Le village de **Barbizon** *(carte 212 D2; informations touristiques: tél. : 01 60 66 41 87)* fut le rendez-vous d'un groupe de peintres paysagistes du XIXe siècle, notamment Charles Daubigny, Camille Corot et Jean-François Millet. Bien que souvent pris d'assaut par les touristes en été, il reste néanmoins un village rural. La rue principale est bordée d'antiquaires et de galeries d'art.

Thomery *(carte 213 E1 ; informations touristiques, tél. : 01 64 70 80 14)*, village niché dans un méandre de la Seine, est réputé pour son chasselas doré. La ville fortifiée de Moret-sur-Loing *(carte 213 E1; informations touristiques: tél. : 01 60 70 41 66)*, immortalisée par les peintres Camille Pissarro et Alfred Sisley, organise un superbe spectacle son et lumière tous les samedis soir de mi-juin à début septembre.

Enfin, **Samois-sur-Seine** (*carte 212 D1)*, situé en plein cœur de la forêt de Fontainebleau, accueille tous les étés le festival de jazz Django Reinhardt. ■

Entrée principale du château de Fontainebleau, menant au célèbre escalier en fer à cheval de la cour du Cheval Blanc.

Office de tourisme
4, rue Royale, Fontainebleau
01 60 74 99 99

Atelier Jean-François Millet
27, Grand-Rue, Barbizon
01 60 66 21 55
Ouvert ts les jours de 9h30 à 12h30 et de 14h à 17h30

Rambouillet et ses environs

212 B2
50 km au sud-ouest de Paris
En voiture : A13, puis A12 à Saint-Quentin-en-Yvelines, puis N10 jusqu'a Rambouillet.
En train : gare Montparnasse jusqu'a Rambouillet, puis bus n° 72

BIEN QUE LE CHÂTEAU DE RAMBOUILLET (ACTUELLE RÉSIDENCE présidentielle) ne soit pas le plus beau d'Île-de-France, il se trouve au milieu d'une forêt magnifique, d'où vous pourrez faire des excursions.

C'est au château de Rambouillet que François Ier mourut en 1547.

Château
Rambouillet
01 34 83 21 21
Fermé mar.
€€

Rochefort-en-Yvelines
212 C2
16 km au sud-est de Rambouillet par D27

Montfort-l'Amaury Office de tourisme
212 B3
26 km au nord de Rambouillet par N10 puis D191
0134868796

LE CHÂTEAU

Le château fut rénové et modifié par ses propriétaires successifs. Louis XVI, qui en fit l'acquisition en 1784, aimait y résider lorsqu'il se rendait à la chasse dans l'immense et giboyeuse forêt avoisinante. Il ajouta plusieurs bâtiments rustiques pour la reine Marie-Antoinette, notamment une laiterie et une bergerie. Depuis 1897, le château est une des résidences du chef de l'État.

Vous pourrez visiter les différents appartements, la laiterie de la reine et la bergerie nationale, et les magnifiques jardins à la française avec leurs grands lacs artificiels. La pièce la plus célèbre du château est sans doute la salle de bains de Napoléon Ier, décorée de fresques de style pompéien. Ne manquez pas le pavillon orné de coquillages, de nacre et de marbre.

LES SITES ENVIRONNANTS

Rochefort-en-Yvelines, situé au sud-est de Rambouillet, n'a quasiment pas changé depuis des siècles. Des escaliers en pierre mènent à l'église Saint-Gilles, d'où l'on peut encore voir une partie des anciennes fortifications du village. Montfort-l'Amaury, qui date du XIe siècle, est l'un des plus beaux villages de la région. Son château domine la colline. ■

L'abbaye des Vaux-de-Cernay

Avec sa nef voûtée, ses lourdes portes en bois, ses objets d'art anciens et ses vieux murs de pierre, l'abbaye des Vaux-de-Cernay *(carte 212 C2, tél.: 01 34 85 23 00)*, fondée en 1148 et située à 10 km au nord-est de Rambouillet, vaut le détour. Cette abbaye cistercienne prospère jusqu'à la fin du XVIIIe siècle a été transformée en hôtel de luxe. Prenez un verre sur la terrasse, qui surplombe les ruines de l'église. ■

Auvers-sur-Oise

AUVERS DOIT SA NOTORIÉTÉ À VAN GOGH, VENU Y PASSER LES DERNIERS mois de sa vie. Plusieurs panneaux représentant de célèbres œuvres du peintre et de ses contemporains, notamment Cézanne, ont été placés à l'emplacement exact où les toiles ont été peintes.

Van Gogh ne passa ici que 70 jours, chez Paul Gachet (médecin et ami des artistes d'Auvers-sur-Oise), mais il travailla avec frénésie et réalisa près de 70 peintures et de nombreux dessins. Il est enterré dans le cimetière local aux côtés de son frère.

Avant l'arrivée de Van Gogh, Auvers était déjà l'une des destinations favorites des peintres paysagistes du XIXe siècle. Charles Daubigny, peintre de l'école de Barbizon, y amarra une péniche – son atelier flottant – en 1857, acquit une maison, et fut rapidement suivi par beaucoup d'autres artistes. Il apporta son soutien à de jeunes peintres comme Renoir, Monet et Cézanne, qui lui rendaient également visite, tout comme Corot et Daumier. Certaines de ses peintures et ses objets personnels sont réunis dans le musée Daubigny, dans la rue du même nom.

Il existe deux autres musées à Auvers : le musée de l'Absinthe (ancêtre du pastis), consacré à l'élixir des poètes, connu sous le nom de « fée verte » et interdit en 1915 ; et le château d'Auvers, qui propose un spectacle audiovisuel de 90 minutes sur les impressionnistes. L'office de tourisme suggère un itinéraire qui englobe l'auberge Ravoux, où Van Gogh mourut le 29 juillet 1890 après s'être tiré une balle dans la poitrine, ainsi que l'église et les champs de maïs qu'il a immortalisés. ■

Église d'Auvers-sur-Oise, **de Van Gogh (1890).**

212 C4
35 km au nord de Paris

En train : gare du Nord jusqu'à Auvers-sur-Oise (*via* Pontoise)

Office de tourisme
rue de la Sansonne
01 30 36 10 06

Auberge Ravoux
place de la Mairie
01 30 36 60 63
Fermé lun. et mi-nov-mi-mars
€

Atelier Daubigny
61, rue Daubigny
01 34 48 03 03
Ouvert mar.-dim. Pâques-nov.
€

Musée Daubigny
rue de la Sansonne
Fermé lun.-mar.
01 30 36 80 20
€

Musée de l'Absinthe
44, rue Alphonse-Callé
01 30 36 83 26
Ouvert mer.-dim. juin-sept., sam.-dim le reste de l'année. Fermé déc.-fév.
€

Château d'Auvers
2, rue de Léry
01 34 48 48 48
Fermé lun.
€

www.auvers-sur-oise.com

La cathédrale de Chartres

Les flèches de la cathédrale sont visibles des kilomètres à la ronde.

DEPUIS PRÈS DE HUIT CENTS ANS, LA CATHÉDRALE DE CHARTRES SE dresse comme un phare au milieu des plaines de la Beauce. Malgré les incendies, les révolutions, deux guerres mondiales et des restaurateurs trop zélés, elle est restée presque intacte depuis le jour de sa consécration, en 1260.

www.ville-chartres.com

212 B2
83 km au sud-ouest de Paris

En voiture : A6, puis A10, et enfin A11 vers Le Mans puis direction Chartres.
En train : gare Montparnasse jusqu'à Chartres

Office de tourisme

place de la Cathédrale

02 37 18 26 26

Page ci-contre : L'arbre de Jessé sur la façade ouest.

Au IVe siècle, une première basilique consacrée à la Vierge est édifiée à l'emplacement actuel de la cathédrale. De nombreux pèlerins s'y rendent pour les vertus miraculeuses des eaux de son puits, selon une vieille croyance des druides. En 876, Charles le Chauve, petit-fils de Charlemagne, fait don du « voile de la Vierge », tunique qu'aurait portée Marie lorsqu'elle donna naissance au Christ, et augmente ainsi le prestige de la ville et le nombre de pèlerins.

Du XIe au XIIe siècle, une série d'incendies détruit les quatre basiliques successives. En 1194, un terrible incendie embrase la ville tout entière. Seuls le portail royal et les tours occidentales de l'église sont épargnés. Tout laissait penser que la précieuse relique avait été brûlée. Mais trois jours plus tard, alors que les ruines fument encore, elle apparaît, intacte, au cours d'une procession organisée par le clergé de la cathédrale. Le miracle est interprété comme un signe de Marie appelant les habitants de Chartres à bâtir une église encore plus grande. Le projet de reconstruction aussitôt lancé aboutit à la superbe cathédrale gothique que l'on connaît aujourd'hui. Bâti presque entièrement en moins de trente ans, au début du XIIIe siècle, ce monument est d'une cohérence architecturale et sculpturale hors du commun.

LES VITRAUX « BLEU DE CHARTRES »

Les vitraux de la cathédrale, avec leur couleur unique dite « bleu de Chartres », sont célèbres dans le monde entier et constituent une collection extraordinairement complète. Le portail royal du XIIe siècle, ses vitraux et sa verrière spectaculaire connue sous le nom de « Vierge bleue » survécurent au grand incendie. Les verrières du XIIIe siècle qui ornent le reste de la cathédrale illustrent des scènes bibliques et historiques où sont représentés chevaliers, paysans, rois, nobles et une foule d'artisans au travail. Elles retracent avec éclat la vie quotidienne et religieuse à l'époque médiévale. Chaque vitrail raconte une histoire qui se lit de gauche à droite et de bas en haut.

STATUES ET LABYRINTHE

Les statues des trois principaux portails complètent l'iconographie de l'église. Le porche nord illustre l'histoire de la Création jusqu'à la chute d'Adam et Ève (de gauche à droite), suivie de personnages de l'Ancien Testament et d'une scène de la Nativité. Le porche sud dépeint des scènes du Jugement dernier.

Malheureusement, des chaises actuellement disposées dans la nef cachent le labyrinthe de pierre le mieux préservé de France. Les pèlerins parcouraient ce labyrinthe de 291 m de long à genoux.

À VOIR ET À FAIRE

Toute l'année, vous pouvez faire une visite guidée de la cathédrale pour découvrir ses vitraux, ses sculptures et son histoire. Vérifiez les horaires d'ouverture selon la saison. S'il vous reste du temps, faites un tour dans la vieille ville. L'office de tourisme suggère un circuit touristique qui englobe l'ancien palais épiscopal, devenu musée des Beaux-Arts et la rivière, qui coule sous des ponts en pierre le long d'un vieux moulin et de maisons à colombage datant de la Renaissance. Un petit train effectue pratiquement le même itinéraire pendant la saison touristique. Ne manquez pas l'église Saint-Pierre, souvent éclipsée par la célèbre cathédrale. Elle abrite également quelques beaux vitraux des XIIIe et XIVe siècles. ■

La maison au crépi rose et aux volets verts s'insérait parfaitement dans le jardin qu'avait imaginé Monet.

Giverny

En 1883, Claude Monet s'installa avec sa famille à Giverny, où il demeura jusqu'à sa mort, en 1926. Sa maison et ses jardins étaient pour lui une éternelle source d'inspiration et il y consacra beaucoup de temps et d'argent.

LES JARDINS

Quelle que soit la saison, le jardin arbore autant de couleurs qu'à l'époque de Monet. Lorsque la famille s'installa à Giverny, il ne s'agissait que d'un modeste verger d'un hectare, clos par de grands murs de pierre. Le peintre le transforma complètement en créant des parterres symétriques et des perspectives et en plantant des massifs dont la couleur changeait tous les mois. Il détestait les jardins à la française et préféra s'entourer d'arcades de capucines rampantes, de rosiers entrelacés et de roses trémières.

Dix ans après son arrivée à Giverny, Monet acheta le terrain situé de l'autre côté de la ligne de chemin de fer dans le but de dévier l'Epte et de créer un bassin et un jardin aquatique. Il se heurta à la méfiance de ses voisins, qui considéraient ce projet comme extravagant, mais finit par obtenir gain de cause. Il fit d'abord creuser un lac artificiel et réalisa un jardin exotique composé de saules, de bambous, de glycines et, bien sûr, de nénuphars. Un artisan local construisit l'élégant pont japonais et une barque flotte encore sur le bassin.

LA MAISON ET L'ATELIER

La maison au crépi rose et aux volets verts accueillit les nombreux amis de Monet. Ce dernier offrait à ses invités des légumes frais provenant d'un jardin potager situé à l'autre bout de la ville. Le peintre supervisait lui-même les menus des repas et consignait dans ses livres des dizaines de recettes que lui donnaient ses amis, notamment Stéphane Mallarmé ou encore Auguste Rodin, qui venaient partager son repas soit dans la cuisine aux carreaux bleus soit dans la salle à manger aux tentures jaunes.

Monet adorait les estampes japonaises et sa collection, dont il s'inspira pour la création de son jardin aquatique, est exposée dans plusieurs pièces de la maison. Sur les murs du modeste salon étaient accrochées des œuvres que le peintre admirait particulièrement, notamment une dizaine de Cézanne, quelques Renoir, huit Manet et quelques Degas. Désormais dispersées dans les musées et les collec-

---

212 B4
78 km au nord-ouest de Paris

En voiture : A13/ E05 depuis le pont de Saint-Cloud, vers Rouen. Sortir à Bonnières, suivre la D201 jusqu'a Giverny. En train : gare Saint-Lazare, direction Rouen, descendre à Vernon, et prendre un bus ou un taxi, ou marcher 4 km

Musée d'Art américain

99, rue Claude-Monet

02 32 51 94 65
www.giverny.org/museums

Fermé mars-nov.

€€

tions du monde entier, ces œuvres ont été reproduites pour recréer le décor de l'époque.

Après la mort du peintre, sa maison fut laissée à l'abandon et, lorsque son fils Michel en fit don à l'Institut de France en 1966, les sols, les poutres du plafond et l'escalier s'étaient effondrés. Il fallut dix ans pour restaurer à la fois la maison et les jardins. Un musée ouvrit finalement ses portes en 1980 et près de 500 000 visiteurs s'y rendent chaque année.

L'entrée se fait par l'immense atelier bâti en 1916 : Monet avait en effet besoin d'espace et de lumière pour peindre les gigantesques *Nymphéas* que lui avait commandés son ami Georges Clemenceau pour le musée de l'Orangerie de Paris (voir p. 140). Aujourd'hui, l'atelier abrite des reproductions d'œuvres du peintre et une boutique.

Pour éviter la foule, venez un jour de semaine (de préférence pas le mercredi). Les cars touristiques partent généralement autour de 16 h mais les jardins restent ouverts jusqu'à 18 h, heure idéale pour s'y promener.

LE MUSÉE D'ART AMÉRICAIN

Le musée d'Art américain, situé à quelques rues de la maison de Monet, vaut également le détour. Vous y verrez des œuvres d'artistes américains qui ont vécu et peint en France de 1865 à 1915. ■

Musée Claude Monet

- 84, rue Claude-Monet
- 02 32 51 28 21 www.fondation-monet.com
- Ouvert mar.-dim. avr.-oct.
- Maison et jardins : €€. Jardin : €

Monet créa un étang en déviant le cours d'une rivière. C'est ce paysage que Monet aimait tant peindre.

Autres sites à visiter

LE CHÂTEAU ET LA FORÊT DE CHANTILLY

Situé en plein cœur de la forêt et entouré de douves, le château de Chantilly est l'un des plus beaux de la région parisienne. En grande partie détruit pendant la Révolution, il a été reconstruit et abrite aujourd'hui la collection d'œuvres d'art réunie par le duc d'Aumale au XIXe siècle qui forme le musée Condé.

Ce qui distingue ce château des autres, ce sont ses grandes écuries (construites entre 1719-1735; cate 212 D4, *tél. : 03 44 57 13 13*), situées dans un bâtiment de pierre monumental où pouvaient tenir autrefois 240 chevaux et 300 chiens. Des démonstrations de dressage sont effectuées en public tous les jours, sauf le mardi. Les écuries abritent aujourd'hui un très intéressant musée du Cheval. Chantilly est également connu pour son hippodrome. Vous pourrez y voir des pur-sang s'entraîner ou assister à une course de chevaux.

À proximité, se trouvent l'abbaye cistercienne de Royaumont *(carte 212 D4, Asnières-sur-Oise, tél. : 01 30 35 59 00)* et l'ancienne cité royale de Senlis *(carte 210 D4)*.
212 D4; Chantilly, 40 km au nord de Paris
03 44 62 62 62 / www.chateaudechantilly.com
Fermé mar. €€ En voiture: prendre la A1 jusqu'à la sortie de Survilliers-Saint-Witz, puis la N17 jusqu'à Chantilly. En train: gare du Nord ou RER D jusqu'à Chantilly-Gouvieux (puis courte marche)

LE CHÂTEAU DE LA MALMAISON

Joséphine acheta ce château lorsque Napoléon était encore Premier consul. Celui-ci trouvait sa résidence officielle, le palais des Tuileries, triste et froide et se retirait à la Malmaison chaque fois qu'il le pouvait. Joséphine conserva la propriété après leur divorce et dépensa énormément d'argent pour orner le château et embellir les jardins, qu'elle dota de la première grande roseraie. Le château est devenu un musée dédié à l'histoire napoléonienne et à l'Empire.
212 C3; 1, avenue du Château, Rueil-Malmaison 01 41 29 05 55/wwwchateau-malmaison.fr Fermé mar. €€ Métro ou RER A jusqu'à la Grande Arche de la Défense, puis le bus 258

LE CHÂTEAU ET LE MUSÉE D'ÉCOUEN

Beaucoup d'œuvres de la collection du musée de la Renaissance d'Écouen viennent du musée de Cluny, à Paris. Le magnifique château fut réalisé au XVIe siècle par plusieurs grands artistes, notamment le Rosso et Jean Clouet. L'aile sud est quasiment restée intacte depuis cette époque. La collection comprend une série de tapisseries du XVIe siècle illustrant l'histoire de David et Bethsabée. 212 D3; Écouen, 19 km au nord de Paris par la N16 01 34 38 38 50 ; www.musee-renaissance.fr Fermé mar. €€ En train: gare du Nord jusqu'à Écouen-Ézanville, puis bus n° 269 ■

Les Quatre Évangiles, un ouvrage du XIIe siècle de l'abbaye de Werden (Allemagne), maintenant au musée de Condé à Chantilly.

Informations pratiques

Le métro.

INFORMATIONS PRATIQUES

PRÉPARER VOTRE VOYAGE

QUAND PARTIR ?

Le choix des dates de votre séjour à Paris dépend de ce que vous recherchez. Certains trouvent qu'à Noël les illuminations donnent à la ville un charme émouvant, d'autres considèrent que janvier et février sont les meilleurs mois car les touristes y sont moins nombreux (certains hôtels pratiquent d'ailleurs des tarifs « basse saison ») et que les boutiques sont à l'heure des soldes.
Paris en avril est superbe, mais le temps peut être froid et pluvieux. Mai et juin sont habituellement des mois très agréables. Le 21 juin, la fête de la Musique fait descendre les Parisiens dans la rue jusque tard dans la nuit. En août, la capitale est très calme, la plupart des Parisiens sont partis en vacances, mais beaucoup de restaurants et de magasins sont fermés.
Pendant l'été, de nombreuses manifestations culturelles sont gratuites, notamment les concerts organisés dans les parcs et jardins de la ville et les cinémas de plein air à La Villette.
Septembre annonce la *rentrée* avec le retour des Parisiens et la reprise de l'activité économique. la ville est ravissante en automne, lorsque les marronniers se parent de leur feuillage couleur rouille. De plus, un dimanche de la mi-septembre, se tient la Journée du Patrimoine, l'occasion de visiter des monuments historiques et des palais nationaux normalement fermés au public.

LE CLIMAT

Les hivers à Paris sont tempérés et pluvieux en général, les printemps et les automnes plutôt frais. Les étés, ni trop chauds ni trop humides, sont le plus souvent très agréables.

Ce qu'il faut emporter
Prévoyez un vêtement pour la pluie quelle que soit la saison et emportez un chandail même en été. Vous aurez aussi besoin de chaussures confortables et étanches, d'une tenue habillée pour sortir le soir.

Une carte bancaire vous sera très utile aussi bien pour vos retraits en espèces dans les distributeurs automatiques que pour tous vos achats. Si vous êtes étranger, assurez-vous que votre carte bancaire est internationale.

N'oubliez pas votre permis de conduire et vos papiers d'assurance.

ASSURANCE

Si vous êtes étranger, vérifiez avant le départ que vous êtes bien couvert pour les soins médicaux, en cas de rapatriement ou de perte/vol d'un bagage ou d'argent.

PASSEPORTS ET VISAS

Pour les ressortissants de nationalité canadienne, le passeport en cours de validité suffit, si le séjour n'excède pas 90 jours (pas de visa exigé) et pour les ressortissants de l'Union européenne, seule la carte d'identité est nécessaire.

REJOINDRE LE CENTRE DE PARIS DEPUIS LES AÉROPORTS

www.adp.fr
Deux aéroports desservent la capitale : Roissy-Charles-de-Gaulle et Orly.

Roissy-Charles de Gaulle
(Au nord de Paris)
Tél. : 01 48 62 22 80
Pour vous rendre de l'aéroport dans Paris, vous pouvez soit prendre un taxi (comptez environ 45 €), soit une navette Air France (qui vous amènera à la porte Maillot ou place de l'Étoile), ROISSYBUS (dessert Opéra) ou encore le RER B qui relie Paris à la banlieue (arrêt aux stations Gare du Nord, Châtelet, Saint-Michel, Luxembourg, Port-Royal et Denfert-Rochereau).

Orly
(Au sud de Paris)
Tél. : 01 49 75 52 52.
Si vous arrivez à l'aéroport d'Orly, vous pouvez prendre soit un taxi (environ 30 €), soit ORLYBUS (station Denfert-Rochereau), ou le RER B et ORLYVAL (station Les Halles) ou encore le RER C et ORLYRAIL (cœur de Paris).

Si vous voyagez en groupe (jusqu'à 8 personnes), des minibus peuvent également être réservés pour votre transfert porte-à-porte :
Airport Shuttle
Tél. : 01 30 11 13 00
www.airportshuttle.fr
(à partir de 22 € par pers., 2 min.)
Airport Express
Tél. : 01 41 71 41 46
www.airportexpress.fr
(23 € par pers./2 pers. et plus)
Paris Shuttle
Tél. : 01 48 40 17 17
www.parishuttle.com
(25 € par pers./2 pers. et plus)
Airport connection
Tél. : 01 43 65 55 55
www.airport-connection.com
(25 € par pers.)

VOUS DÉPLACER

Il n'est pas simple de circuler en voiture dans Paris, les embouteillages sont fréquents et les places de stationnement rares. Il est préférable d'utiliser les transports en commun, qui sont sûrs, propres, rapides et desservent tous les points de la capitale. Les taxis, en dehors des heures de pointe, sont également efficaces.

LOCATION DE VOITURES

Avis, tél. : 08 20 05 05 05
www.avis.fr
Europcar, tél. : 08 25 35 83 58
www.europcar.fr
Hertz, tél. : 01 41 91 95 25
www.hertz.fr
Ada, tél. : 08 25 16 91 69
www.ada-location.com

Conduire en France
Lorsque vous utilisez votre véhicule, munissez-vous de tous les papiers nécessaires. Rappel aux

conducteurs étrangers : à chaque croisement sans feu ni stop, le véhicule qui vient de votre droite est prioritaire et n'a pas à s'arrêter. Ralentissez donc toujours à l'approche d'un carrefour et regardez bien sur votre droite avant de vous y engager. En l'absence de panneau de signalisation, rappelez-vous que la vitesse est limitée : en agglomération à 50 km/h, sur les boulevards périphériques à 80 km/h, sur les routes nationales à 90 km/h, sur les autoroutes à 130 km/h et 110 km/h par temps de pluie.

Si vous avez consommé plus de deux verres de vin, abstenez-vous de conduire.

La ceinture de sécurité est obligatoire pour tous les passagers (y compris pour les passagers à l'arrière du véhicule). Les enfants de moins de dix ans ne sont pas autorisés à s'asseoir sur le siège avant, et doivent impérativement utiliser un réhausseur conforme aux normes de sécurité. Il est interdit d'utiliser un téléphone portable en conduisant.

Si votre véhicule a été immobilisé ou enlevé par la fourrière, adressez-vous au commissariat de police le plus proche.

Dépannage
Europ assistance
Tél. : 01 41 85 85 85
www.europassistance.com
Si votre voiture de location tombe en panne, consultez la documentation. Vous y trouverez le numéro d'appel assistance. Vous pouvez aussi vous adresser à un garage. Si vous n'en trouvez pas, contactez la police au 17 ou la gendarmerie. Sur les autoroutes, des bornes de secours sont placées à intervalles réguliers.

TRANSPORTS EN COMMUN

www.ratp.fr ou www.citefutee.com
Une seule société, la RATP (Régie autonome des Transports parisiens) gère les transports en commun à Paris. Vous avez à votre disposition le **métro,** les **bus** qui, outre le service régulier de jour, proposent un service la nuit avec **Noctambus** (1 h à 5 h du matin), **Balabus** fonctionne de 12 h 30 à 20 h 30, d'avril à septembre, et enfin le **RER** (Réseau Express Régional), conjointement géré avec la SNCF.
Le réseau de la RATP/SNCF est divisé en 8 zones tarifaires : Paris intra muros est ainsi composé des zones 1 et 2. Si vous voulez aller au château de Versailles, vous devrez prendre un ticket de zone 3. Vous avez le choix entre plusieurs titres de transports : le billet à l'unité n'autorisant qu'un seul voyage et pas de correspondance bus-métro, un carnet de 10 billets. À moins d'avoir des déplacements très occasionnels, ce n'est pas la solution la plus économique.
D'autres formules adaptées vous sont proposées dont les tarifs dépendent de leur durée de validité, de leur nombre de zones mais toutes sont valables sur le réseau RATP et avec un nombre illimité de voyage : Mobilis (1 jour) ; carte orange (abonnement hebdomadaire ou mensuel composé d'une carte nominative, d'une photo d'identité et d'un coupon ; Paris Visite (1, 2, 3 ou 5 jours), Carte Musées et Monuments (1, 3 ou 5 jours) donnant accès également à 70 monuments et musées). Vous pouvez vous procurer ces différents titres de transport aux guichets dans les stations de métro, pour certains auprès de détaillants de tabac qui possèdent une enseigne verte représentant un ticket.

Métro (de 5 h 30 à 0 h 30).
Le métropolitain parisien, communément appelé le métro, est facile d'utilisation. Un plan détaillé est affiché dans chaque station. Vous pouvez aussi vous le procurer gratuitement aux guichets. Chaque ligne porte un numéro et un nom composé des deux stations à ses extrémités ; par exemple la ligne 1 (qui traverse Paris d'est en ouest) est La Défense-Château de Vincennes. Ne jetez pas votre titre de transport avant d'avoir quitté l'enceinte du métro. Un contrôleur en veste verte peut demander à le voir. Vous encourez une amende si vous ne pouvez pas le présenter.

RER (5 h 30 à 0 h 45)
Le RER établit la liaison avec Paris. Le ticket de métro est valable pour le RER qui dessert les stations à l'intérieur de la capitale. Pour des déplacements rapides d'un bout à l'autre de Paris, c'est très pratique.

Bus (de 7 h à 21 h en général)
Les tickets de métro sont valables dans les bus (à valider dans l'appareil situé à proximité du conducteur) et pour un seul trajet. Les billets sont également vendus dans les bus, mais uniquement à l'unité. Les arrêts sont signalés sur les abribus ou sur une simple borne sur le trottoir. Dessus figurent à chaque fois le numéro de la ligne (ou des lignes) qui passe à cet endroit, un plan détaillé avec tous les arrêts de la ligne et un plan général du réseau de bus et enfin les horaires de début et de fin de service. Les **Noctambus** (18 lignes) desservent les artères principales. Départ toutes les heures de la rue Saint-Martin et l'avenue Victoria (Place du Châtelet). Le **Balabus**, une ligne touristique en service uniquement les dimanches et jours fériés, entre la gare de Lyon et La Défense.

Taxis
Vous pouvez héler un taxi dans la rue ou aux stations de taxis situées aux principaux carrefours. Si l'enseigne sur le toit est complètement allumée, le taxi est libre. Si elle est éteinte avec une veilleuse en dessous de l'enseigne allumée, le taxi est occupé. La prise en charge dans les gares, les bagages encombrants, un quatrième voyageur (le chauffeur de taxi peut refuser de prendre au-delà de trois personnes) ou un animal (à l'exception des chiens guides) font l'objet d'un supplément. Le pourboire reste à votre discrétion, il représente habituellement 10 % du prix de la course. Lorsque vous commandez un taxi, le compteur se met en route dès

le moment où le chauffeur reçoit votre appel, d'où un coût parfois élevé. Demandez toujours un reçu. Cela peut servir si vous avez oublié quelque chose dans le véhicule ou eu un problème avec le chauffeur. Les tarifs varient en fonction des zones géographiques (Paris intra muros, banlieue) de même qu'un tarif majoré est appliqué après 19 h, les dimanches et les jours fériés.
Toute réclamation doit être adressée à la Préfecture de Police, Service des Taxis, 36, rue des Morillons, 75015, tél. : 01 55 76 20 00 Ⓜ Convention

Radio Taxis
Si vous avez besoin d'un taxi à une date prévue à l'avance, n'hésitez pas à en réserver un par téléphone. C'est souvent quand on en a le plus besoin que soudain, ils deviennent rares !
Alpha-Taxi, tél. : 01 45 85 85 85 www.alphataxi.fr
Blue Shuttle, tél. : 01 30 11 13 00/www.airportshuttle.fr
G7, tél. : 01 47 39 47 39 www.g7.fr
Taxis Bleus, tél. : 0 825 16 10 10 www.taxi-bleus.fr
Taxis Inter, tél. : 01 55 07 89 40
Taxi-Radio-Étoile, tél. : 01 42 70 41 41
City Bird, moto-taxi (avec chauffeur, casque fourni), tél. : 0 826 100 100/www.city-bird.com

TRAINS

www.sncf.com
La **SNCF** (Société nationale des Chemins de Fer) assure les liaisons entre Paris et toute la France. Informations et réservations au tél. : de France , 36 35 ; de l'étranger, 08 92 35 35 35 (de 7 h à 22 h) ; Lignes de banlieue, tél. : 08 91 36 20 20
Les principales gares (chacune avec sa station de métro du même nom) sont la gare de Lyon (en direction du sud-est de la France, Suisse et l'Italie) ; la gare du Nord (dessert Bruxelles, Londres et le nord de la France) ; la gare de l'Est (en direction de l'est de la France) ; la gare Saint-Lazare (vers la Normandie et le nord-ouest de la France) ; la gare d'Austerlitz (vers l'Espagne et le Sud-Ouest) et la gare Montparnasse (vers la Bretagne et l'ouest de la France). Le TGV (Train à Grande Vitesse) vous emmènera à Lyon en deux heures, à Bruxelles en une heure et demie, à Londres en 2 h 50 (avec l'Eurostar via le tunnel sous la Manche) ou à Marseille en trois heures. Il est impératif de réserver pour tous les voyages en TGV ou Eurostar. Avant de monter dans le train, n'oubliez pas de composter votre billet dans l'une des bornes orange (ou les nouvelles jaunes) que vous trouverez sur le quai, sinon vous risquez d'être verbalisé.

EXCURSIONS ET VISITES ORGANISÉES

En bus
Visite de la capitale et de ses monuments (voir aussi Balabus)
Cityrama: 4, place des Pyramides, 75001, tél. : 01 44 55 61 00 / www.cityrama.fr Ⓜ Palais-Royal
Paris Vision: Agence Rivoli, 214, rue de Rivoli, 75001, tél. : 01 42 60 30 01/www.parisvision.fr Ⓜ RER : Auber
Paris l'Open Tour: 13, rue Auber 75009, tél. : 01 42 66 56 56/ www.paris-opentour.com Ⓜ RER : Auber

Promenades à pied
Une sélection de visites, des musées et monuments aux quartiers historiques.
Paris Contact, tél. : 01 42 51 08 40
Paris Walking Tours, tél. : 01 48 09 21 40

Promenades à vélo
Promenades dans différents quartiers et parcs. Certaines promenades à vélo de nuit sont également proposées.
Paris à Vélo, C'est Sympa : 37, boulevard Bourdon, 75004, tél. : 01 48 87 60 01 Ⓜ Bastille
Paris-Vélo : 4, rue Fer à Moulin 75005, tél. : 01 43 37 59 22, Ⓜ Saint-Marcel

Croisière
La Seine
Bateaux-Mouches : Pont de l'Alma, Rive droite, tél. : 01 42 25 96 10/ www.bateaux-mouches.fr
Ⓜ Alma-Marceau
Excursions de 11 h à 22 h
Bateaux parisiens Tour Eiffel : Port de la Bourdonnais, 75008, tél. : 01 44 11 33 44/www.bateauxparisiens.fr Ⓜ Bir-Hakeim
Excursions de 10 h à 22 h 30.
Bateaux vedettes de Paris : Port de Suffren, tél. : 01 47 05 71 29 Ⓜ Bir-Hakeim
Excursions de 10 h à 23 h.
Bateaux vedettes du Pont-Neuf: 1, square du Vert Galant, île de la Cité, tél. : 01 46 33 98 38/ www.marinedebercy.com Ⓜ Pont-Neuf. Excursions de 10 h 30 à 22 h 30.
Batobus: Ce service de bateaux municipal dessert la Tour Eiffel (Ⓜ Bir-Hakeim), le musée d'Orsay (Ⓜ Solférino), le Louvre (Ⓜ Louvre-Palais-Royal), l'Hôtel de Ville (Ⓜ Hôtel de Ville) et Notre-Dame (Ⓜ Cité). Fonctionne de 10 h à 22 h à la belle saison. Tél. : 01 44 11 33 99/www.batobus.com

Les canaux
Canauxrama: 13, quai de la Loire 75019, tél. : 01 42 39 15 00/www.canauxrama.com (sur réservations). Départs du bassin de La Villette, à 9 h 45 et 14 h 45 ; du Port de l'Arsenal à 9 h 45 et 14 h 30. Ⓜ Jaurès
Paris Canal: 19, quai de la Loire, 75019, tél. : 01 42 40 96 97/www.pariscanal.com (sur réservations). Départs quai Anatole-France, près du musée d'Orsay, à 9 h ; Parc de La Villette à 14 h 30. Ⓜ Jaurès

QUELQUES CONSEILS PRATIQUES

LA POSTE

www.laposte.fr
La Poste, le service postal français, possède des bureaux dans chaque quartier.
Poste principale : 52, rue du Louvre, 75001. Ouverte 24 h/ 24, 7 j/7. Tél. : 01 40 28 76 00
Ⓜ Louvre ou les Halles
Les autres bureaux d'arrondissements sont ouverts du lundi au vendredi, de 8 h à 19 h et le samedi matin, de 8 h à 12 h.

Les codes postaux de Paris commencent systématiquement par 75 et se terminent par le numéro de l'arrondissement. Par exemple, 75010 correspond au dixième arrondissement, 75002 au deuxième arrondissement, etc.
Boîtes aux lettres : des boîtes aux lettres de couleur jaune sont situées à l'extérieur de chaque bureau de poste et dans tous les endroits fréquentés de la ville. Veillez à insérer votre lettre dans la fente lui correspondant (Paris / banlieue / autres départements et étranger).

TÉLÉPHONE

Vous pouvez utiliser les cabines publiques dans la rue, vous rendre à un bureau de poste, ou appeler depuis votre hôtel (avec commission) ou d'un café.
Pour les appels d'une cabine téléphonique, achetez une télécarte dans les bureaux de poste, de tabac et les maisons de la presse. Suivez les instructions affichées à l'écran. Certains cafés possèdent des appareils téléphoniques à pièces.
Tous les numéros de téléphone français sont constitués de 10 chiffres. Les numéros sur Paris et la région parisienne commencent par 01. Les quatre autres préfixes nationaux sont 02 pour le Nord-Ouest, 03 pour le Nord-Est, 04 pour le Sud-Est et 05 pour le Sud-Ouest. Les numéros commençant par 08 00 sont gratuits (numéros verts). Tous les autres numéros commençant par 08 sont facturés.
Pour téléphoner à l'étranger, composez 00 suivi de l'indicatif du pays (1 pour les États-Unis et le Canada, 32 pour la Belgique et 41 pour la Suisse).
Pour obtenir le service des renseignements en France, composez le 12. Pour les renseignements à l'étranger, composez le 00-33-12 suivi de l'indicatif du pays (ex. : 1 pour le Canada).

ÉLECTRICITÉ

Le courant électrique en France est alimenté en 220 volts ; un transformateur ou un adaptateur est nécessaire pour les appareils en 110 volts. Beaucoup d'appareils sont munis d'un commutateur qui permet de passer d'un voltage à l'autre, mais il est préférable d'utiliser un adaptateur. Vous pourrez vous en procurer dans les quincailleries ou au sous-sol du BHV, 52, rue de Rivoli, 75004.

MONNAIE ET CHANGE

Banque de France, 39, rue Croix des Petits-Champs, 75001, tél. : 01 42 92 42 42 Ⓜ Palais-Royal
American Express 11, rue Scribe 75009, Tél. 01 47 14 50 00/www.americanexpress.fr Ⓜ Opéra
Depuis le 1er janvier 2002, la monnaie française est l'euro. La France la partage avec onze autres pays européens. Pour les ressortissants de ces pays, inutile de changer leur monnaie qui, même avec la face nationale, est valable en France. Les ressortissants étrangers à la zone euro trouveront des bureaux de change dans les gares, les aéroports et un peu partout en ville. Ils sont signalés par un panneau « Change ». Une commission est prise sur chaque opération de change. La Banque de France offre le taux de change le plus compétitif. L'American Express assure le change et fait bénéficier les clients détenteurs de leur carte, de services supplémentaires.
Les distributeurs automatiques de billets (DAB) permettent de retirer des espèces facilement. Si vous êtes étranger, assurez-vous que votre carte de paiement est internationale.
Les cartes bancaires françaises possèdent une puce d'identification. Les cartes étrangères possèdent ces informations sur une bande magnétique qui peut parfois entraîner quelques problèmes de lecture.
Le retrait en espèces à l'aide d'une carte bancaire est soumis à une commission, mais cela reste néanmoins plus avantageux qu'un retrait dans une banque.

JOURS FÉRIÉS

Le 1er janvier, les dimanche et lundi de Pâques, les 1er et 8 mai, le jeudi de l'Ascension (40 jours après Pâques), le 14 juillet, le 15 août, les 1er et 11 novembre, le 25 décembre.

HORAIRES D'OUVERTURE

La majorité des banques sont ouvertes du lundi au vendredi de 9 h à 17 h. Certaines ferment à l'heure du déjeuner, d'autres sont ouvertes le samedi.
Les grands magasins sont ouverts du lundi au samedi, de 9 h 30 à 19 h ; certains restent ouverts jusqu'à 22 h (un jour dans la semaine). Les boutiques ouvrent à 10 h pour fermer vers 19 h/19 h 30. Beaucoup sont fermées le lundi, certaines le sont aussi à l'heure du déjeuner (entre 13 h et 14 h 30). De plus en plus de magasins ouvrent le dimanche, mais il est préférable de vous en assurer. Les cafés ouvrent très tôt le matin et ce jusqu'à 20 h, 22 h, parfois 2 h du matin. Les restaurants commencent à servir généralement vers midi jusqu'à 15 h, puis de 19 h 30 à 23 h. De nombreux magasins et restaurants sont fermés en août.

DÉCALAGE HORAIRE

La France a une heure d'avance sur celle du méridien de Greenwich (heure GMT).

POURBOIRES

Le service est inclus dans les prix affichés au restaurant. Ceci est indiqué en bas du menu. On laisse habituellement un petit pourboire au serveur surtout si vous avez été satisfait du service.
Pour les porteurs, concierges, guides et coiffeurs, les ouvreuses et le vestiaire, le pourboire est de 1€ à 2 €. Le personnel des hôtels ne perçoit habituellement pas de pourboire, sauf si vous avez demandé un service en dehors de leurs tâches ordinaires.

TOILETTES

L'utilisation des toilettes publiques (les « sanisettes ») coûte 0,50€.

Rares sont celles accessibles aux fauteuils roulants et toutes sont interdites aux enfants de moins de 10 ans non accompagnés. Certaines stations de métro ont des toilettes publiques. Les grands magasins en possèdent également. Vous pouvez aussi aller dans un café et vous diriger vers le panneau « toilettes/téléphone ». C'est souvent gratuit, mais il peut vous être dit – plus ou moins aimablement – que « les toilettes sont réservées à la clientèle ».

OFFICE DE TOURISME

Office de Tourisme de Paris
Bureau central : 127, av. des Champs-Élysées, Tél. 08 92 68 30 00 / www.parisinfo.com Ⓜ Charles de Gaulle–Étoile. Ouvert tous les jours de 9 h à 20 h. Vous trouverez aussi des bureaux de tourisme dans les aéroports et les gares.

PERSONNES HANDICAPÉES

Auxiliaires des Aveugles
71, avenue Breteuil, 75015,
tél. : 01 43 06 39 68
Ⓜ Cambronne

Les Compagnons de Voyage
163bis, av. de Clichy, 75017,
tél. : 01 53 11 11 12.
Paiement à l'heure ; réservation 24 h à l'avance

Le métro est pratiquement inaccessible aux fauteuils roulants, à l'exception de quelques stations du RER. Les stations Cité-Universitaire, Auber et Charles-de- Gaulle-Étoile disposent d'ascenseurs publics. Dans les stations citées ci-après, adressez-vous à un agent de la RATP qui vous accompagnera (une clé spéciale est en effet nécessaire) : Châtelet-Les-Halles, Gare de Lyon, La Grande Arche de La Défense, Porte de Clichy, Denfert-Rochereau, Saint-Michel-Notre-Dame, Porte Maillot, Avenue Foch, Avenue Henry Martin, Boulainvilliers, Avenue du Président-Kennedy et Invalides. Les autres stations ne sont pas aménagées.
La nouvelle ligne de métro Météor est accessible aux fauteuils roulants. Un certain nombre de lignes de bus sont accessibles aux fauteuils roulants, se renseigner au tél. : 0810646464.

Aihrop (tél. : 01 41 29 01 29) propose des véhicules adaptés pour les navettes entre Paris et Roissy Charles-de-Gaulle. (lun.-ven., de 10 h à 15 h ; sur réservation) ou demandez un taxi monospace (type Renault Espace) au moment de la réservation.
Les taxis sont tenus de prendre les passagers à mobilité réduite même s'ils doivent leur prêter assistance, de même qu'ils ne peuvent refuser les chiens guides d'aveugles. Ces voyageurs sont prioritaires dans les files d'attente des aéroports et les gares.
Peu d'aménagements ont été pensés pour accueillir les personnes handicapées dans les hôtels et les restaurants. Les personnes handicapées devront s'assurer qu'ils peuvent les accueillir. « Une pièce accessible » veut dire qu'on peut avoir accès en fauteuil roulant et se déplacer facilement dans la salle. « Adapté » signifie que la salle de bains est aux normes. Attention, les ascenseurs des hôtels sont souvent trop exigus pour un fauteuil roulant. Les chaînes d'hôtels modernes sont souvent mieux équipées.

MÉDIAS

Presse
Les principaux titres de la presse parisienne sont *Libération* (de gauche), *Le Monde* (tendance de gauche), *Le Figaro* (de droite), *France-Soir* et *Le Parisien* (journaux populaires). *Le Journal du Dimanche* est le seul quotidien national publié le dimanche. Vous trouverez facilement la presse étrangère dans les gares et les maisons de la presse. Il existe également de nombreux magazines hebdomadaires d'informations tels *L'Express, Le Nouvel Observateur, Le Point*… Pour l'actualité des spectacles à Paris, procurez-vous *Zurban, Pariscope, Figaroscope, Nova Magazine* ou encore *L'Officiel des spectacles*.

Télévision
Les chaînes nationales accessibles sur le réseau non câblé sont TF1, France 2, France 3, France 5 et M6. Le réseau câblé ou par satellite propose de nombreuses chaînes en français comme Paris Première, TV5, CANAL +, Planète, LCI, Eurosport… ou en langues étrangères (CNN, BBC Prime, MTV, MCM, Eurosport, RAI Uno, TVE 1, Euronews…), auxquelles il faut ajouter les 14 nouvelles chaînes de la TNT, la télé numérique terrestre, (France 4, Public Sénat, W9…).

Radios
À côté des grandes stations généralistes comme France Inter, Europe 1 ou RTL, il existe une foule de stations spécialisées. France Info (105.5 FM) est la station dédiée aux informations en continu ; FIP (105.1FM) propose une grande variété de genres musicaux sans interruption publicitaire ; Radio Nova (101.5 FM) s'adresse à un public branché aimant les sons mixés ; Radio latina (99 FM) pour les rythmes sud-américains ; Skyrock (96 FM) pour le rap et RFM (103.9 FM) pour la variété internationale et le rock ; Radio Classique (101.1 FM) diffuse exclusivement de la musique classique.

LES URGENCES

EN CAS D'ACCIDENT

Police, tél. : 17
Pompiers, tél. : 18
SAMU, tél. : 15 ou 01 45 67 50 50
Centre anti-poison, tél. : 01 40 05 48 48
SOS Médecin, tél. : 08 20 33 24 24
SOS Dentaire: 87, boulevard de Port-Royal, 75013, tél. : 01 43 37 51 00/01 47 07 33 68
Ⓜ Gobelins

PHARMACIE 24 H/24

Pharmacie des Champs-Élysées, 84, avenue des Champs-Élysées, 75008, Tél. 01 45 62 02 41.
Ⓜ George-V
Pharmacie Européenne de la place Clichy, 6, place de Clichy 75009, Tél. 01 48 74 65 18
Ⓜ Place de Clichy

AMBASSADES ET CONSULATS

Ambassade du Canada
35, avenue Montaigne, 75008,
tél. : 01 44 43 29 00
Ⓜ Alma-Marceau

Consulat du Canada
37 avenue Montaigne, 75008,
tél. : 01 44 43 29 16
Ⓜ Franklin D. Roosevelt

Délégation générale du Québec
66, rue Pergolèse 75016,
tél. : 08 00 90 77 77
www.mri.gouv.qc.ca/paris/index.html
Ⓜ Kléber

Ambassade de Suisse
142, rue de Grenelle, 75007,
tél. : 01 49 55 67 00/www.dfae.admin.ch/paris_emb/f/home.html
Ⓜ Varenne

Ambassade de Belgique
9, rue Tilsitt, 75017,
tél. : 44 09 39 39
www.diplobel.org/france/home.htm
Ⓜ Charles-de-Gaulle-Étoile

PERTES

Faites toujours une déclaration à la police afin de faire valoir votre assurance. Si vous êtes étranger, en cas de perte de votre pièce d'identité ou passeport, informez-en immédiatement votre consulat (conservez toujours une photocopie des pages de votre passeport, cela facilitera son remplacement).

Bureau des objets trouvés,
36, rue des Morillons, 75015,
tél. : 08 21 00 25 25.
Ⓜ Convention.

RATP objets trouvés
Tél. : 08 92 68 77 14

Carte de paiement perdue ou volée ? Faites immédiatement opposition auprès de votre établissement financier ou en contactant l'un des centres d'opposition ci-dessous.

American Express : 01 47 77 72 00
Diner's Club : 08 10 31 41 59
Mastercard : 01 45 67 84 84
VISA : 08 92 70 57 05

HÔTELS ET RESTAURANTS

L'un des grands plaisirs de voyager en France est lié à la découverte de sa cuisine extraordinaire et Paris ne fait pas exception. Beaucoup d'hôtels ont une salle de restaurant.

Cartes de paiement
La plupart des cartes bancaires sont acceptées dans les hôtels et les restaurants, celles-ci sont indiquées sur un panneau dans le hall d'entrée. Certains établissements plus modestes n'acceptent que les plus courantes.

HÔTELS

Sauf indication contraire, toutes les chambres des hôtels proposés ci-après sont équipées d'une salle de bains ou d'une douche privée. La TVA et le service sont inclus dans le prix.
Pratiquement, tous les hôtels facturent le petit déjeuner en plus, continental (pain, croissant, beurre, confiture et thé ou café) ou quelquefois un buffet.

CLASSEMENT
★★★★ 4 étoiles sont décernées à un hôtel de luxe avec une salle de restaurant, dans lequel chaque chambre dispose d'une salle de bains privée.
★★★ Dans les hôtels 3 étoiles, un minimum de 80 % des chambres sont équipées d'une salle de bains. On peut prendre le petit déjeuner dans la chambre.
★★ Les établissements 2 étoiles doivent posséder au moins 40 % de leurs chambres avec bains ou douche et un téléphone.
★ Les hôtels 1 étoile offre un service simple et convenable.

Les prix sont donnés à titre indicatif et ne tiennent pas compte de la basse ou haute saison. Si vous venez à la haute saison, mieux vaut réserver à l'avance et confirmer par télécopie. D'autre part, un grand nombre d'hôtels majorent leurs tarifs lors des périodes de salons (Mondial de l'auto, Salon du prêt-à-porter, Première Vision…) Mieux vaut éviter ces périodes pour être tranquille. Un acompte ou le numéro de votre carte bancaire peut être exigé.

RESTAURANTS

Il est recommandé de réserver dans les restaurants. Les plus grands sont souvent réservés longtemps à l'avance et les petits sont vite remplis. En principe, les restaurants dont la liste figure ci-après servent une cuisine française. Sinon, cela est indiqué.

Usage
D'ordinaire, le déjeuner se déroule entre 12 h et 14 h. Le dîner est souvent servi vers 20 h, mais cela peut être 19 h.
Les menus doivent être affichés à l'extérieur des établissements. Les étudier ou comparer les prix avant de faire votre choix fait aussi partie du plaisir. Nombreux sont les restaurants qui proposent un ou plusieurs menus à prix fixe dans lesquels le vin est parfois compris. Sinon (et en général c'est plus cher) vous commanderez chaque plat à la carte figurant dans le menu.
Après le plat principal, les Français mangent souvent de la salade et du fromage. Le fromage précède toujours le dessert. Le pain et l'eau du robinet sont servis gratuitement. Fumer est interdit dans les lieux publics en France mais il existe le plus souvent une salle pour fumeurs. Précisez simplement votre préférence au moment de la réservation.

Cafés-bar
Bien que leur nombre ait diminué au cours des dernières années, le café-bar reste une institution bien française. Ils ouvrent tôt le matin pour servir le traditionnel café crème accompagné de croissants ou d'une tartine (un quart de baguette beurrée) et ne désemplissent pas de la journée. Certains sont réputés pour leur terrasse plein sud, d'autres pour leur histoire ou la qualité de leur clientèle. Ce sont assurément des endroits idéaux pour faire une halte et humer l'air de Paris.

N°		tél.	prix	chambres	restaurant	parking
3	À LA VILLA DES ARTISTES	01 43 26 60 86	€€€	59		
4	ARTUS HÔTEL	01 43 29 07 20	€€€€	25		
16	AU MANOIR ST-GERMAIN-DES-P.	01 42 22 21 65	€€€	32		
47	BALZAC	01 44 35 18 00	€€€€€	70	•	•
66	BEAUMARCHAIS	01 53 36 86 86	€€	29+2s		•
17	BEL-AMI	01 42 61 53 53	€€€€	115		
39	BRIGHTON	01 47 03 61 61	€€€	64+1s		
40	CAMBON	01 44 58 93 93	€€€€	32+8s		
5	COLBERT	01 56 81 19 00	€€€€€	36+3s		
41	COSTES	01 42 44 50 00	€€€€€	80+3s	•	
48	CRILLON	01 44 71 15 00	€€€€€	163	•	
58	DUC DE SAINT-SIMON	01 44 39 20 20	€€€€	34+s		
49	ÉLYSÉES CÉRAMIC	01 42 27 20 30	€€€	57		
18	FERRANDI	01 42 22 97 40	€€€	42		•
50	GEORGE V	01 47 23 54 00	€€€€€	260	•	
34	GRAND HÔTEL JEANNE D'ARC	01 48 87 62 11	€	36		
6	GRAND HÔTEL SAINT-MICHEL	01 46 33 33 02	€€€	46		
19	HÔTEL D'ANGLETERRE	01 42 60 34 72	€€€	27		
20	HÔTEL D'AUBUSSON	01 43 29 43 43	€€€€	50	•	•
21	HÔT. DE BRETAGNE MONTPARNASSE	01 45 38 52 59	€€€	44		
22	HÔTEL DE L'ABBAYE	01 45 44 38 11	€€€€	46	•	
67	HÔTEL DE L'AVRE	01 45 75 31 03	€	26		
7	HÔTEL DE L'ESPÉRANCE	01 47 07 10 99	€	38		
35	HÔTEL DE LA BRETONNERIE	01 48 87 77 63	€€€	29		
36	HÔTEL DES CHEVALIERS	01 42 72 73 47	€€€	24		
8	HÔTEL DES GRANDES ÉCOLES	01 43 26 79 23	€€	50		•
9	HÔTEL DES GRANDS HOMMES	01 46 34 19 60	€€€	32+s		
10	HÔTEL DES JARDINS DU LUXEMB.	01 40 46 08 88	€€€	27		
23	HÔTEL DES SAINTS-PÈRES	01 45 44 50 00	€€€	42		
37	HÔTEL DU BOURG-TIBOURG	01 42 78 47 39	€€€	30		
1	HÔTEL DU JEU DE PAUME	01 43 26 14 18	€€€€	28+2s		
42	HÔTEL DU LOUVRE	01 44 58 38 38	€€€€€	199+s	•	
30	HÔTEL DU VIEUX MARAIS	01 42 78 47 22	€€	30		
31	HÔTEL DE LA PLACE DU LOUVRE	01 42 33 78 68	€€€	20		
11	HÔTEL PARC SAINT-SÉVERIN	01 43 54 32 17	€€€	27		
32	HÔTEL VICTOIRES OPÉRA	01 42 36 41 08	€€€	24		

Tous ces hôtels acceptent le paiement par cartes bancaires internationales.

Indication de prix (chambre double sans petit déjeuner) € moins de 115 €

Les îles · Le Quartier latin · Saint-Germain Montparnasse · Le Châtelet et les Halles · Le Marais et la Bastille · Le Louvre et le Palais-Royal

ascenseur	climatisation	piscine	salle de sports	site internet	fax
•	•			www.villa-artistes.com	01 43 54 73 70
•	•			www.artushotel.com	01 43 29 67 44
•	•				01 45 48 22 25
•	•				01 44 35 18 05
•	•			www.hotelbeaumarchais.com	01 43 38 32 86
•	•			www.hotel-bel-ami.com	01 49 27 09 33
				www.esprit-de-france.com	01 42 60 41 78
•	•			www.hotel-cambon.com	01 42 60 30 59
•	•			www.solmelia.com	01 56 81 19 02
•	•	INT.	•	www.hotelcostes.com	01 42 44 50 01
•	•		•	www.crillon.com	01 44 71 15 02
•				www.paris-trendy.com	01 45 48 68 25
•	•			www.elysees-ceramic.com	01 46 22 95 83
•	•			www.123france.com	01 45 44 89 97
•	•	INT.	•	www.fourseasons.com	01 47 20 40 00
•				www.myhotelinparis.com	01 48 87 37 31
•	•			www.grand-hotel-st-michel.com	01 40 46 96 33
•					01 42 60 16 93
•	•			www.hoteldaubusson.com	01 43 29 12 62
•	•			www.bwbretagnemontparnasse.com	01 45 38 50 39
•	•			www.hotel-abbaye.com	01 45 48 07 86
•				www.hoteldelavre.com	01 45 75 63 26
•					01 43 37 56 19
•				www.labretonnerie.com	01 42 77 26 78
•				www.parishotel.com	01 42 72 54 10
•				www.hotel-grandes-ecoles.com	01 43 25 28 15
•	•			www.hoteldesgrandshommes.com	01 43 26 67 32
•	•		•	www.travel-in-paris.com/jardin-Luxembourg	01 40 46 02 28
•	•			www.hotel-esprit-de-france.com	01 45 44 90 83
•	•			www.hotelrivolinotredame.com	01 40 29 07 00
•			•	www.jeudepaumehotel.com	01 40 46 02 76
•	•			www.hoteldulouvre.com	01 44 58 38 00
•	•				01 42 78 34 32
•					01 42 33 09 95
•	•			www.esprit-de-france.com	01 43 54 70 71
•	•			www.hotelvictoiresopera.com	01 45 08 08 79

€€ de 115 à 150 € €€€ de 150 à 230 € €€€€ de 230 à 300 € €€€€€ + de 300 €

Les Champs-Élysées | Les Grands Boulevards | La tour Eiffel et les Invalides | Le XVIe arrondissement | Montmartre | Autres endroits

N°		tél.	prix	chambres	restaurant	parking
43	INTERCONTINENTAL	01 44 77 11 11	€€€€€	450+s		
24	L'HÔTEL	01 44 41 99 00	€€€€€	24		
25	LA VILLA	01 43 26 60 00	€€€€	32	•	
51	LANCASTER	01 40 76 40 76	€€€€€	60		
56	L'ÉLYSÉE	01 42 65 29 25	€€€	32		
12	LE CLOS MÉDICIS	01 43 29 10 80	€€€	38	•	
2	LE NOTRE-DAME HÔTEL	01 43 54 20 43	€€€	26		
59	LIBERTEL BELLECHASSE	01 45 50 22 31	€€€	41		
13	LIBERTEL QUARTIER LATIN	01 44 27 06 45	€€€	29		
60	LINDBERGH	01 45 48 35 53	€€	26		
26	LUTÉTIA	01 49 54 46 46	€€€€	250+s		
14	LUXEMBOURG	01 43 25 35 90	€€€	33	•	
44	MANSART	01 42 61 50 28	€€€	57		
68	MÉRIDIEN ÉTOILE	01 40 68 34 34	€€€€€	1025+s	•	•
27	MÉRIDIEN MONTPARNASSE	01 44 36 44 36	€€€€€	953+s	•	•
45	MOLIÈRE	01 42 96 22 01	€€€	29+3s	•	
52	MONNA LISA	01 56 43 38 38	€€€€	22		
61	MONTALEMBERT	01 45 49 68 68	€€€€€	56	•	
38	PAVILLON DE LA REINE	01 40 29 19 19	€€€€€	34*	•	•
53	PERSHING HALL	01 58 36 58 00	€€€€€	26		
57	PULITZER-OPÉRA	01 53 34 98 10	€€€	44	•	
62	RAPHAËL	01 53 64 32 00	€€€€€	90		
28	RELAIS CHRISTINE	01 40 51 60 80	€€€€€	51	•	•
69	RÉSIDENCE LE VERT GALANT	01 44 08 83 50	€	15		•
46	RITZ	01 43 16 30 30	€€€€€	187+s	•	
54	ROYAL MONCEAU	01 42 99 88 00	€€€€€	219+s	•	•
29	SAINT-GERMAIN	01 49 54 70 00	€€€	29	•	
63	SAINT-JAMES	01 44 05 81 81	€€€€€	46		•
33	SAINT-MERRY	01 42 78 14 15	€€€	11+1s	•	
15	SÉLECT HÔTEL	01 46 34 14 80	€€	68		
64	SQUARE	01 44 14 91 90	€€€€	22		•
65	TERRASS' HÔTEL	01 46 06 72 85	€€€	101	•	
70	TRIANON PALACE	01 30 84 50 00	€€€€€	180	•	•
55	VERNET	01 44 31 98 00	€€€€€	57+s	•	•

Tous ces hôtels acceptent le paiement par cartes bancaires internationales.

Indication de prix (chambre double sans petit déjeuner) € moins de 115 €

Les îles — Le Quartier latin — Saint-Germain Montparnasse — Le Châtelet et les Halles — Le Marais et la Bastille — Le Louvre et le Palais-Royal

ascenseur	climatisation	piscine	salle de sports	site internet	fax
●	●			www.interconti.com	01 44 77 14 60
●	●			www.1-hotel.com	01 43 25 64 81
●	●			www.villa-saintgermain.com	01 46 34 63 63
●	●			www.hotel-lancaster.fr	01 40 76 40 00
●	●			www.france-hotel-guide.com	01 42 65 64 28
●	●			www.closmedicis.com	01 43 54 26 90
●	●			www.lenotredamehotel.com	01 43 26 61 75
●				www.libertel-hotels.com	01 45 51 52 36
●	●			www.libertel-hotels.com	01 43 25 36 70
●				www.hotellindbergh.com	01 45 49 31 48
●	●			www.lutetia.com	01 49 54 46 00
●				www.hotel-Luxembourg.com	01 43 25 17 18
●	●			www.esprit-de-france.com	01 49 27 97 44
●	●			www.lemeridien-etoile.com	01 40 55 67 88
●	●			www.lemeridien-montparnasse.com	01 44 36 49 00
●	●			www.hotel-moliere.fr	01 42 60 48 68
●	●			www.hotelmonnalisa.com	01 45 62 39 90
●	●			www.montalembert.com	01 45 49 69 49
●	●			www.pavillon-de-la-reine.com	01 40 29 19 20
●	●			www.pershinghall.com	01 58 36 58 01
●	●			www.hotelpulitzer.com	01 53 34 98 11
	●			www.raphael-hotel.com	01 53 64 32 01
●	●			www.relais-christine.com	01 40 51 60 81
					01 44 08 83 69
●	●	INT.	●	www.ritz.com	01 43 16 31 78
●	●	INT.	●	www.royalmonceau.com	01 42 99 89 90
●				www.hotel-saint-germain.fr	01 45 48 26 89
●	●		●	www.saint-james-paris.com	01 44 05 81 82
				www.France-hotel-guide.com	01 40 29 06 82
●	●			www.selecthotel.fr	01 46 34 51 79
●	●			www.hotelsquare.com	01 44 14 91 99
●	●			www.terrass-hotel.com	01 42 52 29 11
●	●	INT.	●	www.westin.com	01 30 84 50 01
●	●		●	www.hotelvernet.com	01 44 31 85 69

* : +13 appart+8 duplex

€€ de 115 à 150 € €€€ de 150 à 230 € €€€€ de 230 à 300 € €€€€€ + de 300 €

Les Champs-Élysées | Les Grands Boulevards | La tour Eiffel et les Invalides | Le XVIe arrondissement | Montmartre | Autres endroits

LES ÎLES

01 – HÔTEL DU JEU DE PAUME

★★★★ €€€€
TÉL.: 01 43 26 14 18
FAX: 01 40 46 02 76
54, RUE ST-LOUIS-EN-L'ÎLE – 75004
Ⓜ PONT-MARIE

Au XVIIe siècle, il y avait près de 300 salles de jeu de paume à Paris. Sur l'île Saint-Louis, l'une d'elles a été transformée en hôtel. Les volumes ont été redistribués avec talent dans un esprit provençal.

02 – LE NOTRE-DAME HÔTEL

★★★ €€€
TÉL.: 01 43 54 20 43
FAX: 01 43 26 61 75
1, QUAI SAINT-MICHEL – 75005
Ⓜ SAINT-MICHEL

Face à Notre-Dame… Des poutres, des chambres rénovées et confortables, des salles de bains en marbre.

LE QUARTIER LATIN

03 – À LA VILLA DES ARTISTES

★★★ €€€
TÉL.: 0143 26 60 86
FAX: 01 43 54 73 70
9, RUE DE LA GRANDE-CHAUMIÈRE – 75006
Ⓜ VAVIN

Cet hôtel est un haut lieu de pèlerinage. C'est là que Hemingway, Man Ray, Modigliani, Beckett séjournèrent. La décoration années 1930 est bien inspirée. Très calme.

04 – ARTUS HÔTEL

★★★ €€€€
TÉL.: 0143 29 07 20
FAX: 01 43 29 67 44
34, RUE DE BUCI – 75006
Ⓜ MABILLON

Un très bel hôtel conçu par un designer de talent. Tons chauds et naturels, éclairages tamisés, des salles de bains très agréables, des chambres très bien agencées.

05 – HÔTEL COLBERT

★★★★ €€€€€
TÉL.: 01 56 81 19 00
FAX: 01 56 81 19 02
7, RUE DE L'HÔTEL-COLBERT
75005
Ⓜ MAUBERT-MUTUALITÉ

Un hôtel de luxe très élégant à deux pas de Notre-Dame. Les salles de réception sont d'une grande classe, le service très soigné.

06 – GRAND HÔTEL SAINT-MICHEL

★★★ €€€
TÉL.: 01 46 33 33 02
FAX: 01 40 46 96 33
19, RUE CUJAS – 75005
Ⓜ LUXEMBOURG

En plein cœur du quartier étudiant, cet hôtel décoré dans un style Directoire propose des chambres agréables et harmonieusement décorées.

07 – HÔTEL DE L'ESPÉRANCE

★★ €
TÉL.: 01 47 07 10 99
FAX: 01 43 37 56 19
15, RUE PASCAL – 75005
Ⓜ CENSIER-DAUBENTON

Un charmant hôtel familial bien tenu et sans prétention. Un très bon rapport qualité-prix.

08 – HÔTEL DES GRANDES ÉCOLES

★★ €€
TÉL.: 01 43 26 79 23
FAX: 01 43 25 28 15
75, RUE DU CARDINAL-LEMOINE
75005
Ⓜ CARDINAL-LEMOINE

Cet hôtel a des atouts incomparables: sa situation, son jardin dans lequel vous pouvez prendre votre petit-déjeuner, ses chambres spacieuses, ses belles salles de bains, et tout cela à un prix très abordable.

09 – HÔTEL DES GRANDS HOMMES

★★★ €€€
TÉL.: 01 46 34 19 60
FAX: 01 43 26 67 32
17, PLACE DU PANTHÉON
75005
Ⓜ LUXEMBOURG

Demandez une chambre avec vue sur le Panthéon. Chambres agréablement décorées.

10 – HÔTEL DES JARDINS DU LUXEMBOURG

★★★ €€€
TÉL.: 01 40 46 08 88
FAX: 01 40 46 02 28
5, IMPASSE ROYER-COLLARD
75005
Ⓜ LUXEMBOURG

Dans une impasse très tranquille, cet hôtel dispose de chambres élégamment décorées dans un style contemporain.

11 – HÔTEL PARC SAINT-SÉVERIN

★★★ €€€
TÉL.: 01 43 54 32 17
FAX: 01 43 54 70 71
22, RUE DE LA PARCHEMINERIE
75005
Ⓜ SAINT-MICHEL

Demandez une chambre avec terrasse, vous ne serez pas déçu…

12 – HÔTEL LE CLOS MÉDICIS

★★★ €€€
TÉL.: 01 43 29 10 80
FAX: 01 43 54 26 90
56, RUE MONSIEUR-LE-PRINCE
75006
Ⓜ CLUNY-LA SORBONNE

Face aux jardins du Luxembourg, ce bel hôtel offre un excellent confort à ses clients. Les salles de réception sont accueillantes, les chambres sont calmes et agréables, les salles de bains très réussies.

13 – HÔTEL LIBERTEL QUARTIER LATIN

★★★ €€€
TÉL.: 01 44 27 06 45
FAX: 01 43 25 36 70
9, RUE DES ÉCOLES – 75005
Ⓜ CARDINAL-LEMOINE

Cet hôtel s'apparente au show-room d'un décorateur. Tout a été spécialement conçu, les lignes sont épurées, les couleurs chaudes, les matières nobles (ébène, lin).

14 – HÔTEL LUXEMBOURG

★★★ €€€
TÉL.: 01 43 25 35 90
FAX: 01 43 25 17 18
4, RUE DE VAUGIRARD – 75006
Ⓜ LUXEMBOURG

Un hôtel très soigné donnant sur un jardin-patio agrémenté d'une fontaine, un mobilier de style XVIIIe, des étoffes à profusion renforcent un sentiment de confort et de raffinement.

15 – SÉLECT HÔTEL

★★★ €€
TÉL.: 01 46 34 14 80
FAX: 01 46 34 51 79
1, PLACE DE LA SORBONNE
75005
Ⓜ CLUNY LA SORBONNE

Une belle verrière, des plantes exotiques, du mobilier design, des salles de bains rénovées… Le Sélect Hôtel dispose d'une décoration contemporaine très soignée.

SAINT-GERMAIN ET MONTPARNASSE

16 – AU MANOIR SAINT-GERMAIN-DES-PRÉS

★★★★ €€€

TÉL.: 01 42 22 21 65
FAX: 01 45 48 22 25
153, BOULEVARD SAINT-GERMAIN – 75006
Ⓜ SAINT-GERMAIN-DES-PRÉS

Face à Saint-Germain-des-Près et des célèbres cafés de Flore et des Deux-Magots, se tient l'élégant Manoir.

17 – HÔTEL BEL-AMI

★★★★ €€€€

TÉL.: 01 42 61 53 53
FAX: 01 49 27 09 33
7/11, RUE SAINT-BENOÎT – 75006
Ⓜ SAINT-GERMAIN-DES-PRÉS

Les amateurs de design seront comblés dans cet hôtel entièrement rénové. Mélange de style, harmonie des couleurs, matières nobles, maîtrise de la lumière... le Bel-Ami est vraiment très chic.

18 – HÔTEL FERRANDI

★★★ €€€

TÉL.: 01 42 22 97 40
FAX: 01 45 44 89 97
92, RUE DU CHERCHE-MIDI 75006
Ⓜ SAINT-PLACIDE

Le Ferrandi est un trois étoiles qui a tout d'un grand hôtel. De belles réceptions richement meublées et décorées en style Restauration, des chambres spacieuses et des salles de bains confortables.

19 – HÔTEL D'ANGLETERRE

★★★ €€€

TÉL.: 01 42 60 34 72
FAX: 01 42 60 16 93
44, RUE JACOB – 75006
Ⓜ SAINT-GERMAIN-DES-PRÉS

Au cœur du quartier des antiquaires et des galeries d'art, cet hôtel dispose de somptueux volumes, un mobilier ancien de belle facture et un jardin-patio très agréable.

20 – HÔTEL D'AUBUSSON

★★★★ €€€€

TÉL.: 01 43 29 43 43
FAX: 01 43 29 12 62
33, RUE DAUPHINE – 75006
Ⓜ ODÉON

Un décor Grand Siècle, une insonorisation parfaite, un service de qualité font de cette adresse, un Must pour les habitués des belles demeures.

21 – HÔTEL DE BRETAGNE MONTPARNASSE

★★★ €€€

TÉL.: 01 45 38 52 59
FAX: 01 45 38 50 39
33, RUE RAYMOND LOSSERAND 75014
Ⓜ GAÎTÉ

À deux pas de la gare Montparnasse-TGV, cet hôtel à la décoration contemporaine dispose de chambres fonctionnelles (mobilier en bois clair, mur jaune paille...) et de belles salles de bains.

22 – HÔTEL DE L'ABBAYE

★★★ €€€€

TÉL.: 01 45 44 38 11
FAX: 01 45 48 07 86
10, RUE CASSETTE – 75006
Ⓜ ODÉON

Autour d'un luxuriant jardin-patio, s'organisent salons et chambres, dans le calme et la volupté. L'accueil est impeccable. Une adresse très romantique...

23 – HÔTEL DES SAINTS-PÈRES

★★★ €€€

TÉL.: 01 45 44 50 00
FAX: 01 45 44 90 83
65, RUE DES SAINTS-PÈRES 75006
Ⓜ SAINT-GERMAIN-DES-PRÉS

Ancien hôtel particulier du XVIIe siècle, cet hôtel s'organise autour d'un patio très agréable. Les chambres sont meublées et agencées avec goût.

24 – L'HÔTEL

★★★★ €€€€€

TÉL.: 01 44 41 99 00
FAX: 01 43 25 64 81
13, RUE DES BEAUX-ARTS – 75006
Ⓜ MABILLON

L'atrium de l'Hôtel est une merveille architecturale et les chambres qu'il dessert sont toutes aménagées avec un goût exquis. Le service est d'un grand raffinement tout comme les petits salons de réception.

25 – HÔTEL LA VILLA

★★★★ €€€€

TÉL.: 01 43 26 60 00
FAX: 01 46 34 63 63
29, RUE JACOB – 75006
Ⓜ SAINT-GERMAIN-DES-PRÉS

La Villa est un hôtel à la déco très harmonieuse. Des chambres à la fois sobres et chaleureuses, des salles de bains magnifiquement agencées.

26 – HÔTEL LUTÉTIA

★★★★ €€€€

TÉL.: 01 49 54 46 46
FAX: 01 49 54 46 00
45, BOULEVARD RASPAIL – 75006
Ⓜ SÈVRES-BABYLONE

Situé au cœur du quartier de la mode, des arts et des lettres, à quelques pas du jardin du Luxembourg, des antiquaires, des musées d'Orsay, cet hôtel est réputé par la qualité de sa décoration et son histoire.

27 – HÔTEL MÉRIDIEN MONTPARNASSE

★★★★ €€€€€

TÉL.: 01 44 36 44 36
FAX: 01 44 36 47 00
19, RUE DE COMMANDANT MOUCHOTTE – 75014
Ⓜ GAÎTÉ

Depuis certaines chambres, vous avez une vue sur tout Paris. Cet hôtel moderne de très haut de gamme offre de belles prestations.

28 – RELAIS CHRISTINE

★★★★ €€€€€

TÉL.: 01 40 51 60 80
FAX: 01 40 51 60 81
3, RUE CHRISTINE – 75006
Ⓜ ODÉON

Dans les bâtiments de l'ancien couvent des Augustins, cet hôtel est un havre de luxe et de volupté. Les chambres sont conçues avec soin et goût du détail, certaines donnent sur un jardin. La salle à manger est une magnifique salle voûtée du XIIIe siècle.

29 – HÔTEL SAINT-GERMAIN

★★★ €€€

TÉL.: 01 49 54 70 00
FAX: 01 45 48 26 89
88, RUE DU BAC – 75007
Ⓜ ODÉON

Cet hôtel vient d'achever sa rénovation et c'est une réussite. Le mobilier ancien côtoie le moderne avec distinction.

LE CHÂTELET ET LES HALLES

30 – HÔTEL DU VIEUX MARAIS

★★ €€

TÉL.: 01 42 78 47 22
FAX: 01 42 78 34 32
8, RUE DU PLÂTRE – 75004
Ⓜ RAMBUTEAU

INDICATIONS DE PRIX
(pour une chambre double standard sans petit déjeuner)

€ < 115 € €€ = 115-150 € €€€ = 150-230 € €€€€ = 230-300 € €€€€€ > 300 €

Cet hôtel, entièrement rénové, offre de belles prestations pour sa catégorie. Un mobilier en chêne clair très design, des éclairages étudiés, des salles de bains en marbre, tout cela dans une rue calme du Marais.

31 – HÔTEL DE LA PLACE DU LOUVRE
★★★ €€€
TÉL.: 01 42 33 78 68
FAX: 01 42 33 09 95
21, RUE DES PRÊTRES-SAINT-GERMAIN-L'AUXERROIS – 75001
Ⓜ CHÂTELET OU LOUVRE

Décoration réussie, mélange d'ancien et de moderne. Les chambres sont agréables et certaines ont une vue sur le Louvre.

32 – HÔTEL VICTOIRES OPÉRA
★★★★ €€€
TÉL.: 01 42 36 41 08
FAX: 01 45 08 08 79
56, RUE MONTORGUEIL – 75002
Ⓜ SENTIER

Dans un des quartiers les plus animés de Paris, cet hôtel offre un décor très soigné et très tendance. Les couleurs et les matières se répondent dans une parfaite harmonie, les lignes sont épurées. Les tarifs sont majorés pendant les salons.

33 – HÔTEL SAINT-MERRY
★★★ €€€
TÉL.: 0142 78 14 15
FAX: 01 40 29 06 82
78, RUE DE LA VERRERIE – 75004
Ⓜ CHÂTELET

Un hôtel qui a une forte personnalité avec son style néo-gothique flamboyant, ses chandeliers, ses ferronneries…

LE MARAIS ET LA BASTILLE

34 – GRAND HÔTEL JEANNE D'ARC
★★ €
TÉL.: 01 48 87 62 11
FAX: 01 48 87 37 31
3, RUE DE JARENTE – 75004
Ⓜ SAINT-PAUL

Au cœur du Marais, une bonne adresse pour ceux qui ne veulent pas se ruiner et goûter les charmes d'un petit hôtel familial.

35 – HÔTEL DE LA BRETONNERIE
★★★ €€€
TÉL.: 01 48 87 77 63
FAX: 01 42 77 26 78
22, RUE SAINTE-CROIX-DE-LA-BRETONNERIE – 75004
Ⓜ HÔTEL-DE-VILLE

Dans un ancien hôtel particulier, à deux pas du musée Picasso, cet établissement offre de vastes chambres décorées avec goût. Une adresse très chaleureuse.

36 – HÔTEL DES CHEVALIERS
★★★ €€€
TÉL.: 01 42 72 73 47
FAX: 01 42 72 54 10
30, RUE DE TURENNE – 75003
Ⓜ SAINT-PAUL

Tout près de la place des Vosges, cet hôtel occupe un bel immeuble du XVIIe siècle. Le service est parfait, la décoration harmonieuse et coordonnée.

37 – HÔTEL DU BOURG-TIBOURG
★★★ €€€
TÉL.: 01 42 78 47 39
FAX: 01 40 29 07 00
19, RUE DU BOURG-TIBOURG 75004
Ⓜ HÔTEL-DE-VILLE

Cet hôtel, entièrement rénové il y a peu, est devenu un véritable écrin baroque. De lourdes tentures, une lumière tamisée par des abats jours à frange… On se croirait dans un décor de théâtre.

38 – HÔTEL PAVILLON DE LA REINE
★★★★ €€€€€
TÉL.: 01 40 29 19 19
FAX: 01 40 29 19 20
28, PLACE DES VOSGES – 75003
Ⓜ SAINT-PAUL

En plus de sa localisation exceptionnelle, ce merveilleux hôtel offre un très haut niveau de prestation ainsi qu'un parking privé, ce qui est appréciable dans ce quartier.

LE LOUVRE

39 – HÔTEL BRIGHTON
★★★ €€€
TÉL.: 01 47 03 61 61
FAX: 01 42 60 4178
218, RUE DE RIVOLI – 75001
Ⓜ TUILERIES OU CONCORDE

Quelques chambres (entièrement rénovées) donnent sur les jardins des Tuileries, à deux pas du Louvre. Compte tenu de leurs dimensions spacieuses et leur vue exceptionnelle, elles offrent un excellent rapport qualité-prix.

40 – HÔTEL CAMBON
★★★★ €€€€
TÉL.: 01 44 58 93 93
FAX: 01 42 60 30 59
3, RUE CAMBON – 75001
Ⓜ TUILERIES OU CONCORDE

Un lieu design apprécié des VIP de la mode. Les éclairages tamisés, les espaces aérés, la propreté méticuleuse des pièces de réception confèrent une agréable sérénité à cette adresse.

41 – HÔTEL COSTES
★★★★ €€€€€
TÉL.: 01 42 44 50 00
FAX: 01 42 44 50 01
239, RUE SAINT-HONORÉ – 75001
Ⓜ CONCORDE

Costes, c'est l'alliance réussie du baroque et du design, du show off et de la discrétion. Ainsi, on ne s'ennuie jamais comme dans les hôtels trop standardisés tout en savourant une paix royale autour d'un superbe patio.

42 – HÔTEL DU LOUVRE
★★★★ €€€€€
TÉL.: 01 44 58 38 38
FAX: 01 44 58 38 00
1, PLACE ANDRÉ MALRAUX 75001
Ⓜ PALAIS-ROYAL

Entre le Louvre, la Comédie-Française et l'Opéra, une bonne adresse de luxe pour un week-end culturel.

43 – HÔTEL INTERCONTINENTAL
★★★★ €€€€€
TÉL.: 01 44 77 11 11
FAX: 01 44 77 14 60
3, RUE CASTIGLIONE – 75001
Ⓜ TUILERIES OU CONCORDE

Récemment rénové, l'Intercontinental est merveilleusement situé et offre d'excellentes prestations.

44 – HÔTEL MANSART
★★★ €€€
TÉL.: 01 42 61 50 28
FAX: 01 49 27 97 44
5, RUE DES CAPUCINES – 75001
Ⓜ OPÉRA OU MADELEINE

Logez en face du Ritz sans vous ruiner. Des suites Grand Siècle ou Napoléon III, des chambres et des salles de bains offrant de beaux volumes, une situation de rêve, l'hôtel Mansart dispose de quelques atouts pour vous séduire.

45 – HÔTEL MOLIÈRE
★★★ €€€
TÉL.: 01 42 96 22 01
FAX: 01 42 60 48 68
21, RUE MOLIÈRE – 75001
Ⓜ PYRAMIDES
Le Molière sort d'un programme de rénovation très réussi. Les chambres sont harmonieuses et très confortables.

46 – HÔTEL RITZ
★★★★ €€€€€
TÉL.: 01 43 16 30 30
FAX: 01 43 16 31 78
15, PLACE VENDÔME – 75001
Ⓜ TUILERIES
Assurément l'un des plus beaux palaces de Paris, chargé d'histoire et d'empreintes de stars.

LES CHAMPS-ÉLYSÉES

47 – HÔTEL BALZAC
★★★★ €€€€€
TÉL.: 0144 35 18 00
FAX: 01 44 35 18 05
6, RUE BALZAC – 75008
Ⓜ GEORGE-V
À deux pas de l'agitation des Champs-Elysées, ce bel hôtel est très accueillant avec sa déco chaleureuse (mur terre de sienne, palmiers dans le grand salon). Les chambres sont somptueuses, les salles de bains en marbre et le restaurant, avec Pierre Gagnaire aux commandes, est l'une des meilleures tables de Paris.

48 – HÔTEL CRILLON
★★★★ €€€€€
TÉL.: 01 44 71 15 00
FAX: 01 44 71 15 02
10, PLACE DE LA CONCORDE 75008
Ⓜ CONCORDE
Un palace avec vue sur l'une des plus belles places du monde… Une adresse très exclusive pour la jet-set.

49 – HÔTEL ÉLYSÉES CÉRAMIC
★★★ €€€
TÉL.: 01 42 27 20 30
FAX: 01 46 22 95 83
34, AVENUE DE WAGRAM 75008
Ⓜ CHARLES-DE-GAULLE-ÉTOILE

Dans un immeuble à la façade Art nouveau due à l'architecte Lavirotte, cet hôtel a judicieusement axé sa rénovation sur ce style.

50 – HÔTEL GEORGE V
★★★★ €€€€€
TÉL.: 01 49 52 70 00
FAX: 01 49 52 70 10
31, AVENUE GEORGE-V – 75008
Ⓜ GEORGE-V
Le George V sort d'un long et luxueux programme de rénovation. Les salles de bains sont particulièrement réussies.

51 – HÔTEL LANCASTER
★★★★ €€€€€
TÉL.: 01 40 76 40 76
FAX: 01 40 76 40 00
7, RUE DE BERRI – 75008
Ⓜ F.D. ROOSEVELT
Le cadre de cet hôtel et de ses chambres est somptueux. Des meubles anciens, des tableaux de belle facture sont mis en valeur par une rénovation harmonieuse. Les chambres sont très grandes, les salles de bains superbement agencées et modernes.

52 – HÔTEL MONNA LISA
★★★★ €€€€
TÉL.: 01 56 43 38 38
FAX: 01 45 62 39 90
97, RUE DE LA BOÉTIE – 75008
Ⓜ F.D. ROOSEVELT
Un hôtel design où volumes, matières, couleur et lumière ont été savamment pensés pour vous offrir la sérénité. Le restaurant Caffe Ristretto est une excellente adresse italienne à Paris.

53 – PERSHING HALL
★★★★ €€€€€
TÉL.: 01 58 36 58 00
FAX: 01 58 36 58 01
49, RUE PIERRE CHARRON – 75008
Ⓜ GEORGE-V
Cet hôtel particulier haussmannien a été transformé en hôtel de luxe très tendance: des chambres spacieuses très bien équipées, un lounge pour boire un verre en écoutant de la musique spécialement mixée, un restaurant tenu par un chef talentueux (Yann Bourgeois).

54 – HÔTEL ROYAL MONCEAU
★★★★ €€€€€
TÉL.: 01 42 99 88 00
FAX: 01 42 99 89 90
37, AVENUE HOCHE – 75008
Ⓜ TERNES

Le Royal Monceau se démarque des autres palaces par son luxe raffiné et discret. Deux restaurants, un jardin, un spa et un personnel très attentionné devraient vous permettre de passer un agréable séjour.

55 – HÔTEL VERNET
★★★★ €€€€€
TÉL.: 01 44 31 98 00
FAX: 01 44 31 85 69
25, RUE VERNET – 75008
Ⓜ GEORGE-V
Le Vernet est un grand hôtel en miniature. Ses 51 chambres sont toutes équipées d'un jacuzzi. Son restaurant gastronomique tenu par Eric Briffard a une étoile Michelin.

56 – L'ÉLYSÉE
★★★ €€€
TÉL.: 01 42 65 29 25
FAX: 01 42 65 64 28
16, RUE DES SAUSSAIES – 75008
Ⓜ MIROMESNIL
Un agréable hôtel, à deux pas du ministère de l'intérieur, qui dispose d'une trentaine de chambres et de 3 suites dont la décoration, inspirée des XVIIIe et XIXe siècles, est délicate et très accueillante.

LES GRANDS BOULEVARDS

57 – HÔTEL PULITZER-OPÉRA
★★★ €€€
TÉL.: 01 53 34 98 10
FAX: 01 53 34 98 11
23, RUE DU FAUBOURG-MONTMARTRE – 75009
Ⓜ GRANDS BOULEVARDS
Un nouvel hôtel dans un quartier qui en compte déjà beaucoup. Pourtant, le Pulitzer est unique car il bénéficie d'une décoration sobre et moderne, d'un patio verdoyant, d'une bonne insonorisation et de salles de bains bien agencées.

LA TOUR EIFFEL ET LES INVALIDES

58 – HÔTEL DUC DE SAINT-SIMON
★★★ €€€€
TÉL.: 01 44 39 20 20
FAX: 01 45 48 68 25
14, RUE SAINT-SIMON – 75007
Ⓜ RUE DU BAC
Un havre de paix sur la rive gauche avec un exquis mobilier

INDICATIONS DE PRIX
(pour une chambre double standard sans petit déjeuner)

€ < 115 €   €€ = 115-150 €   €€€ = 150-230 €   €€€€ = 230-300 €   €€€€€ > 300 €

ancien, un jardin et une très belle salle de petits-déjeuners en sous-sol.

59 – HÔTEL LIBERTEL BELLECHASSE
★★★ €€€
TÉL. : 01 45 50 22 31
FAX : 01 45 51 52 36
8, RUE DE BELLECHASSE
75007
Ⓜ SOLFÉRINO

À deux pas du musée d'Orsay, cet hôtel de style Empire a beaucoup d'allure et des chambres agréables.

60 – HÔTEL LINDBERGH
★★ €€
TÉL. : 01 45 48 35 53
FAX : 01 45 49 31 48
5, RUE CHOMEL
75007
Ⓜ SÈVRES-BABYLONE

Ce petit hôtel plein de charme offre une décoration très chaleureuse, et les chambres rénovées récemment y sont impeccables.

61 – HÔTEL MONTALEMBERT
★★★★ €€€€€
TÉL. : 01 45 49 68 68
FAX : 01 45 49 69 49
3, RUE DE MONTALEMBERT
75007
Ⓜ RUE DU BAC

Le Montalembert est un hôtel de grand standing tout en étant moderne. Les chambres et les salles de bains, décorées avec goût et luxe offrent un maximum de confort.

LE XVIᵉ ARRONDISSEMENT

62 – HÔTEL RAPHAËL
★★★★ €€€€€
TÉL. : 01 53 64 32 00
FAX : 01 53 64 32 01
17, AVENUE KLÉBER
75116
Ⓜ CHARLES-DE-GAULLE-ÉTOILE

Le Raphaël est l'adresse parisienne de ceux qui sont revenus des grands palaces souvent impersonnels. Ici, tout est luxueux, voluptueux et discret. Le service est d'une grande classe.

63 – HÔTEL SAINT-JAMES
★★★★ €€€€€
TÉL. : 01 44 05 81 81
FAX : 01 44 05 81 82
43, AVENUE BUGEAUD – 75116
Ⓜ PORTE DAUPHINE

L'hôtel Saint-James a des airs d'hôtel de ville de sous-préfecture, mais à Paris, dans le XVIᵉ arrondissement, c'est le nec plus ultra. À l'intérieur, vous reconnaîtrez tous les charmes d'un club anglais : des boiseries, une superbe bibliothèque, de confortables sofas…

64 – HÔTEL SQUARE
★★★★ €€€€
TÉL. : 01 44 14 91 90
FAX : 01 44 14 91 99
3, RUE DES BOULAINVILLIERS
75016
Ⓜ RANELAGH

Au sud du XVIᵉ arrondissement, se tient un immeuble en marbre gris qui abrite un hôtel au design contemporain et harmonieux. Les chambres sont grandes, les salles de bains en marbre.

MONTMARTRE

65 – TERRASS' HÔTEL
★★★★ €€€
TÉL. : 01 46 06 72 85
FAX : 01 42 52 29 11
12, RUE JOSEPH-DE-MAISTRE
75018
Ⓜ BLANCHE

À partir du 4ᵉ étage ou depuis la terrasse, la vue s'étend sur tout Paris. Les chambres ont été rénovées et offrent des volumes généreux.

AUTRES ENDROITS

66 – HÔTEL BEAUMARCHAIS
★★★ €€
TÉL. : 01 53 36 86 86
FAX : 01 43 38 32 86
3, RUE OBERKAMPF – 75011
Ⓜ OBERKAMPF

Le propriétaire est architecte et cela se ressent dans la qualité de la décoration. Les chambres sont très agréables, les salles de bains originales et les prix sont doux.

67 – HÔTEL DE L'AVRE
★★ €
TÉL. : 01 45 75 31 03
FAX : 01 45 75 63 26
21, RUE DE L'AVRE – 75015
Ⓜ LA-MOTTE-PICQUET-GRENELLE

Dans ce petit hôtel, vous ne risquez pas d'être déçu. La décoration est harmonieuse, le calme règne sur les chambres qui donnent sur le jardin, les salles de bains sont bien agencées et enfin le rapport qualité-prix est excellent.

68 – HÔTEL MÉRIDIEN ÉTOILE
★★★★ €€€€€
TÉL. : 01 40 68 34 34
FAX : 01 40 68 31 31
81, BOULEVARD GOUVION SAINT-CYR – 75017
Ⓜ PORTE MAILLOT

Ce gigantesque hôtel dans une tour offre une superbe vue sur Paris, mais manque singulièrement de charme.

69 – RÉSIDENCE LE VERT GALANT
★★★ €
TÉL. : 01 44 08 83 50
FAX : 01 44 08 83 69
41, RUE CROULEBARBE – 75013
Ⓜ GOBELINS

Cette belle et calme maison de campagne avec un jardin sur lequel donnent toutes les chambres vous fera immédiatement oublier le stress parisien.

70 – HÔTEL TRIANON PALACE
★★★★ €€€€€
TÉL. : 01 30 84 50 00
FAX : 01 30 84 50 01
1, BOULEVARD DE LA REINE
78000 VERSAILLES
Ⓜ RER C : GARE RIVE GAUCHE GARE RIVE DROITE (DEPUIS GARE ST-LAZARE) OU GARE DES CHANTIERS DEPUIS GARE MONTPARNASSE.

À une demi-heure des portes de Paris, à 5 minutes du château de Versailles, le Trianon Palace propose une alternative intéressante à ceux qui apprécient à la fois le luxe et la vue sur des champs peuplés de moutons. Les installations du spa (piscine, hammam, sauna, salle de sport, salles de massage) sont impeccables et très agréables.

RESTAURANTS

		tél.	métro
	moins de 20 €		
82	**AU PIED DE FOUET**	01 47 05 12 27	Sèvres-Babylone
29	**BISTROT BEAUBOURG**	01 42 77 48 02	Rambuteau
79	**CHARTIER**	01 47 70 86 29	Grands Boulevards
83	**CHEZ GERMAINE**	01 42 73 28 34	Duroc
106	**CHEZ GLADINES (LE)**	01 45 80 70 10	Corvisart
101	**CHEZ TOINETTE**	01 42 54 44 36	Abbesses
45	**L'AS DU FALLAFEL**	01 48 87 63 60	Saint-Paul
103	**L'ÉTRIER**	01 42 29 14 01	Lamarck-Caulaincourt
97	**LE GALILÉO**	01 47 20 91 30	Kléber
46	**LE PETIT FER À CHEVAL**	01 42 72 47 47	Saint-Paul/Hôtel-de-Ville
47	**LE TEMPS DES CERISES**	01 42 72 08 63	Sully-Morland/Bastille
48	**LE TRUMILOU**	01 42 77 63 98	Hôtel-de-Ville/Pont-Marie
27	**POLIDOR**	01 43 26 95 34	Odéon
	de 20 € à 35 €		
01	**MA SALLE À MANGER**	01 43 29 52 34	Pont-Neuf
28	**AU PIED DE COCHON**	01 40 13 77 00	Louvre/Les Halles
49	**AUX BONS CRUS**	01 42 60 06 45	Bourse/Palais-Royal
11	**AUX CHARPENTIERS**	01 43 26 30 05	Mabillon
04	**BALZAR**	01 43 54 13 67	Cluny-La Sorbonne
05	**BOUILLON RACINE**	01 44 32 15 60	Cluny-La Sorbonne
02	**BRASSERIE DE L'ISLE ST-LOUIS**	01 43 54 02 59	Pont-Marie
30	**CAFÉ BEAUBOURG**	01 48 87 63 96	Rambuteau
41	**CHEZ OMAR**	01 42 72 36 26	Filles-du-Calvaire
107	**CLOS MORILLONS**	01 48 28 04 37	Porte de Vanves
80	**I GOLOSI**	01 48 24 18 63	Grands Boulevards
32	**LES DESSOUS DE LA ROBE**	01 40 26 68 18	Châtelet-Les Halles
16	**L'OS À MOELLE**	01 45 57 27 27	Lourmel
17	**LA BASTIDE ODÉON**	01 43 26 03 65	Odéon
33	**LA POULE AU POT**	01 42 36 32 96	Les Halles
06	**LA TABLE D'AUDE**	01 43 26 36 36	Cluny-La Sorbonne
08	**LES PAPILLES**	01 43 25 20 79	Luxembourg
104	**LE TAROUDANT II**	01 42 64 95 81	Abbesses/Blanche
	de 35 € à 50 €		
10	**ALCAZAR**	01 53 10 19 99	Odéon
36	**AU BASCOU**	01 42 72 69 25	Arts et Métiers
78	**AU PETIT RICHE**	01 47 70 68 68	Richelieu-Drouot
105	**AU TROU GASCON**	01 43 44 34 26	Daumesnil
37	**BISTROT DU DÔME**	01 48 04 88 44	Bastille
39	**BLUE ELEPHANT**	01 47 00 42 00	Bastille
40	**BOFINGER**	01 42 72 87 82	Bastille
94	**BON**	01 40 72 70 00	La Muette
12	**BRASSERIE LIPP**	01 45 48 53 91	Saint-Germain-des-Prés

N°		tél.	métro
13	CAFÉ DE FLORE	01 45 48 55 26	Saint-Germain-des-Prés
50	CAFÉ MARLY	01 49 26 06 60	Palais-Royal
56	CAP VERNET	01 47 20 20 40	Charles-de-Gaulle–Étoile
100	CHARLOT	01 53 20 48 00	Place de Clichy
42	GEORGES	01 44 78 47 99	Rambuteau
43	JULIEN	01 47 70 12 06	Strasbourg-Saint-Denis
60	L'ANGLE DU FAUBOURG	01 40 74 20 20	Ternes
62	L'AVENUE	01 40 70 14 91	Franklin D. Roosevelt
87	L'ESPLANADE	01 47 05 38 80	La Tour-Maubourg
18	LA CAGOUILLE	01 43 22 09 01	Gaité
19	LA COUPOLE	01 43 20 14 20	Montparnasse
109	LA RÉGALADE	01 45 45 68 58	Alésia
20	LA RÔTISSERIE D'EN FACE	01 43 26 40 98	Saint-Michel
89	LEO LE LION	01 45 51 41 77	École militaire
22	LE DÔME	01 43 35 25 81	Montparnasse
03	MON VIEIL AMI	01 40 46 01 35	Sully-Morland
09	LE PROCOPE	01 40 46 79 00	Odéon
85	LES ORMES	01 45 51 46 93	Invalides
111	LE TRAIN BLEU	01 43 43 09 06	Gare de Lyon
24	LES BOUQUINISTES	01 43 25 45 94	Saint-Michel
25	LES BOUCHONS DE FR. CLERC	01 43 54 15 34	Saint-Michel
52	MACÉO	01 42 97 53 85	Pyramides
26	PAVILLON MONTSOURIS	01 45 88 38 52	RER Cité-Universitaire
54	PINXO	01 40 20 72 00	Tuileries
72	RENOMA CAFÉ GALLERY	01 47 20 46 19	George-V
53	RESTAURANT DU PALAIS ROYAL	01 40 20 00 27	Palais-Royal
112	RESTAURANT MARTY	01 43 31 39 51	Gobelins
73	RUE BALZAC	01 53 89 90 91	Franklin D. Roosevelt
74	SAVEURS ET SALON	01 40 06 97 97	Madeleine
77	TANJIA	01 42 25 95 00	Franklin D. Roosevelt
	de 50 € à 80 €		
99	BEAUVILLIERS	01 42 54 54 42	Lamarck-Caulaincourt
38	BENOÎT	01 42 72 25 76	Hôtel de Ville
55	CAFFE RISTRETTO	01 56 43 38 38	Franklin D. Roosevelt
14	CLOSERIE DES LILAS	01 40 51 34 50	Vavin
57	COPENHAGUE	01 44 13 86 26	George-V
58	FOUQUET'S	01 47 23 77 20	George-V

Les îles — Le Quartier latin — Saint-Germain et Montparnasse — Le Châtelet et les Halles — Le Marais et la Bastille — Le Louvre et le Palais-Royal

N°		tél.	métro
31	GÉRARD BESSON	01 42 33 14 74	Les Halles
95	GÉRAUD	01 45 20 33 00	Pompe-La Muette
84	HÉLÈNE DARROZE	01 42 22 00 11	Sèvres-Babylone
15	JACQUES CAGNA	01 43 26 49 39	Saint-Michel
61	L'ASTOR	01 53 05 05 20	Saint-Augustin
96	L'ASTRANCE	01 40 50 84 40	Passy
108	LA GRANDE CASCADE	01 45 27 33 51	Porte Maillot
102	LA TABLE D'ANVERS	01 48 78 35 21	Anvers
21	LE CIEL DE PARIS	01 40 64 77 64	Montparnasse
23	LE DUC	01 43 20 96 30	Raspail
64	LE PICHET DE PARIS	01 43 59 50 34	George-V
110	LE PRÉ CATELAN	01 44 14 41 14	Porte Maillot
66	LES ÉLYSÉES	01 44 31 98 98	George-V
88	LES OLIVADES	01 47 83 70 09	Saint-François-Xavier
67	MARIUS ET JEANNETTE	01 47 23 41 88	Alma-Marceau
70	NIRVANA	01 53 89 18 91	Mirosmenil
35	PHARAMOND	01 42 33 06 72	Les Halles
75	SPOON	01 40 76 34 44	Franklin D. Roosevelt
92	VIOLON D'INGRES	01 45 55 15 05	Pont de l'Alma
	plus de 80 €		
93	59, POINCARÉ	01 47 27 59 59	Victor-Hugo
51	CARRÉ DES FEUILLANTS	01 42 86 82 82	Concorde/Tuileries
59	GUY SAVOY	01 43 80 40 61	Charles-de-Gaulle-Étoile
44	L'AMBROISIE	01 42 78 51 45	Saint-Paul
86	L'ARPÈGE	01 45 51 47 33	Varenne
63	LA MAISON BLANCHE	01 47 23 55 99	Alma-Marceau
07	LA TOUR D'ARGENT	01 43 54 23 31	Maubert-Mutualité
90	LE DIVELLEC	01 45 51 91 96	Invalides
34	LE GRAND VÉFOUR	01 42 96 56 27	Palais-Royal
91	LE JULES VERNE	01 45 55 61 44	Trocadéro
65	LEDOYEN	01 53 05 10 01	Champs-Élysées-Clemenceau
81	LUCAS-CARTON	01 42 65 22 90	Madeleine
98	MAISON PRUNIER	01 44 17 35 85	Victor-Hugo
68	MAXIM'S	01 42 65 27 94	Concorde
69	MICHEL ROSTANG	01 47 63 40 77	Ternes
71	PIERRE GAGNAIRE	01 58 36 12 50	George-V
76	TAILLEVENT	01 44 95 15 01	George-V

Les Champs-Élysées — Les Grands Boulevards — La tour Eiffel et les Invalides — Le XVIe arrondissement — Montmartre — Autres endroits

LES ÎLES

01 – MA SALLE À MANGER
26, PLACE DAUPHINE
75001 PARIS
TÉL. : 01 43 29 52 34
€ €
FERMÉ SAM. ET DIM.

Spécialités de poisson et de volaille, au seuil d'une des places les plus calmes de Paris.

02 – BRASSERIE DE L'ISLE SAINT-LOUIS
55, QUAI DE BOURBON
75004 PARIS
TÉL. : 01 43 54 02 59
€ €
FERMÉ VEN., SAM. ET DIM. AU DÉJ.

De la bonne cuisine traditionnelle.

03 – MON VIEIL AMI
69, RUE ST-LOUIS-EN-L'ÎLE
75004 PARIS
TÉL. : 01 40 46 01 35
€ € €
FERMÉ LUN. ET MAR. MIDI.

Cuisine classique mais allégée, dans une belle maison ancienne dont la décoration a été rafraîchie il ya quelque temps.

LE QUARTIER LATIN

04 – BALZAR
49, RUE DES ÉCOLES
75005 PARIS
TÉL. : 01 43 54 13 67
€ €
FERMÉ AOÛT

Une brasserie comme on les aime : simple et efficace dans le service, copieuse et bonne dans l'assiette.

05 – BOUILLON RACINE
3, RUE RACINE
75006 PARIS
TÉL. : 01 44 32 15 60
€ €

Dans un beau décor Art nouveau, une cuisine belge de qualité. Un bon choix de bières et un excellent waterzoï.

06 – LA TABLE D'AUDE
8, RUE DE VAUGIRARD
75006 PARIS
TÉL. : 01 43 26 36 36
€ €
FERMÉ DIM. ET 2 SEMAINES EN AOÛT

Des bons «petits» plats du Sud-Ouest dans une ambiance chaleureuse.

07 – LA TOUR D'ARGENT
15, QUAI TOURNELLE
75005 PARIS
TÉL. : 01 43 54 23 31
€ € € € €
FERMÉ LUN.

Même si sa réputation a baissé (elle a chuté de 3 à 2 étoiles dans le Michelin), la Tour d'Argent reste un des grands noms de la haute gastronomie française. L'ambiance feutrée tout comme la vue sur la Seine et Notre-Dame laissent un souvenir inoubliable.

08 – LES PAPILLES
30, RUE GAY-LUSSAC
75005 PARIS
TÉL. : 01 43 25 20 79
€ €

Carte légère à midi, menu du marché le soir, le tout dans une charmante épicerie fine où les vins sont particulièrement alléchants.

09 – LE PROCOPE
13, RUE DE L'ANCIENNE-COMÉDIE
75006 PARIS
TÉL. : 01 40 46 79 00
€ € €

Par son histoire et son cadre, le Procope est un des endroits mythiques de Paris.

SAINT-GERMAIN ET MONTPARNASSE

10 – ALCAZAR
62, RUE MAZARINE
75006 PARIS
TÉL. : 01 53 10 19 99
€ € €

Ce restaurant, qui appartient à Terence Conran, propose une cuisine cosmopolite et inventive.

11 – AUX CHARPENTIERS
10, RUE MABILLON
75006 PARIS
TÉL. : 01 43 2 30 05
€ €
FERMÉ DIM. ET JOURS FÉRIÉS

Autrefois, c'était un restaurant populaire. Désormais, c'est un restaurant plutôt chic où l'on mange de solides plats classiques.

12 – BRASSERIE LIPP
151, BOULEVARD SAINT-GERMAIN
75006 PARIS
TÉL. : 01 45 48 53 91
€ € €

Une institution de Saint-Germain-des-Prés où se croisent hommes de lettres et politiciens. Cassoulet le jeudi, tête de veau le vendredi et bœuf gros sel pour le week-end.

POUR APPELER DEPUIS L'ÉTRANGER : 00 33 +...

13 – CAFÉ DE FLORE
172, BOULEVARD SAINT-GERMAIN
75006 PARIS
TÉL. : 01 45 48 55 26
€ € €

Un endroit mythique de Saint-Germain-des-Prés.

14 – CLOSERIE DES LILAS
171, BOULEVARD MONTPARNASSE
75006 PARIS
TÉL. : 01 40 51 34 50
€ € € €

Un nouveau chef a amélioré la cuisine de ce bar-brasserie-restaurant de Montparnasse archi-connu, quartier général d'Hemingway, Picasso, Apollinaire et bien d'autres. L'endroit est idéal pour boire un verre au coude à coude avec l'intelligentsia parisienne.

15 – JACQUES CAGNA
14, RUE DES GRANDS-AUGUSTINS
75006 PARIS
TÉL. : 01 43 26 49 39
€ € € €
FERMÉ SAM. AU DÉJ., DIM., AOÛT ET NOËL

Dans un magnifique hôtel particulier soigneusement meublé, cela fait plus de vingt-cinq ans que Jacques Cagna et sa sœur reçoivent les gourmets les plus exigeants. Tous les produits sont sélectionnés avec le plus grand soin.

16 – L'OS À MOELLE
3, RUE VASCO DE GAMA
75015 PARIS
TÉL. : 01 45 57 27 27
€ €
FERMÉ DIM., LUN. ET AOÛT

Avec Thierry Faucher en cuisine, de bons plats du terroir à des prix ajustés.

17 – LA BASTIDE ODÉON
7, RUE CORNEILLE
75006 PARIS
TÉL. : 01 43 26 03 65
€ €
FERMÉ DIM., LUN ET AOÛT

Une cuisine provençale remise au goût du jour.

18 – LA CAGOUILLE
10, PLACE CONSTANTIN-BRANCUSI
75014 PARIS
TÉL. : 01 43 22 09 01
€ € €

Un bon restaurant de poisson, un service sympathique et une terrasse pour les beaux jours.

19 – LA COUPOLE
102, BOULEVARD MONTPARNASSE
75014 PARIS
TÉL. : 01 43 20 14 20
€ € €

Une des brasseries historiques de Paris. Le service et les plats sont à la hauteur de la réputation.

20 – LA RÔTISSERIE D'EN FACE
2, RUE CHRISTINE
75006 PARIS
TÉL. : 01 43 26 40 98
€ € €
FERMÉ SAM. AU DÉJ. ET DIM.

Annexe à prix modérés du restaurant de Jacques Cagna; une cuisine de bistrot créative et une atmosphère bon enfant.

RECOMMANDÉ

21 – LE CIEL DE PARIS
TOUR MONTPARNASSE
33, AVENUE DU MAINE
75014 PARIS
TÉL. : 01 40 64 77 64
€ € € €

Jean-François Oyon s'est installé dans les plus hautes cuisines de Paris. Les saveurs admirablement concoctées par le chef en feraient presque oublier le panorama de ce fascinant 56e étage…

22 – LE DÔME
108, BOULEVARD MONTPARNASSE
75014 PARIS
TÉL. : 01 43 35 25 81
€ € €

Dans cette brasserie très connue de Montparnasse, les poissons sont remarquables et l'ambiance très animée.

23 – LE DUC
243, BOULEVARD RASPAIL
75014 PARIS
TÉL. : 01 43 20 96 30
€ € € €
FERMÉ SAM. AU DÉJ., DIM., LUN. ET VACANCES SCOLAIRES

D'excellents produits, des cuissons parfaites permettant de restituer des saveurs les plus pures ; Le Duc est une grande maison…

24 – LES BOUQUINISTES
53, QUAI DES GRANDS-AUGUSTINS
75006 PARIS
TÉL. : 01 43 25 45 94
€ € €
FERMÉ SAM. AU DÉJ. ET DIM. AU DÉJ.

Une cuisine moderne dans un beau décor. Ne manquez pas les remarquables glaces et sorbets maison.

INDICATIONS DE PRIX (pour un repas, vin non compris)

€ < 20 € | € € = 20-35 € | € € € = 35-50 € | € € € € = 50-80 € | € € € € € > 80 €

25 – LES BOUCHONS DE FRANÇOIS CLERC
12, RUE DE L'HÔTEL COLBERT
75005 PARIS
TÉL. : 01 43 54 15 34
€ € €
FERMÉ SAM. AU DÉJ. ET DIM.

Ce restaurant propose de bonnes bouteilles de vin à des prix raisonnables ainsi qu'une cuisine raffinée.

RECOMMANDÉ

26 – PAVILLON MONTSOURIS
20, RUE GAZAN
75014 PARIS
TÉL. : 01 43 31 29 00
€ € €
FERMÉ DIM. SOIR

Un déjeuner à la terrasse du Pavillon Montsouris par une belle journée de printemps, c'est le bonheur…

27 – POLIDOR
41, RUE MONSIEUR-LE-PRINCE
75006 PARIS
TÉL. : 01 43 26 95 34
€

Un classique de la restauration. James Joyce était un habitué.

LE CHÂTELET ET LES HALLES

28 – AU PIED DE COCHON
6, RUE COQUILLIÈRE
75001 PARIS
TÉL. : 01 40 13 77 00
€ €
OUVERT 24 H/24

Cet ancien bistrot des Halles propose des spécialités du terroir et reste ouvert toute la nuit.

29 – BISTROT BEAUBOURG
25, RUE QUINCAMPOIX
75004 PARIS
TÉL. : 01 42 77 48 02
€

Une atmosphère bon enfant, des plats de bonne tenue pour une addition raisonnable, juste à côté du centre Georges Pompidou.

30 – CAFÉ BEAUBOURG
43, RUE SAINT-MERRI
75004 PARIS
TÉL. : 01 48 87 63 96
€ €

Un endroit design et à la mode pour boire un verre et grignoter.

31 – GÉRARD BESSON
5, RUE DU COQ-HÉRON
75001 PARIS
TÉL. : 01 42 33 14 74
€ € € €
FERMÉ SAM. AU DÉJ., SAM. MI-JUIN À MI-SEPT ET DIM.

Le chef s'ingénie à servir des produits d'une extrême fraîcheur renouvelant ainsi de grands classiques.

32 – LES DESSOUS DE LA ROBE
4, RUE BERTIN POIRÉE
75001 PARIS
TÉL. : 01 40 26 68 18
€ €
FERMÉ SAM. ET DIM. AU DÉJ. ET LUN

Entre l'auberge et le bistrot, ce restaurant sert une cuisine agréablement traditionnelle dans une ambiance très sympathique.

33 – LA POULE AU POT
9, RUE VAUVILLIERS
75001 PARIS
TÉL. : 01 42 36 32 96
€ €
FERMÉ LUN. ET AU DÉJ.

Un restaurant ouvert toute la nuit qui accueille noctambules et gens du théâtre et propose une cuisine traditionnelle.

RECOMMANDÉ

34 – LE GRAND VÉFOUR
17, RUE DU BEAUJOLAIS
75001 PARIS
TÉL. : 01 42 96 56 27
€ € € € €
FERMÉ SAM. ET DIM.

Dans un merveilleux décor Directoire, Guy Martin confirme chaque jour sa grande classe. Le service est attentif et souriant. Patrick Tamisier, le sommelier, ne demande qu'à vous faire sortir des sentiers battus pour trouver le vin idéal.

35 – PHARAMOND
24, RUE DE LA GRANDE-TRUANDERIE
75001 PARIS
TÉL. : 01 40 28 45 18
€ € € €
FERMÉ DIM. ET LUN. AU DÉJ.

Spécialités normandes dans un authentique bistrot Art déco.

LE MARAIS ET LA BASTILLE

36 – AU BASCOU
38, RUE RÉAUMUR
75003 PARIS
TÉL. : 01 42 72 69 25
€ € €
FERMÉ SAM. AU DÉJ., DIM., AOÛT, ET 1 SEMAINE À NOËL

D'excellentes spécialités basques dans un restaurant à l'ambiance chaleureuse.

37 – BISTROT DU DÔME
2, RUE DE LA BASTILLE
75004 PARIS
TÉL. : 01 48 04 88 44
€ € €
FERMÉ EN AOÛT

Spécialités de poisson dans un joli décor. Parfait pour dîner après l'opéra.

38 – BENOÎT
20, RUE SAINT-MARTIN
75004 PARIS
TÉL. : 01 42 72 25 76
€ € € €
FERMÉ SAM. ET DIM.

Dans un décor de bistrot, Benoît propose une cuisine à base de produits d'excellence. Vous découvrirez un admirable poulet en croûte de sel et de merveilleux desserts de grand-mère.

39 – BLUE ELEPHANT
43, RUE DE LA ROQUETTE
75011 PARIS
TÉL. : 01 47 00 42 00
€ € €

Cela fait treize ans que le Blue Elephant régale les Parisiens de cuisine thaïlandaise. Ne manquez pas le Tom Kaa Kaï (potage), la salade de papaye verte et les bouchées vapeur (Dim Sim) ; les curries au poulet (curry vert) ou bien d'agneau (curry brun).

40 – BOFINGER
5-7, RUE DE LA BASTILLE
75004 PARIS
TÉL. : 01 42 72 87 82
€ € €

La grande brasserie parisienne.

41 – CHEZ OMAR
47, RUE DE BRETAGNE
75003 PARIS
TÉL. : 01 42 72 36 26
€ €
FERMÉ DIM. AU DÉJ.

Excellent couscous dans un décor de vieux bistrot.

42 – GEORGES
PLACE GEORGES-POMPIDOU
75001 PARIS
TÉL. : 01 44 78 47 99
€ € €

Au 6e étage du centre Pompidou, le Georges offre des espaces très design et des plats très nouvelle cuisine.

43 – JULIEN
16, RUE DU FAUBOURG-SAINT-DENIS
75010 PARIS
TÉL. : 01 47 70 12 06
€ € €

Le décor Art nouveau de cette brasserie est fabuleux, le service et la carte sont recommandables.

44 – L'AMBROISIE
9, PLACE DES VOSGES
75004 PARIS
TÉL. : 01 42 78 51 45
€ € € € €
FERMÉ DIM., LUN., 3 SEMAINES EN AOÛT

Bernard Pacaud propose dans un cadre très élégant une cuisine classique (trop, au goût de certains).

45 – L'AS DU FALLAFEL
34, RUE DES ROSIERS
75004 PARIS
TÉL. : 01 48 87 63 60
€
FERMÉ VEN. SOIR ET SAM.

Un fallafel parfaitement épicé.

46 – LE PETIT FER À CHEVAL
30, RUE VIEILLE-DU-TEMPLE
75004 PARIS
TÉL. : 01 42 72 47 47
€

Un petit restaurant à la mode où l'on peut dîner jusqu'à une heure du matin.

47 – LE TEMPS DES CERISES
31, RUE DE LA CERISAIE
75004 PARIS
TÉL. : 01 42 72 08 63
€
FERMÉ SAM. AU DÉJ., DIM. ET AOÛT.

Un petit bistrot d'habitués où l'on sert un excellent canard cuit dans sa graisse.

48 – LE TRUMILOU
84, QUAI DE L'HÔTEL-DE-VILLE
75004 PARIS
TÉL. : 01 42 77 63 98
€

Un vieux bistrot sur les quais.

LE LOUVRE

49 – AUX BONS CRUS
7, RUE DES PETITS-CHAMPS
75001 PARIS
TÉL. : 01 42 60 06 45
€ €
FERMÉ SAM., DIM., ET LUN. DÎN.

Un bar à vin établi depuis près d'un siècle. Des plats traditionnels et une ambiance chaleureuse.

50 – CAFÉ MARLY
COUR NAPOLÉON
93, RUE DE RIVOLI
75001 PARIS
TÉL. : 01 49 26 06 60
€ € €

Dans un cadre exceptionnel (vous êtes dans le Louvre…), un café-restaurant à la mode vous propose une carte tout à fait honorable.

INDICATIONS DE PRIX (pour un repas, vin non compris)

€ < 20 € | € € = 20-35 € | € € € = 35-50 € | € € € € = 50-80 € | € € € € € > 80 €

51 – CARRÉ DES FEUILLANTS
14, RUE CASTIGLIONE
75001 PARIS
TÉL. : 01 42 86 82 82
€ € € € €
FERMÉ SAM. AU DÉJ., DIM. ET AOÛT

Spécialités du Sud-Ouest, à base de foie gras et de truffes sous des formes les plus diverses. Excellent.

RECOMMANDÉ

52 – MACÉO
15, RUE DES PETITS-CHAMPS
75001 PARIS
TÉL. : 01 42 97 53 85
€ € €
FERMÉ DIM.

Ce restaurant cosmopolite propose dans un cadre Second Empire, une cuisine créative, des saveurs subtiles et un excellent rapport qualité-prix.

53 – RESTAURANT DU PALAIS ROYAL
110, GALERIE DE VALOIS
JARDINS DU PALAIS-ROYAL
75001 PARIS
TÉL. : 01 40 20 00 27
€ € €
FERMÉ SAM. AU DÉJ., DIM. SEPT.-MAI, ET 1 SEMAINE À NOËL

La cuisine est bonne sans être exceptionnelle, mais sa terrasse dans les jardins du Palais-Royal vaut le déplacement.

54 – PINXO
HÔTEL PLAZZA PARIS VENDÔME
9, RUE D'ALGER
75001 PARIS
TÉL. : 01 40 20 72 00
€ € €
FERMÉ AOÛT.

Une adresse originale, au décor sobre et élégant. Tenu par Alain Dutournier (Carré des Feuillants) propose des recettes « instantanées » (cuisson rapide, facilité de dégustation). Qualité et portions gourmandes évoquant la tradition.

LES CHAMPS-ÉLYSÉES

55 – CAFFE RISTRETTO
97, RUE LA BOÉTIE
75008 PARIS
TÉL. : 01 56 43 38 38
€ € € €
FERMÉ SAM. ET DIM.

Le Caffe Ristretto sous la conduite de Roberto Casavecchia est l'un des rares restaurants italiens de Paris à marier une cuisine gastronomique inventive à un design chic et moderne.

56 – CAP VERNET
82, AVENUE MARCEAU
75008 PARIS
TÉL. : 01 47 20 20 40
€ € €

Annexe de Guy Savoy, spécialisée dans les fruits de mer. Le décor blanc et bleu est très réussi.

57 – COPENHAGUE
142, AVENUE DES CHAMPS-ÉLYSÉES
75008 PARIS
TÉL. : 01 44 13 86 26
€ € € €
FERMÉ SAM. AU DÉJ. ET DIM.

Une institution venue du froid. Le saumon à l'unilatéral est une merveille.

58 – FOUQUET'S
99, AVENUE DES CHAMPS-ÉLYSÉES
75008 PARIS
TÉL. : 01 47 23 50 00
€ € € €

Une adresse culte sur les Champs-Élysées qui a repris un nouveau souffle.

59 – GUY SAVOY
18, RUE TROYON
75017 PARIS
TÉL. : 01 43 80 40 61
€ € € € €
FERMÉ SAM. AU DÉJ., DIM. ET 1 SEMAINE EN JUILLET

Dans un cadre moderne signé Jean-Michel Wilmotte, Guy Savoy vous propose sa fabuleuse cuisine.

RECOMMANDÉ

60 – L'ANGLE DU FAUBOURG
195, RUE DU FAUBOURG-SAINT-HONORÉ
75008 PARIS
TÉL. : 01 40 74 20 20
€ € €
FERMÉ SAM. ET DIM.

L'annexe de Taillevent est une bien belle adresse. Un décor agréable, une cuisine à la fois simple et imaginative et une addition tout à fait raisonnable.

61 – L'ASTOR
11, RUE D'ASTORG
75008 PARIS
TÉL. : 01 53 05 05 20
€ € € €
FERMÉ SAM. ET DIM., AOÛT

Laurent Delarbre, ancien second du Ritz, a donné ses lettres de noblesse à ce restaurant d'hôtel.

62 – L'AVENUE
41, AVENUE MONTAIGNE
75008 PARIS
TÉL. : 01 40 70 14 91
€ € €

En face de chez Dior, une adresse très parisienne où

se côtoie le monde des médias et de la mode.

63 – LA MAISON BLANCHE
15, AVENUE MONTAIGNE
75008 PARIS
TÉL. : 01 47 23 55 99
€ € € € €
FERMÉ SAM. AU DÉJ., DIM. ET AOÛT

Les frères jumeaux Pourcel, célébrés par tous les critiques, sont venus de Montpellier pour redonner une nouvelle vie à La Maison Blanche. Le résultat est à la hauteur des espérances et le Tout-Paris se presse pour y réserver sa table.

64 – LE PICHET DE PARIS
68, RUE PIERRE-CHARRON
75008 PARIS
TÉL. : 01 43 59 50 34
€ € € €

C'était l'un des restaurants préférés du président Mitterrand qui avait la passion des fruits de mer.

65 – LEDOYEN
CARRÉ DES CHAMPS-ÉLYSÉES
75008 PARIS
TÉL. : 01 53 05 10 01
€ € € € €
FERMÉ SAM., DIM. ET AOÛT

Par sa cuisine subtile et équilibrée, Christian Le Squer a redonné une âme à cet élégant pavillon qui donne sur les Champs-Élysées.

66 – LES ÉLYSÉES
HÔTEL VERNET
25, RUE VERNET
75008 PARIS
TÉL. : 01 44 31 98 98
€ € € €
FERMÉ SAM., DIM ET AOÛT

Eric Briffard propose une excellente cuisine de terroir dans ce charmant restaurant d'hôtel.

67 – MARIUS ET JEANNETTE
4, AVENUE GEORGE-V
75008 PARIS
TÉL. : 01 47 23 41 88
€ € € €

D'excellentes spécialités de poissons méditerranéens, préparées sous la houlette de Bernard Pinault.

68 – MAXIM'S
3, RUE ROYALE
75008 PARIS
TÉL. : 01 42 65 27 94
€ € € € €

Ce haut lieu des nuits parisiennes d'avant-guerre a conservé son décor mais a perdu un peu de son aura.

69 – MICHEL ROSTANG
20, RUE RENNEQUIN
75017 PARIS
TÉL. : 01 47 63 40 77
€ € € € €
FERMÉ SAM. AU DÉJ., DIM. ET 2 SEMAINES EN AOÛT

Élégance et tradition sont les mots clés du chef savoyard de ce restaurant. Spécialités de truffes en saison (décembre à mars).

70 – NIRVANA
3, AV. MATIGNON
75008 PARIS
TÉL. : 01 53 89 18 91
€ € € €

Un décor des Mille et Une Nuits, une cuisine indienne revisitée rive droite, ambiance musicale plutôt branchée... Une adresse de fête, aussi dépaysante que chaleureuse.

71 – PIERRE GAGNAIRE
6, RUE BALZAC
75008 PARIS
TÉL. : 01 58 36 12 50
€ € € € €
FERMÉ SAM., DIM. AU DÉJ., MI-JUIL. À MI-AOÛT

Le restaurant de l'hôtel Balzac a conquis les Parisiens par la qualité artistique de sa cuisine. Le style Gagnaire est vraiment inimitable.

RECOMMANDÉ

72 – RENOMA CAFÉ GALLERY
32, AVENUE GEORGE-V
75008 PARIS
TÉL. : 01 47 20 46 19
€ € €

Design contemporain, fumoir-bibliothèque, exposition de photos, mais aussi une cuisine excellente.

73 – RUE BALZAC
3-5, RUE BALZAC
75008 PARIS
TÉL. : 01 53 89 90 91
€ € €
FERMÉ VEN., SAM. AU DÉJ., DIM. DÎN. ET AOÛT.

Johnny Hallyday et l'acteur Claude Bouillon se sont associés pour monter ce restaurant à succès.

74 – SAVEURS ET SALON
3, RUE DE CASTELLANE
75008 PARIS
TÉL. : 01 40 06 97 97
€ € €
FERMÉ SAM. AU DÉJ. ET DIM.

Bonne ambiance dans cet établissement du quartier de la Madeleine. Une cuisine du marché saine et très goûteuse.

INDICATIONS DE PRIX (pour un repas, vin non compris)

€ < 20 € € € = 20-35 € € € € = 35-50 € € € € € = 50-80 € € € € € € > 80 €

75 – SPOON
14, RUE DE MARIGNAN
75008 PARIS
TÉL. : 01 40 76 34 44
€ € € €
FERMÉ SAM., DIM. ET JOURS FÉRIÉS

Alain Ducasse propose un tour du monde des saveurs, et c'est une belle réussite.

76 – TAILLEVENT
15, RUE LAMENNAIS
75008 PARIS
TÉL. : 01 44 95 15 01
€ € € € €
FERMÉ SAM., DIM., ET VACANCES SCOLAIRES

Jean-Claude Vrinat a appelé Michel del Burgo aux cuisines pour revisiter les classiques et créer de nouvelles saveurs. Ce restaurant est une des plus grandes maisons parisiennes.

77 – TANJIA
23, RUE DE PONTHIEU
75008 PARIS
TÉL. : 01 42 25 95 00
€ € €
FERMÉ SAM ET DIM AU DÉJ.

Les gens du show-biz et de la mode se pressent dans ce restaurant marocain au cadre enchanteur.

LES GRANDS BOULEVARDS

78 – AU PETIT RICHE
25, RUE LE PELETIER
75009 PARIS
TÉL. : 01 47 70 68 68
€ € €
FERMÉ DIM.

Dans un magnifique décor 1880, le Petit Riche vous propose des spécialités du Val de Loire.

79 – CHARTIER
7, RUE DU FAUBOURG-MONTMARTRE
75009 PARIS
TÉL. : 01 47 70 86 29
€

Une grande salle, des tables serrées les unes contre les autres, une carte désuète, des prix serrés, un service effectué par des garçons expérimentés, c'est cela Chartier et cela fait plus d'un siècle que ça dure.

80 – I GOLOSI
6, RUE DE LA GRANGE-BATELIÈRE
75009 PARIS
TÉL. : 01 48 24 18 63
€ €

Des produits de qualité cuisinés avec talent et imagination font de ce restaurant italien l'un des meilleurs de Paris.

81 – LUCAS-CARTON
9, PLACE DE LA MADELEINE
75008 PARIS
TÉL. : 01 42 65 22 90
€ € € € €
FERMÉ SAM. AU DÉJ., DIM. ET 3 SEMAINES EN AOÛT

Dans un décor Art nouveau, Alain Senderens, l'un des chefs les plus doués de sa génération, vous fera découvrir d'incroyables saveurs.

LA TOUR EIFFEL ET LES INVALIDES

82 – AU PIED DE FOUET
45, RUE DE BABYLONE
75007 PARIS
TÉL. : 01 47 05 12 27
€
FERMÉ SAM. AU DÎN., DIM., ET VACANCES SCOLAIRES

Petit restaurant familial. Une cuisine du terroir pour des habitués (certains ont leur propre rond de serviette).

83 – CHEZ GERMAINE
30, RUE PIERRE-LEROUX
75007 PARIS
TÉL. : 01 42 73 28 34
€
FERMÉ SAM., DIM. ET AOÛT

Un petit restaurant d'habitués qui viennent déguster l'excellente purée de pomme de terre dans une ambiance familiale. N'accepte pas les cartes de paiement.

84 – HÉLÈNE DARROZE
4, RUE D'ASSAS
75006 PARIS
TÉL. : 01 42 22 00 11
€ € € €
FERMÉ DIM.

Hélène Darroze propose une cuisine du Sud-Ouest revisitée avec talent.

RECOMMANDÉ

85 – LES ORMES
22, RUE SURCOUF
75007 PARIS
TÉL. : 01 45 51 46 93
€ € €
FERMÉ DIM ET LUN

Une étoile Michelin pour ce restaurant très chaleureux servant une cuisine contemporaine et inventive autour des produits de saison. Il est indispensable de réserver : petite salle et prix raisonnables.

86 – L'ARPÈGE
84, RUE DE VARENNE
75007 PARIS
TÉL. : 01 45 51 47 33
€ € € € €

Alain Passard a créé l'événement en mettant les légumes à l'honneur de sa carte. Des saveurs uniques assemblées par un chef magicien.

87 – L'ESPLANADE
52, RUE FABERT
75007 PARIS
TÉL. : 01 47 05 38 80
€ € €

Un restaurant bien décoré (par Jacques Garcia), bien situé (l'esplanade des Invalides), bien fréquenté (bcbg à la mode) et la cuisine est sans prétention ni surprise.

88 – LES OLIVADES
41, AV. DE SÉGUR
75007 PARIS
TÉL. : 01 47 83 70 09
€ € € €
FERMÉ SAM. ET LUN. AU DÉJ., DIM., ET AOÛT

Une adresse nimbée du soleil de Provence : la décoration lumineuse de la salle, la savoureuse cuisine méridionale. Un bénéfique dépaysement.

89 – LEO LE LION
2, RUE DE L'EXPOSITION
TÉL. : 01 45 51 41 77.
€ € €
FERMÉ DIM. ET LUN., FÊTES DE FIN D'ANNÉE ET AOÛT

Poisson et gibier sont les spécialités de ce bistrot 1930. Autre originalité savoureuse : le grill au feu de bois.

90 – LE DIVELLEC
107, RUE DE L'UNIVERSITÉ
75007 PARIS
TÉL. : 01 45 51 91 96
€ € € € €
FERMÉ DIM., LUN., ET NOËL

L'un des meilleurs restaurants de fruits de mer parisiens.

91 – LE JULES VERNE
TOUR EIFFEL, 2E ÉTAGE
75007 PARIS
TÉL. : 01 45 55 61 44
€ € € € €

Avec pour chef Alain Reix (spécialiste du poisson), un restaurant avec une des plus belles vues du monde. Si vous souhaitez dîner dans ce haut lieu, il vous faudra réserver plusieurs semaines à l'avance

92 – VIOLON D'INGRES
135, RUE ST-DOMINIQUE
75007 PARIS
TÉL. : 01 45 55 15 05
€ € € €
FERMÉ DIM., LUN., ET AOÛT

Christian Constant, ancien chef aux « Ambassadeurs » continue dans son restaurant à faire la même excellente cuisine à prix plus doux.

LE XVIe ARRONDISSEMENT

93 – 59, POINCARÉ
59, AVENUE RAYMOND-POINCARÉ
75016 PARIS
TÉL. : 01 47 27 59 59
€ € € € €
FERMÉ SAM. AU DÉJ., DIM. ET LUN.

Avec son talent et sa classe, Alain Ducasse se concentre sur les saveurs du homard, du bœuf et de l'agneau dans un décor magique.

94 – BON
25, RUE DE LA POMPE
75016 PARIS
TÉL. : 01 40 72 70 00
€ € €

Le nouveau restaurant de Philippe Starck est très agréable et vous pouvez y allez sans craindre de faire une entorse à votre régime.

95 – GÉRAUD
31, RUE VITAL
75016 PARIS
TÉL. : 01 45 20 33 00
€ € € €
FERMÉ SAM. ET DIM., AOÛT

Étonnant décor en faïence pour ce bistrot chic qui sert, en saison, de remarquables préparations de gibier.

96 – L'ASTRANCE
4, RUE BEETHOVEN
75016 PARIS
TÉL. : 01 40 50 84 40
€ € € €

Deux anciens de Passard ont parfaitement réussi leur installation. Les critiques dithyrambiques et le bouche à oreille font qu'il est nécessaire de réserver plusieurs semaines à l'avance.

RECOMMANDÉ

97 – LE GALILÉO

14, RUE GALILÉE,
75016 PARIS
TÉL. : 01 47 20 91 30
€
FERMÉ SOIR ET WEEK-END

Une nouveauté très réussie dans le quartier. Des plats méditerranéens de bonne facture servis avec bonne humeur et efficacité.

98 – MAISON PRUNIER
16, AVENUE VICTOR-HUGO
75016 PARIS
TÉL. : 01 44 17 35 85
€ € € € €
FERMÉ DIM.

Ce restaurant est spécialisé dans le caviar, ce qui rend les additions salées.

MONTMARTRE

99 – BEAUVILLIERS
52, RUE LAMARCK
75018 PARIS
TÉL. : 01 42 54 54 42
€ € € €

Typiquement montmartrois : ambiance romantique, décor un peu kitsch, service bon enfant et cuisine sympathique.

100 – CHARLOT, LE ROI DES COQUILLAGES
81, BOULEVARD DE CLICHY
75009 PARIS
TÉL. : 01 53 20 48 00
€ € €

Un refuge pour les amateurs de fruits de mer.

101 – CHEZ TOINETTE
20, RUE GERMAIN-PILON
75018 PARIS
TÉL. : 01 42 54 44 36
€
FERMÉ AU DÉJ. ET DIM.

De la cuisine provençale à un excellent rapport qualité/prix. N'accepte pas les cartes de paiement.

102 – LA TABLE D'ANVERS
2, PLACE D'ANVERS
75009 PARIS
TÉL. : 01 48 78 35 21
€ € € €
FERMÉ SAM. AU DÉJ. ET DIM. AU DÉJ.

Ces deux frères ont leurs fidèles qui apprécient l'originalité de leur cuisine.

103 – L'ÉTRIER
154, RUE LAMARCK
75018 PARIS
TÉL. : 01 42 29 14 01
€
FERMÉ DIM., LUN. ET AOÛT

Agréable petit bistrot de quartier, plats du jour savoureux inscrits sur une ardoise, ambiance chaleureuse et prix modestes.

104 – LE TAROUDANT II
8, RUE ARISTIDE-BRUANT
75018 PARIS
TÉL. : 01 42 64 95 81
€ €
FERMÉ MER. ET AOÛT

Un des meilleurs couscous de Paris et autres spécialités marocaines délicieuses.

AUTRES ENDROITS

RECOMMANDÉ

105 – AU TROU GASCON
40, RUE TAINE
75012 PARIS
TÉL. : 01 43 44 34 26
€ € €
FERMÉ SAM. AU DÉJ., DIM. ET AOÛT

Dans les murs d'un bistrot de quartier, le Trou Gascon propose d'excellentes spécialités du Sud-Ouest.

106 – CHEZ GLADINES
30, RUE DES CINQ-DIAMANTS
75013 PARIS
TÉL. : 01 45 80 70 10
€
FERMÉ AOÛT

De la bonne cuisine basque à petits prix.

107 – CLOS MORILLONS
50, RUE DES MORILLONS
75015 PARIS
TÉL. : 01 48 28 04 37
€ €
FERMÉ SAM. ET LUN. AU DÉJ., DIM. ET 3 SEM. DÉBUT AOÛT

Excellente adresse du quartier, toute de confort simple et de cuisine savoureuse. Atmosphère chaleureuse et sans prétention.

108 – LA GRANDE CASCADE
BOIS DE BOULOGNE
ALLÉE DE LONGCHAMP
75016 PARIS
TÉL. : 01 45 27 33 51
€ € € €
FERMÉ 20 DÉC.-20 JAN.

Ce restaurant Second Empire, merveilleusement situé à l'orée du bois de Boulogne propose surtout des spécialités provençales.

109 – LA RÉGALADE
49, AVENUE JEAN-MOULIN
75014 PARIS
TÉL. : 01 45 45 68 58
€ € €
FERMÉ DIM., LUN. ET AOÛT

D'excellentes spécialités béarnaises à des prix très honnêtes.

110 – LE PRÉ CATELAN
ROUTE DE SURESNES
75016 PARIS
TÉL. : 01 44 14 41 14
€ € € €
FERMÉ DIM. DÎN., LUN., ET 1 SEMAINE EN FÉVRIER

Frédéric Anton, chef talentueux, redonne un nouveau souffle à ce très agréable restaurant, situé au cœur du bois de Boulogne.

RECOMMANDÉ

111 – LE TRAIN BLEU
20, BOULEVARD DIDEROT
BUFFET DE LA GARE DE LYON
75012 PARIS
TÉL. : 01 43 43 09 06
€ € €

Dans un décor rococo classé à l'Inventaire des monuments historiques, Jean-Pierre Hocquet vous propose une cuisine du terroir exemplaire.

112 – MARTY
20, AVENUE DES GOBELINS
75005 PARIS
TÉL. : 01 43 31 39 51
€ € €

Sous la houlette de Thierry Colas, une cuisine de brasserie revisitée avec talent.

SHOPPING À PARIS

Aucune difficulté pour dépenser de l'argent dans ce paradis du shopping où les devantures attirent les regards de tous côtés. Les commerçants ont l'obligation d'afficher les prix de tous les articles exposés de telle sorte qu'il n'y a pas de surprise. La TVA est déductible aux visiteurs originaires de pays hors de la Communauté européenne au-dessus d'un certain montant d'achats chez le même détaillant le même jour. (Demander le formulaire de détaxe au vendeur).

GRANDS MAGASINS

Pour ceux qui souhaitent trouver tout ce qui leur faut dans le même magasin, les deux établissements voisins, Galeries Lafayette et Printemps (Ⓜ Havre-Caumartin ou Chaussée-d'Antin) sont tout indiqués. Le très chic Bon Marché (Ⓜ Sèvres-Babylone) est situé rive gauche. Le BHV (Ⓜ Hôtel-de-Ville) est situé au cœur de Paris. Les magasins Monoprix et Prisunic vendent aussi bien de la nourriture que de l'habillement et des accessoires. Tati a désormais son seul établissement à Barbès et continue d'attirer les foules en vendant des articles à des prix défiant toute concurrence. On trouvera des vêtements au style pimpant et jeune dans des chaînes de magasins comme Kookaï, Naf Naf, Promod, Zara et H&M.

ANTIQUAIRES

Un grand nombre de magasins d'antiquités sont situés à proximité du Louvre et de l'autre côté de la Seine, dans les rues comprises entre le quai Voltaire et le boulevard Saint-Germain (Ⓜ Rue du Bac). C'est là que de très belles boutiques proposent des pièces dignes de musées. Le Louvre des Antiquaires (fermé lun. Ⓜ Palais-Royal) forme un ensemble de 250 boutiques et le Village Saint-Paul (fermé mar. et mer. Ⓜ Saint-Paul) paraît s'être spécialisé dans l'art des années 1950. Il existe également plusieurs marchés aux puces à Saint-Ouen et à la porte de Vanves (ouvert sam., dim et lun.. Ⓜ Porte-de-Vanves) où l'on écoule quelques objets anciens de valeur et quantités de vieilleries. Comme il est d'usage pour tous marchés aux puces, les deux règles sont d'y aller le plus tôt possible le matin et de ne jamais hésiter à marchander.

PARFUMS

Paris est la capitale des parfums. De grands magasins spécialisés proposent quantité de références.

L'Artisan Parfumeur, 24, bd. Raspail, 75007, tél. : 01 42 22 23 32 Ⓜ Rue du Bac et quatre autres boutiques à Paris (liste sur le site www.artisanparfumeur.com). Face aux géants de la distribution et aux grandes marques, un créateur original d'eaux de toilette et de parfums pour la maison. Service personnalisé.

Marionnaud, près de 80 boutiques à Paris (liste des points de vente sur www.marionnaud.com). Des parfums de marque commercialisés avec des réductions de 30% et même davantage.

Guerlain, 68, avenue Champs-Élysées, 75008, tél. : 01 45 62 52 57 Ⓜ Franklin D. Roosevelt. On peut facilement devenir inconditionnel des parfums Guerlain.

Séphora, 70, avenue Champs-Élysées, 75008, tél. : 01 53 93 22 50 Ⓜ Franklin D. Roosevelt. Il existe une dizaine de boutiques Séphora à Paris, à la pointe en matière de parfums et produits cosmétiques. Ouvert jusqu'à minuit.

Shisheido, Palais-Royal, 142, galerie de Valois, 75001, tél. : 01 49 27 09 09 Ⓜ Palais-Royal. Une luxueuse boutique dans laquelle on pourra sentir les créations de Serge Lutens.

VÊTEMENTS

Les grands noms de la mode sont rassemblés rue du Faubourg-Saint-Honoré, avenue Montaigne et à Saint-Germain-des-Prés. Les autres magasins cités ci-dessous ont tous quelque chose de particulier, avec souvent des prix très avantageux pour des articles de marque.

Act 2, 2, rue des Trois-Frères, 75018, tél. : 01 42 54 01 56 Ⓜ Abbesses. Pour l'homme chic qui veut sortir de l'ordinaire.

Alternatives, 18, rue du Roi-de-Sicile, 75004, tél. : 01 42 78 31 50. Fermé lun. Ⓜ Saint-Paul. Vêtements soigneusement sélectionnés, surtout pour les femmes.

Azzedine Alaïa, 7, rue de Moussy, 75004, tél. : 01 42 72 19 19 Ⓜ Hôtel-de-Ville. Un créateur de mode exceptionnel dont les vêtements rendent les femmes très sexy.

Bonnie Cox, 38, rue des Abbesses, 75018, tél. : 01 42 54 95 68 Ⓜ Abbesses. Fringues pour jeunes gens dans le vent.

Chanel, 29, rue Cambon, 75001, tél. : 01 42 86 28 00 Ⓜ Concorde. Un haut lieu du chic parisien.

Christian Dior, 13, rue François-Ier, 75008, tél. : 01 40 73 54 00 Ⓜ Franklin D. Roosevelt. Les créations de Galliano présentées dans un décor fastueux.

Colette, 213, rue Saint-Honoré, 75001, tél. : 01 55 35 33 90 Ⓜ Tuileries. Des vêtements tendance, des gadgets dernier cri. Bar à eaux très fréquenté au sous-sol.

L'Éclaireur, 3*ter*, rue des Rosiers, 75004, tél. : 01 48 87 10 22. Fermé dim. et lun. mat. Ⓜ Saint-Paul. Une sélection de vêtements et d'accessoires de créateurs tels que Dries Van Noten, Clements-Ribeiro et Helmut Lang.

Galerie Gaultier, 44, avenue Georges V, 75008, tél. : 01 44 43 00 44 Ⓜ George V ; 6, rue vivienne, 75002, tél. : 01 42 86 05 05 Ⓜ Bourse. Le prêt-à-porter, des accessoires et des parfums du créateur le plus doué de sa génération.

L'Habilleur, 44, rue de Poitou, 75003, tél. : 01 48 87 77 12 Ⓜ Filles-du-Calvaire. Une sélection de vêtements de marque à prix réduits.

Hermès, 24, rue du Faubourg-Saint-Honoré, 75008, tél. : 01 40 17 47 17 Ⓜ Madeleine. Une vénérable maison qui n'hésite pas à bousculer les standards.

La Marelle, 21-25, galerie Vivienne, 75002, tél. : 01 42 60 08 19. Fermé sam. ap.-midi Ⓜ Bourse. Vêtements haut de gamme et vêtements d'occasion en parfait état de marques telles que Chanel et Dior.

Maria Luisa, 2, rue Cambon, 75001, tél. : 01 47 03 96 15 Ⓜ Concorde. Vêtements signés Helmut Lang, Ann Demeulemeester et autres. La boutique hommes et accessoires est située en face.

Mouton à Cinq Pattes, 8 et 18, rue Saint-Placide, 75006, tél. : 01 45

48 86 26 et 01 42 84 25 11 Ⓜ Saint-Placide. 138, bd. Saint-Germain, 75006, tél. : 01 43 26 49 25 Ⓜ Odéon. Des dégriffés de grandes marques et de nouveaux créateurs à des prix imbattables pour femmes et hommes.

ACCESSOIRES

Agatha, 5, place des Victoires, 75001, tél. : 01 40 39 08 25 (et 18 autres points de ventes à Paris, voir le site www.agatha.fr) Ⓜ Bourse-Sentier. L'incontournable marque de bijoux fantaisie développe depuis peu sa propre ligne de parfums.

Axes et Soirs, 8, rue Caffarelli, 75003, tél. : 01 42 74 43 06 Ⓜ Temple. Chapeaux insolites et autres accessoires sur mesure et sur rendez-vous.

Bains Plus, 51, rue des Francs-Bourgeois, 75004, tél. : 01 48 87 83 07. Fermé lun. et dim. mat. Ⓜ Hôtel-de-Ville. De somptueux accessoires pour le bain et la détente.

Biche de Bere, 4, passage Sainte-Avoye, 75003, tél. : 01 42 72 15 58 (et 5 autres points de vente à Paris) Ⓜ Rambuteau. Création de bijoux fantaisie très originaux, quelques vêtements , linge de maison.

Droguerie, 9-11, rue du Jour, 75001, tél. : 01 45 08 93 27. Fermé dim. et lun. mat. Ⓜ Les Halles. Tissus bariolés, plumes, boutons, perles fantaisie et colifichets rares.

Jamin Puech, 43, rue Madame, 75006, tél. : 01 45 48 14 85 Ⓜ Saint-Sulpice. Deux jeunes et brillants créateurs se sont spécialisés dans les sacs et autres accessoires de mode.

Kabuki, 13, rue de Turbigo, 75002, tél. : 01 42 36 44 34 Ⓜ Étienne-Marcel. Chaussures de créateurs : Dries Van Noten, Dirk Bikkembergs et Vivienne West wood.

ENFANTS

C'est ma chambre, 45, rue des Archives, 75003, tél. : 01 48 87 26 67. Fermé lun. matin. Ⓜ Hôtel-de-Ville. Les parents et leurs enfants seront enthousiasmés par le mobilier et les accessoires.

Jacadi, 17, rue Tronchet, 75008, tél. : 01 42 65 84 98 Ⓜ Madeleine. La maison-mère d'une chaîne de vêtements classiques pour enfants.

Du Pareil au Même, 128, boulevard de Courcelles, 75017, tél. : 01 47 66 56 52. Ⓜ Ternes. La première des boutiques de cette chaîne de vêtements pour enfants, solides et à des prix intéressants.

Petits Petons, 23, rue Tronchet, 75008, tél. : 01 47 42 27 76 Ⓜ Madeleine. Les plus exquises petites chaussures pour bambins que l'on puisse imaginer.

LIVRES ET DISQUES

La Chaumière à Musique, 5, rue de Vaugirard, 75006, tél. : 04 43 54 07 25. Fermé dim. mat. RER : Luxembourg. Disques d'occasion pour amateurs de musique classique.

FNAC, 74, avenue des Champs-Élysées, 75008, tél. : 01 53 53 64 64. Ouvert jusqu'à minuit. Fermé dim. mat. Ⓜ Franklin D. Roosevelt. Ce magasin de cette grande chaîne de distribution est spécialisé en musique. Une autre adresse (136, rue de Rennes, 75006, tél. : 01 49 54 30 00 Ⓜ Montparnasse-Bienvenue) consacre une vaste partie de sa surface aux livres.

Virgin Megastore, 52-60, avenue des Champs-Élysées, 75008, tél. : 01 49 53 50 00. Ouvert jusqu'à minuit. Fermé dim. mat. Ⓜ Franklin D. Roosevelt. Un grand choix de produits culturels en tous genres. Bar-restaurant.

BONNES CHOSES

Barthélemy, 51, rue de Grenelle, 75007, tél. : 01 442 22 82 24 Ⓜ Sèvres-Babylone. Les meilleurs fromages dans une belle boutique.

Berthillon, 31, rue Saint-Louis-en-Île, 75004, tél. : 01 43 54 31 61 Ⓜ Pont-Marie. Les plus célèbres glaces de Paris, également distribuées dans d'autres établissements de l'île Saint-Louis et de Paris.

Fauchon, 26-30, place de la Madeleine, 75008, tél. : 01 47 42 91 10 Ⓜ Madeleine. Les meilleures denrées sont en vente ici.

Mariage Frères, 30, rue du Bourg-Tibourg, 75004, tél. : 01 42 72 28 11 Ⓜ Hôtel-de-Ville. Plus de 400 thés, des services et des gourmandises. Deux autres boutiques dans Paris et des comptoirs (www.mariagefreres. com).

Les Papilles, 30, rue Gay-Lussac, 75005, tél. : 01 43 25 20 79. RER : Luxembourg. Vins et des mets fins.

Poujauran, 20, rue Jean-Nicot, 75007, tél. : 01 43 17 45 20 Ⓜ Latour-Maubourg. Boulangerie réputée pour la qualité de ses baguettes, pour son gâteau au chocolat et son gâteau basque.

DÉCORATION

Boutiques Paris-Musées

Forum des Halles : 1, rue Pierre-Lescot, 75001, tél. : 01 40 26 56 65 Ⓜ Les Halles. 29*bis*, rue des Francs-Bourgeois, 75004, tél. : 01 42 76 65 79 Ⓜ Saint-Paul. Vente d'objets décorés d'après les œuvres d'art des musées de Paris, telles qu'assiettes, verrerie et autres.

La Chaise Longue, 30, rue Croix-des-Petits-Champs, 75001, tél. : 01 42 96 32 14 Ⓜ Palais-Royal. 8, rue Princesse, 75006, tél. : 01 43 29 62 39 Ⓜ Saint-Germain-des-Prés. 20, rue des Francs-Bourgeois, 75003, tél. : 01 48 04 36 37. Fermé dim. mat. Ⓜ Saint-Paul. Accessoires branchés pour la cuisine et la salle de bain.

The Conran Shop, 117, rue du Bac, 75007, tél. : 01 42 84 10 01. Fermé dim. et lun. mat. Ⓜ Sèvres-Babylone. Le domaine du designer Terence Conran, de beaux meubles et accessoires pour la maison.

Dîners en ville, 27, rue de Varenne, 75007, tél. : 01 42 22 78 33. Une des plus belles boutiques de Paris pour l'art de la table.

Galerie VIA, 29-37 avenue Daumesnil, 75012, tél. : 01 46 28 11 11 Ⓜ Gare de Lyon. Une galerie destinée à la promotion des designers français.

Maison de Famille, 29, rue Saint-Sulpice, 75006, tél. : 01 40 46 97 47 Ⓜ Saint-Sulpice. Tout, des gadgets de cuisine à la literie et aux objets décoratifs. Ambiance raffinée.

Matins bleus, 92, rue de Rennes, 75006, tél. : 01 42 22 23 17 Ⓜ Saint-Germain-des-Prés. Des draps de grande qualité.

Muriel Grateau, 37, rue de Beaune, 75007, tél. : 01 40 20 42 82 Ⓜ Rue du Bac. Draps en lin de couleurs variées et services de tables élégants et modernes.

Villa Marais, 40, rue des Francs-Bourgeois, 75003, tél. : 01 42 78 42 40 Ⓜ Hôtel-de-Ville. Mobilier exotique et objets déco.

PAPETERIE

Art du Bureau, 47, rue des Francs-Bourgeois, 75004, tél. : 01 48 87 57 97. Fermé dim. mat. Ⓜ Saint-Paul. Papeterie originale et élégante.

Papier Plus, 10, rue du Pont-Louis-Philippe, 75004, tél. : 01 42 74 57 68 Ⓜ Pont-Marie. Albums, cahiers, livres blancs, emboîtages… De la papeterie chic.

SORTIR À PARIS

Paris, l'une des premières capitales du monde, ne manque pas de lieux de distractions. Les Parisiens adorent sortir et les spectacles affichent souvent complet. Si possible, réservez vos places vraiment à l'avance tant pour le théâtre que pour les concerts, les ballets et l'opéra. Pour tous les détails sur les heures des concerts et les programmes des salles de cinéma, consulter *Pariscope, l'Officiel des Spectacles, Zurban* ou *Nova* en vente dans les kiosques à journaux.

CAFÉS-THÉÂTRES

Café de la Gare, 41, rue du Temple, 75004, tél. : 01 42 78 52 51 Ⓜ Hôtel-de-Ville. Un café-théâtre mythique qui fut le point de départ de belles carrières.

Le Point-Virgule, 7, rue Sainte-Croix-de-la-Bretonnerie, 75004, tél. : 01 42 78 67 03 Ⓜ Hôtel-de-Ville. Un petit café-théâtre très en vogue.

Comédie de Paris, 42, rue Fontaine, 75009, tél. : 01 42 81 32 22 Ⓜ Blanche. Un petit-café théâtre très agéable.

Blancs-Manteaux, 15, rue des Blancs-Manteaux, 75004, tél. : 01 48 87 15 84 Ⓜ Hôtel-de-Ville. Un café-théâtre ouvert tous les soirs qui propose différentes soirées à thèmes.

THÉÂTRES

La Cartoucherie-Théâtre du Soleil, route du Champ-de-Manœuvre, 75012, tél. : 01 43 74 24 08 Ⓜ Château-de-Vincennes, puis navette. Pièces interprétées dans un entrepôt restauré par la troupe d'Ariane Mnouchkine.

La Comédie-Française, 1, place Colette, tél. : 08 25 10 60 80 Ⓜ Palais-Royal. La troupe de Molière est à l'origine de ce vénérable théâtre près du Palais-Royal. On y joue les pièces du répertoire dramatique français et étranger, classique ou non. Les acteurs sont tous remarquables.

Folies-Bergère, 32, rue Richer, 75009, tél. : 08 92 68 16 50 Ⓜ Grands Boulevards. Comédies musicales et spectacles de variétés dans un admirable vieux théâtre.

Odéon-Théâtre de l'Europe, place de l'Odéon, 75006, tél. : 01 44 41 36 36 Ⓜ Odéon. Ce théâtre présente un programme de pièces tant françaises qu'étrangères.

Théâtre de Bobigny, La Maison de la Culture : 1, boulevard Lénine, Bobigny, tél. : 01 41 60 72 72 Ⓜ Bobigny-Pablo-Picasso. Les spectacles d'avant-garde (Robert Wilson, Peter Sellars) forment l'essentiel du répertoire de ce théâtre situé dans la banlieue « populaire » de Paris.

Théâtre du Rond Point, 2*bis*, av. Franklin D. Roosevelt, 75008, tél. : 01 44 95 98 10 Ⓜ Franklin D. Roosevelt. Ancien théâtre de Marcel Maréchal, la troupe de Jean-Michel Ribes y monte des spectacles classiques, des œuvres de Samuel Beckett et de Harold Pinter, pour ne nommer que ces deux-là, mais les auteurs contemporains sont particulièrement à l'honneur. La salle est une ancienne patinoire. Restaurant, librairie.

Théâtre du Vieux-Colombier, 21, rue du Vieux-Colombier, 75006, tél. : 01 44 39 87 00 Ⓜ Saint-Sulpice. Une extension de la Comédie-Française sur la rive gauche, avec un programme mixte de pièces classiques et de pièces contemporaines.

Théâtre national de Chaillot 1, place du Trocadéro, 75016, tél. : 01 53 65 30 00 Ⓜ Trocadéro. Un immense théâtre dirigé par Jérôme Savary qui y monte de fastueuses productions. On donne aussi de petits concerts dans le foyer principal à l'heure des cocktails en semaine ou le dimanche après-midi.

OPÉRA – BALLETS – MUSIQUE CLASSIQUE

Beaucoup d'églises proposent également des concerts et des récitals. Programmes dans *Pariscope* ou Concertsolo (tél. : 01 44 62 70 90), Les Grands Concerts Sacrés (tél. : 01 48 24 16 29), ou Musique Sacrée à Notre-Dame de Paris (tél. : 01 44 41 49 99).

Théâtre du Châtelet, place du Châtelet, 75001, tél. : 01 40 28 28 40 Ⓜ Châtelet. De grands opéras, des concerts classiques et des spectacles de danse figurent au programme de ce magnifique théâtre.

Cité de la Musique, 211, avenue Jean-Jaurès, 75019, tél. : 01 44 84 45 00 Ⓜ Porte de Pantin. Le bel édifice conçu par Christain de Portzamparc abrite l'Ensemble Inter-Contemporain d'avant-garde de Pierre Boulez.

Maison de la Radio, 116, avenue du Président-Kennedy, 75016, tél. : 01 42 30 10 45 Ⓜ Ranelagh ou Passy. C'est la résidence de l'Orchestre national de France et de l'Orchestre philharmonique.

Opéra-Comique, 5, rue Favart, 75002, tél. : 08 25 00 00 58 Ⓜ Richelieu Drouot. Des opéras, des opérettes et des concerts classiques sont exécutés dans ce théâtre, magnifiquement décoré, construit il y a cent ans par Bernier.

Opéra national de Paris-Bastille, 2*bis*, place de la Bastille, 75012, tél. : 08 92 89 90 90 Ⓜ Bastille. Grands opéras et spectacles de danse sont présentés dans cette construction moderne (que les Parisiens adorent dénigrer, en s'y précipitant quand même à chaque occasion).

Opéra national de Paris Palais-Garnier, place de l'Opéra, 75009, tél. : 08 92 89 90 90 Ⓜ Opéra. Dans ce lieu mythique, le Ballet de l'Opéra national de Paris interprète des spectacles inoubliables. Fresques de Chagall au plafond.

Salle Pleyel, 252, rue du Faubourg-Saint-Honoré, 75008, tél. : 01 45 61 53 00. Ⓜ Ternes. La salle des récitals et des concerts de musique classique. Réouverture après rénovation en 2007.

Théâtre des Champs-Élysées, 15, avenue Montaigne, 75008, tél. : 01 49 52 50 50 Ⓜ Alma-Marceau. C'est le siège de l'Orchestre national de France. On y accueille aussi des formations extérieures et des compagnies d'opéra.

Théâtre de la Ville, 2, place du Châtelet, 75004, tél. : 01 42 74 22 77 Ⓜ Châtelet. Une salle de première importance offrant un programme très audacieux de ballets et spectacles de danse par les meilleures troupes du monde entier.

JAZZ

Bilboquet, 13, rue Saint-Benoît, 75006, tél.: 01 45 48 81 84 Ⓜ Saint-Germain-des-Prés. Club de style Belle Époque situé au cœur de Saint-Germain-des-Prés qui existe depuis une cinquantaine d'années. On y dîne au son du jazz new orleans.

Caveau de la Huchette, 5, rue de la Huchette, 75005, tél.: 01 43 26 65 05 Ⓜ Saint-Michel. Un sous-sol enfumé du Quartier latin avec rock des années 1950, boogie-woogie et swing. Toujours très couru.

Duc des Lombards, 42, rue des Lombards, tél.: 01 42 33 22 88 Ⓜ Châtelet. Une ambiance survoltée dans ce club avec des concerts de jazz à partir de 22 h.

Jazz Club Lionel Hampton, Hôtel Méridien: 81, boulevard Gouvion Saint-Cyr, tél.: 01 40 68 30 42 Ⓜ Porte Maillot. Jazz et blues de bonne qualité dans le hall de l'hôtel Méridien.

New Morning, 7, rue des Petites-Écuries, 75010, tél.: 01 45 23 51 41 Ⓜ Château d'Eau. Des musiciens de jazz, de blues ou de tradition africaine ou sud-américaine jouent dans ce bon club enfumé.

Opus Jazz and Soul Club, 167 quai de Valmy, 75010, tél.: 01 40 34 70 00 Ⓜ Louis-Blanc. Du mardi au samedi. Club de jazz et musique soul. Ambiance agréable pour une programmation variée.

Petit Journal Montparnasse, 13, rue du Commandant-Mouchotte, 75014, tél.: 01 43 21 56 70 Ⓜ Montparnasse. Groupes de jazz classique, de jazz actuel ou de musique sud-américaine.

Petit Journal Saint-Michel, 71, boulevard Saint-Michel, 75005, tél.: 01 43 26 28 59. RER: Luxembourg. Une cave où l'on joue du jazz new orleans.

Sunset, 60, rue des Lombards, 75001, tél.: 01 40 26 46 60 Ⓜ Châtelet. Club de jazz en sous-sol où se produisent de bonnes formations françaises et étrangères.

La Villa, 29, rue Jacob, 75006, tél.: 01 43 26 60 00 Ⓜ Saint-Germain-des-Prés. Des concerts de jazz hors-pair dans ce sous-sol confortable d'un hôtel de la rive gauche.

POP ET ROCK

La Cigale, 120, boulevard Rochechouart, 75018, tél.: 01 49 25 81 75 Ⓜ Pigalle. Concerts rock.

Le Divan du Monde, 75, rue des Martyrs, 75018, tél.: 01 42 52 02 46 Ⓜ Pigalle. Différents genres de musique: rock, chanson française, gospel et Europe centrale.

Élysée-Montmartre, 72, boulevard Rochechouart, 75018, tél.: 01 44 92 45 36 Ⓜ Anvers. Un ancien music-hall de Pigalle sert de cadre à de bons concerts de rap et de rock.

Olympia, 28, boulevard des Capucines, 75009, tél.: 08 92 68 33 68 Ⓜ Opéra. Une salle de concerts mythique où se produisent les stars qui veulent un peu plus d'intimité avec leur public.

BARS – NIGHT-CLUBS

De nouveaux bars branchés s'ouvrent toutes les semaines, surtout dans le quartier de la rue Oberkampf, en pleine ascension.

Les Bains, 7, rue du Bourg-l'Abbé, 75003, tél.: 01 48 87 01 80 Ⓜ Étienne-Marcel. Cette discothèque, installée dans un ancien local de bains-douches connaît un vif succès depuis des années. C'est ici, si vous avez le privilège d'être admis à l'entrée, que vous pourrez côtoyer vedettes et top-models du moment.

Barrio Latino, 46-48, rue du Faubourg-Saint-Antoine 75011, tél.: 01 55 78 48 75 Ⓜ Bastille. Sur plusieurs étages, un restaurant, des bars, des lounges, et toujours beaucoup de monde.

Le Baron, 6, avenue Marceau, 75008, tél.: 01 47 20 04 01 Ⓜ Alma-Marceau. Night-club très sélect (150 entrées à la fois seulement) pour des soirées très branchées où l'on croise souvent des personnalités du monde entier.

Le Batofar, 11, quai François-Mauriac 75013, tél.: 01 56 29 10 00 Ⓜ Quai de la Gare. Des concerts live, un petit salon dans le carré du bateau est très agréable pour boire un verre.

Buddha Bar, 8, rue Boissy-d'Anglas, 75008, tél.: 01 53 05 90 00 Ⓜ Concorde. Grand bar-restaurant pour un public jet-set. Une énorme statue du Bouddha y trône.

Le Bus Palladium, 6, rue Fontaine, 75009, tél.: 01 53 21 07 33 Ⓜ Blanche. Entrée libre pour les filles mar.

Le Casbah, 20, rue de la Forge-Royale, 75011, tél.: 01 43 71 04 99 Ⓜ Ledru-Rollin. Le décor bigarré à la marocaine est la principale attraction de ce club-restaurant. Le jazz et l'acid-house alternent avec la musique dance et le disco.

La Chapelle des Lombards, 19, rue de Lappe, 75011, tél.: 01 43 57 24 24 Ⓜ Bastille. Rythmes latino-américains et concerts «live» le jeudi soir dans une ambiance sympathique et décontractée.

Charbon Café, 109, rue Oberkampf, 75011, tél.: 01 43 57 55 13 Ⓜ Parmentier. Ancien dancing, c'est le premier café branché à s'ouvrir dans cette rue. La salle a été complétée avec de simples comptoirs. Endroit à découvrir pour le décor (plafonds surélevés, fresques murales), mais à éviter le week-end en raison de la bousculade assurée.

Chez Richard, 37, rue Vieille-du-Temple, 75004, tél.: 01 42 74 31 65 Ⓜ Hôtel-de-Ville. Bar-restaurant à trois niveaux dans le Marais. Une clientèle nombreuse de yuppies décontractés.

China Club, 50, rue de Charenton, 75026412, tél.: 01 43 43 82 02 Ⓜ Ledru-Rollin. L'endroit approprié pour prendre un verre en bavardant tranquillement. Cadre de style colonial, extrêmement raffiné et proche de la Bastille.

Cithéa, 112, rue Oberkampf, 75011, tél.: 01 40 21 70 95 Ⓜ Saint-Maur. Musique live, jazz et musique sud-américaine du mercredi au samedi soir dans ce petit club avec piste de danse.

Le Comptoir, 14, rue Vauvilliers, 75001, tél. 01 40 26 26 66 Ⓜ Les Halles. Un endroit tout indiqué pour déguster un verre en grignotant des tapas ; décor très mode.

La Coupole, 100, boulevard de Montparnasse, 75014, tél. : 01 43 20 14 20 Ⓜ Montparnasse. Thés dansants sam. ap.-midi, salsa mar. soir, tango et disco ven. et sam. en soirée dans le sous-sol de cette célèbre brasserie Art déco.

Les Étoiles, 61, rue Château-d'Eau, 75010, tél. : 01 47 70 60 56. Ouvert le premier et le troisième dimanche de chaque mois. Ⓜ Château d'Eau. Cet ancien cinéma est voué à la salsa, dont il est donné des leçons tous les dimanches soirs.

La Favela Chic, 18, rue du Fbg du Temple 75011, tél. : 01 40 21 38 14 Ⓜ République. En venant vers 20 h, vous avez une chance d'avoir une table pour dîner. Vers minuit, Jérôme monte peu à peu le son et vous fait danser sur des rythmes brésiliens mixés par ses soins. Fabuleux…

Les Folies Pigalle, 11, place Pigalle, 75009, tél. : 01 48 78 41 77 Fermé lun. Ⓜ Pigalle. Autrefois boîte de strip-tease, cette discothèque attire un public de travestis et de gens ordinaires. Thé dansant gay dim.

Harry's New York Bar, 5 rue Daunou, 75002, tél. : 01 42 61 71 14 Ⓜ Opéra. Un vénérable bar américain où le premier bloody-mary a été concocté. Ambiance décalée.

La Java, 105, rue du Faubourg-du-Temple, 75010, tél. : 01 42 02 20 52. Fermé lun. et mer. Ⓜ Belleville. Immuable depuis 1938, ce vieux music-hall offre de la musique salsa jeu. et ven. soirs, du mambo sam. soir et un thé dansant dim. ap.-midi.

La Loco, 90, boulevard de Clichy, 75018, tél. : 01 53 41 88 88 Ⓜ Blanche. Un public jeune pour cette immense discothèque à trois niveaux.

Les neuf billards, 179, rue Saint-Maur, 75011, tél. : 01 40 40 05 42 Ⓜ Goncourt. Entrée gratuite et prix modestes. Ambiance musicale assurée par des DJs souvent renommés. Excellente ambiance composite, dans la tradition des vrais bistrots parisiens. Parfait pour débuter une soirée.

Lou Pascalou, 14, rue des Panoyaux, 75020, tél. : 01 46 36 78 10 Ⓜ Ménilmontant. L'un des premiers bars dans le vent du quartier de Ménilmontant, juste au nord de la rue Oberkampf.

Le Piano Zinc, 49, rue des Blancs-Manteaux, 75004, tél. : 01 42 74 32 42. Fermé lun. Ⓜ Hôtel-de-Ville. Bar à niveaux multiples où chacun des consommateurs peut venir chanter au micro.

Plaza Athénée, 25, avenue Montaigne, 75008, tél. : 01 53 67 65 00 Ⓜ George-V. Le nouveau bar du célèbre hôtel, redécoré par Patrick Jouin, né dans le giron de Philippe Starck, l'endroit le plus en vogue de la capitale pour des apéritifs mondains et des rendez-vous d'affaires.

Le Pulp, 25, boulevard Poissonnière, 75009, tél. : 01 40 26 01 93 Ⓜ Bonne-Nouvelle. La meilleure musique house de Paris. Réservé aux filles sauf le jeudi où certains hommes peuvent être admis.

Queen, 102, avenue des Champs-Élysées, 75008, tél. : 01 53 89 08 90 Ⓜ George-V. Toujours la discothèque gay la plus en vue de Paris, avec musique mixée maison et soirées à thème qui attirent aussi les hétéros. Un véritable esprit de fête.

Sanz Sans, 49, rue du Faubourg-Saint-Antoine, 75011, tél. : 01 44 75 78 78 Ⓜ Bastille. Un bar-restaurant bondé de jeunes « in » dans un décor de bric-à-brac très séduisant. Les coktails y sont généreux et les prix raisonnables.

Satellit' Café, 44, rue de la Folie-Méricourt, tél. : 01 47 00 48 87. Fermé dim. Ⓜ Oberkampf. Bar de nuit pendant le week-end possédant une énorme collection de disques en tous genres.

Six-Seven, 67, rue Pierre-Charron, 75008, tél. : 01 58 56 20 50. Fermé lun. Ⓜ George-V. Un night-club un peu chic, mais confortable et accueillant.

Le Sous-Bock, 49, rue Saint-Honoré, 75001, tél. : 01 40 26 46 61 Ⓜ Pont-Neuf ou Les Halles. Un grand pub ouvert toute la nuit et servant de quoi se restaurer toute la journée.

La Suite, 40, avenue Georges-V, 75008, tél. : 01 53 57 49 49 Ⓜ Georges-V. Décor splendide, on se croirait dans un clip vidéo. Bar, restaurant, night-club très confortables. Accueil charmant, malgré des prix un peu élevés.

Le Tambour, 41, rue Montmartre, 75002, tél. : 01 42 33 06 09 Ⓜ Sentier-Les Halles. À ne pas manquer : ce bar-bistrot (de 18 h à 6 h 30) rassemble le Tout Paris, toutes catégories confondues. L'ambiance y est très chaleureuse.

Le Why Note, 38, rue Mouffetard, 75005, tél. : 01 45 87 36 09 Ⓜ Mouffetard. Un tout petit bar de la rive gauche avec musique variée.

Wine and Bubbles, 3, rue Française, 75001, tél. : 01 44 76 99 84 Ⓜ Étienne-Marcel-Châtelet. Dans le quartier « branché » de Montorgueil, un sympathique bar à vin et à champagne. On peut aussi y grignoter une assiette de charcuterie ou de fromage.

CABARETS

Ces shows avec danseuses affriolantes sont très dispendieux. Il est préférable d'éviter un repas, souvent médiocre et hors de prix, et se contenter de prendre un verre au bar.

Crazy Horse Saloon, 12, avenue George-V, 75008, tél. : 01 47 23 32 32 Ⓜ Alma-Marceau. Considéré comme le plus érotique des cabarets. Les danseuses portent des noms comme « Kismy Patchwork » et figurent dans des tableaux appelés « Teasing ».

Lido, 116*bis*, avenue des Champs-Élysées, 75008, tél. : 01 40 76 56 10 Ⓜ George-V. Les Bluebell Girls chantent et dansent dans des costumes fantastiques.

Le Moulin Rouge, 82, boulevard de Clichy, 75009, tél. : 01 53 09 82 82/www.moulinrouge.fr Ⓜ Blanche. Les Doriss Girls sont toujours capables de danser le french cancan dans des tenues spectaculaires. Les tours de danse alternent avec des numéros de cirque sur un rythme époustouflant.

Lapin Agile, 22, rue des Saules, 75018, tél. : 01 46 06 85 87 Ⓜ Blanche. Dans le célèbre cadre de ce cabaret, chansons, humour et poésie. Pour les nostalgiques de l'ambiance montmartroise.

Les chiffres **en gras** font référence à une illustration

N

O

P

Crédits photographiques
Abréviations : (h) haut; (b) bas; (g) gauche; (d) droite; (c) centre.

Couverture: (hg/bg), Tony Stone Images. (hd), Powerstock. (bd), Eye Ubiquitous. 1, Spectrum. 2/3, Image Bank. 8, Images. 9, Pix. 10/11, James L. Stanfield. 12/13, James L. Stanfield. 14/15, Pix. 16, AKG. 17, Giraudon. 18, AKG. 19, Rue des Archives. 20/21 Giraudon. 22, Pix. 24, Pix. 25, Roger Violet. 26, Jean-Pierre Verney. 27, Jean-Pierre Verney.28/29 Studio Chadel. 30-31, Robert Harding. 33, James L. Stanfield. 34, Rue des Archives. 35, AKG. 36, Giraudon. 37, little big man. 38/39 Owen Franker/Corbis. 40 AKG. 41, Prod DB, Bela Productions/D.R. 42, Prod DB, Victoires Productions/D.R. 44, little big man. 45, Pix. 47, Pix. 48, Pix. 50(h), Pix. 50(b), Telegraph Colour Library. 50/51, A/W Maltings. 51(h), Pix. 51(b), Pix. 52, CFCL. 53, Pix. 54, Pix. 56/57, James L. Stanfield and Victor R. Boswell, Jr. 58, AA Picture Library K.Paterson. 58/59, National Geographic Society. 60, Pix. 61, AA Picture Library/K. Paterson. 63, Pix. 65(h), little big man. 65(b), AA Picture Library/J.Tims. 67, Giraudon. 68, Pix. 69, Pix. 70, Pix. 71, Pix. 73(h), Giraudon. 73(bl), Pix. 73(br), Bavaria. 74, AA Picture Library/ B.Rieger. 75, AA Picture Library/ K.Paterson. 76, Pix. 77, AA Picture Library/K.Paterson. 80, Pix. 81, AA Picture Library. 82, Pix. 83, Pix. 85(tl), AA Picture Library/ A.Souter. 85(tr), J. Allan Cash. 85(b), AA Picture Library/P.Kenwood. 86(h), Pix. 86(b), Pix. 87, Pix. 88, AA Picture Library/K.Paterson. 89, AA Picture Library/B.Rieger. 90, Pix. 91, AA Picture Library/W.Voysey. 94, AA Picture Library/P.Kenwood. 95, AA Picture :Library/ J.Tims. 97(h), J.Allan Cash. 97(b), AA Picture Library/J.Tims. 98, Giraudon. 99, AA Picture Library/ K.Paterson. 100, little big man. 101, AA Picture Library/ K.Paterson. 102, AA Picture Library/ K.Paterson. 103, Pix. 104, AA Picture Library/ K.Paterson. 106(h), J.Allan Cash. 106(b), AA Picture Library/B.Rieger. 107, Pix. 109 (h), AA Picture Library/ B.Rieger. 109(c), AA Picture Library/ P.Kenwood. 109(b), AA Picture Library/ P.Enticknap. 110, J. Allan Cash. 111, AA Picture Library/A.Souter. 112, Pix. 113, AA Picture Library/ K.Paterson. 115(h), Giraudon. 115(b) Giraudon. 116, AA Photo Library. 118, AA Picture Library/K.Paterson. 119, Pix. 120, AA Picture Library/ K.Paterson. 121, Pix. 124/5, James L. Stanfield. 126(g), Giraudon. 126(d), Giraudon. 126, A/W Maltings. 127, Giraudon. 128, Giraudon.129, Giraudon. 130, Giraudon. 131, Giraudon. 132, Giraudon. 133, Bridgeman Art Library. 134, RMN. 135, RMN. 136, AKG. 137, CFCL/Image Select. 139(h), Giraudon. 139 (bl), AA Picture Library/A.Souter. 139(br), AA Picture Library/T.Souter. 140, Giraudon. 141, Pix. 142, Pix. 143, AA Picture Library/ K.Paterson. 146, AA Picture Library/B.Rieger. 147, Tony Stone. 148, AFP Photo/Pierre Verdy/Corbis. 149(h), Stéphane Cardinale/People Avenue/Corbis. 149(b), AA Picture Library/A.Souter. 150, Pierre Vauthey/Corbis. 151, AA Picture Library/A.Souter. 152, AA Picture Library. 153, AA Picture Library/B.Rieger. 156, Pix. 157, Tom Ives/Corbis. 158, Pix. 160, Giraudon. 161, Pix. 162, AA Picture Library/ K.Paterson. 163, AA Picture Library/J.Tims. 166(all images), Giraudon. 167, Lance Nelson/Corbis. 168, Giraudon. 169, Pix. 170, AA Picture Library/B.Rieger. 171, AA Picture Library/ K.Paterson. 172, Giraudon. 173, Pix. 174(g), Roger Viollet. 174/5, Giraudon. 177, Pix. 178, AA Picture Library/ A.Souter. 179, Pix. 182, AA Picture Library/B.Rieger. 183, Giraudon. 184(g), little big man. 184(d), Edgar Clarck, Musée du Vin.185, AA Picture Library/T.Souter. 186, AA Picture Library. 188, CFCL/Image Select. 189, J. Allan Cash. 190, Pix. 192, Guardian. 193(h), AA Picture Library/ A.souter. 193(b), Bavaria/ Telegraph Colour Library. 194(h), RMN. 194(b), AA Picture Library/A.Souter. 195, J.Allan Cash. 198, Pix. 199, Pix. 200, AA Picture Library/T.Souter. 201, AA Picture Library/ K.Paterson. 202, Pix. 203, AA Picture Library/J.Tims. 204, Pix. 205, Pix. 206, Pix. 207, Pix. 208/9, AA Picture Library/J.Tims. 210, AA Picture Library/B.Rieger. 211, AA Picture Library/D.Noble. 214, Pix. 215, Giraudon. 216, AA Picture Library/D.Noble. 216/7, A/W Maltings. 217(h), J Allan Cash. 217(b), J Allan Cash. 218/9, James L. Stanfield. 219, AA Picture Library/D.Noble. 220, Pix. 221, J Allan Cash. 222, AA Picture Library/B.Rieger. 223, Giraudon. 224, AA Picture Library/D.Noble. 225, Pix. 226, AA Picture Library/D.Noble. 227, AA Picture Library/T.Souter. 228, Pix. 229, Giraudon. 230, Pix. 231, J Allan Cash. 232, Giraudon.

Première institution scientifique et pédagogique à but non lucratif du monde, la National Geographic Society a été fondée en 1888 « pour l'accroissement et la diffusion des connaissances géographiques ». Depuis lors, elle fait découvrir le monde à des millions de personnes par le biais de ses magazines, livres, programmes de télévision, vidéos, cartes et atlas, bourses de recherche, ateliers pour enseignants, matériel scolaire innovant et ses championnats de géographie.
La National Geographic Society est financée par les cotisations de ses membres, des dons et la vente de ses produits éducatifs. Ce soutien est essentiel à sa mission, qui consiste à mieux faire comprendre le monde et favoriser la sauvegarde de notre planète grâce à l'exploration, la recherche et l'enseignement.

Dépôt légal : 1er trimestre 2006

Impression Cayfosa-Quebecor (Espagne)

Paris

est une publication de la National Geographic Society

Président directeur général : John M. Fahey, Jr.
Président du conseil d'administration : Gilbert M. Grosvenor
Premier vice-président et président du Département livres : Nina D. Hoffman
Vice-président et directeur du Département livres : Kevin Mulroy
Directeur artistique : Marianne Koszorus
Directeur des publications des guides touristiques : Elizabeth L. Newhouse
Éditeur : Barbara A. Noe
Direction de la maquette : Cinda Rose
Directeur de la caratographie : Carl Mehler
Édition des cartes : Joseph F. Ochlak
Consultant : K. M. Kostyal
Directeur de la fabrication : R. Gary Colbert
Responsable du projet en fabrication : Richard S. Wain
Coordination éditoriale : Lawrence Porges
Assistante : Kay kobor Hankins

Création et réalisation de AA Publishing
Responsable de projet : Betty Sheldrick
Responsable artistique du projet : David Austin
Éditeurs : Allen Stidwill, Karen Kemp
Graphiste : Mike Preedy, Keith Russel
Responsable de la cartographie : Simon Mumford
Cartographes : Nicky Barker-Dix, Helen Beever
Directeur de la fabrication : Richard Firth
Recherche iconographique Poppy Owen de l'ISI
Cartes dessinées par Chris Orr Associates, Southampton, GB
Illustrations dessinées par Maltings Partnership, Derby, GB

Édition originale
Copyright © 2001, 2005 par la National Geographic Society.
Tous droits réservés.

Édition française
© 2002, 2006 par la National Geographic Society.
Tous droits réservés.

Réalisation éditoriale : National Geographic France
***Direction éditoriale :* Françoise Kerlo**
***assistée de* Marilyn Chauvel**
***Chef de fabrication :* Alexandre Zimmowitch**

Mise à jour : Catherine Grive, Bulle Helardot, Chloe Pham Van Hoa et Olivier Canaveso pour les Éditions de l'Après-Midi

ISBN: 2-84582-175-1
Toute reproduction intégrale ou partielle de l'ouvrage, par quelque procédé que ce soit, est strictement interdite sans l'autorisation écrite de l'éditeur.

Les informations contenues dans ce guide ont été vérifiées avec soin. Il est cependant possible que certaines changent ou aient changé. En aucun cas, la National Geographic Society ne peut être tenue pour responsable de tels changements, erreurs ou omissions. Les choix des sites, des hôtels et des restaurants ont été laissés aux soins de l'auteur; ils ne reflètent pas nécessairement l'opinion de l'éditeur, qui ne peut en être tenu pour responsable.

NATIONAL GEOGRAPHIC
LES GUIDES DE VOYAGE

Dans la même collection :

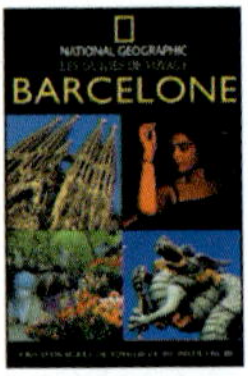

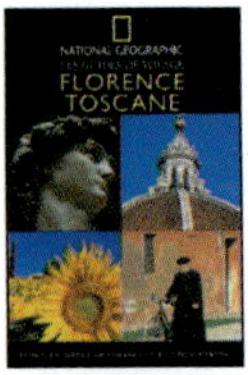

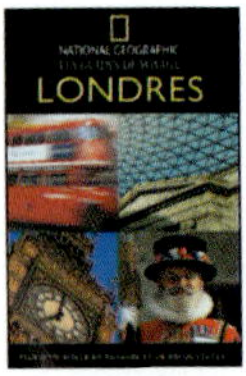

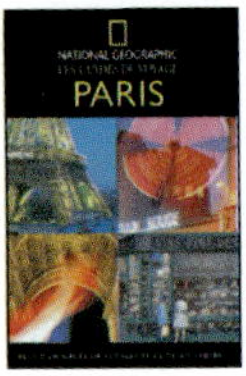

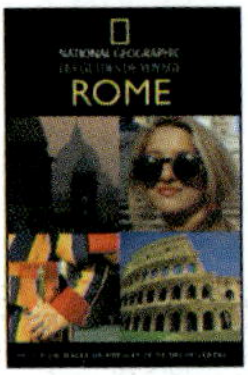

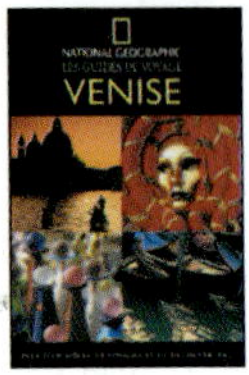

À paraître :
MADRID...

Retrouvez aussi nos autres destinations :

- ALLEMAGNE ISBN : 2-84582-122-0
- AUSTRALIE ISBN : 2-84582-148-4
- CALIFORNIE ISBN : 2-84582-121-2
- CANADA ISBN : 2-84582-077-1
- CHINE ISBN : 2-84582-080-1
- COSTA RICA ISBN : 2-84582-147-6
- CUBA ISBN : 2-84582-079-8
- ÉGYPTE ISBN : 2-84582-066-6
- ESPAGNE ISBN : 2-84582-042-9
- FLORIDE ISBN : 2-84582-076-3
- FRANCE ISBN : 2-84582-040-2
- GDE-BRETAGNE ISBN : 2-84582-087-9
- GRÈCE ISBN : 2-84582-078-X
- INDE ISBN : 2-84582-084-4
- IRLANDE ISBN : 2-84582-105-0
- ITALIE ISBN : 2-84582-039-9
- JAPON ISBN : 2-84582-085-2
- MEXIQUE ISBN : 2-84582-086-0
- PORTUGAL ISBN : 2-84582-124-7
- PROVENCE ISBN : 2-84582-150-6
- SICILE ISBN : 2-84582-149-2
- THAÏLANDE ISBN : 2-84582-067-4